WISCONSIN TRAVEL COMPANION

WISCONSIN TRAVEL COMPANION

A Guide To The History Along Wisconsin's Highways

By Richard Olsenius & Judy A. Zerby

Cartography by
Sona Karentz Andrews, Ph.D.
Department of Geography, University of Minnesota

Bluestem Productions / Mijaz, Inc. Wayzata, Minnesota

Published by Bluestem Productions/Mijaz, Inc.
Box 334, Wayzata, Minnesota 55391

Library of Congress Catalog Card Number: 83-72185
ISBN: 0-9609064-1-X
Printed in The United States of America

10 9 8 7 6 5 4 3 2 1

ACKNOWLEDGMENTS

Writing this page is perhaps one of the hardest jobs connected with The Wisconsin Travel Companion because to thank all of the people who have helped make it possible would take more space than the rest of the book. But as with any in-depth project, there are special people who deserve special notice, and that's what these acknowledgments are all about.

We have been fortunate to have good, reliable people working with us throughout–concerned with the project and dedicated to professionalism. Our editor, Margaret Nelson, a former Wisconsian, took on a formidable task indeed. It was her job to blend the writing styles of two different authors and still have it make sense in the end. Thank you for your patience and good work, Margaret.

Sona Andrews, cartographer extraordinaire, worked with us last year on the Minnesota Travel Companion, yet still agreed to work with us again on the Wisconsin book. Thank you Sona for your very fine maps that help make this book so special.

We'd also like to pay tribute to the reference librarians, both at the Minnesota and Wisconsin State Historical Societies who made our months of research a lot easier. A special thanks to George Talbot and his Iconographic department staff at the Historical Society in Madison. It was there that we culled through thousands of early photographs and started the enormous task of cutting that number down to the eventual 200 used in this book.

Our most heartfelt thanks to all those wonderful folks we met driving the routes to gather additional research and photographs. Many of them opened after-hour doors to their offices and even invited us into their homes.

Finally, a personal note to our families. To Mike (Judy's husband,) who helped print photographs, ran endless errands and filled in for an absentee authoress/wife, my love and gratitude. In exchange for days of unwashed clothes, late dinners and short tempers you, Scott, Chris & Laura were always there. And to Christine (Richard's wife,) who made countless phone calls to coordinate book distribution, assisted with layouts and helped keep my sanity, my love and devotion.

THE AUTHORS

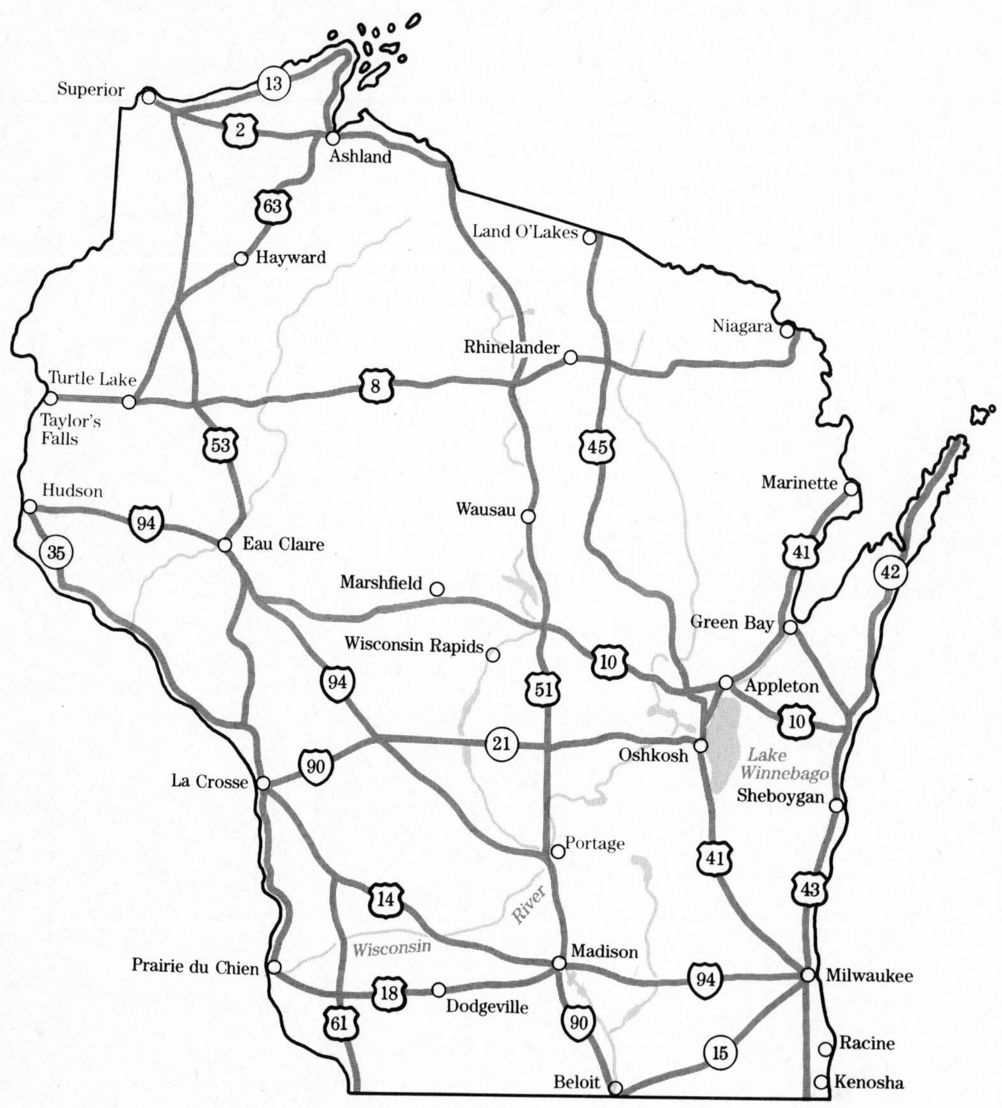
Superior
13
2
Ashland
63
Hayward
Land O'Lakes
Niagara
Rhinelander
Turtle Lake
8
Taylor's
Falls
53
45
Hudson
Marinette
94
Wausau
Eau Claire
35
41
42
Marshfield
Green Bay
Wisconsin Rapids
94
10
51
Appleton
10
21
Oshkosh
Lake
Winnebago
La Crosse
90
Sheboygan
Portage
41
14
43
River
Wisconsin
Madison
Prairie du Chien
94
Milwaukee
18
Dodgeville
61
90
Racine
15
Beloit
Kenosha

TABLE OF CONTENTS

Cover Photo/Virginia Huss De Bruin

INTRODUCTION

A few years ago on a crisp Wisconsin fall day, my wife Christine and I climbed the old fire tower at Bayfield that overlooks the Apostle Islands and Chequamegon Bay. For ten years we had been coming up to sail and explore these quiet islands and we were about to buy some land near the orchards that look down on the bay.

While looking at the reds and yellows of the maples accented against the deep blue of Lake Superior, we decided that to buy land would tie us down. Instead we decided to put our time and money into regional travel books that would highlight the history and landscapes of Minnesota and Wisconsin. From this was born the Minnesota and Wisconsin Travel Companions.

Over the years and thousands of miles, Wisconsin has captured my interest and curosity. Bordered by Lake Superior and Lake Michigan to the north and east and the St. Croix and Mississippi to the west, this state was first traversed along its waterways by Indians moving across the continent after the last ice age. Once the robust voyageurs found their way to Wisconsin's shores, it was only a matter of time before lumbering, railroads, mining, and farming fueled the economy. Immigrants in search of a new beginning, found the rolling Wisconsin land suited to their needs and during the mid-1800's, the towns began to grow. It was my curiosity over who these people were and why they settled where they did, that led to this historical guide.

There is a beauty to Wisconsin that cannot be easily expressed. It can be easily discovered though and each region offers a different feel and has a unique heritage all its own. I hope that this book adds to your appreciation of it. I know for myself, this newly gained knowledge about Wisconsin has forever won me over.

I would also like to thank Judy Zerby, who helped edit the Minnesota Travel Companion and who became a co-writer and publisher of this Wisconsin book.

Keith L. Olsenn

They say you can't go home again – I suppose that's true. But for me, this project was even better, because in writing this book, I had the opportunity to see my home state as I never had before.

Perhaps my initial appreciation for the state came from growing up in Menasha, Wisconsin, where I lived for the first 18 years of my life. During that time, my father, Frank De Bruin, owned a dairy and the whole family was a part of it. When dad drove his truck down the narrow, country roads to pick up milk from the farmers, I rode along, learning early on the importance of agriculture in this state.

As a continuing part of that childhood, every Sunday afternoon my parents and I would stop in to visit relatives, traveling to Little Chute, Hollandtown, Kimberly, and other nearby towns. On vacations we again traveled the state, looking for interesting spots to visit. Many times it would include a new cheese factory my dad had heard about. We covered a lot of ground exploring new places, meeting new people, sharing experiences and, like most childhoods, it was over all too soon.

When I got married and returned to Menasha with my family, I had the chance to share and renew those precious years–each time trying to recapture the feeling of what it was like to grow up here.

Traveling the routes of this book, I had the opportunity to retrace the old roads and find a lot of new ones. I learned how and why the old "Plank Road" I grew up on, got its name and that the lake (Winnebago) I swam in as a kid was once a glacial lake. I met many wonderful people, all anxious to share not only their own histories and experiences, but those of their ancestors as well. They gave me a new appreciation for the state, as I hope this book will in turn do for you. My wish is that after reading it, you will also know what it's like to go home again and will return to Wisconsin many, many times.

Judy A. Zerby

FINAL NOTE: All maps for this book are scaled 1" to 4 miles with north at the top of the page. Each section covers approximately 30 miles. Starting with the opening route of the book (I-94), all routes are laid out south to north and east to west–with the exception of routes 2 and 8. In most cases, references to Chippewa and Sioux Indians are made using their indigenous names–Ojibwe and Dakota. All Wisconsin Historical Society photographs are credited with SHSW.

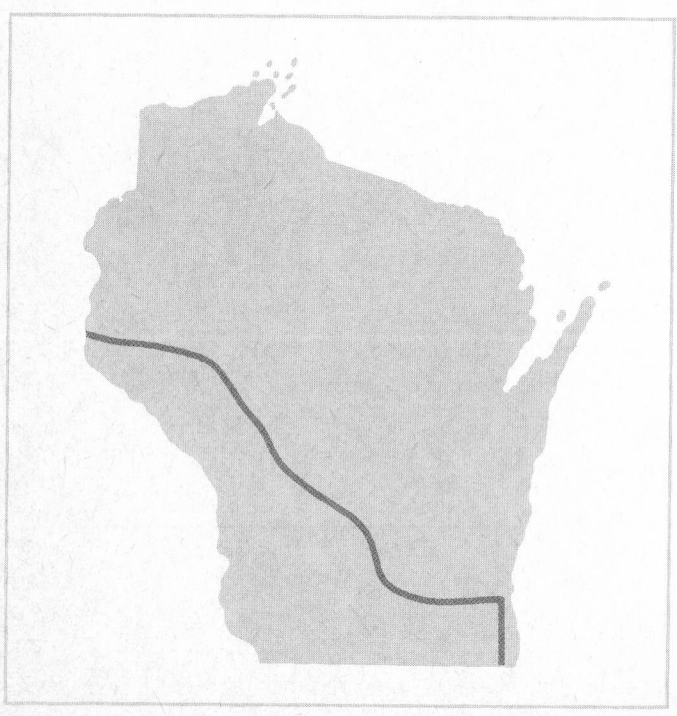

Interstate 94, the longest route in this book, carves a 340-mile swath from the bustling lakeshore towns of Kenosha and Milwaukee, inland to the beautiful Four Lakes Region near Madison, across the important Wisconsin River, and finally ends in the breath-taking St. Croix River valley. Worthy of off-the-road stops are the Aztalan State Park, an ancient Indian village mid-way between Milwaukee and Madison, and the Wisconsin Dells, located about 20 miles east of Portage.

ROUTE I-94, ILLINOIS TO HUDSON

SHSW

Plank roads, an early predecessor to the modern highway system of Wisconsin.

KENOSHA COUNTY, Pop. 123,137

Explorers following area Indian trails in 1834 discovered the Pike River which they translated from the Indian word Kenosha. Kenosha County's most noted trail, the Jambeau, led from Milwaukee along the lakeshore to Gross Point, near Evanston, Illinois. French trader Jacques Jambeau had a cabin on the trail at Skunk Grove, just west of Racine. The well-trod trail was a welcome path to early pioneers.

Captain Gilbert Knapp and two attendants traveled the Jambeau Trail from Chicago in November, 1834 and built a cabin near Racine. They spent the winter here as the first and only white settlers between Milwaukee and Gross Point. The following year Hugh Longwell and six other men came from Michigan and settled at the Pike River's head. A log cabin on the site belonging to Jacob Montgomery and sons marked the county's first permanent settlement.

KENOSHA, Pop. 77,685

This early settlement actually began as the town of Pike River, one mile north of the Kenosha harbor. That thriving village disappeared long ago and nothing remains to mark its location. The Western Emigration Company, organized to buy land on Lake Michigan's western shore, encouraged a group of Hannibal, New York settlers to move here in 1835. Those settlers renamed the town Southport because it was the lake's southernmost port. It incorporated in 1850, assuming the name of Kenosha, an Indian word meaning "pike."

SOMERS, Pop. 7,724

The Felch family moved here in March, 1835, followed by Jacob Montgomery and a few other settlers. A legislative act officially named the town Pike in 1843 but it was changed to Somers in 1851, reportedly because of a wealthy Englishman named Somers who invested heavily in the railroad.

RACINE COUNTY, Pop. 173,132

Jacque Vieau was probably the county's first pioneer, coming here in 1794 and homesteading in Skunk Grove, about

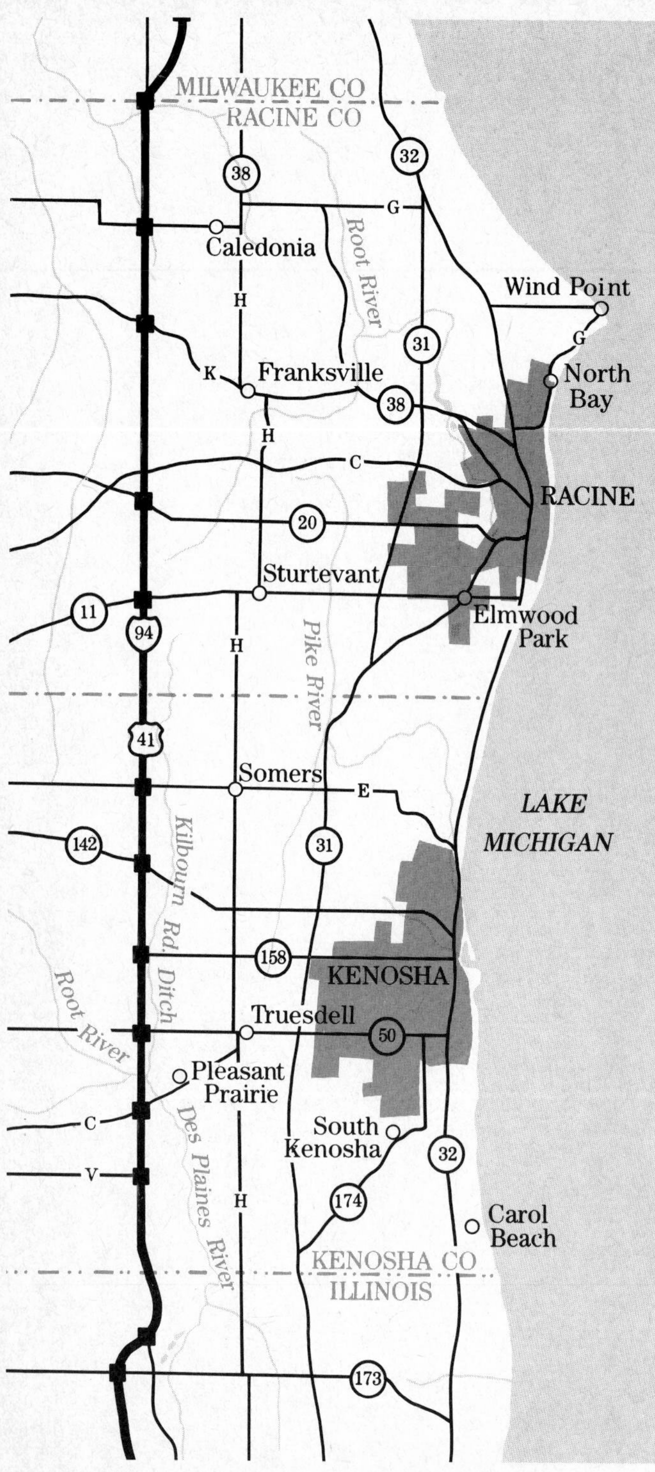

two miles east of present day Franksville. He was well liked by the Indians who called him Jambeau and his cabin and trading post became one of the most important landmarks, receiving many travel-weary pioneers. When whites crowded in and the Potawatomi moved out in 1837 Jambeau sold his land and went with them.

The county's most pressing need that year was the opening of roads. Federal troops had built the Military Road to connect the forts at Chicago and Green Bay before the settlers came. It still exists as County E, crossing the river at the rapids and proceeding up the east side to the lakeshore road, state highway 15. Lack of money prevented further road building until the government road to Janesville and Milwaukee was completed in 1839.

Tangled roots in the river made canoe travel difficult, hence the Potawatomi named it ot-chee-beek or root. A Jesuit priest named St. Cosme gave it the French name for root, Racine, in 1699. The Jesuits believed that "no man could find a better place to send out roots for a prosperous life."

UNION GROVE, Pop. 3,517

Fifteen miles west of Racine on the Chicago, Milwaukee & St. Paul Railroad line, John Dunham built a frame house on 80 acres of land and became Union Grove's first settler in 1838. He remained a short time, then sold out to P.P. Faber. Union Grove incorporated on March 18, 1856 and grew rapidly. By the turn-of-the-century, the town had electric light, a waterworks, telephone and telegraph office, bank, school, flour mill, weekly newspaper, an opera house, pickling works, creamery, hotel and more than 600 residents. The village was reportedly named by Governor Dodge who combined the school's name (Union) with Grove, after the beautiful grove of burr oak trees on the city's west side.

RACINE, Pop. 85,725

Captain Gilbert Knapp, a Yankee skipper on a revenue cutter, landed on the Root River's shores in 1828 and explored the wilderness. Liking what he saw, he vowed to come back and returned in 1833 when Indian land was ceded to the government. Selling his New York business, he went to Chicago and persuaded his friend Gordon S. Hubbard to come along. With an Indian guide they traveled the Jambeau Trail on horseback to Jambeau's trading post and stayed until November, 1834. Settling in a cabin on a high river bluff, Knapp became the true founder of Racine, the "Belle City of the Lakes."

Settlers surged into what was then called Port Gilbert; by the end of 1835, 100 people lived in Racine County. The settlers held a mass meeting to discuss civic problems when the town was platted in 1836. The question of naming the town came up and the names proposed included Kipikawi, Root River and Racine, from an Indian word meaning "river filled with tangled roots." The vote went to Racine when the town was officially organized on December 7, 1836.

FRANKSVILLE

Originally called Skunk Grove, Franksville began as a small switching stop on the Chicago and Northwestern Railway. The town's name was changed for a railway brakeman known only as Frank. Reportedly, Frank would leave the train here to court a girl and it was a standing joke to call the town Frank's Villa, or Franksville.

S.G. Knight surveyed and platted the town in 1874 and Franksville began to grow. Soon after the first settlers arrived, the town had a post office, telegraph and express office, telephone exchange, hotel, blacksmith and wagon shop, cement black factory and sauerkraut plant. By 1915 it had 180 people.

CALEDONIA

This small town a few miles north of Racine was never officially platted and was formerly known as Stearn's Crossing. The name Caledonia, Latin for Scotland, reportedly came from Scottish settlers here.

Pioneers Elam Beardsley and John Davis came here in 1835. Beardsley's wife was the first white woman in the county. A month later, Lucius Blake and family moved here from Niles, Michigan. After a night at Trader Jambeau's post they joined John Davis at a point on the river. After staying with him for a few days, the Blakes staked their claim and built a windowless log shanty with an open door to early settlers in need of housing.

By 1915, the "Polk Gazeteer of Wisconsin" reported that Caledonia's principal businesses were two general stores, a coal yard, harness shop and express office. The post office had three rural routes which supplied daily mail to the surrounding countryside.

MILWAUKEE COUNTY, Pop. 964,988

In its earliest days Milwaukee County was richly forested, inhabited by abundant game, and disturbed only by occasional visits of roaming Indians. The only white men who came here were fur traders going to a Milwaukee trading post which had long been a favorite because of its location at the junction of the Kinnickinnic, Menominee and Milwaukee rivers.

Settlement began about 1833 when settlers came from New England in increasing numbers. One year later, with Wisconsin still a part of Michigan Territory, the Michigan legislature passed an act laying out Milwaukee County. Since settlement was sparse, the county wasn't officially organized until August 25, 1835 with the city of Milwaukee named county seat. By 1836 the county had 2,893 people, half of whom were concentrated around the mouth of the Menominee River.

The name for the county and city came from Mahn-a-waukee, a Potawatomi Indian word meaning "gathering place."

SHSW

Laying bricks on North Main St., Racine, 1901.

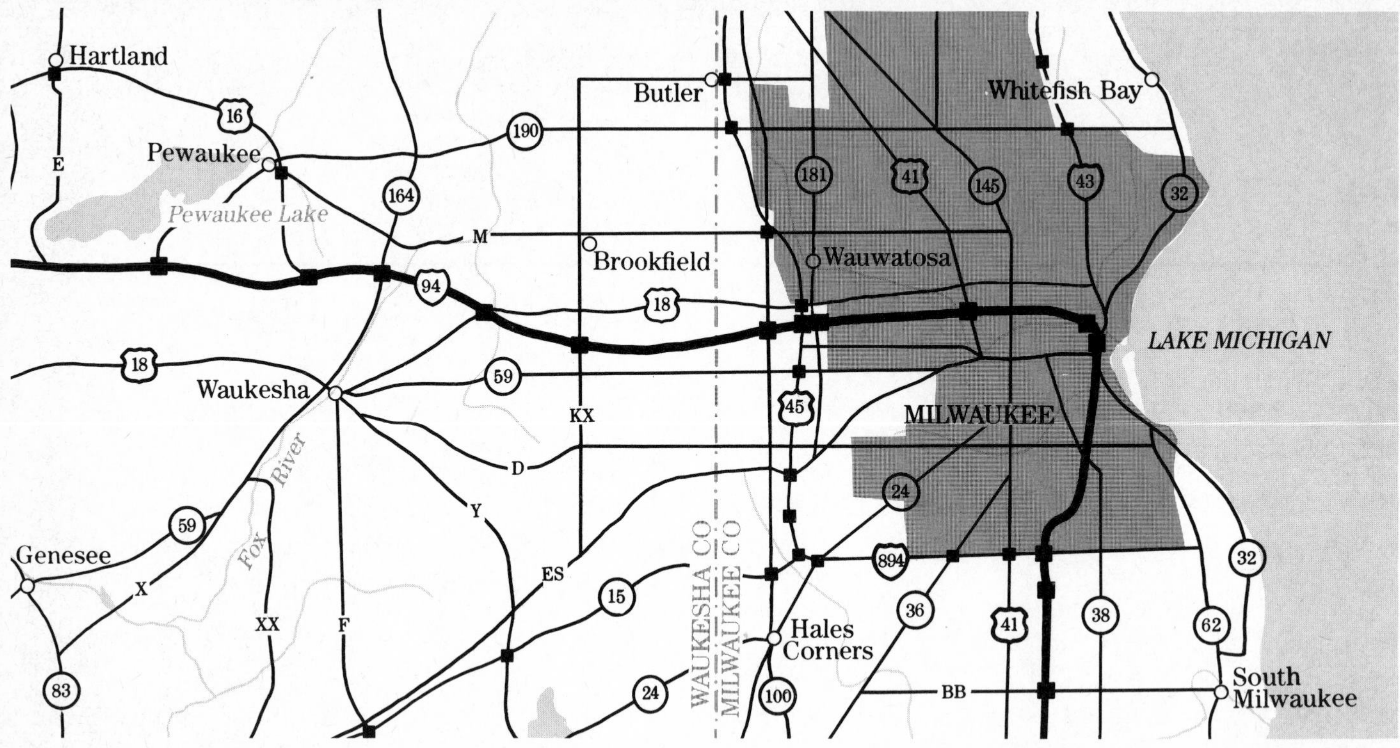

MILWAUKEE, Pop. 636,210

By all rights, Jacques Vieau, Northwest Fur Company agent, should have the title of Milwaukee's first settler. Vieau and his family canoed here in 1795 and were met at the river's mouth by a delegation of Potawatomies, Sauks, Foxes and Winnebagoes. Following their warm welcome, Vieau paddled up the Menomonee River and built a cabin and fur storage house on the valley's south side, in what later became Mitchell Park. Very successful, Vieau's wealth and family grew side by side. He and his wife eventually had 13 children. Ironically, one of Vieau's daughters was later responsible for his losing the title of Milwaukee's founder.

Josette Vieau was fifteen, intelligent and beautiful when Solomon Juneau, a naturalized American of French birth, came to work at her father's post in 1818. Six feet tall, with piercing blue eyes, he was a prime catch for any woman. When Juneau asked for Josette's hand, Vieau readily gave his consent. Because the county had no priest, the Juneaus canoed to Green Bay and were married in a mission church. Soon after their marriage, Juneau established a trading post on the river's east bank. Still there when land speculators arrived to plat the town, Solomon Juneau was credited as Milwaukee's official founder.

By 1845 Milwaukee's population had grown to 10,000 people, more than half of German descent. Because of the fertile soil, an increasing number of German immigrants moved here in the early '50's to pursue farming. The Poles, the city's second largest ethnic group, arrived in the decades following the Civil War and settled chiefly on the town's south side.

Although the early settlers were primarily fur traders and farmers, Milwaukee later became important as a trading and industrial center. The city first achieved great economic importance during the Civil War as a harbor for Great Lakes traffic. At that time Wisconsin farms were an important wheat source for the country. By 1856 the schooner Dean Richmond carried Milwaukee's first transoceanic wheat shipment direct to Liverpool, England. Milwaukee was moving steadily ahead.

In addition to wheat, farmers soon discovered a new source of income—raising crops used to produce Milwaukee's most popular new industry, beer.

WAUKESHA COUNTY, Pop. 280,326

Like all northern and eastern Wisconsin counties, Waukesha was molded from early action of the Superior, Chippewa, Green Bay and Michigan glaciers. The Green Bay and Michigan glaciers accumulated drift along a 150-mile line seen today in the tumultuous Kettle Moraine ridge which passes through southwestern Waukesha County's beautiful

MSHS

Milwaukee, ca. 1900.

SHSW

Chief Yellow Thunder, leader of the Winnebago Indians.

lake region. Landforms from this glacial period can be seen in the Kettle Moraine State Forest (Southern unit) where 70 miles of trails offer a good view of water-filled kettle lakes, conical-shaped hills called kanes, and large ridges of gravel, or moraines, that once covered the area. The lookout point of the Scuppernong Trail provides a breathtaking view of a variety of landscapes.

The lakes of southeastern Waukesha County, including Lake Muskego, the largest, were formed by the same glacial movement that created the Kettle Moraine area. Most of these lakes are longest from northeast to southwest, due to the movement of the Lake Michigan glacier. Almost all, including Lake Pewaukee, are drained by the Fox, the county's principal river which has its headwaters in northeastern Waukesha County, empties into the Illinois River and eventually spills into the Mississippi, as do most of the region's other rivers.

Because of its varied features, deep forest, oak openings, lakes and prairies, Waukesha County was inhabited by both Indians and their predecessors, the Mound Builders. Waukesha was a favorite river crossing and deeply worn trails marked the path of many. The Potawatomi, friends of the Winnebagoes and Menominees, occupied the county when whites first visited. The land was ceded by treaty in 1836 and the Potawatomi were removed to the Missouri River. Several returned from time to time, however, and a large encampment came in 1864, remaining in Winnebago territory for a considerable time under the leadership of Chief Yellow Thunder. Some later became citizens, adopting many white customs.

Most of the Mound Builders' mounds have been destroyed, although sections of some are located in Waukesha. The best preserved sections are on the Carroll College grounds.

Waukesha was named by Joshua Hathaway when he selected this location for a town. Hathaway claimed the name was taken from Wauk-tsha, a Potawatomi Indian word meaning "fox" or "little fox," which also applied to the river along which Waukesha is located.

WAUKESHA, Pop. 50,319

Before the white man came, a large Potawatomi village was located here called Tcheegascoutak, meaning "burnt or fire land." The name reportedly referred to prairie fires which frequently ravaged the open land. The name was translated to Prairie Village by legislative act in March, 1839. However, when W.A. Barstow proposed a flour mill for Prairie Village, people in surrounding towns called it Barstow's Mills. In 1846, the village was once again renamed, this time in honor of the newly organized county.

Early settlers, the Cutler brothers and their employees, John Manderville and Henry Luther, settled Waukesha on May 7, 1834. Coming on horseback from LaPorte, Indiana, they were enchanted with the Fox valley's blooming prairie and scattered groves of oak openings. Finding timber, springs and waterpower, the two brothers and their companions blazed out claims, embracing the Fox River rapids. They raised a few potatoes and a little buckwheat that first summer and the Cutlers returned to Indiana in the fall. Collecting wagons, live stock, equipment and provisions, they returned in the spring of 1835 with their father and two more men. In that way Waukesha's early development and the county's first permanent white settlement began.

SHSW

Hay cutter. Photo/Matthew Whitt.

PEWAUKEE, Pop. 4,637

Before 1837 area land was selling for $500-1,000 per claim and cheap land speculators moved in, hoping to make a quick killing. Later that year, financial panic hit, claims went down to five dollars, and the speculators fled to Milwaukee to work their way by boat back East.

Although Asa Clark made his claim in 1836, after the first settlers, he is considered the father of Pewaukee, largely responsible for the village's growth. In 1838 Clark built a dam and saw mill at Lake Pewaukee's outlet. Two years later, he operated the first quarry and lime kiln and opened the first hotel. That same year he alone platted the village and organized the Congregational Church. In 1845 he built a large, stone flour mill.

Pewaukee received many of the county's early settlers, second only to Waukesha, due, at least in part, to the fact that it was near Milwaukee. Frontiersmen frequently walked 15 or 20 miles to get supplies, then walked home again with the supplies on their backs. At Pewaukee the forest broke into wide oak openings, making cultivating easier for farmers. Later development occurred when the county's first railroads, the Milwaukee & Mississippi and the Milwaukee & Watertown, came though in 1851.

Pewaukee comes from Pee-wauk-ee-win-ick, a Potawatomi Indian word meaning "the dusty place."

SHSW

Delafield, 1884.

HARTLAND, Pop. 5,559

Hartland, located in the beautiful Bark River valley in the heart of the famous lakes region, was once one of Waukesha County's most promising towns. Unsurpassed as a place of business, farmers flocked here from miles away to receive top market price for their produce. Waterpower made saw and grist mills possible.

Hartland's first permanent settlers were Sylvanus and Betsy Warren and their 14 children. Mr. Warren built the town's first mill in 1838 and the town was then called Warren. Four years later, Christ Hershey bought Warren's property and the town became known as Hersheyville. There's no record of why the town was called Hartland when it incorporated in 1892. Potawatomies living here originally called this locale Shabaquanake, meaning "a growing group."

DELAFIELD, Pop. 4,083

Deacon Schuyler came to Delafield in the spring of 1837, followed in September by Albert Campbell. Campbell's house was built of polar poles, including some split into "shakes" in place of shingles. Within a year 25 more immigrants located near Campbell and a town began to grow.

The old territorial road, the main thoroughfare from Milwaukee westward, passed through Delafield in 1838. The route was heavily traveled and brought the county's supplies as well as many new settlers. The first hotel was also opened as a result. Because of major disagreements among the townspeople, however, the later plank road and railroad passed through Hartland and Oconomowoc, instead of Delafield, leading to the town's decline as a major business center. The village was later compensated with the building of St. John's Military Academy, the state fish hatchery, Nashotah Mission and a state tuberculosis sanatorium.

According to early documents the village was called Hayopolis for awhile, then the Indian name Namahbin. In 1843 the town renamed itself for Charles Delafield, a prominent settler from New York who came here in 1843 and erected the first mill.

Nagawicka Lake, one of Waukesha County's largest lakes, is located in Delafield. Three miles long and three-quarter miles wide, the lake reaches a depth of 95 feet and is lined with summer homes and resorts.

OCONOMOWOC, Pop. 9,909

Although many pioneers were lured to California by gold, Charles B. Sheldon, Oconomowoc's first settler, ignored that pull and pursued Oconomowoc's growth instead. Coming here in 1837 he staked a claim along Fowler Lake's east bank on an old Indian trail which is now Main Street. Shortly

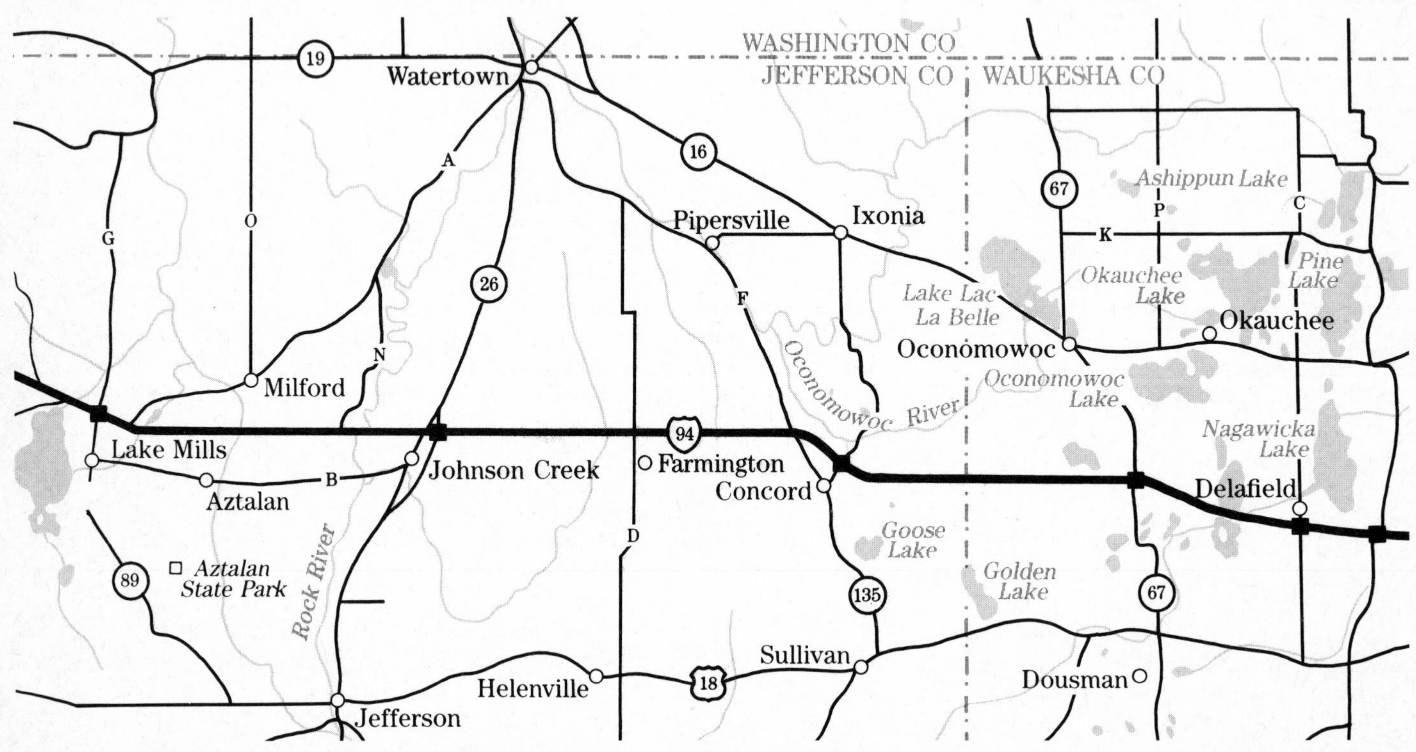

afterward, John S. Rockwell and A.W. Hatch, pioneer merchants from Milwaukee, bought an interest in the claim and jointly employed men to build a dam across the outlet of Fowler Lake. Here they erected a saw mill and later a grist mill.

In its early years Oconomowoc was overshadowed by Summit Corners, where mail was received, and by Delafield, an important point on the territorial road. However, due to John Rockwell's enterprising ways, the town soon prospered as a lumber center.

Oconomowoc is generally considered to be from the Potawatomi word Coo-no-mo-wauk, meaning "gathering of the water." The name is especially appropriate since the region's beautiful water bodies, particularly Lac La Belle and the Oconomowoc River, are among the largest examples of glacial kettles, ancient pits dug out by the retreating ice.

JEFFERSON COUNTY, Pop. 66,152

Jefferson County's land was acquired through treaty in 1833. Two years later the first settlers came from New England. By 1850, German immigrants made up 70-80 percent of the population.

Most of the German settlers here were either farmers or artisans, living mostly on lands west of the Rock River and south of the Scuppernong where there were more oak openings and fewer forests. The Germans had a very thorough approach to farming and paid more attention to their cattle and barns than any farmers around. Their strong knowledge of fertilizer produced bumper wheat crops and their economic influence was felt in many ways.

Although there is some doubt about the location of the first settlement, most reports claim it was in Hebron. There, on Christmas Day, 1835, The Rock River Claim Company staked a half section of land around Bark River's waterpower. David Sargent, left in charge for the winter, was joined the following spring by a blacksmith, Rufus Dodge, and Alvin Foster. Together the three men erected the county's first saw mill. This location was then known as Bark River Mills but changed to Hebron, after a church hymn in 1868.

Early settlers named the county in honor of President Thomas Jefferson.

WATERTOWN, Pop. 12,202

A little off the main route, Watertown is worth notice because it was the site of the country's first kindergarten. Founded in 1856 by Mrs. Carl Schurz, the school was run in the Froebelian method of teaching which Mrs. Schurz brought here from England. She had several children of relatives and neighbors as early pupils, then passed her ideas on to Elizabeth Peabody who became an active disciple of the movement.

SHSW

Watertown Lager Beer pouring contest at local saloon.

A 57-room octagon house, on the same grounds as the kindergarten building, was built in 1854 of solid brick. The largest single family residence of its day, the house was located at the western end of the old Watertown-Milwaukee Plank Road and had a beautiful view of the Rock River and surrounding countryside. Designed and built by John Richards of Hinsdale, Massachusetts, one of Watertown's first mayors, the house was occupied by Richards and his descendants until 1937. It is open daily from 10-5 and admission is charged.

Wisconsin brick cheese also originated here. Jacob Jossi, a German Swiss, began producing the cheese while living in Dodge County, then moved to Watertown where he continued to produce the famous cheese until his death in 1907.

Despite all these firsts, it's the stuffed-goose industry that really made Watertown famous. In 1879 William Stiehm of Johnson's Creek marketed a goose weighing 22 pounds. Until that time the heaviest goose weighed 18 pounds. Geese of 36-38 pounds are sometimes produced today. "Stuffing" geese, a practice of Northern Germany, is a rather simple method. Geese are penned up so they can hardly move, then force fed at short intervals. An immediate weight gain occurs, with the liver developing the most and large layers of fat accumulating throughout the body. For a time, Watertown was the only place in the United States where artificial fattening of geese was practiced. Many restaurants featured Watertown Goose as a house specialty.

An early name for Watertown was Ka-Ka-ree, an Indian word meaning "ox bow," which described the double bend in the Rock River here. Timothy Johnson, Watertown's first settler, originally called the town Johnson's Rapids but later changed the name to honor his hometown in New York state.

JOHNSON CREEK, Pop. 1,136

Watertown's first settler, Timothy Johnson, also came here with Charles Goodhue in 1837 and jointly claimed land where Johnson Creek now stands. Together they erected a dam and saw mill and named their settlement Belleville, after Charles Bell who owned much of the village's land. After mail was misdelivered to Belleville in Dane County, the town was renamed to honor its founder.

In early 1849 Johnson Creek took up the temperance cry. The Auger-Hole Society began in William Graham's wagon shop. Instead of signing a pledge to swear off alcohol, members bored a hole with an auger in a plank leaning against the side of the room and swore not to drink until the hole grew up. If a member ever violated his pledge, he was required to plug the hole with a wooden pin in the presence of his stronger brothers and sisters. The great demand for pins caused such a drain on Graham's supply of wagon timber that the society was forced to disband.

Johnson's Creek had two first-class stave mills and two stores in 1861. One mill belonged to G.C. Mansfield, the other to John Rose. The rest of the village consisted of a brick hotel owned by Charles Bell and a dozen houses. When the railroad arrived in 1859, the town grew rapidly, soon including two churches, three saloons, two blacksmith shops, two shoe shops, two wagon shops, two hotels, an agricultural implement dealer, a cheese factory, lumber yard, school and drug store.

AZTALAN

Timothy Johnson, Thomas Brayton and several companions first discovered what was then called The Ancient City. Traveling for seven days by canoe up the Rock River, the group staked claims in October, 1836, near the Crawfish River. Brayton's 16X20 foot rough log house, was outfitted to accommodate visitors, land seekers and/or hunting parties. Furnishings were made on the spot with an ax, auger and jackknife. Bedsteads were erected in the house corners by boring holes in the logs at a proper width and length for beds, then forcing rails into them. Upright posts reached to the roof in other corners, supporting end and side rails. Brayton's family arrived on July 1, 1837, after the house was completed.

From the beginning, Aztalan had high hopes of becoming Wisconsin's capital. The town had the county's first post office in 1837 and was a leading business and industrial center five years later. However, fate stepped in and Aztalan was a decayed village by the early 1850's. Since Aztalan was on the outdated territorial road, the stage coach disappeared. Hopes rose again when the railroads came, but the Chicago Northwestern Railroad missed the village by five miles in 1859 and again by two miles in 1881 when it completed the Milwaukee to Madison line. The new Wisconsin Central line

SHSW

Excursion of the Wisconsin Archeaological Society to Aztalan site, 1905. Photo/H.R. Clough.

also bypassed Aztalan and the once-thriving city rapidly declined. The Aztalan Baptist Church, built in 1852, is the only building remaining from the pioneer village. The first settlers are buried in the Aztalan-Milford Cemetery.

The village was named in 1836 by Judge N. Hyer who believed it was the original homeland of the Aztec Indians.

AZTALAN STATE PARK

Conical-shaped earth mounds, which archeologists believe are the remains of an ancient Aztec city, mark the entrance to this park. Twelve-foot high posts, part of a restored stockade, are an awesome reminder that this is a prehistoric sight, dating back approximately four centuries, long before Nicolet marked Wisconsin's founding.

In 1836 Judge N.F. Hyer discovered this site which continues to puzzle today's anthropologists. Naming it Aztalan after the Aztec Indians of Mexico, Hyer discovered three pyramidal mounds which appeared to occupy a rectangular area, 21 acres in size and enclosed by a three to five foot ridge. A series of smaller mounds seemed to serve as bastions in the walls of a fortress. Word of the discovery spread rapidly and the curious flocked to the mysterious site. Unfortunately, these fortune hunters and adventurers destroyed many of the original earthworks. The first expert excavation work took place in 1919.

The mound builders were apparently a nomadic tribe from the prehistoric village of Cahokia, near East St. Louis, Illinois. A fairly sedentary people, the tribe lived by growing corn and garden crops and by utilizing the area's animal and vegetable resources. Startling as it is, they evidently also practiced cannibalism.

After moving here, the Aztalanians immediately erected a stockade around the village to protect themselves from native "barbarian" Indians. The walls, 12 feet in the air, were surfaced with a mud and grass mixture to prevent the sun from cracking the mixture as it baked. The effect was much like today's plastered walls. Village houses were constructed in similar fashion.

Evidently, about 1,000 Indians lived in ancient Aztalan, which occupied both banks of the Crawfish River. However, only 22 skeletons have been unearthed in the small percentage of sifted earth. Although evidence shows that the village was burned to the ground and burial mounds revealed scores of impacted arrows and missing heads, the reasons for the violent end are unknown.

Fortunately, Wisconsin's conservation department continues to investigate this vast and unusual archeological find. Their restorative efforts may one day provide answers to the many questions about these ancient visitors.

SHSW

Richard's Octagon House, Watertown, 1870.

LAKE MILLS, Pop. 3,670

Capt. Joseph Keyes, born at Putney, Vermont, came to Wisconsin on a prospecting tour in June, 1836 and founded Lake Mills. He completed a log house in the fall of 1837 and built a saw and grist mill two years later, but life was far from easy. Supplies were scarce and settlers survived for weeks on bullhead and sheephead from the Crawfish River. Flour came from mills in Oconomowoc, Beloit or Rockford, Illinois and liquor was a luxury. An accident involving Keyes is a good example of the hardships many pioneers were forced to endure.

After obtaining about six pounds of flour from Thomas Brayton's place, Keyes was on his way home to Lake Mills. He decided to take a shortcut and ford the river. Somehow Keyes miscalculated the depth, walked into quicksand, and narrowly escaped drowning. The precious flour dissolved and he sat on the bank in tears.

Keyes moved north to Menasha in 1850 and erected one of that town's first saw mills. He was appointed register of the United States land office in 1859 and died in Menasha on September 17, 1874 at the age of 79, one of Wisconsin's most honored and resourceful pioneers.

Lake Mills was named by Keyes, probably because his mill was close to Rock Lake. The name was changed to Tyranena in 1870 but popular sentiment forced the change back to Lake Mills a year later.

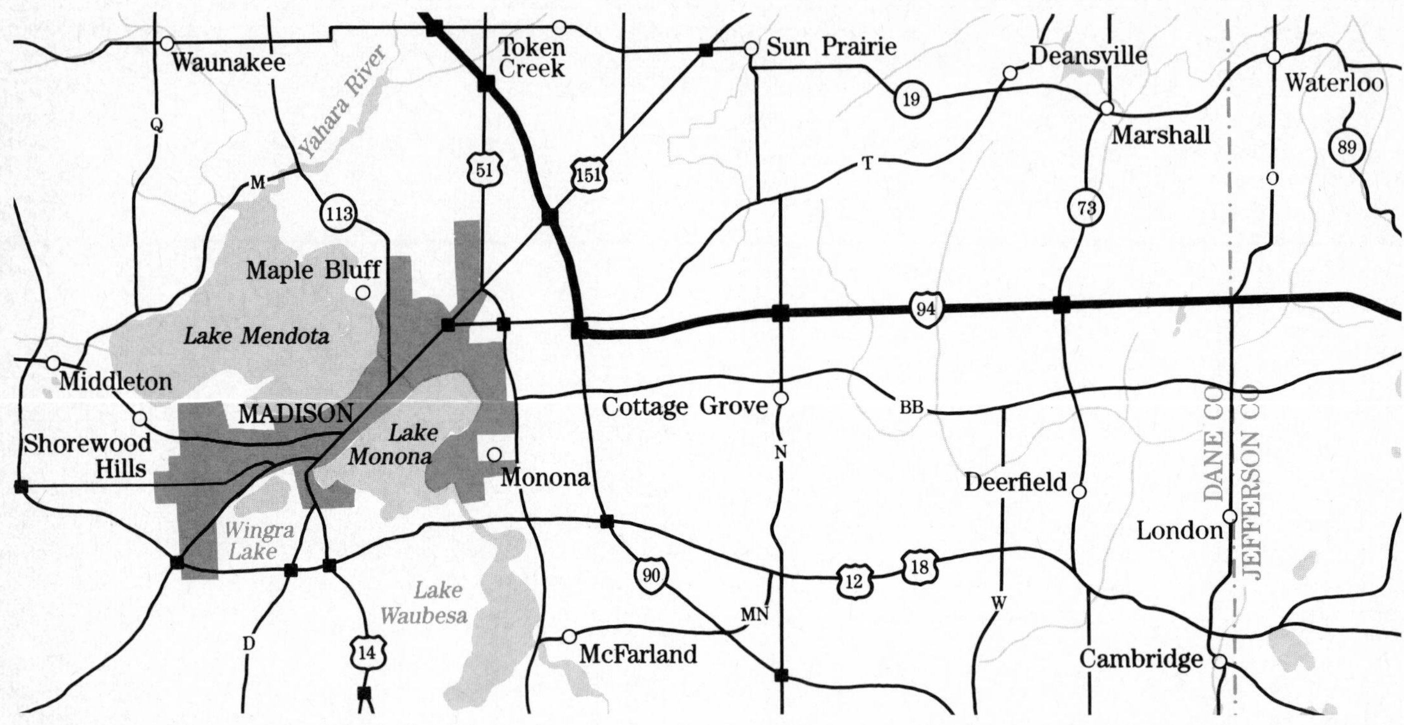

DANE COUNTY, Pop. 323,545

Dane County is made up of rolling hills of rich farmland laid down by ancient glaciers. The Yahara River, a tributary to the Rock River, flows from the Madison-area lakes and is the county's major river. The area's more rugged features, the Blue Mounds, are located in western Dane County and were noticed by English explorer Jonathan Carver in 1766. Carver left his canoe at the Ouisconsin (Wisconsin) River and crossed 15 miles south to the mounds. Climbing to the top of West Blue Mound, he surveyed the treeless prairie that faded into the autumn haze. About that same time Carver noticed that the Sauk Indians extracted large quantities of lead from these hills of a quality as "good as the produce of other countries."

It was this lead that attracted the first settlers in 1828. However, the white man was preceded thousands of years earlier by various Indian nations who maintained camps in the region. The mound builders, a people we know only by numerous mounds left throughout the state, came first. Many mounds resembled animals and were used for religious and burial ceremonies. Later, the Fox, Miami, Illinois, Sauk and lastly the Winnebago claimed these lands. In 1837, the Winnebago signed a treaty ceding all hunting and farming rights east of the Mississippi. Nonetheless, the Yahara Valley's beauty remained a secret during the early 1800's, known only to an occasional miner crossing from Green Bay to the lead mines of Galena and southwest Wisconsin.

Although miners and explorers used the Indian trails that crossed the Four Lakes Region, a need for roads developed with the coming of settlers. More importantly, the U.S. Army needed a supply road to connect Fort Howard at Green Bay to the military outpost of Prairie du Chien on the Mississippi. The Military Road began through Dane County about 1839. A well-worn Indian trail, following a ridge south of the Wisconsin River, was its route from Prairie du Chien to Blue Mounds. From there the road followed a trail northwest of Lake Mendota on its way to Portage. Mile-stakes kept travelers aware of their progress.

The Territory of Wiskonsin (early spelling) was created in 1836 and Dane County was established soon. James Doty, developer of Madison, named the county to honor Nathan Dane, creator of the Ordinance of 1787 which established the Northwest Territories, of which Wisconsin was a part.

BLACK HAWK WAR

After a miserable winter on the Iowa reservations, a band of Sauk and Fox Indians crossed the Mississippi in the spring of 1832. They believed life would return to normal if they returned to their Illinois homeland and peacefully raised crops. Unfortunately, whites saw the Indians only as invaders who were breaking a treaty. A series of tragic events followed, fueled by Indian naivete and a trigger-eager militia. Realizing their mistake, the Indians fled for their lives up the Rock River into Wisconsin, led by an aging Chief Black Hawk. The inept soldiers soon lost Black Hawk's trail in the marshy and largely unmapped Four Lakes Region.

However, soldiers en route to Portage for supplies, discovered Black Hawk and his band by chance. The Army began the chase anew, trying to save face for the humiliation they suffered when losing Black Hawk's trail. In July, 1832, the soldiers finally caught up with Black Hawk as his band tried to cross the Wisconsin River near what is now Sauk City. The Indians held off the soldiers long enough to allow most of the women, children and aged to cross the river, but this battle marked the beginning of the end for the near-starving band. Women and children were put into canoes and braves followed along the shore, but the sick, old and starving who couldn't keep up were left along the way.

This hungry, pathetic band eventually ended up at the mouth of the Bad Axe on the Mississippi, surrounded on all sides. Although Black Hawk tried to surrender to the steamboat Warrior standing off shore, his white flag was met with cannon fire, killing 23. Hoping someone would take pity on the women and children, Black Hawk sent them out in canoes and rafts. Sparing no one, the soldiers killed 150 men, women and children on the river. Black Hawk escaped, but was later captured by Winnebagoes and imprisoned first at Fort Crawford, Prairie du Chien and later at St. Louis. He was eventually paroled. The Black Hawk War, as it came to be called, was the only real confrontation between the Indians and whites of Wisconsin. Black Hawk was quoted as saying, "I loved my towns, my cornfields, and the home of my people..I fought for it."

MADISON, Pop. 170,616

Madison, Wisconsin's capital, is built on a narrow strip between Lakes Monona and Mendota. The University of Wisconsin is located on rolling hills overlooking Lake Mendota on the city's west side.

Early explorers found this lake region "beautiful, but uninhabitable," so the Madison area was left to the Winnebago Indian while the southwest part of the state was settled and mined for lead. After James Doty lost his appointment as federal judge in 1832, he became a land speculator. Appreciating the value of the Four Lakes region from previous explorations, Doty began to buy land. Doty and Steven Mason, Governor of Michigan Territory, owned most of the land between Lake Mendota and Monona. They platted a paper town and named it after James Madison, the fourth President of the United States who died in 1836 when the new town was platted.

With Black Hawk's capture and the death of many of his warriors in 1832, fears of Indians lessened and whites began settling this exciting new area west of Lake Michigan. The Territory of Wisconsin was created in 1836 and the first territorial congress was held in a small frame building at Belmont in southwest Wisconsin. Doty lobbied there to move

SHSW

East Washington St., Madison. Ca. 1890. Photo/E.W. Nielson.

the capital to his newly created town. Ironically, the lobbying took place several months before the first settler had even moved into Madison. That honor went to Eban Peck who moved here with his wife and son and built three log buildings where 122 Butler Street is today. These buildings were the center of activity in Madison for a time.

When work began on the capital, Peck's small hotel and tavern provided rest and refreshment for workers. It also became a stopover for the stage running between Portage and Mineral Point. Eleven years later, the first Madison capital was completed and many of the state's early meetings were held upstairs in the American Hotel. Legislators often complained about holding meeti?gs in the partially completed state house, telling of ice on the walls, frozen inkwells, poor accommodations (many had to sleep on crowded floors) and noise from squealing pigs kept in the basement. Several attempted to move the state government to Milwaukee where it was more "civilized."

Madison grew slowly and was a just a little town of about 40 buildings and 700 residents when Wisconsin became a state in 1848. Pigs, chickens, and cows reportedly strolled the capital grounds by day and residents stalked bear, wolves and deer by night. Leonard Farwell of Milwaukee arrived in Madison in 1847, pledging to shape the town into what a state capital is supposed to be. Streets were laid out and improved, thousands of shade trees were planted, marshes were drained and the decaying wood sidewalks were replaced. A canal was opened between Lakes Mendota and Monona where Farwell built a dam and grist mill. His projects eventually led him into the Governor's seat in 1852.

After 1850, railroads replaced the stage lines that led in and out of Madison and the city grew as the state's service center. Steamboats plied Lake Mendota, parks developed, and some 26 hotels were built to handle the many visitors. By 1916 this quiet area where the Winnebago once hunted and fished had a population of 32,000. That same year the new granite capital was completed, replacing the second capital which had burned in 1904. The capital, with its sections pointing to the four points of the compass, is topped by a dome that can be seen for many miles across the county.

The territorial government of Wisconsin passed a law in 1838 incorporating the University of the Territory of Wisconsin, but it wasn't opened until Wisconsin became a state. The first 20 students entered the old Madison Female Academy building in 1849, the same year 157 acres were purchased along the shores of Lake Mendota as the future university site. The rolling hills overlooking the lake were then a tangle of bushes and trees. The first permanent building, North Hall, was built in 1851 and served for several years as dormitory, classroom, mess hall and faculty living quarters. A new dormitory called South Hall was completed in 1855.

Buildings and courses were soon added but a financial problem developed because of insufficient funding by the state. The 1864 commencement was cancelled since only one student was qualified to graduate and most of the students had withdrawn from school to fight in the Civil War. The University almost went bankrupt and professors were asked to work at half-pay. However, by 1866 the University had reorganized and acquired more than 300,000 acres of land donated by the federal government. Today the University of Wisconsin in Madison has an enrollment of 43,000 students.

FOUR LAKES REGION

A nineteenth-century writer said lakes Mendota, Monona, Waubesa and Kegonsa, were the most beautiful, clear waters he had ever seen. "If these lakes were in any other county except where they are, they would be considered among the wonders of the world...It appears the Almighty intended them for only the children of the forest," he said. But the state's first settler, Ebenezer Brigham, passed across the hills that separate Mendota and Monona Lakes and predicted that a great city would some day be located here.

Before that city began, the lakes did belong to the children of the forest. For many years a large number of effigy mounds have been found near the lakes, attesting to their importance as hunting and camping grounds.

The Winnebago were the last Indian nation to live along these shores. Although white settlers called the lakes by numbers (Mendota was #4), the Winnebago called Mendota Wonk-shek-ho-mik-la meaning "where the man lies." They had large camps with as many as 500 people in a camp, along the lake. Around Lake Mendota, early archeologists became fascinated with the animal-shaped mounds used by earlier Indians to bury their dead or honor their gods. One large bird-shaped mound on the lake's north shore has a wingspan of more than 600 feet. In all, some 1000 mounds have been discovered in the Four Lakes Region. The Winnebago gave up their lands in the treaty of 1836 and slowly moved from the area and most of the mounds were destroyed by farming and Madison's development.

The lakes got their present names from a surveyor who platted the university campus in 1849. Mendota, Dakota (Sioux) for "where the waters mingle," was Lake #4. Monona is also an Indian word, but historians are unsure of its meaning. All Madison lakes lie along the Yahara River valley which drains southward into the Rock River. When glaciers passed through the valley, the debris, boulders and gravel blocked the river, creating this chain of lakes.

SHSW

A view of early Madison across Lake Mendota.

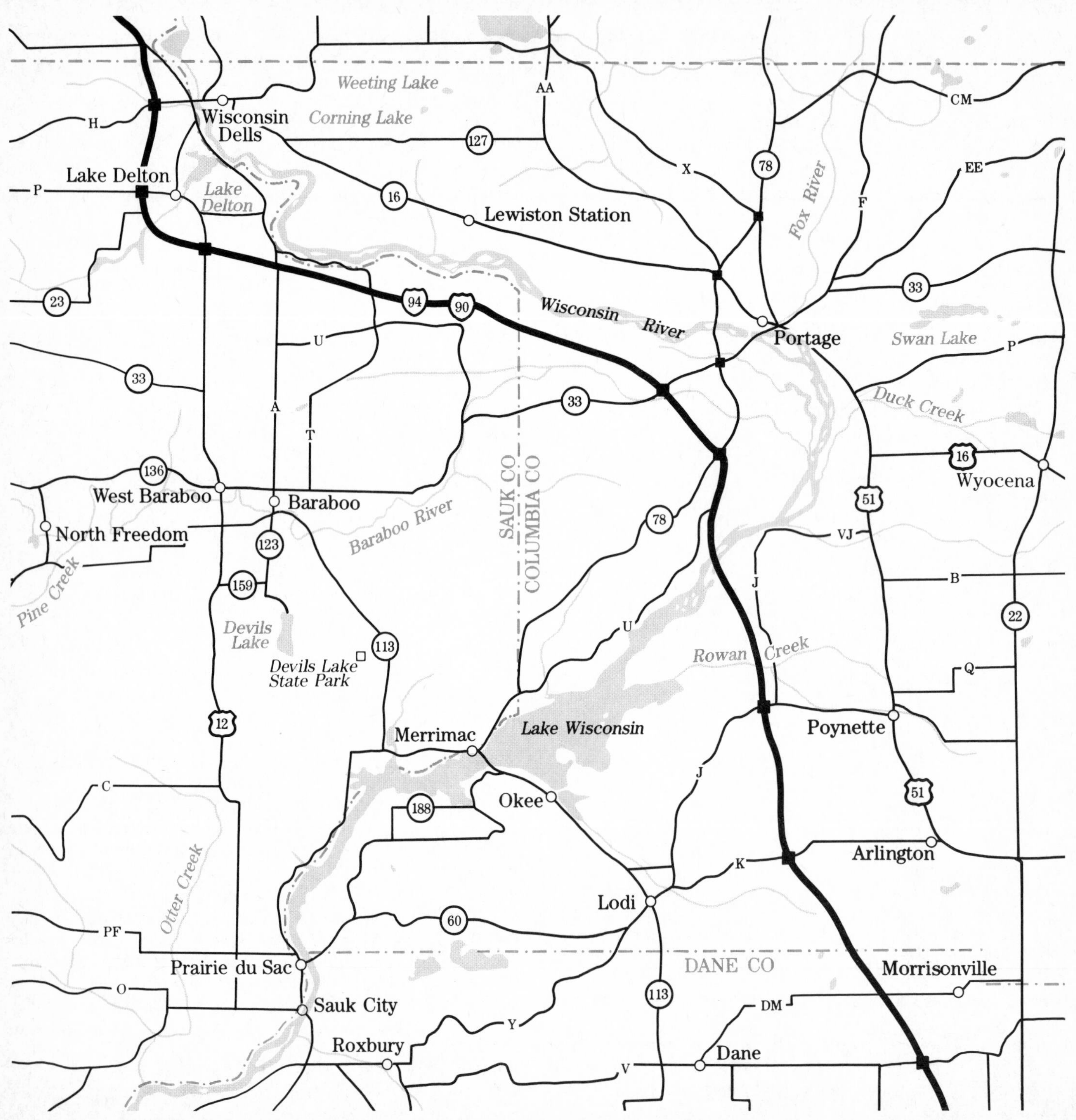

Weeting Lake
AA
CM
H
Wisconsin Dells
Corning Lake
127
78
X
EE
Fox River
F
P
Lake Delton
Lake Delton
16
Lewiston Station
23
94
90
33
Wisconsin River
Portage
Swan Lake
P
U
33
33
A
T
Duck Creek
16
Wyocena
136
West Baraboo
Baraboo
51
78
North Freedom
Baraboo River
SAUK CO
COLUMBIA CO
VJ
123
J
B
159
Pine Creek
22
U
Devils Lake
113
Rowan Creek
Devils Lake State Park
Q
12
Merrimac
Lake Wisconsin
Poynette
C
J
Okee
51
188
Arlington
K
Otter Creek
Lodi
60
PF
Prairie du Sac
DANE CO
Morrisonville
O
113
Sauk City
DM
Y
Roxbury
Dane
V

COLUMBIA COUNTY, Pop. 43,222

Columbia might be considered one of Wisconsin's most important counties for it was here that French explorers Joliet and Marquette discovered a critical link in their passage to the great Mississippi River.

Marquette's party traveled south on the Fox River from Green Bay to the Four Lakes Region in Columbia County in 1673 and stopped here, on the west bank of the Fox, at a large Mascouten Indian village near Governor's Bend in the town of Fort Winnebago, (then Portage County.)

Studying his map, Father Marquette had surmised, "we knew that there was, three leagues from the Mascoutens, a river entering into the Mississippi; we also knew that the point of the compass we were to hold to reach it was west-southwest, but the way is so cut up by marshes and little lakes that it is easy to go astray, especially as the river leading to it is so covered with wild oats that you can hardly discover the channel. Hence we had good need of our two Miami guides who led us safely to a portage of 2,700 paces and helped us to transport our canoes to enter this river.

"The river on which we embarked is called Meskousing (the Wisconsin); it is very broad, with a sandy bottom forming many shallows which render navigation very difficult. On the banks appear fertile lands, diversified with wood, prairie and hill. Here you find oaks, walnut, whitewood and another kind of tree with branches armed with thorns. We saw no small game or fish, but deer and moose in considerable numbers."

Marquette told in his diary that the party crossed the portage a few days after leaving the Mascouten village, launched their canoes on the broad Wisconsin's waters, and began their historic journey to the interior of America. A red granite memorial marks this famous crossing on highway 33 in Portage. The original Marquette-Joliet route is now marked as the Wauona Trail. Wauona is an Indian word meaning "place where one takes up his canoe and carries it."

THE MILITARY ROAD

Early in 1835 Secretary of War Lewis Cass ordered soldiers to "open, lay out and bridge a road" from Fort Howard at Green Bay via Fond du Lac and Fort Winnebago to Ford Crawford, near Prairie du Chien. The actual surveying and road building was supervised by Lt. Centre and James Duane Doty, later governor of Wisconsin. Doty was especially familiar with the Fox and Wisconsin river valleys because he had traveled through the territory years before as secretary to Cass.

The road entered Columbia County from the south near the town of Arlington, continued northeasterly to what is now Poynette, then ran due north to Fort Winnebago.

Although crudely constructed, the road was a great improvement over no road at all. It was built by cutting through timber land, clearing a track about two rods wide (approximately 33 feet), and setting up mile stakes. The stakes were set up with earth mounds on the prairies and with stone, when it could be found. On marshes and other low places, so-called corduroy roads were made by crossing timbers and covering them with brush and earth. Portions of the Military Road can still be traveled along County K in Columbia County near the Fort Winnebago cemetery in Portage.

SHSW

Carrying lunch to a logging crew, ca. 1900.

ARLINGTON, Pop. 440

The first important settlement in this community occurred in 1870 when the Madison & Portage Railroad was built through the eastern section. A depot was located here to provide farmers with facilities to ship grain and stock. A year later Sarah Pierce and David Bullen bought land and platted the village. The first house was built by Winslow Bullen and later George McMillan opened a store in the lower story.

Arlington became a banking and trading center for a very productive agricultural section. In time it contained a grain elevator, farm implement depot, lumber yard and a number of substantial businesses.

William McDonald laid out a smaller village within the town limits in 1846 and called it Inch, but no lots were sold, stores opened or houses built. By 1880, the place was a ghost town and people living in the neighborhood spoke of it as "once being called Inch, but now it's not even half an 'Inch.'"

POYNETTE, Pop. 1,447

James Duane Doty, later Governor of Wisconsin, bought 120 acres of land here in Feburary, 1837 and proceeded to lay out a village called Pauquette, after his friend and widely-known fur trader from Portage. The plat was subsequently vacated, however, and it was 1850 before anything further happened. At that time, a post office application was submitted and due to a clerical error they named it Poynette. No effort was ever made to change the name and when the village was replatted in 1851, it was named after the post office.

Poynette developed as an important trading center and included such establishments as a creamery, feed mill, sorghum factory, grain elevator and salting station for cucumber pickles.

For a number of years, Poynette flourished as a busy flour center, the Lower Mills built in 1858 and the Upper Mill in 1860. A brisk trade was enjoyed by the Lower Mills but when the Madison & Portage Railroad came through in 1870, better brands of flour came to the village than could be supplied by the local plants and growth was halted.

Things started to pick up again in 1871, however, when R.B. Wentworth & Company from Portage built a small warehouse and purchased their grain at Poynette. That summer Hugh Jamieson built a large elevator with a storage capacity of 12,000 bushes and went into the business of buying and shipping. This business later developed into the successful firm of Jamieson Brothers' Company which incorporated here in 1909.

PORTAGE, Pop. 7,896

When the early explorers and fur traders established this post in 1792 the route was marked by Indian trails, not roads. Despite that crude beginning, Portage flourished with the trade of furs, military supplies and wheat brought in through the Fox-Wisconsin waterway.

Nonetheless, many years passed before the first permanent settlers located here. It was a hot, July day in 1837, when Mr. and Mrs. Henry Carpenter moved into Portage. Looking for a place to raise a family and provide themselves with a little income, they decided to build a hotel on the Wisconsin River. A year later, the Carpenters and the rest of the community anxiously watched as the Portage Canal Company begin work on the ill-fated Portage canal. Work on the canal stopped abruptly but only after $10,000 had been spent.

By 1850, 13 years after the Carpenter's arrival, the city had 2,062 people and another 10,000 people, their teams and stock, portaged the Wisconsin River here. The town officially incorporated in April, 1854 naming itself for the important crossing point.

Thirty years after the Carpenters moved to Portage, government engineers finally completed the Portage canal, a project 75-foot wide and two-and-a-half miles long. Unfortunately, the continuing cost of dredging to maintain a channel for large boats in the shallow Wisconsin River proved prohibitive after the canal opened in 1876. That problem, along with increased competition from an improved railroad network, caused river shipments to wane. The Portage canal was closed finally in 1951 but remains a "stagnant reminder of the past."

FORT WINNEBAGO

The Fort Winnebago site had been a natural gathering spot for traders. In 1793, Laurant Barth and his family obtained Indian permission to transport goods at the portage. Soon after arriving, Barth built a cabin on the low land between the Fox and Wisconsin rivers, the first to be built by a white man in Columbia County. Five years later the French-Canadian Jean B. Lecuyer established a fur trading post at what is now Portage.

Finally, in 1820, John Jacob Astor, one of America's first millionaires, established a new fur trading post with Pierre Pauquette, a French-Canadian Indian who was Astor's representative for the American Fur Trading Company. Astor reportedly had much to do with the building of Fort Winnebago at the junction of the Portage Canal and the Fox River.

That location was selected because the narrow neck of land separating the Fox and Wisconsin rivers could be used as a portage between the two. Realizing the importance of this portage for travel and trade, the U.S. government established a military oversight here: ground was broken for Fort Winnebago in 1828.

The Indians felt doomed by the fort and protested accordingly but the military felt Wisconsin's interior waterways were now quite safe, with Fort Howard (Green Bay) at the northeast end of the route, Fort Winnebago at the portage, and Fort Crawford (Prairie du Chien) at the southwestern end.

Temporary barracks were soon built of tamarack logs rafted down the Wisconsin River from Pine Island, some 50 miles away. Stone Quarry Hill provided the stone and chimney bricks were found near the present Wisconsin River bridge. Major David Twiggs and three companies of Fort Howard soldiers completed the military post in Spring, 1830.

The young Jefferson Davis was one of Twigg's first lieutenants. Davis assisted in rafting logs from Pine Island to the fort and later made furniture which folks at the fort christened as original "Davis". He fell in love with Sarah, the daughter of Colonel Zachary Taylor from Ft. Crawford, but she died of malaria three months after their marriage. Heartbroken, Davis left Wisconsin and went south where he led the Confederate Army in the Civil War years later.

Only two buildings remain from this 4,000 acre military

post. The army surgeon's house, overlooking the famous Marquette landing site, is open daily, May-November, from 9 a.m. to 6 p.m. The second building is the Old Indian Agency House, built by the government in 1832 for Indian Agent John Kinzie and his bride, Juliette. This house is fully restored and open every day from sunrise to sunset. A small admission fee is charged at each building. Both are located one mile east of Portage on Highway 33. At the junction of 33 and County K is a white farmhouse, privately owned. From the road you can see a 10-foot stone foundation and a working windmill which mark the center of Fort Winnebago.

One last note about Ft. Winnebago as told by an early pioneer: "The flag-staff was raised at the left-hand entrance of the fort near what was then the Adjutant General's office; at the foot of the staff, a depth of 11 ft., was a box containing a sealed chest having in it the roster of the fort, mementoes, newspapers and several bottles of choice liquor. The discovery of the deposit will someday create no little wonder if not greatly gratify the exhumer." The state historical society's research office has never been notified of such a discovery!

SAUK COUNTY, Pop. 43,469

Formed as part of Dane County in 1840, this county was eventually renamed after the Sauk, or Ozaukee, Indians who once lived here. The name means, "people living at a river mouth" although another source claims the name means "yellow earth," and refers to the body stripes the Indians painted in yellow ochre. Sauk County is bounded by the Wisconsin River and the rugged dells region on the east and by the valleys and hills of the driftless area, a region untouched by

SHSW

Photo/Charland.

The "Dancing Annie," a lumber company wannigan, was the office and supply store for the Chippewa Lumber & Boom Company.

glaciers, on the west. The county's most conspicuous feature is the Baraboo Range, hills which rise gently from the great bend in the Wisconsin River and stretch northward to beautiful Devil's Lake.

The Baraboo River flows to the Wisconsin River from the west, cutting spectacular gorges through the thick sandstone. Seven miles east of Baraboo it flows through a 400-foot deep gorge. The area's limestone outcroppings have yielded many fossils deposited when pre-historic seas covered the continent millions of years ago. In central Sauk County, near Leland, is Natural Bridge State Park, site of an unusual 35-foot sandstone bridge carved by sand and wind erosion.

The first white settlers ventured here shortly after the Winnebago ceded their lands in 1837. However, Archibald Baker and Andrew Dunn settled near Baraboo before the treaty was ratified and Indians burned their crude cabin. Berry Haney, who operated a stage between Mineral Point and Portage, heard that the treaty would be ratified in a year, crossed the river at today's Sauk City and staked his claim. Since Haney knew of the Indian danger, he protected his buildings by constructing them of sod. This location became known as Haraszthy, then Westfield, and finally Sauk City.

Most early settlers worked in the forests, sending logs to the Mississippi lumber mills via the Wisconsin River. The town's first sawmill was built in 1842. Logging was eventually replaced by wheat farming and a number of grist mills developed along the county's rivers and streams. Iron ore was discovered in 1844, mining began about 1855, and a town named Ironton prospered. Smelters and machine shops were built and iron mining was an important part of the county's economy for many years. Ore was also found in the Baraboo Range in 1887 but offered little profit compared to the Penokee-Gogebic mines in northern Wisconsin which opened in the late 1800's.

SHSW

Devils Lake from the west bluff, 510 feet above the lake.

Fearing that settlements north in the Baraboo Valley were becoming politically powerful, Sauk Prairie lobbied to become the county seat. Sauk City and Prairie du Sac were also contenders. Prairie du Sac offered several corner lots to the county and swayed the county commissioners' vote in their favor. However, Baraboo Valley towns were dissatisfied with the outcome and another referendum was held in 1846. A mid-county area was chosen as a compromise and lots were sold to raise money for a courthouse. The new village was first named Adams, but was later named Baraboo after the river that flows through it. The river was named for a French trader who had a post where the Baraboo joins the Wisconsin River.

DEVILS LAKE STATE PARK

This region of Wisconsin was once covered with mountains known as the Archean Range. Similar to the Rockies of today, this range was worn down to a level plain over millions of years and only the Baraboo hills remain.

Wisconsin was covered with ancient seas and a thick layer of sediment was deposited, creating the sandstone that overlies the region. During the more recent ice age, glaciers pushed down intermittently for thousands of years across much of the state. The most recent incursion of these glaciers ended only 10-12,000 years ago and blocked this deep valley which was once a channel of the Wisconsin River. The river was displaced to the east and this valley basin filled with water and became known as Devil's Lake.

The rugged hills and stone formations surrounding the lake were the source of many Indian legends. The Indians knew the lake was deep (at 44 feet, the deepest in Sauk County) and thought it reached down to the demons in the earth. Stories were handed down about giant birds that hurled lightning bolts at the water monsters below, bolts which were the source of energy that shattered the rocks along the surrounding cliffs. Thus the lake became known as Devil's Lake. Winnebago tribes thought more highly of the lake and called it Tawak-cun-chuk-dah, meaning, "holy or spirit lake." Because this area was holy to the Indians, many burial mounds have been found in the park. Some were effigy mounds, formed into shapes of animals they felt were sacred or important. Devil's Lake State Park, created in 1911, is Wisconsin's largest state park and one of its most scenic.

CIRCUS AT BARABOO

Five brothers from Baraboo named Ringling got started in the circus world when they developed a small juggling and musical act in 1882. By 1884, the act was called "Ringling Bros. Grand Carnival of Fun" and toured Wisconsin, Minnesota, Dakota Territory and Iowa. The Ringling's shows were held in concert halls and earned more than $800 that first summer. The next summer they held their first outdoor circus which included nine wagons (no bandwagon) and a 49 X 90 foot tent. Year after year the circus opened the summer touring season in Baraboo and continued to grow in size. In 1888, it was renamed the "Ringling Bros. Stupendous Consolidation of Seven Monstrous Shows" and took to the rails with the development of railroads. The circus soon consisted of 22 railroad cars carrying elephants, horses and other animals. The Ringling's suffered through rainy seasons, train accidents and occasional fights with local men. In 1891 a battle took place between circus workers and local residents in Bolivar, Missouri.

A strong rivalry developed between the Ringling and Barnum & Bailey circuses in the late 1800's. Often the shows played opposite each other, creating strong competition and tense encounters. Each tried to outdo the other with their animal acts. The Ringlings bought out their competition in 1907, but ran the two circuses independently until they were merged into the "Greatest Show on Earth" in 1919. Baraboo served as the winter quarters for the circus until 1918. One interesting event happened in 1911 when the circus was canceled at McCook, Nebraska. The train pulled into town with the animal wagons facing the wrong side: there was no way to unload the animals. In 1915 Al Ringling built a $100,000 theater in Baraboo which he donated to the city. Today it is used as a movie theater.

In 1959, a museum was created in Baraboo to capture the golden years of the circus. The Circus World Museum is located along the Baraboo River at the old winter quarters area of the Ringling Circus and includes 27 buildings that contain circus acts, animals and memorabilia. A circus library houses news items, thousands of photographs, posters and historical data on the world's circuses.

WISCONSIN DELLS, Pop. 2,521

An Indian legend tells of a giant snake that slid down along the path of the Wisconsin River on its way to the Mississippi. The weight of the snake cut and pushed aside the rocks, creating a seven mile chasm which is now one of Wisconsin's major tourist sites. Geologists know that the dalles, a French word meaning "slabs of rock," were created by the Wisconsin River which carved the deep channel through the sandstone plains of central Wisconsin as it drained the retreating glaciers 10,000 years ago.

The gorge ranges from 50 to 100 feet deep with sides so steep that early travelers found it impossible to land a boat. Today the dalles are divided into two parts, Upper and Lower, separated by an hydroelectric dam. The unusual formations are caused by resistant sandstone and the erosive effects of the river. As logging started along the Wisconsin River and its tributaries such as the Lemonweir, boom towns sprang up along its banks. Most logging activity centered at Newport, five miles below the dalles settlement of Kilbourn. (Kilbourn later became known as the Wisconsin Dells.) However, Newport's vitality was diminished in the late 1850's when Byron Kilbourn brought his Chicago, Milwaukee, St. Paul & Pacific Railroad across the Wisconsin River to the town named after him. Kilbourn grew rapidly, while Newport died almost overnight. Many of Newport's buildings were hauled to Kilbourn which became an important logging supply point along the Wisconsin River.

SHSW

Ringling Bros. Circus elephants at Baraboo, ca. 1900.

Over the years, Kilbourn's city fathers realized that the village's name didn't describe the beauty of the dalles. So in 1931, they named it Wisconsin Dells in hopes of attracting more tourists. Their dreams were fulfilled and the area has become highly commercialized, with boat rides, golf courses, motels and many other tourist attractions. In addition, the region has taken on many romantic names. The Jaws of the Dells—two immense rocks that stand on either side of the river—mark the entrance to the gorge. Other names include Chapel Gorge, Echo Cove, Devil's Elbow, Artist's Glen and many more.

Steamer "Dell Queen" in the narrows at the Dells of the Wisconsin River, 1885. Photo/H.H. Bennett.

NEWPORT GHOST TOWN

Five miles south of Wisconsin Dells on the Wisconsin River's west bank is the site of the old village of Newport. Joseph Bailey moved here from Ohio in 1849 and claimed 160 acres along the Wisconsin River, convinced that this was the ideal site for a future town. He, in turn, convinced Johnathan Bowman to help him acquire another 240 acres. Logs were already flowing down through the dalles and steamboats were able to ascend the river this far during high water. It was obvious that the railroad would soon extend into Sauk County so Bailey and Bowman met with Byron Kilbourn, who was president of the rail line and mayor of Milwaukee. The purpose of the meeting was to get assurances that the railroad would cross the Wisconsin River at their new town. After positive indications from Kilbourn, Newport boomed. Lot prices soared and 15 stores, three hotels and even a girl's seminary fashioned after Mt. Holyoke girl's college of Massachusetts were built.

In 1853, the state granted permission to build a dam across the river to harness power for a mill. During this time, Kilbourn secretly bought land north of Newport where he intended to have the railroad cross. His men went so far as to survey this new area at night, making soundings along the river by lantern to check the feasibility of a dam.

Word of Kilbourn's land purchases leaked and Newport settlers panicked. When the railroad reached the river, it was no surprise that the bridge was built north of Newport at the new town of Kilbourn. Within months, many of Newport's buildings were moved to Kilbourn. Bailey, Newport's founder, hung on for awhile, helping pilot log-rafts through the narrow dalles. Byron Kilbourn later became the subject of an investigation in which nearly a million dollars in bribes were paid to acquire favorable railroad grants. The scandal ruined Kilbourn, who later died in Florida.

There is little to remind people that a village of 2,000 once lived here, except for Dawn Manor, a stone mansion located along Lake Delton on County A. It was built in 1855 by Captain Abraham Vanderpoel, a friend of President Lincoln who signed the Wisconsin Constitution.

LAKE DELTON, Pop. 1,158

Three miles south of Wisconsin Dells is Lake Delton. The small village began in 1850 when Jared Fox and the Topping brothers built a dam and sawmill here. Alexander Vosler built a small hotel to house the mill workers and eventually opened a more substantial structure called Delton House. Lake Delton grew around its mill, foundry, stores and post office, and was known for awhile as Loretto, after the postmaster's wife. Referring to the village, an historian wrote, "The locality is an extremely healthy one and death is a rare visitor. But nevertheless in case of accident, the citizens of Delton are supplied with a cemetery."

Kilbourn Railroad Station, ca. 1890.
Columbia County Historical Society

SHSW

Mirror Lake dam and roller mill. Photo/Bert De Koeyer

SHSW

Afternoon picnic at Stand Rock. Photo/H.H. Bennett.

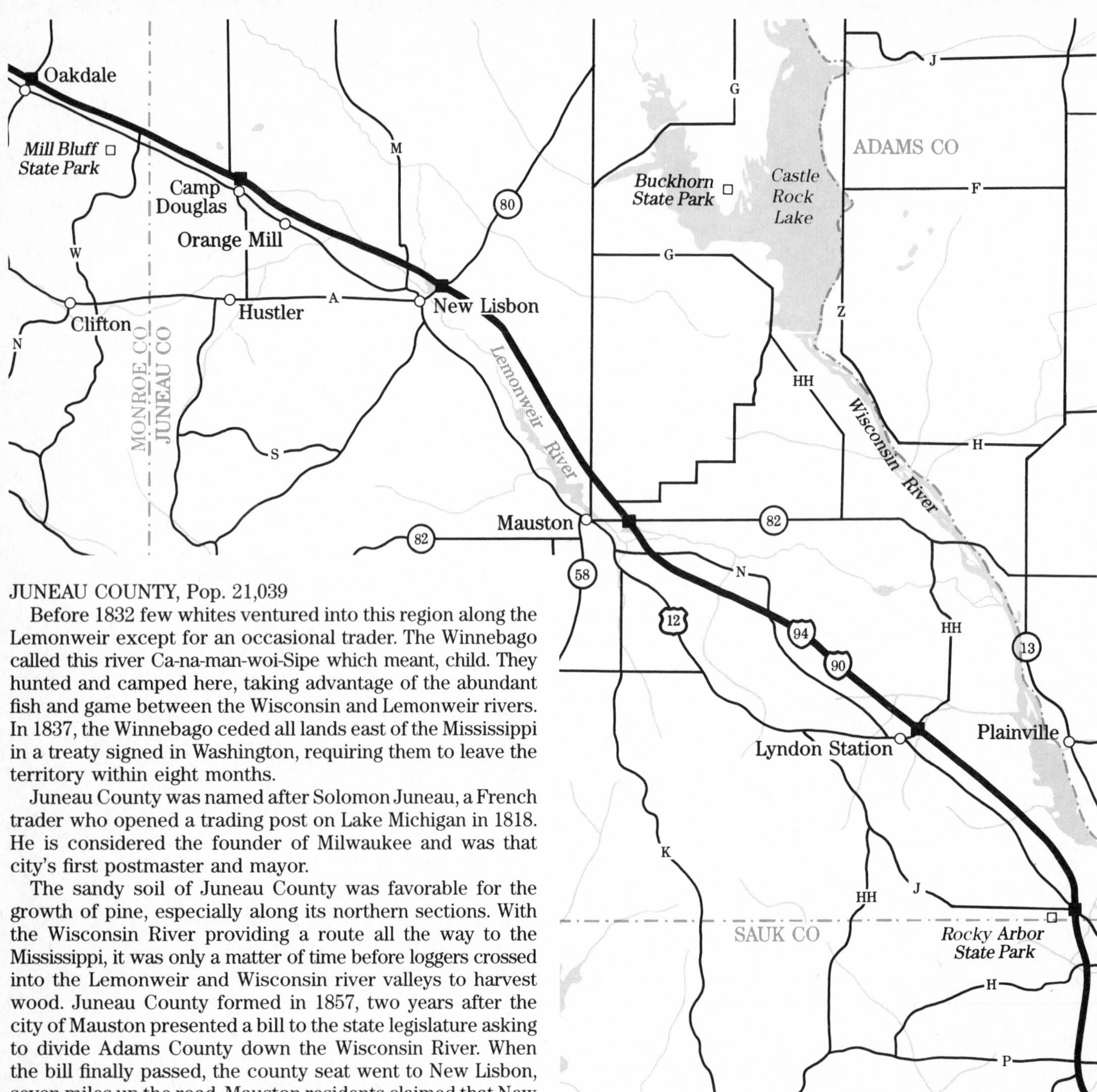

JUNEAU COUNTY, Pop. 21,039

Before 1832 few whites ventured into this region along the Lemonweir except for an occasional trader. The Winnebago called this river Ca-na-man-woi-Sipe which meant, child. They hunted and camped here, taking advantage of the abundant fish and game between the Wisconsin and Lemonweir rivers. In 1837, the Winnebago ceded all lands east of the Mississippi in a treaty signed in Washington, requiring them to leave the territory within eight months.

Juneau County was named after Solomon Juneau, a French trader who opened a trading post on Lake Michigan in 1818. He is considered the founder of Milwaukee and was that city's first postmaster and mayor.

The sandy soil of Juneau County was favorable for the growth of pine, especially along its northern sections. With the Wisconsin River providing a route all the way to the Mississippi, it was only a matter of time before loggers crossed into the Lemonweir and Wisconsin river valleys to harvest wood. Juneau County formed in 1857, two years after the city of Mauston presented a bill to the state legislature asking to divide Adams County down the Wisconsin River. When the bill finally passed, the county seat went to New Lisbon, seven miles up the road. Mauston residents claimed that New Lisbon had unfairly offered corner lots to legislators and the county seat battle continued for several years. In 1859, another vote was taken and 500 more people voted than lived in the county. Mauston claimed fraud and the courts finally awarded it the county government that same year.

LYNDON STATION, Pop. 375

Charles Clemens, a logger, became one of the area's first settlers in 1850. After leaving to serve as a sharpshooter in the Civil War, Clemens returned to Lyndon but found it too crowded for his tastes. He moved to northern Wisconsin and continued to work as a logger.

During the late 1860's, the area around Lyndon Station became known as the "greatest hops district in the United States." Thousands planted the crop, used to flavor beer, and made as much as 50 cents a pound. Each August the countryside was covered with the yellow-green vines clinging to their poles. But the bubble burst in 1868, when the price of hops plummeted to 15 cents a pound and many lost their money.

MAUSTON, Pop. 3,284

In the winter of 1838-39, John La Ronde and Judge S. Walsworth tried to establish a trading post here to sell goods to the Winnebago Indians. Although the Winnebago had given up their lands in a treaty the year before, a number continued to live in and around the Fort Winnebago (Portage) area. The trading post was the only white civilization here until J.B. McNeil and two others decided to log pine along the Lemonweir. They gathered men and supplies and built a dam and mill that began operating the following year. Gen M. Maughs bought the mill in 1848 and finally moved here with his family in 1851 to personally take charge. The town was platted and called Maughstown, but was later shortened to Mauston. Located in the midst of a rich agricultural area, Mauston became a marketing and shipping point when the Chicago, Milwaukee, St. Paul & Pacific came through after 1858.

The Mauston Mill ground 150 barrels of flour a day and used five millstones powered by the Lemonweir River. The town also had the Runkel & Co. Brewery. A historian noted that "Although Mauston stands at the head of the county in temperance and good order...the Runkel Brewery is the most successful business in the village." Mauston also boasted about the county jail built in 1879. Heralded as the state's most secure and complete structure, the jail had hot and cold running water and a furnace that heated the entire building.

NEW LISBON, Pop. 1,390

In the fall of 1837, John Kingston and Samuel Pilkington left Racine on the shores of Lake Michigan to explore the Lemonweir Valley. The Winnebago had signed away these lands that same year and the men saw potential in starting a logging business near the Lemonweir River after hearing rumors of an extensive pine forest. They traveled up the frozen Rock River that December, passed through the lake area that would later become Madison, and bought supplies at a trading post at Portage. On the seventh day of their journey, with supplies running out, they breakfasted on two crackers at a place on the Lemonweir where the Winnebago usually maintained winter camps. The location later became New Lisbon. Surveying the valley, Kingston and Pilkington decided there wasn't enough pine to be profitable so they started their long journey back.

Five years lapsed before any logging actually got started on the Lemonweir. Three men named Smith, Wilson and Allen began cutting trees above New Lisbon in the fall of 1842. They constructed a boom at New Lisbon to catch logs being sent down the river. Wilson built the town's first frame house in 1844 and he was the only one of the three to finally call this place home. Others soon followed, but the main interest was logging and not developing a town. It was 1851 before settlers came here for farming and other endeavors. A post office named Mill Haven was finally established in 1853 and was located a mile south of today's New Lisbon.

When Amasa Wilson got around to platting a village near his mill, the post office was moved here. The new village retained the name of Mill Haven until 1868 when it was

SHSW

Camp Douglas, 1905.

renamed after Lisbon, Ohio. Though farming was increasing along the valley, the Lemonweir mills were New Lisbon's economic base for many years. In addition the town had a flour mill that ground 15,000 bushels of wheat a year and boasted three wagon and sleigh manufacturers. It's location at the junction of two branches of the Chicago, Milwaukee, St. Paul & Pacific Railroad was also important to the village's growth.

CAMP DOUGLAS, Pop. 589

When the Chicago, Milwaukee & St. Paul trains began running between La Crosse and Milwaukee, they needed firewood to keep the steam boilers running. James Douglas set up a woodcutting camp here in 1864 to provide the locomotives with fuel. It was a busy railroad route and Douglas soon had many men cutting for him. Their saws were powered by an unusual treadmill turned by horses.

Douglas had competition a short distance down the tracks from a man named Temple who was also cutting cordwood. Undaunted, Douglas placed a sign along the tracks so engineers would have no doubt that they had arrived at Camp Douglas. Soon there were two signs–one at Camp Temple, another at Camp Douglas.

When the West Wisconsin was built down from Tomah in 1873, it crossed just east of Camp Douglas. Though James Douglas had long departed, the crude collection of homes that had gathered by the tracks moved down to the newly-built depot at the railroad junction. Camp Williams Military Reservation is northeast of Camp Douglas. Started in 1900 it was the birthplace of the Red Arrow Army Division from Wisconsin and Michigan. The 32nd Red Arrow Division fought in France during World War I and in the South Pacific in World War II. Today the field and accompanying airport is used in National Guard training.

MILL BLUFF STATE PARK

A number of buttes and mesas rise above this region's sandy plain similar to the flat-topped ridges and cliffs found on the Great Plains and in areas of the Southwest. These mesas are capped with a resistant sandstone layer which protects the softer stone underneath. When the resistant rock eventually weathers away, the formation slowly becomes a rounded hill. East of Sparta, there are several of these old buttes and mesas, which are now in the final stage of erosion as rounded hills. The buttes range from 100 to 300 feet in height. This area is typical of Wisconsin's topography before the ice ages. Mill Bluff State Park includes some of these prominent mesas and has 21 wooded campsites.

MONROE COUNTY, Pop. 35,074

Monroe County was formed in 1854 and named after James Monroe, the fifth president of the United States. It is part of the driftless area which was not crossed by glaciers so the county's streams and rivers have more mature valleys than many other areas of Wisconsin. Because so much of the county is drained by rivers and streams, there are few lakes.

This region of steep hills and ridges is known as coulee country. A range of hills running north and south through central Monroe County formed a barrier to the railroads and a 3,000 foot passage eventually had to be tunneled through the ridge.

The Fox Indians once lived along these valleys but moved further south along the Mississippi River during 1700's. Then the Winnebago Indians expanded their territory from the Green Bay area. In a treaty signed in 1837, the Winnebago gave into pressure by the whites and ceded all their Wisconsin lands. However, many of them refused to leave the state for reservations in the west.

The county's first settler, Esau Johnson, came up the Kickapoo River in 1842 following a rumor of oil in this region. There wasn't any oil, but Johnson fell in love with the Kickapoo Valley. Eager to get his family, he hollowed out a tree, made some paddles and canoed back down to Crawford County to get them. The county was surveyed in 1849 and settlement began to increase when a new state road was built through here the same year. The road ran from Prairie du Chien through La Crosse, Sparta, then to Black River Falls, Eau Claire and finally Hudson. Shortly after that, another road was built following an old Indian trail from Portage down through Sparta and on to the Mississippi.

These roads helped farmers and settlers who had previously traveled by river or slow-moving oxen down to Prairie du Chien or La Crosse for their mail and supplies. When Monroe County was separated from La Crosse County in 1854, Sparta became the county seat.

A large amount of marsh land in Monroe County was placed under cranberry cultivation. The marshes have to be ditched, drained and flooded during the proper times of the season. The cranberry is one of the last fruits in the fall to be picked and during the autumn months, the bogs are occasionally flooded to protect plants from frost.

OAKDALE

When the railroad came through, a small village formed around a section house and became known as Leroy Station. When their letters and parcels were delivered to Elroy, 25 miles to the south, the town changed its name to Oakdale after a nearby stand of oak.

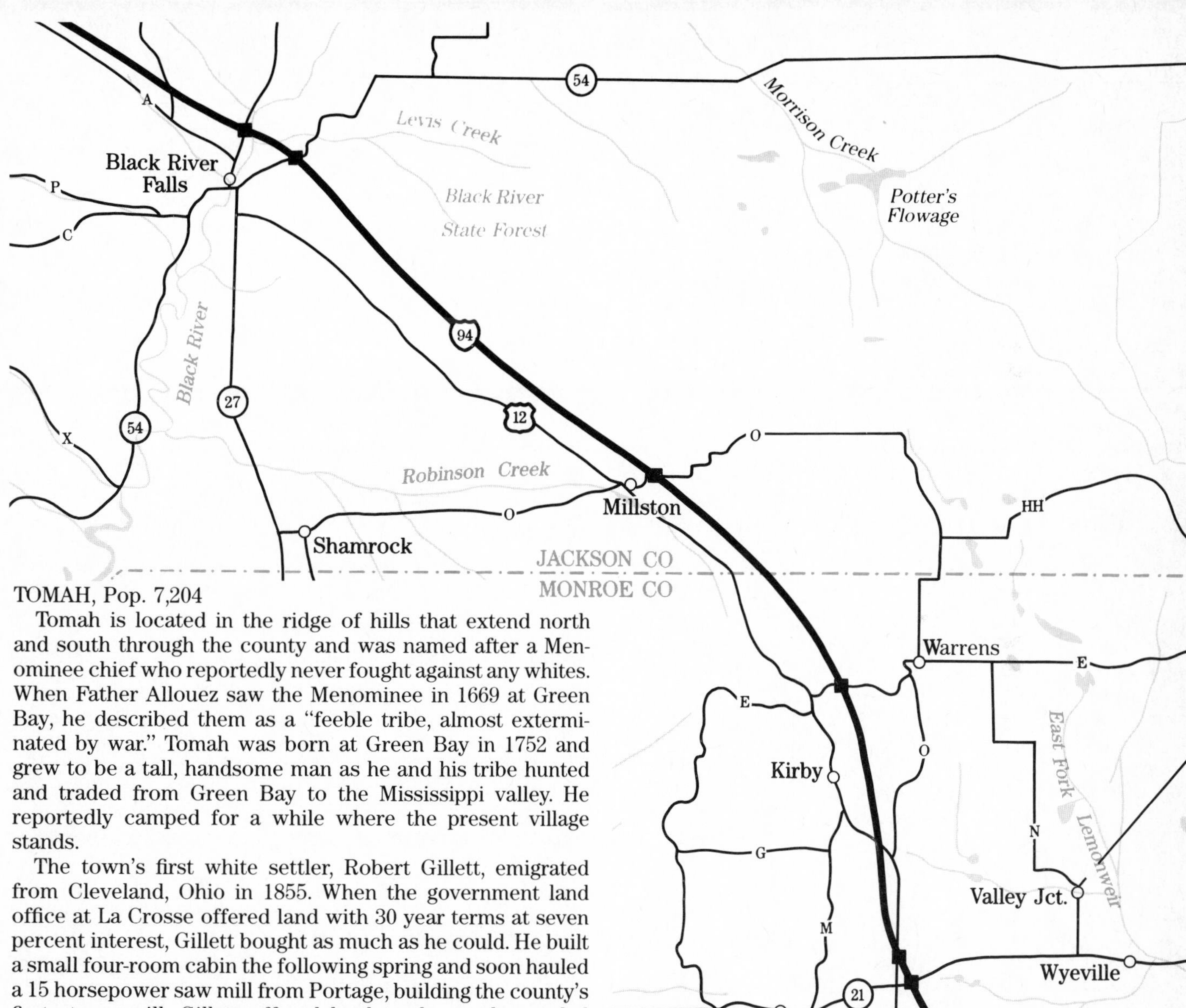

TOMAH, Pop. 7,204

Tomah is located in the ridge of hills that extend north and south through the county and was named after a Menominee chief who reportedly never fought against any whites. When Father Allouez saw the Menominee in 1669 at Green Bay, he described them as a "feeble tribe, almost exterminated by war." Tomah was born at Green Bay in 1752 and grew to be a tall, handsome man as he and his tribe hunted and traded from Green Bay to the Mississippi valley. He reportedly camped for a while where the present village stands.

The town's first white settler, Robert Gillett, emigrated from Cleveland, Ohio in 1855. When the government land office at La Crosse offered land with 30 year terms at seven percent interest, Gillett bought as much as he could. He built a small four-room cabin the following spring and soon hauled a 15 horsepower saw mill from Portage, building the county's first steam mill. Gillett offered land to those who settled nearby and his small crude barn housed a school and, in 1857, the first church service. The school soon got its own log cabin, but had only eight students in attendance.

Settlers who wanted government land had to improve the property, which meant building a cabin. Many built the simplest of shelters, using poles to hold a thatch roof, then went to the La Crosse land office with a friend who verified that they had indeed built a house and lived in it. Many obtained land for speculation without expending much energy.

Tomah's business district began in 1857, when the first store and blacksmith shop were opened. The first town officers were elected and held meetings in a village house, paying the owner $3 for its use. The Milwaukee & St. Paul Railroad reached here in 1858 and within a few months connected Tomah with the Mississippi and Lake Michigan. At this point, in 1859, residents finally convinced the government that they needed a post office. Another boost to the local economy came when the Tomah & Lake St. Croix Railroad Company was built from Tomah to Hudson. It was completed to Hudson in 1871. That same year Jay Cooke's financial empire collapsed. Cooke had his hand in railroad projects from Superior to Washington state and his collapse and the failure of his railroad reportedly had a devastating effect on Tomah, which took many years to recover.

The large Veterans Medical Center located at Tomah is a complex which began as a one-building Indian school in 1890. Tomah is also the hometown of Frank King who originated the nationally distributed comic strip "Gasoline Alley" in 1918. King's comic strip centered around America's fascination with the automobile and whose characters aged in real time.

TUNNEL CITY

This small settlement was founded around the Blue Ridge Trail, a stage road which connected the small towns of the La Crosse River Valley during the 1850's. When the railroad reached up from La Crosse, the grade here was too steep to cross. Landowners north of Tomah offered land to the railroad and they decided to cross the ridge there instead. For awhile, the trains slowly climbed the hills to the small collection of buildings at this stage stop which later became known a Tunnel City. The passengers were then hauled by wagon across the crest, to a train waiting on the other side. Someone eventually decided to put a capstan at the top, using oxen to turn it, and pull the small train over the top of the hill. Nonetheless, the need for a tunnel was obvious and work began on a 1,700 foot long passage. Hand tools and wheelbarrows were used and the first of three tunnels was not completed until 1859. They were called 1,2, and 3. Number 3, located near Sparta, is the longest at 3,800 feet and cost $1 million which was prohibitive in those days.

WARRENS, Pop. 300

Located near the East Fork of the Lemonweir River, this village got its start when the Tomah & Lake St. Croix was completed to here in 1863. George Warren and James Gamble built a saw mill which became known as Warren's Mill. Around 1890 the village was renamed Warrens.

JACKSON COUNTY, Pop. 16,831

Jackson County has a varied topography of forests, hills, and prairie. The central plains of Wisconsin lie in the eastern part of the county, about 15 miles east of Black River Falls. This region of level ground has areas of sand and scrub timber which resembles the West in some places. The occasional ridge, butte or mesas give an un-Wisconsin like feel to the land. A number of marshes also dot this area and cranberries grow wild.

In southwest Jackson County lies the coulee country of the Mississippi and Black River valleys, an area untouched by glaciers. Here the streams and rivers have eroded a region of valleys and narrow ridges unaltered by the ice age. The word coulee describes a valley where water runs only during wet seasons.

When French trappers traveled along the Black River, they found Winnebago Indians living in the region. They thought that the Winnebago had once lived on either Pacific or Gulf coasts because their name means "men from the strong-smelling water." The fertile Black River Valley marked the northern boundary of their territory. To the north were the Ojibwe who continued to force the Dakota into Minnesota during the early 1700's. The Winnebago Nation eventually fell to the pressure of whites who wanted more land opened for logging and settlement. In a treaty signed in 1837, the Winnebago ceded all lands east of the Mississippi and promised to move to reservations in Iowa. From there they were removed to two different locations in Minnesota, then displaced to Nebraska and the Dakotas.

The county was formed in 1853 and named after Andrew Jackson, the seventh president of the United States (1829-1837). Black River Falls, which developed around sawmills on the Black River, was named the county seat and became the area's trade center. The Tomah & Lake St. Croix Railroad crossed diagonally through the county in 1869 and was completed to the St. Croix River at Hudson in 1871. It later became known as the West Central, the Chicago, St. Paul, Minneapolis & Omaha and finally the Chicago & Northwestern. Before the Interstate was built, the main route through west-central Wisconsin was U.S. 12 which paralleled the railroad northwest from Lake Delton.

MILLSTON

This small hamlet was once the home of Hugh Mills who owned many acres of timber here. Mills built a large house that houses loggers for a time during the lumber era. When the Tomah & Lake St. Croix Railroad was built through here in 1871, local Indians referred to this place as Big Gut Station, in reference to Mill's large stomach.

BLACK RIVER FALLS, Pop. 3,434

In 1818 Joseph Rolette led an expedition from Prairie du Chien into Winnebago territory. He finally stopped at the falls on the river the Indians called Black and built a small log mill, but he was soon driven off by unhappy Indians who burned his mill. It was 21 years before another settlement was attempted.

In the spring of 1839, Jacob Spaulding and the Wood brothers left Prairie du Chien for Rolette's old mill site. Upon arriving, they first built a large double cabin for themselves and their workers on the south bank of Town Creek. About 40 Indians came to visit Spaulding, led by Chief Menominee. After staying at the camp for a few days, the Indians came to the point of their visit. They wanted the white men to leave. With careful maneuvering, Spaulding and his crew got the Indians on one side of the cabin before drawing their guns, holding them at bay. Without further discussion the Indians departed.

During the winter of 1840 food ran low and everyone except Spaulding left camp. Spaulding survived by subsisting on elk and deer, but was thrown off the mill by the Wood brothers when they returned in the spring. With the help of the Prairie du Chien sheriff, Spaulding returned and was reinstated as a partner.

SHSW

Black River Falls, ca. 1890. Photo/ C.J. Van Schaick.

SHSW

Newly-arrived immigrants at Black River Falls.

Barron County H.S.

Waiting for the train at Stout's Spur, 1911.

That next spring, trouble brewed again. Mormons from Nauvoo, Illinois, came to the Black River Falls area and began cutting trees on Spaulding's property for a church they were building back in Illinois. Upset, Spaulding armed his men and forced the Mormons off his land. Feeling wronged, the Mormons sent to Nauvoo for men and guns, but they backed off when they learned that soldiers from Prairie du Chien would side with Spaulding and his men. They suddenly left the settlement for Illinois in 1844 when they learned that their leader, Joseph Smith, had been killed in Carthage, Illinois.

Black River Falls developed and remained a lumber town for many years. When the La Crosse land office opened in 1848, transfers were made to settlers at $1.25 an acre. Since logging 40 acres could make the owner $2,000 in profit, there was great incentive to exploit the area. Supplies for the growing number of logging crews were originally brought up the Black River from Prairie du Chien and consisted mostly of pork, flour, whiskey and tobacco. Flat-bottomed keel boats, about 60 feet long by five feet wide, were used and broad-shouldered men poled the boat against the current. It requiring about four days to make the trip. The loggers were most pleased with the supply of liquor and according to one historian, "Inebriety was the rule, sobriety the exception."

Lumbering was clearly the emphasis at Black River Falls. Up to 1847 the only real construction was a 18 x 26 boarding house where, 30 to 40 men slept each night in spoon fashion. That was also the year of the flood. The Black River overflowed its banks after a June rainstorm and most of the mills and booms were swept away. It took weeks to sort out everyone's logs from the tangled log jam downstream.

When the mail route was opened to Stillwater, Minnesota from Prairie du Chien in 1850, a branch office was opened at Black River Falls. It was run out of Albert Tuttle's house, the first house in town to wear a coat of paint. By this time a road connected Black River Falls, Hudson and Sparta. In 1857, when the court house was nearly completed, someone burned it down. It was 1862 before another was built. This structure included a jail which had one cell for women prisoners, one for the insane, one for the mild-type and one for those prone to violence. About this time a number of men were drinking in town and decided to dig up two blocks of main street with a plow. The melee ended when they broke into a feed store and poured oats and flour over each other.

By 1860, Black River Falls had only 500 people and most were involved with lumbering. That same year a fire started in the bowling alley and engulfed most of the town. "No one can realize the horrors of that night, nor the scene of gloom which greeted the gaze of citizens with the dawn...desolation was heaped up full and running over," wrote an eyewitness. But the village rebuilt and the population doubled in one year. The village included the Albion mill, a planing mill, the Spaulding carriage factory and an opera house for plays and lectures. Iron ore was smelted at Black River Falls in 1856 and later in 1886, but the ore was not best quality and the process was too expensive to be profitable.

At Bell Mound rest stop, a path leads to the top of 180 foot Bell Mound which offers a panoramic view of Black River State Forest and the open-pit mine where low-grade iron ore is extracted. This operation was started in 1969 and shipped 2,800 tons daily for a time.

FOREST FIRE

South of Black River Falls the Interstate crosses a forest that was decimated in a fire that started on a windy afternoon in April, 1977. The fire crossed the Interstate in three different locations and by the time the fire burned out, 17,600 acres and 14 homes had been destroyed. The aspen and oak are already growing up through the charred stumps and this region will hardly show evidence of a fire in 50 years.

SHSW

George Hull's mill at Hixton, ca. 1880.

HIXTON, Pop. 364

John L. Hicks and several friends started out from Galesville in the spring of 1854 intending to walk to Minnesota for a new beginning. Millions of acres of Minnesota land had been opened for settlement in 1851 by treaties signed with the Dakota Indians. However, when Hicks camped for the night along the headwaters of the Trempealeau River, he decided that this shallow valley would be his home. His friends continued on while Hicks built a 12 x 16 foot shack that he lived in for some months.

A number of farmers followed Hicks to the valley and the little hamlet became known as Hixton, the shortened version of Hick's Town. But the town didn't start to grow until the Green Bay & Western came here en route to the Mississippi to ship wheat coming off the Minnesota fields. The gently sloping Treampealeau River valley provided the perfect rail route for crossing the rugged coulee country. Hixton was able to support two flour mills during the 1870's.

OSSEO, Pop. 1,474

Several Richland County farmers moved here in 1857 after it was rumored that the railroad would come through this part of Trempealeau County. A village was platted into 116 blocks. W.H. Thomas was one of the first to settle here and the hamlet had only a few shanties and a small hotel for the first few years. One side of Thomas' house was a small general store, the other side was the school where four girls took their lessons. The post office was a bit south at Beef River Station, a stage-stop on the Sparta to Eau Claire route. The post office shared space in a weathered log cabin with a saloon and Silkwood, the postmaster, kept all the mail in his desk drawer.

The post office was moved to Osseo from the Beef River Station in 1867 and the stage line was diverted to the main village as a result. There are a few interpretations of the meaning of the name Osseo. One is that an early settler took the Spanish word oso meaning "bear," to name the town. Others say the name is of Indian origin from the word ossi, meaning "stony place or place of river and stone." The word Osseo is also used in Longfellow's "Song of Hiawatha."

To Osseo's disappointment, the railroad didn't reach here from Fairchild until 1887. It was a small line built and owned by N.C. Foster of Fairchild. In 1891, Osseo was destroyed by fire, but was rebuilt shortly after. More recently, in 1922, Clyde Van Gorden wired together 1000 wet cell batteries to provide the first amateur radio broadcast of WTAQ. This 200 watt station, with an antenna strung from a windmill, carried a piano and cornet duet by Frank and Camilla Smith.

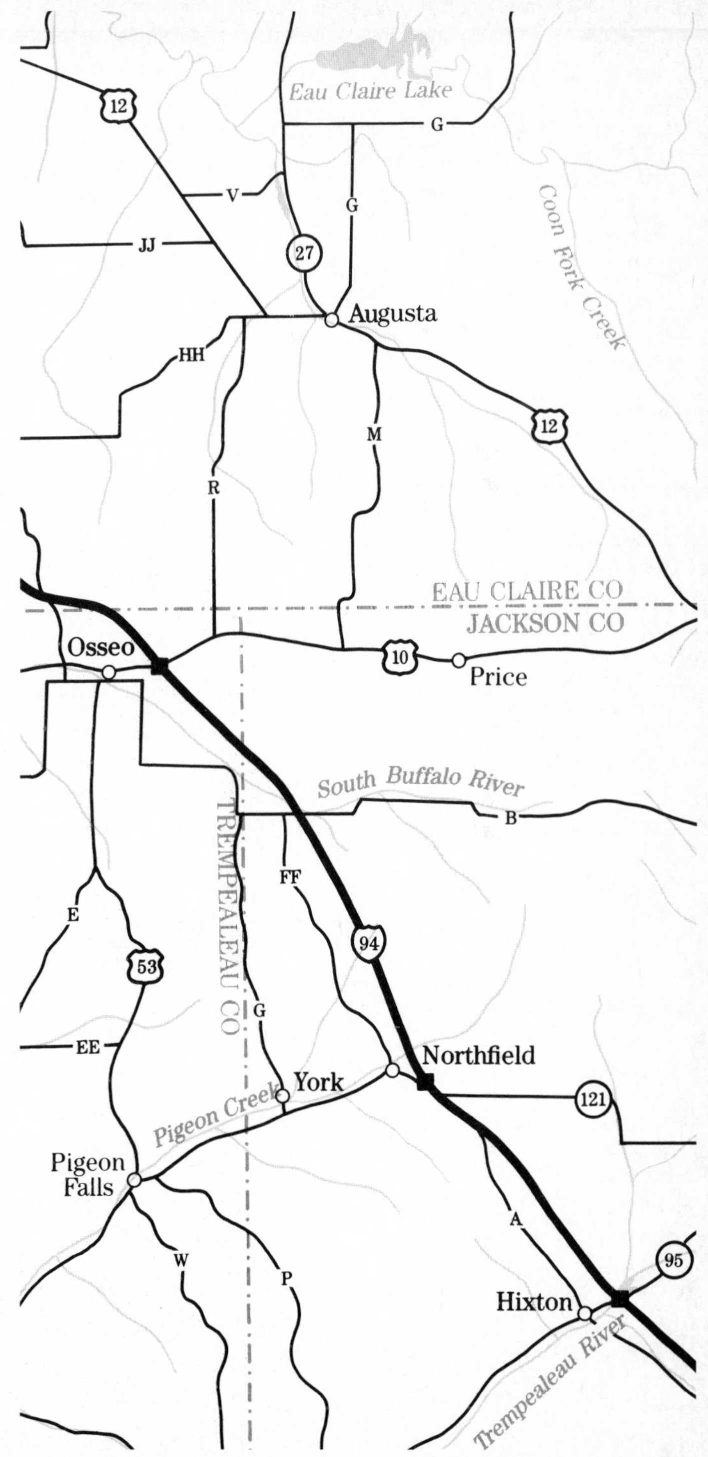

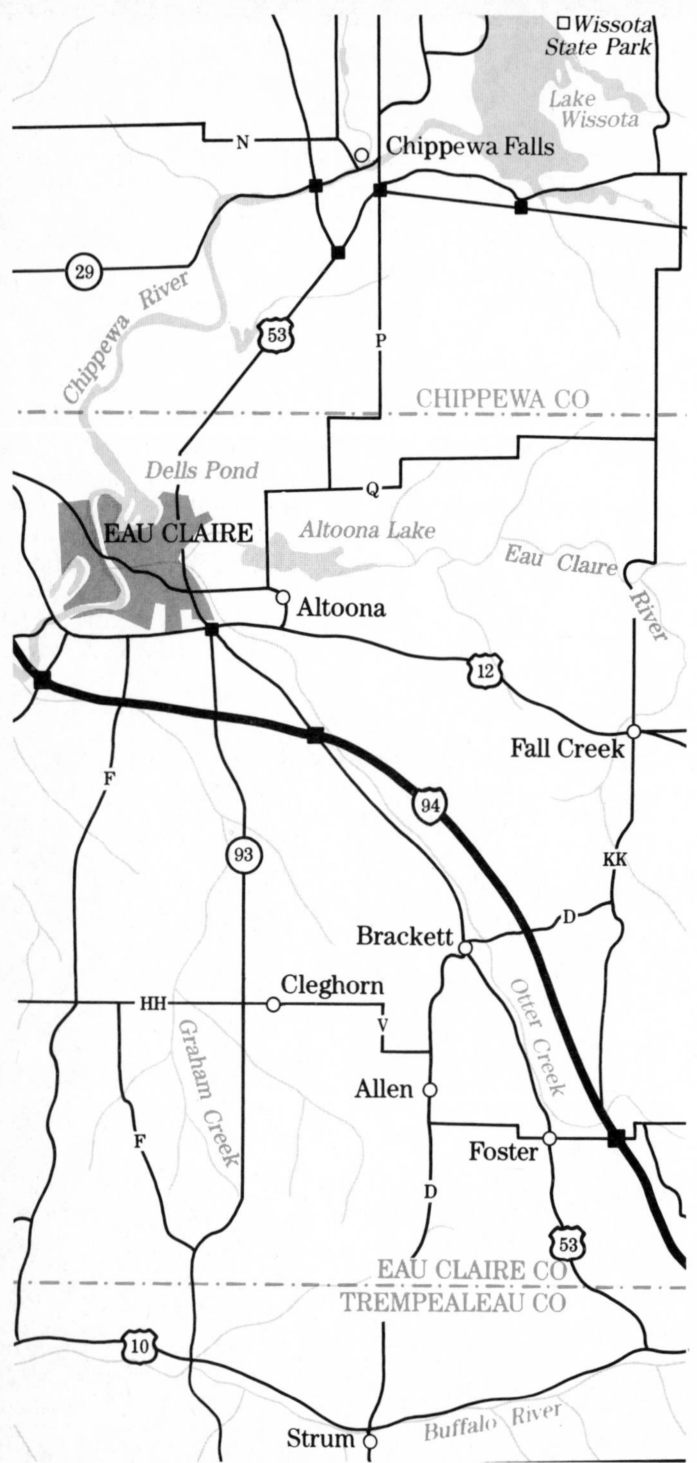

EAU CLAIRE COUNTY, Pop. 78,805

This region of Wisconsin became the buffer zone between the Dakota Indians to the west, the Ojibwe to the north and the Winnebago tribes of the east. The treaty which better defined these Indian lands was carried out at Prairie du Chien in a council with these nations in 1825. The waterways of northwestern Wisconsin were used as boundaries. Carver on his travels through here in the 1700's referred to the Chippewa and Eau Claire rivers as the Roads of War, because of the continual fighting between the Dakota and Ojibwe and their use of the rivers to carry out raids against one another.

The county was named after the Eau Claire River, which has been known by other names. It was labeled as the Rufus River on 18th century maps, but the Ojibwe called it Wah-yaw-con-ut-ta-gua-yaw-sebe which translated into "Clearwater River." When the proposed city was platted in 1855, settlers felt the name Clearwater was too plain. Hence they renamed the river in its French version to Eau Claire.

The county's first whites were most likely Radisson and Groseilliers, French adventurers who traveled down from Lake Superior around 1656. Father Hennepin, a Jesuit priest, claimed to have entered the Chippewa River while held captive by Dakota Indians in 1680. Another Frenchman, Le Sueur, ventured up the Chippewa briefly in search of copper and furs, but the first Englishman to write about this area was Jonathan Carver who explored the Chippewa River in 1767.

The fighting between the Dakota and Ojibwe made any travel here dangerous. Eight years after the Winnebago ceded their Wisconsin lands in 1837, settlement began. The settlers weren't farmers, but men interested in the tall pine of the Eau Claire and Chippewa valleys. The state legislature officially organized Eau Claire County in 1856 with a total population of 100 and the small village of Eau Claire was named the county seat. The county's first murder trial occurred in 1858 when two German roommates had a fatal fight over who would wash the dishes.

FOSTER

This small collection of homes was first named Emmett in the 1850's by area homesteaders. Then Nathaniel Foster, a wealthy eccentric who lived 18 miles east in Fairchild, began a building campaign there that became the talk of the region. Starting in 1875, Foster organized a lumber company and built a hotel, steam sawmill, grain elevator, feed mill, a 350-seat opera house, and, in 1895, one of northwest Wisconsin's larger retail stores. It is no wonder that Emmett quickly changed its name to Foster when he ran a railroad line up to the little hamlet. Though the railroad was called the Fairchild & North Central, people referred to it as the Foster & Nobody Else's line.

CLEGHORN & BRACKETT

Farming began here in the 1850's and a small trading center was started and named after Lewis Cleghorn, a local settler. There is little to note about Cleghorn except that Nathaniel Foster's railroad once connected it to Foster and Fairchild. For a time, local farmers shipped grain from this point.

Brackett was named after James M. Brackett, postmaster of Eau Claire starting in 1878.

EAU CLAIRE, Pop. 51,509

When Jonathan Carver paddled up the Chippewa River in 1766, he described a prairie land where large herds of buffalo and elk roamed, but also a land shadowed with fighting between the Ojibwe and Dakota. Where the Eau Claire and Chippewa rivers join, the prairie gave way to a forest of pine, beech, maple and birch.

A French trader named Le Duc probably lived here along the river in 1784, trading with the Ojibwe. Disliked by the Ojibwe, he eventually moved down the Chippewa to trade with the Dakota after Le Duc collecting two Ojibwe scalps to gain favor with the Dakota. It was 1832 before historians note another trader in this region. Louis de Marie, his Ojibwe wife and eight children left Prairie du Chien that year and headed for Chippewa Falls. On their way up the Mississippi, they noted the dead from the Bad Axe massacre lying along the shore. Marie moved his post in and around the Chippewa Valley for several years as he successfully traded with the Indians.

Though some logging was done on the Chippewa and over on the Red Cedar River, the first actual settlement at the confluence of the Chippewa and Eau Claire rivers wasn't until 1845. With little money, Arthur and Stephen McCann and Jeremiah Thomas located here in makeshift shanties. They spent the river logging along the Clearwater River (Eau Claire), then joined forces with Simon and George Randall to build a mill. They spent an entire season working on the mill before placing out a boom to collect the logs they had cut along the Chippewa. In June 1847 their efforts and investment were swept away in a flash flood.

About this time others were drawn by this forested region's potential and started to make their way to Eau Claire. In 1849-50 a road was built from Prairie du Chien through Sparta, Black River Falls, Eau Claire and eventually over to Hudson. Most settlers continued on past the tough little lumber hamlet of Eau Claire to the St. Croix prairies and open lands of Minnesota. The hamlet, originally known as Clearwater, eventually changed its name to the more romantic sounding French version, Eau Claire.

SHSW

The "Ida Campbell" unloads at Eau Claire, 1875.

Courtesy of Leinenkugel Brewery

The Leinenkugel bottlers, north of Eau Claire at Chippewa Falls.

Beginning in 1850, new homestead laws opened most of northwest Wisconsin's land for settlement. Supplies of pork and flour came up from Galena or Prairie du Chien for the settlers and speculators. Since Eau Claire's business was lumbering, there were few stores or retail businesses in this town of 100 men before 1855. Growth was slow as California and Minnesota attracted most new settlers. The Mississippi was still the great waterway and for many the trip up the Eau Claire was too difficult. A stage between Eau Claire and Lake Pepin cost $3 one-way.

When the county formed in 1856, a rumor circulated that a railroad would be built from Portage through here to Hudson on the St. Croix. As one historian noted, "the most wild and visionary schemes" were indulged in. In any case, villages organized and developed on the three separate banks of the river and were known as Eau Claire, Eau Claire City and North Eau Claire. Stores, homes and Churches were built and money was invested in mills, while the rich pineries of the Chippewa and Eau Claire valleys provided the economic base. In 1872, the three separate villages incorporated as Eau Claire.

It is estimated that half of Wisconsin's pine was in forests drained by the Chippewa River. In 1871, 112 lumber camps operated along the river and cut 247 million feet of timber each year, leading all other Wisconsin rivers by a good margin. As intensive lumbering continued, disputes developed over rights on the Chippewa River. Members of the Beef Slough Company, located at the mouth of the Chippewa, wanted the river undamned, allowing free movement of their logs down to their collecting booms. The dams and booms at the Chippewa Falls and Eau Claire were unacceptable to them. Tensions existed between the Eau Claire mills and the Beef Slough Company through much of the 1880's.

In the spring of 1867, two Beef Slough men named Bacon and Davis, with others, tried to smashed their spring drive of logs through the booms at Eau Claire. Their purpose was to open the Chippewa once and for all, making it a straight shot for logs being sent to their booms at Beef Slough. A posse of 250 Eau Claire men armed with shotguns prevented destruction of the Eau Claire milling operations.

Besides the tension between opposing lumber companies, work in the mills themselves was extremely hard and the hours long. In 1881, 1,800 workers of the Eau Claire Lumber Company walked off their jobs and held rallies demanding a 10-hour day. Their motto was "ten hours or no sawdust." The state militia, called out by Gov. William Smith, camped here for several days to maintain peace and the conflict became known as the Sawdust War.

The West Wisconsin Railroad which was rumored to come here in 1856 didn't become a reality until 14 years later. When the tracks were finally laid into town, 10,000 Chippewa Valley people turned out for the celebration. In addition to the train the taxpayers had something special to celebrate: county officials had craftily avoided funding most of the rail construction through the county by inserting in the contract that they "may" and not "shall" pay a subsidy for their portion of the line.

At the turn-of-the-century, after the forests were stripped of what many had thought was an inexhaustible supply of white pine, most of the Eau Claire's 22 mills closed down. Some converted their lumber mills over to paper milling, utilizing the more abundant and cheaper grade of pulpwood that had been untouched. Today Eau Claire is a diversified manufacturing and agricultural trading center.

ALTOONA Pop. 4,393

This city was known as East Eau Claire when first platted in 1881 and had only two houses. The settlement developed after the Chicago, St. Paul, Minneapolis and Omaha Railroad (Chicago and Northwestern) established a machine shop and round-house here. When the village received its city charter in 1887, it renamed itself after a Pennsylvania town.

DUNN COUNTY, Pop. 34,314

Dunn County was named for Charles Dunn, Chief Justice of the new Wisconsin Territory during 1836-48. The land here is gently rolling, shaped 10-12,000 years ago by glacial action and then overgrown by a thick forest of basswood, oak, maple, ash, and elm. The county's predominate feature as seen from the Interstate is the Red Cedar River's steep, narrow valley. It was along the Red Cedar that the Ojibwe traveled to their hunting camps. Later the Red Cedar carried millions of feet of lumber to the huge Menomonie mills.

The American Fur Company of Jacob Astor made the white man's first incursion into the region's forests when his men came up the Red Cedar in 1820 to log for a short time. In 1829, soldiers from Fort Crawford, Prairie du Chien, cut logs along the Red Cedar, then rafted them down to their fort. Despite those loggers, Dunn County's settlement didn't begin until two men named Wilson and Knapp bought into a mill located where Wilson Creek and the Red Cedar River converge. Here began the important Knapp-Stout lumber company around which Menomonie grew.

When Dunn County was created in 1854, the county seat was the small logging village of Dunnville (no longer visible), a few miles up from the confluence of the Red Cedar and Chippewa rivers. Dunn County included the Pepin area at one time and lawyers traveling from Pepin to Dunnville eventually tired of the long trip and petitioned the legislature to create Pepin County. When Pepin County broke off in 1858, Dunnville was no longer centrally located. After Dunnville's wooden courthouse burned in 1858, the lumber town of Menomonie became the county seat.

Settlers flocked to Dunn County during the 1860's, with most coming from New York. By 1880, at least 18 mills operated along the Red Cedar, Hay, Eau Galle, and Chippewa rivers, providing work for many of the new arrivals. However, most of the mills shut down when the pine was depleted from the northern part of the county and the hardwoods from the western part. By 1900, the county's future rested with agriculture and manufacturing. Flour was important for a period, providing the logging camps with bread. The county's rich clays also sustained a brick-making industry that produced 30 million bricks in 1906. During the 1920-30's, dairying provided most of the Dunn County farmer's cash income, outstripping the production of other Chippewa Valley counties.

ELK MOUND & RUSK

These two villages formed around the Tomah and Lake St. Croix Railroad when it was built through here in 1870. Nei-

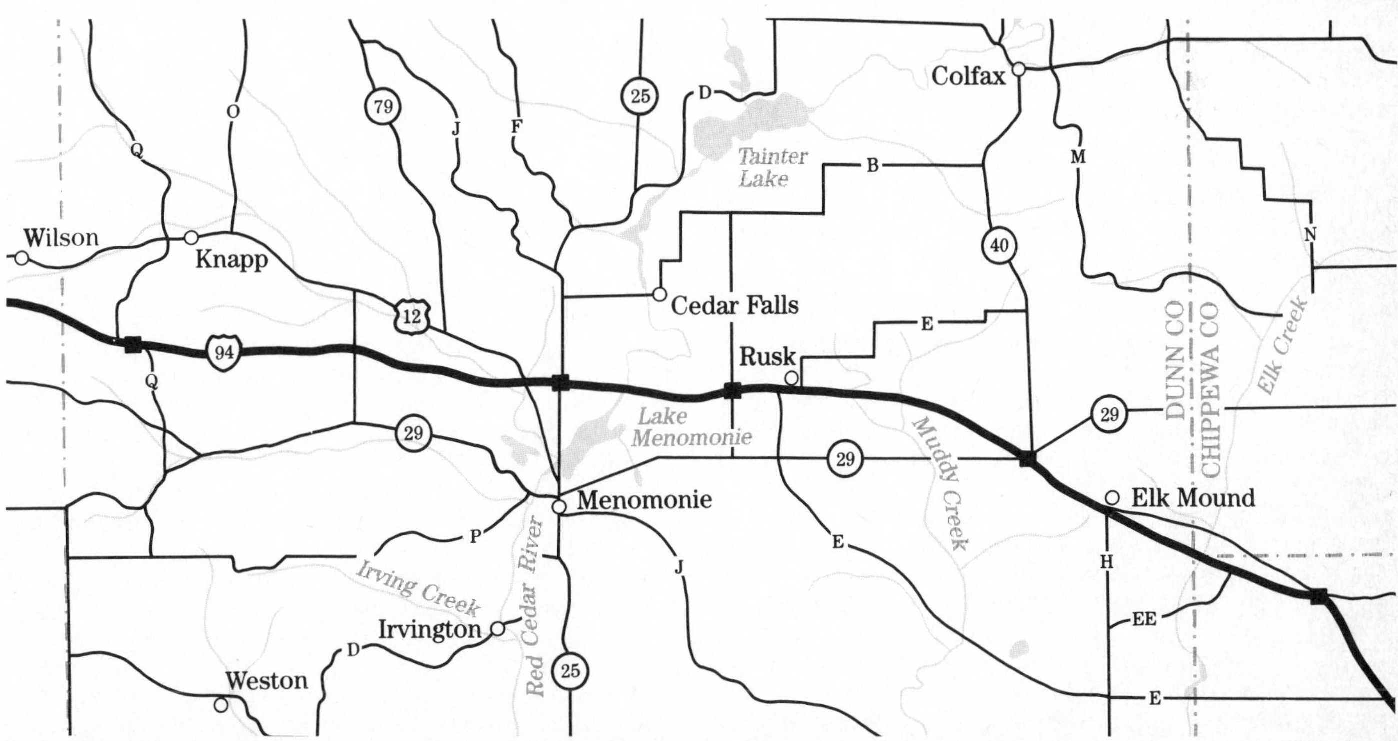

SHSW

The Knapp Stout & Company lumber mill at Menomonie, 1900.

ther village was much more than a post office, general store and a small business or two in its early years. Rusk only had about 40 inhabitants during the late 1880's. Elk Mound is named for a 1200-foot bluff near Muddy Creek from which the Ojibwe watched for the movements of their enemy the Dakota during the early 1700's. Elk were also occasionally seen feeding on the top of this grassy knob.

MENOMONIE, Pop. 12,769

Not long after white men began traveling into Indian lands, they were attracted to the pine forests of the Chippewa and Red Cedar river valleys. A Kentucky man, Hardin Perkins, built a mill on the Red Cedar in 1822, but a flood washed it away as it was nearing completion. Since the Dakota and Ojibwe had protested the mill, Perkins gave up. It wasn't until 1828, when a Judge Lockwood promised whiskey and beads, that the Indians allowed some logging here. With some assurance of safety, James Lockwood built a small mill where Perkins had started his. The Lockwood mill was the Chippewa Valley's first and Menomonie grew around it. Logs cut and milled here were used to rebuild Fort Crawford at Prairie du Chien.

Hiram Allen, a Vermont native, came to the Red Cedar area in 1833. He purchased the Lockwood Mill two years later, then ran the mill, maintained a supply store and built another mill. The mills on Gilbert and Wilson creeks prospered for the next dozen or so years, despite changing ownerships, fires and rebuilding. When Capt. William Wilson traveled through here with his Indian guide, he was impressed with the vast pine forests and decided to buy into the mills. Returning to Fort Dodge, Iowa, Wilson interested a friend, John Knapp, in joining him in this venture. In the summer of 1846, Wilson, Knapp and Lorenzo Bullard took their families up the Chippewa to the Red Cedar River and began the first permanent settlement of Menomonie, an Indian word for wild rice.

Having ceded their lands, the Ojibwe watched as their ricing beds were flooded by small dams built to help float logs to the mills. One historian simply treated the displacement of the Indians by writing, "With time and the advancement of civilization, the redskins disappeared." During the 1800's, the Winnebago, Sauk, Fox, Ojibwe, and Dakota had all been displaced or put into reservations by treaties and forced inducements.

In the meantime, others bought into the successful Wilson, Knapp mill and the operation came to be known as the Knapp, Stout & Company. During the 1860's the lumber company grew into one of the Wisconsin's largest lumber corporations, with self-sustaining camps ranging along the Red Cedar and Chippewa rivers. The company owned more than 100,000 acres with 1,500 men working in the forests and mills. Knapp, Stout & Company had company farms to produce wheat and vegetables for their crews and provided hotels, a company store, newspaper and even moral attitudes by banning the purchase or sale of liquor. Because of the liquor ban, Menomonie was reportedly without crime.

After logs were milled at Menomonie, rafts of lumber were floated down the Chippewa to Reads Landing on the Mississippi, then on to St. Louis. The Menomonie mills continued at full capacity for 30 years until 1900 when the pine and hardwoods forests were finally depleted.

At the same time Knapp, Stout & Company's impact went beyond Menomonie providing a start for some of Wisconsin's northern villages. The economic void left in Menomonee after the mills closed was eventually filled by dairying, light manufacturing and the growth of Stout State University. Lumberman James Stout founded the college in 1903 to train teachers in industrial and household arts and the state took over the college's administration in 1911. Brick manufacturing began in Menomonie during the early 1880's and within a few years a number of brickyards, with a annual capacity of 30 million bricks, operated here.

DUNNVILLE (Ghost Town)

Dunnville began when Samuel Lamb built a modest house and tavern in 1850. Located south of Menomonie where County Y crosses the Red Cedar River, Dunnville marked the furthest point Mississippi riverboats could ascend the Chippewa River. Supplies for the growing Knapp, Stout & Company mills were unloaded here and carted to Menomonie. Several hundred people lived here during the 1850's, working in the quarry, creamery or saw mill or handling supplies.

The Colburn House Hotel was built, followed by the Tainter Hotel a few years later and a stage carried passengers between Dunnville and Menomonie, 12 miles north. When Dunn County was formed in 1854, this thriving village became the county seat. However four years later, Menomonie was a larger city, Pepin County was created and Dunnville was displaced as the county seat. After the courthouse burned in 1858, Dunnville declined and eventually died. The last lumber raft left the aging settlement in August, 1901 and all who wanted to ride were allowed to climb aboard. Today, all that is left of Dunnville are a few old buildings, including the Colburn and Tainter Houses.

KNAPP, Pop. 419

When the Tomah & Lake St. Croix came through in the early 1870's, Omer Cole and John Bailey settled here. The small depot was called Knapp Station after John Knapp, a principal owner of the powerful Knapp, Stout & Company. When the St. Croix railroad bridge connecting Wisconsin and Minnesota was completed in 1872, a Minneapolis barrel company located here to take advantage of the hardwood forest region west of Menomonie and Hudson. A general store and a cultivator company also located here. More than 2.5 million pounds of goods were shipped from Knapp each month during the 1880's—an indication of the manufacturing once done here.

SHSW

Chicago, Milwaukee & St. Paul Railroad employees and wives, 1895.

ST. CROIX COUNTY, Pop. 43,872

When Fort Snelling was built in 1819 by today's St. Paul, it offered trade opportunities and protection from the Indians and interest in the St. Croix Valley heightened. Some Fort Snelling officers purchased land along the St. Croix and later sold in 1855 to Philander Prescott who laid out the town of Prescott. Joseph Brown, also from Fort Snelling, was one of the St. Croix Valley's first white settlers. He established himself at Stillwater, cut logs at Taylors Falls in 1836 with permission from the Dakota Indians, and sold whiskey and supplies to the Indians. The settlers began arriving in larger numbers starting in 1837, when the Ojibwe and Dakota gave up their St. Croix lands.

But many looked over the area and thought the climate was too severe and that only pine and wild rice could grow here. As a result, settlement was slow. When St. Croix County was established in 1840 (including most of northwestern Wisconsin) only 58 people voted in the election to make Joseph Brown's Stillwater warehouse the county seat. When Wisconsin was established in 1848, most of the region's 600 settlers expected the state boundary to be over at the Mississippi instead of the St. Croix River.

As loggers cleared the land, early St. Croix County farmers found that the soil was very fertile. Many took up wheat farming and St. Croix, Buffalo and Trempealeau counties led the state in wheat production from 1879-1899. By 1900, however, wheat had given way to corn, hay and oats to feed the cows of the growing dairy industry. During the county's peak wheat years the Willow, Apple and Kinnickinnic rivers had provided power for numerous grist mills. During the 1850's more than 70 mills hugged the shores of the fast-moving Apple River in the county's northern section. Today, the Apple River attracts large numbers of tourists who float down its waters on tubes.

WILSON & HERSEY

Like other towns along the Interstate, Wilson owes its beginnings to the vast hardwood forests of eastern St. Croix County. It was named after William Wilson who moved up from Menomonie to start a mill. Before the train from Tomah to Hudson came through here, donkeys dragged logs over ice-coated roads to Wilson's mill.

The Tomah & Lake St. Croix Railroad reached Hudson in St. Croix County from the lumbering centers of Eau Claire and Menomonie in 1871 and small milling centers developed around the railroad wherever supplies and men could be found. The railroad later changed its name to West Wisconsin and was taken over, like many western Wisconsin lines, by the Chicago, St. Paul, Minneapolis & Omaha Railroad. This line is now run by the Chicago & Northwestern Railroad.

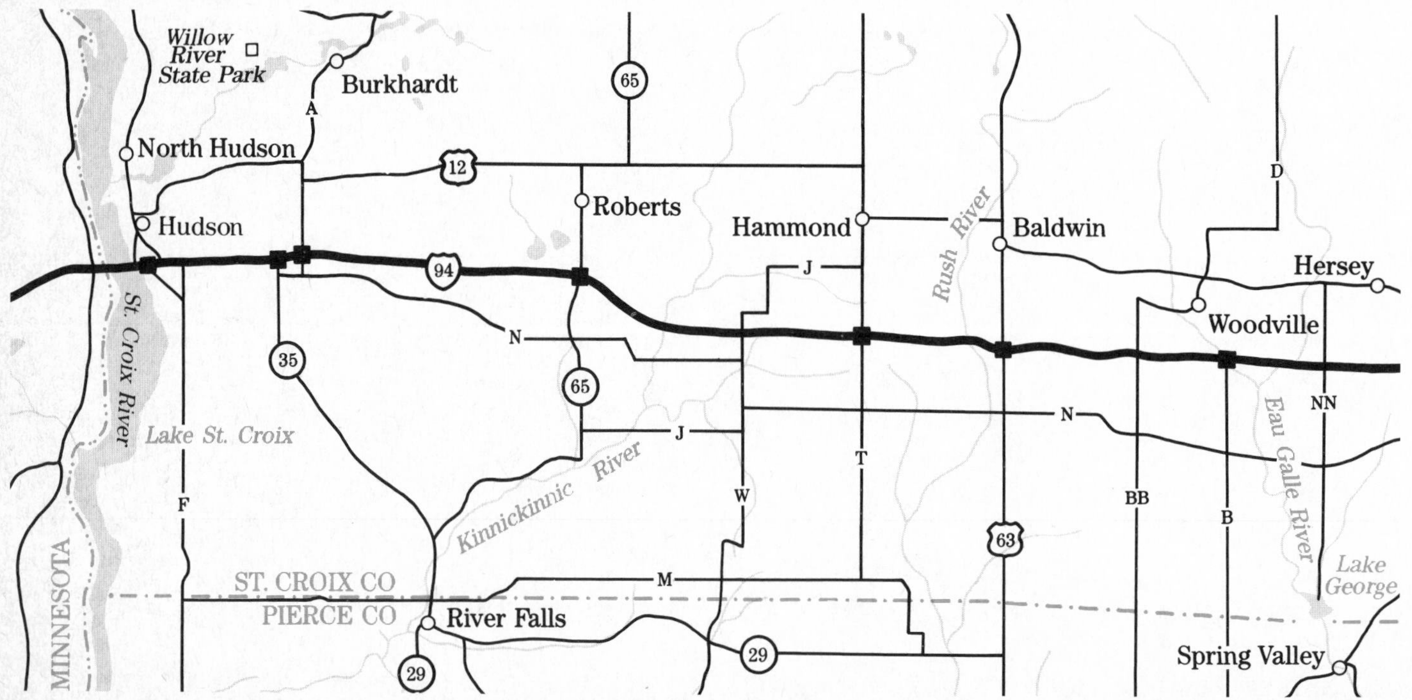

Hersey, named after Samuel Hersey, an early settler, grew around a lumber mill, a basket factory, schoolhouse, and barrel factory. The village once had 340 residents and many complained about stumps scattered along main street. It also had one hotel and a stage that ran twice weekly to Maiden Rock on the Mississippi. In the late 1800's, Hersey encouraged farming so it could survive as a market center and not fade away after the lumber boom ended.

WOODVILLE, Pop. 725

This small village formed around the Chicago, St. Paul, Minneapolis & Omaha Railroad depot in 1876. Its name probably reflects its location, once in the center of a dense forest of hardwoods called the Big Woods. This mature forest covered the land from Menomonie to the St. Croix bluffs and on into Minnesota. Woodville grew around saw mills located along the Eau Galle River which means "river of the gravel banks." The largest mill was the Woodville Company, but most logging activity ended when the mills closed down in 1892. In the 1870's Wildwood thrived south of Woodville where stages crossed the river en route to Menomonie.

STAGECOACH ROUTES

South of I-94, close to County N, was the stage route that connected Eau Claire to Hudson during the 1860's. It followed an Indian trail through the Big Woods and prairie openings and was relatively comfortable for travelers. An inn, located where the trail crossed the Eau Galle River, provided rest and food for both passengers and horses. It was also the site of Wildwood, a settlement which included a brick factory, woodworking mill, some iron mining, a smelter, furnace and shot tower. The stage went out of business in 1871 when the Chicago, St. Paul, Minneapolis & Omaha Railroad came through, but Wildwood continued to grow around the brickyards and logging. However, logging eventually extended too far away from Wildwood to be profitable and the town died.

BALDWIN, Pop. 1,620

When the Tomah & Lake St. Croix reached here in the summer of 1871, the section house and small houses were named Clarksville after the local shipping agent. However D.A. Baldwin soon bought the railroad and changed its name to West Wisconsin. Locals thought they'd please Baldwin by renaming the town after him.

When Baldwin was incorporated in 1874, residents of Hammond were upset because part of their city was incorporated into Baldwin. The state legislature finally settled the matter in Baldwin's favor. However on a Sunday in April, 1884, a fire swept through the town, destroying many of the buildings. Nine years later another fire destroyed four business blocks. Finally the town learned its lesson and rebuilt with brick.

SHSW

The Jones Family. Photo/ C.J. Van Schaick

As wheat farming increased in the county, Baldwin became a shipping point. Without streams to provide waterpower, the town used steam to run its mill. Nearby hardwood forests provided wood for making steam. When wheat production shifted to the Dakotas at the turn-of-the-century, many mills closed down or were moved. Wisconsin and Minnesota wheat farmers were paying for years of not rotated crops which depleted the soil's nutrients. Bugs and disease were becoming more common and Wisconsin farmers began a transition to the production of milk and cheese products.

HAMMOND, Pop. 991

A Boston land company that intended to start a settlement here, finally gave up the idea in 1855 and turned the land over to Mann, Hammond & Company. Hammond, from Waukesha near Milwaukee, started a mill which provided others with incentive to settle. According to one story, 50 new settlers had a Fourth of July picnic at which they raised the flag, gave speeches about the area's bright future, and watched the wolves eat the leavings as they left on their wagons.

John Thayer arrived here in 1856 and ran the post office from his small hotel, the Pioneer House. It burned in 1877 but was rebuilt by its new owner, Edward Gardiner, and renamed the Gardiner House. The hotel was noted for its fine horse stables, run in connection with the hotel much like parking lots located next to today's motels. When the train came through in 1871, Hammond became a shipping point for area wheat farmers.

ROBERTS, Pop. 833

Roberts was founded a mile north of the present village but moved its buildings down to the tracks when the train came through in 1871. It was named for a railway official.

BURKHARDT & WILLOW RIVER STATE PARK

Christian Burkhardt, a German, came up the Willow River in 1868 and established a mill and elevator at a picturesque site once known as Bouchea after Peter Bouchea of Hudson. Burkhardt's mill was one of the county's largest during the late 1800's and one of the region's first mills to use a new roller process which produced a purer, whiter flour from the hard spring wheat. Burkhardt also built a large mansion, which today is used as a nursing home. The village that developed on his property was also on the Omaha line built from Hudson to Ashland in the late 1800's. Burkhardt, who unsuccessfully resisted having the town named after him, was also interested in generating electricity and his operation sent the first electricity to Hudson in 1893.

SHSW

Overlooking Hudson and the St. Croix Valley, 1870.

The mill shut down in 1931 and 13 years later the village made national news when the entire town was sold to a co-op. The state later bought the Burkhardt area, and developed it as a state park. Three dams along the Willow River have created lakes within the 2,700 acre park. A one-mile walk from the campsite leads back to the picturesque Willow Falls where the water plunges 100 feet into a limestone basin. During the logging era on the St. Croix River, there was so much debris and trash along the shoreline that most picnickers journeyed up the Willow to picnic at these falls.

HUDSON, Pop. 5,434

Situated in the St. Croix River Valley is the old town of Hudson. Before the valley's white pine attracted speculators, fur traders were the main travelers along these waters. Some Frenchmen reportedly had a post here in the late 1700's, but Louis Massey and Peter Bouchea became the first settlers when they stopped along the St. Croix south of the Willow River. Massey, a French-Canadian who worked as a riverman, helped in the American Fur Company's posts and farmed near Fort Snelling before he came here.

Massey and his wife (Bouchea's sister) arrived in two canoes that were lashed together and stuffed with their belongings. Bouchea was a fur trader who had worked for the American Fur Company in the Apostle Islands. After a few other whites arrived, they decided their collection of log houses needed a name. Joel Foster who had recently fought in the Mexican War suggested Buena Vista, Spanish for "beautiful view." The closest supply point was down at Red Rock (Newport) where they bought their pork and flour, but the trail was difficult. Since steamboat supplies were unpredictable, most settlers shot their own game.

Bouchea later said that he had killed more than 125 deer and 15 elk during one of those early falls. There were so many deer and elk skins that they had little monetary value. Massey, a colorful character called "Uncle Massey" by his friends, lived out his life at Hudson and was almost 100 years old when he died in 1887.

A few years after Massey, Bouchea and others had arrived, another group of settlers started a village on an adjoining 20 acres and named their rival hamlet Willow River. Because of their river location, these early pioneers were sure both villages would outstrip St. Paul as a future metropolis. Little money was spent advertising their charms though and the towns grew slowly. In 1851, the state forced the two villages to join under the name Willow River. The Buena Vista settlers were unhappy, so in compromise the village was renamed Hudson.

As settlement increased, a government land office opened here in 1849 and Hudson became the primary steamboat stop for those wanting to farm in St. Croix and adjacent counties. By 1872, railroads had reached east from Tomah and west from St. Paul to the barrier of the St. Croix River. A bridge obviously had to be built. As the piles were being driven into the riverbed, angry loggers came down from Stillwater and stole the equipment, claiming the span under the bridge would be too small to float their log rafts through. A compromise was reached after the Stillwater loggers threatened to pull the piles out as fast as they were driven in. For many years this was known as the Battle of the Piles.

Logging, so vital to the valley during the latter 1800's, was also important to Hudson's development. Just north of the I-94 bridge on the level terrace near the marina, the Hudson saw mill operated from 1849 to 1917. As farmers increased their acreage, grist mills were also in demand. The first such mill was built in 1853 on the Willow River, two miles out of Hudson, by Caleb Greene and Charles Cox who called their flour "Paradise." D.A. Baldwin, a railroad promoter who helped establish North Hudson, also owned two mills at the mouth of the Willow River. A major industry began at North Hudson when the West Wisconsin railroad moved its repair shops here in 1872. Today the old shops are being occupied by new businesses.

Crossing the wide St. Croix was always an obstacle for those who wanted to trade or visit at St. Paul. Early crossing were by ferry which started operation in 1849. Rope was used to pull the ferry across until a steam engine was put on board. In 1913, the first interstate bridge connecting Hudson with Minnesota was completed as a toll road. However, motorists feared the bridge because it was at the bottom of a steep hill which included a series of sharp turns through Hudson. The town later bought and operated the bridge until a free bridge was built in 1951 where the Interstate now crosses the river. The toll during the 1930's was 15 cents for car and driver and a nickel for each passenger.

ST. CROIX RIVER

The St. Croix River, which begins near Solon Springs, Wisconsin, was an important route for early explorers and traders who crossed from Lake Superior to the Mississippi and St. Croix valleys. A short portage from the Bois Brule River brought them to the St. Croix. Daniel Greysolon sieur Duluth was probably the first white to pass into the St. Croix Valley when he explored this region for France in 1680. It was on this trip that Duluth heard from Dakota hunters that a white man named Father Hennepin had been captured along the Mississippi and was being held near Lake Mille Lacs in Minnesota. Duluth pressured the Indians into releasing Hennepin and shortly after the two men had their historic meeting not far from here.

This picturesque pine and prairie region was covered by an inland sea millions of years ago. The waters deposited many feet of limestone that is seen today along some of the valley's bluffs. Similar deposits are found across much of the United States and geologists call this sandstone the St. Croixian Series. When the glaciers melted 10-12,000 years ago, waters from Glacial Lakes Duluth, the predecessor of Lake Superior, carved down through the sandstone and lava creating this valley. Near St. Croix Falls, the river has cut a narrow gorge through the tough resistant stone.

For many years, the St. Croix Valley was the dividing line between the warring Dakota and Ojibwe. Neither dared camp here fearing a swift raid from the opposite shore. The Dakota called this river Hoganwahnkay-kin, meaning "the place where fish lie." The French preferred another name. The explorer Le Sueur first called this the St. Croix, French for "Holy Cross," after he discovered a cross over the grave of a voyageur who had perished and been buried near the river. The St. Croix, approximately 170 miles long, begins near the Solon Springs portage and empties into the Mississippi at Prescott. The broadening of the river at Stillwater is called Lake St. Croix and is caused by silt deposited by the Mississippi across the mouth of the St. Croix at Prescott.

Lake St. Croix provided a place to gather logs sent down from the Upper St. Croix pineries during the 1850's. Booms were built to collect the logs and identify their individual markings so as to credit the loggers upstream. From these booms, the logs were either cut into lumber or rafted together and floated to mills downstream on the Mississippi. As many as 600 men worked these booms. The largest was the St. Croix Boom Company which started north of Stillwater in 1856. Sawmills also flourished along the St. Croix: during the last half of the 1800's, more than 100 mills operated along the river.

Steamboats running supplies to the camps and mills operated all the way to St. Croix Falls. However, railroads eventually took the steamers' trade and by 1914 the logs had stopped flowing down to the booms. After that, a more subdued period returned to the river. Today, the scenic waters of the Upper St. Croix River are part of the National Wild and Scenic River System, with the regional headquarters located at St. Croix Falls.

SHSW

Many lumber rafts left the St. Croix for mills on the Mississippi.

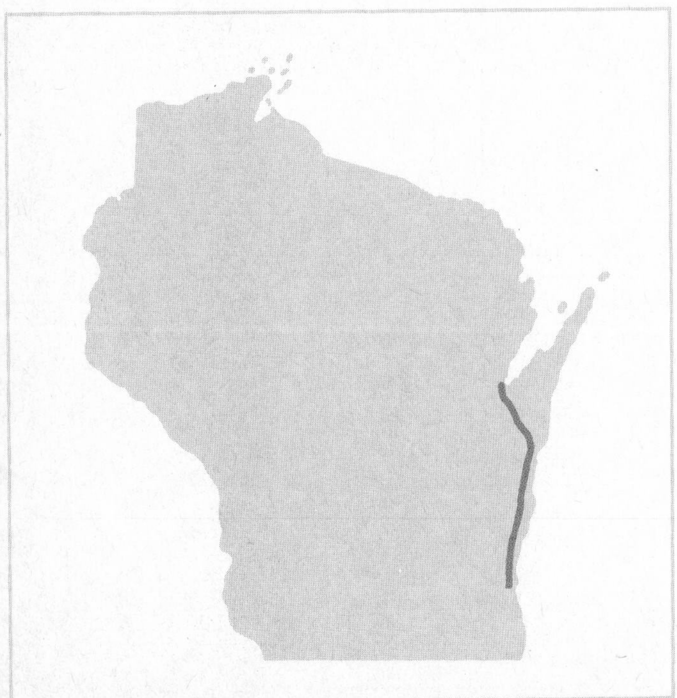

Interstate 43, the oldest interstate in Wisconsin, hugs the shore of Lake Michigan 115 miles from Milwaukee, the home of Bavarian brewmasters to Green Bay, the home of the NFL's Green Bay Packers. Down along the lakeshore, near Port Washington, you'll have a chance to discover the ghost town of Ulao, once a vital port of call for the Great Lakes sailing ships.

ROUTE 43, MILWAUKEE TO GREEN BAY

SHSW

Unusual ice formation on Lake Michigan.

MILWAUKEE COUNTY, POP. 964,988

Elsewhere in this book we have discussed the Indians, settlers, and industries of early Milwaukee County. Here, because Interstate 43 follows the Lake Michigan coastline, we'll discuss that lake's role in the early history of the county and the state.

LAKE MICHIGAN

When the glaciers retreated about 10,000 years ago, the debris being pushed before them was deposited at the furthest point of the glacial advance. The result is known as an end moraine. Milwaukee sits upon such a moraine, low hills of sand and gravel left by a massive tongue of ice which once swept down over all of Lake Michigan. The Lake Michigan shoreline today retains that sand and gravel in its sandy beaches, bedrock cliffs, rocky islands and dune fields.

These glacial deposits provided the fertile soil of eastern Wisconsin's agricultural region, and the lake provided a modifying influence on the area's climate. Early immigrants flocked here to farm, enriching the culture and founding the communities of Luxemburg, Belgium, Poland, Wales and Germantown.

The Lake Michigan shoreline from Chicago to Door County, Wisconsin is relatively straight with only a few broad areas. The beaches are generally narrow and much of the coast consists of steep, wave-cut, drift or clay bluffs which sometimes rise 60 feet above the lake. There are several good dune areas, including the Terry Andrae State Park near Sheboygan, and many rocky shores, including those at the Harrington Beach State Park north of Port Washington. In short, Lake Michigan has enough geological variety to satisfy any interest.

We begin our Lake Michigan tour just north of Milwaukee's suburbs in Ozaukee County, a part of Milwaukee County until 1836.

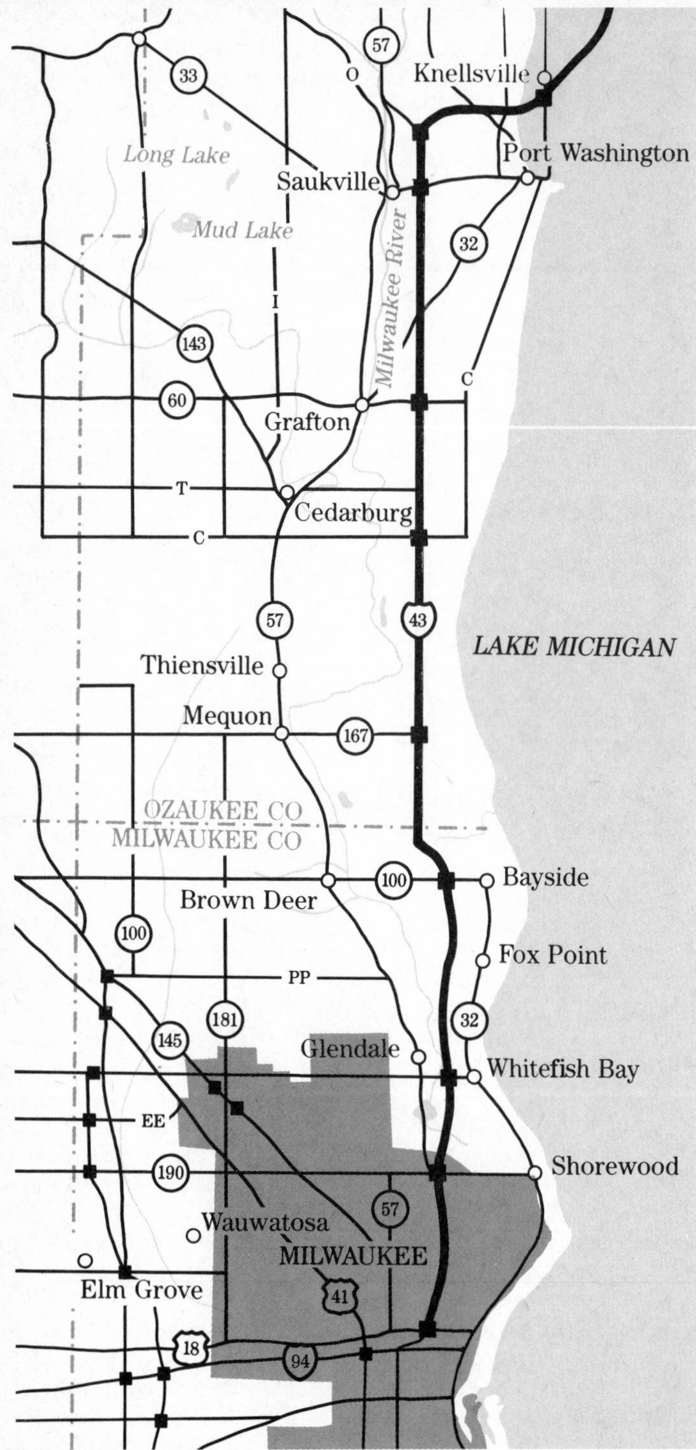

OZAUKEE COUNTY, Pop. 66,981

Early visitors here discovered that the lake had many clay bluffs, some rising up to 60 feet in places. Further inland was a rich land of cultivated fields and forests of black oak, maple and beech. The Milwaukee River and Cedar Creek ran through the county, promising abundant waterpower. Attracted by all this natural beauty, the Potawatomi Indians frequently hunted and fished here. Eventually, however, they retreated to a region south and west of the Milwaukee River and the county's permanent white settlement began.

Worcester Harrison (commonly referred to as "General") was the first settler. He came from Michigan City, Indiana, in December of 1835 and was immediately drawn to an area near the Lake Michigan shore at the mouth of Sauk Creek, the present city of Port Washington.

Except for Harrison, the county's first first permanent settlers built homes at Mequon, which was within ox team distance of Milwaukee, the market for their prospective crops.

GRAFTON, Pop. 8,381

Established in 1842, this town had the honor of being home to the county's first lawyer. H.G. Turner arrived in 1844 and later became county judge.

In the early days, Grafton, Hamilton, Cedarburg, Saukville, Waubeka and Newburg were all industrial centers, with saw mills, flour mills, and small woodworking plants.

GHOST TOWN

Just 20 minutes north of the last Milwaukee suburbs lies the ghost town of Ulao. Although few physical remnants remain, this once-thriving town has a rich, varied and somewhat ironic history.

Although the town has been deserted since the last Mormon settlers lived here in 1856, it was an important port of call along the lake in its heyday.

Ulao was platted in 1847 on top of a high bluff on Lake Michigan's sandy shore. James T. Gifford of Elgin, Illinois decided this location was an ideal outlet for farmers who were cutting timber inland and looking for a market. Gifford built a 1,000-foot long pier at the bluff's foot, then constructed chutes to slide timber from the top of the bluff to the waiting vessels below. He also built a saw mill and warehouse on the site.

Three miles of road were built from the bustling town to the west side of the Milwaukee River. Timber was cut, stumps removed and the road graded into the state's first turnpike (now County Q). As plans for the town expanded, Gifford took on associates who also settled here.

The project's timing was perfect. Competition from other harbor developments along Lake Michigan had not yet begun and woodburning steamers were abundant. A large side-wheeler could burn up to ten acres of timbered land in one journey. Gifford sought to meet their needs.

Everything went well for the next three years. Then in 1850, for some unknown reason, Gifford sold his interest to a Great Lakes captain named John Howe. Howe's sister, Jane, also moved here with her husband, Luther Guiteau. Their son, Charles, grew up to be extremely high strung. Here we pick up the tale as cited in "Ghost Towns of Wisconsin."

"As he grew older, Charles drifted around, attempting unsuccessfully to obtain government positions. Finally, in 1880, he badgered the Secretary of State, under the newly-elected President Garfield, to appoint him Ambassador of Austria. He became such a nuisance that he was finally barred from the White House. Then in July of that year, he bought a revolver for $15, and went to the Washington railroad station, where the President of the United States was leaving to attend a class reunion. The forty-four year-old Guiteau, pulled out his gun, shot and killed Garfield..."

After the Civil War, the wood that Ulao depended on was depleted, lake-going vessels now stopped at the improved Port Washington harbor and the once-thriving town became nothing more than farms and a deserted beach.

You can still visit the Ulao site on County Q. Stop at the Ghost Town Tavern and ask for directions to the Guiteau family's brick home and the private home site that was once the Mormon Church. About a quarter mile further east, is the bluff overlooking Lake Michigan where it all began. Remnants of the old road are still visible. Take the path down to the beach and listen closely for the sound of waves crashing against the thousand-foot pier.

PORT WASHINGTON, Pop. 8,612

This town, the county's first settlement, received the prestigious title of county seat. When General Harrison settled here, he named the town Wisconsin City, but soon discovered that many other towns were also using that name. He changed it to Washington, appropriate to the promise of the budding metropolis, and it was altered to Port Washington in 1844.

When Harrison moved in, he purchased and cleared 16 acres of land where he built a tavern, two stores, several dwellings and a saw mill. A wide circle of acquaintances soon came and helped Harrison develop a thriving new town. Abraham Lincoln reportedly once thought of opening an office here but couldn't visit the town because of an early spring flood.

SHSW

Vacationers stroll the bluff-lined shores of Lake Michigan.

A Great Lakes excursion steamer at a Lake Michigan port of call.

In 1837, financial panic ended the town's growth and most residents moved away. For five years, the General was the only soul in town. Finally, activity picked up when speculators moved in to develop the town's port in 1842. Besides its natural beauty, the town had the advantage of a natural harbor and investors rushed in to build piers which would provide the new shipping interests with shelter.

LAKE MICHIGAN TRAGEDY

Two major Great Lake steamboat accidents occurred within sight of Port Washington. The first, in 1856 involved the loss of the Niagara.

Captain Fred Miller and the Niagara had left Collingwood on September 24 with about 300 passengers. Two days later, while four miles off Port Washington, the ship began to burn. Three schooners noticed the trouble and went out to help while the steamer Traveler headed over from a point 10 miles away. Flames spread quickly and 150-185 people died despite efforts to improvise rafts. By the time the Traveler arrived, only the captain and a few passengers who had jumped into the water could be rescued.

The second tragedy occurred exactly one month later and almost in the same spot. The Toledo, an American Transportation Company steamboat, was bound from Buffalo, with European immigrants heading for farming communities on Lake Michigan's western shore. Eighty persons were on board.

The ship docked at Port Washington's Blake Pier, discharged passengers and freight, took on wood for fuel and was preparing to put out again when a sudden storm came up, churning the lake's waters into a fury. Since the pier didn't provide adequate shelter and the ship had already cleared to leave, the captain pushed out. The storm's violence increased. Before the ship was 20 rods (330 feet) out, it was apparent she was in difficulty. She drifted shoreward. Efforts to drop anchor were useless as her links were caught in the opening of the ship's bow. She continued to drift, finally striking the beach's sandy bottom where she fell to pieces. Only three people on board were saved, including Aquilla Gifford, a 20 year-old deck hand who had also survived the Niagara tragedy.

The Toledo, one of the lake's largest propeller craft, was uninsured. Parts of her cargo, valued at $100,000, were picked up for miles along the beach for many years after the crash.

The Toledo's anchor was recovered by a fishing crew in 1900 and kept as a memorial. It can be seen in the Port Washington cemetery where the victims also are buried.

HARRINGTON BEACH STATE PARK

Seven miles north of Port Washington are the rocky shores of Harrington Beach State Park. The park's wild beach and lowland forest are a refreshing break from your drive. Quarry Lake, an inland lake within the park, is an abandoned limestone quarry ringed by marsh cedars. The White Cedar Swamp Nature Trail offers a view of how Lake Michigan's shoreline looked before development. The park, open from April 1 to December 1, extends one mile along Lake Michigan and has a half-mile sandy beach. Picnicking is allowed but no overnight camping.

BELGIUM, Pop. 892

The 1860 federal census showed 2,204 German families in Ozaukee County, including 431 Luxembourgers. The Luxembourg families arrived between 1845 and 1848 and occupied such a large percentage of the town that they decided to name it Luxembourg, after their homeland. However, when they sent that name to Washington, a secretary mistakenly assigned it to a town in in Kewaunee County and named this town Belgium.

The immigrants came here in poverty. Economic conditions in Luxembourg were critical, due to political tension between Germany and France. The iron and zinc mines that later employed many had not yet been developed.

The Homestead Act enabled these settlers to buy virgin farming land at $1.25 per acre. Most of the Luxembourgers purchased 70-75 acres, devoting their major efforts to dairying and later diversifying to small grains, including flax for the Milwaukee breweries. Produce for canning was also later profitable. A cannery is still located here.

The Luxembourgers were exceptionally thrifty, as the following story relates.

A Luxembourg farmer went to the bank to pay off his mortgage, carrying a bucket of money in his arms. When the cashier finished counting it she said, "Sir, there must be some mistake. Your mortgage is $7,000 and there's $10,000 here." The Luxembourger paused, then said, "Oh, I guess I brought the wrong bucket."

Most of the town is still of Luxembourg descent.

SHEBOYGAN COUNTY, Pop. 100,935

This picturesque county has three distinct features making up its natural beauty. The most unique is a range of gravel hills in the western section known as kettles.

Thousands of years ago, when glaciers moved their icy tongues over this area plowing out the Winnebago and Michigan lake beds, they carried along great quantities of gravel and sand. As the ice masses melted, they left behind huge dome-shaped knolls and strange bowl-like indentations. Huge

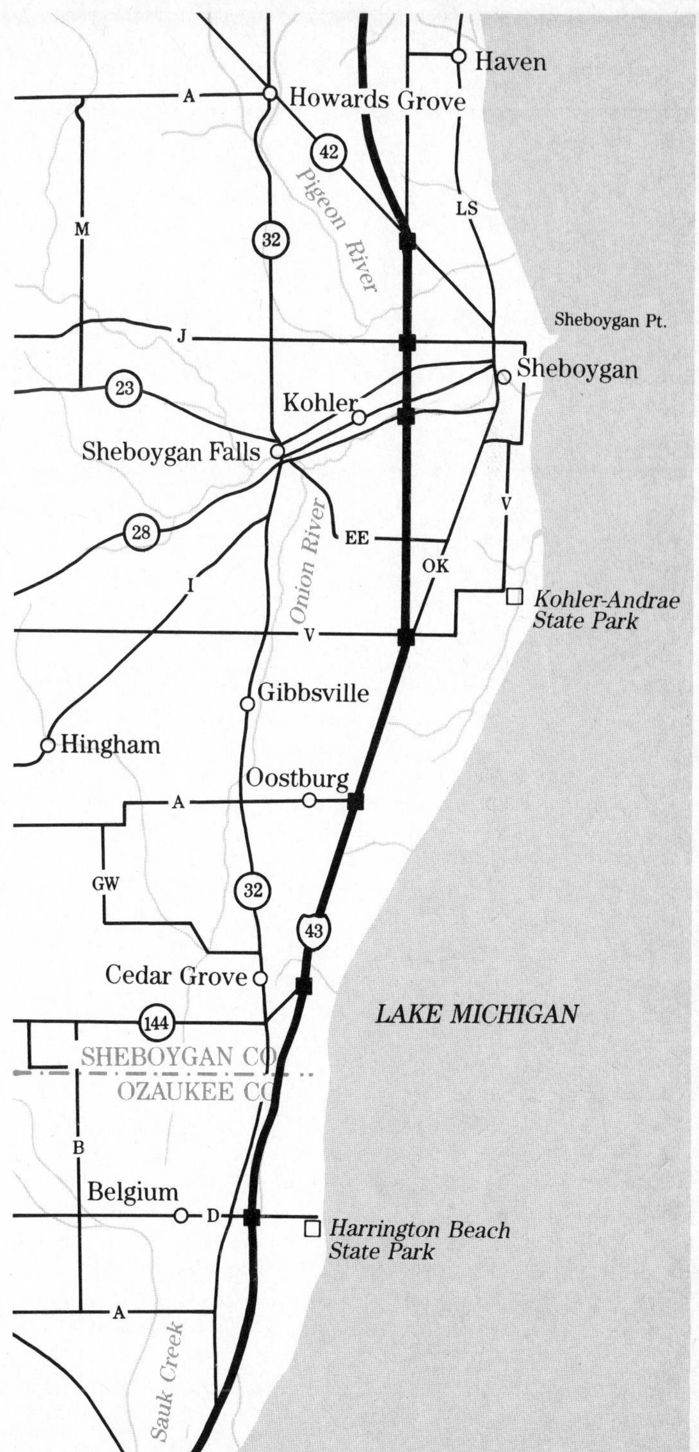

forests grew over the floors of these valleys, extending up the steep slopes to crown the hill tops. The impression left is of a vast natural amphitheater. Here in Sheboygan County, in the Kettle Moraine State Forest, you will see these formations in a more perfect form than anywhere else in the world.

The county's second distinct feature is Lake Michigan, the largest fresh water body lying wholly in one state. The clean, glittering lake shore was a favorite path of Indians and early whites who waded through the shallow water, over sand bars, to cross the numerous streams which discharged here.

Abrupt bluffs, 40-60 feet high, come close to the water north of Sheboygan, but south of the city the shore is low, wide and covered with sand dunes. This sand dune shore, best seen at Kohler-Andrae State Park, is the county's third distinct feature and remains as wild and picturesque as in prehistoric days. Within the park the undulating sea of sand piles up in heaps and ridges sometimes 30-40 feet high. Year after year, the wind blows in from the lake and the dunes march forward, slowing engulfing adjacent farm lands. This quiet and lonely spot is a favorite retreat for nature lovers, hikers and collectors of Indian relics.

The broad farming country of the early settlers stretches between the lake and Sheboygan County's kettle areas. The rolling landscape is dotted with farmhouses and herds of black and white cattle which graze on the grassy slopes and meadows.

Together, the Kettles, the lake and the sand dunes provide one of the most varied landscapes in the state.

CEDAR GROVE, Pop. 1,420

Although this is one of the county's oldest villages, little is known about its origin. According to land documents, the earliest claim was made by Gerthinderk Ta Kolste on November 3, 1846. The first post office was established three years later with Sweezy Burr as postmaster.

When the railroad came through here in the late 1800's, a lively controversy developed between the town's north and south ends about where the depot should be located. The south won.

The town's name refers to an extensive growth of cedar trees nearby.

OOSTBURG, Pop. 1,647

As with many small villages, the railroad's presence here spurred Oostburg's growth. When the Lake Shore Railroad was completed from Milwaukee in 1873, there was no settlement here. The original station, an old box car resting on the ground, was located about one and one/half miles further south.

Peter Daane, the village's founder, operated a store in a small settlement near the present highway 141, about two miles southeast of here. Daane heard that the railroad would bypass his area because an agreement could not be reached on the depot and promised to GIVE the railroad a depot if they moved the station a mile and a half north.

With the aid of friends, Daane built the depot as well as a grain and produce warehouse and a general store nearby. The town soon became remarkably successful and took its name from Daane's hometown in the Netherlands.

Most people here are Hollanders and worship in four churches, often in Dutch. The town has no dance halls or movie theaters and everything closes on Sunday, including the gas stations.

KOHLER, Pop. 1,651

Kohler, the county's newest village, of the county, is commonly known as a "model village" and an industrial area.

The Kohler Company located here is the county's largest manufacturer and one of the state's most important. Founded in 1873, the company was originally a foundry and is now best known for its plumbing ware. The plant was organized in 1888 at Sheboygan, but moved to its present site 11 years later.

Kohler was officially organized in 1912 and named after the company's original owner, John M. Kohler, an Austrian. The company built the village to provide neat, pleasant living conditions for its workers. Houses are sold to employees at cost and families are assisted in their purchase by a low cost, monthly rental plan. Most houses were built in colonial and modern English styles, with a pleasing variety of design. The town plan was established by public ordinance. All streets are paved, tree-lined and follow the land's natural contour. Considered a garden village, it is a distinctive American community.

SHEBOYGAN, Pop. 48,085

Sheboygan's site was recognized early as an ideal spot to build a city. A natural harbor, plentiful fish from Lake Michigan and the Sheboygan River, and pine and hardwood forests close by, added up to a near-perfect area. Few pioneers came to the county without first stopping in Sheboygan.

William Paine, an Englishman, came here in 1834 and built a saw mill on the river. Later General Harrison put up a cabin on the river's south side but he and Paine soon lost their property for failing to file proper claims. Thus the first settlers were hardly there long enough to be considered permanent.

SHSW

South 12th St., Sheboygan, 1871.

The village's plat was filed in the winter of 1835 by William Trowbridge. Houses were quickly built and the town grew rapidly.

Sheboygan had high hopes of becoming the leading commercial and maritime center along Lake Michigan's western shore. For many years, the Sheboygan port was a busy place, its docks and wharfs lined with vessels taking on and discharging freight and passengers. In 1845 there were 75 steamboat arrivals and departures; three years later, there were 525. No one dreamed that railroads would one day drive ships off the lakes.

In the 50's, agricultural exports, especially wheat, increased greatly as farmers raised more and more for outside markets. The flour trade, closely identified with the wheat trade, flourished after several mills were built. Dean & Crossett built a grist mill on the river's south side near its mouth in 1851. Grinding the first grain on December 29, it was the city's first manufacturing enterprise to use waterpower.

Sheboygan is based on the Chippewa Indian word Jibaigan which means "passage or waterway between lakes." The

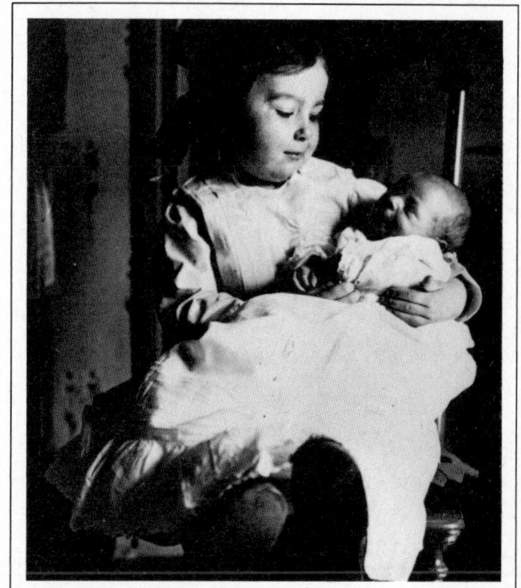

SHSW

Photo/ C.J. Van Schaick

Sheboygan River, with its source near Lake Winnebago, was a favorite and convenient travel route for Indians canoeing between the upper Fox and Lake Winnebago to Lake Michigan. Others think the word Sheboygan came from Sheub-wan-wan-gum, an Indian word meaning "rumbling waters."

OLD WADE HOUSE

A few miles west of Sheboygan on highway 23 is the lovely Wade House, a century-old stagecoach inn. The house was built by frontiersman, Sylvanus Wade, in 1851, from lumber cut on the site. Roofed with handhewn cedar shakes and furnished with handmade furniture, it cost a modest $300.

Wade watched Wisconsin build plank roads in the mid-nineteenth century, and soon became a busy promoter of the Sheboygan-Fond du Lac route. Although the roads were crudely designed and often murderous to cross in early spring, they were much better than the rough Indian trails that preceded them and allowed stagecoach lines to conveniently transport people cross-country.

Since the trip from Sheboygan to Wade House took nearly five hours at best, Wade knew his inn would be a welcome respite to teams and travelers alike. His doors were open for 90 years.

Now restored to its original condition by the Kohler Foundation, Old Wade House is open to tourists daily from May 1 to October 31.

MANITOWOC COUNTY, Pop. 82,918

Like much of the Midwest, Manitowoc County was almost an impenetrable wilderness for early settlers. Pine was the prevailing timber and whole forests grew along the Manitowoc River. Elm, beech, maple and other hardwoods also grew abundantly but later fell to aggressive lumbermen. Wild rice and grasses in the marshes would one day yield to waving fields of grain and cultivated farmland.

The county is well-watered from its principal stream, the Manitowoc, for which it was named. The river winds 45 miles, eventually emptying into Lake Michigan. Good waterpower was easily available and eight mills once operated along the river which was navigable by canoe almost to Lake Winnebago. The county's next largest streams are the Twin Rivers, the Neshoto and the Mishicott, which unite a few feet from Lake Michigan. Waterpower was utilized along these streams as well as along the Sheboygan River.

Permanent settlement began in 1836 when Jacob W. Conroe purchased several hundred acres of land and built a saw mill in Manitowoc Rapids. However, events a year earlier had brought the area's first visitors. Gold deposits were rumored near Kewaunee and a metropolis was expected to develop quickly. Three surveyors looked over the area and spread the rumor. Two years later, a land office opened to sell lots. Four villages, Manitowoc, Manitowoc Rapids, Two Rivers and Neshoto, sprang up simultaneously. A grand rush for the

SHSW

Sunday buggy ride.

"yellow jackets" began in Kewaunee (now a part of Kewaunee County) with swamp land selling for $500 an acre. Unfortunately, the gold didn't pan out and capitalists withdrew their money and their confidence from Kewaunee.

The Indian name for the county's main river was Munedowk, meaning "river of bad spirits." It was later spelled phonetically as Manitowoc.

CLEVELAND, Pop. 958

Until the first post office was established here in 1885, Cleveland was known as Centerville Station because the railroad depot lay half-way between Sheboygan and Manitowoc.

W.N. Adams was the town's first settler, arriving in 1847. Within a few months, the land was occupied by immigrants from Saxony, Germany and Prussia.

Cleveland has the tragic distinction of being the county's first town to record a murder among whites. It involved a romantic triangle between three suitors. Msrs. Gerken, Eichof and Egloff were all vying for one woman's hand. When Gerken won, the others plotted his death. On his way home one night, Gerken was struck in the back of the head with an ax. His body was concealed under a bridge where it was discovered several days later. Egloff and Eichof were soon arrested and put in jail but they escaped into the wilderness a few months later. Thirty-three years after that one of the men returned for a visit but was not arrested.

NEWTON, Pop. 2,332

Named after a Revolutionary War hero from South Carolina, Newton was established during the county's transformation from lumbering to agriculture. That change was due in great measure to the arrival of a large number of German farm laborers and handymen.

The political struggles of the 40's brought many professionals here, including journalists, lawyers and doctors. A journalist named Valentine Wintermeyer built a saw mill near Silver Lake and could reportedly "rip off" poetry and lumber with equal ability. His partner, C.Keil, was involved in an amusing incident. After killing a pig on his property one day, Keil didn't know how to remove the bristles. He finally proceeded to clean it using shaving soap and a razor.

MANITOWOC, Pop. 32,547

Because of its location on Lake Michigan's border, Manitowoc County's industrial and economic life has always been influenced by its geographical location.

Early trade here was handled by schooners which traveled up and down the lakes, bartering at various ports and bringing in supplies from the urban centers. However, the villagers were isolated when the Manitowoc River froze in winter. Only

SHSW

Manitowoc outer harbor, ca. 1900

when the first steamer came through again did they feel in touch with civilization. Consequently, many citizens worked feverishly to secure government aid to improve the harbors.

Benjamin Jones is considered the father of Manitowoc and its first permanent settler. He came here as a land speculator for Jones, King & Company of Chicago and platted the town in 1836. The company then carved out a city from the large tamarack forest which skirted the river near the foot of Sixth and Seventh streets. Shanties were built for the men and a large tract of land was cleared with trees used to build buildings in town or saved as steamboat wood.

No perceptible growth occurred here until the late '40's when a large number of German, Irish, Norwegian and Bohemian immigrants arrived. They were mostly farm laborers, mechanics and tradespeople and were commonly known as "Forty-eighters."

No regular roadways led into Manitowoc except for a few Indian trails, including the best known, the old Sauk trail which follows the lakeshore. You can imagine the delight of the early pioneers when the Milwaukee & Green Bay Railroad steamed into town in 1870. Teams no longer had to struggle through the dense woods between here and Milwaukee. Increased markets brought increased growth and by 1900 Manitowoc's population was about 12,000.

BRANCH

This town, at the mouth of the Branch River, was settled by E. Lenaville who built a saw mill in 1838 and leant his name to the small community. Its name was officially changed to Branch when the post office was established in 1857.

FRANCIS CREEK, Pop. 538

From this point on, the route gradually turns away from the lake and enters more of the county's farm communities.

This village was originally known as French Creek and was originally located on the Green Bay Road, an early mail route, just north of Manitowoc. There Joseph Paquin, probably the town's first settler, built a tavern which was frequented by mail carriers. The post office later changed the town's name to Francis Creek because Wisconsin had another French Creek post office. When rural free delivery started here, this post office was closed. When it reopened in 1917, the government gave it the name Axelyn. A young schoolteacher named Leo Meyer petitioned to change the town's name back to Francis Creek and when he later drowned on a school picnic, his request was honored posthumously.

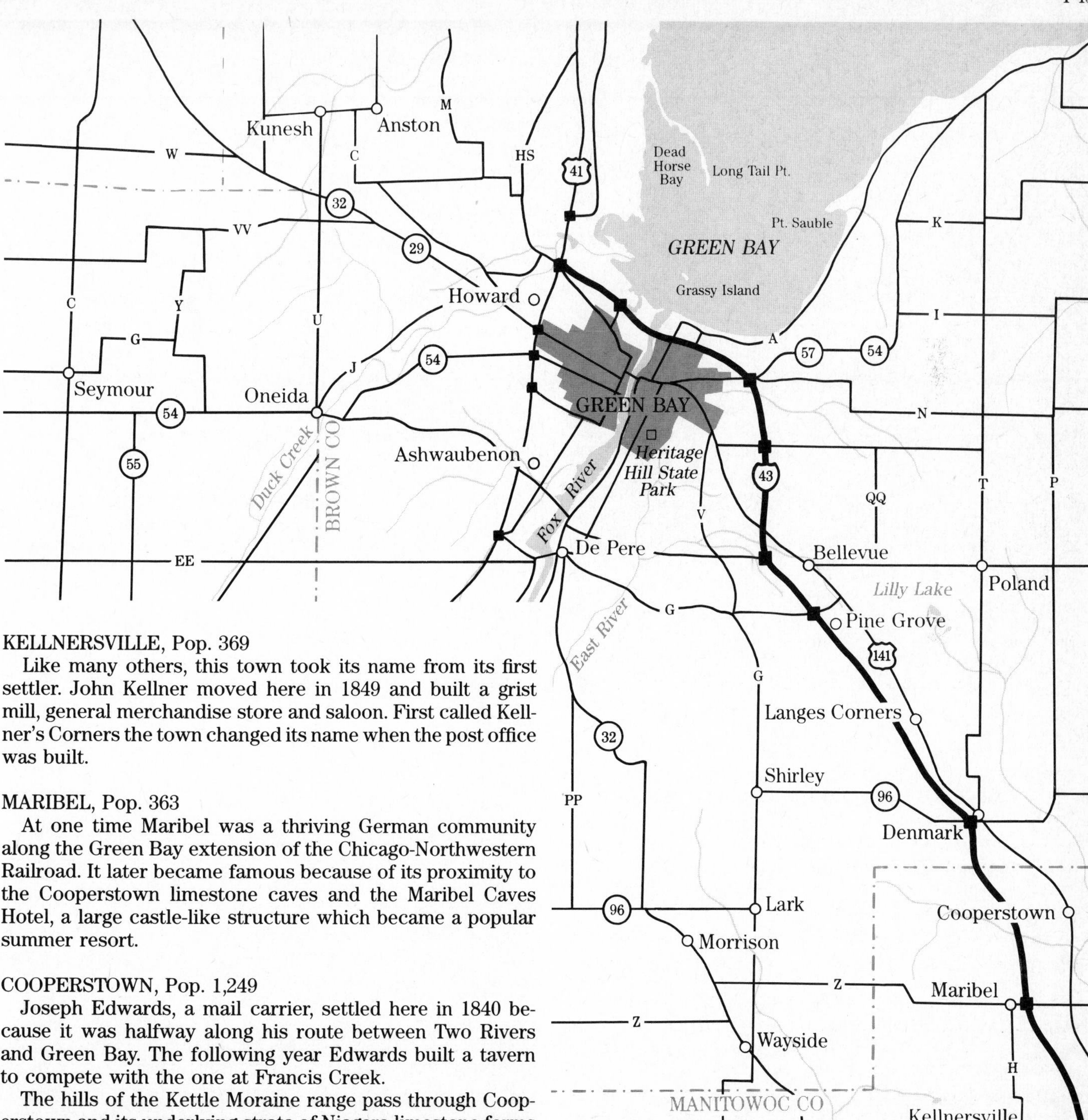

KELLNERSVILLE, Pop. 369

Like many others, this town took its name from its first settler. John Kellner moved here in 1849 and built a grist mill, general merchandise store and saloon. First called Kellner's Corners the town changed its name when the post office was built.

MARIBEL, Pop. 363

At one time Maribel was a thriving German community along the Green Bay extension of the Chicago-Northwestern Railroad. It later became famous because of its proximity to the Cooperstown limestone caves and the Maribel Caves Hotel, a large castle-like structure which became a popular summer resort.

COOPERSTOWN, Pop. 1,249

Joseph Edwards, a mail carrier, settled here in 1840 because it was halfway along his route between Two Rivers and Green Bay. The following year Edwards built a tavern to compete with the one at Francis Creek.

The hills of the Kettle Moraine range pass through Cooperstown and its underlying strata of Niagara limestone forms several horizontal caves, known as the Cooperstown Caves.

SHSW

Early mail carrier. Photo/Matthew Witt

BROWN COUNTY, Pop. 175,280

Millions of years ago a shallow sea lay over the North American continent. An accumulation of mud and sand lay in the sea, eroded from the unsubmerged parts of the continent. Remains of marine animals covered its bottom, depositing shells and lime mud. After much time had passed, the lime mud hardened into limestone, the shells into fossils and the clay mud into shale.

Within Brown County there are three different limestone formations. The first, known as Galena limestone, lies in ridges along the county's west side and traces can be found in the quarries at Duck Creek in Green Bay. East of this limestone bed is a band called the ledge which is seldom seen at the surface except at the foot of the cliffs on Green Bay.

The most beautiful formation lies along a ridge which begins east of Horicon and stretches north through Door County. It contains several huge chasms where waterfalls tumble from protruding rocks, and scores of caves which were home to rattlesnakes and wildcats for years. The ice age wore down this softer shale but the hard limestone remained, forming the valley now occupied by Green Bay, the Fox River and Lake Winnebago.

Soil and loose rocks from the retreating glaciers formed depressions without outlets known as kettles because of their resemblance to large bowls. You can see good examples of these kettles around Baird's Creek. Later retreats of ice filled the valley with water. At first the resulting lake found an outlet along what is now the Upper Fox River into what is now the Wisconsin River at Portage. Sand and gravel ridges formed by waves remained and were used by the Indians as convenient travel routes. The shifting water lines in Green Bay and at Long Tail Point indicate that the deposition continues.

When Lake Michigan reached its present level, the deep valleys were filled with a thick sand and gravel clay. Much of Brown County contains large quantities of this red clay which is often used for making bricks. The Fox River cut a deep channel at Wrightstown but smaller streams created narrow, steep-sided gullies. Erosion still goes on and can be seen anywhere along Lake Michigan's western shore. (For more information on Brown County see p216)

DENMARK, Pop. 1,475

Well-watered by the Neshoto River, the Denmark area has always contained plenty of rich farmland. An early cheese factory was owned and operated here by D. Benecke in 1876.

Denmark was settled by Danes who originally named it Copenhagen after their homeland's capital. When the post office was built the town became Denmark.

LANGES CORNERS

Well into Wisconsin's dairy region, this little town is made up of a small group of homes clustered around a cheese factory.

PINE GROVE

Once a trading center for neighboring farms, this town is named for a grove of tall pine trees located between the Catholic church and public school.

BELLEVUE, Pop. 4,101

Although Bellevue is predominantly Belgian, the town's first settler was a German named Platten, who came here in 1842. Mostly a dairy farming community, it is watered by several small streams which empty into the East River, the boundary between Allouez and Bellevue.

Red Banks, 1897. Site of Jean Nicolet's discovery of Wisconsin.

Looking across Fox River to Green Bay waterfront. Photo/F. Straubel.

GREEN BAY, Pop. 87,899

Green Bay was actually the beginning of Wisconsin.

When Jean Nicolet discovered this area, he believed he had found a new passageway to China. Met by Winnebago Indians, Nicolet came ashore in a brightly colored, Chinese robe and brandished two pistols, presenting a formidable sight to the unsuspecting tribe. Subsequently, on the Red Banks of Green Bay in 1634, Nicolet claimed the land in the name of Samuel de Champlain and New France (Canada). Because of his discovery and Green Bay's location between the Great Lakes and the Fox River, this region was called the Gateway to the Midwest.

One hundred years after Nicolet's discovery, the state changed hands between three masters; the French, British and finally, the Americans. By the mid-1800's, Green Bay had evolved from a scattering of Indian camps to a healthy cluster of white settlements. The first permanent settler was Charles de Langlade (known as the Father of Wisconsin) who moved here in 1765 to what he called "a heavily mosquito-infested swamp."

Despite De Langlade's unkind remarks, industries and the people to run them sprang up everywhere. During 1855 alone, 350,000 board feet of lumber and 168,000 barrels of flour were shipped out of Green Bay, an average of three steamboats per week.

By 1900 the town had seen a plethora of roads—poorly-cut Indian trails, rough-hewn plank roads, the government-designed Military Road and finally, the iron, railroads.

Remnants of Green Bay's past have been faithfully restored here in a state park called Heritage Hill. This park, located at the junction of highways 172 and 57, keeps the past alive with costumed interpreters and a hands-on policy. You can barter with a fur trader, dip candles, ride in a horse-drawn carriage, listen to a brass band in the Victorian bandshell and generally enjoy a taste of your heritage. Special events are held throughout the year, climaxed by a two-week Christmas festival which starts the Friday after Thanksgiving.

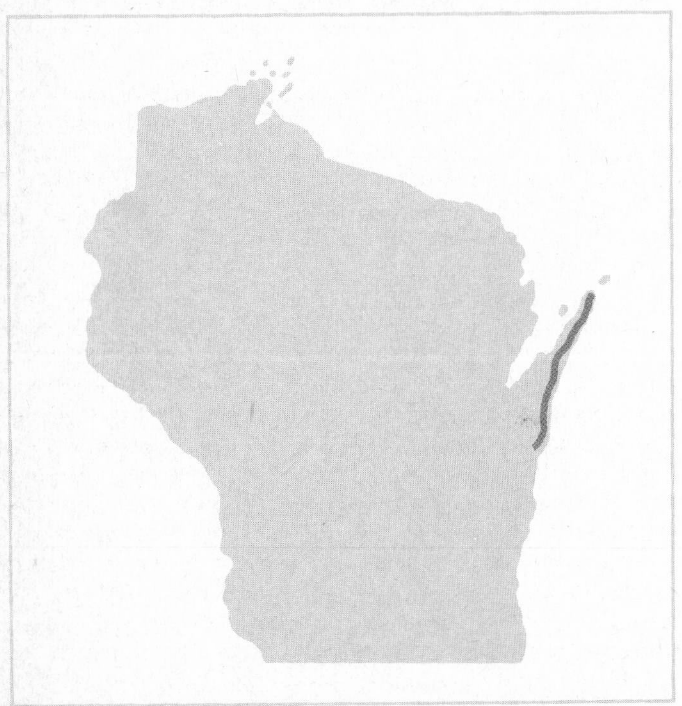

State 42, covering a total of 95 miles, has the prestige of running straight through Door County, one of the state's most popular tourist areas. This county, which creates a teapot-shape to the state, offers a natural, quiet beauty with recreational opportunities of every kind included in five state parks. At the peninsula's tip is Washington Island, home of this country's oldest Icelandic settlement.

ROUTE 42, TWO RIVERS TO ROCK ISLAND

Door County Historical Museum

Illinois couple picnic in Door County.

MANITOWOC COUNTY, Pop. 82,918

Travelers here may notice a heavy red clay covering this county. It was deposited thousands of years ago by retreating glaciers. Glacial Lake Chicago, an earlier body of water much larger than Lake Michigan, formed at the southern edge of the Michigan lobe, a long tongue of ice from the Wisconsin Glacier. As the glacier slowly retreated northward, it deposited this clay on the lake bottom.

After the lake drained, the remaining clay mixed with other glacial materials, then re-worked into a red till which was later deposited across the county's terminal moraines, or ridges. The clay in certain parts of the county, notably near Manitowoc, is an unusual light variety which early settlers made into cream-colored bricks, resulting in a thriving new industry.

The first permanent settlement began at Manitowoc Rapids in 1835 after eastern prospectors were impressed with the area and rapidly purchased hundreds of acres there. Jacob and John Conroe of Middlebury, Vermont canoed from Green Bay in Spring, 1836, and became the first white settlers. Jacob brought 30 men with him to build a mill with lumber he purchased at $20 a thousand plus five dollars to freight it from Chicago. The mill was quite successful and the only one in the county to survive the 1837 financial panic.

Manitowoc County takes its name from the river running through it and comes from the Indian word Munedowk meaning "spirit land," or "river of bad spirits."

TWO RIVERS, Pop. 13,354

John Arndt and Robert Eberts moved their families to Two Rivers in 1837, establishing the area's first permanent settlement. Together, they erected a log house and sawmill. Two more settlers arrived later that year, but a widespread financial panic prevented further development. The town's prosperity came later, when lumbering was firmly established.

Most of Two River's early success in lumbering was due to Deacon Smith who moved here on September 24, 1845. Smith bought the Eberts' mill and ran it successfully, as well as serving the town as pastor, doctor, druggist and counsel.

Two Rivers reportedly had the county's first brewery. Malt was ground with hand rollers and beer was transferred to Manitowoc twice a week by row boat on Lake Michigan.

The town gets its name from its location between the North and South Twin Rivers.

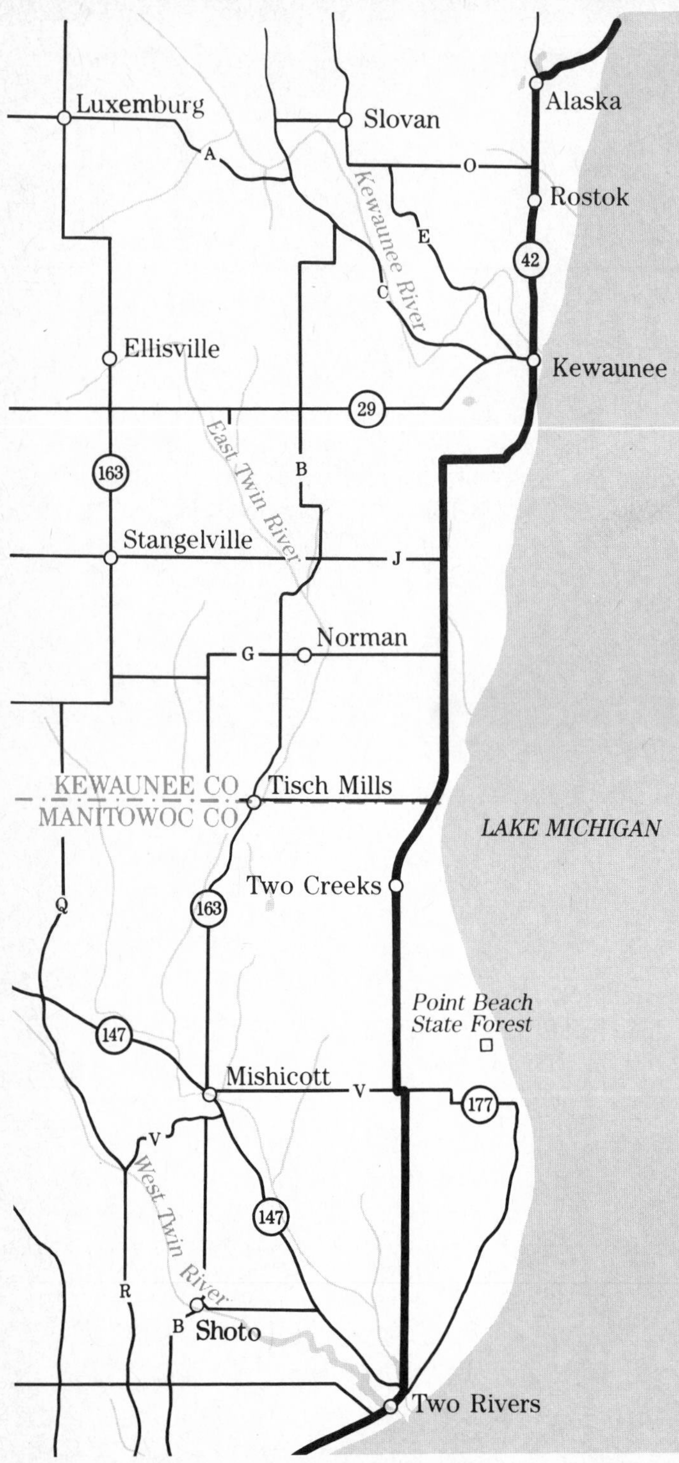

POINT BEACH STATE FOREST

A six mile sandy beach along Lake Michigan is a major attraction of this forest, located just north of Two Rivers. In addition, Rowley's Point, named after the first permanent settler in Two Creeks, has a one of the largest and brightest Coast Guard lighthouses on the Great Lakes with a beam that can be seen 19 miles. Remnants of some of the 26 lake vessels which were wrecked before the light was erected are on display.

Point Beach Forest contains many acres of the towering white pine that once made Wisconsin's lumber industry so successful. Self-guided or ranger-led hikes follow trails through the woods and along glacial lake ridges with marshy land between. Picnicking and camping are allowed and recommended.

TWO CREEKS, Pop. 489

Jacques Vieau, a Northwest Fur Company agent, came to Two Creeks in 1795 in a mackinaw boat manned by 12 men and heavily loaded with goods. Once on shore, Vieau and his family followed an old Indian trail nine miles southwest to the present Jambo Creek. He established a trading post there and subsequently returned to Two Creeks.

The bay here, once known as Sandy Bay, was later called Rowley's Point for Peter Rowley who built the town's first house. The settlement, organized in 1860, was also named for Rowley. One year later residents voted to change the name to Two Creeks.

Because of the abundant hemlock bark here, the Milwaukee firm of G. Pfister & Company established a large tannery in 1860. In time, this business developed to large proportions, laborers were imported and a thriving village resulted. A saw mill was also built at this time, along with 30 houses and a pier into the lake to receive wood products.

As the forests were depleted, the hemlock bark supply and the town's population also dwindled. By 1910 only 575 people remained, half German, half Bohemian.

TWO CREEKS BURIED FOREST

When the Wisconsin Glacier retreated through this area some 12,000 years ago, the meltwater raised the level of ancestral Lake Michigan enough to flood the Two Creeks forest, partially burying it under its sand. Standing trees were snapped off or uprooted by the glacier's icy lobes and the entire 25-acre forest was covered with 12 feet of glacial clay, sand, gravel and boulders. Later, Lake Michigan's waves eroded the shore cliffs, exposing the original glacial layers and uncovering trees with 11,850 year-old bark. Now a part of the Ice Age National Scientific Reserve, this forest is world fa-

SHSW

Sturgeon Bay excursion vessel.

mous among geologists searching for data on the ice age. Interpretive facilities aid the amateur in understanding this fascinating period of Wisconsin history.

KEWAUNEE COUNTY, Pop. 19,539

Kewaunee County is well watered, with its eastern boundary along Lake Michigan and fed by the Kewaunee and Ahnapee rivers. The geology here is made up of Racine and Niagara limestone, Cincinatti shale, and beneath that, Galena limestone, all formations which dip toward the lake, providing good drainage throughout the county. The fertile clay and sand soil is good for wheat, oats and dairying.

Montgomery & Peterson, a Chicago firm, actually made Kewaunee County's first real settlement in 1837. Soon after they arrived, the firm built a mill on the Kewaunee River about three miles from its Lake Michigan outlet. Unfortunately, the company was unable to stock the mill with winter supplies and workmen deserted it the following year. It remained uninhabited until 1843 when the new owners found the mill dam broken and nearby houses burned down by Indians who had made this a summer fishing resort.

KEWAUNEE, Pop. 2,801

Joshua Hathaway, a prosperous land developer, purchased lots here in 1836 and was commissioned by the district surveyor to lay out the town. He arranged the area in wide avenues averaging 75 feet, with 50X150 foot lots. Six blocks on the lake front were reserved for parks, commons, and boulevards. Lots started selling that fall and a rumor of gold found on the premises produced a great rush, with property at a premium. Hathaway sold a piece of land to Governor Doty for $15,000. When the gold fever ended, it was valued at $3,000. Not a single nugget was found and the land speculators moved on.

Kewaunee incorporated on April 30, 1873. Joshua Hathaway christened the town and county with a Chippewa Indian word meaning "prairie hen."

ALASKA

When the post office was established here in 1959, the town honored itself with the name of the newest state, acquired the same year.

ROSTOK

Originally settled by Czechoslovakian immigrants, Rostok was named after a city in Bohemia.

ALGOMA, Pop. 3,656

This little city lies along both sides of the Ahnapee River (which originally leant its name to the town) and overlooks Lake Michigan.

In 1876 the city allocated $80,000 to extend its piers and improve the natural harbor, which was only one foot deep. The goal was to create an inner harbor and a navigable channel, 12 feet in depth, to enter it. When completed, the project had cost $100,293.45 and the channel was seven feet deep.

Joseph McCormick was the first white settler to come here. He arrived from Manitowoc in 1834, sailing nine miles up river to an island which later took his name. After prospecting several days, McCormick returned to Manitowoc spreading tales of the heavily-timbered land and fertile soils. Nevertheless, the town did not grow to any degree until 1851.

One year later the Citizen, a Manitowoc vessel, began making regular trips here bringing food and supplies to the growing pioneer settlement. The first steamboat, the Cleveland, landed here in 1856 with a large number of eager settlers. A new school house and bridge were soon built and the town incorporated on April 1. In 1899, the city was renamed Algoma, an Indian word meaning "park of flowers."

DOOR COUNTY, Pop. 25,029

Jutting out on a 70-mile-long peninsula between Green Bay and Lake Michigan, this county draws an incredible number of summer visitors each year. It is not surprising that the peninsula has more state parks (five) than any Wisconsin county or that Door has been nicknamed the Cape Cod of the Midwest. In addition to its natural beauty, the Door is famous for the important role it played in Wisconsin's early history.

Door County, once the home of two important Indian tribes, also became known as the threshold to the west. It was here, in 1634, at the base of the peninsula in Green Bay, that Jean Nicolet sailed into the Winnebago Indian village at Red Banks and claimed the land for New France. This discovery led Father Marquette to the great Mississippi River and the beginning of settlement in the west.

POTAWATOMI INDIANS

After the Winnebagoes left their settlement at Red Banks and fled to Lake Winnebago, the Potawatomi moved into Door County. Their village, named Mechingan, was located a half mile north of the present day Jacksonport. The always friendly Potawatomi offered shelter to other tribes who needed it and around 1650 their village was flooded with 4,000 inhabitants including many fugitives from an Iroquois war in Canada.

Life among the Potawatomi was almost ideal before the white settlers came. They had no class distinctions, no slavery, no drunkenness (white men brought the first liquor) no poverty (everything was communal) and no disease. Living in fairly comfortable surroundings, the Indians supported themselves by hunting and fishing in nearby woods and streams. They had a simple life with simple needs.

The Potawatomi left Door County as a result of treaties in 1836. As a memorial to them, the Door County Historical Society has erected a tall, figurative totem pole on the golf course just inside Peninsula State Park. It marks the center of the Potawatomi's early dominion and includes the grave of its last leader, Chief Simon Kahquados.

WHITE SETTLEMENT

Increase Claflin, Door County's first white settler of record, located his early dwelling near Little Sturgeon Point on March 19, 1835. Claflin erected a log cabin within this unknown wilderness and lived, mostly in peace, until he moved to Fish Creek in 1844.

Several more whites came to the area after Claflin had lived here successfully for a number of months. Soon they were clearing land and forming little communities. But life wasn't easy on this peninsula. Even after raising a successful crop, it was difficult to get it to market: Green Bay, the nearest trading spot, was 50 miles away. Farmers had to make the long, arduous trip on foot through the woods or by coasting on the water in a small, open boat.

FORESTVILLE, Pop. 455

The first white settlers here came on the Ahnapee River which runs through town. The James Keogh family, for example, came from Ahnapee (Algoma) to Forestville by boat in 1852. A saw mill was built and a steamer and two barges, owned by J. Fetzer & Co., freighted the area's forest products down river to Green Bay.

Forestville became the third town in Door County in April, 1857, and organized the following year.

MAPLEWOOD

German and Irish settlers named this town after the area's many maple trees.

POTAWATOMI STATE PARK

As with all Door County parks, the 1,200-acre Potawatomi State Park has much to see. The park's overlooks and observation tower provide views all the way to Upper Michigan on a clear day. Miles of blacktop roads within the park are available for biking and a chance to hear more than 50 varieties of songbirds. Hiking trails lead to Sturgeon Bay. Swimming is not allowed but the fishing is excellent.

ICE AGE TRAIL

A rare opportunity to discover remaining evidence of prehistoric glaciers exists in a 1,000-mile-long hiking trail here. For the last 15 years, private citizens have worked to complete the Ice Age Trail which begins in Potawatomi State Park and ends in Interstate Park, on the Minnesota border. A 950-mile biking trail is also available, offering another unique perspective of the geological features found along its path. Detailed maps are available and interpretive centers can provide more information.

A federal bill signed into law in 1980 designates the Ice Age Trail as one of only eight National Scenic Trails which include the Appalachian and Pacific Crest Trails.

STURGEON BAY, Pop. 8,847

This arm of Green Bay got its name from the Menominee Indians who thought the bay's outline resembled the sturgeon fish common to its waters.

In its earlier years, Sturgeon Bay, the county seat, was known only as a trading post. In time, settlers moved into the area and built log cabins along the Bay's east banks. Peter Rowley settled here first, locating on the west bank in 1835. He lived alone for four or five years, clearing the land and fishing in the bay. Then one day he suddenly pulled up stakes and moved to Kewaunee. Nothing further is known of him.

In the Fall of 1856, Assemblyman Ezra B. Stevens drew up a bill to organize the town under the name of a Spanish city called Otumba. Several efforts were made to change the name; it was also known as Graham and later Tehema, but neither became permanent. Local residents knew that this area was well-known as Sturgeon Bay, and made the name official on February 13, 1860. An early spring drive here is not only beautiful, but provides something to take home–cherries, one of Sturgeon Bay's leading industries. Door County produces million of pounds of the famous Red Tart cherries each year, making it the nation's third largest cherry producer.

More recently, Sturgeon Bay has developed a reputation as the largest shipbuilding port on the Great Lakes. Some 3,000 skilled craftsmen turn out a variety of ships including the 1,000 foot superlakers which carry cargo on the Great Lakes. Since 1968 the Bay Shipbuilding Company has built 32 vessels on a 7,000-ton floating dry dock. Tours are not permitted but visitors can view yard activity from surrounding streets.

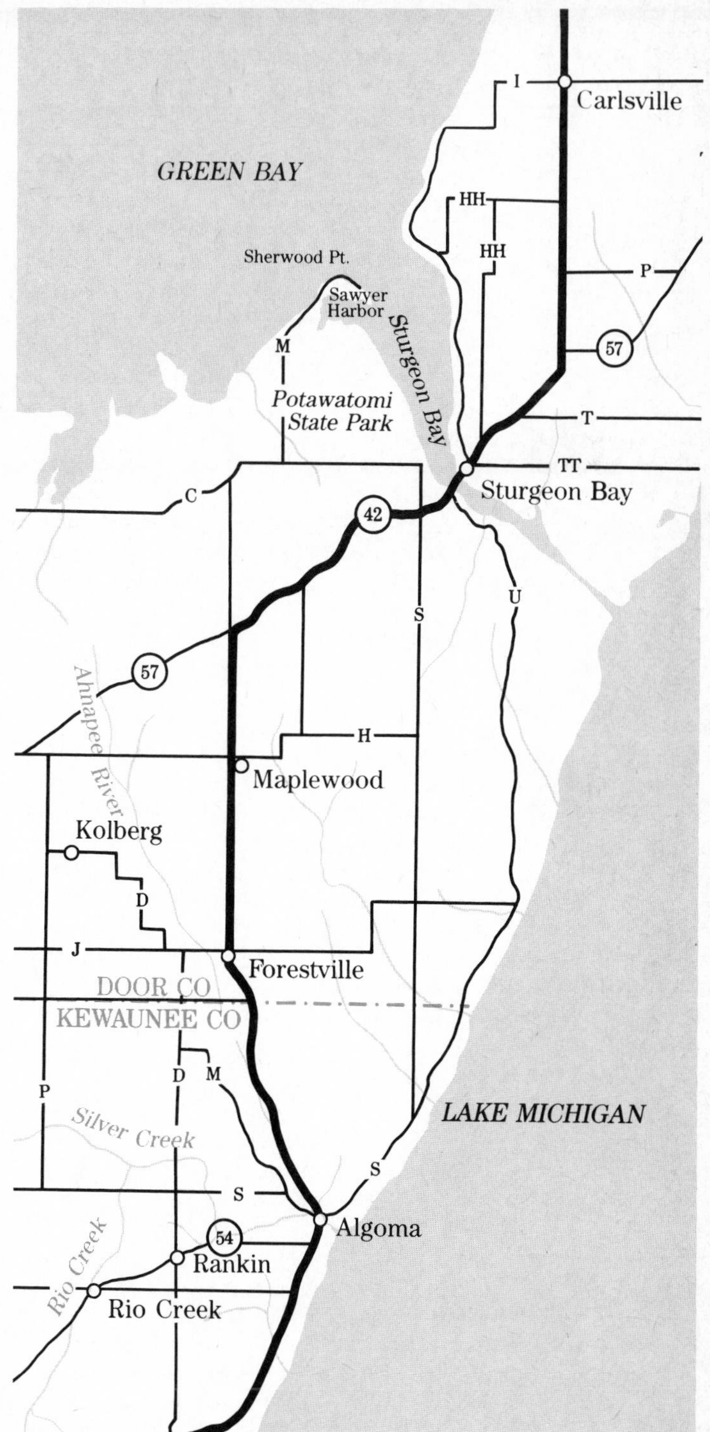

SHSW

Sturgeon Bay to Egg Harbor mail & passenger sleigh.

A ship canal connects Sturgeon Bay with Lake Michigan, but for thousands of years before it was constructed the only means of crossing was via a portage trail. This trail, the oldest known highway in the west, is called the Marquette Trail because Father Jacques Marquette and Louis Joliet were the first known white men to carry canoes over it.

The Door County Museum on 4th and Michigan Avenues and the Sturgeon Bay Marine Museum at Sunset Park, give the traveler an inside look at the region's early history.

THE GREAT FIRE OF 1871

Perhaps no other year will be remembered as much in the annals of Door County, or any northwestern Wisconsin county, as the year 1871. During that year a series of natural disasters threatened to wipe out most of the county and the loss was evenly divided between water and fire. Hundreds of lives were lost on the lakes from shipwrecks strewn at intervals from Chicago to Buffalo. On land, forest fires raged furiously due to the particularly dry summer. But the most serious disaster of all occurred in October, 1871 and few homesteads escaped.

Though no one is certain what started the blaze—a spark from some land clearer's log heaps or the smouldering coals of a camp fire—once started the whole territory was a powder keg. Small fires started across the bay in mid-September spread slowly throughout the northwest counties. The forests, corduroy roads, fences, wood structures, even the swamps were reduced to ashes. The air was thick with smoke, making even breathing difficult. At night the sunset was replaced by an ominous dark red glow. Finally, on October 7, the fire got a new start and became a tornado of flame. On the morning of October 8, a gust of fiery wind jumped Green Bay and rushed inland. The cries of birds mingled with other frightened animals and falling timber. A little town known as Williamsonville was completely destroyed by fire. Portions of the road leading into town were blocked with smouldering trees nine deep. Burned bodies of animals and people were stacked together in heaps. Of the 80 or so people that lived in Williamsonville, only 17 survived.

A drenching rain finally smothered the blaze but not before 1200 people were killed, 7,500 were left homeless and some of the area's richest farmlands were burned into barrenness forever.

CARLSVILLE,

Carlsville provides a good initiation to Door County. With slides, light and sound effects, the "Door County Experience" provides a superb multi-media show of the area from past to present. Admission is charged.

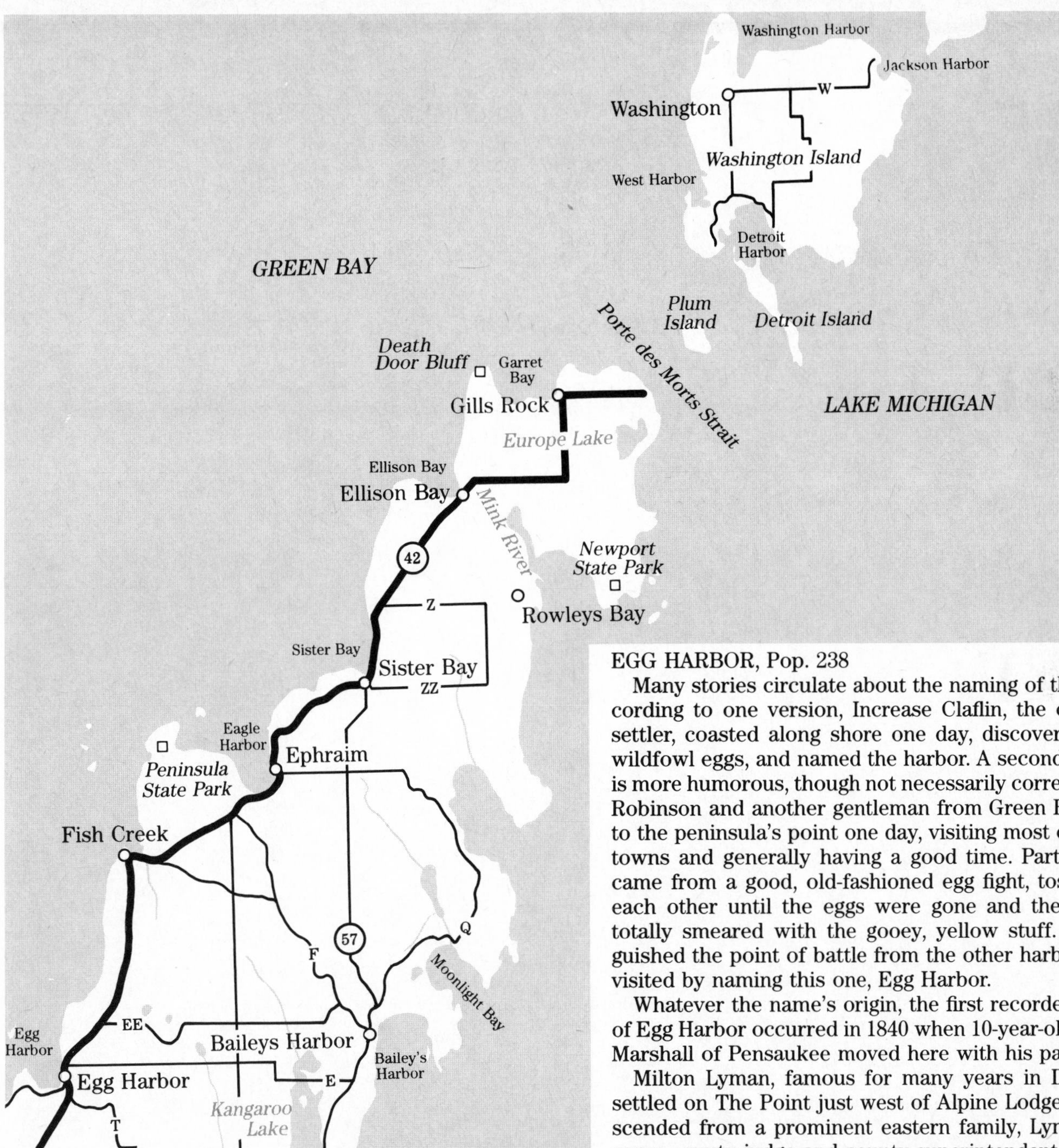

EGG HARBOR, Pop. 238

Many stories circulate about the naming of this town. According to one version, Increase Claflin, the county's first settler, coasted along shore one day, discovered a nest of wildfowl eggs, and named the harbor. A second explanation is more humorous, though not necessarily correct. A Colonel Robinson and another gentleman from Green Bay sailed up to the peninsula's point one day, visiting most of the harbor towns and generally having a good time. Part of their fun came from a good, old-fashioned egg fight, tossing eggs at each other until the eggs were gone and they were both totally smeared with the gooey, yellow stuff. They distinguished the point of battle from the other harbors they had visited by naming this one, Egg Harbor.

Whatever the name's origin, the first recorded settlement of Egg Harbor occurred in 1840 when 10-year-old Ransselaer Marshall of Pensaukee moved here with his parents.

Milton Lyman, famous for many years in Door County, settled on The Point just west of Alpine Lodge in 1853. Descended from a prominent eastern family, Lyman later became county judge and county superintendent of schools.

FISH CREEK,

Increase Claflin, generally regarded as the first white set-

SHSW

Frozen hull of the Kate E. Howard on Lake Michigan shore.

tler, moved here in 1844 after living on Little Sturgeon Point. However, Asa Thorp who bought property here in 1853, became the town's real promoter.

Thorp had come from the east with his father and eventually landed in Milwaukee. He learned to make wooden butter tubs as a boy and worked his way out of Milwaukee by making wooden wares for the new settlers. One day Thorp was approached by a stranger as he sat in front of a store repairing tubs. The stranger asked Thorp to come with him to Rock Island and make fish barrels instead. He told Thorp that Rock Island had no county or state organization, no taxes and no lawyers or preachers. What they did have was lots of fish and lots of money.

Thorp left for Rock Island by steamer in 1845, but most of the area's fishermen had already left. However, as they passed Increase Claflin's newly built cabin the steamer's captain told Thorp that this place badly needed a pier. Thorp returned in 1853, built the pier and employed many men to cut cordwood for passing steamboats. Fish Creek soon became an important business center.

Door County Historical Museum

U.S. Coast Guard Station, Door County

SHSW

Great Lakes excursion steamer takes on passengers at Alsag Anderson's dock in Ephraim harbor.

PENINSULA STATE PARK

At 3,760 acres this is truly the largest and most popular state park on Door County. It offers 467 campsites and all the related activities. Besides the Eagle Lighthouse, an historic landmark built in 1868, the park has an unique evening program. Using regional and national themes, the University of Wisconsin-Green Bay Heritage Ensemble performs musical productions covering subjects from the Great Lakes to famous Americans. A small admission fee is charged.

EPHRAIM, Pop. 319

A village with this name was originally located near Ft. Howard in Green Bay, but several members left that community in 1851 and moved to the east shore of Sturgeon Bay. In 1853 the group (mostly of Norwegian descent) finally settled the present village—as a communistic colony.

The settlers jointly agreed that each homeowner could have one lot fronting the water and another in the rear if desired. The lots were priced at $4.00 each and every one was sold by the end of the year. Ephraim's pioneers consisted of 18 people including five couples, four unmarried men and four children. Thomas Goodletson's house, built in 1857, still stands and is open to the public free of charge.

The settlers didn't let a Sunday pass without community worship or a day without gathering to sing hymns. In 1859, they built the first church on the Door County peninsula.

Located at the northern end of town is the Anderson store and dockhouse. Aslag Anderson, a Norwegian millwright, built the store and dock in 1858. This complex served as a transportation center from the sailing days through the steamship era of the the 1920's. Years of graffiti have been etched into the sides of the building now used as a gift shop. The complex was restored in 1952.

Ephraim is nestled along a beautiful scenic harbor with two New England-stlye church steeples and a picturesque hotel dominating the skyline.

SISTER BAY, Pop. 564

Increase Claflin named much of this peninsula, including Sister Bay. Claflin, who sailed these waters often, noticed that two bays in this area were quite close together and similar in appearance, then named them Little Sister Bay and Big Sister Bay. The Sister Islands offshore are a breeding ground for herring gulls and terns.

ELLISON BAY

Government surveyors recorded this bay on their 1865 maps and named it after John Ellison who promoted the settlement. The Indians called this Joe-Sahbe-Bay after the son of Neatoshing also known as Mishicott.

NEWPORT STATE PARK

Just across the peninsula from Ellison Bay is the beautiful Newport State Park, offering sand beaches and crysal clear water along Lake Michigan's coastline. Although only 13 primitive campsites are currently available, 26 miles of hiking trails and a large picnic area make this an ideal place for a day's outing.

GILLS ROCK

This area's original occupants, the Potawatomi Indians,

named this region Wahya-quakah-mekong meaning "head of the land," a fitting name for the tip of the peninsula.

According to one history of Gills Rock, a man named Allen Bradley came here in the 1830's and impressed everyone with his brute strength. A giant of a man, he measured four feet around his chest, had extremely broad hands and wore Indian moccasins because no shoes would fit. Once, on a bet, "Old Bradley" carried a 250-pound man around a room until the man begged to be released.

The town was named for Elias Gill who came here in the '70's to reap the bounties of the area's forests. Older Wisconsin maps noted this as Hedgehog Harbor.

Often called the tip of the thumb, Gills Rock is still a Scandinavian fishing village. You will see many small boats here, their nets drying in the sun. Whitefish caught in these waters are used in the famous Door County fish boils.

WASHINGTON ISLAND

When pioneers came here Washington Island was covered by a deep forest and had long been a favorite spot of the Indians. In fact, it was first named Potawatomi Island for the tribe which occupied it. Today it is rich with archaelogical evidence of their ancient cities, cemeteries and cornfields.

Amos Sanders bought this island in 1849 and became the town's first chairman when it was organized. Though not heavily populated, the island and the town continued to grow and prosper. Icelandic pioneers settled here in the mid-1800's making this the oldest Icelandic settlement in the United States. Approximately 550 permanent residents live on the island today.

This island was also the destination of the first ship to sail the Great Lakes, the Griffin, which explorer Robert La Salle built at Niagara Falls and sailed to the west in search of furs. La Salle financed an expedition exploring the course of the Mississippi with the money from their sale. On September 18, 1679, after loading pelts here, the Griffin hoisted anchor and set out to sea, never to be heard from again.

Two ferries currently provide daily summer service from Gills Rock to the Island. Once on the island, 100 miles of scenic roads offer complete facilities from modern to old-world charm and a chance to explore this unique part of Wisconsin history.

ROCK ISLAND

When Jean Nicolet made his famous voyage to Red Banks at Green Bay, he passed this island's northern shore just as Indians had for many years. In that sense Rock Island, not Green Bay, was actually the first place white men visited in Wisconsin.

Door County has a shoreline of about 250 miles, excluding the small bays and inlets along the way. Scores of hidden shoals and several dangerous passages line the shore and made Green Bay's sudden squalls and Lake Michigan's big storms literally murder for unsuspecting crafts. In 1872, the Griffin and 99 other vessels were lost or wrecked while going through Porte des Morts Strait or "Death's Door." Thus, Door County got its name.

SHSW

Ferryboat landing at Gills Rock, 1929.

SHSW

A small gaff-rigged schooner.

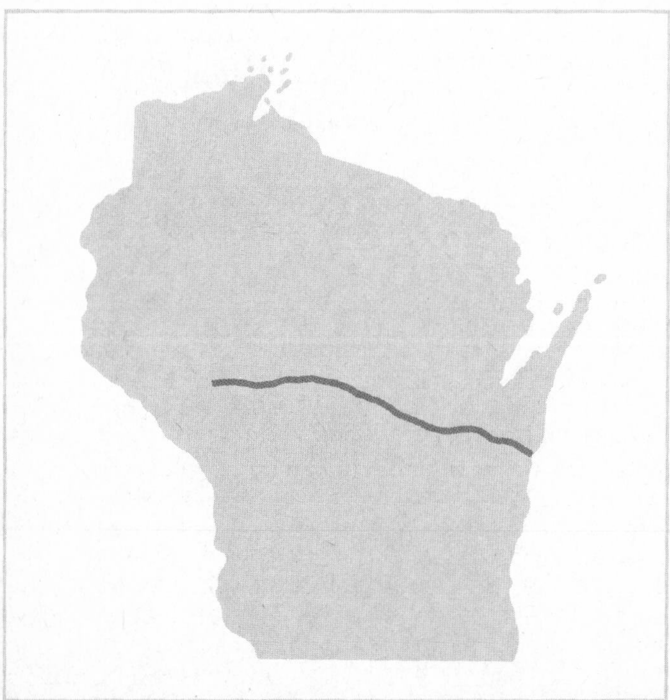

U.S. 10 travels approximately 185 miles from the city of Manitowoc hugging the coast of Lake Michigan, through the sandy soil of mid-Wisconsin and finally, to the hilly, western Uplands. One of the prettiest lookout points in Wisconsin is located along this route in High Cliff State Park, near Forest Junction. On a clear day you can see all the way across Lake Winnebago–a total of 30 miles.

ROUTE 10, MANITOWOC TO PRICE

A cold December morning in Manitowoc Harbor, ca. 1897.

MANITOWOC COUNTY, Pop. 82,918

Almost from the beginnqng, Manitowoc's economic and industrial life has been influenced by its geographical location. With its eastern border along Lake Michigan, much of the first transportation in and out of this county was conducted over the lake. Consequently, the area was almost totally isolated when the lake froze over during the winter. With that in mind, most early activity centered around the county's harbors. Improving the natural harbor made it easier for larger ships to get in and out, bringing in settlers and much-needed supplies and allowing ships to take out lumber, which was rapidly becoming an important industry.

Eastern land developers, coming here in 1835, considered Manitowoc County an ideal location for a lumber industry; pine was abundant in the surrounding forests, the Manitowoc River was an excellent source of waterpower and lumber markets were opening up all along the lake shore. Back in Middlebury, Vermont, Jacob W. Conroe heard about this prospective industry and decided to quickly move west and get into it. Bringing 30 men with him to build a mill, Conroe arrived in Spring, 1836 and became the county's first permanent settler. The settlement was originally named Conroe, but later became Manitowoc Rapids.

Shortly after Conroe arrived, a chartered schooner came from Green Bay with lumber and supplies to establish a camp. Conroe persuaded the schooner's captain, Joseph Edwards, to stay on and Edwards soon built a scow (flat-bottomed boat with square ends) which enabled his crew to ship lumber down river into the bay where it was loaded on to sailing vessels bound for distant markets.

MANITOWOC, Pop. 32,547

Benjamin Jones, the founder of Manitowoc, came here as a land speculator with the Chicago firm of Jones, King & Company as early as 1835. He made a claim on about 2,000 acres including all land south from the mouth of the Manitowoc River for three miles and west from the lake to the present western city limits. In 1836 Jones, King & Company sent a five-man crew to clear the site for a new town. They began by clearing an area in the large tamarack forest which skirted the river near the foot of the present Sixth and Seventh streets. Stakes were driven to divide the lots as platted. After establishing company headquarters, Jones, King & Company contracted Jacob Conroe, who had established a saw mill at the Rapids, to sell them all the lumber he could manufacture for $20 per thousand so they could build the town. The following year, Jones, King & Company sent 40 more men to Manitowoc to help erect buildings and continue clearing the vast forest. Two of the workers had families and their dwellings became the city's first permanent houses.

In the spring of 1838 J.P. Clark of Detroit came to Manitowoc with a crew of 20 men, a complete set of fishing apparatus and a schooner named the Gazelle. He planned to set up a fishing business on a large scale and was soon doing just that. Fish were plentiful and Clark's men frequently caught as many as 150 barrels of whitefish in one haul. Clark continued his business for 15 years, amassing a small fortune. Though not as prosperous as it once was, the fishing industry which Clark began still plays an important role in Manitowoc's economy.

Two severe cholera epidemics hit Manitowoc, one in 1850, another in 1854, and all but a few of the most stubborn settlers left. Several years later the city began growing again, thanks to a brand new industry—shipbuilding. The industry expanded along with commerce on the Great Lakes and the largest plant employed about 2,500 men at its peak. The boom lasted until 1890 when iron vessels began replacing wooden ones and Manitowoc could not keep up with the larger manufacturing centers.

Between 1848 and 1856 this area grew rapidly, as a large number of immigrants moved here. Germans, Bohemians and Norwegians—mostly farm laborers, mechanics and tradesmen—settled some of the now unincorporated towns around Manitowoc.

WHITELAW, Pop. 649

This small town, formerly known as Pine Grove Siding, developed around 1872 when the Chicago & Northwestern Railroad stopped here. The town reportedly changed its name to honor a railway officer. The village originally included a large flour mill, a lumber yard, creamery, Catholic church and school, cigar factory, cement factory and various other shops. It was predominantly German.

CATO

Jonas C. Burns, a printer, founded Cato in 1845 when he moved into the nearby forests in order to apply his printing skills to a related but highly illegal profession, counterfeiting. Burns was arrested one day while pedaling his wares in the countryside, making him the town's first felon as well as its first settler!

After Burns' arrest, Cato fell into the hands of John Harris, land promoter. Little is known about him, except that the town was known as Harrisville until he left the area. In 1855 the town was officially organized and Alanson Hickok, the town chairman, named it Cato in honor his New York hometown.

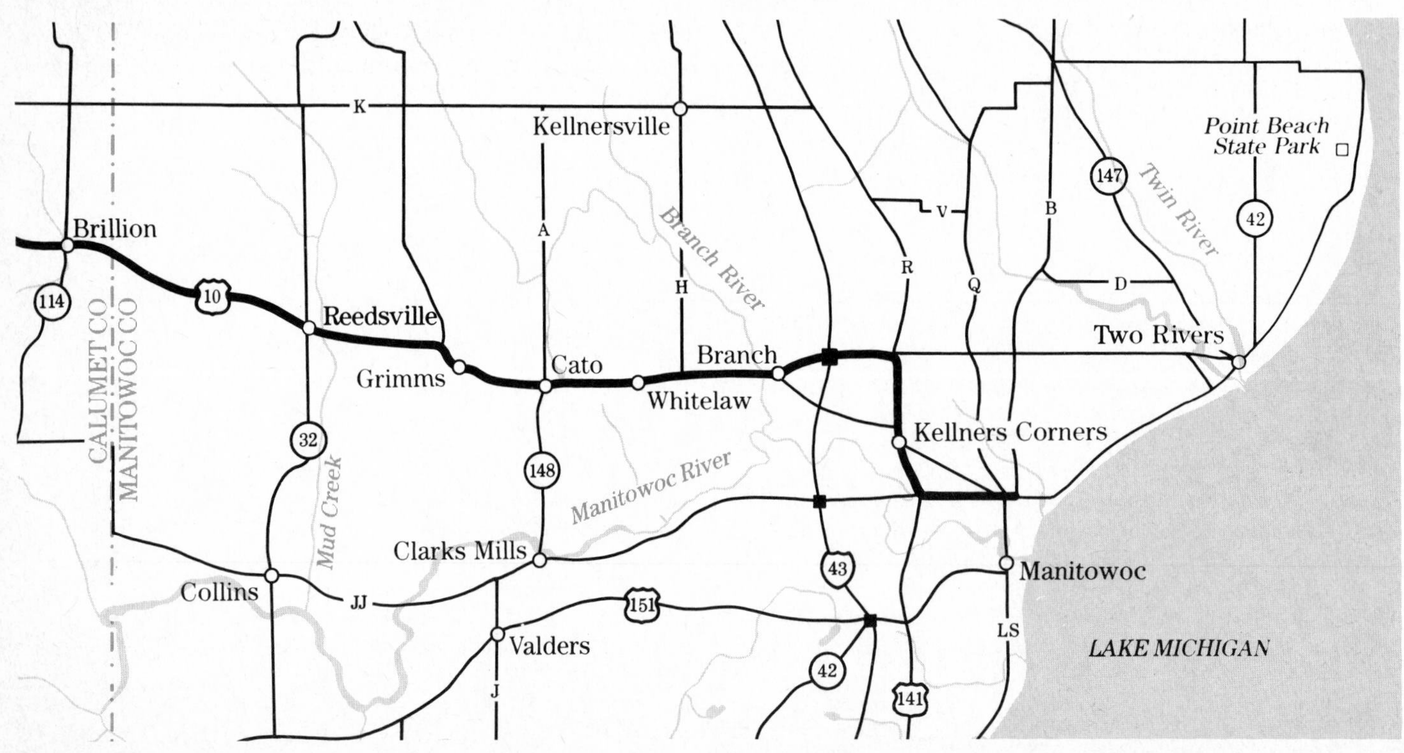

EARLY ROADS

Two important roads—the Calumet and the Menasha Road—were laid out through Cato around 1850. Hearing of the success of plank roads in the East, Wisconsin Governor Tallmadge approved a state charter to build these new "ultra" roads through selected counties of the state, including Manitowoc County.

Since timber was plentiful, plank roads were relatively cheap to build as well as durable, practical and safe. Built of aged oak, they were said to last at least eight years before needing major repairs. Horses could pull three times the weight on these roads because of reduced friction and planks were less slippery than the crushed stone being laid elsewhere. At their high point in the 1850's, about 2,000 miles of wooden roads had been laid.

Construction of the roads was a complicated process. First, a foundation called a sleeper layer was put down, consisting of 13 to 20 foot logs cut in half and embedded in trenches parallel with the road, then tamped down so that the top was at ground level. Planks, mostly eight feet long and three inches thick, were then placed across the sleepers. In some places each plank was secured with spikes, in others, only the fifth plank was secured, and still others secured no planks. Where possible plank roads had two lanes on separate beds. All were elevated so water could drain off and the tops were finished with a thin layer of fine gravel.

At first these roads were unregulated and private. Then in 1854 the government imposed a one percent tax on road revenue. In 1858, a government statute regulated tolls at booths set up along ten mile intervals on the road. The fee was two cents a mile for a vehicle drawn by one or two animals, one cent for every horse and rider, and two cents for every "score of neat cattle." Persons attending church services or funerals, on military duty or appearing in court, passed free.

Plank roads were not a long-term success, primarily because they weren't profitable. Although it was illegal to evade the tolls most travelers made wide detours around the toll booths and booth keepers frequently embezzled tolls. In addition, farmers found that their horses got stiff on long journeys. Planks didn't keep as long as had been projected and were often needing repair. Plank roads were rapidly declining by 1860 and most were abandoned by the end of the century. Nonetheless, the roads played a useful, if somewhat limited, role in the state's development.

GRIMMS

When the Chicago & Northwestern Railroad passed through Manitowoc County, this town named itself after Jacob Grimm who owned the depot property. Besides the railroad, this small settlement had one of the largest lime kilns in Wisconsin. Lime deposits found and manufactured here were noted for their fine quality.

REEDSVILLE, Pop. 1,134

Reedsville began as the 56-block property of Judge George Reed of Manitowoc who purchased it in 1854. It was known as Mud Creek, after the small stream which runs through town, until Reed's death in 1883 when it was renamed in his honor.

SHSW

Corduroy roads replace well-worn Indian trails.

The town developed quickly. One of its first settlers, a French-Canadian named James Dumass, came from Green Bay with his Menominee wife in 1854 to build a saw mill for Judge Reed. It was the town's main industry for many years. Later settlers included Germans, Bohemians and Irish who tilled the soil in the ways of their homeland.

An interesting aspect of Reedsville history involved cattle fairs held on the last Wednesday of the month, which attracted crowds by the thousands. On fair day all roads leading to town were choked for miles with pedestrians, vehicles and livestock. Booths lined the main streets which were rented to transient merchants selling clothing, boots, shoes, pots and kettles and wagon loads of fruits. Everyone wanted a piece of the action; patent medicine peddlers, gamblers, horse jockeys, gypsies, even pickpockets. Local merchants protested in vain, except for the the saloon keepers who reportedly did a thriving business.

The Chicago & Northwestern Railroad Company chugged through here in 1872 infusing new life. Reedsville incorporated 20 years later and continues to be a thriving business center for the western part of Manitowoc County.

CALUMET COUNTY, Pop. 30,867

Like many northern Wisconsin counties, Calumet County was covered with a heavy growth of pine in its early days. The pine was soon removed by extensive lumbering, leaving a rich soil, easy to cultivate and ripe for agriculture. As a result, the county developed around a profitable dairying and cheese-making industry. At one time, 30 successful cheese factories were operating throughout the county. Stockbridge led in the industry, but the whole region bordering the lake was actively involved.

Calumet County was named by the Menominee Indians for their village along the east shore of Lake Winnebago (now the town of Calumet in Fond du Lac County.) The name is said to mean "pipe of peace." The county insignia includes two crossed peace pipes and the motto "We extend the calumet."

The county was originally settled by two bands of Indians, the Stockbridge and the Brothertowns. In the winter of 1834 two or three families from each band lived in the dense forest and used a few Menominee trails as their roads. The Indian villages lay primarily along the east bank of Lake Winnebago and supplies came in by boat up the lower Fox. These two tribes cut the first trees, cleared the first land, and erected the first dwellings. Many stayed on after the first white settlements began.

The Brothertowns and the Stockbridge, two New York Indian tribes, originally settled in Green Bay around 1822. The two tribes obtained land along Lake Winnebago in 1831 but real settlement didn't begin until 1833. The Indians couldn't officially organize a town because they weren't American citizens but each tribe assumed the town system of government and lived like any other pioneer. The Brothertowns even employed a white settler, Moody Mann, to build them a grist mill which became the standard of its class for miles around. The Stockbridge built similar mills and residents of Oshkosh and Fond du Lac had all their milling done there for many years.

In 1834 other whites followed Mann into the county to set up homes. John Dean, a former lieutenant of Jefferson Davis at Fort Winnebago, came with several comrades-in-arms. Soon after their arrival, the Military Road was cut through and the county's population swelled. The growing white settlement gradually crowded the Indians away from the lake shore. However, on March 3, 1843, an act of Congress granted the Indians full rights of citizenship with title to their land, the towns of Brothertown and Stockbridge were officially organized, and the Indians and whites lived as one.

BRILLION, Pop. 2,907

Early records show that William McMullen, Sr. and his two sons settled here in the fall of 1855. Most of their early activities involved clearing the heavy timber that covered this area. One year later they were joined by German immigrant Christopher Horn who was later elected town treasurer. Originally known as Spring Creek, the name Branden was suggested when the town organized in 1856. Because of a similar name in Fond du Lac County, Postmaster T.N. West suggested that the settlement be named Pilleola, a combination of his daughter's first names. The Post Office Department found this name too difficult and selected Brillion.

Like most of Calumet County, Brillion's growth developed around the railroad. The Milwaukee, Lake Shore & Western railway extended its line through here in 1871 connecting Brillion with other parts of the county and enabling it to grow swiftly.

SHSW

A light moment in an early Wisconsin farm field.

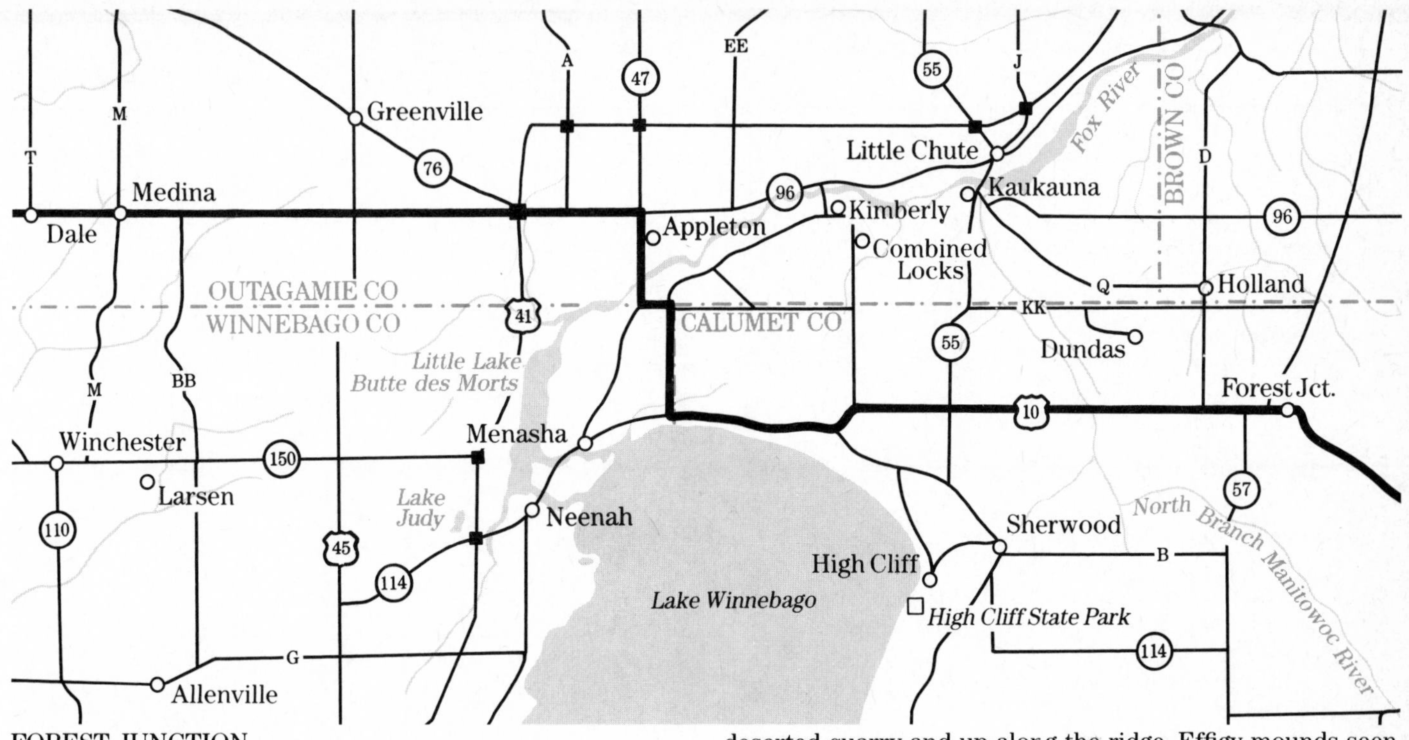

FOREST JUNCTION

This little town was established in 1871 about the same time the Wisconsin Central Railroad entered Calumet County. Thirty acres belonging to Mrs. Charlotte Quentin were soon platted and named Forest. A short time later, 80 more acres opposite Mrs. Quentin's property was platted as Baldwin after its owner. Two years later, when the Lake Shore & Western Railroad came through, the post office officially named the whole area Forest Junction.

HIGH CLIFF STATE PARK

Six miles west of Forest Junction, then a few miles south on County Road M, is High Cliff Park, one of the prettiest lookout points in the state. In the early 1800's Chief Red Bird, leader of the Winnebagoes, would stand at the top of the cliff telling his children about the good life beyond the lake's calm waters. Red Bird called this lake Wiskooserah meaning "water by the flowering banks." On a clear day you can see at least 30 miles from the lookout point. A 12-foot statue of Red Bird honors the peacemaker.

The historical society is housed in what was once the main building of the Western Lime and Cement Company which ran the limestone quarry here in the 1870's. Today you can hike the Indian Mound Trail through the lime kiln's rugged deserted quarry and up along the ridge. Effigy mounds seen on the trail were constructed 500-1,000 years ago by Woodland Indians. Most are in geometric or animal shapes and four resemble panthers, including one mound 285 feet long. Built as a religious symbol by the Indians, the mounds deserve respect.

OUTAGAMIE COUNTY, Pop. 128,726

The Fox River Valley, including Outagamie County, was a pivotal point for every voyageur, explorer, or missionary who ever ventured into the state. Jean Nicolet first set foot in Green Bay in 1634 leading the way for missionary Father Claude Jean Allouez who made a portage in 1670 at Kakaling (Kaukauna,) and whose mission of St. Marks (probably near Leeman) opened settlement in the county.

The Fox Indians made Calumet County their primary home in the mid 1600's and were heavily engaged in open warfare with whites primarily due to fraudulent French fur trade. Canadian troops made repeated incursions into the county to settle the fights. A fierce battle near Appleton almost annihilated the Fox tribe. (For more information see Buttes Des Morts p.??) Survivors withdrew toward the Mississippi River, clearing the way for the Menominees, who were friendly to the whites and remained in Outagamie until 1836 when they ceded lands to the government by treaty.

Grignon House, Kaukauna, Wi. 1890 Photo by H.C. Tanner.

Outagamie County's earliest white settlers, Dominick and Paul Ducharme and Augustin Grignon, located here in the 1790's. (The log house that Grignon built in Kaukauna in 1837 is the oldest standing house in the state.) However, the greatest influx of population came in the 1840's with the establishment of Lawrence University in Appleton. The name Outagamie is an Indian word meaning "dwellers on the other side of a stream." It was given by the Chippewa Indians to their ancient enemies the Foxes.

One of Outagamie County's greatest assets is its agricultural base. Although it grew slowly, the dairy industry boomed during the 1880's and has dominated the county's agricultural economy ever since. By 1944 Outagamie County farmers made their total income from milk. In fact, for many years Outagamie County's cattle out numbered its residents!

In 1871 Wisconsin suffered its worst natural disaster and Outagamie County was nearly destroyed. A forest fire at Peshtigo spread so quickly that the entire 30-mile strip from Appleton to Menominee, Michigan, was in danger of devastation. Not one town in the county escaped. Property loss was enormous. Whole neighborhoods were swept by fire. Appleton's business interests were hit hard but the fires were fortunately extinguished before they reached the area's newest and most productive industry—the paper mills. Statewide statistics on the fire, which occurred the same night as the famous Chicago fire, listed 1,152 persons dead, 1,500 persons seriously injured and more than 3,000 homeless.

APPLETON, Pop. 53,531

Situated on both banks of the Fox River, Appleton was first settled in 1848 by the John F. Johnston family. Their house, the first permanent home within the village, had many uses over the years, serving as a hotel, hospital, church, Sunday school and post office.

The Fox River provided waterpower and a means of transportation to early settlers and new mills along the river soon turned out a variety of wood products including shingles, lathes, barrels, sashes, doors and chairs. A flour mill processed wheat which was rapidly becoming the area's major farm crop. Before long the Richmond brothers used the waterpower for a paper mill—a rather daredevil scheme in those days. The territory was prospering with men of good will and capital, and on April 14, 1853 the area's first settler, John F. Johnston, became president of the newly formed village of Appleton. Settlers soon overflowed into three separate villages—Appleton, Grand Chute and Lawesburg—but eventually the three consolidated into Appleton which officially incorporated as a city on March 2, 1857. It was named after the father-in-law of the president of Lawrence University, a distinguished institution around which the town was built.

On September 30, 1882, Appleton became the site of the world's first water-driven, hydro-electric plant as well as of the first house in the world to use electric power. A replica of the plant is located at 807 South Oneida Street.

MEDINA

On April 12, 1848, William Young came here and erected a shanty which soon became a popular stopping point for travelers going north. Young built a larger frame house to accommodate the visitors and in 1855 built a still larger dwelling which became known as Young's Corners. Eventually the area grew into Medina which was officially organized in 1851 and named after an Ohio town.

DALE, Pop. 1,620

It is believed that no white man lived here before December, 1847, when three railmakers, Arthur C. Minto, John Stanfield and Thomas Swan built a cedar log shanty to shelter them during the winter. Despite that shelter, the village was primarily farm land until the Wisconsin Central Railway arrived in 1872. Shortly after, the town was platted and John Leppla became the first postmaster.

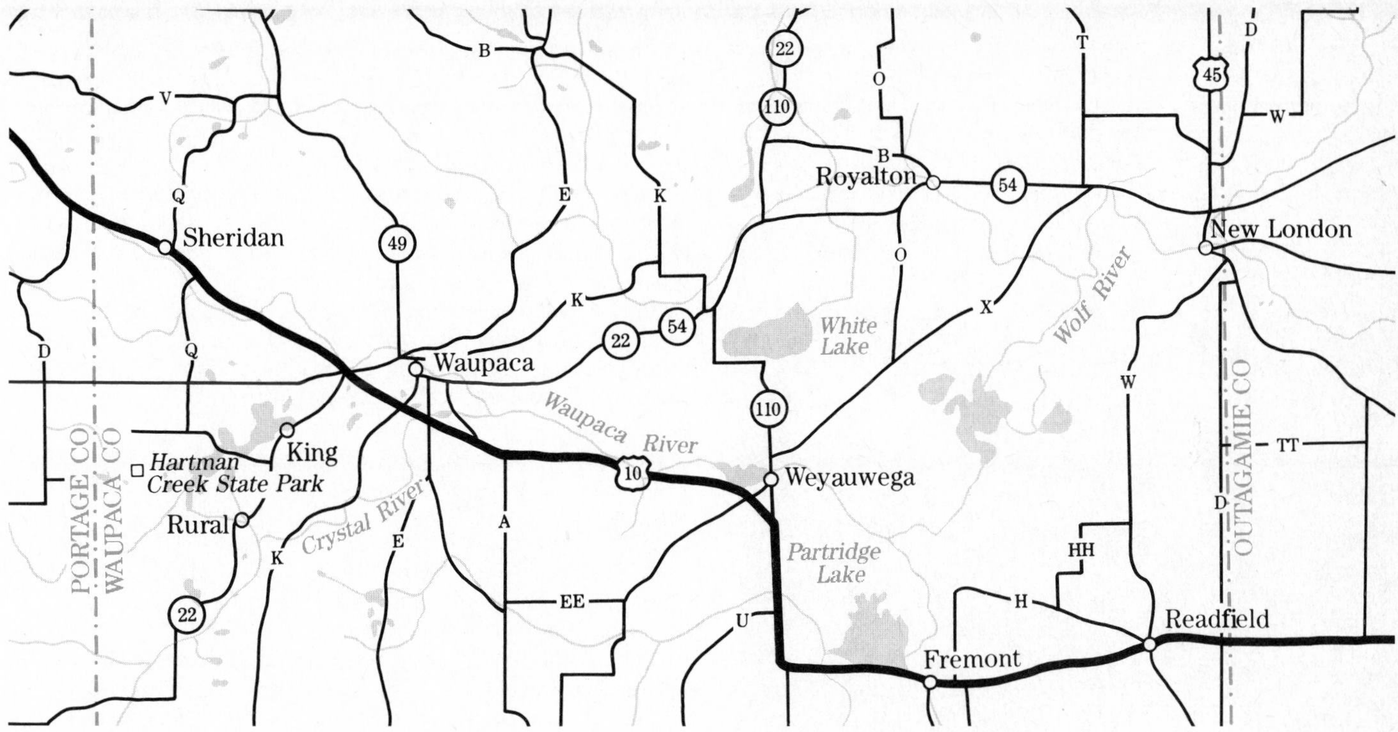

WAUPACA COUNTY, Pop. 42,831

Evidence of the county's earliest settlers can still be seen today in the marked clearings and scores of mounds on the islands of White Lake and the beautiful Chain-'O-Lakes region west of Waupaca. These locales, once the flourishing villages of Menominee Indians, represent the best of Waupaca County's natural beauty. Most of the county's towns were named by or in honor of the Indians, including Waupaca or the Indian word Waubuck Seba meaning "tomorrow" or "pale water." The little town of Weyauwega was named after a Menominee leader whose skull now rests in the Smithsonian Institution.

In 1843 Alpheus Hicks, the first white settler, came to Waupaca County from Oshkosh. He landed near the present site of Fremont and was the county's only permanent settler until 1848 when the Menominees signed a treat, ceding all lands to the government. A short time later Robert Grignon was granted a quarter section of land near the mouth of the Wolf River and promptly erected a saw mill, beginning a prosperous new industry for the county.

Because Waupaca County once lay just within the tiber region's southern boundaries, its early importance rested with the lumber industry. The Wolf River, running through the southeastern part, became the main water highway for the 400 million feet of logs taken annually from the thickly wooded lands to the north. Saw mills and lumber factories were scattered throughout the county and the Wolf was soon responsible for the growth and vitality of nearly every village along its path.

READFIELD

Early settlers Johann and Fredericke Huebner moved here from Milwaukee in the 1850's to quarry the nearby limestone. They settled in the heavy unbroken forest just east of the Wolf River but after a log fell just short of their new baby they decided this was not a safe place to bring up their child and moved out. However, attention was later drawn here by stagecoach travelers passing through Readfield on their way from Green Bay to Stevens Point and because Readfield was a stop on the original mail route from Menasha to Waupaca.

In 1854, with the population increasing, residents named the town after Charles Readfield, county register of deeds. That same year Readfield became Caledonia Township's first post office and John Littlefield was named postmaster.

FREMONT, Pop. 510

Before the railroads came, Fremont promised to become a thriving village because its sturdy bridge across the river was the best crossing for miles. Although some of the earliest settlements began on the river's east side, the village's main section gradually extended toward the outlet of Partridge Lake where the first saw mills were built.

The town's first dwelling was erected in 1849 by D. Gorden. Two years later W.A. Springer moved from Little River, located near the mouth of Partridge Lake, and laid out a village which he named Springer's Point. Years later, in 1888, it was incorporated with the village of Fremont, reportedly named after Colonel John Fremont who explored California and fought in the Mexican War.

SHSW

Sunday morning shave in lumber camp.

Fremont prospered as a lumber camp during the 1890's but the last log was driven down the Wolf River in 1911. Today, people come to Fremont in the summer to fish the Wolf for pike which spawn in the swamps upstream.

WEYAUWEGA, Pop. 1,549

This city and its industry were born at the same time. In 1848, Amos Dodge, James Hicks, M. Lewis and Henry Tourtelotte obtained rights to the city's waterpower which was provided by the lake and the Waupaca River. A year later they started building a saw mill and dam, but because of financial problems, the project was completed by James, Walter and Jacob Weed. These same men later developed other mills which contributed to the town's prosperity. In 1851, when it looked like Weyauwega would become the county seat, the Weyauwega House, a large hotel with bar, was built. Hotel Marlyn was built the following year.

Finally, in 1856, Weyauwega was incorporated as a village. Its name honors an Indian chief and means "here we rest." The town's growth continued with arrival of the Soo Line in 1871. Later, as agriculture in the north expanded, Weyauwega became well known as a farm trading center.

WAUPACA, Pop. 4,472

Sometime in mid-July, 1849, Waupaca received its first white settlers, W.B. and Joseph Hibbard and E.C. Sessions. Journeying north from Plymouth up Lake Winnebago, the trio crossed the Wolf River and discovered the rich opportunity for waterpower here. Returning to Plymouth, they spread word of the fine location and brought back a number of eager settlers. After setting up a rather crude dwelling, Hibbard traveled down to Lind for supplies and met a General Taylor whose party was searching for the "Vermonter's Camp," as Waupaca was then called. They returned to the site and the town was officially organized two years later. The name Waupaca is of Indian derivation and has many meanings including "where one waits to shoot deer," "pale water," and "white sand bottom."

In 1855 James Lathrop built a grist mill on the Crystal River a few miles south of town to serve most area farmers. The spot became known as Little Hope because the railroad built its depot on the site of today's Waupaca, bypassing the mill by three miles. Little Hope and the original grist mill, now open to the public and called the Red Mill Colonial Shop, still stand just off County K.

As other northern towns turned their attention toward lumbering, Waupaca's growth centered around potatoes. Although local farmers still market potatoes, Waupaca is now an important tourist spot. Just west of town, a 23 chain-o-lakes keeps fishing and boating enthusiasts coming back summer after summer. The entire chain is spring-fed, cold and clear, offering many varieties of fish as well as long, leisurely canoe excursions.

SHERIDAN

Established in January, 1865, this town was settled primarily as a station stop for the Wisconsin Central Railroad. It was originally named Sessions Prairie, but changed to Sheridan in honor of Civil War General Philip H. Sheridan, a famous cavalry leader and Indian fighter.

Four potato warehouses were once located here, filling 430 rail cars to New York in 1889. U.S. 10 was relocated south of Sheridan in 1968 and only local traffic now passes through this once vital area.

PORTAGE COUNTY, Pop. 57,420

The county's early history centers around lumbering on the Wisconsin River. The first log driving here occurred when logs for Fort Winnebago at Portage were rafted down river from a small island further north. That logging operation was directed by Major Twiggs, later a famous Mexican War general, and Lt. Jefferson Davis, West Point graduate and future head of the Confederate Army.

Although troops came in the fall of 1828 and drove the lumber the following spring, two years passed before major lumbering operations began. At that time Daniel Whitney of Green Bay obtained a permit from the War Department, which controlled such matters, to build a saw mill and cut timber in what was then Indian territory. He finally erected his mill in 1832 at Whitney's Rapids, just below Point Bas. More mills followed, much to the Indians' dismay. A treaty was finally made with the Menominees in 1836 at Cedar Point on the Fox River. In that treaty Governor Dodge declared that the Indians' title would be restricted to a six-mile-wide strip of land along the Wisconsin, running 40 miles upstream from Point Bas to what is now Wausau. Exploring parties immediately went up the river and during 1837-39 every eligible place on the Wisconsin River as far as Big Bull Falls was occupied.

The tract of land relinquished in the treaty was surveyed in 1839 and offered for sale in 1840 at Mineral Point. The Wallace Rowan family heard of this prime lumbering area and claimed a quarter section of the land in what is now Poynette (now a part of Columbia County,) becoming Portage County's first permanent settlers. Rowan built a double log house and began trading with the Indians. Located along the military road between Prairie du Chien and Fort Howard in Green Bay, Rowan frequently entertained travelers and his house became known as Rowan's Inn.

Portage County, organized in 1836, originally covered only the land around Fort Winnebago and Portage. The county and city received their names from the portage on the Fox-Wisconsin rivers which early French explorers referred to as le portage. Plover, the county seat, was known as the "Shootinest City in America" because of the lumberjacks and rivermen who spent their off-seasons there.

AMHERST, Pop. 477

This small village was established about the time the Wisconsin Central Railroad laid tracks through here. Early settlers Judge Gilbert Park and Adam Uline proposed naming the village after a town in Nova Scotia where they had spent their boyhood.

In 1859 the annual town board meeting was held at the home of Peter Grover, who, with Asa Bancroft had built a grist mill on the Tomorrow River in 1858, making them the first permanent settlers in Amherst Junction. After adding a fully operational dam and much needed machinery, the mill became known as the Johnson Feed Mill and Elevator. A shell of the original building still stands along the river banks.

Amherst today has a community of about 60 Amish families who bought the area's smaller farms and maintain turn-of-the-century traditions.

Stevens Point H.S.

Market square saloon in Stevens Point.

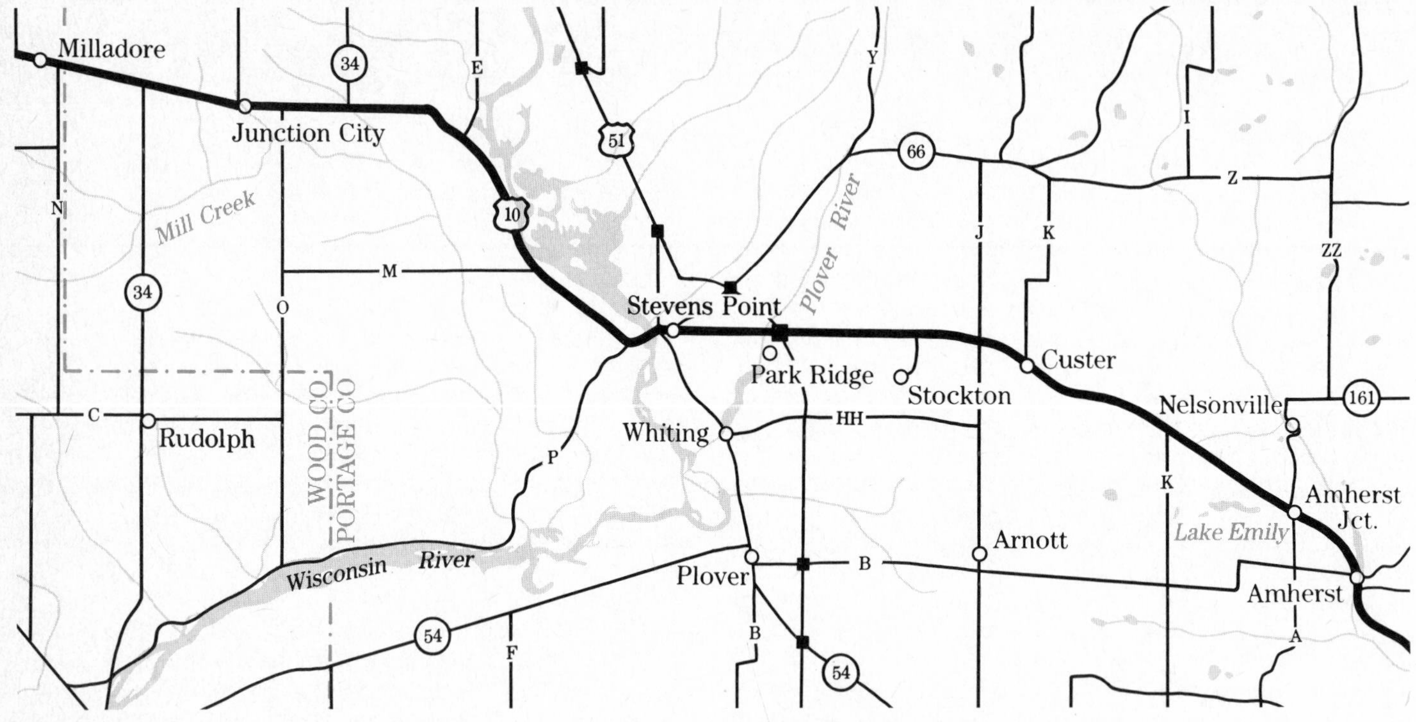

AMHERST JUNCTION, Pop. 225

To accommodate area potato growers the Green Bay & Minnesota Railroad formed a junction with the Wisconsin Central (Soo Line) in 1871 about one mile northwest of Amherst. The spot became known as the Virgin Spur but the small village was commonly called Junction. Because the Grover family held considerable local property, the town chose the name Groversburg for a time before changing to Amherst Junction.

The small village had many advantages as a shipping point for produce and most farmers took advantage of it. Half a dozen potato warehouses were located here around 1881 and filled 300 carloads in one season.

CUSTER

The first post office was established on December 12, 1876 with Leonard Van Hecke as postmaster. Van Hecke was probably the town's first settler and named it after General George Custer who was defeated at the battle of the Little Big Horn that same year.

Local farmers raised wheat which they cut by hand. Later hops became a big cash crop, selling for 25 cents per bushel. Many girls from Stevens Point picked hops at harvest and ended the season with a big dance.

STEVENS POINT, Pop. 22,970

The Wisconsin and Plover rivers form a natural basin here and Stevens Point stands in the middle. Founded in 1839 by George Stevens the "Point" was a convenient stopover for lumbermen rafting logs on the long haul up river from Wisconsin Rapids to Mosinee. However, nearby forests couldn't supply enough timber for large-scale logging operations and Stevens Point never became an important lumber city despite a dozen saw mills during the rush. The Point and Portage County reached their present growth and prosperity with development of the paper and agriculture industries. With the arrival of the Wisconsin Central Railroad in 1871, the Point turned from a small, backwoods town into an intellectual civic center. That same year Nicholas Jacobs and his wife opened up the Jacobs House, a hotel popular with passing farmers who could get a fine dinner here for 25 cents. A barn behind the hotel could accommodate 50 teams and hay was available for an additional 10 cents.

The Point's public square on the west end of main street was once known as the "Potato Capital of Wisconsin." This two block long, brick-paved marketplace has been an active market ever since Mathias Mitchell donated it to the town in 1847. Summer or winter, the Thursday and Saturday markets were a colorful beehive of activity as well as a valuable business asset. Farmers hawked their wares, talked about farm crops and prices, then discussed politics in the taverns at night. Many spoke Polish since a large number of Poles had immigrated to Portage County. A few farmers still bring crops to the square during the summer, but now they have to pay parking meters in the municipal lot across the street.

JUNCTION CITY, Pop. 523

When the Valley Railroad (Chicago, Milwaukee & St. Paul) intersected with the Wisconsin Central (Soo) Line in 1874, a village called Junction was almost inevitable. George Oster, the first postmaster, suggested the name when the post office was established here in 1874 but citizens liked Junction City better. When the village incorporated on May 9, 1911, the name stuck.

The town's first store opened in 1876, owned and operated by Thomas Mathews. "The Stevens Point Journal" reported that "one year earlier there was only two log shanties, now there are two depots, two saw mills, a hotel, boarding house, saloon, three dwellings and a schoolhouse." In 1877 a two-story hotel/depot combination was built which became known as Russell House.

WOOD COUNTY, Pop. 72,799

The Wisconsin River, falling one hundred feet along a 15-mile course here, was primarily responsible for early settlement. Because of this great source of water power, the first Wood County settlements located themselves along its banks from Whitney's Rapids at Nekoosa, north to Wisconsin Rapids. Before long, choice mill sites were pushing back the formidable wilderness.

Daniel and David Whitney and A.B. Sampson built a saw mill on the river just opposite Nekoosa in 1831, marking the county's first settlement. A second saw mill was built a short time later near Port Edwards by Sam Merrill and his partner, Grignon.

Settlements along the river continued to grow in size and importance in the 1840's with most mill sites later developing into present-day cities or villages.

Wood County officially organized in 1856 as lumber industries pushed into the forest located along either side of the river. Joseph Wood who came here from Illinois in 1848 and settled in Grand Rapids (now Wisconsin Rapids,) introduced a state legislature bill which detached this county from the existing Portage County. Wood later served one term in the legislature, one year as county judge and was finally elected mayor of Grand Rapids. The county was named after him.

MILLADORE, Pop. 240

When George Hooper homesteaded here in October 1872, there were no other permanent settlers. However, Hooper discovered an old dwelling by the side of the railroad tracks which one source claims was originally inhabited by James Brennan who worked for the Wisconsin Central line here in 1870. The abandoned building had several rooms, including two living rooms and others apparently used for passengers and freight. Hooper staked his claim and eight years later built the first saw mill which operated until all the nearby timber was gone.

One year after Hooper arrived, a Bohemian named Martin Bretel moved here and set up a blacksmith shop. In 1875 John Blenker moved in and built a saw mill, general store and the Blenker Hotel. More settlers followed rapidly; the town was platted in 1877 and officially organized as Mill Creek. Since Wisconsin already had a post office with that name, citizens were asked to choose another that resembled the original. They chose Milladore, as it has been called ever since.

Stevens Point H.S.

Stevens Point "Journal" office. Building draped to mourn death of President Ulysses S. Grant in July, 1885.

BLENKER

Until the railroad came through in 1884, this was mostly logging country. The town was named after John Blenker who moved here from the neighboring Milladore, opened the first store and became postmaster.

AUBURNDALE, Pop. 641

Settled primarily by the English, the town was reportedly named for the auburn hair of the children of John Connor, the town's most prominent resident.

Early French fur traders came here to trade with the Chippewa, Sioux and Winnebago Indians who lived along the Big and Little Eau Pleine rivers. The Chippewa and Sioux fought a fierce battle at Smokey Hill just north of town.

The first white settler, William St. Thomas, moved here in 1871, clearing land and erecting a shanty in a nearby clump of trees. John and Robert Connor came in May of the same year, purchased large areas of land, platted the town and built the first general store. John became the first postmaster in June, 1873.

Auburndale had two saw mills that year and a great influx of settlers interested in logging. When the Wisconsin Central (Soo Line) Railroad was competed, the village grew in size and importance. It had 30 dwellings, five general stores, a blacksmith shop, saw mills producing millions of feet of lumber per year, three churches and one tavern when incorporated in 1881.

Today, Auburndale is a shadow of its former self and dairying has replaced lumbering. The Soo Line still runs parallel to the town and a Connor is still the most prominent resident—president of the Auburndale bank.

MARSHFIELD, Pop. 18,053

This town is actually the second Marshfield in Wisconsin history. The first was established in 1868 by Louis and Frank Rivers who built a tavern here to serve railroad construction gangs. Four years later the Wisconsin Central (Soo Line) cut a swath through the forest, stopping directly in front of the Rivers' tavern and making Marshfield stop 32. Although Marshfield had no main street, a depot stood somewhat shakily in the midst of felled stumps and trees. Other railroads soon entered the county, including the Omaha, Princeton and branch lines. By 1887, Marshfield had a saw mill, furniture factory, stave and hub factory, boiler works, harness shops, nine hotels, 19 saloons and two newspapers—one in English, the other in German. The logging business attracted many French-Canadians who lived in a part of Marshfield called French Town.

At the height of its prosperity, on June, 27, 1887, Marshfield was engulfed by a great fire. A locomotive passing through

SHSW

An Auburndale farm family displays their bountiful harvest.

town sparked the Upham Company's lumber piles to start the blaze and a strong wind fanned the flames. Horse drawn fire engines galloped towards Marshfield from Stevens Point, Spencer and other settlements but when they got to town their hoses burned off at the hydrants and their wooden ladders quickly caught fire. By nightfall the greater part of Marshfield was smouldering in ashes. No one was killed in the fire but most of the 250 businesses and homes were lost. The town's mayor, W.H. Upham, (later Governor of Wisconsin) lived a few blocks from the business district and his home was spared. When residents asked if Marshfield would rebuild, he said, "If the flag in front of my home is raised on the morning of the 28th, we will." Promptly at 6 a.m. the stars and stripes went up.

Within a few years, a new Marshfield was built; brick buildings replaced frame, cheese making and dairying replaced lumbering, and an early advertisement boasted, "Like Phoenix, we have come out of the ashes, with a full stock of Dry Goods, Groceries, Boots and Shoes..."

The town was reportedly named for John J. Marsh, a New Yorker who owned most of the town and gave his name to it. Governor Upham's 1884 mansion still stands, a fitting memorial to the past. Tours are available on Sundays and Wednesdays from 11:30 a.m–4:00 p.m.

CLARK COUNTY, Pop. 32,910

Named after revolutionary hero George Rogers Clark, this county was first visited by white men when a party of French and Canadian trappers employed by the American Fur Company arrived in 1836 on the East Fork of the Black River. Here they established a temporary post and began wilderness expeditions in search of Indian villages, especially Chippewa. Norbert St. Germaine, a 16-year-old packer, was with the traders who are credited as Clark County's first permanent settlers even though they didn't stay long.

Next in line were Mormons, seeking timber to build their tabernacle at Nauvoo, Illinois. These religious people came up the Black River in 1841, established Black River Falls, cut logs from the vast forests and floated them down the Black and Mississippi rivers to their final destinations. A stream near Black River Falls is named after Jonathan Cunningham, a Morman who slipped into the icy water and was drowned while running logs with his companions. For a time Mormon activities flourished here but many Mormans moved back to Nauvoo after several troubled years.

Most early settlers were connected with lumbering. The mill employees and those who rafted timber down the river had no interest in abandoning their chosen pursuits to grub out a living among the stumps. It was simpler for lumbermen to buy supplies than to raise them. When the county was organized in 1854 there were about 25 homes on occupied land extending along the Black River and its tributaries from the mouth of the East Fork to the present site of Greenwood.

Just west of Neillsville, a small wayside provides a spectacular view of the moraines or deposits left by the receding glaciers. The mounds northwest of Neillsville are of great geographical significance: they are believed to be nunataks, hills which projected through the ice sheet so their tops were not touched by the glacier.

LYNN

Early founders George Ure and Gottlieb Sternitzky moved here from Chicago in 1856 when Ure paid $300 for 80 acres of land now worth 30 or 40 times that much. A short time later Bartemus Brooks and his three sons moved here along with Fredrick Yankee, his four sons and Archibald Yorkston. As was the custom, these early pioneers soon banded together to purchase supplies, traveling to Sparta by team once a year to buy flour.

Lynn developed as a station on the branch line of the Chicago, Milwaukee and St. Paul Railroad which crossed the Omaha Railroad a half mile down the road. The two lines, built at the same time, created much rivalry and frequent dissension between construction crews. Both railroads dreamed of being a through line to the northern Lake Superior country. The St. Paul reached the crossing first, chained an engine to the tracks, and had a carload of armed men guard the right-of-way. Excitement ran high for several days, although no violence occurred. Ironically, the Wisconsin Central pushed a line through to Ashland about the same time and the St. Paul never completed its line, although it maintained the right-of-way at the junction.

GRANTON, Pop. 882

Like its neighbor, Lynn, this little village was settled in 1856. Granton's first settler was Eli Williams who came to this area along the banks of O'Neill Creek on a war claim. Because of that war the town was named after General Ulys-

SHSW

Clark County lumberjacks haul logs through the dense Northwoods to the Black River.

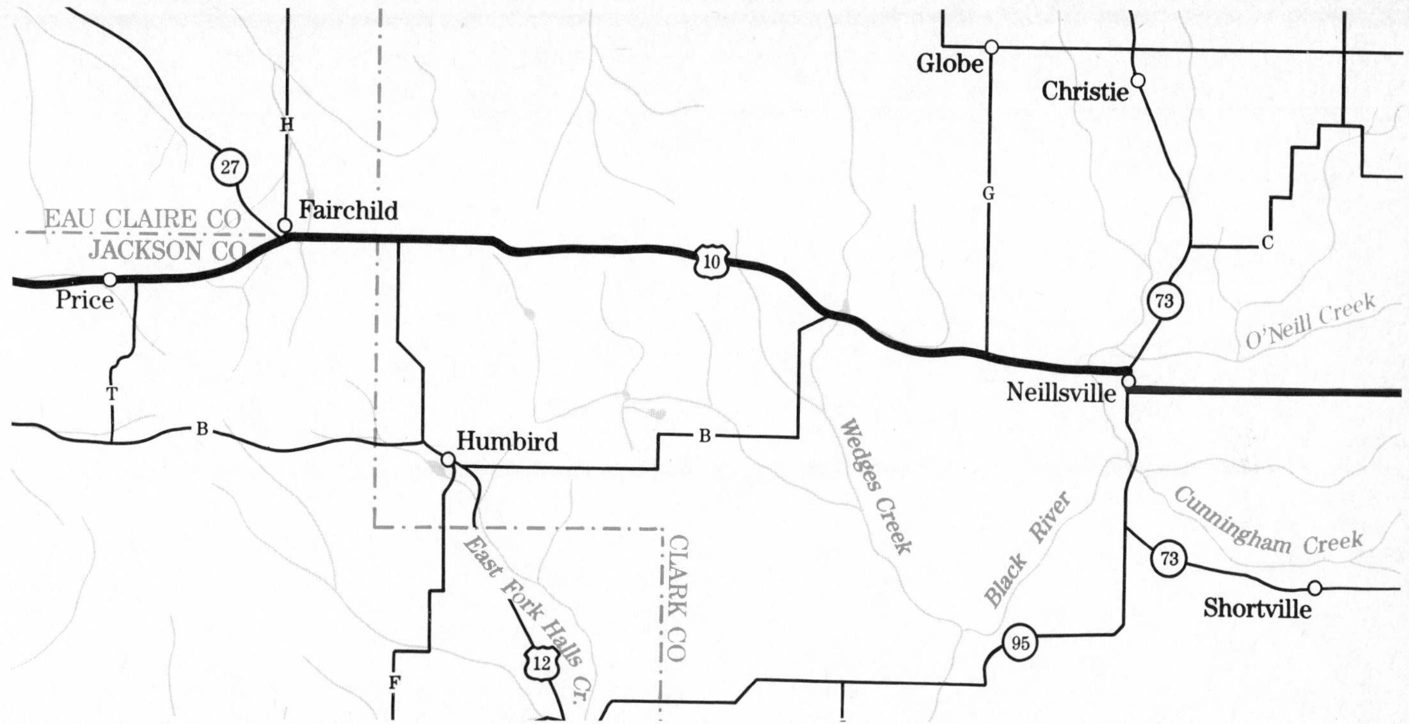

ses S. Grant. A year after Williams came, Nelson Marsh moved in, establishing the first tavern and post office on the site of the old Neillsville-Stevens Point stage line. Later this area was developed into the hamlet of Mapleworks.

In the spring of 1890 Marsh's son Vet assured Granton's prosperity. The Chicago, St.Paul/Minneapolis and Omaha railroad was pushing through this area and wanted to locate its station a half mile east of the existing town because a larger spring there would provide plenty of water for the railroad at a lower cost. Marsh quickly bought up a 60-acre tract and persuaded railroad officials to build on the present site. Granton was officially platted on November 22, 1890 and incorporated 12 years later with a population of 316.

NEILLSVILLE, Pop. 2,780

The first and largest town in Jackson County was founded in 1844 by New Yorker James O'Neill. In 1839, through a shared business venture with his brothers Henry and Alexander, O'Neill carefully investigated an area three miles below Black River Falls. Liking it, he built a saw mill on the east side. Five years later he returned, accompanied by a number of laborers. Together they blazed their way through the brush, coming overland to the present town site in an ox-drawn wagon. The two-day trip marked the first road through the county.

Immediately after arriving, O'Neill built an 18X24 log house, the first in the county, and a crude log saw mill with one upright saw near the present O'Neill Creek north of town. It was a convenient site. Logs were easily floated down the creek to the mill where the men combined the lumber into rafts in 10,000-foot units. When the lumber reached Black River Falls it was combined into units of 40-50,000 feet and rafted to the Mississippi, then on to Burlington, Iowa where it eventually sold for an average of $10 per thousand feet.

O'Neill found a virtual wilderness here. Game was so plentiful that he could shoot deer from the door of his log cabin. Wolves frequently chased deer into the clearing, but they often escaped by hiding in the dam behind the mill.

Neillsville grew slowly. In the fall of 1866 the village had only a few dozen buildings scattered over a limited area including the saw mill, a blacksmith shop, a dilapidated frame hotel called the Hubbard House, a general store, a printing office, post office, drug store, a few scattered homes and O'Neill's two-story dwelling. The current post office stands on the site of the O'Neill House.

Neillsville began to prosper in the 1870's. Brick store buildings were built, three passenger trains ran through town each day in both directions, and the town soon became the main distribution center for important dairying and stock raising industries. A handsome city jail, built in 1876, still stands as

SHSW

Travelers find their journey slowed on an early road near Fairchild.

the home of the county historical society. Neillsville, the county seat of Clark County, incorporated in 1882.

EAU CLAIRE COUNTY, Pop. 78,805

This Wisconsin region became the buffer zone between the Dakota Indians to the west, the Ojibwe to the north and the Winnebago tribes of the east. The treaty which better defined these Indian lands was carried out at Prairie du Chien in 1825 and used the waterways of northwestern Wisconsin as boundaries. Carver traveled through here in the 1700's and referred to the Chippewa and Eau Claire rivers as "Road of War," because of continual fighting between the Dakota and Ojibwe.

The county was named after the Eau Claire River, which has been known by many other names. On early 18th century maps, it was labeled as Rufus River, but the Ojibwe called it Wah-yaw-con-ut-ta-gua-yaw-sebe, meaning "Clearwater River." When the proposed city was platted in 1855, it was decided that Clearwater was too plain and the river was renamed with its French version, Eau Claire.

The first whites to come here might have been Radisson and Grosseliers, French adventurers who traveled from Lake Superior about 1656. Father Hennepin, a Jesuit priest, claimed to have entered the Chippewa River while held captive by Dakota Indians in 1680. Le Sueur, another Frenchman, ventured up the Chippewa briefly in search of copper and furs. But the first Englishman to write about this area was Jonathan Carver who explored the Chippewa River in 1767.

Travel in this region was dangerous because of the fighting between the Dakota and Ojibwe and it was eight years after the Winnebago ceded their Wisconsin lands in 1837 that settlement in the county begin. These were not farmers who settled here, but men interested in the tall pine of the Eau Claire and Chippewa valleys. Eau Claire County was officially organized by the state legislature in 1856 with a total population of 100. The small village of Eau Claire was named the county seat. The first murder trial in the new county came in 1858 when tow Germans living together had a fatal fight over who would wash the dishes.

FAIRCHILD, Pop. 577

Named after Lucius Fairchild, the first man to serve three terms as Governor of Wisconsin, this village began taking shape during his first term in 1865. That same year, A. McClanathan, James Hobart, and several other early settlers cleared the bushy lowlands for what would one day be a busy agricultural community.

Three years later, the West Wisconsin railway pushed into Fairchild and beyond. Then, in 1870, a Mr. Van Auken built a steam saw mill here, probably the first of its kind in the country. Because of the area's abundant hardwoods, the mill flourished until it was forced to close in 1874.

In 1879 Fairchild celebrated its 4th of July in an unusual way. The postmaster contributed funds to buy dynamite. A number of eager boys celebrated the day by blowing stumps out of the street—about 300 in all. That night a splendid bonfire ended the festivities.

Fairchild was officially incorporated in 1880 with a population of about 800. That same year Nathaniel C. Foster, one of the village's most influential citizens, erected an elevator and feed mill, followed a few years later by an opera house and hotel called the Fairchild House. Foster also built a steam mill which employed about 260 men.

Fairchild was almost destroyed in 1895 by a tremendous fire which began when a kerosene lamp in the village drug store exploded. Flames ignited the building and spread quickly to adjacent frame buildings, destroying all 23 buildings in the business district except for the opera house, the Methodist church and one residence. The town rebuilt with grim determination and N.C. Foster opened the Big Store retail establishment which soon made Fairchild the largest trading center in northwestern Wisconsin.

However, Foster continued to make most of his money from a successful lumber company valued at $500,000. To increase the efficiency of his operation, he built a railroad, the F. and N.E. ("Foster's and Nobody Elses") from Fairchild to Owen, the only railroad ever constructed without being mortgaged. After Foster's death in 1923 his home was donated to the village. The site is now a park.

JACKSON COUNTY, Pop. 16,831

This county is varied with forests, hills, and prairie. In the eastern part, about 15 miles east of Black River Falls, are the central plains of Wisconsin. In some places this region of level ground has the appearance of Wyoming with sandy areas and scrub timber. The occasional ridge, butte or mesas give an un-Wisconsin feel to the land. A number of marshes also dot this area and cranberries grow wild. Southwest Jackson includes the coulee country of the Mississippi and Black River valleys, an area untouched by glaciers during the ice age where the streams and rivers have eroded over thousands of years, creating a region of deep valleys and narrow ridges. A coulee is a valley where water runs only during wet seasons.

The county was formed in 1853 and named after Andrew Jackson, the seventh president of the United States (1829-1837). Black River Falls, which developed around saw mills on the Black River, was named the county seat and became the area's trade center. The Tomah & Lake St. Croix Railroad crossed diagonally through the county in 1869 and was completed to the St. Croix River at Hudson in 1871. The railroad later became known as the West Central, the Chicago, St. Paul, Minneapolis & Omaha and finally the Chicago & Northwestern. Before the Interstate highway was built, the main route through west-central Wisconsin was U.S. 12 which followed railroad right-of-way west from Lake Delton.

When French trappers hunted along the Black River, they found Winnebago Indians. The Winnebago may have once lived along either the Pacific or Gulf coasts because their name means "men from the strong-smelling water." The fertile Black River valley marked the northern boundary of their territory. To the north were the Ojibwe, who continued to displace the Dakota Indians into Minnesota during the early 1700's. As the whites pressured to open more lands for logging and settlement, the Winnebago fell to the pressure. In a treaty signed in 1837, they gave up all their lands east of the Mississippi and promised to move to reservations in Iowa. From there the Indians were removed to two different locations in Minnesota, before they were displaced to Nebraska and the Dakotas.

PRICE

Only a handful of houses, a corner bar and a Lutheran church remain in the small village of Price, just north of Highway 10, to mark what was once a thriving farming and logging community. It included a large potato warehouse and a pickle factory operated by the Libby Company.

Lumberman Steve Foster came to town around the turn-of-the-century and developed a business which was so successful that the Chicago Northwestern railroad was soon running four passenger trains and two freight trains through town daily. The one-way fare from Price to Osseo was 36 cents.

A co-op creamery built in Price in 1909 had more than 100 customers at one time. The town also included a live stock yard, machine shop, blacksmith, church and school.

It was named after the Price Lumber Company of Black River Falls, which was heavily engaged in lumbering in the area.

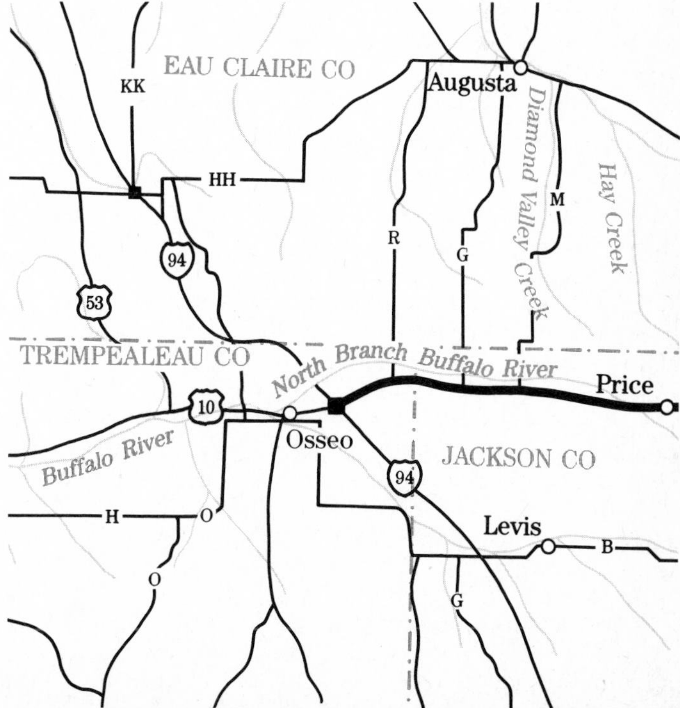

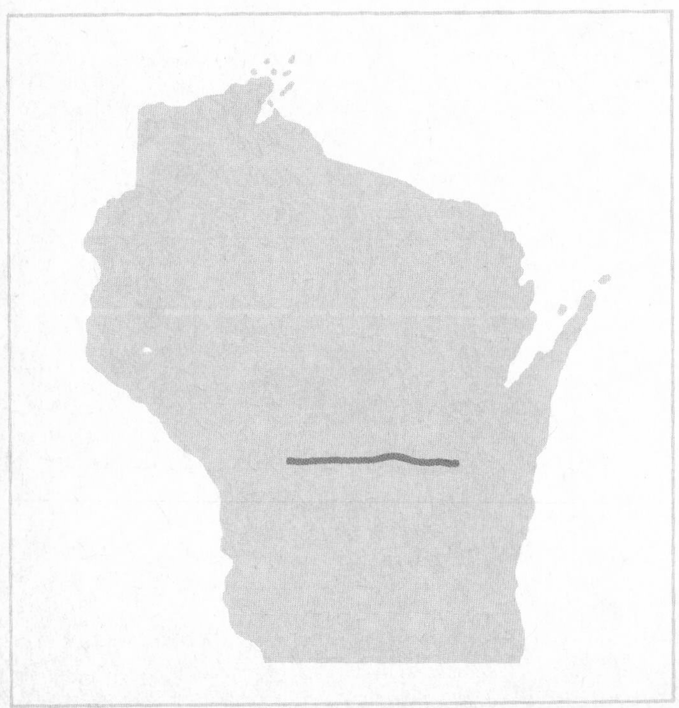

State 21 follows a relatively straight, two-lane course 105 miles out of the fertile Fox River Valley to the low cranberry marshes of south central Wisconsin. Starting at Oshkosh, home of the Experimental Aircraft Association (E.A.A.), one of the top 100 tourist attractions in America, this route also passes Roche-A-Cri State Park, marked by an enormous flat-topped rock jutting 300 feet above the trees.

ROUTE 21, OSHKOSH TO NECEDAH

SHSW

Photographer C.J. Van Schaick captures a special moment.

WINNEBAGO COUNTY, Pop. 131,732

For more than 200 years fur traders, French explorers and Jesuit missionaries roamed this rich, fertile Fox River valley, charting their courses along Lake Winnebago. By 1836 a few settlers were scattered around the county, but migration was heaviest in southern Wisconsin where lead was being mined. Winnebago County began four years after the county officially organized in 1846. Migration increased rapidly as word spread of this beautiful river country. In one year Winnebago County's population increased from 732 to 2,787.

Many of the first cities sprang up along waterways. As they grew, agricultural and manufacturing industries clustered around Lake Winnebago and the Lower Fox River and the cities of Neenah, Menasha, Appleton and Oshkosh became home to some of Wisconsin's largest and most successful businesses.

OSHKOSH, Pop. 49,678

George Johnson, the area's first permanent white settler, came here in 1833 via the old mail route between Fort Howard and Fort Winnebago. Near the present W. Algoma Street Bridge (near the foot of Lake Butte des Morts), Johnson established a trading post consisting of two log cabins and the village of Algoma, an Indian word meaning "sandy place," began.

Johnson's first neighbors came three years later when the Indians officially ceded this territory to the government. Governor Dodge and two associates, Webster Stanley and Chester Gallup, crossed the Fox at Knaggs' Ferry and immediately claimed an angle of land between the Fox River's north bank and Lake Winnebago which would become the future city of Oshkosh. In 1837 this small community became known as Athens.

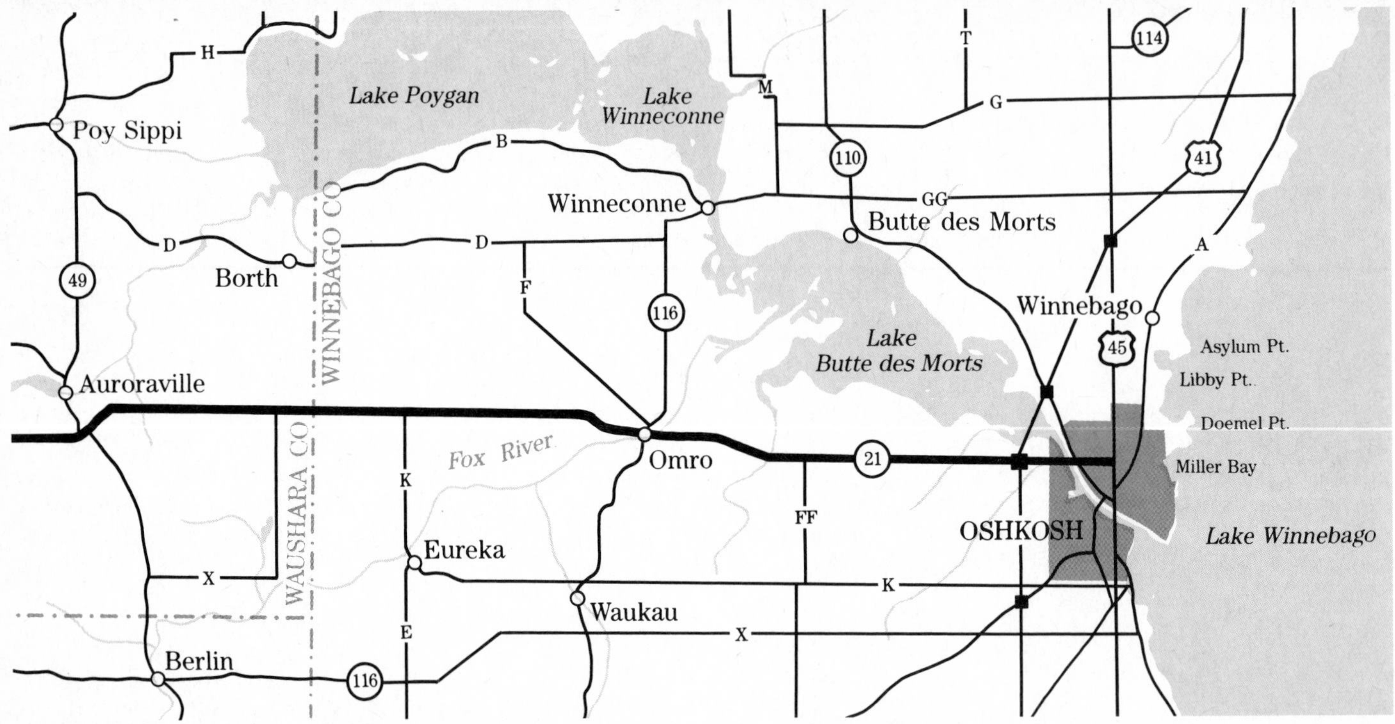

For the next ten years Athens and Algoma were lumber rivals. The big question was which would absorb the other. By 1847 Athens had been renamed for the famous Menominee Indian Chief Oshkosh and the rivalry continued with the building of two steam saw mills-one in Oshkosh, the other in Algoma. That same year Oshkosh became the county seat. It incorporated six years later with a population of 2,500 and finally, in 1856, with its population increasing rapidly, Oshkosh absorbed Algoma as a part of its fifth ward.

Unfortunately, Oshkosh was plagued with a series of fires. The last, in 1875, destroyed most of the downtown business district and more than 200 homes. Two people were killed and property damage was valued at two and one-half million dollars. Despite the setback, Oshkosh rebuilt immediately and continued to thrive thereafter. A few homes built before the fire can be seen downtown.

As the lumbering business prospered in northern Wisconsin, the state's southern cities found a way to share the wealth. Before long Oshkosh was one of the Northwest's chief lumbering centers, thanks largely to the Wolf River.

The Wolf, navigable for 150 miles, made it possible to float northern pine from the northern forests through Winnebago County to Lake Winnebago. Oshkosh lumber mills were soon manufacturing 100 million feet of lumber per year and over one hundred million shingles which, combined with the sashes and doors produced, was enough to fill more than 15,000 railroad cars in one year.

Although wood is still the city's major industry, a variety of goods including Oshkosh B'Gosh overalls, four-wheel drive trucks, marine motors, machine axles and tents help its economy thrive. A 1952 addition, the Experimental Aircraft Association (EAA), brings several thousand visitors to Oshkosh each year to see the August air show and the new EAA Museum. During the EAA Fly-In, the Oshkosh airport is famed as the busiest in the world!

OMRO, Pop. 1,684

Sometime before 1845, Charles Omro moved here and put up a log hut which later became a trading post. However, Edward West, builder of the Appleton Canal, is generally regarded as the first white settler in Omro, known then as Butte des Morts, an Indian word meaning "Hill of the Dead."

West bought 500 acres of land, erected two log cabins, and cut a wagon road through the forest to move his family here in spring, 1845. Soon after his arrival, saw mills, grist mills, hotels, and a general store were built. The town was officially organized in 1847 and West became town supervisor. The town's name changed to Bloomingdale a year later but has been known as Omro since 1852.

The village grew rapidly after the St. Paul railroad arrived in 1861 when Omro's economy was no longer dependent on the irregular river traffic.

The religious community, particularly the spiritualist movement, also flourished. For approximately 20 years, between 1877 and the turn of the century, Omro was Wisconsin's leading spiritualistic center and its leaders were known around the world. The seven original members soon grew into the 100-member First Spiritualist's Society of Omro. The Society built a $2,500 hall, established the Children's Progressive Lyceum Sunday School and brought in celebrated speakers from all over the country. The Omro group flourished for many years, but following hostile reaction from local church groups was finally superseded by a new state organization with headquarters in Milwaukee.

WAUSHARA COUNTY, Pop. 18,526

Waushara, from an Indian word meaning "good land," is a fitting name for this area of fertile soil and numerous lakes and rivers.

Most early visitors to Wisconsin came through Waushara County via the Fox River. Explorer Jean Nicolet traveled this route as early as 1634 and Sieur Radisson visited the Mascoutin and Winnebago Indians in the Fox and Wisconsin river regions 25 years later. The Fox, the county's largest river, offered early settlers unlimited opportunities for fishing and manufacturing.

Another excellent source of fish was the Pine River which drains the northeastern half of the county, ending in Lake Poygan. A local newspaper of the day reported that "there were so many fish near the dam at Poysippi, that people were catching them with their bare hands and throwing them into their wagon boxes as fast as they could pick them up."

Many early settlers came from Syracuse, New York and were coopers or makers of wooden tubs or casks. With plenty of excellent timber, the coopers were always busy. Many went out in the winter, chopped a tree down and made a barrel on the spot. These barrels were always in demand; many were used for the new berry crop, cranberries.

CRANBERRY COUNTRY

Well-drained Waushara county provided settlers with the perfect soil to raise cranberries, a brand new crop which soon became one of Wisconsin's most productive new industries. Settlers in Berlin were the first in the country to develop the new crop. The wild harvest was considered so important in 1850 that laws were enacted to ensure proper ripening of the berries. Anyone who picked them before September 20 was fined $50.

Edward Sacket became one of the most successful cranberry producers. Immediately after arriving here, Sacket improved his 700 acres of land by copying methods used in the East. He cleared brush, built dams and dug ditches to regulate flooding. After building a large warehouse on an island outside of town, Sacket set up housing for his workers in a former county courthouse which he had moved to another nearby island. Finally, he built a plank road to connect the two islands.

In 1865 Sacket sold 938 barrels of berries in Chicago for more than $13,000. News of the potential wealth spread rap-

SHSW

John Kaminski, first licensed pilot in Wisconsin with his Curtis bi-plane, 1912.

idly and the cranberry boom began. Four years later the Sacket marsh harvested a $70,000 crop. The local newspaper called development of the cranberry industry "magical."

AURORAVILLE

Because of its location Auroraville was a favorite stopping point for farmers from the county's north and northwestern towns who worked in Berlin. A fountain, which has stood on the town's main street for many years, offers a cool drink to thirsty travelers.

Several cranberry marshes were located here from 1860 to 1870 and many Indians came from the Keshena reservation to pick fruit for $2 per day. Auroraville took its name from the township it resides in.

REDGRANITE, Pop. 976

The John C. Williams, William F. Chipman and John H. Dedrick families moved here in 1848, a few years before the village was organized. Land was cheap because the red granite top soil was unsuited for raising crops. However, before long the town realized the granite's real worth and settlement grew. Granite quarries sprang up, employing hundreds of local men. Workers were often kept busy hauling paving blocks to Berlin. Before the Chicago & Northwestern railroad came through in 1901, blocks were hauled in heavy lumber wagons 12 miles along a muddy road.

The town's name, taken from the red granite mined here, is all that remains of the once busy quarries. Today, one of the original quarries is a water-filled pit which serves as an old-fashioned swimmin' hole.

WAUTOMA, Pop. 1,629

Phillip Green moved to Wautoma, built a log house and started a tavern in the winter of 1848. He lived alone here for two years until a Mr. Atkins came into the new settlement with the Shumway brothers. Since the county was rich with pine the men built a saw mill and storehouse which they christened "Shumway's Mills." Because of the brothers' interest in the community, the village was named Shumwaytown.

Three years later the village was platted and organized, including the Shumway land which had been purchased by William Everhard. A year later, Everhard and G.W. Smith built a grist mill and the town changed its name to Wautoma, meaning "land of Tomah" after an early Indian chief. It was a banner year. The population increased, another general store was built and Wautoma became the new county seat. Court was held above the Marble and Curtis general store.

Wautoma continued to grow until the need for a railroad became obvious. Unfortunately the railroad never came.

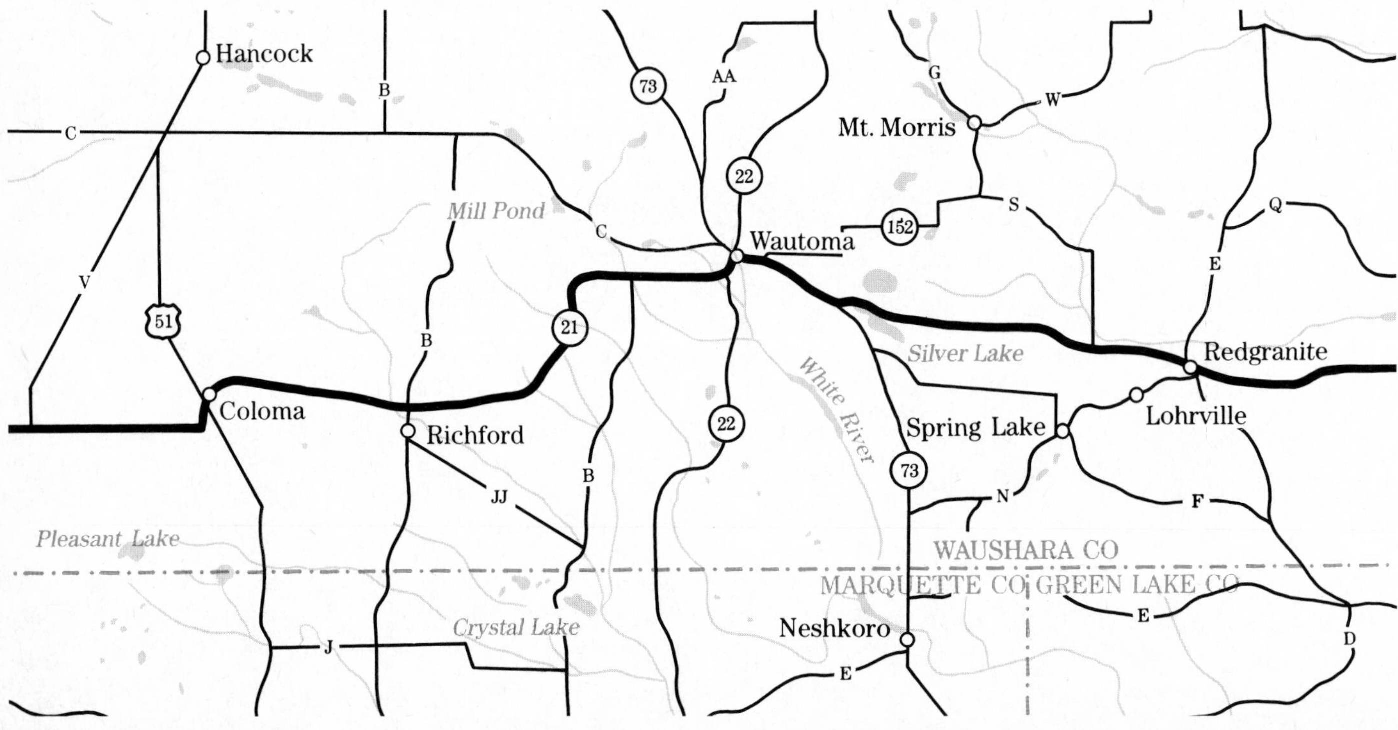

Fall cranberry harvest

RICHFORD, Pop. 404

This town was named by the many settlers who came here from Richford, a town in northwestern Vermont. John Hall, the earliest settler, came in 1850 with his wife and five children. Shortly after their arrival, one of Hall's sons and a son-in-law, Joseph Rue, built a dam and saw mill which became quite successful within one year.

One of Richford's most prominent men in those days was Hall's brother-in-law, a Mr. Woodruff. Trading land for goods, Woodruff moved here soon after the Halls and built a store, tavern, hotel, blacksmith shop, saw mill and grist mill. In 1857 he became town chairman and the town's name was changed from Adario to Richford. Although Woodruff owned most of the town, he later went bankrupt and died of consumption in 1864.

COLOMA, Pop. 367

When Coloma was organized in 1858, it was called Coloma Corners, a name chosen by Charles White, the town's first settler. White had just returned from the California gold fields and named the town for the first California town to discover gold. In 1877 the Wisconsin Central railroad (later the Soo Line) came through here, but totally ignored the town, stopping two miles down the road instead. Subsequently, a new depot and village sprang up along the railroad lines and was called Coloma Station. The railroad and highway still run through the center of town, parallel to the main street.

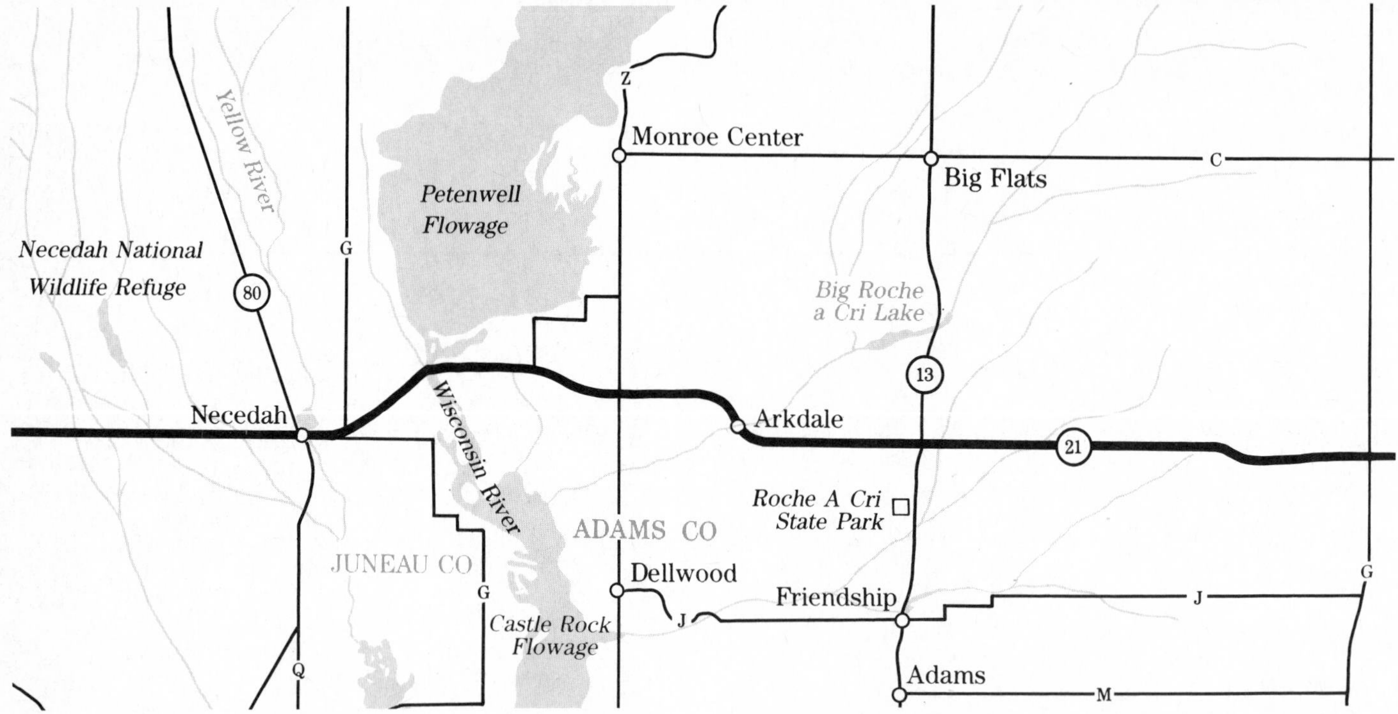

ADAMS COUNTY, Pop. 13,457

Early lumbermen, en route to the northern pineries, considered Adams County a good point to stopover and pick up needed supplies. A trading post opened in 1838 near New Haven to meet their needs and this was the only establishment between Fort Winnebago and Stevens Point for years. Jared Walsworth, a man of considerable frontier experience and the county's first permanent settler, ran the post. Five years later, the Walsworth "tavern" as it was known, became the birthplace of J.S. Pardee, the first white child born in the county. The county officially organized in 1848 and was named in honor of John Adams, the second President of the United States.

Agribusiness is currently the important industry in Adams County. Cash crops of potatoes, peas and beans bring about 14 million dollars annually.

ROCHE-A-CRI STATE PARK

Once a rocky island in ancient Glacial Lake Wisconsin, this 410-acre, semi-wilderness park was named by early French explorers. The big, flat-topped rock juts 300 feet above surrounding woods and was named Roche-a-Cris, or "Crevice in the Rock," because of its large cleft. At the rock's base are early Indian petroglyphs (stone etchings) discovered by surveyors in 1851. The park is located a few miles south of the intersection of highways 21 and 13.

FRIENDSHIP, Pop. 744

A few miles south of Roche A Cri, on highway 13, is Friendship, the county seat. In 1854 H.M. Whitney filed an 80-acre claim in the center of Adams County just south of Roche A Cri. The Whitney tract, now covered by Friendship, was then an unbroken forest. As settlers moved in, they named the town for their old home, Friendship, New York. Officially founded in 1856, Friendship began as a railroad settlement when the Wisconsin Central decided to chart a course through here. However, two men foiled the railroad's plans by buying up property on the planned right-of-way, then asking $75 per acre for land not worth five. The railroad refused to buy and moved their stop a few miles south. A new settlement sprang up near the station and called itself Lower Friendship (now the town of Adams.) A bitter rivalry developed between the two villages and continues to this day.

ARKDALE

Arkdale was settled about 1853, primarily by Norwegian/Danish settlers. Ole Karnes chose this land because of good oak trees and was one of the first to move here. High water caused the Karnes family to wait seven weeks before crossing a creek to their new wilderness homestead.

In the 1860's, the town was called Vinje, after a village in Norway, then later changed to Dellwood and finally Arkdale.

JUNEAU COUNTY, Pop. 21,039

Before 1832, this region along the Lemonweir Valley saw few whites except for an occasional trader. The Winnebago called this river Ca-na-man-woi-Sipe, which meant, "child." They hunted and camped here, taking advantage of the numerous fish and game that existed between the Wisconsin and Lemonweir rivers. In 1837, a treaty was signed in Washington whereby the Winnebago ceded all their lands east of the Mississippi and were to leave the state within eight months.

Juneau County was named after Solomon Juneau, a French trader who opened a trading post on Lake Michigan in 1818. He is considered the founder of Milwaukee and became that city's first postmaster and mayor.

Juneau County's sandy soil was favorable for the growth of pine, especially in the north. With the Wisconsin River providing a route all the way to the Mississippi, it was only a matter of time before loggers crossed into the Lemonweir and Wisconsin river valleys to harvest wood. Juneau County formed in 1857, two years after Mauston presented a bill to the state legislature asking to divide Adams County down the Wisconsin River. When the bill was finally passed, the

SHSW

Lemonweir flour mill built in 1852.

SHSW

Logging supply boat working the Wisconsin River, 1913.

SHSW

Main St., Necedah, 1882.

county seat went to New Lisbon, seven miles up the road. Mauston residents claimed that New Lisbon unfairly offered corner lots to legislators. The county seat battle continued for several years. In 1859, when another vote was taken, 500 more people placed ballots than were known to live in the county. Mauston claimed fraud and the courts finally awarded the county government to Mauston that same year.

NECEDAH, Pop. 773

The Winnebago Indians named this town, situated at the base of a high bluff on the Yellow River, Necedah, or "Land of the Yellow Waters." It was first explored by white men in 1843 when all Yellow River territory belonged to the Indians.

Five years later the Indians ceded all of their lands east of the Wolf River to the U.S. government and Thomas Weston and J.T. Kingston came to Necedah. As was the custom, the two men staked claims by blazing a tree on either side of the river and carving their names and the date on them. After building a rough log shanty, they returned to their homes in Grand Rapids (now Wisconsin Rapids) and formed a saw mill company.

Settlement began that summer when Weston's crew drove 700,000 feet of logs from Grand Rapids down to the proposed mill in Necedah. By June, 1849, they had cleared six acres from the base of the bluff to the water's edge, adjacent to the present dam. Lumber for permanent buildings soon came down the Wisconsin River from Grand Rapids. More settlers moved in and 11 families were making Necedah their home by 1852.

The town was an important lumbering center in its early years. Sixty-five million feet of logs were sawed annually, then shipped down the Yellow River and into the Wisconsin River, where most of it was sold at Galena, Illinois, bringing $11 to $12 per thousand feet. The Necedah Lumber Company shipped out 900 cars of lumber in the first nine months after one railroad came to town in 1881. In all, 18 miles of railroad cars were loaded with native hardwoods such as red and white oak, elm, maple, ash, basswood and birch.

NECEDAH WILDLIFE REFUGE

Once poorly-drained swampland unsuited for farming, this 40,000-acre site was set aside in 1939 as a permanent wildlife refuge and soon became well known for its large deer herds. In 1946 the herd numbered nearly 5,000 and more than 1,600

Frank White Belly, George Home Crow and Joe High Eagle.

deer were harvested during a gun hunting season. Since then, gun and bow and arrow seasons have been an annual event at the Necedah Refuge.

Visitors in early spring or fall can observe the 10,000 geese and ducks which migrate to this safe place annually. A refuge manager will direct visitors to special areas of interest and self-guided auto tours are available.

MONROE COUNTY, Pop. 35,074

Formed in 1854, this county was named after James Monroe, the fifth president of the United States. It is part of the driftless area which was not crossed by glaciers, so the streams and rivers have more mature valleys then other portions of the state and the region is known as coulee country. Because so much of the county is drained by rivers and streams, there are few lakes.

A range of north-south hills through the center of the county formed a barrier to the railroads. Because of these hills, the railroads eventually had to tunnel 3,000 feet through the ridge.

The Fox Indians once lived along the county's valleys, but moved further south along the Mississippi River during the 1700's. They were followed by the Winnebago Indians from the Green Bay area. In a treaty signed in 1837, the Winnebago gave into pressure by whites and ceded all their Wisconsin lands. For many years, however, a number of Winnebago refused to leave the state for reservations in the West.

The county's first settler, Esau Johnson, came up the Kickapoo River in 1842 on a prospecting trip, following a rumor that the region had oil. There wasn't any oil, but Johnson fell in love with the Kickapoo Valley. In a hurry to get his family, he hollowed out a tree, made some paddles and canoed back down to Crawford County. When the county was surveyed in 1849, settlement began to increase, helped by a new state road built through the county that same year. It ran from Prairie du Chien through La Crosse, Sparta, then to Black River Falls, Eau Claire and finally Hudson. Shortly after that, another road was built following an old Indian trail from Portage down through Sparta and on to the Mississippi.

These roads helped the farmers and settlers who either traveled by river or slow-moving oxen down to Prairie du Chien or La Crosse for their mail and supplies. When Monroe County was separated from La Crosse County in 1854, Sparta was named the county seat.

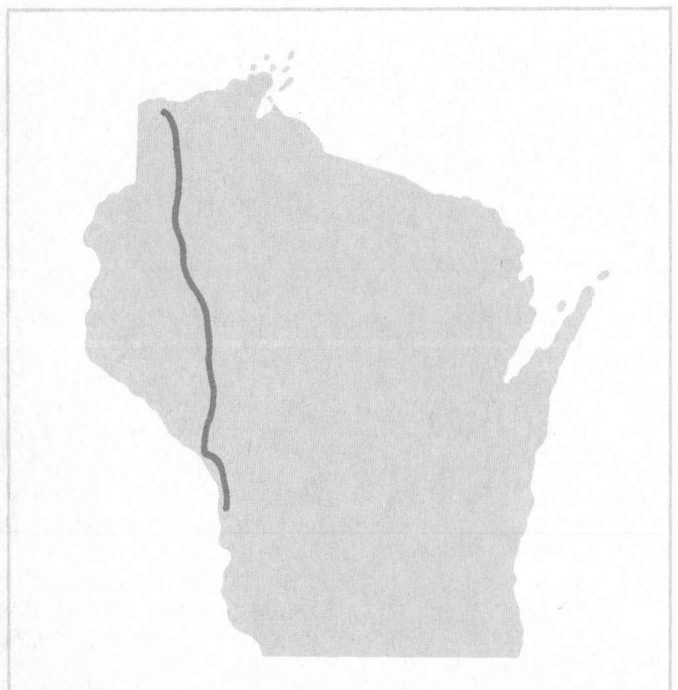

U.S. 53 passes 235 miles from the coulee country of the Mississippi River Valley, into the important early logging regions of Eau Claire and Chippewa Falls. In the north as it passes the lake region, it crosses the famous St. Croix-Brule River portage which was an early highway for Indians and explorers.

ROUTE 53, LA CROSSE TO SUPERIOR

SHSW

An afternoon ride to the Black River. Photo/ C.J. Van Schaick.

LA CROSSE COUNTY, Pop. 91,056

La Crosse County is a region of deep fertile valleys and rolling hills eroded over many years by streams draining into the Mississippi and La Crosse rivers. The sand and limestone bluffs on either side of the Mississippi rise to 500 feet. These sedimentary rocks contain shells and other ancient marine fossils laid down by a giant sea that covered most of the North American continent millions of years ago. During the more recent glacial melting, 10-12,000 years ago, the La Crosse and Mississippi rivers began cutting their valleys through these rocks. The Mississippi Valley was once much deeper than it is today, but after the glaciers retreated and the river slowed, the Mississippi filled with silt to its present level.

A prehistoric people used the river to move into the region after the last ice age. Indian nations followed but it wasn't until 1680 that a Franciscan priest, Father Hennepin, became the first white to pass through this area. Except for fur traders who followed Hennepin, La Crosse County wasn't settled until 1841 when the nearest towns were Prairie du Chien and Galena, Illinois. Milwaukee was still a small village and Chicago's population was only 5,000. La Crosse County was officially organized in 1851 but its present boundaries weren't set until 1918. French traders watched the Indians play a game with sticks and a deerskin ball and called it La Crosse. When exploring here in 1766, Jonathan Carver noted that the opposing goals were 600 yards apart and that up to 300 men played the game. Carver said they played with such ferocity that many were injured.

LA CROSSE, Pop. 48,347

Winnebago Indians once lived on this level, sandy prairie at the confluence of the Mississippi, La Crosse and Black rivers. During the early 1800's French traders came to the Winnebago camps to trade guns, powder, knives, blankets, shirts and whiskey for the Indians' furs. Eventually this treeless prairie, ten miles long and three miles wide, became known as Prairie La Crosse. Though the Winnebago ceded this land and all others east of the Mississippi in 1837 in exchange for reservations, many refused to leave. In 1841, Nathan Myrick, 18-years-old, came to the Prairie La Crosse area to trade with the Winnebago who were still there. He arrived with only ten cents and a load of trade-goods and anxiously waited for ten days before the Indians came to him. After that Myrick "had plenty good trade." He built a crude trading post on Barron's Island, called Pettibone Park today, and also cut cord-wood for steamers venturing up the Mississippi. In 1842 he moved his post to the mainland at Prairie La Crosse.

Myrick wrote about a cold winter morning where, "The weather was cold and that night a blizzard sprung up. The next morning was the bluest I ever experienced; I was sick, homesick, and it was the only time I wished myself back home in the East (New York)." He persevered and over the next few years the Prairie La Crosse post became the central trading spot from the Black to the Bad Axe River. Myrick traded with important Indians such as Chief Winneshiek and Chief Decorah.

In 1844 Myrick and Scooter Mills went up to the pineries of the Black River to cut and float logs down to La Crosse. From here the lumber was floated down to St. Louis. All traveling was done on the Mississippi until 1845 when the first overland trip was made in eight days from Prairie du Chien to Black River Falls. In 1848, when the Winnebago were forcibly removed from this region, Prairie La Crosse's white population was only 30.

The government made area land available that same year, but settlement was slow until the early 1850's. During this time, a number of settlers from New York and Vermont came and established grist mills, saw mills, and a newspaper whose early purpose was to promote this new town. Prairie La Crosse soon became the county seat and over the next 40 years was an important Mississippi lumber town. Lots sold for about $40 and a number of buildings were constructed during the 1850's. Obviously, it did not immediately become the big city its promoters wanted!

A number of German and Norwegians immigrated here during the late 1850's, attracted by work in the pine forests of the Black River area. By 1856 this village of Germans, New

Englanders and Norwegians had grown to 3,000 and felt it was sophisticated enough to drop Prairie from its name. Historian J.A. Renggly once wrote, "that drifting down the great (Mississippi) on a radiant morning, the voyager will recall nothing more varied in his travels than the city of La Crosse. The home of savages less than 50 years ago, it is now the home of wealth, enterprise, education and refinement."

La Crosse was more than a good riverport (1,569 boat arrivals in 1857) and lumber center. The railroad connection to Milwaukee in 1858 assured the city's success. When the Civil War stopped river traffic below Ohio, La Crosse became an important rail-link for products moving east and west. By the time logging ended in the Wisconsin pineries at the turn-of-the-century, other industries—including four large breweries—had developed to sustain the town. Today La Crosse is a diversified industrial and agri-market center.

SHSW

Trempealeau reflected in the waters of the Mississippi, 1890.

ONALASKA, Pop. 9,249

With La Crosse a short distance south, few settlers came here except for an occasional lumberman or hunter. When William G. Rowe decided to start a business in 1851, he purchased a small house in La Crosse, loaded it on a wagon and moved it up the prairie. His main purpose was to run a tavern for loggers. Others soon began settling around Rowe's tavern and by the late 1800's, 300 people were situated around the post office, school and train depot. According to one report the town got its name from a line of poetry Rowe frequently quoted which referred to a distant Alaskan fishing village with a similar name.

Stretching out below Onalaska is the Upper Mississippi River Wildlife and Fish Refuge, a 200,000-acre refuge created in 1924 which runs from Wabasha, Minnesota to Rock Island, Illinois. Its purpose is to protect the natural habitat of the important central Mississippi flyway.

MIDWAY

Once known as Midway Station, this small village formed around the railroad which came through in the early 1870's. The hamlet once had a blacksmith shop, a frame hotel, store and grain elevator with a capacity of 10,000 barrels.

HOLMEN, Pop. 2,411

This village began when Frederick Anderson built his blacksmith shop next to Halfway Creek in 1860. Before that,

SHSW

The steamboat "Northwestern" on its way to Lake Pepin, 1873.

Halfway Creek was a resting stop for travelers heading up the rugged trail to Black River Falls. Although the town was originally known as Frederickstown and Cricken, the village postmaster requested a change in honor of a Mr. Holmen who surveyed this region in 1851. Holm is also a Norwegian word referring to low, fertile land which borders water.

The Caseberg Mill Company harnessed Halfway Creek's waters in 1876 and ground flour from wheat, corn and buckwheat for local farmers over several decades. A rafting pin factory was also located here and its pins were used to help tie rafts of logs shipped on the Mississippi. At one time Holmen boasted a two-story hotel, meat market, a creamery, ice-harvesting and its first doctor who came in 1883.

TREMPEALEAU COUNTY, Pop. 26,158

This beautiful region is part of the Upper Coulee County, a land of high prairie where streams have cut deep coulees through the sandstone on their run down the Mississippi Valley bluffs.

Although many trappers passed through here, Nicholas Perrot was the first to reside in this county. He reportedly spent the winter of 1685 camped two miles above the present village of Trempealeau, then moved up to Lake Pepin the following spring.

The French were determined to establish a post among the Dakota Indians and in 1731 sent Rene Godefrey sieur de Linctot to winter near a large bluff situated in the Mississippi River bottoms. The Dakota called this bluff Pah-hah-dah or "mountain separated by water." The French called it la montagne qui trempe a l'eau, meaning "the mountain which is stepped in water." From this French phrase came the word Trempealeau.

The Dakota and Winnebago occupied these lands and traded with the French, followed by the English and finally the Americans. From these Mississippi bluffs the Indians watched the rapid change and new technology the whites brought up the river. The first steamboat, the Virginia, steamed past Trempealeau Mountain in the spring of 1823 on its journey up to Fort Snelling.

James Reed, James Dousville and a colorful trapper named Augustin Rocque are considered the first settlers to move into the county. James Reed brought his family up from Prairie du Chien in 1840 and settled at what was first known as Reed's Landing, then as Montoville and later as Trempealeau. Trempealeau County was officially formed in 1854 with the county seat at Galesville, but the county government later moved to Arcadia and finally to Whitehall in 1877.

GALESVILLE, Pop. 1,239

In the winter of 1852-53, Trempealeau County was sparsely settled with a population of only 75. That February B. Heuston and Catharine Davidson married at Trempealeau and then built a cabin to the east at the Opening, a spot along the shallow gorge of Beaver Creek which later became known as Galesville.

During the summer of 1853 Judge Gale became frustrated with his attempts to establish a college in La Crosse and decided to develop a new town and college. He traveled the rolling coulee country 17 miles north of La Crosse looking for a place to start his town, build a mill and establish his school. Fording the Black River, he journeyed up Beaver Creek to where the waterpower would be ideal for his mill, purchased 2,000 acres, and platted Galesville. Gale's brother-in-law, Dr. William Young, the town's first doctor, actively promoted Galesville throughout the area. When Trempealeau County was organized in 1854, the town was named the county seat despite the fact that only rugged trails led to it.

A number of settlers came here in 1854 as work began on the mill. Unfortunately it was destroyed in a flash flood and another was started. A year later, Galesville's population was only 30. A writer describes Galesville's early days as ones of "strange scenes, queer characters, eccentric experiences and sadness." However, it grew rapidly over the next several years.

The Commercial Hotel was built, as well as a courthouse, flour mill, blacksmith and general store.

During this time, Judge Gale was busy looking for subscribers to his college which he had tentatively named Yale University. In 1858 there was enough money to lay the foundations for what would be called Gale College. Early historians noted that the university grounds rested on the edge of Beaver Creek valley and included two Indian mounds that were 35 and 75 feet in length. One mound resembled a bear, the other a horse.

Gale College taught a good selection of courses, including Latin. After the first class graduated in 1865, Gale stepped down as president. Unfortunately the railroad bypassed Galesville, decreasing its importance as a marketing center. The county seat was moved to the new metropolis of Arcadia in 1876 and to Whitehall the following year. A branch of the Chicago & Northwestern finally reached Galesville in 1883—too late to have a major impact.

Gale College was closed in 1903 and the buildings housed a two-year Lutheran college until 1939. The Brothers of Mary bought it as a training school in 1941 and run it today as an ecumenical retreat house. The buildings are set on a picturesque hillside and Judge Gale's grave is located under a stand of fir trees behind the buildings.

LAKE MARINUKA

The few lakes in Trempealeau County tend to be created by dams, including Lake Marinuka, the county's largest lake, which is created by the Galesville mill dam. The lake was named after Marie Nounka, an Indian princess who was the daughter of Chief Winneshiek and granddaughter of the famous Winnebago Chief, One-Eyed Decorah. She died at Galesville in 1884 at 82 and was buried at the head of the lake. According to Indian rites she was buried at midnight with her head pointing north. Her grave has been moved twice: once because someone built a barn too close to it, the second time in the early 1900's when the fire department needed the spot. Today her grave is located in a park off County Road T, on the lake's northwest side. A concrete teepee marks that spot, close to a cool spring that feeds into the lake.

North of Galesville, U.S. 53 winds through a hilly coulee country of forests and dairy farms.

DECORAH'S PEAK

About two miles east of Galesville one hill sits prominently in the band of hills that run north and south. The Indians used this peak to send smoke signals to call their tribe together or to alert for possible trouble.

Decorah had his small village on the Black River, about a mile and a half below the peak, where the tribe fished, hunted and raised corn. One night in the early 1800's a band of Dakota Indians attacked Decorah's camp. Many were killed and Decorah escaped to a small cave on the nearby hill. The following morning the weary Decorah journeyed on foot to Prairie du Chien, seeking help from the soldiers at Fort Crawford.

ETTRICK, Pop. 462

This small farming village formed when Norwegian farmers settled here in the 1870's. Nonetheless, it was named by the Scottish postmaster after a forest region in Scotland. Iver Pederson opened the first store in 1870, a multi-purpose building with the basement used as a saloon, the main floor as a general store and the top story for a church. The town also had a creamery, flour and woolen mill and in the early 1900's floated bonds for construction of a cooperative railroad between Ettrick and Blair. The line, called the Ettrick and Northern Railway Company, had twice daily passenger and freight service but was unprofitable after truck shipping and highways developed.

SHSW

Indian women in the studio of C.J. Van Schaick.

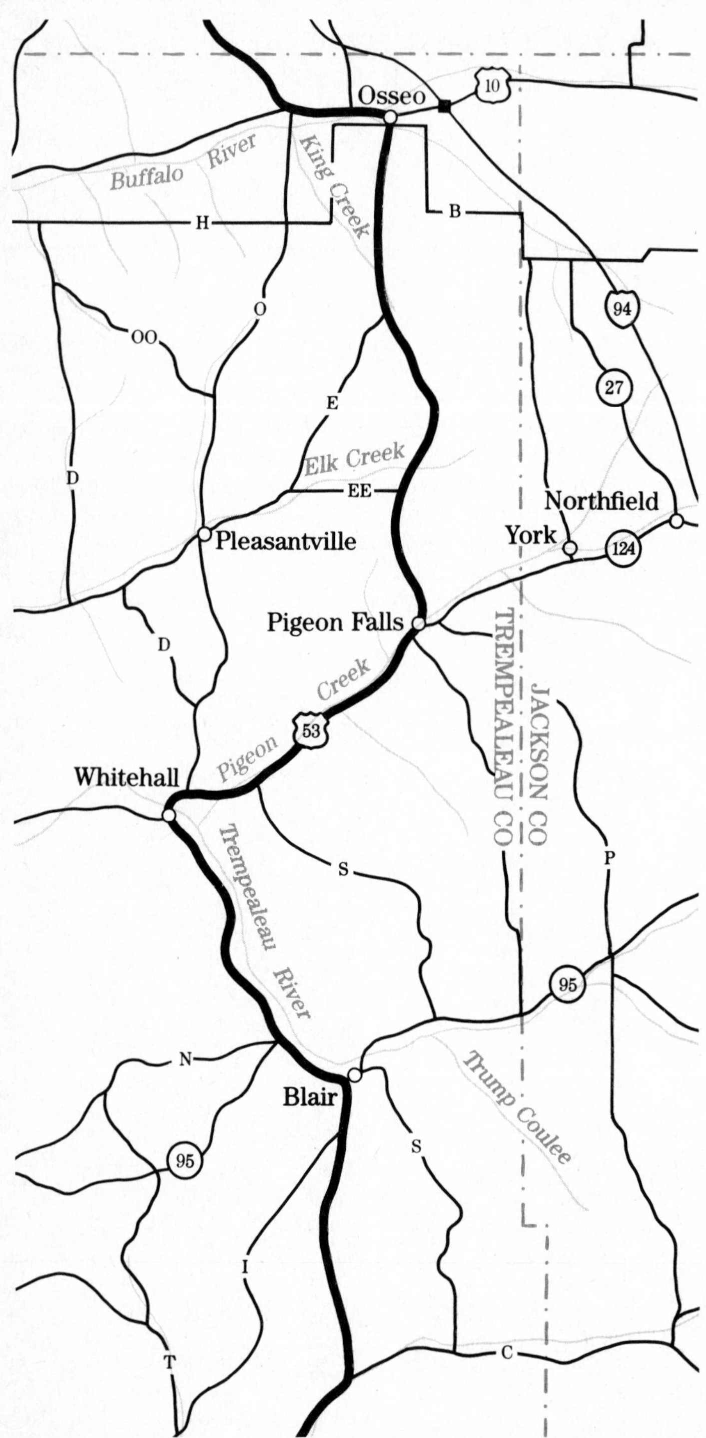

BLAIR, Pop. 1,142

For many years, Blair was little more than a grist mill settlement in the Trempealeau River valley. It was called Porterville after a local family until the Green Bay and Western Railway Company followed the river valley down to the Mississippi in 1873 where this small community lay in its path. The town changed its named to Blair after John Blair, one of the railroad stockholders, and regular train service was established in January 1874 connecting Green Bay on Lake Michigan with Winona on the Mississippi. Almost overnight, Blair became an important trading and shipping center.

The town also has a darker side to its history. One of Wisconsin's few lynchings took place here in 1889 when Jacob Olson, a convicted arsonist, returned here after being released from prison. A mob of 50, including Olson's wife and son, tried to convince him to leave. When he refused, the mob tied Olson up and left him swinging from a tree. His wife and son were convicted of murder and 50 others were fined for rioting.

A mill pond has been created on the Trempealeau River here near a beautiful park and small camp ground.

INDIAN AGRICULTURE

Each spring Winnebago women broke up the ground with heavy spades and planted pumpkins and what was called "squaw corn." They cultivated with crude hoes, keeping weeds from crowding out the young plants. The mature corn was picked, hulled, dried and ground in wooden bowls into powder which was made into bread or a thick soup. Corn was also cooked on the cob by putting heated rocks and green corn into holes. After cooking, the corn was cut from the cob and dried under the sun. It could then be stored for years and was a staple in soup.

WHITEHALL, Pop. 1,530

This picturesque area of rolling hills in the Trempealeau Valley was settled in 1855 by farmers Benjamin Wing and Ole Knudson. The area became known as Whitehall, after a town in Illinois, but settlement was slow until the railroad was built along the Trempealeau River in 1873. When he learned that a station would be built here, Henry Ketchum bought land and had E.T. Earl plat 14 blocks in 1873. Earl is considered Whitehall's first resident. He selected his homesite on a day when it was 30 below zero with an impossible wind. Earl built a warehouse with a partner that cold winter, and made the first wheat transaction that January for $1 a bushel.

That following summer, settlers began arriving and needed a place to stay while they selected a farm or home site. The Empire Hotel and a furniture store were built to serve them.

With a new railroad, local farmers found a ready market for their products. After the harvest of '74 some 225,000 bushels of wheat were shipped from Whitehall over the Green Bay and Western Railroad. Hardware stores, a tailor shop, tannery, an enlarged Empire Hotel, a newspaper called the Messenger, and the new Whitehall Mill were all signs of a healthy village. Another sign was the town's successful effort to move the county seat from Arcadia to Whitehall in 1877. Anticipating the move, Whitehall built a two-story courthouse for $1,200.

PIGEON FALLS, Pop. 338

Cyrus Hine explored Pigeon Creek in the summer of 1865 and decided that this narrow channel lined with high banks would be a good place for a mill. That fall he built his mill and a shop for carding wool, or brushing wool to prepare it for spinning. Hine's mill was later replaced by the Ekern Company flour mill.

North of Pigeon Falls a wayside overlooks the region's rich farmland. It is appropriately called Buena Vista.

OSSEO, Pop. 1,474

Several Richland County farmers moved here in 1857 amidst rumors that the railroad would come through this part of Trempealeau County. A village was platted into 116 blocks. W.H. Thomas was one of Osseo's first settlers but for the next few years the hamlet had only a few shanties and a small hotel. One side of Thomas' house was a small general store, the other was a school where four girls were the first students. The post office was a bit south at Beef River Station, a stage stop on the Sparta to Eau Claire route. The post office shared space in a weathered log cabin with a saloon and Silkwood, the postmaster, kept all the mail in his desk drawer.

The post office moved to Osseo from Beef River Station in 1867 and the stage line was diverted here as a result. There are a few versions of how Osseo got its name. One is that an early settler named Field used oso meaning "bear" to name the town. Others say the name is from ossi, an Indian word meaning "stony place or place of river and stone." The word Osseo is also used in Longfellow's "Song of Hiawatha."

To Osseo's disappointment, the small railroad owned by N.C. Foster of Fairchild didn't reach here from Fairchild until 1887 because it went first to Strum, Eleva and Mondovi. Osseo was destroyed by a disastrous fire in 1891 but was rebuilt shortly after. More recently in 1922, Clyde Van Gorden reportedly wired together 1000 wet-cell batteries to provide the first amateur radio broadcast in this region. WTAQ, the 200-watt station with an antenna strung from a windmill, carried a piano and cornet duet by Frank and Camilla Smith.

A new state trail, Buffalo River Trail, is under development and is to follow the railroad grade from Mondovi to Fairchild.

SHSW

Railroads played an important role in the development of towns along the Trempealeau River Valley.

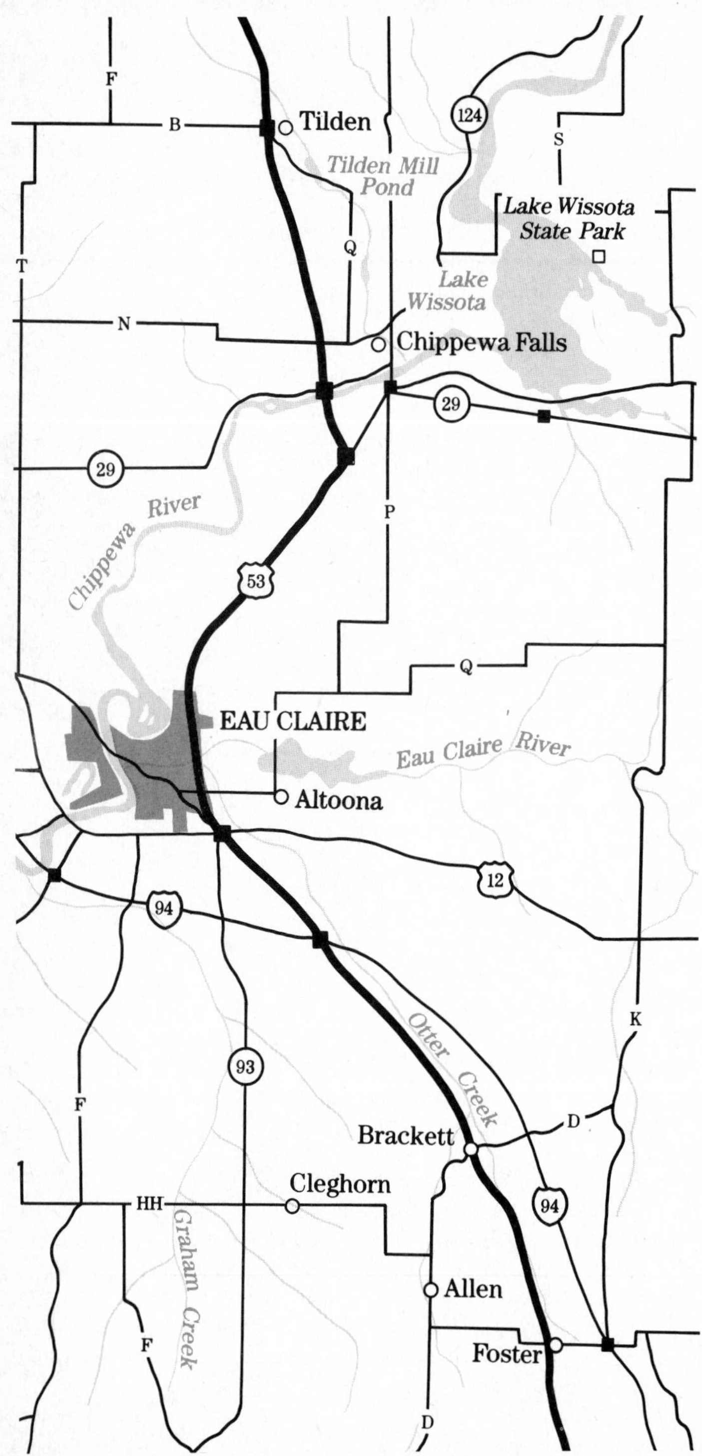

EAU CLAIRE COUNTY, Pop. 78,805

As the road enters Eau Claire County, the coulee county is left behind. Eau Claire County is crossed by the Chippewa and Eau Claire rivers, both of which played an important part in Wisconsin's history.

This region of Wisconsin became a buffer zone between the Dakota Indians to the west, the Ojibwe to the north and the Winnebago of the east. The treaty defining these Indian lands was made at Prairie du Chien in 1825 and used the waterways of northwestern Wisconsin as boundaries. Traveling through here in the 1700's Carter referred to the Chippewa and Eau Claire rivers as the Roads of War because of the continual fighting between the Dakota and Ojibwe and their use of these rivers.

The county was named after the Eau Claire River which on early 18th century maps was labeled as the Rufus River. The Ojibwe called it Wah-yaw-con-ut-ta-gua-yaw-sebe which translated into Clearwater River but early settlers felt the English version too plain. When the proposed city was platted in 1855, the river was renamed in French to Eau Claire.

The first whites to visit here might have been Radisson and Groseilliers, the French adventurers who traveled down from Lake Superior around 1656. Father Hennepin, a Jesuit priest, claimed to have entered the Chippewa River while held captive by Dakota Indians in 1680. Another Frenchman, Le Sueur, ventured up the Chippewa briefly in search of copper and furs. But Jonathan Carver was the first Englishman to write extensively about this area when he explored the Chippewa River in 1767.

Obviously, fighting between the Dakota and Ojibwe made travel here dangerous. It was eight years after the Winnebago ceded their Wisconsin lands in 1837 before settlement begin in Eau Claire County. The first settlers were men interested in the area's tall pine. The state legislature officially organized the county in 1856 with a population of 100 and the small village of Eau Claire was named the county seat. The county's first murder trial was in 1858 when two Germans living together had a fatal fight over who would wash the dishes.

FOSTER

This small collection of homes was first named Emmett in the 1850's by area homesteaders. Nathaniel Foster, a wealthy eccentric living 18 miles east in Fairchild, began a building campaign there that became the talk of the region. Starting in 1875, he organized a lumber company and built a hotel, steam saw mill, a grain elevator, a feed mill and a 350-seat opera house. In 1895 he built one of the larger retail stores in northwest Wisconsin. It is not surprising that when Foster ran a railroad line up to Emmett it quickly changed its name

Farmer displays bountiful cabbage crop.

to Foster. Though the railroad was called the Fairchild & North Central, the story goes that most people referred to it as "Foster & Nobody Elses."

CLEGHORN & BRACKETT

Farming began here in the 1850's and a small trading center was started and named after Lewis Cleghorn, a local settler. There is little to note about Cleghorn except that Nathaniel Foster's small railroad line once connected it to Foster and Fairchild. Local farmers once shipped grain from this point.

Brackett was named after James M. Brackett, the Eau Claire postmaster from 1878.

EAU CLAIRE, Pop. 51,509

When Jonathan Carver paddled up the Chippewa River in 1766, he described a prairie land where large herds of Buffalo and Elk roamed a land shadowed by conflict between the Ojibwe and Dakota. Where the Eau Claire River joins the Chippewa, the prairie gave way to a forest of pine, beech, maple and birch.

A French trader named Le Duc probably lived along the river here in 1784, trading with the Ojibwe who disliked him. He eventually moved down the Chippewa to trade with the Dakota, reportedly taking along two Ojibwe scalps to gain favor with the Dakota. Another trader wasn't noted here until 1832 when Louis de Marie, his Ojibwe wife and eight children left Prairie du Chien and headed for the falls on the Chippewa River. On their way up the Mississippi to the Chippewa, they saw dead bodies from the Bad Axe massacre lying along the shore. Marie moved his post throughout the Chippewa Valley for several years as he successfully traded with the Indians.

Though some logging was done on the Chippewa and over on the Red Cedar River, the first actual settlement didn't form at the confluence of the Chippewa and Eau Claire rivers until 1845. With little money, Arthur and Stephen McCann and Jeremiah Thomas located here in makeshift shanties and spent the year logging along the Clearwater River (Eau Claire). They joined forces with Simon and George Randall to build a mill the next year and spent an entire season on the mill before placing out a boom to collect the logs they had cut along the Chippewa. That summer their investment was swept away in a flash flood.

Despite that misfortune, others were drawn to Eau Claire by the potential of this forested region. In 1849-50 a road was built up from Prairie du Chien through Sparta, Black River Falls, Eau Claire and eventually over to Hudson. Most settlers continued on past the tough little lumber hamlet of Eau Claire to the St. Croix prairies and open lands of Minnesota. Originally known as clearwater, the village changed

SHSW

Eau Claire, 1870.

its name to the more romantic sounding French version, Eau Claire.

Beginning in 1850 new homestead laws opened most of northwest Wisconsin for settlement. Supplies of pork and flour came up from either Galena or Prairie du Chien for the settlers and speculators. Eau Claire's business was lumbering and prior to 1855 the town of 100 men had few stores or retail businesses. Growth here was slow since many settlers were attracted to California and the open prairies of Minnesota. The Mississippi was still the great waterway, but the trip to Eau Claire was too difficult for many. A stage between Eau Claire and Lake Pepin had a one-way fare of $3.

When the county formed in 1856, a rumor circulated that a railroad would be built from Portage through here to Hudson on the St. Croix. One historian noted that settlers indulged in "the most wild and visionary schemes." In any case, the village organized and developed on the three separate banks of the rivers and the sections were known as Eau Claire, Eau Claire City and North Eau Claire. Churches and mills were built, while the rich pineries of the Chippewa and Eau Claire valleys became the growing town's economic base. In 1872, the three separate villages incorporated as the city of Eau Claire.

SHSW

Sleeping quarters on a Chippewa River logging raft.

Historians estimate that half of Wisconsin's pine was located in forests drained by the Chippewa River. In 1871, 112 lumber camps operated along the river and cut 247 million feet of timber each year, leading all other Wisconsin rivers by a good margin. As intensive lumbering continued, disputes developed over rights on the river. Members of the Beef Slough Company, located at the Chippewa's mouth, wanted the river left undamned so their logs could move freely down to their collecting booms. They felt the dams and booms at Chippewa Falls and Eau Claire were unacceptable. Tensions between the Beef Slough Company and the mills at Chippewa Falls and Eau Claire continued through much of the 1880's.

In the spring of 1867, two Beef Slough men named Bacon and Davis and a number of workers tried to smash their spring log supply through the Eau Claire booms. They wanted to open the Chippewa once and for all, making it a straight shot for their logs to Beef Slough at the Mississippi. They were stopped by a posse of 250 Eau Claire men armed with shotguns who were determined to prevent destruction of the Eau Claire mill.

In addition to those tensions, work in the mills was extremely hard and the hours long. In 1881, 1,800 Eau Claire Lumber Company workers walked off their jobs and held rallies demanding a ten-hour day in what was known as the Sawdust War. The motto was "ten hours or no sawdust." Gov. William Smith called out the state militia which camped here for several days maintaining peace.

The train rumored to come here in 1856 finally came in 1870. A great celebration—including 10,000 people—awaited the West Wisconsin Railroad when it came into town. The taxpayers had something special to celebrate. County officials had craftily avoided funding most of the county's rail construction by inserting in the contract that they "may" pay a subsidy for their portion of the line rather than "shall,"

At the turn-of-the-century, the forests were stripped of what many had thought was an inexhaustible supply of white pine and most of Eau Claire's 22 mills closed down. Some converted to paper milling, using the more abundant and cheaper pulpwood that had been untouched. Today Eau Claire is a diversified manufacturing and agricultural trading center.

ALTOONA Pop. 4,393

Once known as East Eau Claire, this town was platted in 1881 with two houses. A settlement eventually developed after the Chicago, St. Paul, Minneapolis and Omaha Railroad (Chicago and Northwestern) established a machine shop and roundhouse here. Chartered in 1887, it renamed itself after a Pennsylvania town.

CHIPPEWA COUNTY, POP. 51,702

At the turn of the century a writer said, "The climate of the (Chippewa) valley is exceptionally good, protected as by the forests surrounding it. It is not so cold as the prairies south and west of the state, and there is much less bleak wind from the north. Sleighing is generally good in the winter. Spring comes early, and with warm growing summers and lovely autumn, there is nothing to be desired in this regard." Another historian wrote that the Chippewa River Valley is "a weird, wild district," and "haunted by spirits or is the scene of many thrilling incidents." The valley history abounds with stories of Indians, explorers, trappers, and loggers who traveled this water highway.

Though Father Hennepin reportedly visited here in 1680, followed by Carver in 1766, these pine lands were mostly uninhabited by whites until Louis De Marie traded with the Indians at Eau Claire in 1832. He moved up river to the large falls on the Chippewa the following year. Those early years centered around the valuable furs of the beaver and other native animals. After the Revolutionary War the United States government forbid foreigners from fur trading on American soil, giving impetus to John J. Astor's American Fur Company. His agent H.L. Dousman, located at Prairie du Chien, and encouraged the Chippewa Valley Indians to trap as much as they could. Astor and his men made great fortunes while the Indians quickly learned the white man's profit motive. As the lower Mississippi's need for lumber grew, there was pressure to settle and log the Chippewa Valley.

A large part of northern Wisconsin broke off from the huge Crawford County to establish Chippewa County in 1845 but it wasn't until 1853 that Chippewa County was fully organized with Chippewa Falls as county seat. The 1850 census recorded 615 settlers in the county, mostly loggers. With wheat prices and land values climbing, many Canadian, German and Norwegian settlers immigrated here beginning in 1855. However it wasn't until most of the east coast pineries were depleted in the 1880's that the Chippewa Valley's expansive white pine forests were exploited. In the next 20 years, 14 billion feet of lumber were cut throughout the valley. By 1911 the forests were gone and most mills had permanently closed their doors.

RAFTING DOWN THE CHIPPEWA

After the logs were cut and planed into lumber at Chippewa Falls and Eau Claire, rafts of lumber 200 feet long and 60 feet wide were taken down river by an 11-man crew. The men used 12-foot oars to guide the fronts and backs of the rafts around bends and sand bars. Each raft carried the flag of the mill it came from. Since the crew had to eat, a cook went along, piling sand on one end of the raft to make a cook fire. Depending on the Chippewa's current, the run down to Reads Landing on the Mississippi averaged 12-15 hours. The crew then left the raft and walked back to camp. Later they were able to take a small steamer to Eau Claire. When the Milwaukee railroad was built from Wabasha to Chippewa Falls, they rode the train.

CHIPPEWA FALLS, Pop. 11,845

When Indian boundaries were established at Prairie du Chien in 1825, the treaty required the government to establish a trading post and blacksmith near the falls on the Chippewa River. Lyman Warren and his wife were in charge of the two-story log house which was an important American Fur Company trading post until the Indians ceded their lands east of the Mississippi by treaty in 1837, opening the Chippewa Valley to the public. Though the Dakota and Ojibwe gave up rights to this land, they continued to hunt and camp here for many years . About that time, Jean Brunet led Hercules Dousman, General Sibley, Colonel Aiken and Lyman Warren to build the first mill at the Falls. Brunet was a French-born dealer in logging supplies and boats who taught the Indians to work iron. An expert river navigator, he also piloted the first raft from Chippewa Falls to Prairie du Chien. But financial times on the river were difficult and Brunet worked for many years to make the mill pay. After his partner, Warren, died in the winter of 1843-44, Brunet gave up and sold out. He died in 1877, a short distance up river at Cornell, which was once known as Brunet Falls.

Hiram Allen took over the old Brunet mill in 1846 and the mill began to profit despite devastating floods and financial uncertainties. When a lumberjack named Tim Hurley started Chippewa's first saloon here in 1849, it became headquarters for "all the gamblers and roughs in this section."

Unfortunately, a group from Hurley's saloon lynched an Indian because the Indian defended his wife from attack. More than 1,500 Indians gathered at Hurley's bar demanding justice. Four whites volunteered to turn themselves in for trial at Prairie du Chien. They made the trip, but were released when no one at Prairie du Chien came forward to file a complaint. To be sure, they never returned to the Falls.

Development at the Falls was slow. The first frame house wasn't built until 1850 and mail was sporadically carried up river from Wabasha until 1855 when once a week delivery was established. Hiram Allen finally surveyed and platted the town in 1856 but as late as 1854 Indians camped at what became Spring Street. During those lumbering days, Chippewa Falls was a town of adventurers, lumbermen, and drifters looking for excitement and fortune. At one point the Falls had more than 75 saloons and most deals were made over a whiskey bottle. The influx of new settlers included many women and most of the men reportedly discarded their Indian wives to find a new bride.

It was hard to get to the Falls. Until the 1850's the only routes were over rough trails or via an exhausting paddle against current of the Chippewa River. Stage roads were eventually developed during the 1860's and in 1875 the Chippewa Falls and Western Railroad connected the city with the outside world. Later in 1880's other railroads were also completed to Chippewa Falls.

The late 1880's also saw the first woolen mill established here. It was first known as the Chippewa Falls Woolen and Linen Mill Company, then as Crystal Spring Mills. There wool was carded, washed, dyed and woven into mackinaws, or short plaid coats, wool battings and blankets. At the turn-of-the-century, Chippewa Falls also became an important shoe manufacturing center, with six companies producing shoes for national distribution. Also located here at one time or another were six cigar factories, a broom factory and two breweries. Today the Jacob Leinenkugel Brewery, founded in 1867, is Chippewa Fall's oldest industry. Leinenkugels was first sold only locally but due to its popularity is distributed throughout the Midwest. In 1873, it was one of more than 4,000 small breweries in the United States. Today there are fewer then 40 family breweries in operation.

Chippewa Falls also had its share of snow, fires and floods. In 1857 the snow was so deep that many horses and cattle starved and travel was impossible. When one family's food ran out, they had only their neighbor's generosity to rely on. Most of the town burned in 1869 and all the bridges between Chippewa Falls and Eau Claire were torn away in the great flood of 1884.

The 1880's was also the time when Fredrick Weyerhaeuser came to Wisconsin and developed the Mississippi River Lumber Company. After buying the mill at Chippewa Falls, he made it into one of the largest mills under the name of Chippewa Lumber and Boom Company. It occupied ten acres, was powered by 500-horsepower water wheels and at its peak cut 325,000 feet of lumber and 100,000 shingles per day. Weyerhaeuser was an expert in getting maximum productivity out of his men and the forests. Everything was cut, slashed and floated down to the mills except hardwood trees. They were not considered valuable since they wouldn't float high enough down the shallow streams. When Weyerhaeuser moved westward, he left behind a denuded Chippewa Valley.

Located just east of Chippewa Falls is Lake Wissota, created by hydro-electric dams backing up the Chippewa and Yellow rivers. On the east side of the lake is Wissota State Park, built up along the high hills that line the lake. There

SHSW

Chippewa Falls log drivers on bateaux, ca. 1908.

are 81 secluded campsites and a picnic grounds that overlooks the lake from a high bluff.

BUILDING THE LOG CABIN

Building a log cabin was one of the first things a new settler did. He began by choosing trees of the same diameter, then cutting them into 12 to 15 foot lengths. He notched each end of the log so they would lie flat and reenforce each other. On the day of the raising, the settler tried to gather enough people to help him lift the logs to make the walls, which were about eight feet high. Then the space between the logs was chinked with mud. Shingles were cut from oak and windows were made of glass, greased paper or deer skin. A wooden latch was fixed to the door which was opened from the outside by pulling on a piece of leather. At night the door was locked by pulling in the string although the expression was that the "latch string was always hanging out" for neighbors. In the security of their cabin settlers spent the night cooking, repairing important tools and listening to the wolves.

TILDEN

The area around Tilden was the first land farmed in the county. A German, George Meyer, went to Eau Claire to start a farm in 1848, but Hiram Allen advised him to go north near Hay Creek. Taking Allen's advice, Meyers came here, cleared land and had a succession of excellent wheat crops. He eventually sold out to a farmer named Henneman and the Rheingans, Muller, Simons and Hartmann families soon moved here. The village was laid out and platted in the 1890's and at one time had a saloon, general store, creamery, blacksmith shop and school. St. Peter's Catholic Church begin by holding services in a small cabin in 1859.

Tilden was named after Samuel J. Tilden, a Democratic presidential candidate who was the supposed winner of the 1876 election. However, a bipartisan committee (the Republicans held a one-seat edge) examined the vote and declared Rutherford B. Hayes, a Republican, the 19th President.

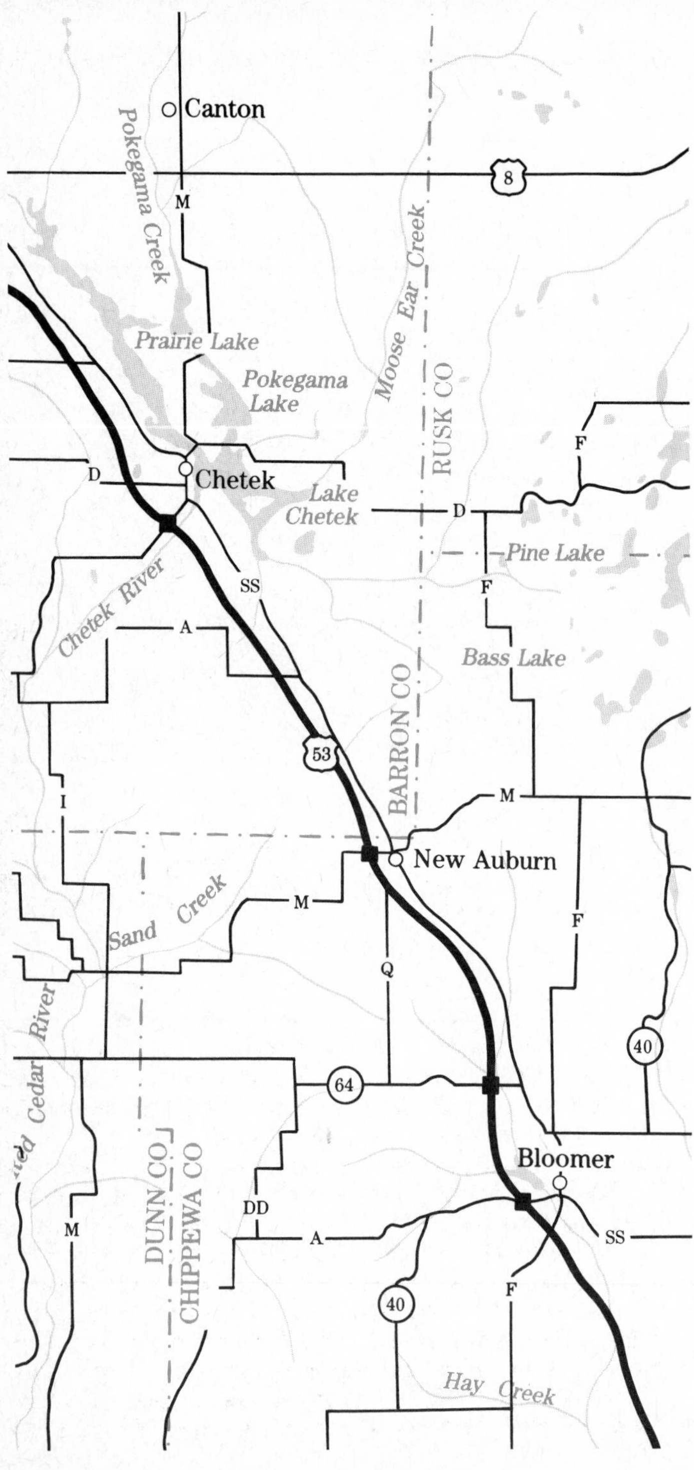

BLOOMER, Pop. 3,342

His agents convinced Jacob Bloomer, a well-to-do businessman, that this spot along the Chippewa River was ideal for a mill. He brought a work gang here during the summer of 1848, but had tired of the project by winter and sold his partially completed dam and mill to Hiram Allen of Chippewa Falls. One of Bloomer's men, Tim Hurley, left for Chippewa Falls where he opened its first saloon. Sylvester Van Loon, an emigrant from New York, was the first actual settler. He built a cabin 14 by 36 feet with a shingle roof here in 1855. Van Loon was set for winter, until his hay supply was destroyed by fire. He then sold his oxen so his other livestock could make it through the winter. Van Loon and his family survived on venison during that first winter: the snow was so deep that the deer could hardly move and Van Loon approached them on snowshoes and clubbed them over the head. Van Loon stayed on to become the postmaster and run a small general store and others followed. The village was known as Vanville until it was officially platted in 1867 and changed to Bloomer. Most farmers here cleared land to raise wheat. Flour milling became Bloomer's mainstay until potato farming became popular and Bloomer became a shipping point. Eventually dairy farming and a creamery that handled half a million pounds of milk daily became the town's economic base. Its first brewery was built here in 1875 by Wendland and Adler. The last case of beer came off the line in 1947 and was shipped to England under the name of Buckingham Ale. The brewery's decaying brick building is located on the town's east side and the mill can be seen where the creek is dammed. Bloomer has recently titled itself the "Rope Jumping Capital" of the world because of a school rope jumping program started by the late Wally Mohrman. Each year Bloomer schools hold a rope jumping exhibition.

NEW AUBURN

Wheat, corn and dairy farmers were attracted here in the 1850's. When David Cartwright and his son hauled a steam saw mill here from Eau Claire in 1875, they saw some indication that the Chicago, St. Paul, Minneapolis and Omaha Railroad would be built through here. The small hamlet became known as Cartwright's Mill and they cut wood logs and made spokes for wagon wheels. The mill changed hands several times and an extensive lath and planing mill was constructed in 1882. Five years later, the York Iron Company mined coal here for their furnaces at Black River Falls. Over the years the village has been known as Cartwright's Mill, Cartwright and Auburn. It was finally named New Auburn in 1904.

SHSW

Indians working quarry, location unknown.

BARRON COUNTY, Pop. 38,730

Numerous glaciers spread over Barron County for an on-again, off-again, period that lasted more than 100 thousand years. The latest glacier to affect Barron County, the Wisconsin stage of glaciation, ended 10,000 to 12,000 years ago. Only certain sections of the glacier extended here: one area of northwest Barron was covered by the St. Croix lobe; the northeast part by the Chippewa lobe. Irregular hills, called terminal moraines, formed along the edges of these glacial flows.

An unusual feature found in a few locations in Barron County are outcroppings of a reddish stone called catlinite, more commonly known as pipestone and similar to that found at the national monument at Pipestone, Minnesota. The Indians fashioned this soft stone into pipes that were used for religious and ceremonial purposes. Early Barron County settlers also discovered an extensive collection of mounds, built by early Indians who moved into this region after the ice age. Many of these mounds were examined in the 1890's, and time and farming have obscured or destroyed most of them.

SHSW

Indians in studio of photographer C.J. Van Schaick, River Falls.

This land, drained by many clear-running streams, was rich in game and wild rice. The Dakota and Ojibwe, enemies since the Ojibwe first came into the Lake Superior region after the 1500's, fought for many years over these hunting and wild ricing lands. The Ojibwe slowly won control over this area and when Indian territories were formally drawn up by the Treaty of 1825, they became this land's rightful owners. Just a few years later they gave up their lands to the whites for reservations.

Ojibwe Indian trails led through much of Barron County and were also used by whites as they explored the area. There is some evidence that the French maintained a post just south of Rice Lake. In the 1880's, villagers dug up some old logs that might have been part of a stockade built by traders during the 1700's. But the region around Barron County wasn't opened to white settlement until after the Ojibwe ceded their lands south of Lake Superior in 1837. When a land office opened at St. Croix Falls in 1848, a number of lumbermen became interested in this region.

The name Knapp, Stout & Company is inseparable from the early history of Barron County. The logging company began in 1846 when Captain William Wilson and John Knapp bought a small mill at what later became the city of Menomonie. Others joined the partnership, including Henry Stout, and the company made massive land purchases from the government at $1.25 an acre. In 1879 they purchased 100,000 acres in the area from Cornell University and the Northwestern & Omaha railroads. It was Wilson who eyed the land in Barron County in 1848 when he was searching for farmlands to raise wheat, pork, potatoes and vegetables for their logging crews. Wilson called this open area of south central Barron County, Prairie Farm. When the Knapp, Stout & Company reached its peak, it was farming 6,000 acres of land in Barron and Dunn counties. The company expanded logging operations into Barron County in 1860, starting a logging camp at a place later known as Barron village. They built a camp eight years later at what is now Rice Lake and another at Chetek a few years after that.

In the 1870's Knapp, Stout & Company were considered the world's largest logging operation. But they left in their wake devastated forests whose stumps and slash fueled forest fires which raged across the region. Shortly after 1890 lumbering declined and Knapp, Stout & Company began disposing of their cut-over land by advertising bargain prices in Scandinavia and the eastern United States. Many people took up the challenge and agriculture became increasingly important to the county. Wheat and potatoes dominated at first, but dairy farming and dairy products eventually sustained the Scandinavian and German farmers.

The county was known as Dallas County up to 1869 when it became Barron to honor Henry D. Barron, a politician who represented the region. Unfortunately, the county's early records were lost when County Treasurer James Bracklin and his files fell out of a boat into the Red Cedar River. Bracklin was saved, but his files weren't. (This county description is repeated on U.S. 8. & U.S. 63)

CHETEK, Pop. 1,931

Situated near a chain of lakes, Chetek was once the site of ancient Indian camps. These Indians, possibly ancestors to the once vast Dakota nation, built many burial mounds in this region. The Dakota Indians hunted and fished here before they were displaced by the Ojibwe who pushed in from the northeast during the 1700's. When the first white settlers arrived, they noted that many Ojibwe camped along the shores of Lake Chetek. Chetek is an Ojibwe word meaning, "swan on a lake."

The village of Chetek began as a logging camp for the Knapp, Stout & Company in 1870. A saw and planing mill was constructed and operated here until the supply of white and jack pine ran out around 1888. However, most of Chetek's businesses began with the railroad's arrival in 1882. During the celebration over the arrival of the line, the railroad workers became drunk and out of hand and farmers ended up chasing most of them out of town.

The numerous Chetek-area lakes attracted many vacationers. During the summer, the train was loaded with wealthy residents of Eau Claire, Menomonie and Chippewa Falls who built cabins and clubhouses here. On the lake's west side symposiums and talks were held on newly cleared grounds. Promotional booklets were printed and distributed in southern states such as Texas and Louisiana extolling the region's merits.

Ojibwe Indians working rice fields.

CAMERON, Pop. 1,115

Cameron first began with a small collection of homes about a mile and a half south at a place known as Holman's Crossing, where the Chippewa division of Chicago, St. Paul, Minneapolis & Omaha was constructed in 1878. Six years later the Soo Line passed north of the small village on its way east and the town moved its buildings on sleds and wagons to the junction of the two railroads. At one time, residents of North Cameron could take any of 12 different passenger trains going north, south, east or west. L.C. Stanley, the area's original owner, named Cameron after his friend, a state senator from La Crosse.

The region was heavily settled by Scandinavians who first came to work in the logging camps in the last half of the 1800's. Most supplemented their meager incomes by farming during the summer, then resumed work as loggers or railroad workers during the fall and winter.

Many Indian trails crossed the area and early settlers discovered many burial mounds, gardens and campsites. Fascinated, the settlers opened a number of the mounds in search of artifacts and found arrowheads, cooking utensils and other objects. Unfortunately, most of the mounds have been destroyed by farming, lake cabin building or the erosion of time.

About eight miles northeast of Cameron the Indians quarried an outcrop of pipestone, a reddish clay that can be easily carved with a knife and fashioned into pipes and instruments. This quarry and another at Pipestone, Minnesota, were the major sources for this important ceremonial stone. According to one story, all the Ojibwe braves who knew the location of this pipestone quarry were killed in a battle with the Dakota. For years the Ojibwe searched the Barron County hills looking for this small quarry. Also located near Cameron was a large cranberry bog and wild rice bed. Knapp, Stout & Company built a dam across the creek in the 1860's, creating an artificial lake that flooded the shallow wetlands. When the loggers left and the dam was demolished, this area reverted back to a marsh.

RICE LAKE, Pop. 7,691

Rice Lake was also an important Indian camping region. Here the Indians gathered wild rice, a grain which grew in the lake's shallow waters. Women did most of the work, gathering the rice from canoes. One pushed the canoe forward with a pole while another gathered the grain with two sticks. One stick held the stalks over the canoe while the other hit the tassels, knocking the grain into the canoe. The rice was then parched over a fire and placed in moose skin. The men usually walked on the skin until the hulls came off. An average Indian family collected about five bushels in a

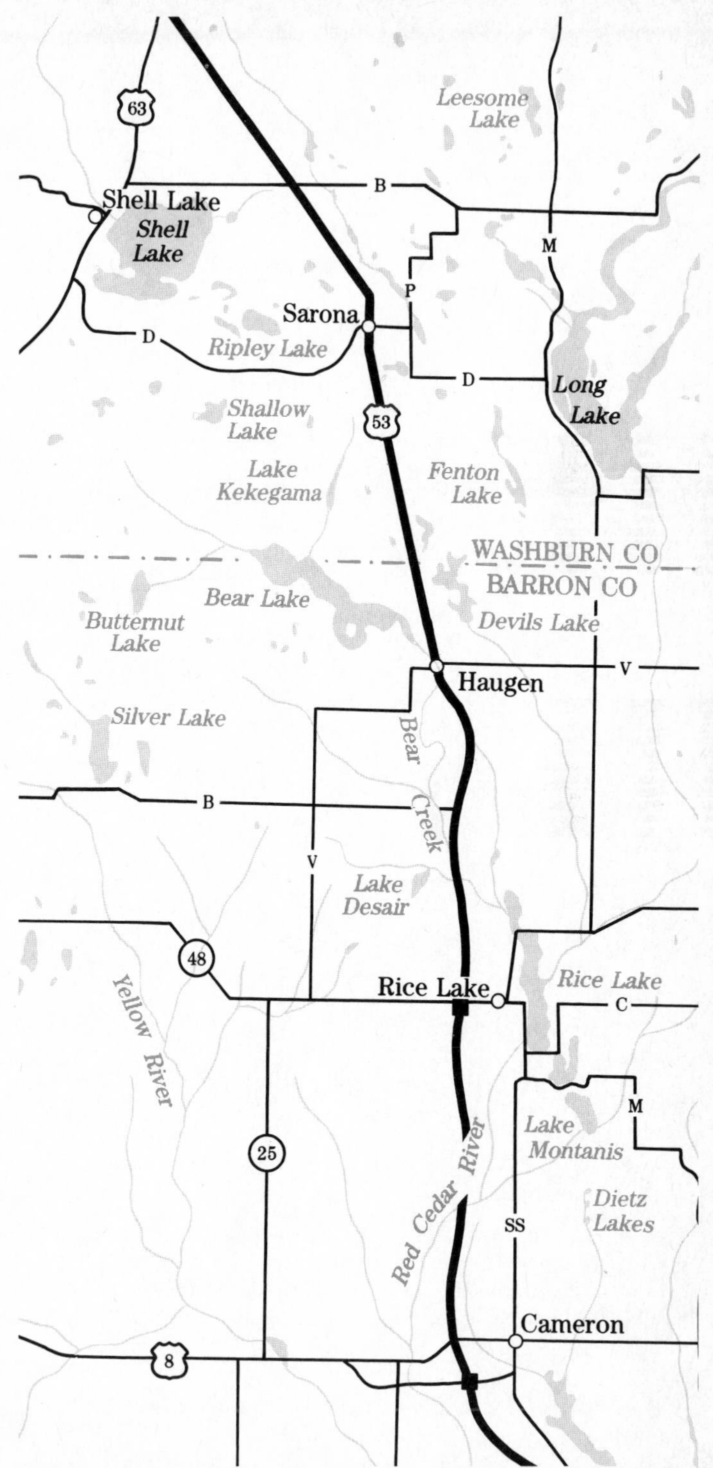

season and was paid about four dollars per bushel.

Captain Thomas Wilson and James Bracklin saw this region of marshes, pools and rice beds of the Red Cedar River in 1858 and realized its potential for sending logs to their Menomonie mills. At that time, the Ojibwe still had a large camp on the lake. Ten years later Knapp, Stout & Company established a logging camp here and started to cut the pine. Work also began on a dam which raised the Red Cedar River, flooding the rice beds and forcing the Indians to look elsewhere for wild rice.

M.W. Heller, who came with his family to run the Rice Lake mill in 1871, is considered the first permanent settler. He also built the first store, hotel and blacksmith shop. In 1872 he set aside Saturday afternoons at the mill to grind flour for the growing number of settlers. During this time the town was known as Rice Lake Mills. The county seat was moved to Rice Lake for a year in 1873, before Barron mustered enough votes to get it back. Laws were rigidly enforced here and some 14 prisoners were reportedly kept in two cells in the winter of 1890. In addition, a woman was supposedly jailed for committing adultery.

The Rice Lake Lumber Company was formed when the railroad reached here about 1882. The new lumber company bought large tracts of pine lands along the Red Cedar River and built a new sawmill which had an average capacity of 35,000,000 feet per year during the late 1880's. Knapp, Stout & Company also used Rice Lake as a regional base for their 25 area logging camps. They even ran a small steamer, Lady of the Lake, to pull logs across Rice Lake to be floated down to Menomonie. Rice Lake continued to grow with the addition of a small brewery, barrel stave company, numerous stores and shops. One interesting company started here in 1918 was the New Idea Potato Company which occupied more than 12,000 square feet of factory space. Today, Rice Lake is a regional retail center, with a substantial income from the tourist industry. The mills are gone and cabins now line the lake which once contained the Indians' shallow rice beds.

SHSW

Cameron, 1907.

HAUGEN, Pop. 251

Named after a state senator, Haugen was settled by Bohemians who came here to farm the cut-over land left by the lumber companies. At one time Haugen residents had an organized society called the Western Bohemian Brotherhood Association. Many considered themselves open-minded and started a debating organization called the Bohemian Free Thinkers. When the railroad was completed through the village in the spring of 1883, Haugen was only a whistle-stop. James Smith, credited with opening the first store, also ran the post office. The town eventually added a bank, a box factory, a lumber yard, four general stores, two billiard halls, a barber shop and a potato warehouse. In the early 1900's, its population was almost double what it is today.

WASHBURN COUNTY, Pop. 13,174

This county wasn't formed until 1883 when it separated from Burnett County along the St. Croix. It was named after Cadwallader Washburn, governor of Wisconsin for three terms starting in 1872. The county and its history centers around the village of Shell Lake (See Route 63).

SARONA

Four Knapp, Stout & Company lumber camps worked this area, floating logs across Bear Lake and down Bear Creek to the Rice Lake mills, until 1899 when the pine was almost gone. The last Bear Lake log drive was during the summer of 1900, about the time a German Mennonite farming colony settled here. The train had already been built through and had a rail shanty here they called Bashaw. Not particularly fond of the name, area farmers tried to rename the small hamlet Sauerville, after Frank Sauer, one of the colony's founders. Since Sauer didn't want a town named after him, the colony combined his name with Sharon, a biblical reference to a place with abundant pastures, and came up with Sarona.

SHSW

Within a few decades, loggers had stripped most of northern Wisconsin's pineries.

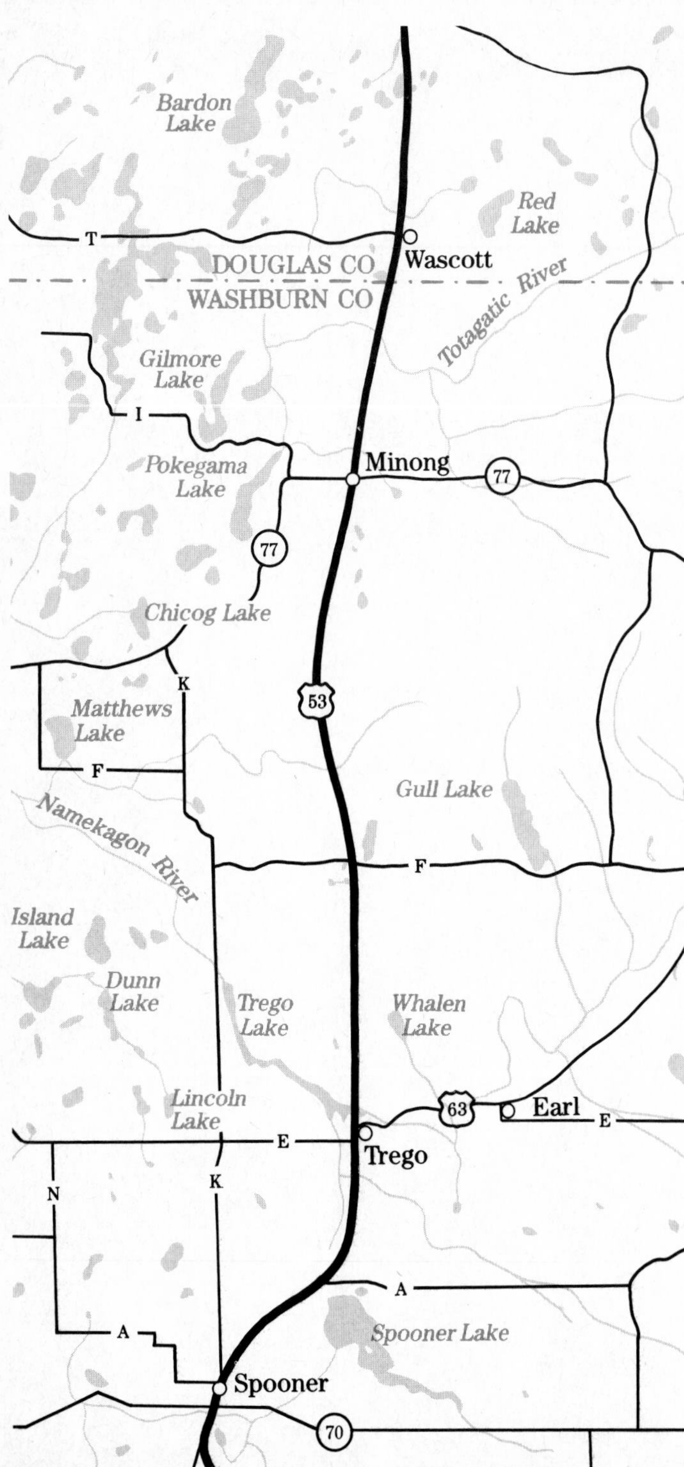

SPOONER, Pop. 2,365

Lumber baron Fredrick Weyerhaeuser pressured the railroad to come into this pine forested area to ship out his logs. In 1880 tracks were laid northward from Shell Lake to a small station and village called Chandler, 1.5 miles north of today's Spooner. Lots sold well and settlers expected Chandler to become an important railroad shipping point. Gravel pits used by the railroad to construct its line to Ashland were also located nearby. Unfortunately for Chandler, another railroad line extended from Rice Lake, crossed the Omaha Line to the south and became known as Chicago Junction. The depot was moved from Chandler to Chicago Junction for a few months, then to a new village called Spooner that was forming between Chandler and the Junction.

The railroad named the town for John Coit Spooner, a railroad attorney who spent much of his career trying to prevent the return of undeveloped railroad property to public domain. He was also a state senator for a few terms during the late 1800's but resigned his term amidst a scandal that his campaign was financed with an illegal $50,000 fund. He continued his corporate law practice in New York and rarely returned to Wisconsin. The town is also the site of a Ptate Agricultural Experimentation Station that pioneered work in the late 1880's on shelter-belts and windbreaks to slow erosion in these sandy soil regions.

TREGO

After the railroad was built up to Ashland by way of Hayward in 1882, the crews returned here to Superior Junction to connect the railroad with Superior. In 1902 the town's name was changed to Trego. When the railroads were built across northern Wisconsin, they were divided into six-mile sections which were maintained by a small rail crew. More often, the crew built a small shack. New settlers found these section houses a convenient place to build near, so small communities developed there. Sidings were often built so the lumber companies could load their logs on to flat-beds. Eventually a post office was needed and the hamlet would be named.

One local historian claims Trego's name is a shortened version of saying that from here trains can go in three different directions. Others say Indians named the junction as they watched train load after train load of logged trees shipped down to the mills.

NAMEKAGON RIVER

The Namekagon River is a winding, rock strewn river that begins east of Cable in Namekagon Lake. During the last part of the 1800's, the river was used to drive logs down to the St. Croix River and on to the mills at Stillwater. The Veazie

SHSW

A logging train of the Chippewa Logging and Boom Co. removes pine from the Thornapple River region. Photo/Charland.

dam, once located near Trego, was only one of many built along the river. It operated from 1878 to the turn-of-the-century to maintain the stream's level for logging purposes.

The Ojibwe had many hunting and fishing villages along this picturesque river. They named the river Namekagon, which means "home of the sturgeon." Today it is part of the St. Croix National Scenic Riverway system, a 260-mile network of undeveloped riverway which Congress set aside in 1968 to protect some of the Midwest's most wild and undeveloped river areas. More information on how to access this system is available at the riverway's headquarters in St. Croix Falls or at the Interpretive Center on U.S. 63 just north of Trego.

MINONG

This is a Chippewa word meaning, "pleasant valley," or "where the blueberries grow."

WASCOTT

A clear-running spring was discovered when the railroad was built through here in 1883. Water was needed for the steam-driven trains so a tank and pump were built at the spring, along with a small house for the operator. A railroad section house was also moved here for a man named Peter Heinz. Eventually, a few settlers moved near here, a post office opened, and a box car was left for a depot. A stone depot was built in 1922. The town once had the longest rail siding between Spooner and Superior. First called 20-Mile Junction, because of its distance from Trego, the village changed its name to honor W.A. Scott, an official of the Chicago & Northwestern Railroad.

SHSW

Spooner, 1905.

DOUGLAS COUNTY, Pop. 44,421

As highway 53 heads north to Lake Superior it passes into a part of Douglas County which slopes down to the Superior Lowland, an area once covered by a large glacial Lake known as Glacial Lake Duluth, the predecessor to Lake Superior. The Douglas County Copper Ridge rims the lowlands from five to twenty miles south of the lake and marks the old glacial lake's southern shoreline. The streams that flow down this ridge into Lake Superior are not very long, but in their brief journey, many have cut gorges 40-100 feet deep through the forest floor. The county's main rivers are the St. Louis, Nemadji, Bois Brule and the Black rivers. A 160-foot waterfall, the highest in the state, is located on the Black River at Pattison State Park which is ten miles south of Superior on State 35.

Of these rivers the Bois Brule River is especially important because it was a major river link to the Wisconsin and Minnesota interiors through a two-mile portage to the St. Croix River near Solon Springs. Before the white man came and started logging, most of Douglas County was covered with pine forests which provided the Dakota and Ojibwe Indians with mink, otter, bear and deer furs. The Dakota Indian occupied this region alone until the late 1600's when the Ojibwe nation were pushed out of the eastern United States by the warring Iroquois and migrated to the Lake Superior hunting lands. Because the Ojibwe had frequent contact with the French on their travels westward, they acquired guns and became more sophisticated in their fighting techniques. They were a strong and able foe who slowly pushed the Dakota from Wisconsin, then forced them out of northern Minnesota in the mid-1700's.

A French explorer, Daniel Greysolon Duluth, was the first white to venture inland from Lake Superior on the Bois Brule River in 1680. With four other men, Duluth portaged over to the St. Croix River that led them to the Mississippi and began an extensive French fur trading business, collecting furs from the Indians in exchange for European goods.

Control of this region changed from the French to English in 1763 and it wasn't until after the War of 1812 that the United States government decided to stop the smuggling of British goods across U.S. land. When this region was made a Wisconsin Territory in 1818, most of northern Wisconsin was part of a large county called Michilimackinac, but only a few traders lived here. The American Fur Company began mining Copper Ridge for copper in 1846, but soon abandoned the project because the ore was low quality.

At one time or another, Douglas County was part of Crawford, Chippewa, St. Croix and La Pointe counties. Few were interested in this county's pine and Lake Superior port until

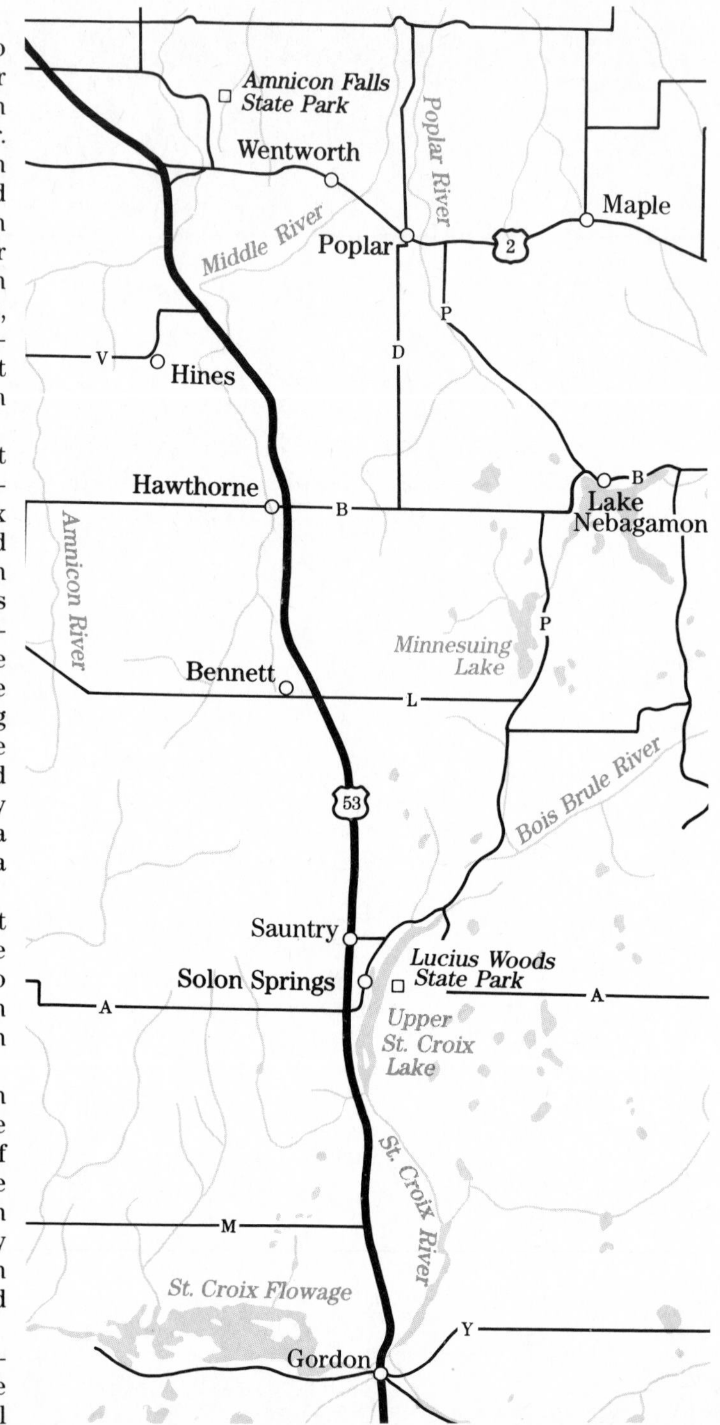

after Wisconsin became a state in 1848. In 1854 La Pointe County was split and the eastern portion was called St. Louis County. Soon St. Louis was renamed Douglas County after Stephen A. Douglas, one of the early developers of the city of Superior. Despite the new name, the county's total population in 1855 was 385.

In the county's early days, fur trade and lumbering provided most of the money and work. The forests near Lake Superior were logged first, starting around 1873. The county's southern part was logged when the railroad reached up through the St. Croix watershed in 1883 from the lumber towns of Eau Claire and Chippewa Falls.

GORDON

In the fall of 1860 Antoine Guerdon banked his canoe where the Eau Claire River joins the St. Croix, at a place the Ojibwe called amick, meaning "beaver." Guerdon had come from La Pointe on Lake Superior to trade with the Ojibwe since he had been told that many Ojibwe camped here. Guerdon purchased land, built a cabin and store, and traded food and goods for Indian furs. Gordon, as he was soon called, also provided a stopping place for the courier who took mail between St. Paul and Bayfield. An educated and religious man, he built a small cabin here to teach the Indian children how to read and write and he held services on Sundays. A church was built in 1874 and Franciscan Fathers from Bayfield occasionally came to lead services.

The town began to thrive. Two hotels were built to accommodate the increasing number of travelers along the mail route to Bayfield. When the railroad was looking for right-of-way to lay its tracks in 1882, Gordon deeded the rights through his little town. When logging began, the village became a supply point for Weyerhaeuser crews working in the woods. At one time there were more than 16 dams on the nearby rivers constructed by the St. Croix Dam Company. When opened during the spring rush, the dams carried the winter's cut of logs down to St. Croix Valley mills. Antoine Gordon died in 1907 at 98, about the time logging ended here and the camps were deserted. He is buried under a tall pine in a cemetery overlooking the Eau Claire River where he stopped his canoe. His gravestone is in the form of pine logs.

In later years the village had a pickle factory and a bowling alley, as well as a number of other stores built when U.S. 53 was completed in 1922. Gordon was also known for the blueberries which grew here and were shipped by rail to other parts of the state. A state nursery has been located near here since 1933 with most labor provided by a nearby state prison camp.

SOLON SPRINGS, Pop. 590

First known as White Birch, this area developed around logging. It also became a favorite summer tourist spot boosted by dependable train service when the railroad came through in the 1880's. At one time the town had three hotels but they burned after 1912. Tom Solon, a entrepreneur, liked the spring water here and developed a commercial bottling plant. The Solon Springs bottled water was distributed across the Midwest and helped put the town on the map. The town changed its name to Solon Springs around 1896.

Solon Springs was reportedly the site of the largest load of logs skidded at one time, 35,240 feet in all. Located next to town is the 41-acre Lucius Woods State Park, with one of the few virgin stands of pine left by the loggers. The park has camping facilities and borders the beautiful Upper Lake St. Croix. It was named after Nicholas Lucius who operated the town's first store.

BOIS BRULE & ST. CROIX RIVERS

The Bois Brule River, which is French for "half-burned wood," provided traders, explorers and missionaries with a path to the St. Croix and Mississippi River valleys for 200 years. Most historians agree that the first white man to complete the journey down the Brule-St. Croix waterway was Daniel Greysolon Sieur Duluth in 1680. His mission was to find the Mississippi's source and to make peace between the warring Dakota and Ojibwe nations for France.

The source of the Brule and St. Croix is in a muskeg swamp located a short distance northeast of Solon Springs. The portage between the two rivers is about two miles. When Rev. William Boutwell passed here in 1832 he reported that the portage was burned over and the first few miles of the Brule were intolerable because of the maze of new undergrowth. Boutwell wrote that, "This highway led to two or three posts and yet you would hardly suppose a rat could even pass." The two mile path, first used by Indians, is the divide where water either drains northward into Superior or southward through the St. Croix River into the Mississippi, finally emptying into the Gulf of Mexico. Traders used the route until about 1886 when it was replaced by improved trails, roads and the railroad.

The actual portage follows a steep ridge and has a resting spot midway. The old trail is hard to follow because of the growth of grasses and brush, although scouts and WPA workers cleared much of the route in the 1930's and erected plaques to mark it. The Brule River is the home to several species of trout. In fact, before there were fishing regulations, thousands of pounds of trout were netted out of the river.

There is an Ojibwe legend concerning Winneboujou, a spirit

or Manitou, said to have lived in the Eau Claire lakes region. Winneboujou was a master at working a forge. He hammered under the moonlight and his booming sounds could be heard by the Indians up and down the Brule valley and as far east as the St. Croix River. The glow from his forge fires lit up the sky. The Ojibwe felt Winneboujou brought good fortune, while the Dakota reportedly feared Winneboujou and his power. During the summer, he was to have lived near the source of the Brule River and St. Croix rivers.

BENNETT

Charles Anderson, Bennett's first settler, came here in 1881 to work on the railroad's right-of-way. The camp was located about a mile north of the present village. Anderson later returned with his family and became a blacksmith. As soon as the railroad was completed, logging firms such as the Sauntry Logging Company began harvesting the large stands of white pine. From Bennett, they built spurs into the forest to haul out lumber and loaded it on flat-cars. The train was Bennett's only connection to the outside world for many years. Highway 53 was improved and paved in 1922. During this time Richard Bennett, a real estate agent, moved here and began selling cut-over land to people interested in farming. French Canadians and Scandinavians were the first takers. About 1900, after the large lumber companies had moved on, smaller mills sprung up at Bennett. Early farmers working the cut-over land were hard pressed to raise enough hay for their oxen or plow horses, and grow enough vegetables and cut enough wood to last through the winter.

The Bennett Hotel was built in the early 1900's along with a Catholic and Lutheran church, the depot, and a two-room school house. A hoop and barrel stave operation was located here for several years, making and shipping butter tub parts throughout the Midwest.

HAWTHORNE

Resting beside the Middle River, this hamlet formed around a small shack which housed the telegraph office of Joe Ackerman and Louis Efaw. Only an Indian trail led through here until the Chicago, Minneapolis, St. Paul & Omaha Railroad was built in 1881-82. Once the trains were running, lumbering began. The Dunlap Company began first, followed by a man named Phillips who built a mill a bit north on the Middle River. His dam provided enough power to cut 50,000 feet of lumber daily. The Weyerhaeuser organization built a rail spur east from Hawthorne to extract pine from the Lake Nebagamon region and a turntable at Hawthorne reversed the trains for the return trip.

Three general stores competed for trade at Hawthorne and it wasn't uncommon to have 300 lumberjacks roaming the streets looking for a good time during lumbering's boom years. Reportedly named after a logger, this was a good-sized village, including two large hotels, a creamery, several saloons, a pool hall, three stores, several restaurants, a barber shop, school and two saw mills. Most of it was destroyed one day in the early 1900's when a locomotive started a fire in the Bonnell sawmill. The town did little rebuilding, since the logging boom was over and there was little reason to remain.

SHSW

Prospecting for copper south of Superior, 1899.

AMNICON RIVER

Amnicon is an Indian word meaning, "spawning ground." An 825-acre park forest ed with white and Norway pine, is located on the Amnicon River just north of U.S. 2. At the park, the Amnicon flows through a series of cascades and waterfalls before emptying into Lake Superior six miles away. There are 40 campsites located in the park.

SUPERIOR, Pop. 29,571

Superior sits on a level terrace at the head of Lake Superior. The Indians and early white settlers considered this location a good place to camp because the natural harbor protected them from sudden storms on the lake. The harbor was formed by lake currents and wave action that pushed sand down along the shoreline and heaped it into a sand spit ten miles long. The St. Louis River, which fills the bay behind the sand bar, broke through at the Minnesota and Wisconsin points, creating a natural entry into what is known as St. Louis Bay. (Duluth opened a channel on its side of the harbor in 1870 as competition for harbor shipping increased.)

In 1661 Radisson and Groseilliers explored the bay, having learned about it from the Ojibwe. Jean Claude Allouez ventured here in 1667 from his small Indian mission on Chequamegon Bay, but it was Daniel Greysolon Sieur Duluth who paddled up the St. Louis in 1679 to try to make peace between the warring Dakota and Ojibwe and establish a trading post. The French had little to gain in fur trading if the Indians were at war. Duluth established a trading post on the Minnesota side of the St. Louis River and called it Fond du Lac, meaning "head of the Lake." For the next 150 years, the French, British and Americans maintained trading posts here, carrying pack after pack of knives, blankets, guns and whiskey inland along the St. Louis River to trade for the mink, beaver, wolf and bear furs and skins which made fashionable European hats and coats.

Active settlement began at Superior when speculators heard that the Sault Ste. Marie canal was going to be built to link Lake Superior with the east. When Daniel Robertson, editor of the Minnesota Democrat, and his friends, Judge Daniel Baker and Rensselaer Nelson of St. Paul, heard the news, they packed their bags and made the difficult journey over Indian trails to claim land on both sides of the Nemadji River. Two other groups came that winter and made claims along Superior Bay. Two of these groups consolidated their 4,000 acres and called themselves the "Proprietors of Superior." Several politicians from Washington also promoted a city here: streets such as Breckenridge, Corcoran and Douglas are named in their honor.

A government surveyor, George Stuntz, surveyed the land here in the summer of 1853. As he canoed along St. Louis Bay and viewed this flat land covered with birch, pine, spruce and fir, he discovered a man named Conners building a house on what later became Conner's Point. By the following spring 250 new settlers were calling Superior their home. To take advantage of the harbor and promote shipping, a pier was built 800 feet into the lake. A hotel called the Superior House was also opened. In 1854 a military road connected Superior with St. Paul, bringing in settlers on the newly-

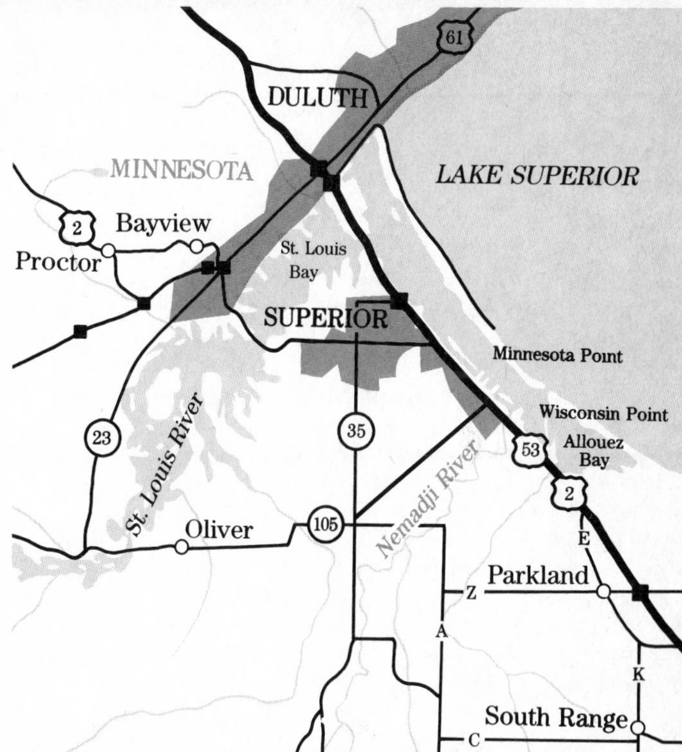

formed stage lines. During the following three years, some 2,000 lots with prices as high as $2,000 were sold. The "Proprietors" handled some $4,000,000 in transactions, mostly from speculators who did not intend to move here.

The next major effort was to have the railroad connect Superior with the population center of St. Paul. A new plan seemed to be hatched every month. In all, at least 10 different proposals were made to connect Superior by rail. The financial Panic of 1857 had a stifling effect on Superior, as well as Duluth, at that time a little village on the other side of the bay. Superior had a population of about 3,000 prior to the panic but was quickly reduced to 500. Duluth had only a few hardy souls and Beaver Bay was the only other settlement along the lake's north shore.

Little growth took place here for the next two decades. There was little incentive for settlers and no reason for a railroad to invest in a line to Superior.

The first real chance for a railroad came in 1870 when the Lake Superior & Mississippi Railroad was chartered to come from St. Paul to Superior. Instead, its tracks went into Duluth, bringing a rush of settlers and business there and marking the beginning of an intense rivalry between Duluth and Superior which still exists. When Duluth planned to enlarge its harbor entrance so ships could avoid the seven-mile trip down to the Wisconsin Cut, Superior filed an injunction to halt the dredging. They filed on a Friday and the injunction was to take effect the following Monday. Over the weekend Duluth workers made a great effort to build a manmade channel: by Monday a small steamboat passed from Duluth harbor into Lake Superior.

Superior finally got its rail connection in 1881 when the Northern Pacific crossed from Duluth on its way to Ashland, spurring new growth in Superior. When ore was found on the Vermillion Range in Minnesota's Arrowhead and near Ashland on the Gogebic Range, the value of the Twin Ports of Superior and Duluth was realized. Lumbering, ore and flour milling made Superior Wisconsin's second largest city at the turn of the century. Finnish settlers came first, followed by Scandinavians and Poles. Ship arrivals increased from 21 in 1883 to more than 900 by 1890. Newly-designed whaleback boats were built in the Superior shipyards as fast as possible to carry ore and grain to the eastern mills of Ashtabula, Cleveland, Toledo, Buffalo, Detroit and Chicago. The "Meteor," the only remaining example of the whaleback boat, is berthed in sand along St. Louis Bay in Superior.

The Duluth-Superior rivalry continued over iron ore shipments, but the Mesabi ore was closer to Duluth and much of the ore was shipped from there. Nevertheless, Superior built one of the world's largest groupings of ore docks and was shipping more ore than Duluth during the 1930's. It has been said that both World Wars were won by Minnesota's iron mines, with help from Superior's docks. Duluth residents called the Superior docks necklaces, because their lights sparkled across the harbor at night.

Today, the grain elevators, ore docks and shipyards are a monument to Superior's growth. However, like other Great Lake cities, the economies of Superior and Duluth are now trying to adapt to changes affecting the steel industry.

SHSW

A natural spring in northwestern Wisconsin.

LAKE SUPERIOR

From the city of Superior one can see dark hills that run behind Duluth and then along the North Shore. These hills were once the shoreline of a previous lake, Glacial Lake Duluth, which was much larger than today's Lake Superior. This huge basin was formed by a succession of glaciers which pushed down from the northeast, carving an ever-widening channel. Coupled with continental drift—a pulling apart of the north and south shores—the basin became a giant collector for water from the melting glaciers. As the lake overflowed, much of the water drained south through the St. Louis River, Bois Brule and other south shore streams, carving out the St. Croix Valley and contributing to the deep Mississippi Valley at Prescott.

Lake Superior was a highway for 17th century voyageurs who came west to trade for the rich furs of the Dakota and Ojibwe Indians. Great summer gatherings were held to exchange goods at Fond du Lac (a village near the mouth of the St. Louis River), La Pointe on Chequamegon Bay, and at Grand Portage on Minnesota's North Shore. The Indians, who had previously hunted only for their own needs, were surprised that these "men with hats" would give knives, guns and whiskey for furs. Nevertheless, the foreign goods motivated the Indians to supply all the furs they could trap to the traders. As the fur trading network grew, the Bois Brule and St. Louis rivers became important south shore routes.

Both the Ojibwe and Dakota Indians were in this region when fur trading began, although the Ojibwe eventually pushed the Dakota into Minnesota. Conflicts between these two nations over ricing and hunting rights spanned two centuries until the Dakota were removed from Minnesota after the Sioux Uprising of 1862.

The Ojibwe called Lake Superior, Kitchigumi, meaning "Great Water." The French called it, Lac Superieur, since it lay at the beginning of the great inland lake chain. Traders crossed the lake in birchbark canoes but developed a larger canoe, the Montreal, which carried 12 men and their supplies. As trade increased, larger boats were built to sail under the lake's roughest conditions. During the late 1700's those larger sailing vessels resupplied the fur companies operating throughout the Northwest.

The first steamboat appeared on the lake in 1841, but the opening of the Sault Ste. Marie canal in the early 1850's

SHSW

Looking south on Tower Ave., Superior, 1889.

brought major shipping to the lake and hastened development of Superior and Duluth. In the 1890's a cigar-shaped ore carrier called a Whaleback, appeared on the lake to serve the Mesabi Iron Range. Passenger ships and cruise ships also began making regular calls at the lake ports, and became a fashionable, elegant, way to see this rugged north region.

After World War II, ship travel declined as cars and planes provided quicker, more efficient, travel. Today, cargo carriers flying the flags of many nations cross the lake from the St. Lawrence Seaway. Large ore boats also cross between the North Shore taconite shipping ports and steel mills on the lower lakes. Despite some pollution from shoreline industries and cities, Lake Superior, the largest freshwater lake on earth, is still once of the world's cleanest. The balance is fragile though since Superior requires 190 years to completely exchange its water.

NEMADJI RIVER

This short stream begins in Minnesota and runs rapidly down the Superior Highlands, cutting ravines 25 to 100 feet deep before emptying into Superior Bay. The state's highest waterfall is located at Pattison State Park on the Black River, one of the Nemadji's tributaries. The waterfall drops 160 feet into a sandstone gorge. The park marks the southern limits of the Lake Superior Lowlands, at one time Glacial Lake Duluth's southern shore. The park is 13 miles south of Superior on State 35.

SOUTH RANGE

Beginning in 1881 a small community developed here around the railroad line that was built from Eau Claire to Superior. Several stores were built, including one with a dance hall on the top floor. An adjoining saloon was the main attraction of the Grand Central Hotel which was built for railroad passengers as well as loggers who worked the northern Douglas County forests. Two lumber mills were located west of South Range at a place called Slab Town and a tram took boards back to South Range to be finished at the planing mill. Two copper mines were also started near here around 1900 but proved unprofitable and were closed. The town rests on Lake Superior's southern ridge which is known as the Douglas Copper Range or South Range.

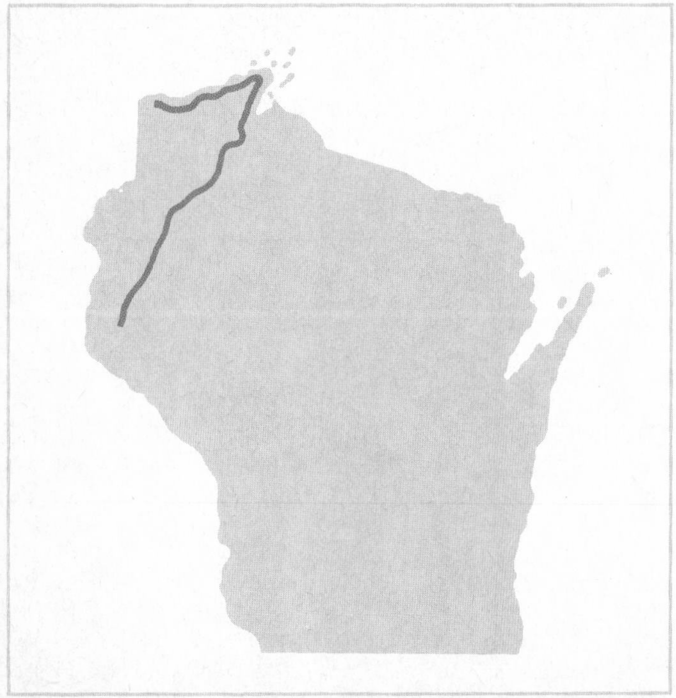

U.S. 63 leaves the farmland of northwestern Wisconsin and crosses into the lakes region. It parallels for a time, the Namekagon River, part of St. Croix National Wild and Scenic River system. Near Ashland this route continues on State 13, into the beautiful Bayfield Peninsula. Along the shoreline, a string of picturesque fishing villages have formed. Today many of the Apostle Islands are preserved as part of the Apostle Island National Lakeshore system.

ROUTE 63 & 13, TURTLE LAKE TO BAYFIELD

SHSW

Family picnic. Photo/Dr. Joseph Smith

BARRON COUNTY, Pop. 38,730

Numerous glaciers spread over Barron County during an on-again, off-again period lasting more than 100,000 years. The latest glacier affecting parts of Barron County—the Wisconsin stage of glaciation—ended 10,000 to 12,000 years ago. Only certain sections of the glacier extended here: an area of northwest Barron County was covered by the St. Croix lobe; the northeast part by the Chippewa lobe. Irregular hills, called terminal moraines, formed along the edges of these glacial flows.

Outcroppings of a reddish stone called catlinite, or pipestone, are one unusual feature of the county. It is similar to the pipestone found at the national monument at Pipestone, Minnesota which the Indians fashioned into pipes for religious and ceremonial purposes. Early Barron County settlers also discovered an extensive collection of mounds built by the Indians who moved into this region after the ice age. Many of these mounds were examined in the 1890's but time and farming have obscured or destroyed most of them.

This land, drained by many clear-running streams, was rich in game and wild rice. The Dakota and Ojibwe, enemies since the Ojibwe first came into the Lake Superior region after the 1500's, fought for many years over hunting and wild ricing territory. The Ojibwe slowly won control here and were considered the rightful owners of this land when Indian territories were formally drawn up by the Treaty of 1825. However, not many years later, the Ojibwe gave up their lands to whites and left for reservations.

Ojibwe Indian trails led through much of Barron County and were used by the first whites to explore the area. The Bayfield Trail passed through Rice Lake on its way to the Chippewa River and connected with the Superior Trail at Prairie Lake near Cameron.

Evidently the French maintained a post just south of Rice Lake. In the 1880's villagers dug up old posts that were probably part of a stockade traders built during the 1700's. Despite that early trading, the Barron County region didn't open to white settlers until after the Ojibwe ceded these lands in

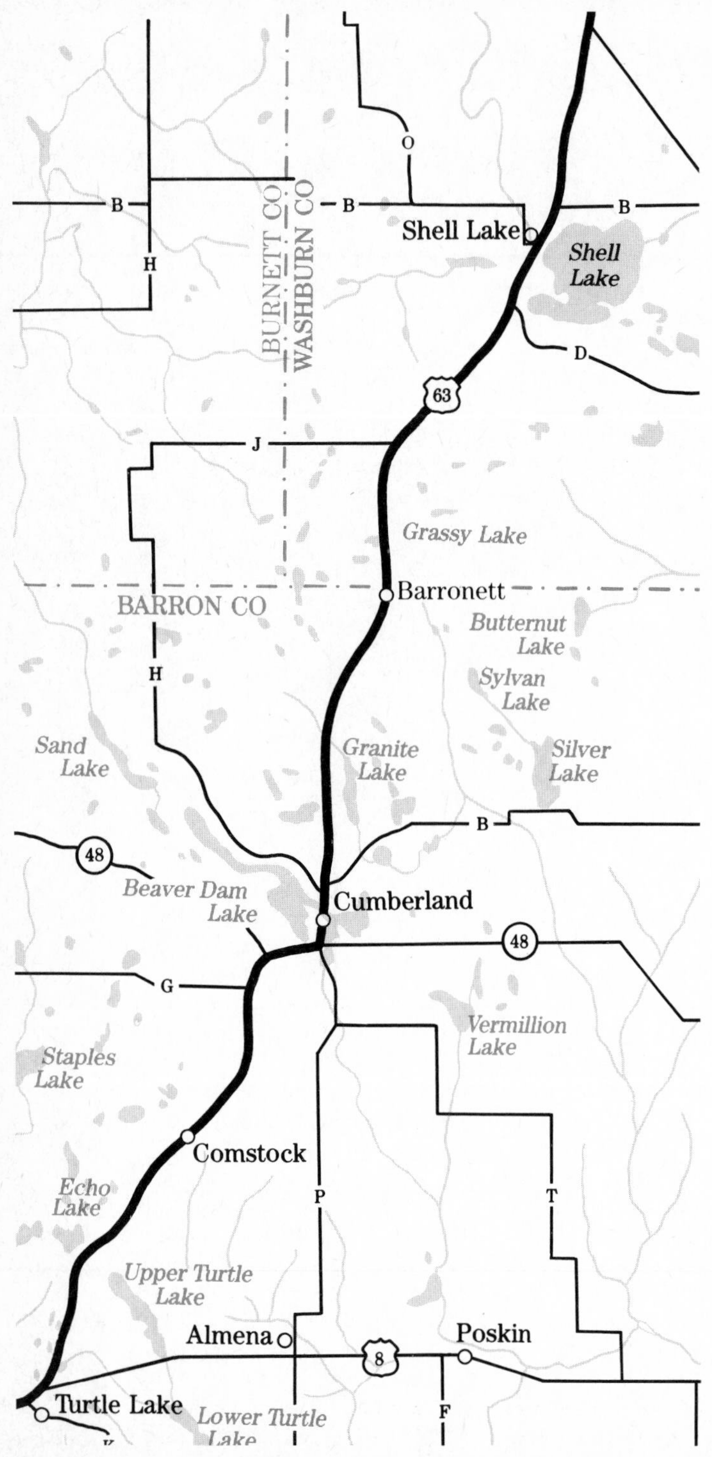

1837. When a land office opened at St. Croix Falls in 1848, many lumbermen became interested in western Barron County near Turtle Lake and Prairie Farm.

The name Knapp, Stout & Company is an inseparable part of Barron County's early history. The logging company began in 1846 when Captain William Wilson and John Knapp bought a small mill at what later became Menomonie. Others joined the partnership, including Henry Stout, and the company bought massive amounts of land from the government at $1.25 an acre. In 1879 they purchased 100,000 acres in the area from Cornell University and the Northwestern & Omaha railroads. Wilson first eyed the Barron County land in 1848 when searching for farmlands to raise wheat, pork, potatoes and vegetables for the company's logging crews. He called this open area of southcentral Barron County, Prairie Farm. At its peak the Knapp, Stout & Company was farming 6,000 acres in Barron and Dunn counties. They expanded logging operations into Barron County in 1860, starting a logging camp at a place later known as Barron. They had a camp eight years later at what is now Rice Lake and another a few years after that at Chetek.

In the 1870's Knapp, Stout & Company were considered the world's largest logging operation. Unfortunately, they left in their wake devastated forests whose stumps and slash provided fuel for fires which raged across the region. Shortly after 1890, lumbering declined and Knapp, Stout & Company disposed of their cutover land by advertising bargain prices in Scandinavia and the eastern cities of the United States. Many people took up the challenge and agriculture became increasingly important. Wheat and potatoes dominated at first, but dairy farming and dairy products sustained the Scandinavian and German farmers.

The county was known as Dallas County up to 1869 when it became Barron to honor Henry D. Barron, a St. Croix Falls politician who represented the region. Unfortunately, the county's early records were lost when County Treasurer James Bracklin and his files fell out of a boat and into the Red Cedar River. Bracklin was saved, but his files weren't. (This county description is repeated on U.S. 8.)

TURTLE LAKE, Pop. 762

This fertile region of farms and dairy herds was once surrounded by a vast pine forest that drew lumberman to southern and eastern Barron County along the Red Cedar and Yellow rivers. By 1878 the St. Paul, Minneapolis, Chicago and Omaha Railroad was constructed through here to Cumberland and a few years later it ran up to the important ports of Superior and Ashland. With the coming of the railroad, Turtle Lake seemed a good place to build a mill.

A settler named Richardson had steam-powered saws which attracted many loggers to Turtle Lake, almost half were Indians who had wigwams at Upper and Lower Turtle lakes. Once this hamlet became a stop on the Omaha line, C.W. Haskins built a hotel even though the town's only other buildings were its two saloons. Mail began to arrive and Richardson became postmaster. The village was briefly known as Skowhegan after Richardson's hometown in Maine.

About that time the giant Knapp, Stout & Company began logging near Upper & Lower Turtle lakes. From there, they floated logs down Turtle and Hay creeks to their Menomonie mills. With supplies coming from St. Paul by train, they requested a train stop at their lakeside camp and Skowhegan soon became Turtle Lake.

Long winters with wheat stranded on Lake Superior's frozen shores at Duluth and Superior made it necessary to develop an east-west connection with the Minneapolis wheat mills. In 1884 the Soo line began work on a railroad connecting the important Sault Ste. Marie shipping center with Minneapolis and St. Paul. Turtle Lake grew as a junction point of two important railroads of northern Wisconsin. The Omaha and Soo companies shared a depot but not without problems. In April, 1901, trains from each line plowed into one another at the crossing, rammed the depot, and burned it down. A few people were injured, but no one was killed. A new depot was built and a better signaling system was developed!

The Richardson mill, which had gone bankrupt, and a nearby shingle factory were both moved around 1890 to the growing city of Barron. With the mills gone and logging declining, farming became more important to Turtle Lake's economy. A creamery was established in 1900 but farmers were not well-organized and the business failed. The Almena creamery also took milk from the Turtle Lake area, but a new owner of the Turtle Lake Creamery bought a carload of milk separators and gave them to farmers in return for cream. His ploy worked and faith in the Turtle Lake Creamery grew. In 1916 the Turtle Lake Co-op Creamery bought it for $14,000.

At one time Turtle Lake had five hotels, two banks, two oil supply depots, two photograph galleries, a harness and shoe shop, tailor, livery barn, theater, and other small shops. It also had a pea canning company and a Gedney's pickle station which collected cucumbers from local gardens and shipped them by rail to Chaska, Minnesota.

LAKE SUPERIOR HIGHLANDS

About 700 million years ago Wisconsin and the surrounding area were part of a mountain range stretching from Canada through northern Michigan, Wisconsin and Minnesota which looked much like today's Rocky Mountains. The fossils

Turtle Lake Library

Turtle Lake school room, 1909.

and granites found in these hills are among the world's oldest.

Difficult as it is to imagine, the tall mountains were worn away by wind, rain and snow to a level plain which geologists call a peneplain. This entire region eventually sank and was covered by seas for millions of years. These seas deposited an overlying layer of sediment, creating sand and limestone. Again this land lifted and the seas drained. Eventually northern Wisconsin's surface was shaped by glaciers that repeatedly moved down over the region for hundred of thousands of years, with the last glaciers retreating 10,000-12,000 years ago. In geologic time, the formation of Lake Superior, the growth of white pine, and the arrival of Indians and white man is recent history.

COMSTOCK

In 1848 the region north of Turtle Lake was being logged by Capt. Andrew Tainter of the Knapp, Stout & Company, whose mills were located at Menomonie on the Red Cedar River. Andrew Swamby arrived here in 1874 and started a general store to supply loggers working nearby. Soon after a mill was started at Crystal Lake. When Swamby opened a post office in a corner of his store, the small hamlet was named Comstock for an area judge.

The Comstock Co-op Creamery, established in 1907 with working capital of $3,000, became one of Barron County's early successful cooperatives. For 13 years the small dairy processed 981,166 pounds of cream and 354,487 pounds of butter a year. Today it is a cheese factory.

When the Chicago, St. Paul, Minneapolis & Omaha line came through here Comstock grew little since the commercial centers of Turtle Lake and Cumberland were nearby. Nevertheless, a bank was started in 1918 with $10,000 in assets. Two years later a Comstock boosters club was organized with 100 members whose purpose was to provide "clean amusement and entertainment for all." More recently, two local boys, Ben and John Peterson, won gold and silver medals for wrestling in the 1972 Olympics at Munich, Germany.

A mile north of Comstock, a post office was established in 1880 near the Omaha tracks. It was named after the Sprague brothers who operated a small saw mill here. At one time, there were a number of homes along the tracks. A church and district school were built, but the hamlet faded when logging ended and the Sprague Mill closed. The school still stands east of the highway and has been a private home for many years.

CUMBERLAND, Pop. 1,983

In the mid-1800's the Beaver Dam Lake area was the Indian camp of Pon-gee Rau-gen, or Little Pipe as the whites called him. The lake bordering the camp was called "Che-wa-cum-ma-towangok," or "lake made by beavers." The Ojibwe nation had given up their claims to northern Wisconsin in an 1837 treaty, but many Indians continued to live and hunt in the area since white settlers didn't come until 1874. After settlers came and began cutting trees, the Indians moved to the Lac Court Oreilles reservation southeast of Hayward. Little Pipe stayed on, living by the lake, until one day in 1895 when he died while out in his canoe.

In the fall of 1874 two Norwegians, O.A. Ritan and R. H. Clotheir, came up from Hersey in St. Croix County to homestead. They visited the lake, but returned home unsure if they should make the move. On the way home they ran into surveyors for the proposed North Wisconsin Railway and learned that the line would probably run by Beaver Dam Lake. That same winter, Ritan and a man named Dahlby returned with their families and built a small cabin where they all finished out the winter. Other settlers followed and all survived by fishing and hunting deer, partridge and bear. Indians visited the early settlers, sometimes asking for food and other times just socializing. The first white child born in Cumberland was called "lily of the woods" by the Indians. Little Pipe even brought the baby a pair of moccasins.

The railroad intended to come through Cumberland the following summer, but law suits over their land grant slowed progress. For three years, with only trails connecting them to the outside world, the settlers made laborious trips to Barron or Rice Lake for supplies. When the train finally reached Cumberland in 1878, spirits soared. More than 300 new settlers arrived within a year. When the railroad workers went on strike, Italian strike breakers were brought in and many settled here and sent for their families. The village was called Lakeland for awhile, but the president of the North Wisconsin section of the Omaha line owned a good share of the land and renamed it after his hometown of Cumberland, Maryland.

Located near a chain of lakes, logging became the town's main economy. At one time during the 1880's, Cumberland had more lumber mills than any other village in Barron County. Logs were cut in a 12-mile radius and floated to Beaver Dam Lake. According to some historians, Cumberland was one of Wisconsin's toughest logging towns. A phrase "Cumberland, Hurley, Hayward and hell," was popular and there is some proof to back it up! In 1884 there were 24 saloons in a town of under a thousand. However, during the next two years city fathers started to clean up the town. A law was passed limiting the town to five saloons and a tax was even applied to dogs in hopes of reducing the large numbers that roamed the streets.

In the following years Cumberland flourished around lumbering and the railroad and had numerous stores, banks, churches, a hospital, potato warehouses, creamery, a canning company, pickle factory and telephone company. During the early 1900's, even a rumor of oil circulated. An oil company agent came through town with a homemade device which supposedly detected oil. With such positive indication of oil underfoot, the state granted permission to drill. Cumberland's hopes of becoming an oil town soon fizzled and many lost their money on worthless leases and options. The town has also been noted for the many Swedish turnips or rutabagas grown in the region. They even have a fall festival honoring the vegetable.

BARRONETT

Once known as Foster, this village was a stop on the Chicago, St. Paul, Minneapolis & Omaha railroad. The Barronett Lumber Company cut ten million feet of lumber annually when it operated a saw mill here during the late 1800's. Besides lumber, a brickyard located near Barronett produced four million bricks each year. As this railroad village attracted more settlers, a hotel, bank, creamery, church and blacksmith shop were built. The tracks were recently torn up and the old Stella Cheese building lies in disrepair along the vacated right-of-way.

WASHBURN COUNTY, Pop. 13,174

This county formed in 1883 when it separated from Burnett County and was named for Cadwallader Washburn. Washburn was elected one of Wisconsin's first Republican congressmen in 1854 and became Governor of Wisconsin for three terms starting in 1872. The county and its history revolves around the village of Shell Lake.

SHELL LAKE, Pop. 1,135

Shell Lake, after which the village is named, has had at least two other names during the last 200 years. The Ojibwe called it Mokokeses Sahkiagin since they considered it barren, with no fish or wild rice to attract them. Only frogs inhabited the soft muddy shore, hence the Indian name which means "frog's navel." When the railroad surveyed the area, this small village was known as Summit because its elevation of 1242 feet is relatively high for Wisconsin. Eventually it became known as Shell Lake because it is shell-shaped.

Ellwood Thomas, the first white settler, built a trading post here around 1872. Since logging was beginning on the Yellow River a few miles north, Thomas built his post to trade with loggers as well as Indians who did not live on the Lac Court Oreilles reservation. This band of Ojibwe, the "Lost Tribe," was not eligible for government subsidies because it refused to enter the reservation.

The arrival of the Omaha railroad from Barronett in 1879, along with development of Weyerhaeuser's Shell Lake Lumber Company, stimulated the town's rapid growth. Built by the lake, the mill operated here from 1881 to 1900. Hotels replaced tar-paper shacks and wooden row houses sheltered the German and Swedish mill workers. For a while only Swedish was spoken at the local Swedish Lutheran church.

As the lumber operation grew, 800 men worked in the mill or in the forests. Stumps were removed from main street and a boardwalk was built. Unfortunately, many loggers came to town wearing their calk boots with spikes that tore up the new walks. Because the lumber company needed a more efficient way to bring out logs, a narrow gauge railroad called the Crescent Springs Railroad was built. It had 25 miles of track around Shell Lake and over to Sarona and other places where wood was plentiful. Many villagers road the train around the lake to picnic or pick berries in the woods. When it was discontinued, many of the county's roads were built on the railroad's right-of-way (County Road D).

The lumber company also used a steamboat to raft logs across the lake to the mill. The boat, the Crescent, eventually rotted on shore, although its anchor was found in the muck many years later and hauled to the city park for display. When the mill closed in 1902, many workers followed Weyerhaeuser's empire west, leaving many shops, houses and saloons vacant. Some houses were moved into the country by farmers working the cut-over land. Slowly, Shell Lake recovered from the mill's closing by becoming a railroad shipping point for area farmers. It also grew as vacationers came to the area by train.

One of the city's more unusual laws was drafted in 1916, making it illegal to skin a skunk within city limits. The city also voted to pay the Catholic church $1 every time the church bell was used to alert the volunteer fire department.

Fourth of July Celebration to Shell Lake, ca. 1880.

Washburn County H.S.

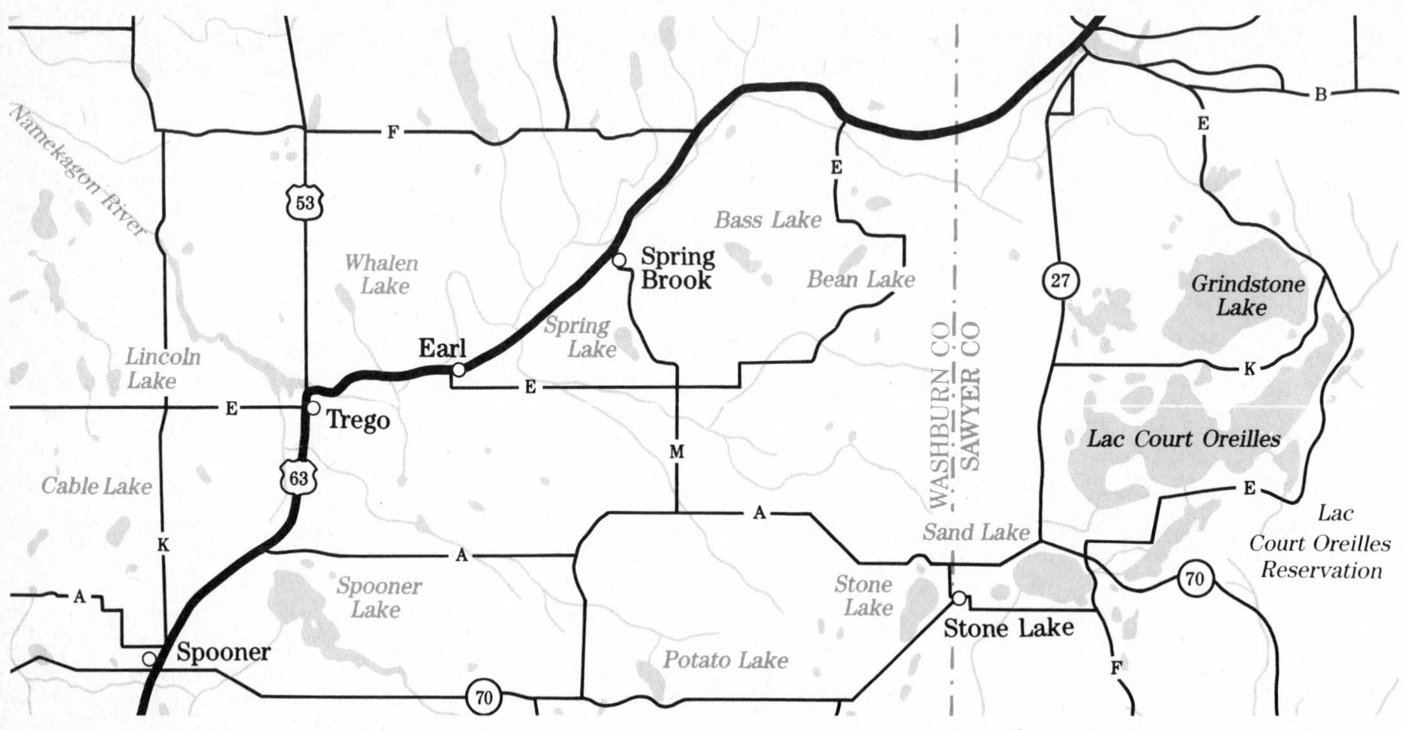

SPOONER, Pop. 2,365

Fredrick Weyerhaeuser pressured the railroad to extend its service into this pine forested area because there were no decent streams to float his logs. Tracks were laid northward from Shell Lake in 1880, a small station was built, and the village of Chandler was platted 1.5 miles north of today's Spooner. Lots sold well because buyers expected Chandler to become an important railroad shipping point. The gravel pits the railroad used for construction of its line to Ashland were also located near here. Another railroad line soon reached up from Rice Lake and crossed the Omaha line below Chandler at a point called Chicago Junction. The depot was moved from Chandler to Chicago Junction for a few months, then moved to the new village of Spooner just south of Chandler.

The railroad named Spooner for John Coit Spooner, their attorney who spent much of his career fighting the return of undeveloped railroad property to public domain. Spooner was also a state senator for a few terms during the late 1800's but resigned amidst a scandal that he financed his campaign with an illegal $50,000 fund. He continued his corporate law practice in New York and rarely returned to Wisconsin.

Spooner was also the site of a State Agricultural Experimentation Station that pioneered work during the late 1880's on shelter-belts and windbreaks to check erosion in these sandy soil regions.

TREGO

In 1882, after the railroad was completed to Ashland via Hayward, crews returned here to Superior Junction and began connecting the railroad to Superior. In 1902 the town's name was changed to Trego. When railroads were built across northern Wisconsin, the roads were divided into six-mile sections with each section maintained by a small rail crew. A small shack was built most often and new settlers found these section houses convenient places to build near. Eventually, small communities developed at these section houses and sidings were often built so the lumber companies could load their logs on flat-beds. In time a post office was requested and the hamlet was named.

One local historian claims Trego's name is a shorthand version of saying "from here trains can go in three different directions." Another story is that Indians gave the junction its name as they watched one train load of logged trees after another go down to the mills.

NAMEKAGON RIVER

The Namekagon River is a winding, rock strewn river that has its beginnings east of Cable in Namekagon Lake. During the late 1800's, the Namekagon was used to drive logs down to the St. Croix River and on to the Stillwater mills. The Veazie dam, once located near Trego, was only one of many built along the river. It operated from 1878 to the turn-of-the-century, maintaining the stream's level for logging purposes.

The Ojibwe had many fishing and hunting villages along this picturesque river. They named the river Namekagon which means "home of the sturgeon." Today the Namekagon River is part of the St. Croix National Scenic Riverway system, a 260-mile network set aside by Congress in 1968 to protect some of the Midwest's most wild and undeveloped river areas. More information on how to access this system is available at the St. Croix Riverway headquarters in St. Croix Falls or at the Interpretive Center on U.S. 63 just north of Trego.

EARL & SPRINGBROOK

Earl began as a small trackside post office when the Chicago, St. Paul, Minneapolis and Omaha line was built through here in 1882. It was named Earle after the man who built the railroad bridge over the marsh and creek at the nearby Veazie logging settlement. George Veazie built a large dam here that backed up the Namekagon River, raising its level eight feet higher than today and creating enough water current to rush logs to the St. Croix River. The Veazie dam was used until it was blown up around 1901. The "e" on Earle, was eventually dropped.

Springbrook was known as Namekagon until about 1900 when the post office changed it. A number of houses were built along the tracks near the small depot. In addition, there was once a cream-buying depot here where farmers shipped to creameries down the track.

Barron County H.S.

Sunday afternoon ride on a railroad handcar.

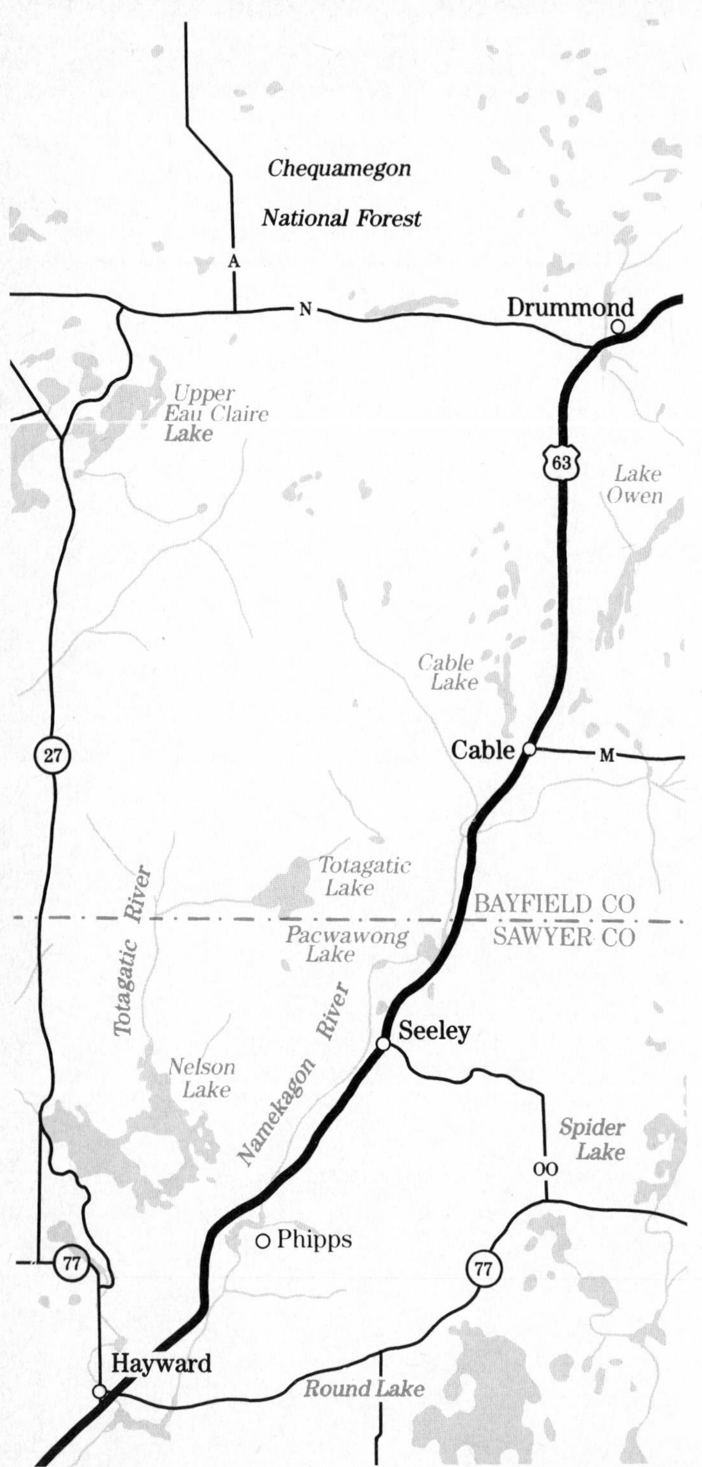

SAWYER COUNTY, Pop. 12,843

Millions of years ago, this region of Wisconsin consisted of towering mountains not unlike the Rockies of today. Slowly, but consistently, the mountains were worn away and covered by vast seas that spread across the continent. Eventually the land emerged again from the sea, covered by sediment and countless numbers of shells and fragments of marine life. More recently, a series of glaciers swept across northern Wisconsin for thousands of years. The last glacial intrusion, called the Wisconsin stage of glaciation, ended 10,000 to 12,000 years ago.

This glacier shaped the land of northern Wisconsin into rounded hills and valleys. At the same time, the Namekagon River drained the melting waters and eroded down through the sedimentary rocks to the bedrock of the old mountain range. As the glaciers continued to melt, large ice-blocks and debris were deposited along its edges, forming the many lakes that stretch across northwest Wisconsin.

With the glaciers gone, the barren but rich soil grew shrubs, and vegetation formed in small ponds to create marshes. Young aspen and willow forests slowly covered the land, and after hundreds of years the more mature pine forests spread across the state.

Sawyer County's white settlements began in the late 1850's. When logging started along the St. Croix in 1838, interest in Namekagon's white pine forests was kindled. Some cutting was done along the river in the 1870's, but wholesale logging began when Hayward built his mill in 1883. However, even with all this activity in the forests, there were only 2,400 permanent residents in Sawyer County when it was formed in 1883. Eight years later, the population had only grown to 3,400. After the mills closed at the turn-of-the-century, the cut-over land was ravaged by fire. Slowly, settlers claimed the stump fields for farming. Finally, during the Depression, the Civilian Conservation Corp (CCC) camps worked to re-forest the area's desolate land.

Sawyer County was named after Philetus Sawyer, one of northern Wisconsin's great lumber barons. After beginning work in a Vermont lumber mill at age 17, Sawyer came to Wisconsin in 1847 and showed his genius at investing his money and reorganizing financially troubled companies. He bought choice tracts of pine forests and later resold them to freewheeling lumber companies at a good profit. Sawyer also organized the Omaha railroad which was built through the county. During much of the latter 1800's, he was one of Wisconsin's dominant Republicans, serving in Congress as a two-term U.S. Senator. He lost an election in 1893 after being accused of misappropriating funds and bribery. He died seven years later.

LAC COURT OREILLES INDIAN RESERVATION

This county was first occupied by an Indian culture called the Mound Builders, an ancient people who built mounds in the shapes of animals or other symbols where they buried their dead or held religious rites. Many mounds were built in the Lac Court Oreilles area, near or in sight of water. Unfortunately, early settlers and builders destroyed many of these effigy mounds before extensive surveying was done in 1914. As a result, in spite of detailed research, little is known about these people except that they occupied this region after the glaciers retreated. They were probably ancestors of the Dakota Indians who lived in this region before the Ojibwe forced their way here. This was an important area of lakes and marshes, with abundant wild rice, game and materials for shelter. In addition, a waterway led from Lac Court Oreilles, via a short portage, to the Namekagon River.

The oldest Indian settlement was at the isthmus between the Big and Little Lac Court Oreilles lakes. As French fur traders pushed into the Wisconsin region during the 1700's, so did the Ojibwe. The Dakota resisted and the Dakota and Ojibwe fought over hunting and ricing lands for years. However, the Ojibwe, with modern guns and experience, slowly forced the Dakota to Minnesota's southwest prairies.

The French named this area Lac Court Oreilles, meaning "short ears." They may have coined the name because Indians here did not hang heavy articles from their ears to elongate their earlobes as Indian nations to the east often did.

The first Ojibwe band to remain at Lac Court Oreilles came here to hunt and decided to stay with the spirit of one of their children who died here. Radisson and Groseilliers, the French explorers who were the first whites to reach the interior of northern Wisconsin, journeyed to Lac Court Oreilles as early as 1660-1661 and spent the winter. Snow was so deep that hunting was impossible and the Frenchmen watched many Indians starve while coming close to death themselves. When Jonathan Carver was crossing from the Mississippi on his way to Lake Superior in 1767 on a British mission to find a northwest passage to the Pacific Ocean, he counted 40 homes with large gardens at the Ojibwe village at Lac Court Oreilles.

As the British expanded their influence here after taking possession from the French in 1760, they established a Northwest Company trading post along the Namekagon River, two miles below today's Hayward. It was opened in 1784 by Michel Cadotte who later managed the La Pointe post on Lake Superior for John J. Astor's American Fur Company. John Corbin operated a post at the Indian village of Reserve during the early 1800's and became one of the area's important men.

By the early 1820's, whites were pressing for rights to all of Wisconsin. By 1837 the Ojibwe had forfeited title to their Wisconsin lands and were required to move to Minnesota reservations. However, many refused to go. During the winters, this "Lost Tribe" received little government help and faced incredible hardships. In 1872, President Millard Fillmore returned their ancestral lands to them in a 69,000-acre reservation after 150 Indians died eating spoiled government meat. Unfortunately, 15,000 acres were eventually taken away and the reservation was denuded of its trees during the 1880's logging era. In 1923 an electricity-generating dam on the Chippewa River raised the water level behind the dam 35 feet, flooding many of the Indians' ricing beds, grave sites and homes in a 26 square-mile reservoir. Although the Ojibwe protested, their lands were condemned and homes moved to a town called New Post. Today, some 800 Indians live on the reservation.

HAYWARD, Pop. 1,698

Anthony Hayward made his move when the Chicago, St. Paul, Minneapolis & Omaha railroad was constructed north from Trego in 1880. Hayward worked for a mill in Ashland County but wanted his own mill. The railroad was willing to sell him vast tracts of white pine and he selected a site for his mill on level land in the Namekagon Valley. Hayward's vision was clear, but he was short of cash and contacted two lumbermen, Robert McCormick and William Laird, an associate of Weyerhaeuser, the lumber magnate.

Hayward snowstorm, 1922.

They approved his plan and loaned Hayward $60,000 to form the North Wisconsin Lumber Company in 1883. By the time the first logs went through the massive new saws, the town of Hayward already had about 1000 residents. Logging camps were scattered throughout the woods and logs were skidded out on roads iced down with water during the winter. By spring thaw, most of the logs had been piled along rivers and streams backed up by dams. When the dams were opened, the light floating pine washed down to the Hayward mills. It was at this time, in the 1880's, that towns like Hayward and Hurley got their bawdy reputations. Hundreds of loggers came into town with their pockets full of a season's pay to find companionship, alcohol and a good time. Most left considerably poorer than when they arrived.

By 1884, Robert McCormick had formed the Sawyer County Bank with the help of Fredrick Weyerhaeuser. Two years later McCormick bought out Hayward's interest in the North Wisconsin Lumber Company and the Hayward mill held the record daily production run for northern Wisconsin. With the mills operating at peak efficiency, the stacked lumber stretched on for blocks. With one lumber business, McCormick became very rich and was called the Earl of Namekagon. He took pride in the development of Hayward and promoted the need for a library, an opera house, parks, paved streets and electricity.

Hayward sold out because he was bored with just making money. He moved to the Penokee-Gogebic Range to try his luck in iron mining. Unfortunately, he was a big loser when the speculating bubble burst during a financial panic. Hayward then moved his family to Washington state to try his hand in banking and mining, but he lost his money in bad investments. In 1898 he continued his search for money and fulfillment by chartering a steamboat and heading for the Alaska gold rush. This time he almost died of scurvy when his boat got caught in ice and was locked in for the winter. There is nothing left in Hayward of the man after whom the town is named. His mansion burned after he left for the Wisconsin iron range and his mill burned to the ground in 1922. Today, Hayward is the center of a resort region that extends 30 miles in all directions.

JOHN F. DIETZ

Starting in 1904 a drama unfolded 30 miles southeast of Hayward that captured the attention of Americans across the United States. It centered around John Dietz, the son of a German immigrant, who became a turn-of-the-century folk hero for the working man. Dietz moved up to the wilds of Sawyer County from Rice Lake in 1899 and squatted on land along the Brunet River owned by the Weyerhaeuser Chippewa Logging Company. While living along the Brunet, he worked as a dam watchman regulating the flow of water and logs. Five years later, Dietz moved a few miles east to the Thornapple River and purchased 160 acres. At the same time he submitted a bill for $1,700 to the Chippewa Logging Company for his duties at the dam site. The bill was not honored and Dietz became involved in a fight to collect the money.

John Dietz in detention, 1911.

As it turned out, Dietz' new land on the Thornapple River had a dam run by Weyerhaeuser's company. In the spring of 1904, white pine was almost logged out along the tributaries that flowed into the Chippewa River, and rumor had it that this might be the last drive down the Thornapple. Sitting above the Cameron Dam were millions of feet of pine ready to be floated down the Thornapple. However when the crews came to the Cameron Dam to start the drive, they found Dietz with a no trespassing sign and a rifle. He demanded the pay owed him plus a small royalty for all logs that passed his dam. The logging company got an injunction against Dietz at Hayward with no problem since almost everyone there worked for the lumber industry. In the meantime, Dietz released the water at the dam, leaving the valuable pine high and dry for another season.

The story is complex and spans many years but for the next few years Dietz, his wife Hattie and their six children held off sheriff's deputies, federal marshals and various peacemaking groups from the lumber interests. Dietz became obsessed with his rights as a landowner and at getting what he felt was owed him. The national media picked up the story and played it as the small man vs. the lumber conglomerates. The timing was right since many Wisconsin residents were unhappy with how the powerful lumber trusts had stripped the land. Dietz became a working man's folk hero and his picture and stories of his family holding the dam made good reading. The law and order interests would not relent, but they didn't enjoy their laughing-stock status either and were determined to oust Dietz. He continually refused to answer court orders and successfully avoided a number of attempts to arrest him. Armed men filled the woods and many rifle shots were exchanged, but the dam remained open and Weyerhaeuser's pine rested in the marshes.

In the fall of 1907, the Weyerhaeuser interests gave in and offered Dietz his $1700 if he would let the logs above his dam be salvaged. Three years later, at the nearby village of Winter, Dietz shot a man in a fight. Many wanted the "crazy revolutionary" arrested and brought to trial once and for all. Shortly after, deputies ambushed three of Dietz's children near the Dietz farm. Two of the children were shot and a third escaped into the woods. A week later 33 Sawyer County deputies surrounded the Dietz farm and opened fire on the family. When the shooting stopped, Dietz was slightly wounded and one deputy was dead. Fearing for his family, Dietz finally laid down his rifle.

Once again he made headlines and defense money was organized. Out on bail he traveled to the region's major cities speaking against the establishment. He finally went to trial in 1911 for the murder of deputy Oscar Harp and, though it was never clearly established who pulled the trigger or if Harp was even shot by his own men, Dietz was convicted of murder and sentenced to life in prison. Ten years later a sympathetic Wisconsin Governor, John Blaine, pardoned Dietz. Aging rapidly, he joined his wife in Milwaukee but was still consumed with the whole affair, even claiming that Harp wasn't dead and rocks were in his coffin. Dietz died suddenly in 1924 and was buried at the Meadow Creek Cemetery in Rice Lake.

PHIPPS, SEELEY, LEONARD'S SPUR

Phipps, like other stations along the Omaha Line, prospered when the railroad was built through here in 1880. Older than Hayward, Phipps was the destination of loggers who hauled supplies and timber down the crude roads cut through the forest. Named after W.H. Phipps, an administrator on the Omaha railroad, it had two hotels and a few shops catering to the lumberjacks.

Seeley, another railroad village, is named after T.B. Seeley, a railroad employee. The main logging camp of a lumber contractor named Colbrath was located near Seeley. However, long before loggers came here, Ojibwe Indians camped along the shallow broadening of the Namekagon River at a place some called Puch-wa-a-wang and other's knew as Odabossa's village. It was a well-known camp, visited by many explorers and traders. Henry Schoolcraft, who discovered the source of the Mississippi, wrote about it when he passed here in 1831. Located on a small rise of land, it overlooked some of the area's most productive ricing beds, and had numerous gardens of potatoes, corn, and squash.

Like most northern timber areas, this land was controlled by large companies such as the North Wisconsin Lumber Company in the 1880's. The loggers built a dam which created Pacwawong Lake and drowned the rice beds. Nearby burial grounds were plowed under for farm land.

John Dietz farmstead, 1907

SHSW

Lumber camp vicinity of Cable, 1906

LEONARD'S SPUR

A small hamlet was established around the railroad in 1881 on the Bayfield-Sawyer County. Some logging camps were located nearby and Leonard's Spur became a small resupply depot and post office. It also had a small mill and a logging spur that ran up Big Brook. The beautiful Namekagon River flows west of the highway and the old railroad bed parallels the road on the east.

BAYFIELD COUNTY, Pop. 13,822

In 1845 both Bayfield and Ashland counties were part of a larger county, La Pointe, which had its county seat at the trading village of La Pointe on Madeline Island. In 1858, county residents voted to move the county government over to the growing village of Bayfield. La Pointe residents protested and created their own county, joining forces with the city of Ashland to exclude the Bayfield mainland. La Pointe and Ashland Counties separated in 1860, but it wasn't until 1866 that the name Bayfield was applied to the county. It is named after Lieut. Henry R. Bayfield of the British Navy who did the first extensive surveying of Lake Superior from 1823 to 1825. Bayfield County was extensively logged during the late 1800's, with most of the pine floated to Lake Superior via south shore streams. Near Cable, in the southern part of the county, loggers used the Namekagon River to float logs down to mills on the St. Croix. Today, tourism is one of the county's major industries.

CABLE, Pop. 227

The Omaha line, extended here in 1881, was the catalyst that kept the small town of Cable going in its first two years.

Supplies were brought here to prepare for continuing the line to Ashland. Cable was named after the engineer that brought in the first train. Cable had quite a reputation as a rowdy lumber and railroad town during those first few years. Makeshift shanties, small stores, and many saloons were built, but once the tracks to Ashland were completed Cable almost died. With slash and logging debris surrounding the town, it was inevitable that a fire would sweep into town, destroying all the boom town's old saloons, hotels and houses. The rebuilt village of Cable is based on an economy supported by tourists, skiers and fishermen who seek trout in the winding Namekagon River. The area's downhill ski industry grew around the nearby Telemark ski area.

From Trego to Cable, U.S. 63 is built on broad terraces of the Namekagon River which were cut by the glacial river's fluctuating levels. Naturally, the Namekagon was the early highway which allowed loggers to float their pine to the big mill at Hayward. Two miles north of Cable the highway crosses part of the 838,000 acre Chequamegon National Forest which stretches from the Bayfield Peninsula down into north central Wisconsin.

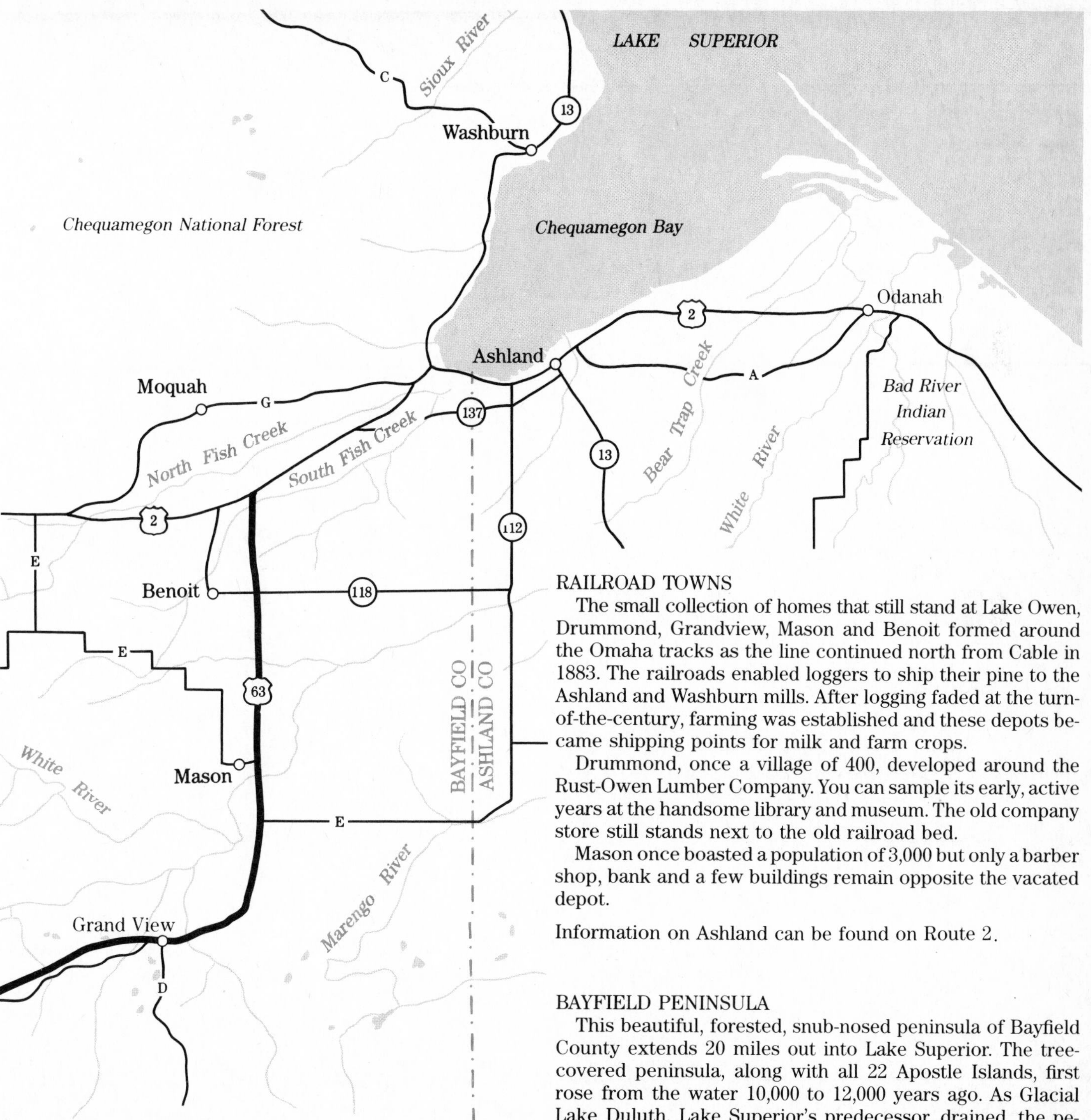

RAILROAD TOWNS

The small collection of homes that still stand at Lake Owen, Drummond, Grandview, Mason and Benoit formed around the Omaha tracks as the line continued north from Cable in 1883. The railroads enabled loggers to ship their pine to the Ashland and Washburn mills. After logging faded at the turn-of-the-century, farming was established and these depots became shipping points for milk and farm crops.

Drummond, once a village of 400, developed around the Rust-Owen Lumber Company. You can sample its early, active years at the handsome library and museum. The old company store still stands next to the old railroad bed.

Mason once boasted a population of 3,000 but only a barber shop, bank and a few buildings remain opposite the vacated depot.

Information on Ashland can be found on Route 2.

BAYFIELD PENINSULA

This beautiful, forested, snub-nosed peninsula of Bayfield County extends 20 miles out into Lake Superior. The tree-covered peninsula, along with all 22 Apostle Islands, first rose from the water 10,000 to 12,000 years ago. As Glacial Lake Duluth, Lake Superior's predecessor, drained, the peninsula's rolling hills rose 600 to 825 feet above it.

Many of the hills resulted when glacial deposits piled upon the red sandstone underlying this area. Pine eventually covered the peninsula and attracted lumbermen who logged here extensively during the late 1800's. Today a dense forest of pine, spruce, and hardwoods cover the peninsula and is part of the 83,000-acre Chequamegon National Forest.

In the early 1900's there was considerable pressure to preserve the Apostle Islands and the peninsula. Isle Royale, off of Superior's North shore, was made a national park, but the islands were overlooked. It wasn't until 1970 that 11 miles of shoreline and 18 of the 22 Apostle Islands became part of the National Lakeshore Park system. The park's goal is to preserve the beautiful beaches, rock formations, caverns and water-eroded cliffs along the shore and islands for everyone to see and use. A hiking and ski trail along the shoreline from Red Cliff to Sand Bay is planned for the future. Camping is also available. The Park Service in the old Bayfield Courthouse has more information.

Highway 13, which primarily follows the edge of the peninsula, is a lightly traveled, out-of-the-way route with several old fishing towns to explore. Lake Superior's many moods can be easily experienced here.

BARKSDALE

The rusting, padlocked gate west of this small collection of lakeside homes was once the entrance to the Dupont Barksdale explosives plant. The plant, named after its manager, Hamilton Barksdale, was built in 1905 when dynamite was in demand at the iron and copper mines in northeast Wisconsin and on Michigan's Upper Peninsula. The World Wars continued the need and the Barksdale plant became the world's largest dynamite producer. The plant closed in 1971 after it became unprofitable.

WASHBURN, Pop 2,080

This city, situated on a rise of land overlooking Chequamegon Bay, was named after Cadwallader Washburn, Governor of Wisconsin from 1872-74. Washburn was one of the first Wisconsin officials to be sent to Washington as a Republican after the Republican Party was founded in Wisconsin in 1854. He also founded the famous Washburn-Crosby

Bayfield H.S.

Washburn, ca. 1880

SHSW

Ole Emerson lumber camp bunkhouse, Bayfield Co., ca. 1900.

Flour Mill in Minneapolis.

The city of Washburn began long after Bayfield and Ashland were thriving villages. It got its needed push when the Chicago, St. Paul, Minneapolis & Omaha railroad arrived here in 1883. A local paper summed up Washburn, "There are no romances of Indian lore in the history of (Washburn), no poetical inspirations. When Washburn was platted, it was strictly for business purposes." The town's banner year was 1891 when three large newly-built saw mills provided most of the city's jobs and income. The mills reportedly cut 100 million feet of lumber yearly until the peninsula's pine was depleted around 1900. On a calm day sawdust from the Washburn, Ashland and Bayfield mills covered Chequamegon Bay. The railroad also built a large elevator on the bay, and shipped large quantities of oats, corn, wheat, rye and flax from the Washburn docks. Coal was arriving at the docks as produce was departing, and the resulting congestion often had shipping at a standstill!

Electric lights came to Washburn when an electric generating plant was built in 1891. A promotional piece about the town said, "Incandescent lights are used quite numerously by private parties, which gives the city a decidedly metropolitan air."

Bayfield County was known as La Pointe County until 1866. Bayfield was the county seat until 1892 when the booming town of Washburn won the title. Shortly before 1900 the lumber industry began logging itself out of existence. The grain and other products that once used Washburn's long docks found overland shipment by trains and trucks more efficient. The dream of having farmers work large tracts of cut-over land never materialized because of the marginal topsoil and short growing season. Contrary to early newspaper accounts that Washburn was more interested in business than anything else, the city now looks to tourism as its most important industry.

The regional office of the Chequamegon National Forest is located in Washburn. This forest was set aside as the second growth covered traces of the lumbering era. It has three sections, with much of the central Bayfield Ridge in the northern section. Information on camping, trails and skiing is available from the district ranger's office in Washburn.

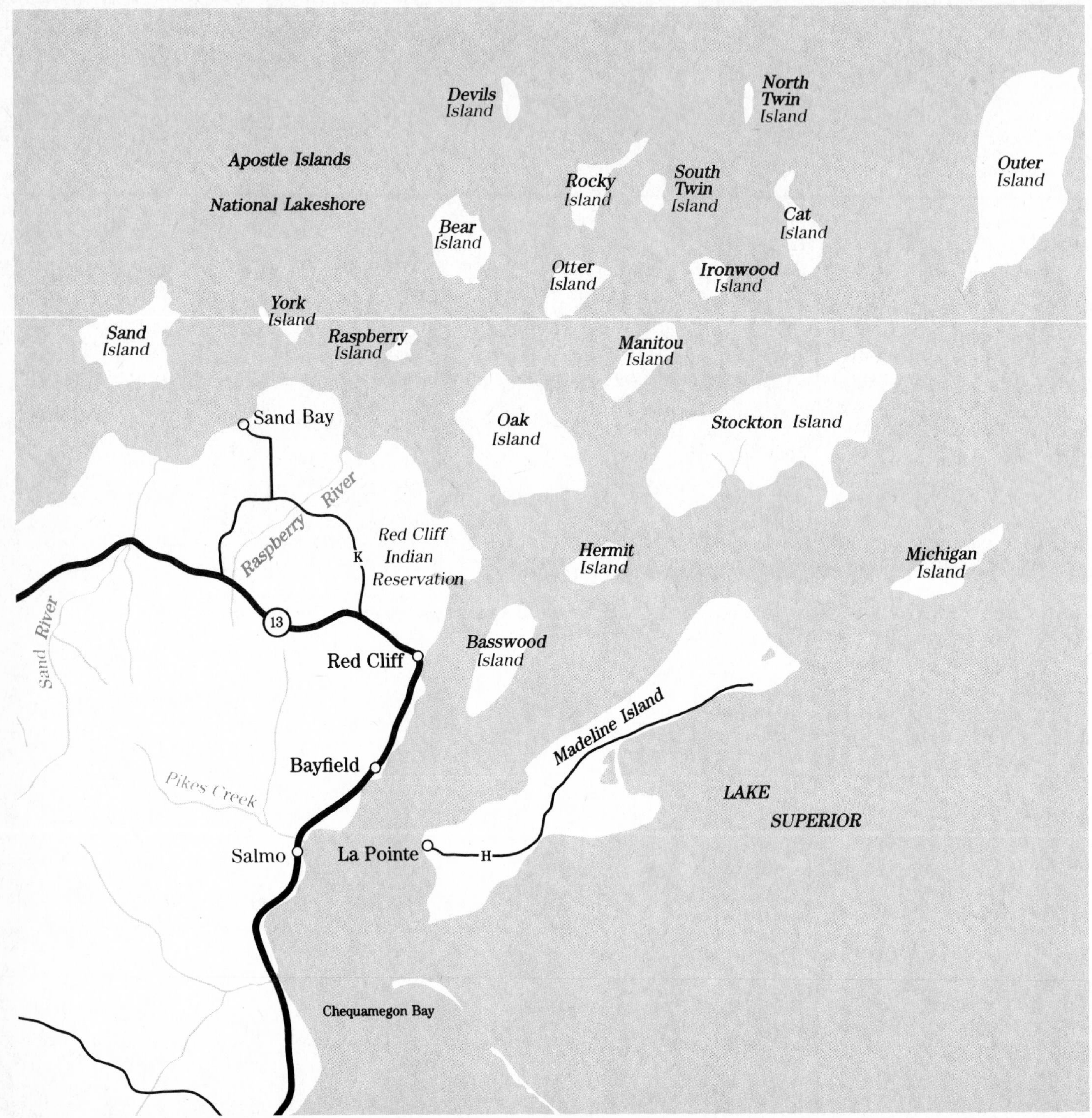

Devils Island
North Twin Island
Apostle Islands
National Lakeshore
Rocky Island
South Twin Island
Outer Island
Cat Island
Bear Island
Otter Island
Ironwood Island
Sand Island
York Island
Raspberry Island
Manitou Island
Sand Bay
Oak Island
Stockton Island
Raspberry River
Red Cliff Indian Reservation
K
Hermit Island
Michigan Island
Sand River
13
Basswood Island
Red Cliff
Madeline Island
Bayfield
Pikes Creek
LAKE SUPERIOR
Salmo
La Pointe
H
Chequamegon Bay

Bayfield H.S.

Booth docks at Bayfield, ca. 1900

BAYFIELD, Pop. 778

When the British Navy's Lt. Henry Bayfield began charting Lake Superior's depths in 1823 it was soon evident that a deep-water harbor could be developed here, protected by the Apostle Islands. However, the land belonged to the Ojibwe until 1854 when they gave it up in a treaty signed across at La Pointe on Madeline Island. That treaty opened the road to settlement for Henry Rice, a St. Paul promoter and personal friend of Lt. Bayfield, who formed the Bayfield Land Company in 1856. Bayfield was platted the following year. A railroad charter was obtained to connect the Chequamegon Bay with St. Paul, but the main effort was to build a pier since travel overland was then confined to rugged trails. As Rice promoted his new town, people arrived via the St. Paul to Bayfield trail or by the schooner Algonquin. In one short year the hillside town grew to almost 100 homes and more than 100 people. Indians carried mail from Superior to Bayfield, an 85-mile trip which averaged five days.

Before long, in 1858, Bayfield flexed its political power and won an election to move the county seat from La Pointe to Bayfield on the mainland. A complicated battle began between the "islanders," and the "mainlanders," resulting in a splitting of the county in 1860. The islanders joined with Ashland to become Ashland County which still retains jurisdiction over most of the Apostle Islands. Bayfield became the county seat of La Pointe County, which was renamed in 1866 in honor of Lt. Bayfield. In part of a seemingly perpetual battle for county seats across Wisconsin, Bayfield lost its title when Washburn was voted county seat in 1892. Bayfield's efforts to build a new brownstone courthouse were in vain. It was stripped and vacated and is now used by the National Park Service and the Bayfield Historical Association which runs a museum.

By 1880 lumber companies began surveying the forests near Bayfield. When the Chicago, St. Paul, Minneapolis & Omaha Railroad reached Bayfield in 1883 it created another important outlet for the saw mills that had begun to operate here. The large Pike and Knight mills employed 125 workers who ranged over the peninsula and out to the islands for their logs. Though the railroad was important, most of the Bayfield lumber was loaded on boats bound for Manitoba and Chicago. There was talk that Bayfield would one day be more important than Chicago.

Besides lumber, Bayfield had another resource. A sedimentary rock found on the mainland and islands called brownstone, was a high strength building stone that was easily quarried. R.D. Pike began developing quarries in 1868 and shipped large amounts of these brown blocks to build houses, courthouses and churches throughout the Great Lakes region, including the Bayfield Courthouse. In the next two decades these quarries helped build many of the fashionable "brownstone houses" of New York City and Chicago.

In addition to logging and quarrying, the whitefish, lake trout and herring of Superior were also attracting people. In 1870 a French-Canadian named Frank Boutin started a fishery in Bayfield which eventually employed 150 men and shipped 12,000 barrels of fish a season. The Booth fishery, started here in 1880, at one time employing 500 men. The Indians' simple hooks and dip nets were replaced by mackinaw boats and long nets. Eventually gasoline engines replaced sails, powerful winches reeled in thousands of feet of gill-nets, and the harvest of Lake Superior Whitefish, chubs and herring increased annually until it peaked with 25 million pounds in 1941. Later, unrestricted fishing, coupled with the destructive sea-lamprey and pollution from the saw mills, all but destroyed the lake trout.

In recent years, Lake Superior's fish population has experienced a strong comeback, thanks to strict fishing laws and a successful war against the lamprey. Nevertheless, the fishing industry today is a fragment of what it once was, survived by a small fleet in Bayfield still run by the Boutin and Booth Companies.

Bayfield peaked as a commercial city and tourist center between the 1880's and 1910. Money flowing into town during that time built many of the Queen Anne style homes which give Bayfield its charm today. The large and grandiose Island View Hotel was built overlooking the harbor in 1883 to handle the many tourists arriving by train. The three-story Island View had 80 sleeping rooms, reception rooms, a large dining room, hot and cold water, a barbershop and more. A promotional brochure touted, "An atmosphere that makes guests feel they are back in the eastern cities." Excursion steamers loaded with vacationers lined the pier.

Bayfield began to fade with Ashland's growth as a shipping, logging and rail center and the birth of Washburn and its lumber mills. The Island View Hotel burned in 1913 and 11 years later the last of Bayfield's lumber mills closed.

Tourism is now the town's key industry. Situated at the base of the beautiful chain of Apostle Islands, Bayfield has a distinct advantage in vying with other Lake Superior communities for tourist dollars. During its short season, boaters come from all over the Midwest to cruise the crystal clear waters around the islands, explore the wilds of Superior via boat, or ferry over to historic Madeline Island.

A 50-block area was included in the U.S. Park Service's Register of Historic Districts in 1981, on Bayfield's 125th anniversary. An excellent booklet cataloging the unique collection of 19th century homes is available from the University of Wisconsin's Sea Grant Institute. During the fall, you can pick apples at the picturesque apple orchards above Bayfield with Lake Superior's deep blue haze as a back-drop.

SHSW

Indian annuity payments at La Pointe, 1852.

LA POINTE, MADELINE ISLAND

Pushed west to the Great Lakes by conflicts with the Iroquois, the Ojibwe, stopped at the relatively secure Chequamegon Bay region and soon made their central home on the island they called Moniqwunakauning, meaning, "home of the golden-breasted woodpecker."

They are thought to have moved to the island starting in the 1500's or 1600's. Stories tell of cannibalism during the lean winter months when 15,000 or more Ojibwe crowded onto the 14-mile-long island. This cannibalism, practiced by medicine men who selected young children for the ritual, ended when Ojibwe villagers protested and executed their medicine men. Fear of the dead children's spirits caused the superstitious Ojibwe to leave the island and it was many years before they returned.

The Jesuit priests Allouez and Marquette preached to the Indians between 1665 and 1669 at the head of Chequamegon Bay where Ashland is now located. Father Allouez named this bay region La Pointe de Chequamegon. Almost 30 years later, in 1693, Pierre Le Sueur established Madeline Island's first trading post because he felt the island was more secure from the raids by Dakota Indians.

During the warm summer months, robust voyageurs brought in furs they had collected from Indians in Minnesota and Wisconsin via the St. Louis, Bois Brule and Bad rivers. They exchanged the furs for knives, clothing, blankets and other items they could trade with the Indians. When fur prices dropped in Europe in 1689, the post was closed. The French reoccupied the island around 1720 and constructed a new post closer to the present town of La Pointe. It was then that the name La Pointe begin to signify this particular settlement. In 1727, La Ronde took charge here, possibly building a small mill and doing limited farming. The post was again vacated during the French and Indian War, but Alexander Henry started trading here as part of the Northwest Company a few years after the English took control of the area in 1760. The English then ran the fur business from here until they lost the territory in the War of 1812. In 1816 the existing post became part of the American Fur Company under Michael Cadotte's management. The island is named after Cadotte's Ojibwe wife whom he called Madeline.

The American Fur Company post supplemented its fur trading by commercially fishing Superior. Using gill nets, they were quite successful, shipping one million pounds of whitefish, herring and trout to eastern markets in peak years. The fish market dried up in 1841 and the American Fur Company went under in 1842.

The Ojibwe Indians signed a treaty at the American Fur Company's old headquarters in 1854, giving up all lands adjoining Lake Superior. The Catholic Ojibwe were moved to the Bad River Reservation and the Protestant Indians were assigned to the Red Cliff Reservation. Although it is difficult to follow the region's history through the many different nations and peoples who have occupied the island, Chequamegon Bay takes on new meaning when you sense its importance as a travel and trade center during those early years.

Today Madeline Island is the only developed island of the Apostles, with a year-round population of about 100. The old trading post at La Pointe is now a Wisconsin Historical Society museum. Near the marina is the old La Pointe cemetery where Michael Cadotte is buried, as well as Chief Buffalo, who was present at the 1854 treaty signing. During the summer, ferry service is available for those interested in driving the 14 mile-long island or camping at Big Bay State Park. During the winter, propeller-driven ice sleds carry children to the mainland for school until the ice is safe for cars.

SHSW

La Pointe, Madeline Island, 1898. Photo/S.W. Bailey

SHSW

Indian graveyard at Catholic cemetery in La Pointe, 1910.

APOSTLE ISLANDS

Before the glaciers ground out the deep basin of Lake Superior, the Apostle Islands were little more than hills separated by streams. The glaciers deepened the valleys and scraped the tops off the hills. When the lake filled, more than 22 hills remained above the water's surface. Some shoal areas are thought to be islands but have eroded and now lie below the water's surface.

Ojibwe legend attributes the Apostle Islands to Winneboujou, an Indian god who hunted deer near his homeland on the Brule River. He followed fresh tracks to the Bayfield region, shot all his arrows at the elusive prey, then watched as the deer swam away into Lake Superior. Angrily, Winneboujou threw rocks at the deer, creating the Apostle Islands.

Most of the islands have steep shores with sandstone ledges eroded into caves and other interesting shapes. The pine-covered islands attracted loggers who cleared them of most trees during the late 1800's. Today the land is again overgrown with aspen, birch, pine and an undergrowth of ferns and forest plants. Fox, coyote, mink, beaver and white-tailed deer inhabit the islands along with bald eagles, ducks, loon, gulls and terns.

The unidentified person who named the Apostle islands believed there were only 12 islands. They were originally named the Federation Islands by Henry Schoolcraft, the man who discovered the source of the Mississippi, when he passed them during the Cass expedition in 1820. He named the individual islands after the states and territories.

When logging reached here, most of the islands were clear-cut and their logs rafted back down the channels to the Bayfield, Washburn and Ashland mills. As shipping increased, lighthouses were needed to guide boats during the night or rough weather. The first lighthouse was built on Michigan Island in 1857 and others followed on other islands. The Devils Island lighthouse had particularly rough duty since it took the brunt of lake storms. When men arrived at the lighthouse in spring, they often had to chop their way into the frozen structure and it took the whole summer before the thick walls warmed. Brownstone quarrying was carried out on Stockton, Basswood and Hermit Islands starting in the late 1880's, but the quarries were closed after the turn-of-the-century when steel and other construction materials became popular for larger buildings. Today the islands are primarily a recreational source, with many part of the Apostle Island National Lakeshore.

LONG ISLAND

This narrow spit of sand was connected to Chequamegon Point as recently as the early 1800's. Early explorers wrote of portaging across this land to the head of the bay where Ashland is today. Long Island, only a quarter mile wide at its widest point, is slightly over six miles long and 10 feet at its highest elevation. It supports pine and grasses as well as an unmanned Coast Guard lighthouse and is a favorite lunchstop for boaters.

HERMIT ISLAND

This small island with a four-mile shoreline was named Minnesota Island until it was renamed after a recluse who lived here about 1850. When the hermit was found dead in his cabin many Bayfield residents boated out to look for his buried treasure, but only a few coins were found. Rumors have also circulated about British bullion supposedly buried here. Sandstone was quarried on the island's southeast side in the late 1800's.

BASSWOOD ISLAND

This small island, once covered with basswood, was the first Apostle Island to be quarried for sandstone. The Superior Sandstone Company came here in 1868 and Basswood stone was used to build the Milwaukee Court House. The quarry, on the island's south side, was worked until 1900.

STOCKTON ISLAND

Second in size only to Madeline Island, this picturesque island of sandy beaches, trails, marshlands and forest is a favorite camping and anchoring spot. The early French called the island Presque Isle, now the name of the point which juts from the island's southeast side. That point was connected to Stockton Island after hundreds of years of wave action created a sandbar between the two. A National Park Ranger Station on Presque Isle Bay provides information on campsites and trails. A beautiful, crescent-shaped, sand beach, blueberries and a 30-acre marsh lie on the opposite end of the point from the ranger station. Trails varying from one-half to two miles in length connect the two. From Presque Isle Bay you can take a four-mile trail to the old quarry on the southwest side of the island. The Park Service and a private charter boat takes campers out to the island.

GULL ISLAND

Connected by only a shallow rocky shoal to Michigan Island, is Gull Island. This piece of rock is the smallest of the Apostle Islands and is a nesting spot for gulls. Over half of the nesting gulls in the island chain nest here and the island is off limits to humans. Eagle Island is another small island that attracts a high number of nesting gulls.

Bayfield H.S.

Excursion to the Apostle Islands, date unknown.

RED CLIFF INDIAN RESERVATION

The Ojibwe Indians, also known as Chippewa, were part of a large Indian migration which arrived in the Lake Superior region during the 1500's. The main impetus for the move west was a continuing conflict with the Iroquois of the East. But Ojibwe found the Dakota already occupying this region and conflict existed between the two nations for the next few hundred years.

As French voyageurs journeyed into this fur rich territory the Ojibwe were, for the most part, friendly and willing to trade. The Dakota, who had little contact with the white man, his weapons or way of fighting, had trouble resisting the onward push of the Ojibwe who were better armed as a result of close contact with the French. For many years the Ojibwe were based in the Chequamegon Bay and Madeline Island in particular. As the Ojibwe pushed into northwestern Wisconsin and Minnesota, the Dakota gave up much of their hunting land. In 1750, a three-day battle at Minnesota's Mille Lacs Lake began the Ojibwe's reign over northern Wisconsin, Minnesota and Canada.

By the 1850's there was pressure to open northern Wisconsin for logging and settlement. The U.S. Government called a treaty session in 1854 at La Pointe on Madeline Island. Here the Lake Superior Ojibwe ceded their vast hunting grounds in exchange for reservations at Red Cliff, Bad River and Fond du Lac in Minnesota. The Red Cliff Reservation, originally 14,000 acres, today totals about 7,000 acres and has 600 Ojibwe residents. The Red Cliff Band is now developing their Lake Superior land to attract tourists. They run a campsite, marina and Indian center which is open for viewing Ojibwe art and crafts.

SAND ISLAND

Called Massachusetts Island by Henry Schoolcraft and Wababiko-miniss by the Indians, Sand Island finally took its name from the sandy beaches and shoals that surround it. The westernmost of the Apostle Islands, it was the home of a popular resort colony begun during the late 1800's. Francis Shaw, the island's first settler, was a Civil War veteran who received this land as a bonus because the U.S. Government didn't have money to make cash payments to all its veterans. A school was run for island residents for a short time around 1910.

Sand Bay, located across the shallow channel on the mainland, has an information center for the Apostle Island National Lakeshore as well as a picnic area and campsites. It also has a beautiful beach where you can see the hazy north shore of Minnesota or a sailboat anchored for the night.

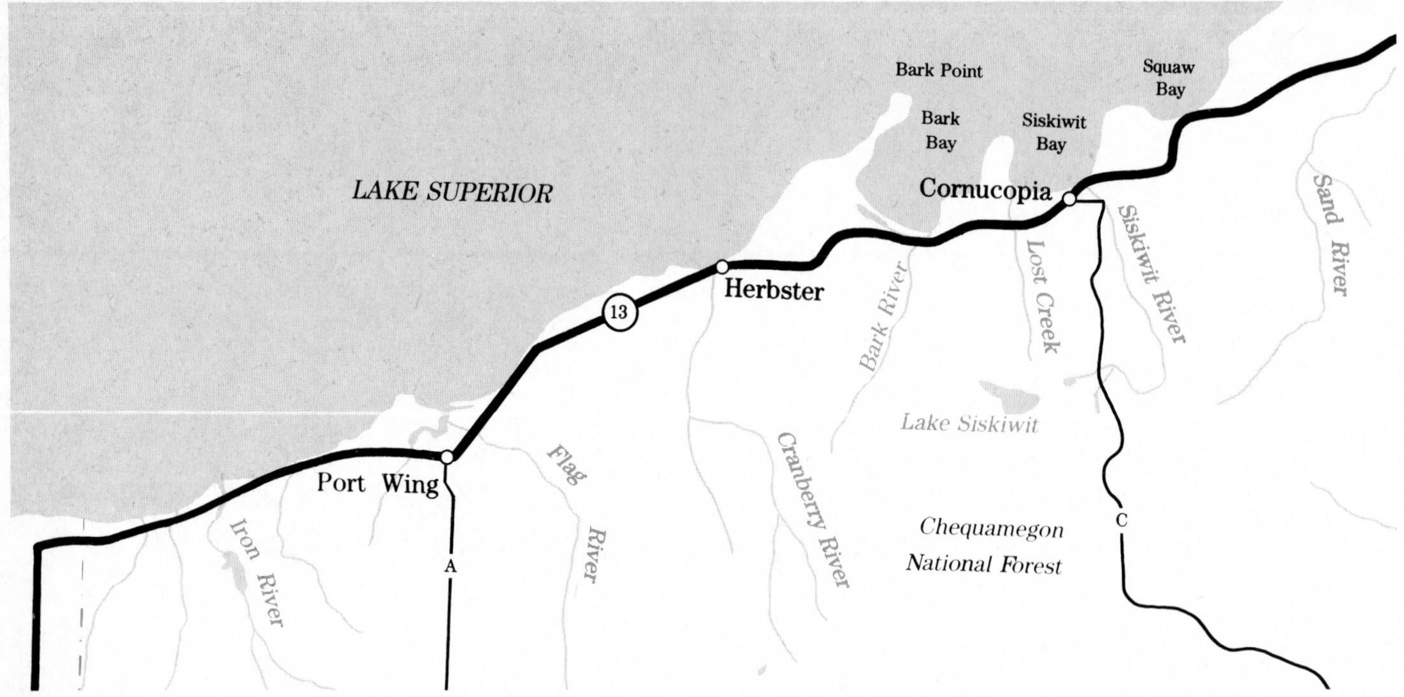

CORNUCOPIA

This old fishing village, located on Siskiwit Bay where the small Siskiwit River comes out of the hills, is Wisconsin's northernmost community. Minneapolis lawyer T.J. Stevenson, speculating that a railroad line would reach here, platted the village and named it after the wide variety of vegetables grown by local farmers. Though the railroad was never built, lumbering provided work for the Polish and Czechoslovakian settlers. They soon built the Russian Orthodox Church with its octagonal tower which is still located at the end of Erie Avenue. When lumbering declined about 1900, many settlers turned to Lake Superior for their income. At one time Cornucopia had a large fleet of fishing boats seining for trout, whitefish and herring. The harbor was active with boats moving in and out and reels of nets being constantly mended. About one-half mile east of town on County Rd. C is the picturesque Siskiwit Falls, a series of rock shelves over which the river flows to Superior.

The Ojibwe called Cornucopia's bay Siskawekaning, meaning, "where the fish can be caught."

HERBSTER

This hamlet along the Cranberry River was named after William Herbster, a camp cook for the Cranberry Lumber Company which had a camp here. Herbster was probably honored because he was one of the few who could read the logger's letters to them. Located south of the highway is the old log gymnasium still used by the school. Townspeople claim it is the only log structure used in the Wisconsin school system.

PORT WING

During the late 1800's Finnish immigrants began moving from the copper mines on the Upper Peninsula of Michigan down along Lake Superior's south shore. Some worked the iron mines of the Gogebic Range, others tried farming the country's marginal soil, and still others tried fishing in summer and working in the forests in winter.

Axel Johannson boated along the shore from Duluth to the Flag River in 1891 and started what would become known as Port Wing. A short time later a small community grew up around a saw mill and post office. Education was a major concern. Instead of having several one-room classes scattered around the area, Port Wing built the first consolidated school system in Wisconsin in 1903. Residents also developed one of the region's first public school buses using a horse and wagon to pick up the children.

The school was recently torn down and only the school bell remains. At the point where the Flat River flows into the small harbor you can see the rotting pilings where steamers

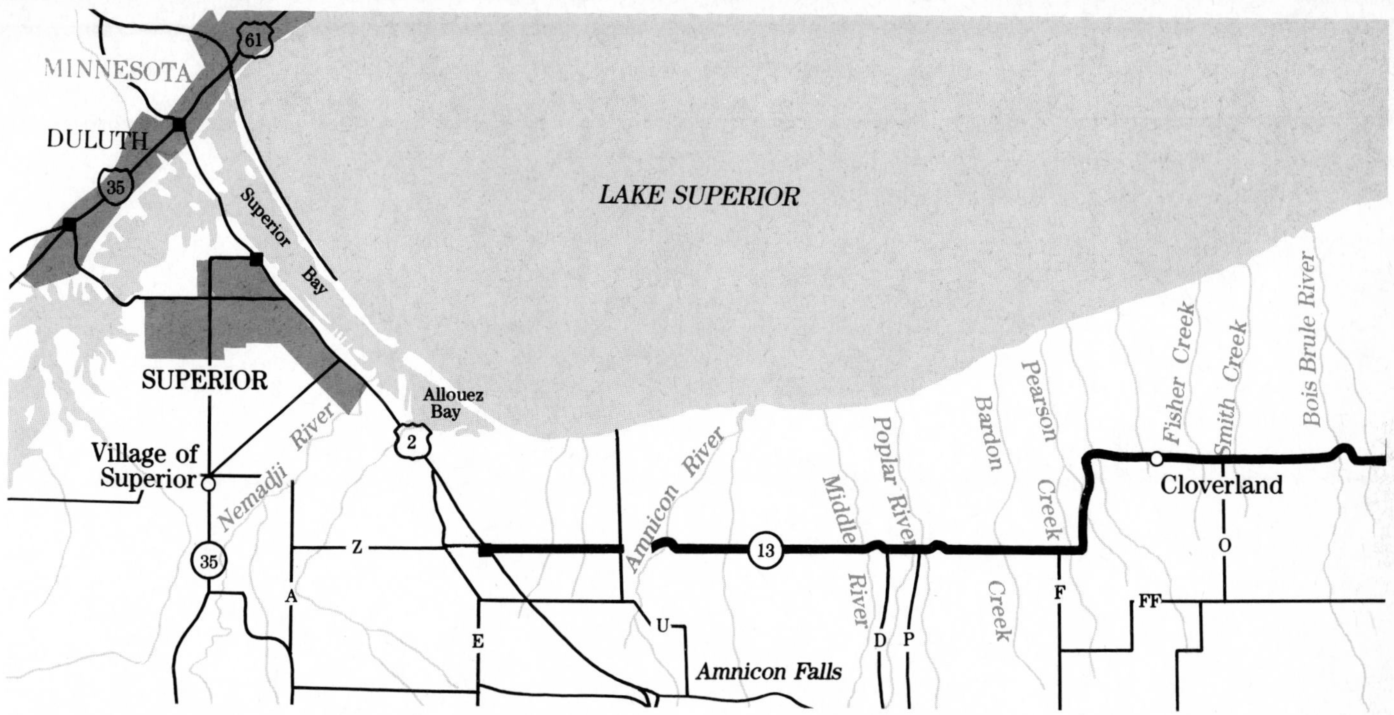

and barges once took on wood from the mill and sandstone from a nearby quarry. This harbor provides one of the few protected south shore anchorages from Superior to the Apostle Islands.

BOIS BRULE RIVER

The Bois Brule was an important waterway used by the early French, British and American traders on their way to the short portage to the St. Croix River.

The hamlet of Clevedon was once located at the mouth of the Brule, approximately five miles north. This was originally the site of an Indian village, but around 1873 an Englishman named Samuel Budgett tried to start a town here by rewarding his faithful employees with land.

The town was named after his Clevedon Estate in England. With some effort, residents improved the harbor in the marshy area of the river, attempted fishing, and built a small stave and lath mill. Some residents even planted fruit trees and did small-scale farming, but the town couldn't sustain itself and within a few years many had left.

Today there is little evidence of Clevedon. In any case, the drive to the mouth of the Brule is worth the effort. The road ends at a small park on a rise overlooking Lake Superior and the marsh adjoining the Bois Brule. You can imagine traders arriving from the Sault on their journey into the interior of the St. Croix River Valley. It is interesting to envision that through a short portage one can canoe from here down to the Gulf of Mexico.

Meadowlands and stands of second and third growth poplar lie between valleys carved by short streams. The old Cloverland township school sits next to the small Rest Haven Cemetery.

DAVIDSON MILL

Pine was logged here during the 1890's with a number of early homesteaders helping their meager farm income by working as loggers for 50 cents a day. Many logs were floated down the Iron, Poplar and Amnicon rivers to be rafted over to Superior for milling. After much of the land was cleared, many farmers tried raising wheat, oats and barley. A Finn named Jaako Tapola, later known as Jacob Davidson, saw profit in grinding local crops into flour. Starting in 1900 Davidson spent two years building an eight-wing Finnish-style windmill (Holland style windmills have four wings), and cutting mill-stones from rocks found along the Amnicon River. The mill, which operated until 1918, ground 40 barrels of flour per day when in full swing.

The 164-acre Amnicon State Park is located two miles south of the mill on county U. Camping is available and trails follow the cascading Amnicon River.

Route 2 crosses 95 miles from Superior, Wisconsin to Hurley. East of Superior, one can catch glimpses of the dark outline of Lake Superior's north shore.
U.S. 2 also crosses the Brule River, an important route for early explorers crossing into the interior of Wisconsin and Minnesota.

ROUTE 2, SUPERIOR TO HURLEY

The remains of an early Lake Superior lighthouse built on Wisconsin Point at Superior Bay, 1897.

DOUGLAS COUNTY, Pop. 44,421

The northern part of Douglas County slopes towards Lake Superior and is called the Superior Lowland. It was once covered by a large glacial lake, Glacial Lake Duluth, which preceded Lake Superior and was hundreds of feet deeper. The Douglas County Copper Ridge rims the lowlands from five to twenty miles south of Lake Superior and was the glacial lake's southern shoreline. The streams flowing down this ridge into Lake Superior are not very long but many have cut 40 to 100 foot deep gorges through the forest floor. The St. Louis, Nemadji, Bois Brule and Black rivers are the county's main rivers. A 160 foot waterfall, the highest in the state, is located on the Black River at Pattison State Park, 10 miles south of Superior on State 35.

The Bois Brule River is especially important to the state's history, having provided one of the major river links to the interior of Wisconsin and Minnesota through a two-mile portage to the St. Croix River.

Before the white man began logging, most of Douglas County was covered with pine forests which provided the Dakota and Ojibwe Indians with mink and otter fur and bear and deer skins. This region was occupied by the Dakota until the late 1600's when the Ojibwe nation was pushed from the Lake Huron region by warring Iroquois. Because of frequent contact with the French, the Ojibwe acquired guns and became more sophisticated than the Dakota in their fighting techniques. The Ojibwe pushed the Dakota from their Wisconsin hunting grounds into northern Minnesota and then out of northern Minnesota in the mid-1700's.

Daniel Greysolon Duluth became the first white explorer to venture inland from Lake Superior in 1680. With four other men, Duluth traveled the Bois Brule River, portaged to the St. Croix River, and eventually made it to the Mississippi. The French developed an extensive fur trading business, bartering European goods for the Indians' furs.

The French lost this region to the English in 1763, but it wasn't until three years after the War of 1812 that the United States government stopped the smuggling of British goods through the new U.S. land. When this region became a Wisconsin Territory in 1818, most of northern Wisconsin was part of a large county called Michilimackinac and only a few traders lived there. For two years starting in 1846, the American Fur Company brought miners here to extract copper, but they abandoned the project because of the ore's low quality.

Over the years, Douglas County was part of Crawford County, Chippewa County, St. Croix County and a county called La Pointe. It wasn't until after Wisconsin became a state in 1848 that people became interested in the county's pine and its Great Lakes' link to the East Coast. In 1854, La Pointe county was split and the new county to the east was called St. Louis. It was soon renamed after Stephen A. Douglas, major holder of a company formed to create a new town in the Lake superior wilderness. Naturally the town would be named Superior. Though the county had a new name, Douglas County's total population in 1855 was 385.

SHSW

Superior, WI, ca.1889

Fur trade and lumbering provided work for people living near the new village of Superior. The region closest to Lake Superior was logged from about 1873 to 1885 and southern Douglas County was logged when the railroad reached through the St. Croix watershed in 1883 from the lumber towns of Eau Claire and Chippewa Falls.

SUPERIOR, Pop. 29,571

Superior sits on a level terrace at the head of Lake Superior. The Indians and early white settlers considered this location a good place to camp because the natural harbor protected them from sudden storms on the lake. The harbor was formed by lake currents and wave action that pushed sand down along the shoreline and heaped it into a sand spit ten miles long. The St. Louis River, which fills the bay behind the sand bar, broke through at the Minnesota and Wisconsin points, creating a natural entry into what is known as St. Louis Bay. (Duluth opened a channel on its side of the harbor in 1870 as competition for harbor shipping increased.)

In 1661 Radisson and Groseilliers explored the bay, having learned about it from the Ojibwe. Jean Claude Allouez ventured here in 1667 from his small Indian mission on Chequamegon Bay, but it was Daniel Greysolon Sieur Duluth who paddled up the St. Louis in 1679 to try to make peace between the warring Dakota and Ojibwe and establish a trading post. The French had little to gain in fur trading if the Indians were at war. Duluth established a trading post on the Minnesota side of the St. Louis River and called it Fond du Lac, meaning "head of the Lake." For the next 150 years, the French, British and Americans maintained trading posts here, carrying pack after pack of knives, blankets, guns and whiskey inland along the St. Louis River to trade for the mink, beaver, wolf and bear furs and skins which made fashionable European hats and coats.

Active settlement began at Superior when speculators heard that the Sault Ste. Marie canal was going to be built to link Lake Superior with the east. When Daniel Robertson, editor of the Minnesota Democrat, and his friends, Judge Daniel Baker and Rensselaer Nelson of St. Paul, heard the news, they packed their bags and made the difficult journey over Indian trails to claim land on both sides of the Nemadji River. Two other groups came that winter and made claims along Superior Bay. Two of these groups consolidated their 4,000 acres and called themselves the "Proprietors of Superior." Several politicians from Washington also promoted a city here: streets such as Breckenridge, Corcoran and Douglas are named in their honor.

A government surveyor, George Stuntz, surveyed the land here in the summer of 1853. As he canoed along St. Louis Bay and viewed this flat land covered with birch, pine, spruce and fir, he discovered a man named Conners building a house on what later became Conner's Point. By the following spring 250 new settlers were calling Superior their home. To take advantage of the harbor and promote shipping, a pier was built 800 feet into the lake. A hotel called the Superior House was also opened. In 1854 a military road connected Superior with St. Paul, bringing in settlers on the newly-formed stage lines. During the following three years, some 2,000 lots with prices as high as $2,000 were sold. The "Proprietors" handled some $4,000,000 in transactions, mostly from speculators who did not intend to move here.

The next major effort was to have the railroad connect Superior with the population center of St. Paul. A new plan seemed to be hatched every month. In all, at least 10 different proposals were made to connect Superior by rail. The financial Panic of 1857 had a stifling effect on Superior, as well as Duluth, at that time a little village on the other side of the bay. Superior had a population of about 3,000 prior to the panic but was quickly reduced to 500. Duluth had only a few hardy souls and Beaver Bay was the only other settlement along the lake's north shore.

Little growth took place here for the next two decades. There was little incentive for settlers and no reason for a railroad to invest in a line to Superior.

The first real chance for a railroad came in 1870 when the Lake Superior & Mississippi Railroad was chartered to come from St. Paul to Superior. Instead, its tracks went into Duluth, bringing a rush of settlers and business there and marking the beginning of an intense rivalry between Duluth and Superior which still exists. When Duluth planned to enlarge its harbor entrance so ships could avoid the seven-mile trip down to the Wisconsin Cut, Superior filed an injunction to halt the dredging. They filed on a Friday and the injunction was to take effect the following Monday. Over the weekend Duluth workers made a great effort to build a manmade

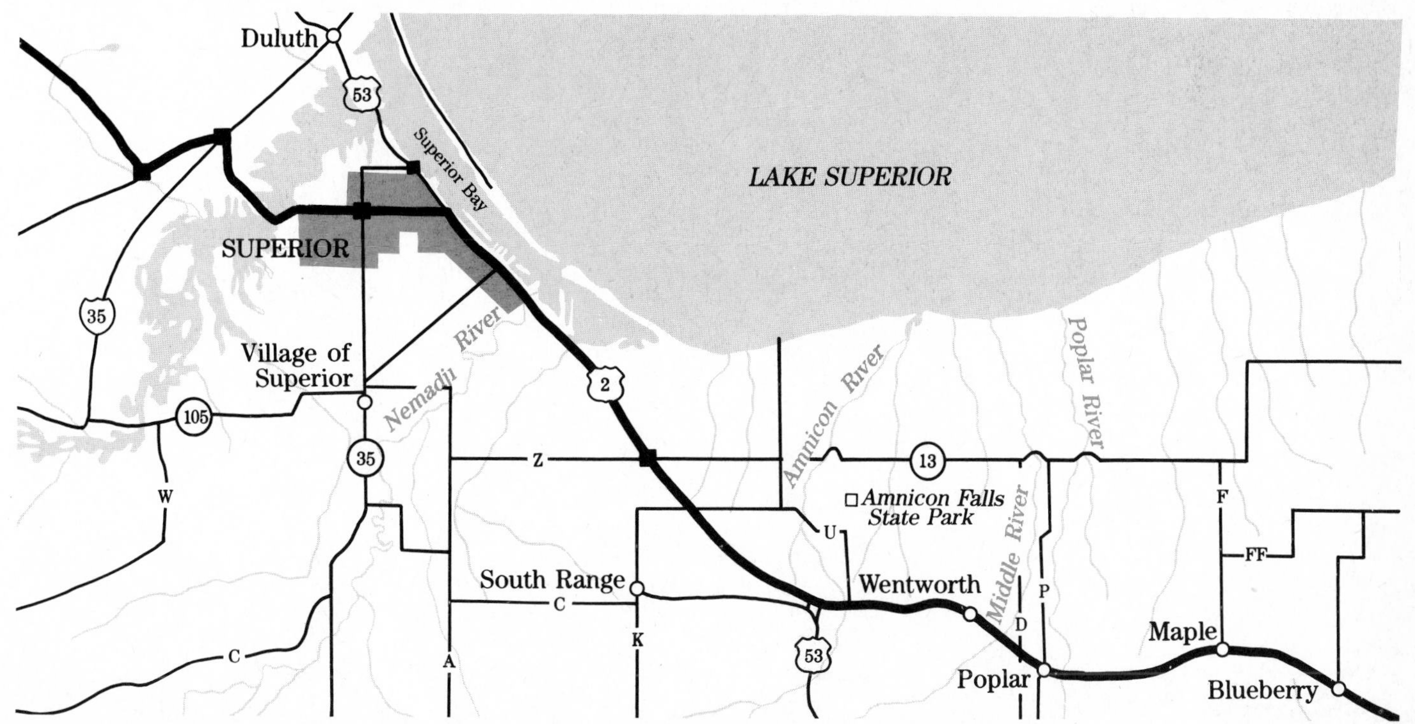

channel: by Monday a small steamboat passed from Duluth harbor into Lake Superior.

Superior finally got its rail connection in 1881 when the Northern Pacific crossed from Duluth on its way to Ashland, spurring new growth in Superior. When ore was found on the Vermillion Range in Minnesota's Arrowhead and near Ashland on the Gogebic Range, the value of the Twin Ports of Superior and Duluth was realized. Lumbering, ore and flour milling made Superior Wisconsin's second largest city at the turn of the century. Finnish settlers came first, followed by Scandinavians and Poles. Ship arrivals increased from 21 in 1883 to more than 900 by 1890. Newly-designed whaleback boats were built in the Superior shipyards as fast as possible to carry ore and grain to the eastern mills of Ashtabula, Cleveland, Toledo, Buffalo, Detroit and Chicago. The "Meteor," the only remaining example of the whaleback boat, is berthed in sand along St. Louis Bay in Superior.

The Duluth-Superior rivalry continued over iron ore shipments, but the Mesabi ore was closer to Duluth and much of the ore was shipped from there. Nevertheless, Superior built one of the world's largest groupings of ore docks and was shipping more ore than Duluth during the 1930's. It has been said that both World Wars were won by Minnesota's iron mines, with help from Superior's docks. Duluth residents called the Superior docks necklaces, because their lights sparkled across the harbor at night.

Today, the grain elevators, ore docks and shipyards are a monument to Superior's growth. However, like other Great Lake cities, the economies of Superior and Duluth are now trying to adapt to changes affecting the steel industry.

LAKE SUPERIOR

From the city of Superior one can see dark hills that run behind Duluth and then along the North Shore. These hills were once the shoreline of a previous lake, Glacial Lake Duluth, which was much larger than today's Lake Superior. This huge basin was formed by a succession of glaciers which pushed down from the northeast, carving an ever-widening channel. Coupled with continental drift—a pulling apart of the north and south shores—the basin became a giant collector for water from the melting glaciers. As the lake overflowed, much of the water drained south through the St. Louis River, Bois Brule and other south shore streams, carving out the St. Croix Valley and contributing to the deep Mississippi Valley at Prescott.

Lake Superior was a highway for 17th century voyageurs who came west to trade for the rich furs of the Dakota and Ojibwe Indians. Great summer gatherings were held to exchange goods at Fond du Lac (a village near the mouth of the St. Louis River), La Pointe on Chequamegon Bay, and at Grand Portage on Minnesota's North Shore. The Indians, who had previously hunted only for their own needs, were surprised that these "men with hats" would give knives, guns and whiskey for furs. Nevertheless, the foreign goods motivated the Indians to supply all the furs they could trap to the traders. As the fur trading network grew, the Bois Brule and St. Louis rivers became important south shore routes.

Both the Ojibwe and Dakota Indians were in this region when fur trading began, although the Ojibwe eventually pushed the Dakota into Minnesota. Conflicts between these two nations over ricing and hunting rights spanned two centuries until the Dakota were removed from Minnesota after the Sioux Uprising of 1862.

The Ojibwe called Lake Superior, Kitchigumi, meaning "Great Water." The French called it, Lac Superieur, since it lay at the beginning of the great inland lake chain. Traders crossed the lake in birch bark canoes but developed a larger canoe, the Montreal, which carried 12 men and their supplies. As trade increased, larger boats were built to sail under the lake's roughest conditions. During the late 1700's those larger sailing vessels resupplied the fur companies operating throughout the Northwest.

The first steamboat appeared on the lake in 1841, but the opening of the Sault Ste. Marie canal in the early 1850's brought major shipping to the lake and hastened development of Superior and Duluth. In the 1890's a cigar-shaped ore carrier called a Whaleback, appeared on the lake to serve the Mesabi Iron Range. Passenger ships and cruise ships also began making regular calls at the lake ports, and became a fashionable, elegant, way to see this rugged north region.

After World War II, ship travel declined as cars and planes provided quicker, more efficient, travel. Today, cargo carriers flying the flags of many nations cross the lake from the St. Lawrence Seaway. Large ore boats also cross between the North Shore taconite shipping ports and steel mills on the lower lakes. Despite some pollution from shoreline industries and cities, Lake Superior, the largest freshwater lake on earth, is still once of the world's cleanest. The balance is fragile though since Superior requires 190 years to completely exchange its water.

NEMADJI RIVER

This short stream begins in Minnesota and runs rapidly down the Superior Highlands, cutting ravines 25 to 100 feet deep before emptying into Superior Bay. The state's highest waterfall is located at Pattison State Park on the Black River, one of the Nemadji's tributaries. The waterfall drops 160 feet into a sandstone gorge. The park marks the southern limits of the Lake Superior Lowlands, at one time Glacial Lake Duluth's southern shore. The park is 13 miles south of Superior on State 35.

SOUTH RANGE

Beginning in 1881 a small community developed here around the railroad line that was built from Eau Claire to Superior. Several stores were built, including one with a dance hall on the top floor. An adjoining saloon was the main attraction of the Grand Central Hotel which was built for railroad passengers as well as loggers who worked the northern Douglas County forests. Two lumber mills were located west of South Range at a place called Slab Town and a tram took boards back to South Range to be finished at the planing mill. Two copper mines were also started near here around 1900 but proved unprofitable and were closed. The town rests on Lake Superior's southern ridge which is known as the Douglas Copper Range or South Range.

AMNICON RIVER

Amnicon is an Indian word meaning, "spawning ground." An 825-acre park forest ed with white and Norway pine, is located on the Amnicon River just north of U.S. 2. At the park, the Amnicon flows through a series of cascades and waterfalls before emptying into Lake Superior six miles away. There are 40 campsites located in the park.

POPLAR, Pop. 569

Settlement began here when Eugene Brainerd homesteaded within a broad stand of poplars that had grown up after the pine was logged. The small settlement was located along the Bayfield to Superior road which was in use after the Civil War. Lumbering was the settlers' main source of income and a saw mill was eventually built, along with a brick factory, cooperative creamery and seasonal pea cannery.

In the mid-1800's, when Poplar was a stop on the railroad between Superior and Ashland, the section house became a school and 19 students attended. The all-purpose section house also served as the telegraph office, depot and post office (a brown bag hung from a nail in which people searched for their own mail.) The dusty and often muddy highway wasn't paved until 1932.

More recently, Poplar has taken great pride in Richard Bond, a World War II fighter pilot and local boy, who was called the "American Ace of Aces" after downing 40 Japanese fighters. A replica of the P-38 Bong flew in the South Pacific is on display a block north of town near the public school. He died in 1945 while test flying a new generation of jet-fighter, the P-80 Shooting Star.

Looking north on the drive between Poplar and Maple you can see the dark outline of the Superior Uplands of Minnesota's north shore. This was the early shoreline of Glacial Lake Duluth and includes some of the oldest surface rocks on this continent.

MAPLE

This small community was founded in 1880 when a Finnish immigrant, Abraham Harju, couldn't find work in Superior. Frustrated, Harju rowed a boat along Superior's south shore to the Poplar River, followed the river inland as far as he could, found a spot he liked and built a cabin. French-Canadian loggers called the area south of Harju's cabin Little Canada, but other Finns arrived after Harju, making them the community's dominate nationality. When a school opened two miles north of Maple in 1885, the teacher had problems communicating with the Finnish-speaking children. The area's one-room schools were consolidated in 1921 at the corner school which is still used today. During lumbering's boom years a small hotel and several cooperative stores existed here. The first church was a Catholic parish at the hamlet of Blueberry. Loggers removed most of the pine from the Maple area and a stand of maple trees grew in its place, giving the village its name.

Ashland H.S.

The once-vital coal and oar docks of the Ashland and Superior harbor.

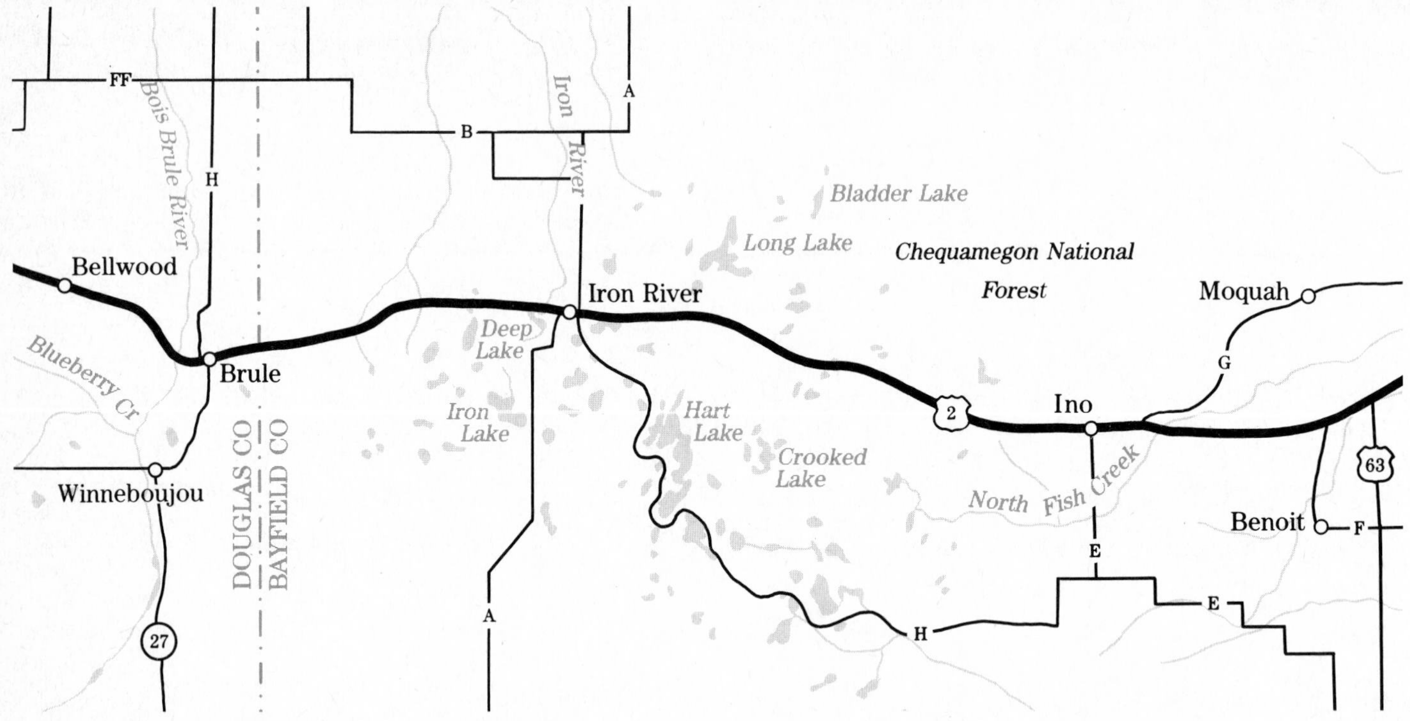

BRULE VILLAGE & BOIS BRULE RIVER

For many years the Brule River provided an Indian crossing between Lake Superior and the St. Croix Valley. From the point where the highway crosses the river, it is 18 miles through thick forest and underbrush to the portage separating the Brule from the St. Croix. Daniel Greysolon Sieur Duluth was probably the first white man to travel the river when he explored the region for France in 1680.

The Dakota, who first occupied this area, called the river Nemitsakonet. The Ojibwe, who forced the Dakota from these lands during the 1600's, called this river Mis-a-ho-da which meant "burnt pines" and the French called it Bois Brule, which has a similar meaning. The French considered the river so important that they built small forts at each end.

The Brule flows in a channel that once drained Glacial Lake Duluth south to the St. Croix River. Now the Brule, colored brown by the bogs and marshes it drains, flows into Lake Superior and provides some of the South Shore's best trout fishing.

South of Brule, at an old railroad station called Winneboujou, one of the area's last battles between the Dakota and Ojibwe took place in 1842. The Dakota retreated after heavy losses and only ventured back along the river in small raiding parties.

An old Ojibwe legend tells how Winneboujou, an Ojibwe god, forged weapons from copper which he found in the hills south of Brule. When the ice of Lake Superior expanded and made booming noises on cold winter nights, the Indians believed Winneboujou was pounding at his anvil. The northern lights that flickered across the sky were said to be from the fires of his forge. Legend has it that Winneboujou killed many Dakota braves while defending his people.

Brule became the center of the lumbering operations that began here after 1850. Logs were cut, skidded out to the river on iced-over trails and dumped. Dams along the river were opened during the spring rush so the logs could float out to Lake Superior where they were rafted together and taken to mills in Duluth and Superior. One of the worst log jams in the river's history occurred in 1903. Logs backed up the river and jammed 50 feet high in some places. After several days of blasting, pulling with horses, and otherwise trying to pry the mess apart, the logs flowed again.

When the train came through in the early 1880's, Brule began to grow. Homes were built, along with a large stable for the logging teams, a post office, hotels, church, school and of course, saloons. The first hotel was owned and run by Grandma Miller who eventually sold it. It burned, was rebuilt, and one day suddenly collapsed. Fires were common in Brule. Several burned through town in those early days, fueled by the debris left by the loggers. All the original buildings have been destroyed.

Many early settlers homesteaded just north of Brule in a Finnish community they called Waino. Antoine Dennis, son of a fur trader, is considered Brule's first resident. Dennis was a mail runner on the road between St. Paul, Superior and Bayfield. This road was built during the Civil War at the same time the Union Army built a bridge across the Brule. Like many lumber towns, Brule's businesses faded away as the logging era ended.

President Calvin Coolidge brought new fame to this little community in 1928 when he made his summer White House along the Brule. He visited at the Pierce estate for 88 days, relaxing and testifying to the river's excellent trout fishing. Fredrick Weyerhaeuser, lumber magnate of the northwest, had an estate on Lake Nebagamon while his lumber companies clear-cut the forests during the late 1800's.

BAYFIELD COUNTY, Pop. 13,822

In 1845 Bayfield County and Ashland County were part of a larger county called La Pointe which had its county seat at the trading village of La Pointe on Madeline Island. By 1858 Bayfield had grown and had enough votes to move the county government there. In protest, La Pointe residents created their own county and joined with Ashland to exclude Bayfield. La Pointe and Ashland Counties separated in 1860, but it wasn't until 1866 that the county was named Bayfield. It is named after the British Navy's Lieut. Henry R. Bayfield, who did the first extensive survey of Lake Superior from 1823 to 1825. Bayfield County was extensively logged during the late 1800's with most pine floated to Lake Superior via south shore streams. In the southern part of the county near Cable, loggers used the Namekagon River to float logs down to the mills on the St. Croix. Today, tourism is one of the county's major industries.

IRON RIVER

The Ojibwe called this river Medicine Springs, but it was called Iron River by workers who constructed the railroad across it in the 1880's. John Pettingill, anticipating that the area would soon be filled with lumbermen, settled and established a small store in 1887. Loggers soon began building camps throughout northern Wisconsin. A saw mill was established and Pettingill expanded his operations by building a hotel where he reportedly had 150 people staying one night.

A few years later in 1897, former U.S. Senator Dwight Sabin began promoting the idea of a new railroad to cross into the county's interior, connecting Iron River with Washburn on Chequamegon Bay. Sabin reasoned that the railroad would service farmers who would work the cleared land after the loggers left. He got Bayfield County to underwrite a good portion of this 34-mile stretch, but cash always seemed to

SHSW

Early northwoods camping excursion.

be short when it was time to pay the workers. The only item the company freely gave workers was a chewing tobacco called "Spearhead and Battle Axe." Before the train ever rolled it was known as the Battle Axe Line, not as the Washburn, Bayfield & Iron River Railroad.

When completed the railroad made two daily trips between Iron River and Washburn. The line consisted of nine engines, two passenger cars and 408 freight cars. Unfortunately, the Battle Axe had problems: it never made a profit and eventually defaulted on its bonds. The Northern Pacific bought it, reduced service to three times a week, and eventually closed down the line. In 1927 the tracks were torn up.

A number of Scandinavian settlers came from the copper mines of the Upper Peninsula of Michigan to the Iron River area. Most took up farming, supplying produce or milk to the cannery or creamery established here. Today, only a few brick buildings remain on Main St. Lodged on the rock under the Iron River bridge are the sheet metal ruins of an old hydroelectric plant which once charged batteries for the 12-volt electric systems that existed in the area.

MOQUAH

Local legend tells of a lumber foreman who returned to camp one evening and found it torn up by a foraging bear. An Indian with the foreman called out Moquah, Ojibwe for bear, and the settlement had its name. After the Keystone Logging Company removed the pine, an enterprising man, James W. Good, bought much of the land around Moquah, surveyed it into lots, and sold them to Czechoslovakian and Polish immigrants around 1907. He built two houses near the railroad tracks and allowed newly arriving settlers to stay with him.

The first depot was only a box car but had "Moquah" proudly painted in bold letters on its side. One Moquah resident wrote about Bob Scott, the railroad's section foreman who was stationed here. "We all loved him (Bob Scott). He lived here with his wife and daughter. They were a novelty to us with their store bought clothes and food though. Although they did raise a nice garden and had a couple of cows, they still represented city folks (to us)."

Moquah was only a flag-stop on the Northern Pacific line.

Ashland H.S.

Hardy pioneers brave a Wisconsin winter.

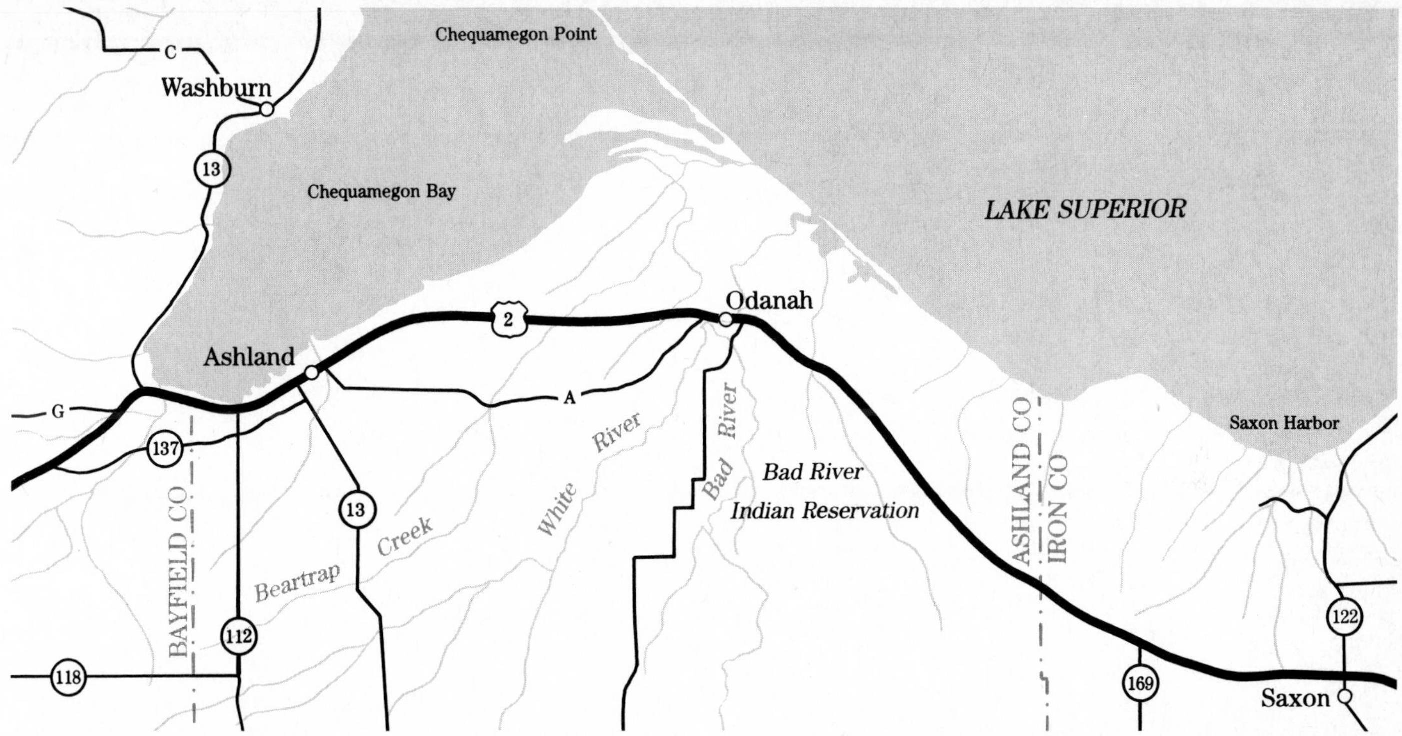

If the train wasn't flagged to stop, mail was hung from a post so the mailman on the 6:15 train could snare it with a hook. Most early Moquah settlers either farmed or harvested and milled the lumber left behind by the loggers. Today Moquah is little more than a bend in the road, with a few buildings and a tavern located near the tracks. Nonetheless, County Road G is a beautiful drive through rolling hills covered by fields and forest.

ASHLAND COUNTY, Pop. 16,783

Ashland County is the most northerly of Wisconsin counties since it includes 21 of the 24 Apostle Islands. Ashland, Bayfield and Douglas counties were all part of a county called La Pointe dating from 1845. But Ashland County was created in 1860 with the county seat at Madeline Island's La Pointe, the oldest European settlement in Wisconsin.

EARLY ASHLAND

Sitting at the head of Chequamegon Bay, Ashland is the site of Wisconsin's first crude structure built by white men. It was raised by French explorers Radisson and Groseilliers about 1659 on their second trip into Lake Superior. They portaged across the sand spit of Chequamegon Point, beached their canoes near where Ashland would form nearly 200 years later, and built a small log house near an Indian village called Agami-Wikedo-Subiwishen. The Ojibwe called this protected bay, Sha-gawau-mikong, which means "place of shallow water."

Radisson and Groseilliers returned to Montreal after a short stay but their boat overturned en route and they lost their records and license to trade here. As a result, their furs were confiscated. They considered this a gross injustice and returned to Europe where they switched loyalties to the English. The English formed the Hudson Bay Company after hearing the explorers' accounts of the furs and game here. In 1865 a French Jesuit Priest, Claude Allouez, came along Lake Superior and into Chequamegon Bay where he constructed a rustic chapel of tree bark at Ashland. Besides preaching to the Ojibwe, Allouez met with Sauk, Fox and Kickapoo Indians who came to visit this white man's unusual chapel. By 1665 Chequamegon Bay's development as a trading center for Indians had become so important that some 4,000 Indians were camping, hunting and trading here. Allouez stayed for four years before being replaced by Father James Marquette, who while teaching Christianity to the Indians, developed a growing curiosity about their stories of the "Father of Waters," the Mississippi. Two years later Marquette left the mission and joined Louis Joliet on a trip down the Wisconsin River where they became, in 1673, the first whites to see the Upper Mississippi. Between 1679, when the French gave up many of their missionary activities, and the

1830's furs were the region's main economy. The French, English and Americans all maintained posts here at different times.

FOUNDING OF ASHLAND

Asaph Whittlesey and George Kilbourne rowed across Chequamegon Bay in 1854 to form a city. They climbed the shore at the end of the bay, chopped down an ash tree, and named this small clearing Whittlesey. It was renamed Ashland in 1860. A number of settlers soon arrived to claim government lands. Steamers such as the Sam Ward, Superior, and others began to call at the small village at the head of the bay. Settlers had high hopes for Ashland's growth, but the nationwide monetary crisis in 1857, followed shortly by the Civil War, made Ashland a deserted village. Even Whittlesey moved away, leaving only one family in town.

Fortunately, Ashland's future brightened in 1871. Rumors circulated that a railroad would be built up to the bay to help remove the vast white and Norway pine forests. Mining fever also took hold when iron ore was discovered on the Penokee-Gogebic Range, an iron-bearing highland which crosses southeast of Ashland and northeastward into the Upper Peninsula of Michigan. Many of the original settlers rushed back to town, including Whittlesey. A newspaper began, a telegraph was connected, and 200 buildings were built almost overnight. Asaph Whittlesey drove the last spike when the Wisconsin Central reached here in 1877, connecting Ashland on Lake Superior with Lake Michigan. Other railroads followed, including the Northern Pacific in 1884 and the Milwaukee, Lake Shore and Western in 1885. By 1886 iron ore was leaving new docks built on Ashland's shores. The entire output of the Gogebic Range was shipped from Ashland's docks for the steel mills of Gary, Indiana and other Great Lakes foundries.

At the same time Pennsylvanian coal was arriving to be unloaded at the new coal docks at Ashland, which once ranked seventh as a coal distribution center in the country. This vital energy source was bound for businesses and homes of northern Minnesota, the Dakotas, Michigan and Wyoming. Quarrying was also done near Ashland for brownstone, a fashionable building stone used throughout the East and Midwest in the early 1890's.

Despite all the other resources, the saw mill was king at Ashland during the late 1800's. At least nine mills were located along the lake. Trains brought in carloads to be cut and planed while the harbor was filled with lumber boats ready to take the wood to eastern ports. All the activity subsided when the forests gave out around 1900 and coal was displaced by oil and gasoline. Ashland's docks fell into disuse and only rotting pilings remain to tell of Ashland's former greatness. Plaques near the lake mention Radisson, Groseilliers and Whittlesey. From the shore you can still see the Apostle Islands outlined in a light haze but the bulk carriers stop here no more.

Located on Ashland's south side is Northland College which was founded in 1892 to provide high school education to children living in the area's isolated lumber camps. It became a college in 1906 and today houses the Sigurd Olson Environmental Institute which holds workshops and funds research in an effort to preserve the environmental quality of Lake Superior.

ODANAH & BAD RIVER INDIAN RESERVATION

This reservation and village were created by a treaty signed at La Pointe in September 1854 when the Ojibwe gave up claim to their lands in the Lake Superior Region. The village is named Odanah, the Ojibwe word for "town." Situated at the junction of the White and Bad Rivers, it is the trading center for the approximately 850 Ojibwe living on the reservation.

During the late 1800's, a white-owned saw mill worked the Odanah forests, running 24 hours a day. Many Indians worked there, but the company abruptly moved out when the forests were depleted, leaving the Ojibwe with this barren land. A second growth has covered most of those scars and pulpwood is now being logged.

Located north of Odanah is the Kakagon & Bad River Slough, a region of marshes and backwater channels which was open water until years of current and wave action created the protective spit of sand across Chequamegon Bay. Ojibwe legend credits the slough and Chequamegon Point to Nanabozho, an Ojibwe god who built a dam across the bay when trying to capture the great beaver. The legend led to the name Sha-gawau-mikong, meaning, "shallow water or place of beaver dam."

One of the Great Lakes' most significant wildlife areas is located behind this sand-bar. During the migratory season, geese, whistling swans, many breeds of ducks and 240 other species of birds stop to rest and feed in this 10,300-acre slough. During the summer more than 100 species are known to nest in the tall slough-grass and wild rice beds. The waters here also contain smallmouth bass, perch, northern and walleyed pike. In fact, the Kakagon River takes its name from the Ojibwe for "home of the walleyed pike." Deer, bear and small mammals make their homes on the higher ground.

Thanks to the Ojibwe, the 17 miles of Lake Superior shoreline on their reservation is still very close to its natural state. In the fall, the Ojibwe harvest about 6,000 pounds of rice from the slough which they sell or use themselves. Though technically a grain, and not a rice, "wild rice" has become a delicacy for people around the world.

SAXON, Pop. 362

Saxon began as a lumbering town in the 1880's when the Chicago and Northwestern was built through here. The small hamlet became a flag-stop known as Siding Four. When the Duluth and South Shore was constructed in 1885, the name was changed to Dogwood. The current name reportedly comes from a Frenchman who was in charge of loading mail sacks onto the train. Every day he would yell "sacks on" in his heavy French accent. Eventually his phrase caught on and the town changed its name to Saxon.

See route U.S. 51 for Iron County and Hurley.

(right) Chequamegon Hotel, a major tourist stop in the early 1900's.
(bottom) Loading a sailing vessel on the Ohio Coal Co. docks. at Ashland Harbor.

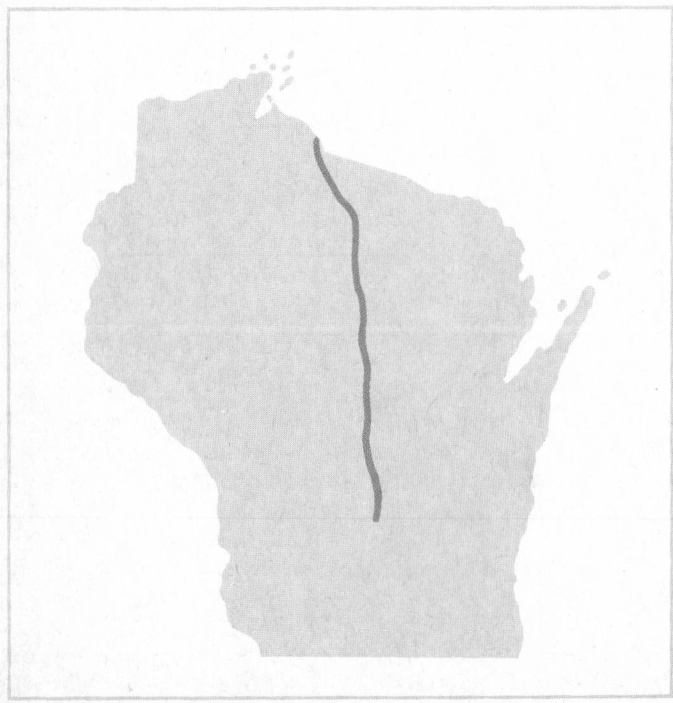

U.S. 51 cuts a path 225 miles through the heart of Wisconsin. Butting up against I-94, this route leads with the city where Father Marquette and Louis Joliet made their famous "portage" which led to the discovery of the Mississippi River. In the "north country," near Merrill, is Grandfather Falls, site of the biggest log jam in Wisconsin history. Here 80 million feet of timber piled up to heights of 20 feet or more.

ROUTE 51, PORTAGE TO HURLEY

SHSW

The abundant white pines attracted railroads northward encouraging new settlement.

COLUMBIA COUNTY, Pop. 43,222

Columbia is important in Wisconsin history for it was here that French explorers Joliet and Marquette discovered a critical link in their passage to the great Mississippi River.

In 1673, Marquette's party traveled south on the Fox River from Green Bay to the Four Lakes Region in Columbia County. Here, on the west bank of the Fox, they stopped at a large Mascouten Indian village near Governor's Bend in the town of Fort Winnebago (then Portage County.)

Studying his map, Father Marquette had surmised, "we knew that there was, three leagues from the Mascoutens, a river entering into the Mississippi; we also knew that the point of the compass we were to hold to reach it was west-southwest, but the way is so cut up by marshes and little lakes that it is easy to go astray, especially as the river leading to it is so covered with wild oats that you can hardly discover the channel. Hence we had good need of our two Miami guides who led us safely to a portage of 2,700 paces and helped us to transport our canoes to enter this river.

"The river on which we embarked is called Meskousing (the Wisconsin); it is very broad, with a sandy bottom forming many shallows which render navigation very difficult. On the banks appear fertile lands, diversified with wood, prairie and hill. Here you find oaks, walnut, whitewood and another kind of tree with branches armed with thorns. We saw no small game or fish, but deer and moose in considerable numbers."

Marquette reported in his diary that the party crossed the portage a few days after leaving the Mascouten village, launched their canoes on the broad Wisconsin's waters, and began their historic journey to the interior of America. A red granite memorial marks this famous crossing on highway 33 in Portage. The original Marquette-Joliet route is now marked as the Wauona Trail. Wauona, an Indian word for portage, meant "place where one takes up his canoe and carries it."

THE FOX AND WISCONSIN RIVERS

Most relics and records of the first people of this land suggest that Indian habitations and migrations were largely

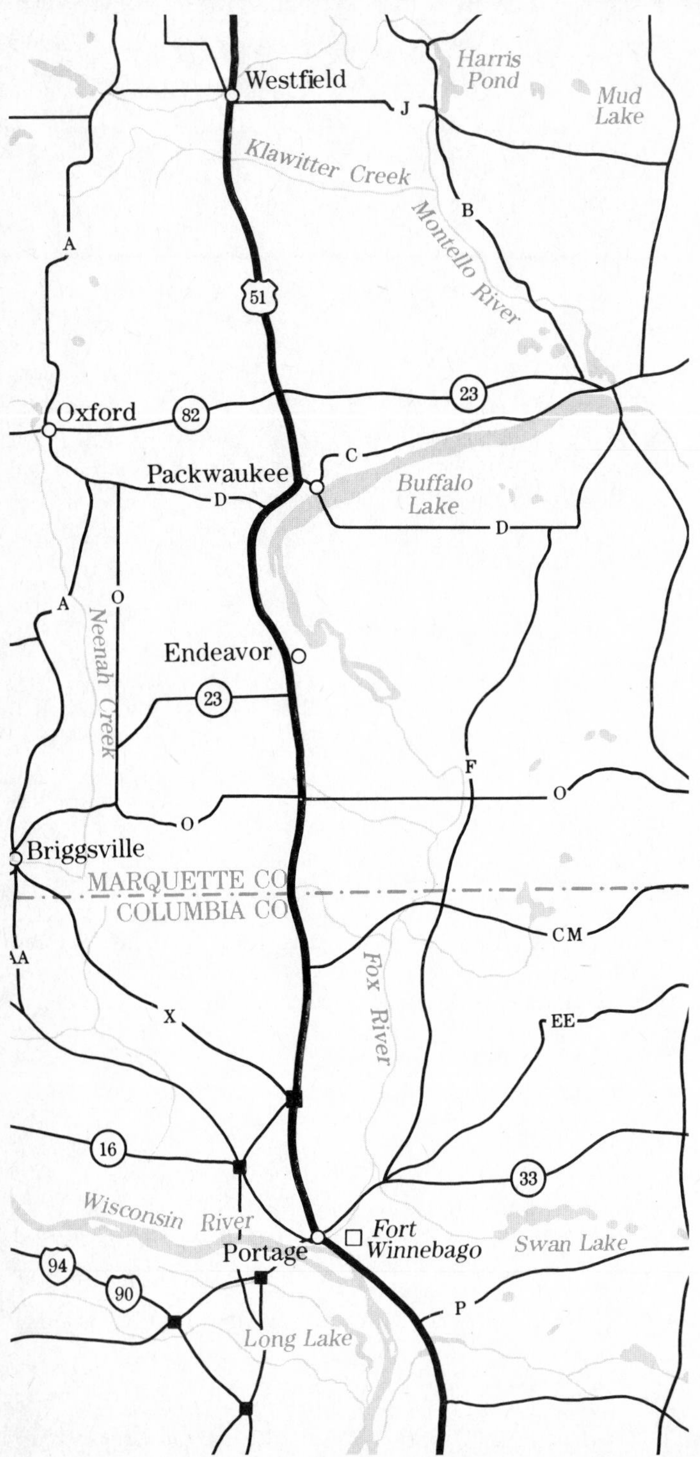

guided by the waterways. The old villages, forts and early settlements were usually not far from present-day streams. In Columbia County, the Fox and Wisconsin rivers were the most influential of these waters. (For more information on the Fox and Wisconsin please see Index.)

EARLY INDIAN TRIBES

The Mascoutens are believed to be the first Indians discovered in this county. Samuel de Champlain, French explorer and founder of Quebec, Canada, wrote that this tribe "hunted, fished and warred in a region many leagues beyond Lake Huron." The Hurons translated the name Mascouten as "Fire Nation." Later scholars said it was derived from Muskoutenec, or prairie, and translated it as "Men of the Prairie," or "prairie people." Whatever the meaning, the Mascouten tribe had numerous villages in what was then Portage County but maintained hunting grounds along the Fox River well into what is currently Columbia County.

Although the Mascoutens were the first tribe sighted in this area, the Winnebago were the only Indians who actually lived in Columbia County. A strong and patient tribe, they founded several villages which flourished here for years. The largest of these was located just two miles south of the portage. Consisting of more than 100 lodges, it was led by their principal chief, De Korra, said to be the grandson of Sebrevoir de Carrie, a French army officer who had been a fur trader among the Winnebagoes. White settlers viewed De Korra as a noble and respected chief who caused them little trouble—until the Winnebago Uprising of 1827.

De Korra's troubles began with another Winnebago chief named Red Bird, who led the uprising. The militia seized De Korra after the attack at Prairie du Chien, and held him hostage for Red Bird. They sent a young Winnebago back to the village to inform the tribe. Several days passed with no word of Red Bird's whereabouts. As the day of De Korra's execution neared, he asked Colonel Snelling for permission to bathe in the river, as was his custom. Snelling said he would gladly grant him that privilege and any other if De Korra promised not to leave town. De Korra solemnly made that promise, noting that he would sooner lose a hundred lives than break his word. Set at liberty, he remained until execution day. That morning, General Atkinson arrived with troops from Jefferson Barracks, Missouri (the Army's western headquarters), cancelled the execution order and permitted De Korra to return to his home above the portage.

A few months later, Red Bird and his band approached the portage point of the Fox River, unarmed, and surrendered to the military. He died later of a self-imposed starvation. A monument marks the spot of his surrender in Portage.

Soon after the completion of Fort Winnebago in 1830, De Korra's village began to disintegrate. When the title to the land was ceded in 1837, little remained. The last of the Winnebagoes left Columbia County on a forced march by U.S. troops, just two days before Christmas, 1873.

Although no Indian battles were ever fought in this county, the Winnebago Uprising led by Red Bird called attention to the exposed condition of white settlers and travelers in southern Wisconsin, particularly along the Fox and Wisconsin river valleys.

FORT WINNEBAGO

The area where Fort Winnebago was built had been a natural gathering spot for traders. In 1793, Laurant Barth and his family obtained Indian permission to transport goods at the portage. Soon after arriving, Barth built a cabin on the low land between the Fox and Wisconsin rivers, the first to be built by a white man in Columbia County. Five years later the French-Canadian Jean B. Lecuyer established a fur trading post at the present site of Portage.

Finally, in 1820, John Jacob Astor, one of America's first millionaires, established a new fur trading post with Pierre Pauquette, a French-Canadian Indian who acted as Astor's representative for the American Fur Trading Company. Astor reportedly had much to do with the building of Fort Winnebago.

The post was located at the junction of the Portage Canal and the Fox River because of the narrow neck of land separating the Fox and Wisconsin rivers which was used as a portage between the two. Realizing the importance of this portage for travel and trade, the U.S. government decided to establish a military oversight on this spot. Ground was broken for Fort Winnebago in 1828.

The Indians felt doomed by the fort and protested accordingly. But the military felt Wisconsin's interior waterways were now quite safe, with Fort Howard (Green Bay) at the northeast end of the route, Fort Winnebago at the portage, and Fort Crawford (Prairie du Chien) at the southwestern end.

Temporary barracks were soon erected of tamarack logs rafted down the Wisconsin River from Pine Island, some 50 miles away. Stone Quarry Hill provided the stone and chimney bricks were found near the present Wisconsin River bridge. Major David Twiggs and three companies of Fort Howard soldiers completed the military post in spring, 1830.

The young Jefferson Davis was one of Twigg's first lieutenants. Davis assisted in rafting logs from Pine Island to the fort and later made furniture which folks at the fort christened as original "Davis". Davis fell in love with Sarah, the daughter of Colonel Zachary Taylor from Fort Crawford but

SHSW

Portage Canal, 1905

she died of malaria three months after their marriage. Heartbroken, Davis left Wisconsin and went south where, years later, he would lead the Confederate Army in the Civil War.

Only two buildings remain from this 4,000 acre military site. One is the army surgeon's house overlooking the famous Marquette landing site. The Surgeon's Quarters are open daily, May-November, from 9 a.m. to 6 p.m. The second building is the Old Indian Agency House. Built by the government in 1832 for Indian Agent, John Kinzie and his bride, Juliette. This house is fully restored and open every day from "sunrise to sunset." A small fee is charged at each building. Both are located just one mile east of Portage, on Highway 33. At the junction of 33 and County K is a white farmhouse, privately owned. From the road you can see a ten-foot stone foundation and a working windmill which once marked the center of Fort Winnebago.

THE MILITARY ROAD

Early in 1835, Secretary of War Lewis Cass, ordered soldiers to "open, lay out and bridge a road" from Fort Howard at Green Bay via Fond du Lac and Fort Winnebago to Ford Crawford, near Prairie du Chien. The actual surveying and road building was supervised by Lt. Centre and James Duane Doty, later governor of Wisconsin. Doty was especially familiar with the Fox and Wisconsin river valleys because he had traveled through the territory years before as secretary to Cass.

The road entered Columbia County from the south near the town of Arlington, continued in a northeasterly direction to what is now Poynette, then ran due north to Fort Winnebago.

Although crudely constructed, the road was a great improvement over no road at all. It was built by cutting through timber land, clearing a track about two rods wide (approximately 33 feet), and setting up mile stakes. The stakes were set up with earth mounds on the prairies and with stone, when it could be found. On marshes and other low places, "corduroy" roads were made by crossing timbers and covering them with brush and earth. Portions of the Military Road in Columbia County can still be travelled along County K which also marks the spot of the Fort Winnebago cemetery.

EARLY SETTLEMENT

The Military Road brought Columbia County's first white settlers. In 1836, the Wallace Rowan family bought 40 acres of land on the road near the present city of Poynette, then built a double-log house later known as the Rowan Inn, big enough to accommodate travelers and a tavern. On the adjoining land, Rowan raised corn, potatoes, oats and vegetables for man and beast.

The Rowans had no neighbors until the 1840's, when the rapidly growing lumber industry enticed settlers from southern Wisconsin and northern Illinois into the county. The most significant population increase came in 1847, one year after the county officially organized, when 50 potters and their families from Staffordshire, England, moved into the northeast section of the county. The immigrants came under the auspices of the Potter's Joint Stock Emigration Society and Savings Fund, an English organization which encouraged the purchase of lands in the western states. Families sent over were determined by ballot. Each member holding a share in the Society (equivalent to one pound sterling) was allowed a choice of 20 aces of land which they agreed to cultivate and build on. In all, these 134 persons settled 1,640 acres of Columbia County land.

PORTAGE, Pop. 7,896

When the early explorers and fur traders established this post in 1792, the route was marked by Indian trails, not roads. But even with its crude beginning, Portage flourished with the trade of furs, military supplies and wheat brought in through the Fox-Wisconsin waterway. However many years passed before the first permanent settlers located here.

It was a hot, July day in 1837, when Mr. and Mrs. Henry Carpenter moved into Portage. Looking for a place to raise a family and provide themselves with a little income, they decided to build a hotel on the Wisconsin River. A year later, the Carpenters and the rest of the community anxiously watched as the Portage Canal Company begin work on the ill-fated Portage canal. Work on the canal stopped abruptly but only after $10,000 had been spent.

By 1850, 13 years after the Carpenters arrived, the city's population had reached 2,062. During that year an estimated 10,000 persons, their teams and stock, portaged the Wisconsin River here. The town was officially incorporated in April, 1854, taking its name from its important crossing point.

Thirty years after the Carpenters moved to Portage, government engineers finally completed the 75-foot-wide, two-and-a-half-mile long, Portage canal project. However, after the canal opened to large boat traffic in 1876, the continuing cost of dredging to maintain a large enough channel in the shallow Wisconsin River proved prohibitive. That problem, along with increased competition from an improved railroad network, caused river shipments to wane. Finally, in 1951, the Portage canal was closed. It remains a "stagnant reminder of the past."

MARQUETTE COUNTY, Pop. 11,672

About the time that the Military Road was finished, Marquette County was formed from Brown county. The first of seven county seats was in the town of Marquette, which shared the county's name, chosen in honor of Jacques Marquette, the French Jesuit explorer who passed through this region in 1673.

The Fox River runs through this county from north to south, widening out near the town of Packwaukee to create Buffalo Lake. The lake covers more than 14 miles of the county and once provided hundreds of Winnebago and Menominee Indians with ample supplies of wild rice and game.

The first permanent settlers in Marquette County were H.F. Owen and J.I. O'Blanis who came to Buffalo in 1848.

ENDEAVOR, Pop. 335

Endeavor began in 1890 as the site of Reverend R. L. Cheney's revival camp. Cheney later decided the camp was the ideal location for a Christian Endeavor Academy and built Cheney Hall on a hill overlooking the roadway. The town and the academy grew together. In its 23 years, Cheney Hall graduated missionaries, pastors, teachers and businessmen. The academy was removed in 1913 and today Cheney Hall (now called Logan Hall) houses the town's grade and high school.

PACKWAUKEE, Pop. 998

John Noyes made the first government land entry in the county in this little village on May 11, 1836. For several years in the late 1800's, Packwaukee promised to become the chief business point of the county, due to its location on the Fox River and the Wisconsin Central Railroad. It was the only town with river and railroad communications and it also served as a major shipping and exchange center. Little remains today of this once bustling town.

The town was named for a friendly Winnebago chieftain.

WESTFIELD, Pop. 1,033

In the late 1800's, Westfield was just a small, unincorporated town of about 400 people. However the town's location in the center of a large agricultural district and position on the Wisconsin Central Railroad line soon made it a large shipping point for produce and stock.

The earliest settlers came here in 1849 from Westfield, N.Y., hence the town's name. Robert Cochrane and his brother built the town's first house; a log structure 16X24 feet on the banks of Duck Creek where they boarded 15 mill hands and kept a hotel. Robert was later appointed postmaster, and, H.B. became one of the town's first three supervisors when it was organized in 1854.

WAUSHARA COUNTY, Pop. 18,526

When French explorers first came to this region it was occupied by Mascouten and Winnebago Indians. The name Waushara reportedly comes from a Winnebago chief known as Big Fox whose name was later corrupted to Waushara, which meant "foxes."

As the Winnebago and Mascouten moved south, the Menominee tribes took over and controlled all of Waushara County by government mandate until 1848. No white settlement was allowed. Then, October 18, 1848, the Indians signed a treaty at Lake Poygan, ceding the county's land to the U.S. White settlers soon came here and two Mexican war veterans, Isaac and William Warwick, made the first claim.

The Warwicks came to the town of Marion in September, 1848, and erected a log shanty eight feet by ten feet, covering it with sod. Isaac later drove two yokes of oxen into Stevens Point where he obtained lumber for a more substantial dwelling.

Angered by their arrival in Marion, the Indian Agent and Menominee chief ordered the Warwicks to leave. Before they could leave, however, the chief rescinded his order in exchange for the Warwicks breaking up some of his land so he could more easily plant a field of corn.

Things went smoothly after that and by 1855, four years after Waushara was officially organized, the county population had reached 5,541, including many settlers from New York. By 1860, several foreign nationalities were present, with Germans the most prevalent.

PHYSICAL FEATURES

The eastern section of Waushara County has a very fertile soil, and by 1860 contained 135,702 acres of farm land, with

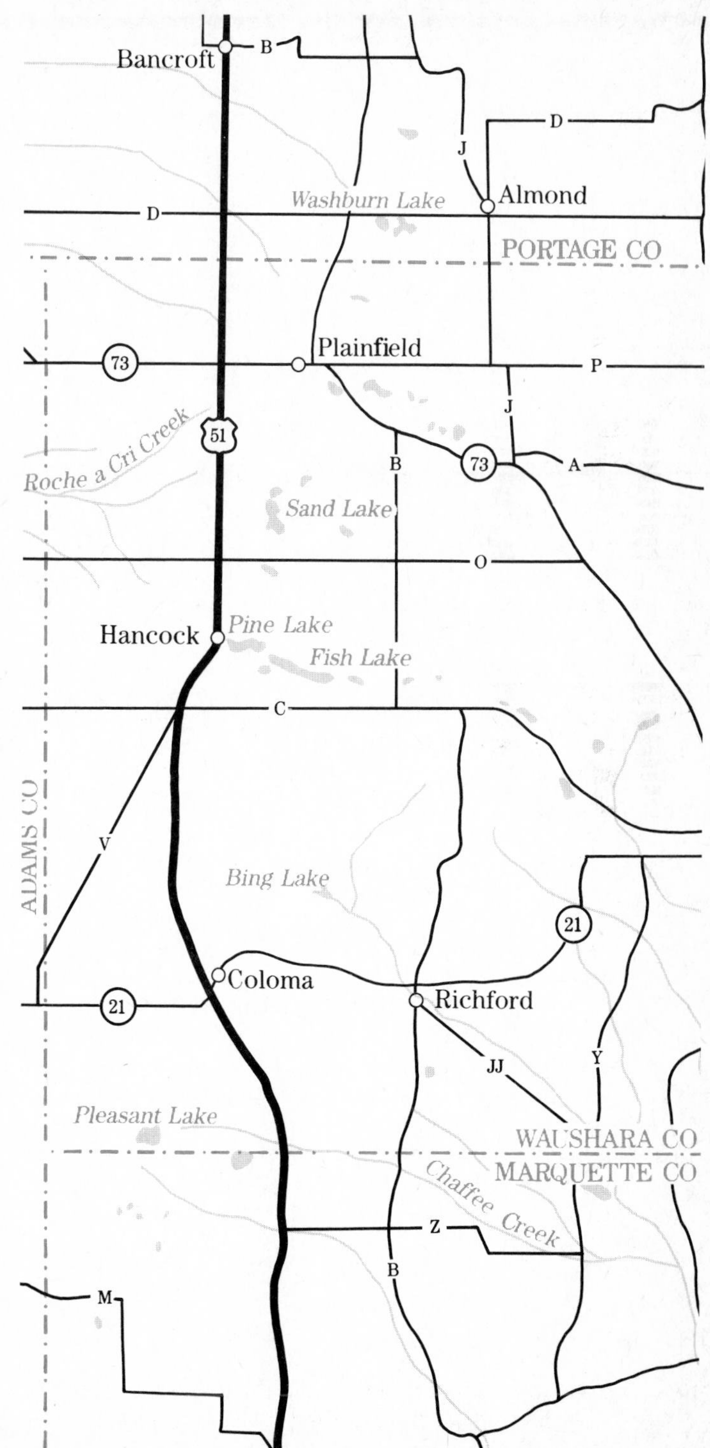

SHSW

Cranberry Pickers west of Junction City, 1887.

wheat and Indian corn ranking highest in production. By the turn of the century, farm acreage increased to 373,842 acres and crops included wheat, barley, rye and buckwheat. Parts of the county also proved perfect for growing shiny, red cranberries, a tart fruit which was a staple in the Indian diet. They also used the brightly colored cranberry juice as a medicine and a dye. In 1850, white settlers in Berlin, Wisconsin were the first in the U.S. to develop the cranberry crop commercially.

COLOMA, Pop. 367

This tiny village, named after the California town where gold was discovered, was officially organized in 1858 as Coloma Station. In 1877, the Wisconsin Central Railroad whistled its way through the village, becoming the first rail company in the county. (For more about Coloma see Route 51 on page 95)

HANCOCK, Pop. 419

The village of Hancock was originally called Sylvester after the first settler who erected a small house here in 1850. Years later the house was used as a hotel and tavern.

PLAINFIELD, Pop. 813

An early thriving town, Plainfield was also on the Wisconsin Central Railroad line. The first settler, William Kelley, came into the village in 1848 when it was known as Norwich.

Four years later E.C. Waterman moved into town and erected a 16X12 shanty to be used as a house and hotel. Waterman then laid out the village, offering free lots to any settler who would promise to live on his land. In 1855, when the post office was established, Waterman became postmaster. He then suggested the village be renamed Plainfield, in honor of his earlier home in Vermont. His original house was later enlarged and became the nucleus of the Plainfield House which later burned and is now the site of a bowling alley.

PORTAGE COUNTY, Pop. 57,420

In its early years, Portage county was closely tied to the lumber industry. In fact, the first log driving on the Wisconsin River occurred in 1828, when lumber from a Portage County island was driven 50 miles south to be used to build Fort Winnebago at Portage.

The lumbering business actually began in 1831 when Daniel Whitney, from Green Bay, obtained a permit from the War

Department which controlled such operations, and built a saw mill at Whitney's Rapids, below Point Bas. Five years later, a second mill was built at Grignon's Rapids. The Menominee Indians complained vigorously to government agents about the mills until they signed a treaty in 1836 at Cedar Point, ceding Indian title to a six mile-wide strip of land along the Wisconsin River, from Point Bas 40 miles upstream to what is now Wausau.

The great demand and high price for lumber at points along the lower Wisconsin stimulated business in the northern pineries. Exploring parties immediately went up river and occupied every eligible dam and mill site on the river as far as Big Bull Falls (Wausau) from 1837-39. The fame of the Wisconsin pineries spread far and wide and settlement was rapid. Yet, when nearly all the mill sites were taken, only about 30 persons had actually settled in the county.

The Wallace Rowan family was the first to locate in the original county of Portage (now Columbia County). Rowan settled a quarter section of land near what is now Poynette on June 6, 1836. There he built a double log house and began trading with the Indians. His house, later called the Rowan Inn, was on the Military Road between Prairie du Chien and Fort Howard via Fort Winnebago and became a popular stopover for travelers.

The name Portage was taken from the Indian word Wauona, meaning "where one takes up his canoe and carries it."

BANCROFT, Pop. 200

This little town took its name from a pioneer Methodist pastor, Rev. Warren G. Bancroft, who came here after the Civil War. The village grew chiefly because of the railroad and a post office was established here on May 17, 1876.

Wausau County Historical Society

The Jolley family at Big Bull Falls, 1866.

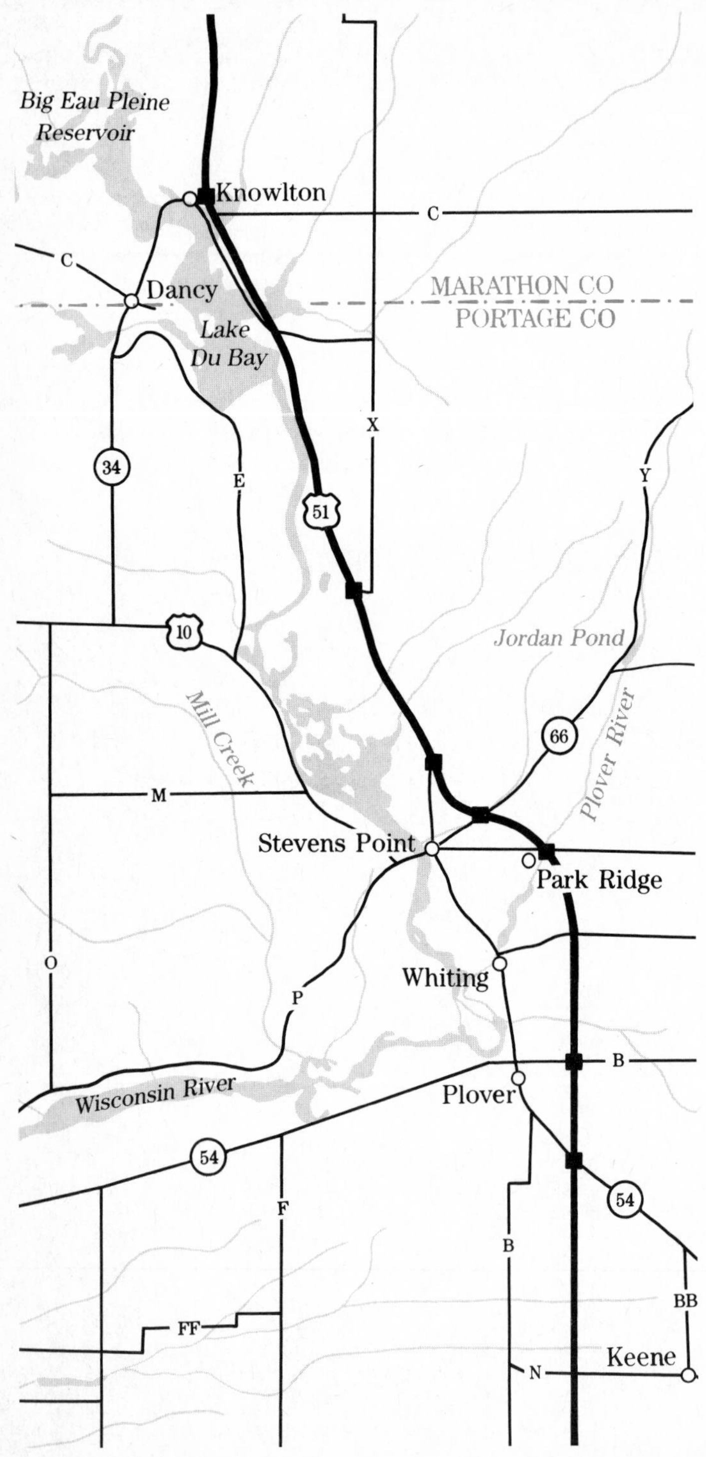

PLOVER, Pop. 5,310

This village was formerly the county seat of Portage and one of the first places settled on the upper Wisconsin River. Originally called Plover Portage, it was here that canoes were taken out of the river and portaged around Conant's Rapids or across the county to the Wolf River on the east or the Black River on the west.

Although located nearly a mile from the river, the town was on the route between the Grand Rapids and the eastern bend of the river, where the Little Plover entered, and its tavern was a popular stop. Moses M. Strong laid the village in 1846. It was so level and handsomely plotted that by the summer of 1857 not a house could be rented in town. Plover declined when the county seat was moved but prospered again when the railroads moved in and the country filled with farms.

S.D. Clark manufactured syrup from sorghum in town. Clark started his business in 1880 and made 700 gallons of syrup that first year. In 1881, he collected 3,000 gallons. Farmers brought in cane for the syrup from up to 15 miles away and averaged about $37 per acre for their crop. The syrup retailed for 50 cents per gallon.

STEVENS POINT, Pop. 22,970

Andrew Mullarkey, an immigrant from County Connaught, Ireland, was the first man to record a land entry in the future city of Stevens Point, but the honor of the town's name went to George Stevens. In 1839, Stevens used the point of the peninsula on the Wisconsin River, at the foot of modern Main Street, to launch supply canoes for his journeys north to Big Bull Falls (Wausau). In 1840 he built a saw mill at that point, a logical place for a lumbering center to develop. Located at the end of a waterway filled with innumerable falls and rapids of white water and at the foot of more than 20 miles of smooth, navigable water, Stevens Point soon became known as the Gateway to the Pineries.

By 1856, 40 wagon loads of goods were arriving at Stevens Point every day. River pilots were then Kings of the River and wages ran from $5 to $15 a day. Stevens Point was the principal depot of the lumbering trade for the Upper Wisconsin and sources show that by 1858 100,000,000 board feet of lumber "slid through the sluice-way of the Shaurette dam at Stevens Point on its way down river". Isaac Ferris, memorable river pilot king, died in 1862 and was buried on the river's west bank opposite the Whiting-Plover Paper Company.

The Point's public square has played an important part in the city's development as a trade center. Deeded to the village in 1847 by Mathias Mitchell, it served as a remembrance of his New England heritage. Great open markets were held there monthly by farmers with record potato crops to sell. As late as 1950, potatoes still accounted for 50 percent of Portage County's crop income.

Railroads also had an influential impact on business in Point. In November, 1871, the first train of railroad cars came into Stevens Point from Menasha with Daniel Phelps as engineer. A throng of people greeted them at the depot shouting, "Hurrah for the cars of progress." With repair shops that employed 170 men, the Wisconsin Central was the most important industry in the city for almost 30 years.

FIRST COUNTY DOCTOR

Dr. John Phillips held office in his house in Stevens Point and made calls by horseback or snowshoes. He competed with Grandma and her doctor book as well as the traveling quack. Accidents were numerous, especially on the river, and by necessity, the pioneer physician amputated crushed feet, set broken bones, and performed emergency operations in his office or on the patient's kitchen table. After the railroad came, surgical cases were often transported to Fond du Lac—on a mattress in the baggage car.

PARK RIDGE, Pop. 643

Aptly named after the ridge that follows the west bank of the historic Plover River, Park Ridge incorporated on January 25, 1838, at an election in what was later known as Viertel's Garage. The village apparently wanted to call itself Plover Hills as the document of incorporation was written with this name throughout. Later it was scratched out in ink to make the village Park Ridge, then spelled as one word, Parkridge.

MARATHON COUNTY, Pop. 111,270

As early as 1836, the year Wisconsin became a Territory, the Menominee Indians, with treaty rights to this section of land, complained that the white men were lumbering here. Consequently, President Andrew Jackson sent Territorial Governor Henry Dodge to investigate the situation and negotiate with Chief Oshkosh. As a result of these negotiations, the U.S. government purchased a strip of land from the Indians, three miles wide on both sides of the Wisconsin River and as far north as Wausau, extending 48 miles into Indian country.

Marathon County developed slowly at first, partly because much of its land was better suited to lumbering than to agriculture, but largely because of difficulties communicating with the settled, southern part of the state.

In 1850 this county was set off from the northern part of Portage County by legislative act and named for a Greek battlefield called Marathon. Wausau was, and still is, its county seat.

In square miles, Marathon is the largest county in Wisconsin. Located in the only hilly section of central Wisconsin, the county is drained by the Wisconsin River, whose chief tributaries are the Eau Pleine, Little Eau Pleine, Rib and Eau Claire rivers.

In its earliest days, Marathon County was covered by a large stand of virgin timber which attracted great lumbering interests. George Stevens came to what is now Wausau in 1837 or 38 and erected a saw mill and dam one year later. Not long after, other lumbermen came to the region and established themselves wherever they could make use of the rivers' waterpower for their mills. Supplies for the lumber camps came primarily from Galena, Illinois and were transported via the Wisconsin and Mississippi rivers. A sled road cut between Wausau and Stevens Point was the only means of overland transportation until the South Line and Wausau Plank Road Company was organized in 1855.

Portage County Historical Society

Market day at Stevens Point public square, ca. 1900.

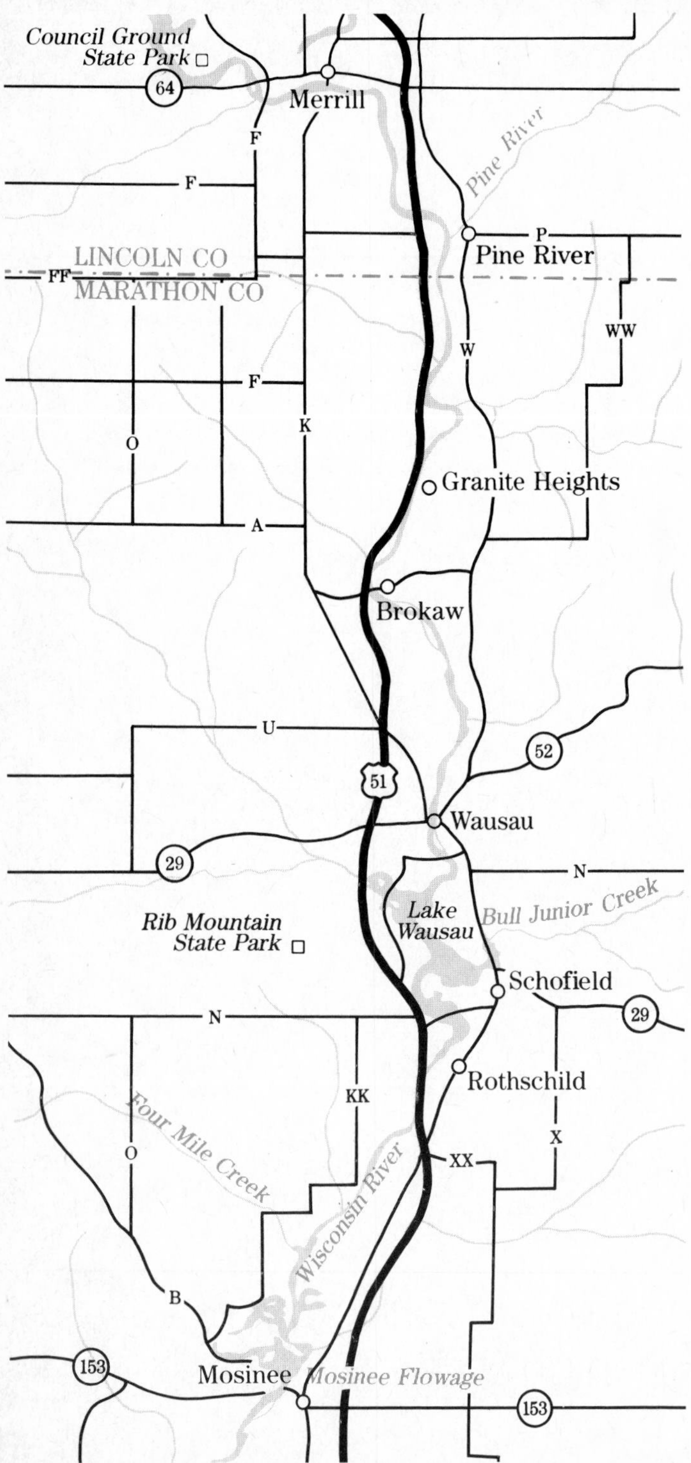

MOSINEE, Pop. 3,015

Mosinee is located at the head of slack water above Stevens Point at what is called Little Bull Falls. As early as 1836, area explorers chose that name for the Falls because the swift rapids sounded much like the gentle lowing of a bull. Sometime later, Postmaster Truman Keeler objected to the name for the town because he thought it was vulgar for ladies to write it on their letters. A trapper named Connor renamed the town in honor of Old Chief Mosinee and the citizens approved.

Winnebago Indians lived here when the town was organized in 1856. Mozinee meant "cold land" to them. However, in 1857, when the first white settlers came, Chippewa Indians were living here in great numbers and their meaning for Mozinee was "moose."

The Mosinee Paper Company on the Wisconsin River is the town's main employer today.

ROTHSCHILD, Pop. 3,338

An early historic account traces the village's beginning to 1909 when a group of Wausau businessmen built a pulp and paper mill here on the Wisconsin River. The Weyerhaeuser Paper Company is located here now and employs approximately 500 people.

In the early days of Rothschild, a man living alone in an old shack here was commonly referred to as the Baron de Rothschild. Rumor had it that he was a member of the Rothschild family who had run away to be alone in the wilderness. Supposedly, the town was named after him.

SCHOFIELD, Pop. 2,226

Known as Eau Claire in the mid-1840's, the town's earliest known settler was John Du Bay who came here to build a saw mill. Dr. William Scholfield came here a few years later from Mineral Point to purchase lumber needed to fence his farm. Captivated with the countryside, Scholfield moved here in 1858, built his own saw mill, laid out the village, erected homes, established a store and several shops to keep the mill in good repair. The village was named in his honor, although the post office later dropped the "l" from the name.

WAUSAU, Pop. 32,426

Platted in 1852 and incorporated ten years later, Wausau had always been seen as a strategic point for capturing business and trade.

In Wausau's earliest days, a band of 800 Chippewas made their living by gathering tree sap from the maple groves just north of Wausau and making it into syrup. The process included the use of birch bark boilers to heat the sap over extremely low fires. Later, more efficient kettles were obtained from agents of the fur companies.

George Stevens, the father of Stevens Point, came to Wausau in 1837 and two years later erected a saw mill and dam. Not long afterwards, other lumbermen came to the region and established mills wherever they could take full advantage of the waterpower from the Wisconsin River. At one time, Wausau had 14 saw mills in operation within the city limits.

In the fall of 1881, the river rose to a dangerous height due to an unusually heavy rainfall. During the night of September 29, more than 500 men in teams worked to weight down the guard lock with rocks and fill it in on the east end. Then, at three a.m. on September 30, the upper boom on the river gave way. Some 60,000,000 feet of logs crashed down upon the jamb piers by the lower divide. Proving equal to the emergency, however, the piers withstood the awful pressure that piled the logs 25 feet high along the solid bed of the river. By noon, water 15 inches above the low water mark rushed over the west end of the guard lock and cut away the track of the Lake Shore. Railroad bridge foundations were washed out, delaying trains up river by as much as two weeks. Mills and houses were submerged and the stone dam completely carried away. The roar of the rushing waters could be heard for miles and the sight at Big Bull Falls of the hurling, tossing timbers crashing into the foam-crested waves was a spectacle never seen again.

These same falls were responsible for the early name of the town, Big Bull Falls. As it became more settled, residents selected the Chippewa Indian word Wausau, which meant "far away."

Wausau Historical Society

Wausau, 1865. Covered bridge over Big Bull Falls.

Wausau Historical Society

Old Ladies Knitting Club, 1880-90.

RIB MOUNTAIN STATE PARK

When Marathon County was established just a few trees topped Rib Mountain and you could only get to the top by climbing hand over hand. Today, thanks to reforestation and an active Kiwanis Club, Rib Mountain is a beautiful state park located four miles south of the junctions of highway 51 and 29.

Its hard quartzite rock enables Rib Mountain to survive as one of the world's oldest "mountains". Spectacular vistas from a 60-foot observation tower, long hiking trails marked with interesting geological information, several wooded campsites, and a good downhill ski area make this one of Wisconsin's most popular parks.

BROKAW, Pop. 298

Brokaw, a small village incorporated in 1906, is located just off highway 51 on County WW and was previously a part of the township of Texas.

Brokaw's importance centered around a dam built in 1880-81 at a cost of $100,000. The dam was erected at this spot across the Wisconsin River to produce slack water which would facilitate the dividing of logs for the Wausau mills and points below. Without the dam, the current was too swift to divide the logs.

By 1899, Brokaw owed its existence largely to the Wausau Paper Mill Company. Although many of the workers lived in Wausau and took a special Chicago, Milwaukee & St. Paul train, called the Scud to the mill, a larger majority lived in Brokaw in houses built by the company. The paper mill erected a clubhouse and church specifically for its employees. Brokaw is still a company town with no services of any kind available in the village.

Martin Hobart is considered the first farm settler though he was mainly a logger by trade. A strong influx of German immigrants came to Brokaw after 1870 and still remain the backbone of this town.

SHSW

View of Rib Mountain from the Wisconsin River, 1920. Photo/W.I La Certe

LINCOLN COUNTY, Pop. 26,311

Established out of a part of Marathon County in 1874, this county was named in honor of President Abraham Lincoln.

Lakes, several hundred in number,take up more than one-half of Lincoln County. The lakes of the Lac du Flambeau Indian Reservation form the headwaters of the Wisconsin River, which flows south into the mighty Mississippi. All that waterpower made possible the county's first and most important industry—logging.

One of Lincoln County's most unique features is its courthouse in Merrill. The land was purchased in 1900, ground broken in 1901, and the building completed in 1902 following widespread labor trouble from the industries furnishing the building materials. Total cost was $119,882. Built in colonial style, the ground dimensions are 98X125 and the tower is 156 feet tall. Entrances open into a beautiful rotunda, 32 feet in diameter with a height from floor to roof of 50 feet. The handsome tile floor is laid out in an exquisite mosaic design. The courthouse is easily visible as you pass over the highway 51 bridge into town.

MERRILL, Pop. 9,578

The history of Merrill as a settlement began in 1847 when Andrew Warren began construction of a dam across the Wisconsin River here. O.B. Smith, one of the men responsible for building the dam, walked all the way from Chicago to Wausau with a party of 13 since no railroads traveled north of Chicago.

Ten years later, in 1857, Warren invested heavily in what was called the "Horicon" railway scheme. The plan was for a railroad to run from Milwaukee via Horicon and Berlin through to Merrill. Like a great many others, Warren permitted his interest in Merrill's future to overcome his prudence. Mortgaging his interest in the mill, he turned the proceeds over to the railroad's promoters. The railroad scheme proved a fiasco; the stock was all sold and paid for in the East but the road never came through. Farmers along the proposed right-of-way had mortgaged their land also. Titles to such properties were affected for years afterwards. With the collapse of the project, Warren returned to Illinois. Nothing further is known of him.

In the meantime, the name of this settlement went through a series of changes. Originally Warren had christened the rapids on the dam site Jenny Bull's Falls. This was later changed to Jenny Falls and soon after to simply, Jenny. Finally in 1883, the town incorporated and was renamed Merrill, in honor of S.S. Merrill, the general manager of the Chicago, Milwaukee & St. Paul railroad.

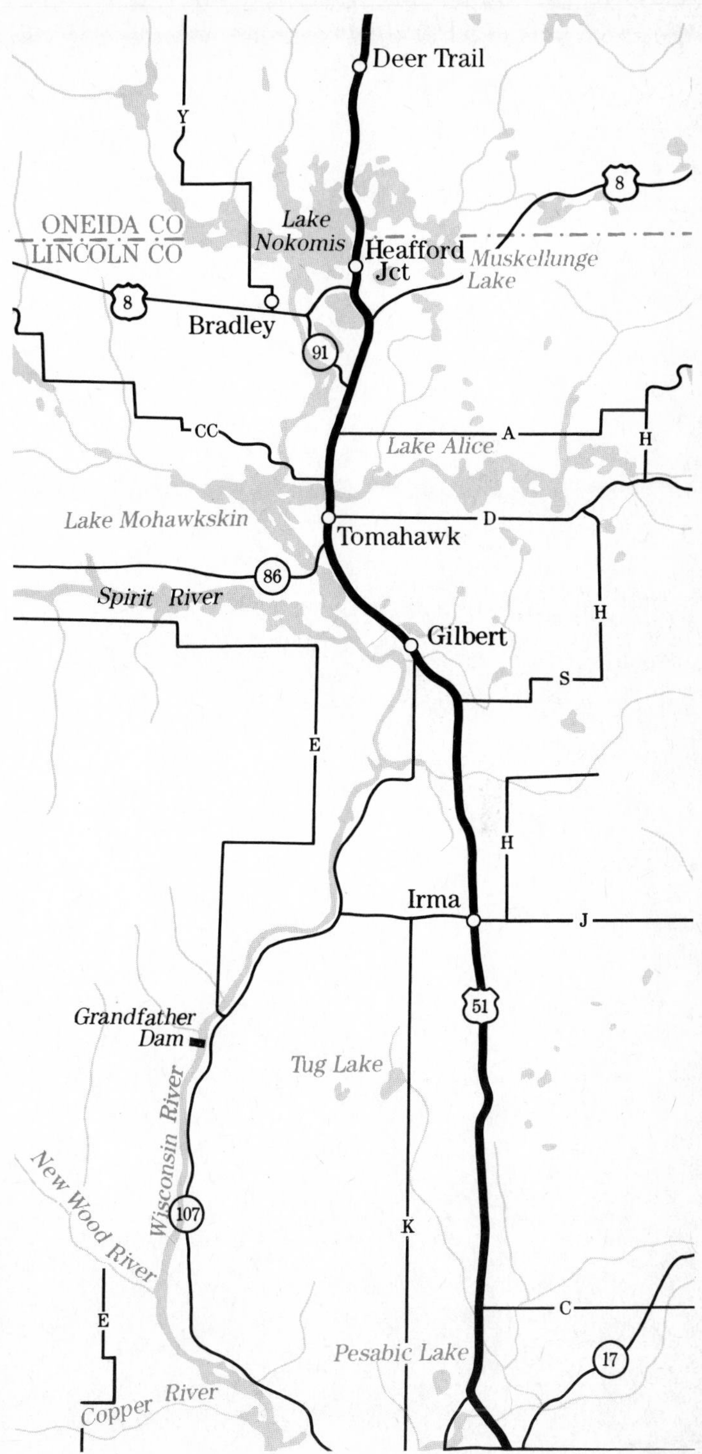

Merrill is situated at the confluence of the Wisconsin and Prairie rivers; its streams divide the town into three major portions.

IRMA

C. C. Munro and his family came to Irma in 1881 to homestead. Standing on the main street, all that they saw was a dense forest. Thinking it a good way to make a living in this new land, Munro built a saw mill so that new settlers could build their cabins with lumber instead of logs.

Officially laid out in 1887 as Courtland, this town on the Chicago, Milwaukee & St. Paul railroad was later named Irma, in honor of the depot agent's daughter.

SHSW

Irma, 1900.

TOMAHAWK, Pop. 3,527

The village of Tomahawk developed slowly. Prior to 1886, this area was practically wilderness, the sole mark of civilization being a tavern kept by Germaine Bouchard on the north side of the Wisconsin River and the west side of the Tomahawk. Bouchard had owned this land since 1858 and also operated a ferry here. Indians favored this site for hunting and named it Tomahawk.

In 1886, as a result of the Tomahawk Land and Boom Company, the town started to grow. The company laid out the site for the city in Spring, 1887; on September 15, 1887, the tracks of the Wisconsin Valley division of the Chicago Milwaukee & St.Paul Railroad reached Tomahawk, and the first train came into town on October 8. Saw mills and other industries sprang up at once, and by 1890 the population had risen to 1,816. A year later Tomahawk incorporated with 2,000 residents.

HEAFFORD JCT.

This town has been primarily a railway junction since the Soo Line ran its first train through town in 1885. Tracks were later laid for the Marinette, Tomahawk & Western railroad from just near Heafford to Tomahawk. This line was meant to join the Grand Trunk railway but the financier died and the project was never completed.

The Chicago, Milwaukee and St. Paul railroad came through here in 1890 and the town was subsequently named after its first depot agent.

SHSW

The Chicago, Milwaukee & St. Paul Railroad reached Tomahawk in 1887.

ONEIDA COUNTY, Pop. 31,216

Like most counties in northern Wisconsin, Oneida developed primarily because of the lumber industry. It was lumbermen who cleared the primeval forest which covered most of this vast territory and eventually opened it for farming.

The first logging north of the Tomahawk River was done at Rhinelander, in Winter, 1857-58. The heaviest stand of white and Norway pine lay just north of here in a belt 18 miles wide and 40 miles long, estimated to contain nearly 700 million feet of pine and 300 million feet of hemlock. In addition, a large tract of birch, birdseye maple and curly maple lay just 12 miles northeast of Rhinelander and was an excellent inducement for hardwood mills. In later years, a stand of more than 50,000 acres of spruce attracted the attention of pulp and paper making industries.

The lumber boom began, appropriately, on New Years Day, 1858, when a crew from Helms & Company in Stevens Point cut out the first tote road from Grandfather Bull's Falls to Eagle Lake on the Eagle River. That winter they banked 20,000 logs at Eagle Lake and drove them to Mosinee to be sawed. With each season, the work gathered momentum until about 20 camps were procuring supplies at Rhinelander in Winter, 1885-86. In the Eagle River district the cut was estimated at 58 million feet. By 1908, the great northern pineries were all but depleted and by 1931 less than 15 percent of the logs and lumber used in Oneida County came from within its borders.

Oneida County took its name from an Indian word meaning "granite people", and was officially formed in January, 1887. The population was 5,010, with 3,665 native-born and 1,345 foreigners, primarily Canadians and Scandinavians.

HAZELHURST, Pop. 780

Hazelhurst is located on the west shore of Lake Katherine, one of the most beautiful bodies of water in this lake region and a tributary to the Big Tomahawk Lake. As with most of these northern Wisconsin towns, Hazelhurst owes its origin to the lumber industry. For 20 years it was the home of the Yawkey-Lee Lumber Company Yawkey-Lee brought many lumberjacks and mill men here in 1887 and by 1900 the town's population reached 1,052. Mrs. Yawkey reportedly named the town, choosing it because "hurst" was an old Saxon term for thicket and she was impressed with the many clumps of hazel brush growing in the village.

MINOCQUA, Pop. 3,328

Surrounded by a chain of five lakes, Minocqua was famous for its beauty. It was built on what would have been an island except for a narrow belt of land at the eastern point con-

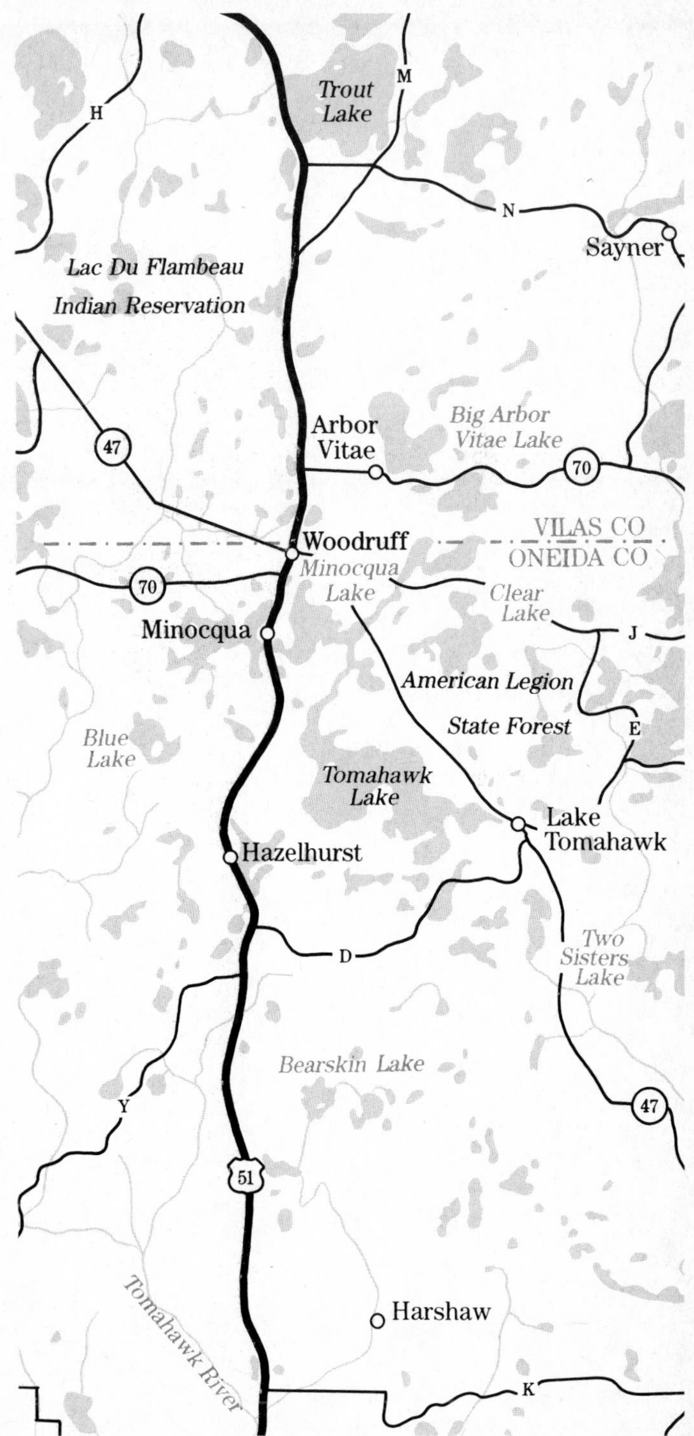

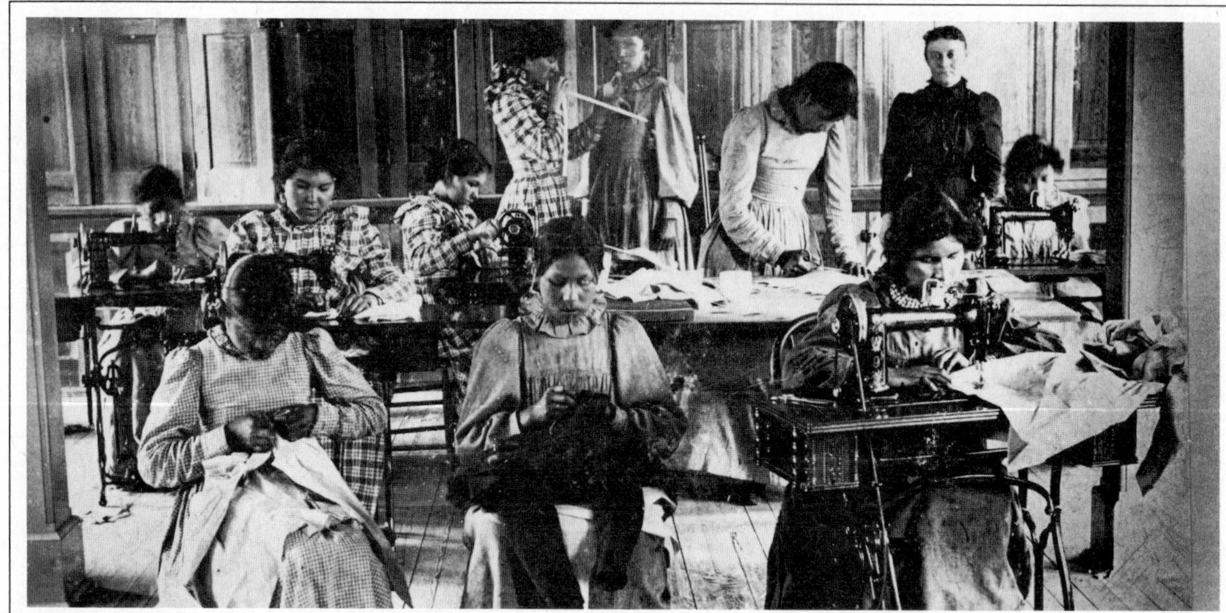

SHSW

Sewing class at Lac du Flambeau school for Indian children, 1895.

necting it to the mainland and was situated on the Chicago, Milwaukee & St. Paul railroad line.

The Flambeau Trail, which was cut through here during the Civil War, connected the head of Tomahawk Lake with the Military Road from Milwaukee to Ontonagon on Lake Superior. The region had always been a great hunting and trapping ground and John Jacob Astor who later built Fort Winnebago established a trading post along this route.

In the spring of 1888, Captain S.W. Ray arrived in the village and found a number of Sioux Indians living in eight wigwams and a small log hut on the present site of St. Patrick's Church. Their chief was called Noc Wib. Settlers in town called him Chief Minocqua, and soon the village became known as Minocqua. The Indian name has two meanings, "noon-day rest" and "good woman."

Fur trapping and lumbering, the biggest commercial ventures in the area, were followed by farming until the mid-30's. Forests now cover almost 80 percent of the Minocqua area and today it is best known as a vacation and recreation spot.

WOODRUFF, Pop. 1,458

This village on the banks of Mud Lake, sometimes called Snake Lake, began in 1888 as the homestead of Antoine Toussaint.

The town's name came out of the early lumber camps located at Three Lakes and Eagle River and operated by the Woodruff-Macquire Company When the Chicago and Northwestern Railroad company was building its line north, they established a terminal near Muskonegan Creek to unload supplies. The railroad men used the phrase, "for Woodruff," and the village later adopted the name.

LAC DU FLAMBEAU INDIAN RESERVATION

French for "lake of the flaming torches," this land was given to individual Indians under the General Allotment Act of 1887. However, the government held the reservation in trust for 25 years, permitting outsiders to log off timber and depriving its Indian owners of the only valuable property they had. By 1914, when lumbering had ceased, the Indians were left unemployed on denuded land. Eventually each Indian received a small tract, virtually worthless for farming and not large enough for grazing or forestry. Studies made by the National Resources Board show that about 32 percent of the reservation's 70,000 acres are swamplands. The land on the reservation is very sandy but is good for clover and potatoes.

Most of the Indians have been allotted 80 acres and the present generation of Lac du Flambeaus are small house holders. While some of them cultivate gardens, many are not interested in more extensive farming, preferring to earn seven dollars a day as guides to summer tourists. The Indians today also make articles from birch bark and buckskin.

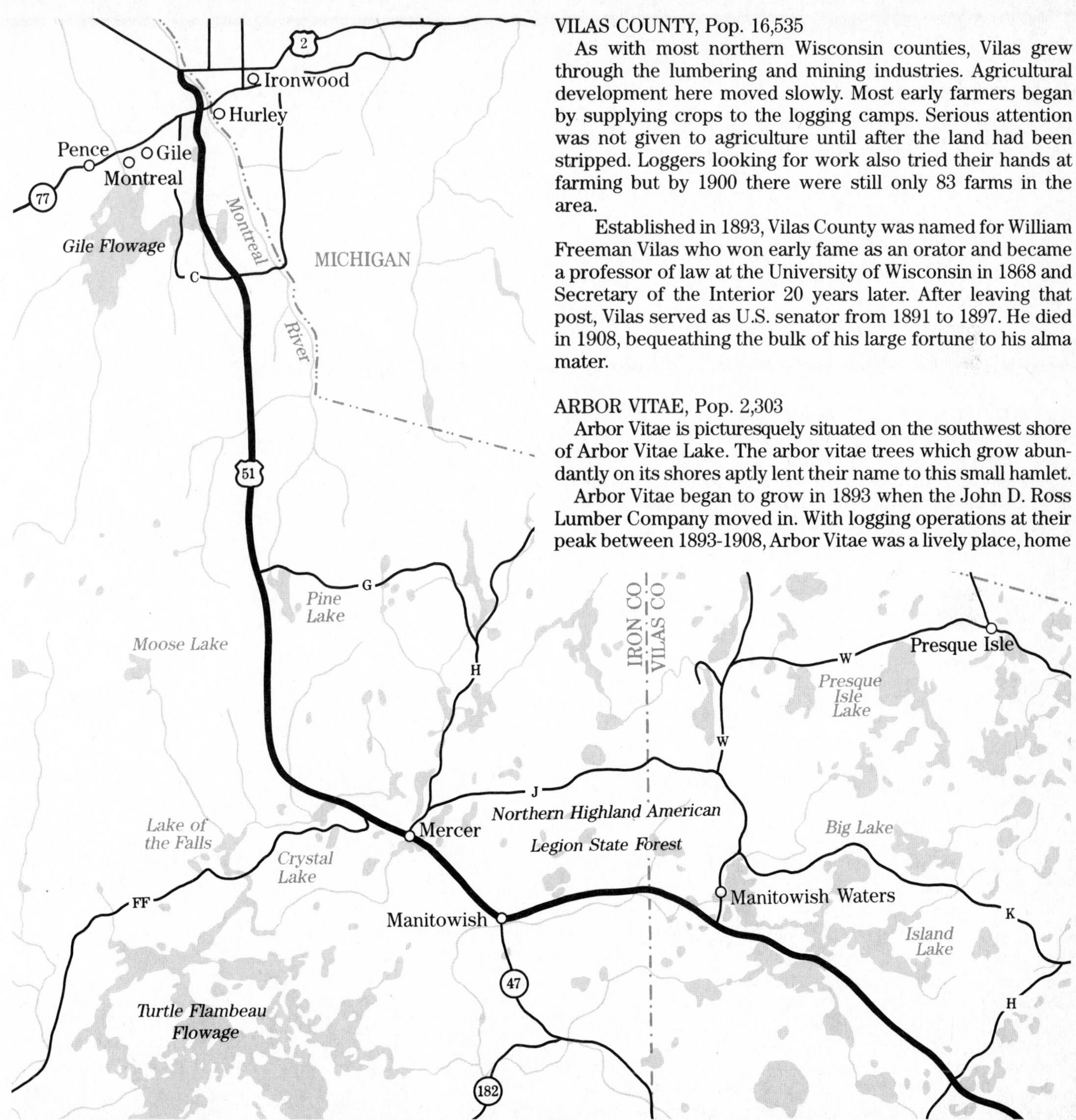

VILAS COUNTY, Pop. 16,535

As with most northern Wisconsin counties, Vilas grew through the lumbering and mining industries. Agricultural development here moved slowly. Most early farmers began by supplying crops to the logging camps. Serious attention was not given to agriculture until after the land had been stripped. Loggers looking for work also tried their hands at farming but by 1900 there were still only 83 farms in the area.

Established in 1893, Vilas County was named for William Freeman Vilas who won early fame as an orator and became a professor of law at the University of Wisconsin in 1868 and Secretary of the Interior 20 years later. After leaving that post, Vilas served as U.S. senator from 1891 to 1897. He died in 1908, bequeathing the bulk of his large fortune to his alma mater.

ARBOR VITAE, Pop. 2,303

Arbor Vitae is picturesquely situated on the southwest shore of Arbor Vitae Lake. The arbor vitae trees which grow abundantly on its shores aptly lent their name to this small hamlet.

Arbor Vitae began to grow in 1893 when the John D. Ross Lumber Company moved in. With logging operations at their peak between 1893-1908, Arbor Vitae was a lively place, home to some 200 families and a total population of over 1,200. The village had a clubhouse for dances, a Young Men's Association, a Woodmen's hall, a ball park and a good general store. The people were happy and loved their small community. They moved with great reluctance when the lumber operations were finished.

MANITOWISH WATERS, Pop. 625

Named in 1939, rather late in the settlement years, Manitowish Waters was originally known as Flambeau, a French word meaning "Torch Lake." The town was within the Indian village of the same name which is now a part of the Lac du Flambeau Indian Reservation.

Like most towns in this region, Flambeau witnessed the restless activities of the lumberman. As a result it had become the center of a great logging operation by 1855. Herrick & Stearns, a Michigan firm, came to town with a government contract to cut Indian timber, organized the Lac du Flambeau Lumber Company, and put in logging gangs, a saw mill and store. Their work kept them quite busy until 1913 when all the lumber was finally cut and they closed their doors forever.

The state legislature removed this township from the Lac du Flambeau area in 1927 and renamed it Spider Lake. In 1939 the name was changed again to Manitowish Waters based on a corruption of a Chippewa word meaning evil spirit.

IRON COUNTY, Pop. 6,730

The years just before the turn-of-the-century were a time of great excitement for Iron County. Logging operations and iron ore discoveries in the Penokee Range gave rise to a boom era of speculation and rapid development. To the earliest residents in the sparsely populated north, it must have seemed that civilization was finally on its way, riding the spur line out from Ashland, carried along in the pay envelopes of hardworking miners and loggers.

But a good mill can require up to ten timbered acres a day to keep operating and it wasn't long before most of the mature stand of pine and much of the hardwood was gone. The ore deposits lasted somewhat longer, but the boom era was over long before the last mine finally closed. Though the ore cars groaned over the tracks to Ashland and the hewn timber choked the streams in springtime, little profit was left behind in Iron County. A few got rich, but none who lived here.

Success was often measured in small bushels: one remotely situated farmer reportedly spent two and one half days carrying his crop to market—a lumber camp. His year's crop was 30 bushel of potatoes, for which he received 35 cents a bushel. In 1854 and 1858, the federal government offered subsidies to farmers who settled for cheap land, hoping this would open the north for settlement.

At the turn of the century, a state forester reported on conditions left behind by the logging operations. "Of over 17 million acres of timber in the northern counties, 8 million were cut-over lands, largely burned over and waste brush; one-half of it as nearly desert as can be in the climate of Wisconsin."

MINING ON THE RANGE

The railroad reached the city of Ashland by 1880, about the same time the mining boom began to take shape on the Penokee/Gogebic Range. The first mining machinery was brought to Iron County overland by the Hayes brothers who began a mining site on the Montreal River, later called the Germania Mine.

The ore mined out of the Penokee Range was of a very high grade, containing up to 66 percent iron ore. It came out of two types of rock; soft rock referred to as "dirt" mining, and hard rock, called simply "rock", which required a different technique of drilling and blasting. Hard rock mining paid better because the danger of contracting emphysema or silicosis was very high.

The vast Mesabi Range in Minnesota was discovered in 1890 and was outproducing both the Gogebic and Penokee sources by the turn-of-the-century. The lower grade ore was easier to mine by the strip method and the sheer quantity of the Mesabi deposits soon made it the nation's foremost iron producing area.

The mines and the logging industry created a demand for small truck farming operations, forming the nucleus for agriculture in the county, but it wasn't until after 1910 that farming the cut-over stumpland became popular.

Mining operations continued at normal output until the 1960's, when several of the major mines shut down. The high costs of mining the ore as well as competition from foreign and domestic sources, made it impossible for the Penokee Range mines to survive. The last to close was the Carey mine in 1965.

WATER RESOURCES

The continental divide lies a few miles south of the Penokee Range. North of the divide lies the watershed of the Great Lakes. To the south, rain and melting snow force the waters to flow into the Mississippi River. The Lake Superior watershed is drained principally by the Potato and Tyler Fork rivers, which flow into the Bad River and the Montreal River and then directly into Lake Superior. The North Fork of the Flambeau River drains most of the Mississippi watershed in

Iron County. The southeast portion of the county is included in the Wisconsin Highland Lake District which has as many lakes per square mile as any place on earth.

MANITOWISH

The Indians believed there were evil spirits in the waters here and thus the name Manitowish, meaning "evil spirit."

MERCER, Pop. 1,425

An early lumberman, Dan Shea, was sent here by the Brooks and Ross Lumber Company of Merrill to build a dam and start logging operations. Two tote roads were built and settlers slowly moved into the area as logs were moved out. The town was later named after John Mercer, one of northern Wisconsin's earlier prominent timbermen.

HURLEY, Pop. 2,015

The legendary town of Hurley grew up in the days of the early loggers and miners. It is reportedly named for Judge M.A. Hurley, a Wausau lawyer who owned a prominent iron ore mine.

In 1886, crowded with loggers and miners of every character and nationality, Hurley reeled with a spirit we now appreciate only in the movies. Released from their grueling work in the mines, the men swept down on Hurley in the hundreds, determined to get drunk and raise a little hell. With men and money on the loose, gambling, vice and saloons (65 on Silver Street alone), made a quick and profitable appearance. In 1919, Michigan's prohibition laws resulted in even more business. Hurley soon gained a national reputation for drinking, gambling, prostitution and frequent law violations.

Through it all, a few strong men, like Robert Burton, matched their enthusiasm for the future of the iron range with a desire to see Hurley become a thriving metropolis of the north. Burton moved Hurley toward that goal by building the palacial $100,000 Burton Hotel in 1886. It was a grand structure; four stories high, with a huge ballroom, 96 guest rooms, carved panelled bar and fresh flowers on every dining room table.

Unfortunately, hard times in 1897 forced Burton to trade his hotel to Myron Ross of Chicago, a former mail carrier who gave three million cancelled postage stamps for the hotel. The trade shocked the town and the hotel never regained its original stature. Rundown for lack of use and maintenance, it soon became a rooming house and later a warehouse for the Badger Distillery.

Finally, on the morning of February 2, 1947, fate dealt the Burton House its last blow. A fire swept through the once-fabulous "House of a Thousand Windows", and Burton House was reduced to a memory of a bygone era.

SHSW

Tobacco farmer nearly hidden by his crop. Hurley, 1895.

U.S. 45 runs 145 miles from the lush, Lake Winnebago countryside in east-central Wisconsin to the densely forested, lake-studded, northern resort area. Here on route 45 at Lac Vieux Desert, you will find the headwaters of the Wisconsin River, a prime waterway in the discovery of the Mississippi and the beginning of Western expansion. This route takes you through Neenah, home of Kimberly, Clark & Co., makers of "Kleenex."

ROUTE 45, OSHKOSH TO LAND O'LAKES

SHSW

Pastoral view of Wisconsin countryside. Photo/Paul Vanderbilt.

WINNEBAGO COUNTY, Pop. 131,732

Fur traders, French explorers and Jesuit missionaries roamed this county for more than 200 years, searching for the rich, fertile Fox River valley and charting their course along the shores of Lake Winnebago. A few settlers were scattered about Winnebago County by 1836, but migration was heaviest in southern Wisconsin where lead was discovered and mined. Four years after the county officially organized in 1846, migration increased rapidly as word got out about this beautiful river country. In one year the county's population increased from 732 to 2,787.

Many early cities sprang up along the waterways and agricultural and manufacturing industries clustered around Lake Winnebago and the Lower Fox River. The cities of Neenah, Menasha, Appleton and Oshkosh became the centers of some of Wisconsin's largest and most successful businesses.

LAKE WINNEBAGO

Lake Winnebago was the first thing named in Wisconsin. An early map referred to it as Lac des Puans, French for "Lake of the Winnebago" or the more unpleasant "stinking water". Father Hennepin may have named it more accurately when he called it Kitchigamie, or "large lake" on his map of 1697. At 28 miles long and ten miles wide, Winnebago is the largest body of fresh water in any one state. It was formed in the early days of the glaciers. Glacial lake sediment known as Glacial Lake Oshkosh once extended from the present shores of Green Bay southward to Lake Winnebago, deposited by impounded meltwater from a retreating glacier. As Green Bay freed itself of ice, Lake Oshkosh spilled northward via the Fox River, eventually emptying into Lake Michigan. After Lake Oshkosh drained, several bodies of water were left behind, including Lake Winnebago. At its maximum level, Glacial Lake Oshkosh stood 65 feet above the present lake.

As the Lower Fox River leaves Winnebago, it breaks into two channels surrounding Doty Island in Neenah. The two channels then descend over ten-foot rapids into Little Lake Butte des Morts, creating Neenah and Menasha's waterpower. Before the railroads, Lake Winnebago was also the link between all settlements along its shores.

WINNEBAGO INDIANS

The first Indian tribe in Wisconsin was the Winnebago, a branch of the Dakota (Sioux) tribe. The Winnebagoes' early village, under the guidance of Chief Four Legs, was located on Doty Island, in the current cities of Neenah and Menasha. When French explorer Jean Nicolet visited Wisconsin in 1634 he referred to these peoples as Gens de mer, or "People of

the Sea." The Algonquin Indians (of which the Fox were a tribe), called them Wennibegouk, or "Men of the Salt Sea."

For a long time, the Winnebagoes ruled all the neighboring Algonquin tribes, but in the early part of the 17th century, an alliance of their subject tribes and two wars with the Illinois Indians almost exterminated the Winnebagoes and they never regained their former power. On August 11, 1827, the Winnebagoes concluded a treaty at the Little Butte des Morts, by which the Winnebago, Menominee and New York Indians ceded their lands in the Fox valley to the United States. Later, in November, 1837, all of the Winnebago lands east of the Mississippi were also ceded to the U.S. by treaty. In 1840, U.S. troops came to Portage to remove the Indians. After being relocated in parts of Iowa, Minnesota and Dakota, they were finally placed on 128,000 acres of the northern part of the Omaha reservation in eastern Nebraska.

OSHKOSH, Pop.49,678

Augustin Grignon and James Porlier established a trading post at the village of Buttes des Morts (then within the Oshkosh limits) in 1818 but most sources cite Webster Stanley and Henry Gallup as the first settlers here in 1836.

Stanley and Gallup were among the settlers who met in George Wright's kitchen on a wintry day in 1840 to discuss the city's future. At that time the area was divided into two parts; Athens on the river's north side, Brooklyn on the south. A majority vote combined both areas into the present city of Oshkosh, an Indian word for "brave" and also the name of the Menominee Indians' chief.

The city incorporated in March of 1853 and became a leading lumber center. Both sides of the Fox River were lined for miles with saw mills, sash, door and blind factories, and manufacturing centers of every kind. The city's public buildings reflected its material prosperity—until a disastrous series of fires began.

A TRAGIC HISTORY

From the beginning, Oshkosh was known as the Northwest's leading lumber center, manufacturing some 100 million feet of lumber per year and over 100 million shingles. But the biggest lumber center also carried the biggest risk of fire.

The first fire occurred in May, 1859, sweeping the main business street, Ferry, for nearly a quarter of a mile. However, the city was rebuilt in less than six months, although it had only a third of its original population. Then on May 9, 1874, a second fire started in the Spalding & Peck lumber yard destroying $50,000 worth of property. Unbelievably, two months later another fire roared over a mile-long district on Upper Main and North Division streets, destroying all buildings and killing the city treasurer. Again, less than a year later, a third fire sprang up in the Morgan Brothers' mill. Assisted by a gale wind, it burned the western portion of the second ward and the southeast portion of the first, destroying the railroad depot, post office, opera house, almost all of the prominent business houses, and 200-300 private residences. At one point, the whole area was in flames at the same time. Sweeping northward, the fire moved just enough to meet the line of the previous burnt-out area and there it was held. The loss included two people dead and a property damage estimated at two and one-half million dollars. In the face of such tragedy, citizens reflected the origin of their town's name and bravely rebuilt.

EDITOR'S NOTE:

Since highway 45 bypasses Neenah, Menasha and Appleton, only brief descriptions will be included here. Please refer to Route 41 for more complete information on these important Fox River valley towns.

NEENAH, Pop. 23,272

While Oshkosh was developing its reputation in lumber, Neenah, to the north, was rapidly becoming the county's biggest paper mill center. Surprisingly, Neenah was once known as Flour City.

When the George H. Mansur family moved into this area, known then as Winnebago Rapids, in August, 1843, they found a ghost town, containing 34 block houses, a saw mill, grist mill, wing dam and canal, blacksmith shop and a wealth of iron, plows, shovels and tools. The deserted town of Winnebago Rapids lay quiet as death along the forest shores of a wide river, tumbling over the Puant rapids from the broad Lake Winnebago into Little Lake Buttes des Morts.

Originally part of a Menominee Indian reservation, the saw and grist mills had been built by the government to be operated by the Indians who often left them unattended as the work was unsuited to their way of life. Without the Indian help, the government was forced to abandon the project. Then in 1838, smallpox wiped out most of the Indians. The survivors soon left the Rapids area and the settlement fell into decay.

Mansur came to town on the heels of this disaster and set to work repairing the old mills which he managed successfully until 1844. The following year Governor Doty built his log house on the island and took up residence here. Settlers continued to pour in to the area and the first village plat of Neenah was recorded on September 8, 1847.

A year later, Harvey L. Kimberly came here from New Haven, Connecticut and entered into partnership with his brother, John. Although the Kimberly name is best associated with Kimberly Clark and the birth of Kleenex, the Kimberlys made the original claim in one of the leading flour mill centers of the West.

The Neenah Flouring Mill was built by the Kimberlys in 1850 from hewn oak timber cut on Lake Winnebago's north shore and hauled to the site over the ice. The Kimberly family owned and operated the mill for 33 years until it was destroyed by fire in 1903.

In 1856, when Winnebago Rapids incorporated as Neenah, four flour mills were operating. Two more (the Falcon Mills) were established in 1856-57 and 11 mills eventually operated at the same time. The last mill was built in 1879.

Neenah might still be known as Flour City but for the thriving town of Minneapolis, Minnesota, which began offering more competitive prices. The flour industry fell off and Neenah soon assumed its current renown as the Paper City. (SEE ROUTE 41)

FOX INDIANS

Fox Indians, upset by the continuing nuisances of white men in 1730, started to demand tribute from all traders who passed the lake. One night, Sieur Pierrie Morand, a fur trader who was losing a lot of business because of this, rounded up 800 volunteers and came to the lake, covering soldiers in his trading canoes as if they were goods. Tricking tribal members to come forward in anticipation of gifts brought for them in the canoes, the hidden soldiers leapt up and slaughtered all who were present. Then, making a detour to the Fox village, the soldiers killed the remaining tribe of men, women and children, in just one hour's time. Lake Butte des Morts is reportedly the common burial ground of the Fox tribe, according to a valley legend.

Indian mounds found in west Menasha were the longest serpent effigies ever discovered. Perhaps the best known burial mound was the one located one and one-half miles west of Little Lake Butte des Morts, and another just west of the old Henry Race farm. The Butte des Morts mound was eight foot high and 50 feet in diameter. It was the great hope of Dr. Increase Lapham, one of Wisconsin's early archeologists, that this mound be preserved for all time. However, in 1863, the Chicago and Northwestern Railroad constructed a bridge across the lake, and the famous Hill of the Dead was used for fill along the railroad embankments. The famous spot is part of Fritze Park in the Town of Menasha.

MENASHA, Pop. 14,728

Although Charles Doty, the Governor's son, was intimately connected with this city from the outset, Curtis Reed is considered the founder of Menasha. Reed was responsible for the development of Menasha which he encouraged all his life. The Menasha Conservator published the following description of Reed: "He is rather indifferent in regard to his personal appearances, is social with his friends, hates a mean man and a mean act intensely, will sacrifice his own fortune for the prosperity of the town, expecting to make it up some future time..." A prime example of Reed's character involved control of Neenah-Menasha's waterpower.

In 1847 Governor Doty successfully lobbied for a legislative act granting him and his associates, Harvey Jones and Harrison and Curtis Reed, permission to dam one channel of the island separating Neenah and Menasha. It was hoped the dam would provide a navigable waterway to Green Bay via the Fox River, encouraging commerce and population. However, to accomplish that, it was necessary to select one of Lake Winnebago's two channels. Curtis Reed and Doty both favored the north channel, Menasha. Harvey Jones preferred Neenah. Both sides fought bitterly for the prize.

A boat was hired to take interested persons to inspect the channels, but the Menasha factions persuaded the captain to favor their interest and he did. When the captain ran along the south channel, or Neenah, "he caused he boat to strike boulders and snags, seemingly imperiling the safety of those on board and demonstrating the dangers of that channel." Returning via Menasha, passengers were treated to smooth sailing. It is unclear whether the final outcome was determined by the boat ride or the financial pressure.

Harvey Jones offered to pay $24,000 to construct the proper dam, ship canal and lock, at no charge to the government. Curtis Reed went further and offered $24,000, plus an extra $5,000 for repairs as necessary. Reed and Menasha won, but ill feelings over this project set the stage for future discord between the cities and they have gone their separate ways ever since.

OUTAGAMIE COUNTY, Pop. 128,726

Situated along the great water highway between Lake Winnebago and Green Bay, Outagamie land consists of rolling uplands and gently sloping valleys. Limestone formations prevail throughout the county; the Fox River's channel is heavily bedded with limestone, causing its very hard water.

Pierre Grignon and Dominick and Paul Ducharme were the first permanent settlers of what is now Outagamie County. They homesteaded in Kaukauna as early as 1790 and the house built by Grignon's son Augustin in 1837 still stands as the state's oldest.

Many Outagamie County settlers came from New York. Germans were most numerous among the foreign nationalities. The greatest influx of settlers came in the 1840's primarily because Lawrence University was established in Appleton.

This area belonged to Brown County when the Wisconsin Territory was organized in 1836, but the Legislature set it off as a separate county called Outagamie in 1852. The name used by Chippewa Indians to refer to the Fox tribe, means "dwellers on the other side of a stream."

Grand Chute was named county seat, but it became a ward of Appleton when that city incorporated in 1857. For that reason, Appleton is now county seat.

SHSW

Looking east from the Menasha public square.

SHSW

Steamer "Cornucopia" loads hides at Hammond Bros. warehouse in Appleton, 1872. Lawrence University on bluff.

Outagamie County was almost destroyed by fire in 1871 when all of northeastern Wisconsin turned into a roaring inferno from the Peshtigo forest fire, the state's worst single disaster. (SEE PAGE 221).

APPLETON, Pop. 128,726

The founding of Lawrence University was the founding of Appleton. The town's original name, Grand Chute, was changed to honor Samuel Appleton, father-in-law of Amos Lawrence, who founded the university. The fine educational institution attracted a thriving settlement. Although Lawrence had wanted the university to be located somewhere along the Fox River, his choice of Appleton drew much speculation.

Except for Kaukauna and Little Chute, Appleton's water-power is greater than that at any other point. Lake Winnebago, Poygan and Butte des Morts which have streams draining a 300-mile territory inland are the sources for this power.

Water of a different sort created Telulah Driving Park in the southeastern section of Appleton. Quite a famous summer resort area once existed here on the south banks of the Fox, thanks to the popularity of the mineral spring.

According to Indian legend, Telulah was a beautiful Fox princess who had two lovers, one she favored, the other favored by her father, a Fox chief. A running contest was held to determine the appropriate suitor. The race started far up river and Telulah awaited the winner at the largest sulphur springs.

Her father's choice won and Telulah was thus betrothed to him. Brokenhearted, she sat weeping beside the spring and was seen there so often that the spring and later the whole park became known as Telulah's Spring.

Appleton was also home to Ehrich Weiss, better known as Harry Houdini, and author Edna Ferber.

GREENVILLE, Pop. 3,310

In April, 1848, John Culbertson of Madison, Indiana, left his home and settled here with his four sons. The countryside was bathed in green and Culbertson honored the town by calling it Greenville.

HORTONVILLE, Pop.2,016

Hortonville also dates back to 1848, the year A.E. Whorton, a New Yorker, settled here and built a saw mill. Later, Whorton moved further west and established New San Diego, California.

Hortonville was on the line of the Milwaukee Lake Shore and Western Railroad Company, an important transportation asset.

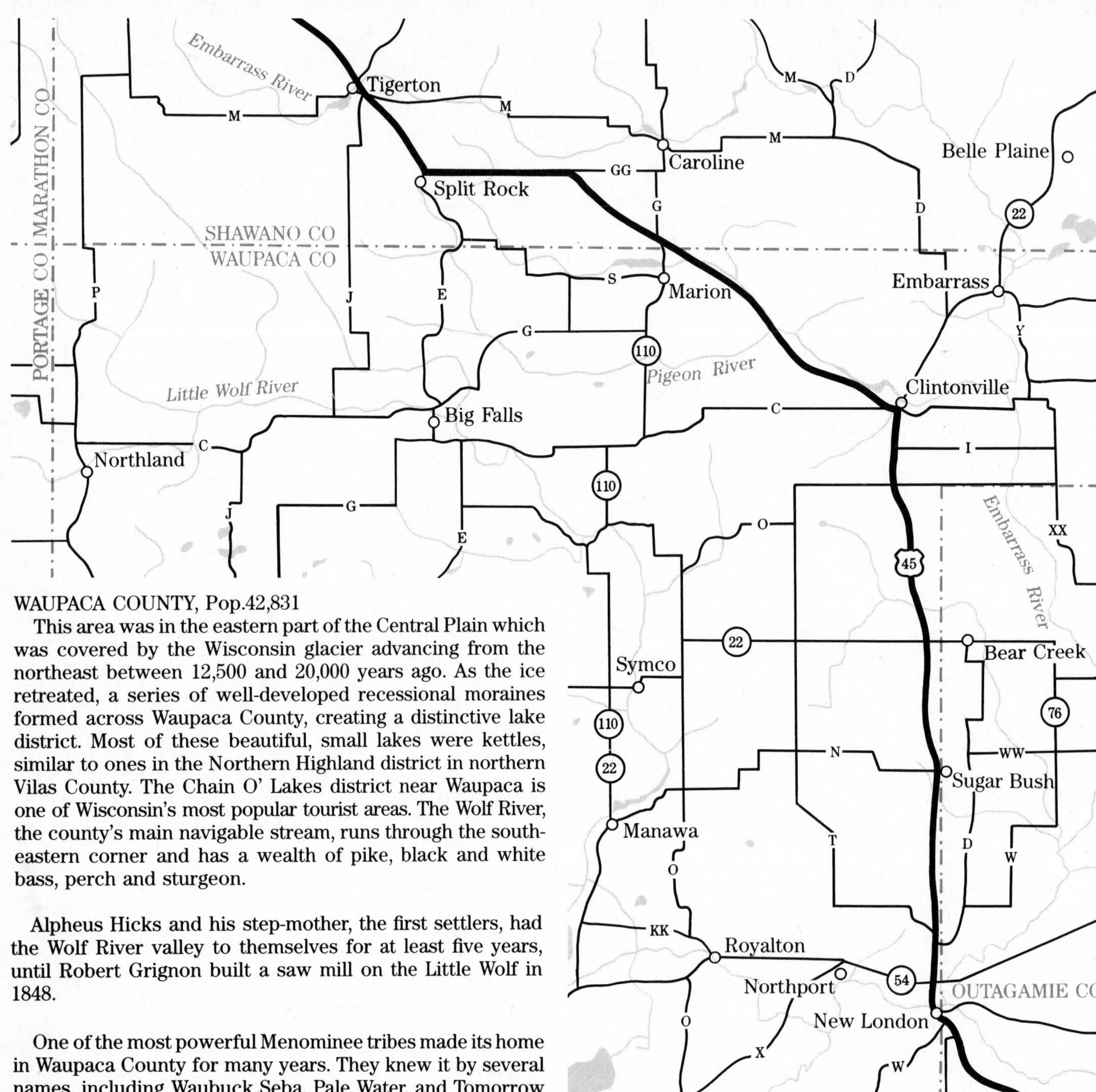

WAUPACA COUNTY, Pop.42,831

This area was in the eastern part of the Central Plain which was covered by the Wisconsin glacier advancing from the northeast between 12,500 and 20,000 years ago. As the ice retreated, a series of well-developed recessional moraines formed across Waupaca County, creating a distinctive lake district. Most of these beautiful, small lakes were kettles, similar to ones in the Northern Highland district in northern Vilas County. The Chain O' Lakes district near Waupaca is one of Wisconsin's most popular tourist areas. The Wolf River, the county's main navigable stream, runs through the southeastern corner and has a wealth of pike, black and white bass, perch and sturgeon.

Alpheus Hicks and his step-mother, the first settlers, had the Wolf River valley to themselves for at least five years, until Robert Grignon built a saw mill on the Little Wolf in 1848.

One of the most powerful Menominee tribes made its home in Waupaca County for many years. They knew it by several names, including Waubuck Seba, Pale Water, and Tomorrow River. The Menominees reportedly believed that white men would one day possess the future–the tomorrow of the land.

NEW LONDON, Pop. 4,941

In the spring of 1848 J.G. Nordman staked a claim two miles south of present day New London on a title he received as a soldier in the Mexican War. He planted corn the following year.

Three years later Lucius Taft made a claim embracing most of what is now New London. He stayed here, actively developing the area, until 1897. The town was originally named Johnson's Landing, but Reeder Smith, another early developer, later renamed it New London after his father's Connecticut birthplace. The town is also known as the Mouth of the Embarrass.

LUMBERING CENTER

For a time nearly all pine timber was driven as logs to the Fox and Wolf river junction, then tugged up to Omro and other towns above to be sawed into boards. There were so many risks in booming timber and rafting it through Lakes Poygan, Buttes des Morts and Winnebago, that lumbermen were discouraged and decided to manufacture lumber near the pinery itself. For that purpose, the lumber companies looked for a well-located town to act as supply depot and a central access point. New London soon became the center of navigation on the Wolf River. Later, its prominence as a steamboat and lumber center made it the logical point for railroads to enter the county.

BEAR CREEK, Pop. 820

Bear Creek, located one mile east on state highway 76, was first settled by Welcome Hyde in 1854. Hyde originally came to this unsurveyed wooded area off the Embarrass River to locate a logging camp. Since an Indian trail was the only thoroughfare west of the Wolf River, it took Hyde and an eight-man crew five days to cut a supply road from the mouth of the Embarrass 20 miles to his logging camp. His team was the first driven north of New London. Hyde's nearest neighbor was eight miles away and his two sons were the town's only children for three years. In 1856 the Hyde children had the distinction of being the sole pupils in Mrs. Williams high school. Literally a "high" school, it was in the attic of the L.E. Phillips' house, entered and exited via a ladder.

CLINTONVILLE, Pop. 4,567

Clintonville's first house, a log cabin with a blanket for the door, was built by Norman and Lydia Clinton of Menasha in 1855. A great bee keeper, Clinton discovered many bee trees along the little stream that empties into the Pigeon River. He named the stream Honey Creek, a name it still carries.

The Clinton's son Urial was the town's first postmaster and Justice of the Peace, and built Clintonville's first saw and grist mill, store and hotel.

Although the Milwaukee, Lake Shore & Western Railway

SHSW

Lumberjacks proudly exhibit a large skid of logs from the northern pineries.

SHSW

Railroad crew checking the line. Photo/ C.J. Van Schaick

didn't reach Clintonville until almost 25 years later, the town's future was never doubted by those who labored sturdily to make it a thriving village. Clintonville incorporated in 1887.

Timbers from the Clinton house are buried under the front sidewalk of the Clintonville Tribune.

MARION, Pop. 1,348

Marion, on the north branch of the Pigeon River, developed around its waterpower. In 1856 J.W. Perry and his son Stephen built the first saw and grist mills. Not surprisingly, the little settlement was long known as Perry's Mills. When the Milwaukee, Lake Shore & Western Railroad reached here in the early 70's, county surveyor Frank Door named it Marion after his hometown of Marion, Ohio. Others say patriotic citizens renamed the town after Francis Marion, the famous Revolutionary War general.

SHAWANO COUNTY, Pop. 35,928

The territory that is now Shawano County was purchased from the Indians during 1831-48, but it was the spring of 1843 when Samuel Farnsworth sent an expedition up the Wolf River to build a saw mill at the outlet of Lake Shawano. That same summer Charles Wescott broke up land and raised potatoes on what was later known as the Old Shawano Farm.

Although the 1853 act organizing the county spelled the name as Shawanaw, a legislative act changed it to Shawano in 1855 and that became official in 1864. The most popular theory about the name's origin is that it came from the Chippewa Indian word, jawanong or sh-aw-a-nong, which applied to the lake within its borders and is believed to mean "of the south". Later it was pointed out that there was an Indian chief named Shawano, or Shaw-wa-no-din, signifying south wind. Residents believed the name meant pure water.

Settlement was slow because mill owners tried to keep prospective farmers away, fearing loss of the more lucrative lumber business. Shawano County contained a great, inexhaustible pine region and most logs were sent to the large mills at Oshkosh. Valuable timber still remains along the Wolf and Embarrass rivers.

INDIAN RESERVATIONS

Shawano County presently includes two Indian reservations, the Menominee and Stockbridge/Munsee. When the Menominee ceded their land in 1852, the government removed the tribe to a 232,400 acre reservation on State 55 with Keshena the main reservation village. The old Military Road once passed through the reservation following Wolf River's eastern bank. The Menominee tribe is unique to the extent that they are the oldest known continuous residents in Wisconsin and still remain an exclusively Wisconsin tribe.

The Stockbridge-Munsee Indians, long an English-speaking tribe, were once neighbors of the eastern Mohegans and Pequots Indians. Their 17th century settlement at Stockbridge, Massachusetts, was one of the earliest reservations in the country. Currently, the Stockbridge/Munsee tribe lives on 11,520 acres of land ceded by the Menominee in 1856 along the Red River southwest of the Menominee reservation.

SPLIT ROCK

Split Rock's name came from railroad surveyors who found a large split rock dead center on the right-of-way through town. Two tall pine trees still shelter the rock along the side of the tracks.

Once a booming logging center of five taverns, a general store, saw mill, grain elevator and post office, Split Rock now has just one tavern and one source's estimate of "50 people, 100 cats, and five dogs that I know of."

TIGERTON, Pop.865

Tigerton, incorporated in 1896, was once a thriving little town, thanks to the extensive coal kilns located just north of town at Whitcomb. Run by the Chicago Rolling Mills, the kilns hired hundreds of men from neighboring villages. A Wisconsin directory states that Tigerton was named about 1865 after Tiger Creek which flows into the Embarrass River. The creek was said to have a section of fast whitewater that roared like a tiger.

WITTENBERG, Pop.997

Rev. E.J. Homme came here in 1879 because of his deep concern for the early settlers and accomplished his dream of servicing orphans, the aged and needy Indians. Homme encouraged his friends and family to move here and Wittenberg's population included 40 families by 1885. Homme's orphanage received homeless children from all over the Upper Midwest and the financial demands of the orphanage, home for the aged and church, forced him to raise money by running a farm, publishing three newspapers, operating four schools, raising and selling garden seeds and a patent medicine he made called Wittenberg Drops. He also convinced the Milwaukee, Lake Shore & Western line to change the town's name from Carbonero to Wittenberg.

Homme died in 1903 and is buried here. His Home for Boys still operates north of town.

ELAND, Pop.230

E.H. Rummely, an officer of the Milwaukee, Lake Shore & Western Railway Company, platted and named this town in 1888. The eland is a variety of antelope found in Central Africa and Rummely probably chose the name because of the area's vast herds of wild deer.

BIRNAMWOOD, Pop. 688

Incorporated in 1895, the town was officially named in 1884 when the first permanent saw mills were built. A story is told of a young college student who rode the North Shore Railroad to the end of the line in a caboose. Large piles of brush were burning along the right of way and the student left the caboose to investigate. A tall blanket-wrapped Indian was watching the flames and the young man reportedly said, "Heap big fire." The Indian replied, "Heap big burn-em-wood." The young man, a student of Shakespeare, remembered a quote from Macbeth about the Great Birnamwood and thought it a great name for a town. It was named Birnamwood on the map and has never changed.

ANIWA, Pop. 273

Aniwa incorporated in 1899. Its name came from an Ojibwa Indian derivative meaning "superiority."

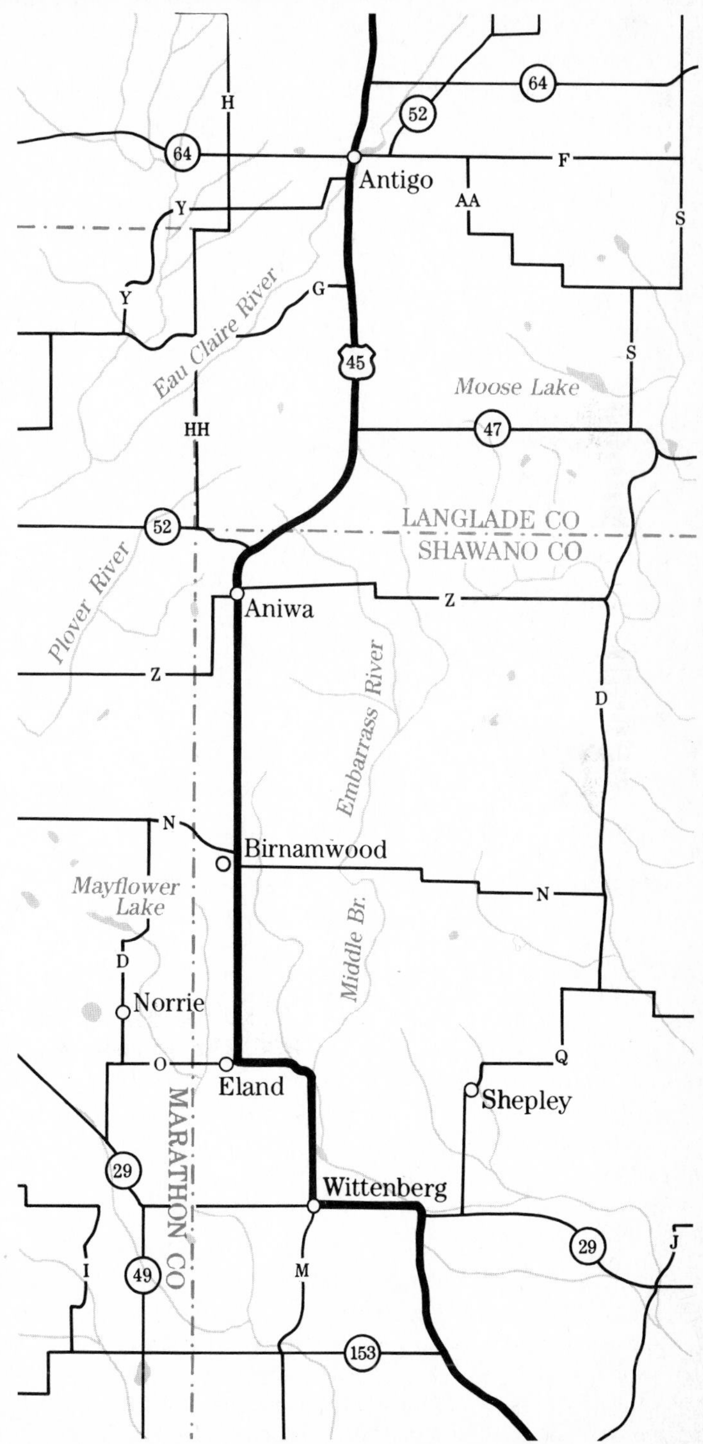

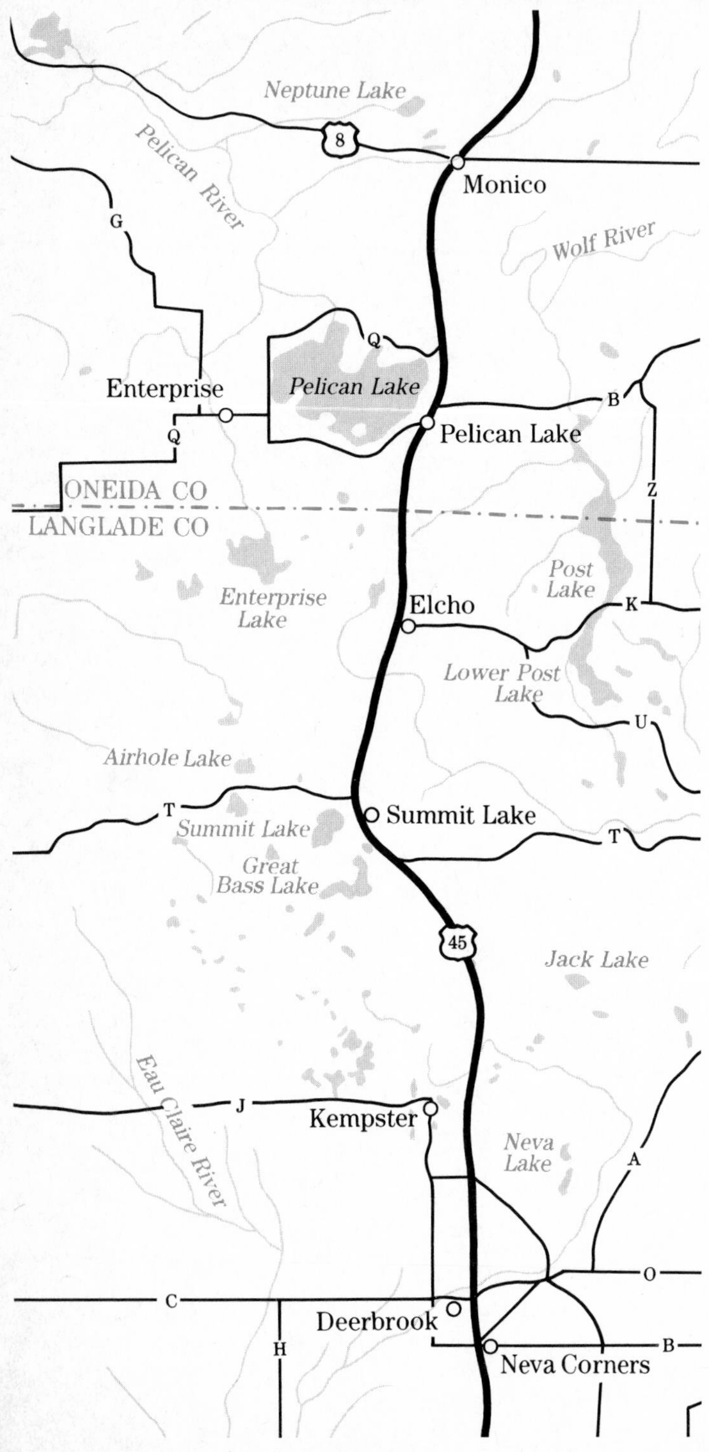

LANGLADE COUNTY, Pop. 19,978

Langlade County lies very near Wisconsin's geographical center. Its largest rivers, the Wolf and Eau Claire, along with numerous creeks, smaller rivers and rivulets, drain and water the entire county. The county was covered by glaciers during two distinct periods and each left its mark on the land's surface. The southwest land is gently rolling, indicating the older glacial period. The rest of the county is rolling and more irregular, the result of a more recent glacial action.

Until 1855 Langlade was literally nature's paradise; a virgin forest where cattle fed upon a thousand hills and fish and game thrived in streams and glacial lakes.

Originally a part of the Northwest Territory, settlers first came here to stay in 1870 and it was 1881 when the county was established. Squire A. Taylor, the county's founder, was a well-educated and progressive citizen of the then-township of Lily who engaged in lumber and logging operations for many years. Langlade County was officially attached to Shawano County until it acquired 1,000 inhabitants and was named New County. A year later Langlade County changed its name again to honor Sieur Chas. De Langlade, a brave leader of the French and Indians who some called Wisconsin's first citizen.

EARLY ROADS

When settlers came into Langlade County on foot or horseback in 1853, the first roads were Indian trails which ran from place to place by the best, though not the shortest, routes. The trails were used until 1885 and roads weren't straightened until long after section lines were surveyed.

The famous Military Road was the most historic and important road in Langlade County. The Wisconsin legislature laid out the road on April 4, 1864 to transport military forces from Fort Howard, Green Bay, to Fort Wilkins, Michigan. It entered the county in section 32, township 31, range 15E and ran northwesterly through Elton, Langlade and Ainsworth townships. More than any other wagon road, the "old militaire" opened up a vast expanse of Wolf River country to early traders and stimulated eastern Langlade County's great lumber industry.

Although the road's stated intent was for military purposes, well-known lumber barons called it a land and timber conspiracy because together with 86,215 acres of railroad-controlled land, it seriously hampered their reign over the area.

ANTIGO, Pop. 8,653

Until 1877, two streaks of rust and a right-of-way—the Milwaukee, Lake Shore & Western's iron trail through the dense unbroken forest—was the only evidence of civilization in this area. But that year, F.A. Deleglise moved here with his family, platted Antigo, and achieved his life ambition to found a city. The area's exceptional soil quality and quick adaptation to agriculture drew Deleglise here. Antigo's name was taken from Nequi-Antigo-Seebeh, a Chippewa name for "Spring River," referring to the balsam evergreens lining its shores.

COUNTY SEAT FIGHT

During Antigo's early settlement, residents continually had problems with the neighboring city of Shawano. Shawano citizens were afraid that they would lose much of the Wolf River lumber business to Antigo. As it turned out, Antigo ultimately surpassed Shawano as a business and commercial center. In the meantime, however, Shawano did everything possible to stunt Antigo's growth, including inducing the state legislature to attach Antigo and New County to Shawano County for judicial and county purposes in 1879. That action bound Antigo, hand and foot, to Shawano.

Twenty miles of woods separated Antigo from the Wolf River meeting place of the town board, a board which was antagonistic toward Antigo. Therefore, the citizens decided to overthrow the board and elect sympathetic officers who would allow this city its right to grow. They kept very quiet before election day, leading their opponents to think that they would not vote. However, on the eve of the 1879 election, Antigo citizens camped out along the road and went into town late on election day to vote. The surprise factor worked. The Antigo slate won by fewer than 100 votes.

DEERBROOK

Most pioneer settlers in this area emigrated from Bohemia, settled at Manitowoc, then purchased land here in Neva township. Wencel Smetana, John Novak and Charles Mosher came in 1879, taking seven days to travel from Manitowoc. A single pair of oxen hauled all of their worldly belongings in a rough wagon over extremely poor roads.

Deerbrook, situated on the Chicago & North Western railway's main line, was named by Edward Dawson, timber cruiser and prospector. Dawson camped near the Eau Claire River one day and watched deer "drink their fill" each morning just as the sun peeped over the hills proclaiming a new day. He called this place Deerbrook and it's been known as that ever since.

SUMMIT LAKE, Pop. 197

Officials of the Milwaukee, Lake Shore & Western Railroad called this village Summit because Summit Lake is the highest (1,726 feet above sea level) body of water in Wisconsin.

The first homesteaders came with the railroad, including W.J. Empey who came from Elmhurst in 1881 and built the first hotel. Wm. Pool, associated with Smith Brothers of Oshkosh, built a saw mill here in 1884 to accommodate lumbering, the principal pioneer industry of the time.

SHSW

Area friends help with barn raising.

ELCHO

The earliest white men to pass this way were French missionaries who traveled into the heart of the north woods via the Wolf River waterway and the Lake Superior Trail. B. F. Dorr, Antigo's city engineer and county surveyor, surveyed and platted this rich timber land in 1887. Dorr owned most of the land, having purchased it from the government for $1.25 per acre. Loggers used to wool flannel remembered him for his ever-present white shirt.

Thorwald Solberg, a Norwegian, opened Elcho's first general store in 1886 and was also the first postmaster. He had previously lived on a homestead in Antigo.

Elcho is an Indian word meaning "Welcome."

ONEIDA COUNTY, Pop. 31,216

Situated in Wisconsin's Northern Highland region, Onedia County contains some of the state's oldest rocks and is the southernmost extension of the vast Canadian shield. True to its highland label, this gentle upland slopes away from an elevation about 1,700 feet above sea level.

All of the major river systems in Wisconsin and Minnesota originate here, before flowing into Lake Superior, Lake Michigan, or the Mississippi River. Two parts of the Northern Highland are densely dotted with glacial lakes: one in Polk County, the other in Vilas and Oneida counties. Few parts of the world contain so many lakes with so little intervening

SHSW

Three Lakes, ca.1920

land. Oneida County, for example, has more than 800 of Wisconsin's 9,000 lakes and hundreds of bogs and marshes mark the sites of former lakes.

The county took its name from the Oneida (Granite People) Indians, a New York branch of the Iroquois who came to Wisconsin in the early 19th century.

LUMBERING IN ONEIDA COUNTY

Oneida County's settlement and development has generally been tied to the lumber industry. It was lumberman who cleared the primeval forest and opened the way for the farmer.

The first logging in the county was north of the Tomahawk River in the winter of 1857-58 at Rhinelander, the county seat. A belt of white and Norway pine, 18 miles wide by 40 miles long and the heaviest in the state, was located just north of the city and large tracts of birch, birdseye and curly maple were located to the northeast, offering great incentive to hardwood mills. Spruce was also plentiful for pulp and papermaking. By the early 1890's up to eight mills operated around Rhinelander, felling 700 million feet of log timber per year at their peak. Such activity soon exhausted the supply, however, and operations slowed considerably by 1904. Lumber barons moved away as the timber was depleted, leaving a gigantic land control problem in their wake. By 1931 just 24,000 acres remained of the original timber stand.

MONICO, Pop. 291

When the Milwaukee, Lake Shore & Western Railroad came into Rhinelander in October, 1882, there were just a few railway shanties at the junction point of Monico. Activity picked up the following year when the Wisconsin Sulphite Fibre Company bought most of the town site and built a factory to remove bark and decay from pulpwood before shipping it on to pulp mills at Appleton. The future looked bright and the town was platted on April 24, 1883.

The following fall the sulphite plant was torn down and a new one with five rotary boilers was established. Early intentions were to develop a paper mill but the mill burned down a few years later. Instead of rebuilding, the company gave up their plans, sold out their interests and left the village. Ed Squier of Rhinelander bought the site and sold it in lots to different parties.

Fire was the village's chief enemy as many local establishments were destroyed by fire and never rebuilt. As late as October, 1920, fire destroyed two stores, the post office, restaurant and seven or eight residences. Just three years later, the railway depot burned to the ground.

An early surveyor of the town, B.F. Dorr, reportedly named the town after Monaco, the principality on the French Riviera. He knew more about surveying than spelling, however, and missed the correct name by one letter.

PELICAN LAKE, Pop. 3,387

As with most neighboring towns, Pelican Lake's growth was stimulated by the Milwaukee Lakeshore & Western Railroad's arrival in 1882. Lumberjacks of so many different nationalities settled here that descendants called themselves the League of Nations. Rivermen passing by were impressed with the number of pelicans nesting along the lakeshore and named the town and lake accordingly.

GAGEN

Little is known of this area except for a few accounts of how Gagen got its name. According to one story, it was named for an early pioneer, Daniel Gagen. However, another account claims Gagen is derived from the Ojibwe Indian word gagego, meaning "no."

THREE LAKES, Pop. 1,864

Twenty years before Three Lakes was a town, Hi Polar operated a trading post on what is now Virgin Lake. The post was a drop point for mail along the Military Road from Green Bay to Ontonagon, Michigan (now Highway 32) part of which still passes through Three Lakes in the Nicolet National Forest.

The community of Three Lakes and its name began when the Lake Shore Traffic Company surveyed this area for a right-of-way. Pushing their way north toward Michigan, the railroad was largely responsible for the town's growth, opening this rich timber area to eager settlers. In 1881, land company surveyors found a lake surrounded by large maple trees and called it Maple Lake. Following the range line they located a second lake which they named Range Line. One mile further north, they crossed the town line and found another lake which they called Town Line Lake. The Milwaukee Lakeshore and Western Railroad also noted the lakes when it brought supplies through here for the lumber camps and called the station Three Lakes. The town was organized in 1897.

CLEARWATER LAKE

Throughout northern Wisconsin, railroads pushing through the vast forest to logging camps needed supply stops and towns grew around their depots. Clearwater, named after a large, clear lake in the area, was one such town.

According to one report, a Mr. and Mrs. Heddin owned most of the original land which was used to establish a Catholic camp. The town's population was approximately 85 people at the turn-of-the-century and a post office was established in 1905.

VILAS COUNTY, Pop. 16,535

The Wisconsin Magazine of History (Autumn, 1953) reported that "the earliest recorded documents suggest that the first white men in this area were the early French traders, missionaries and voyageurs who visited Lac Vieux Desert, a beautiful lake lying on the Wisconsin-Michigan boundary. Being the source of the Wisconsin River, it lay on the route of these early travelers who were en route from the Great Lakes to the Wisconsin and Mississippi rivers. It is widely believed that it may have been a stopover place as early as

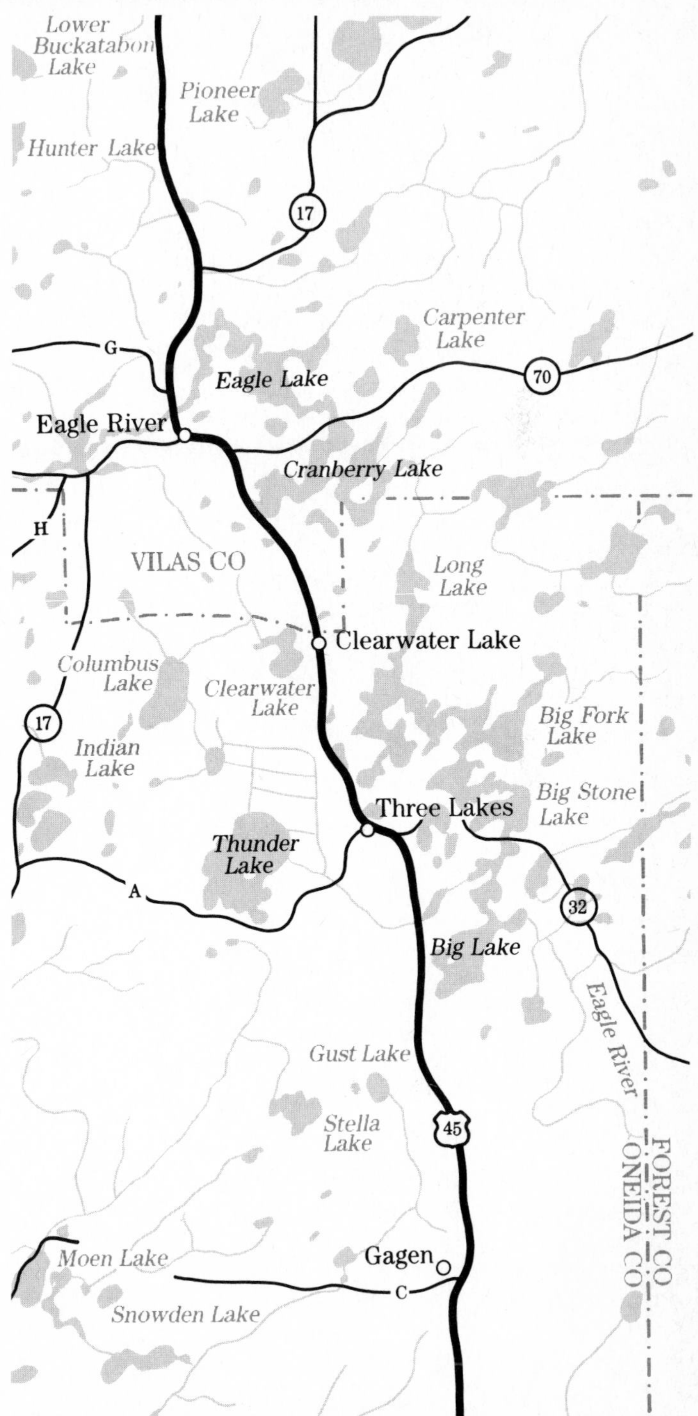

SHSW

Carving out Fifth Ave., Antigo, 1882.

the 1600's. We do know that the early French gave the lake its name which means "old or deserted planting ground."

Area roads were laid out to serve the first Vilas County settlements which mainly occurred along Lac Vieux Desert's southwest shore and Eagle Lake's east shore. The Draper family came to Lac Vieux Desert first, in 1852. Three years later, the Helms and Fox families settled at Eagle Lake and began trading with the Indians. They also established a bank and post office and cut the first pine logs to be floated down the Wisconsin River. Their site was known as Kee-Mi-Con.

Vilas County received its name from a very honorable man—William F. Vilas. A Vermont native, Vilas moved to Wisconsin in 1851 and graduated from the University in 1858. He attained the rank of lieutenant colonel during the War of Secession and later became postmaster general of the United States (1885-88); Secretary of the Interior (1881-91) and U.S. Senator (1891-97). He died in August, 1908, leaving the bulk of his large fortune to his alma mater.

When Vilas County was structured from Oneida County in 1893, it had two towns: Minocqua and Eagle River, the county seat. Other towns soon developed but they were always very small, with the chief business a general store supplying surrounding farmers.

EAGLE RIVER, Pop. 1,326

Most Vilas County villages owed their origin and fortunes to the lumber industry. When logging operations flourished, the villages did too. Conversely, when the timber boom ended, some towns also died. Eagle River, county seat and largest supply depot, survived it all. It continued to profit years later, as it does today, by encouraging a busy, summer tourist trade.

The village lies chiefly on the south bank of Eagle River, so called, some say, because of the many eagles that built nests in the adjacent forest. Eagle nests can still be seen throughout Vilas County. A highway sign marks the site of one on Highway G, approximately six miles out of Eagle River.

Eagle River's rise dates from the Milwaukee, Lake Shore & Western Railroad in 1883, although a few pioneers appeared in the vicinity 20 years before that, including James Hall who settled with his family on Eagle Lake's northern bank, about three miles from town. After the railroad came through, John O'Connor arrived here to pursue a logging operation. Although O'Connor founded the village, it was platted in the name of his wife, Ann. By 1886 the town had three general stores, a hotel, meat market, barber shop and restaurant. The Gerry Lumber Company was established that year and nearby lumber camps required $75,000 worth of supplies every season, contributing to Eagle River's prosperity.

Writing in 1898 Father Goepferd said, "For years the camps were many; the mills ran night and day; wages were high; there was activity and abundance in every store and department, and the 'Lake Shore' had its hands and cars full to ship out products of industry and supply the inhabitants with the necessities of life. Every house was crowded. It was Eagle River's golden age."

CONOVER, Pop. 826

Aside from lumbermen, only two or three settlers lived here when Conover officially organized in 1907; the Reed Brothers, Charles and Gust, were the first. The village was named after Seth Conover from Plymouth who built the first summer resort and hotel on Big Twin Lake in 1883.

LAND O'LAKES, Pop. 803

Like Conover, Land O'Lakes was set off from Eagle River on Jan. 3, 1907. At that time the town was called State Line because it was located on the line constituting the northern boundary between Wisconsin and Michigan.

Rudolph Otto came here about 1878 and built one of the best single-rotary saw mills in northern Wisconsin which he operated for many years until his death. An Eagle River pastor held occasional services for lumbermen and their families at a Catholic mission which was established here in 1889. Land O'Lakes was considered the township headquarters in 1908 because it had a two-room school house and a town hall.

The State Line depot, built half in Michigan and half in Wisconsin, was moved to Michigan in 1907 due to Wisconsin's eight-hour law. Due to the many railroad accidents occurring through carelessness, this ruling (overturned the following year by the Supreme Court,) made it illegal for a Wisconsin railroad worker to put in more than eight hours in one working day (typical work days ran 10-12 hours.) When the depot burned to the ground in 1928, a new building was erected on the old site, again one-half in each state. Because there were other State Line post offices in Minnesota and Mississippi, the town officially became Land O'Lakes in 1926.

MILITARY ROAD

The most important military road in this area was the one from Fort Howard at Green Bay to Fort Wilkins at the mouth of the Ontonagon River on Lake Superior. The U.S. Government gave Michigan and Wisconsin a land grant in 1863 to transport supplies, ammunition and mail. The road took nine years to build and though intended for military purposes soon became an important route for food and supplies to this area and to Upper Michigan iron and copper mining towns.

Mail was transported along this route regularly by men traveling by foot in summer and dog team in winter. When the road was too bad for the dogs, drivers took sacks of papers and hung them on a tree where they stayed until the next summer or until another dog team, not as heavily loaded, could accommodate them.

The road was also used to drive cattle from southern Wisconsin to Lake Superior. The trading posts hired men to cut marsh hay for these cattle and stack it along the trail at half-day intervals. Although the marshes were numerous enough to supply the cattle it was sometimes necessary for them to carry their own food, strapped onto their horns just out of reach.

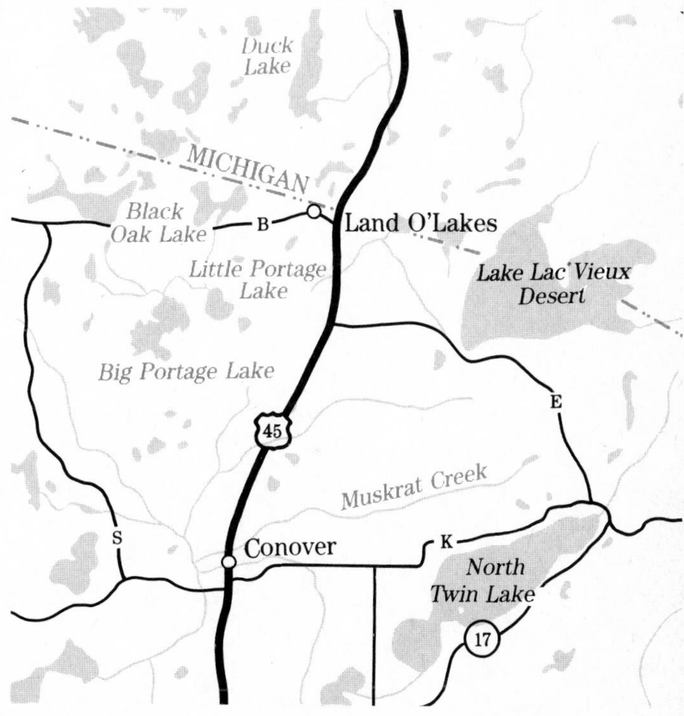

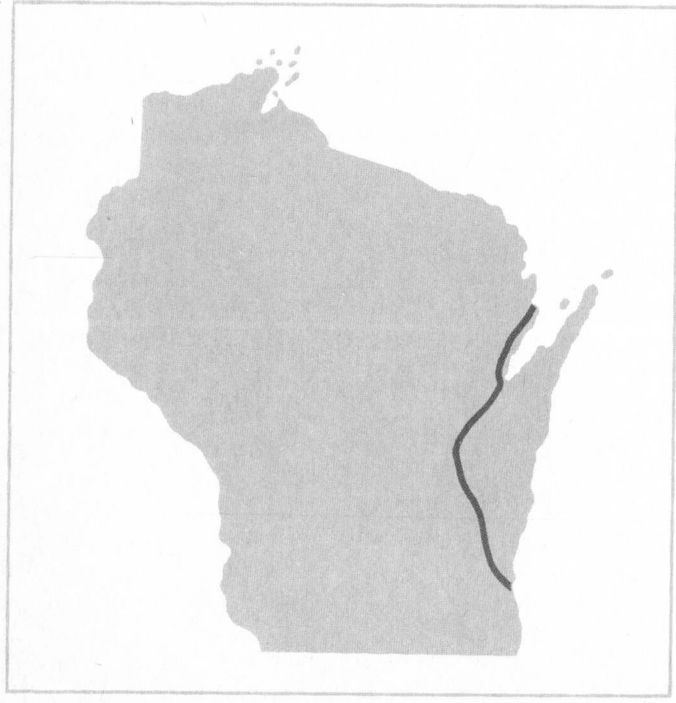

U.S. 41 stretches 185 miles along the early route of missionaries, fur traders and explorers. Winding northward through kettle moraine country, this heavily-traveled route passes flat, fertile farming communities, industrial towns on the Fox River and ends in the once, lumber-rich areas of the north. Route 41 includes the site of Red Banks, located near Green Bay, where Nicolet discovered Wisconsin in 1634.

ROUTE 41, MILWAUKEE TO MARINETTE

SHSW

Produce from the Menomonee River Boom Company garden, 1895.

MILWAUKEE COUNTY, Pop. 964,988

In its earliest days, Milwaukee County was richly forested, inhabited by abundant game and disturbed only by occasional visits from roaming Indian tribes. The only white men who came here were fur traders going to a Milwaukee trading post which had long been a favorite because of its location at the junction of the Kinnickinnic, Menominee and Milwaukee rivers.

Permanent settlement began about 1833 when settlers came in increasing numbers from New England. One year later, with Wisconsin still a part of Michigan Territory, the Michigan legislature passed an act laying out Milwaukee County. Since settlement was sparse, the county wasn't officially organized until August 25, 1835 with Milwaukee as county seat. By 1836 the county had 2,893 people, half of whom were concentrated around the mouth of the Menominee River.

The name for the county and city came from a Potawatomi Indian word Mahn-a-waukee meaing "gathering place."

MILWAUKEE, Pop. 636,210

By all rights, Jacques Vieau, a Northwest Fur Company agent, should have the title of Milwaukee's first settler. Vieau and his family canoed here in 1795 and were met at the river's mouth by a delegation of Potawatomies, Sauks, Foxes and Winnebagoes. Following their warm welcome, Vieau paddled up the Menomonee River and built a cabin and fur storage house on the valley's south side in what later became Mitchell Park. Very successful, Vieau's wealth and family grew side by side. He and his wife eventually had 13 children. Ironically, one of Vieau's daughters was later responsible for his losing the title of Milwaukee's founder.

Josette Vieau was fifteen, intelligent and beautiful when Solomon Juneau, a naturalized American of French birth, came to work in 1818 at her father's post. Six feet tall, with piercing blue eyes, Juneau was a prime catch for any woman. When Juneau asked for Josette's hand, Vieau readily gave his consent. Because the county had no priest, the Juneaus canoed to Green Bay and were married in a mission church. Soon after their wedding, Juneau established a trading post on the river's east bank. Still there when land speculators arrived to plat the town, Solomon Juneau was credited as Milwaukee's official founder and called it Milwaukie, a spelling that persisted for many years. Juneau's home, located at Wisconsin and East Water streets, became the government building.

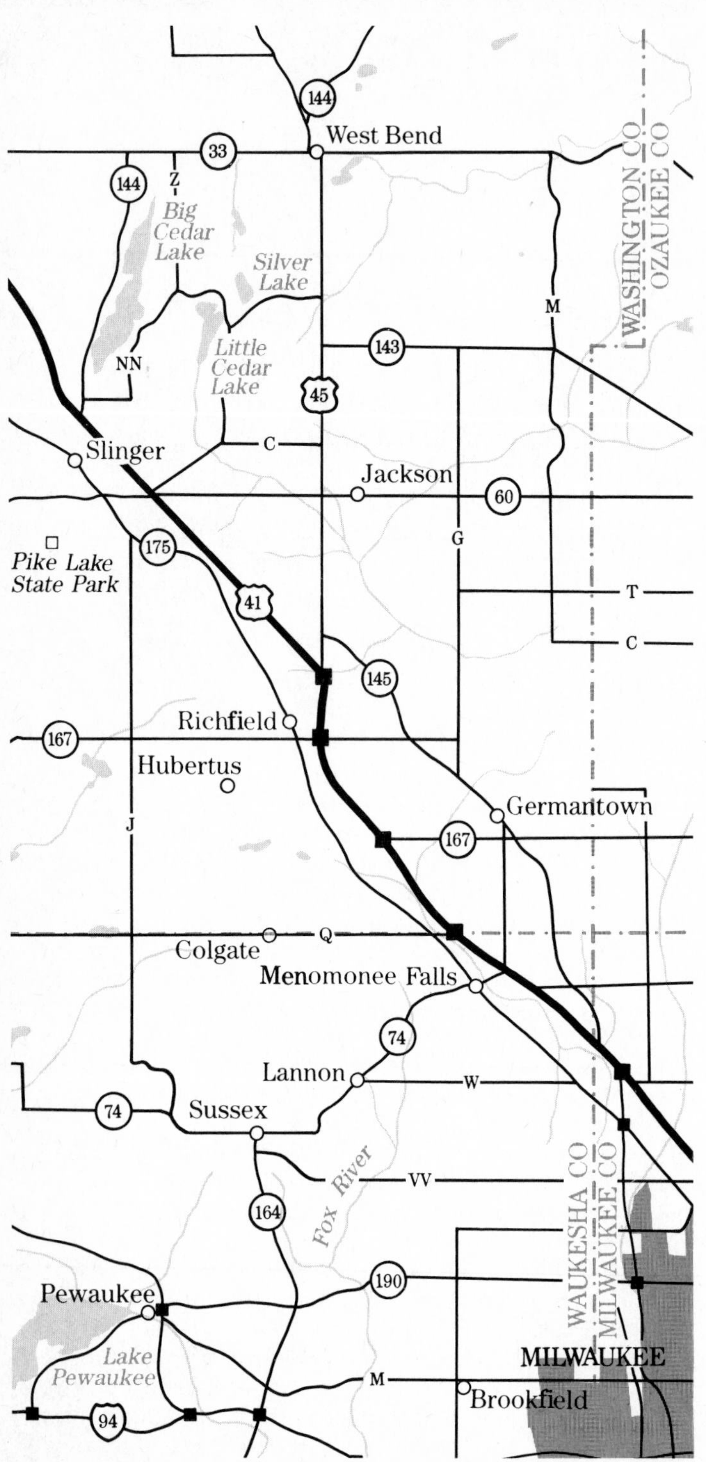

By 1845 Milwaukee's population had grown to 10,000 people, more than half of German descent. Because of the fertile soil, an increasing number of German immigrants moved here in the early 1850's to pursue farming. The Poles, the city's second largest racial group, arrived in the decades following the Civil War and settled chiefly on the town's south side.

Although the early settlers were primarily fur traders and farmers, Milwaukee later became important as a trading and industrial center. The city first achieved great economic importance during the Civil War as a harbor for Great Lakes traffic. At that time Wisconsin farms were an important wheat source for the country. By 1856 the schooner Dean Richmond carried Milwaukee's first transoceanic wheat shipment direct to Liverpool, England.

In addition to wheat, farmers soon discovered a new source of income—raising crops to produce Milwaukee's most popular new industry, beer.

"THE BEER THAT MADE MILWAUKEE FAMOUS"

Ironically, Milwaukee's first brewers were British, not German. When the men from Wales moved into Milwaukee they produced a brew much like a strong ale, porter or stout and quite unlike what we now know. Their process, top fermentation, used a yeast that floated to the top and was then skimmed off. This method produced beer with quite a kick, but it didn't keep well. By the 1840's Bavarian brewmasters had developed a bottom fermentation process with a much better preservation quality and began producing it in Milwaukee. Pabst, Schlitz and Blatz, the three earliest companies to use this method, began in remarkably similar ways.

Jacob Best arrived first, in 1844, and started making beer with his brother and son. Frederick Pabst later married the Best's niece, then eventually bought out and took over the firm. John Braun started the second brewery in 1846. When Braun died, his foreman, Valentin Blatz, bought the business and eventually married Mrs. Braun.

August Krug started the third brewery in 1849. When Krug died, his bookkeeper, Joseph Schlitz, wed Krug's widow and ran the brewery with Krug's nephews, the Uihleins, who eventually became sole owners. Now for that famous slogan. The Schlitz brewing company actually bought the slogan "the beer that made Milwaukee famous" from a smaller brewery. The price? Five thousand dollars.

HOW MILWAUKEE GOT ITS NAME

Milwaukee got its nickname as Cream City as early as 1869 because it was considered a major center for making light-

SHSW

East Water St., Milwaukee, ca. 1900.

colored bricks.

The precise origin of Milwaukee is not so easily determined and has been explained many ways over the years. In 1649 Father Hennepin thought the area should be called Millecki or Melchi, meaning "good land." Twenty years later John Buisson de Cosme referred to it as Milwarkik or "great council place." Later, Lt. James Gorrel called this place Milwauky, or "good earth." And as recently as the early nineteenth century, Milwaukee was called Mahn-a-waukee Seepe, or "gathering place by the river." Mana-wau-kee was said to have been a root the Indians used for medicinal purposes. Most thought this was the only place it grew and the Chippewa would trade one beaver skin for a finger-size piece.

The town's present spelling and meaning were probably established in 1884 when Joshua Hathaway took an Indian derivation meaning "gathering place by the river." The Potawatomi Indians used this place where the Menomonee and Kinnickinnic rivers meet as a council grounds long before the white man came here.

WAUKESHA COUNTY, Pop. 280,326

Although travelers on U.S. 41 get only a brief glimpse of this county, the first settlers saw a picture of true natural beauty. The heavily-timbered forests alternated with park-like oak openings and green prairie meadows, providing a variety lacking in today's cultivated fields.

Like all northern and eastern Wisconsin counties, Waukesha was molded from early action of the Superior, Chippewa, Green Bay and Michigan glaciers. The Green Bay and Michigan glaciers accumulated drift along a 150-mile line, seen today in the tumultuous Kettle Moraine ridge which passes through southwestern Waukesha County's beautiful lake region. Landforms from this glacial period can be seen in the Kettle Moraine State Forest (Southern unit) where 70 miles of trails offer a good view of water-filled kettle lakes, conical-shaped hills called kanes and large ridges of gravel, or moraines, that once covered the area. The lookout point of the Scuppernong Trail offers a breathtaking view of a variety of landscapes.

The word Waukesha (Wauk-tsha) was never written in English until 1846 when it was inscribed on an oak tree in Rochester (Racine County). Joshua Hathaway, who selected this location for a town, chose the name, claiming it was Potawatomi for "fox" or "little fox." The name also applied to the river which flows through the town.

MENOMONEE FALLS, Pop. 27,845

Menomonee, a Potawatomi Indian word meaning "wild rice," is located on the tumbling rapids of the Menominee River which runs through town. Frederic Nehs founded the village in 1843 when he realized the potential of the area's waterpower and bought 700 acres of land. German friends and immigrants followed Nehs and soon opened a bottling plant, flour mill, sugar beet factory and ginseng plant. Nothing remains today of these original industries and most townspeople work in nearby Milwaukee.

WASHINGTON COUNTY, Pop. 84,848

Washington County's surface was primarily shaped by prehistoric glaciers. Massive sheets of ice stretched their icy tongues from Canada south to the Ohio and Missouri rivers. For about 150 miles, the rims of two glaciers, the Michigan and Green Bay, either touched each other or were separated by accumulations of moraine (large ridges of gravel.) The results can be seen in the Kettle Moraine State Forest.

Washington County today is mostly level or gently rolling, a part of the great Wisconsin plateau. The sandy soil is mixed with plenty of humus and at the time of early settlement was covered with rich vegetation, providing good farming conditions.

The county's nickname might be "The Land of the Five Rivers." You might compare it to the Punjab country in northwestern India. Not only do five rivers flow through this county, but all of them—the Rock, Rubicon, Oconomowoc, Menomonee, and Milwaukee—spring from its soil. The Rock, Rubicon and Oconomowoc originate on the west side of the watershed formed by the moraines; the Menomonee and Milwaukee are on the east side.

HOLY HILL

A short drive west on highway 167, about seven miles inside Washington County, brings you to Holy Hill, one of the earliest sites Father Marquette explored. The road meanders through a deep valley and continues through tamarack and cedar swamps until it finally ends in the large rounded hills of the kettle moraine country. A castle-like church and Carmelite Father's monastery are at the crest of the hill.

SHSW

Carmelite Monastary at Holy Hill

Many tales surround this monastery's history, but the best known includes the story of the miraculous cure of Francois Soubris. According to the legend, Soubris, a Quebec monk, had read of this place in an old French diary written by Father Marquette. Marquette had discovered this lofty cone-shaped hill in 1673 on his memorable voyage to the Mississippi River. Climbing the summit, he had erected a cross and dedicated the spot as holy ground forever.

Soubris had been unfaithful to his vows and journeyed to this spot from Chicago for atonement, taking Marquette's manuscript and a rough map with him. Soubris was paralyzed by a serious illness en route and reached the end of his pilgrimage in this crippled condition. Climbing the slope on hands and knees, he spent the night praying for the use of his limbs. When morning came, he rose from his knees with youthful vigor, the paralysis gone forever.

On the spot where he was reportedly cured, Soubris built a rough chapel where he prayed several times a day. Along his path, now sharply defined from use, Soubris erected crosses at which he performed penance on his bare knees. Hearing of his cure, large numbers of people traveled to the hill to seek relief from their ailments. Soubris remained in the area for seven years, then mysteriously disappeared. Some say that the ghost of Soubris can sometimes be seen kneeling at the crosses on a dusky evening.

RICHFIELD, Pop. 8,390

Philipp Laubenheimer was born in Hess-Darmstadt, Germany and migrated here with his wife and seven children in 1842. The town was subsequently named Laubenheimersville in his honor. The Laubenheimers camped beneath a spreading tree for two weeks until their log house was finished. Soon Mrs. Laubenheimer and one child died, but Laubenheimer remained in the town and later built a tavern on the old Fond du Lac road.

The Richfield House, built in 1904, has recently been restored and contains a fine local restaurant.

KETTLE MORAINES

The chain of hills traversing this county from northeast to southwest were created from prehistoric debris dumped there from the edges of the Green Bay and Michigan glaciers. These ranges were called kettle moraines because they were piled up in huge caldron-like bowls, their sides consisting of ice walls, 100 or more feet high. The continuous melting on the rims of these glaciers produced an enormous amount of water which could only be drained through the kettle. Debris piled up, creating a range of gravel hills that ran nearly parallel to each other. There is an impressive view of this moraine from a hill one-half mile west of Slinger.

SLINGER, Pop. 1,612

B. Schleisinger Weil, a German-Alsatian, founded this village. Weil bought a great deal of government land in December, 1845, and platted 527 acres for the village. He then built a house and later a store which contained everything a settler could need. In return, homesteaders brought him everything their land would produce, eventually creating one of the most important markets for miles. Ten years later, the tracks of the La Crosse Railroad were laid through town, largely due to Weil's efforts. Appropriately, the village was then called Schleisingerville. At the request of its citizens, the name was changed to Slinger in 1921 for the sake of brevity.

ALLENTON

This little village sprang up after the Wisconsin Central railroad came through in the early 1880's. Its earlier name, Dekorra Station, was soon changed to Allenton. The village founders included the Ruplinger brothers who built a stave factory here in 1882 and J. Bertschy who built the first grain elevator the same year.

KETTLE MORAINE STATE FOREST

An abundance of early glacial features are preserved in the 43,000 acres of the Northern and Southern units of the Kettle Moraine State Forest. Several self-guided nature trails at Mauthe and Long lakes, in the Northern unit, offer a good opportunity to see and understand the different formations. Access to the Northern unit is through Kewaskum, located on State Highway 28 approximately 10 miles from its intersection with Highway 41.

DODGE COUNTY, Pop. 74,747

Previous to the white man's arrival, large portions of this county were occupied by the Winnebago Indians, but only one main village called Maunk-shak-kah, or White Breast was located here. The character of Dodge County provided all that the early natives needed; a wealth of game and fish, herds of buffalo and fertile cornfields.

Early pioneers Luther A. and John W. Cole, heard of this wealthy prairie and moved to Johnson's Rapids (now Watertown) in December, 1836. The following January the Cole brothers built a log cabin where they kept what they called "bachelor's distress." Luther spent his time clearing land and preparing the ground for spring seeding, while John was "maid of all work," and did the cooking and washing. During the summer and fall of 1837, the Coles worked on a saw mill and dam belonging to Charles F. Goodhue & Son where their later interest soon centered.

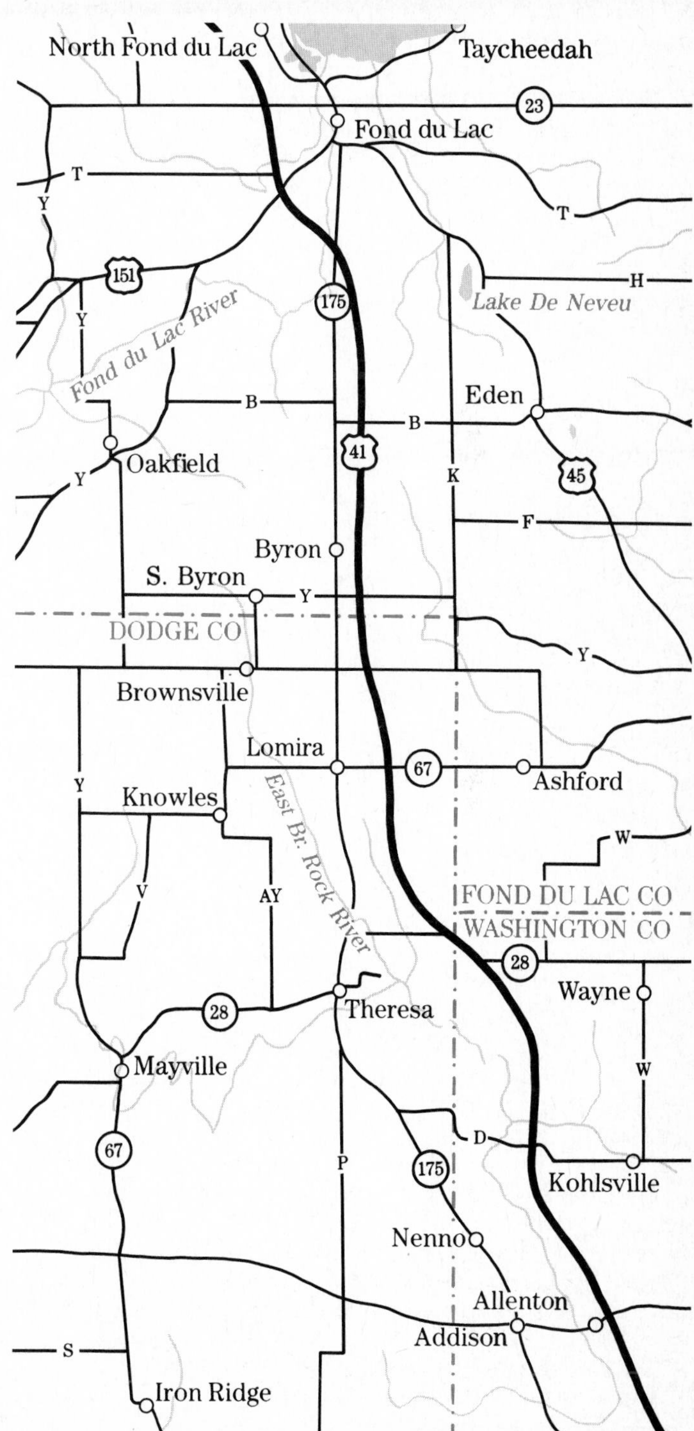

Because the Cole dam was located in Jefferson County, the first permanent settler was really Jacob P. Brower. Brower moved to Dodge County in March, 1838 and built a cabin near Fox Lake. The following June he moved in his family from Green Bay. Here in the strange wilderness country with the Indians their only neighbors, the Browers claimed 200 acres of land and built a double log house on the west side of the river, midway between the old dam and bridge.

Dodge County was officially separated from Jefferson County in March, 1844 and named in honor of Henry Dodge, the Governor of the territory of Wisconsin.

THERESA, Pop. 766

This village lies just off Route 41, along Highway 28. Located on a bend of the Rock River, Theresa was always a busy little trading center and a productive agricultural community. Its residents were largely farmers. Little is known of the first settlers who probably arrived in the early 1840's. An important early arrival was Solomon Juneaü, the founder of Milwaukee who came here in 1849 with his son. The village was subsequently named after Juneau's mother, Theresa. He lived here for several years, buying up government land on which he built a saw and grist mill. Impressed with this area's beauty, Juneau built his home on a hill overlooking the Rock River. In recent years it has been restored and can be visited today.

In 1849, the same year Juneau moved here, Dr. Valentine Miller, a German native, also settled in Theresa. Miller, one of the county's pioneer physicians, was trained at Heidelberg University and practiced medicine here for many years.

MAYVILLE, Pop. 4,338

Continuing on highway 28 about ten miles, you will find Mayville, a village which began as an early trading post. It was named for Chester and Eli P. May who settled here in 1845. That same year ore was found in Mayville and the first smelter was built in 1848-49. The smelters eventually reached a capacity of 800 tons per day, but operations were finally shut down in 1928.

A Bavarian brewmaster operated two small breweries, the Ziegler and the Steger Brewing Companies, from Mayville's early days until Prohibition. Local beer was usually brewed in the winter because the hot summers spoiled the fermentation process. When the beer was done, it was kegged and put in underground cellars. Some of these cellars still remain in the Mayville/Horicon area.

An old settler reported that the Mayville tavern continued to sell beer even after Prohibition—with the aid of a two-way faucet! Strangers in the tavern were sold near beer from the faucet's right side. Regulars, served from the left side, received the full-bodied and stronger Wildcat beer, a private Bavarian recipe.

HORICON MARSH WILDLIFE AREA

Six miles beyond Mayville on highway 28, is the Horicon Marsh, a must stopover, particularly in the fall. This area, covering 31,653 acres, is famous for the numerous geese that pause here on their annual fall migration. In October and November upwards of 200,000 geese reportedly feed here.

According to a state historical marker the marsh "was carved out some 10,000 years ago by the Wisconsin glacier. Gradually the Rock River made deposits which slowed its current and spread its water over this marshland. To promote lumbering, transportation and agriculture, white pioneers built a dam here in 1846. Horicon Lake, covering 51 square miles, became famous for hunting and fishing. Then in 1869, the dam was removed, restoring the old marsh."

Through the years, various development schemes have changed the marsh's character. For more than 20 years conservationists fought to reclaim the area's natural beauty. They won the battle on July 16, 1941, when the marsh was officially set aside as the Horicon National Wild-Life Refuge. Horicon means "clear water."

LOMIRA, Pop. 1,446

Back on Route 41, Lomira, originally called Springfield, was once one of the county's most prosperous villages. Before the white man, it was the temporary home of Chief Blackhawk's son who camped here while blazing a trail from Milwaukee to Green Bay.

Information is scarce regarding the town's early history, but John Foltz is known to have been the first settler here in 1844. He was soon joined by Samuel Kinyon, a New York native who came that spring. A true pioneer, Kinyon chopped and cleared timber from his 170-acre land, shot deer for food and traded with the Indians. Upon his arrival, provisions were scarce and Kinyon was forced to haul his supplies from Rock County more than 100 miles away.

Warren Marston, who moved here with his parents in 1847, later became prominent in the state. He was elected county clerk in 1873 and later served in the Wisconsin legislature.

Route 41 passes through Lomira's oldest section since most of the village moved east of its original site when the Wisconsin Central railroad lines shifted in 1871.

There are two versions of how the town got its current name. One old settler claimed it referred to the low land and mire area around the village; thus the name Lomira. According to the other story, an early family named Schoonover

SHSW

Schoolgirls hamming it up.

had a daughter Elmira who was quite a popular young lady. The village was renamed in her honor, with an adjustment to the current spelling.

FOND DU LAC COUNTY, Pop. 88,952

Fond du Lac County once lay on the dividing line between an immense hardwood and pine forest which extended north to Lake Superior, and a vast prairie which stretched west to the Rocky Mountains. Today, the county is split into two distinct parts north and south by a limestone ridge which runs from Calumet to Byron. The ridge's eastern section has many glaciated regions, including the Ice Age Reserve, a nine-unit, 32,500-acre area set aside by the federal government to preserve Wisconsin's prehistoric features. Part of the reserve runs through Pike Lake State Park near Slinger.

The western ridge has great quantities of limestone and creates a formidable barrier between the two sections. This half also has extremely fertile soil and excellent springs which provide good drainage and make it one of the country's finest dairying counties.

Fond du Lac County takes its name from its location at Lake Winnebago's southern tip. The three French words literally mean "the foot of the lake." The county was probably named by French traders who dealt with Indians near here.

LAKE WINNEBAGO

Lake Winnebago is the largest body of fresh water wholly within one state and the most striking physical feature of Fond du Lac County. It is a remnant of Glacial Lake Oshkosh which spread southeast from Canada to Lake Michigan and deposited its meltwater here.

Winnebago, elevated 162 feet above Lake Michigan, is about 30 miles long north to south and eight to fifteen miles wide east to west. Early settlers thought the quantities of fish taken from this lake—mostly suckers, bull-pouts, catfish and sturgeon—were incredible. Most fish were sold in Fond du Lac during 1859 for ten cents a bushel but suckers and bull-pouts went for 25 cents per sleigh load to pig farmers who needed them for feed.

Lake Winnebago, only 21 feet at its deepest point, is not very cold in summer but freezes early and to a great depth in winter.

SHSW

Fond du Lac, 1900.

RIVERS

Fond du Lac County might well be called the birthplace of rivers, for it is the source of more rivers and creeks than any other Wisconsin county. Perhaps even more remarkable, streams flow from here in all four directions. Of the seven rivers beginning here, only the east and west Branches of the Fond du Lac River lie wholly within the county. The West Branch, largest of the two, has three principal sources—at Metomen, Ripon, and Rosendale. It unites with the East Branch in Fond du Lac, a half-mile before emptying into Lake Winnebago. The East Branch has its principal source in Oakfield, where it is called Seven Mile Creek.

EARLY SETTLEMENT

Prominent Green Bay citizens founded Fond du Lac County. A joint stock association was formed in November, 1835, to buy and sell real estate at or near the head of Lake Winnebago in what was then Brown County. James D. Doty, later Governor of Wisconsin, was the company's largest stockholder with 46 shares. By January 1, 1836, the company owned 3,705 acres of land in what is now Fond du Lac. That spring the company built a double log house on the east side of Brooke Street to provide entertainment for travelers and began a permanent settlement. The county's first house, it was named the Fond du Lac House.

That June, Colwert Pier became the area's first permanent settler. Coming from Green Bay, Pier reached Fond du Lac House and stayed there managing the house as a tavern until his brother and family joined him on March 11, 1837.

BYRON, Pop. 1,681

Byron was organized in 1846 and named after a village in Genesee County, New York. The first residents were primarily farmers, but the stone quarries later dominated the land. Some large quarries can still be seen just off Highway 175.

FOND DU LAC, Pop. 35,863

Explorers had always assumed that a village would develop here around the harbor at the foot of Lake Winnebago. Thanks to Dr. Mason C. Darling it did.

When Darling came here from Sheboygan in 1838 following the Pier brothers arrival two years earlier, Doty gave him land south of the Fond du Lac Land Company's property. A short time later, Darling broke his farm acreage into lots which he sold quite cheaply and sometimes even gave away. He also gave land to the county so that they might build a courthouse, church and school. The town incorporated on March 1, 1847 and Darling was chosen the first village president because of his enthusiasm for the town. Later he became the first mayor.

Fond du Lac, which had existed only on paper when the Pier brothers came here in 1836, grew to 15,308 people by 1875. By then, the thriving metropolis contained 19 public schools, a German and English academy, 18 churches, six banks, one monthly, five weekly and two daily newspapers, 12 hotels, four separate railroad lines, four foundries and machine shops, four sash, door and blind factories (including the largest in the world), 10 saw mills, two flour mills, a wagon factory and various other institutions and manufacturing interests.

An octagon house at 276 Linden Street, listed on the National Register of Historic Sites, is a fine, restored example of Fond du Lac's early architecture. It was built by Isaac Brown in 1856 and later occupied by his son Edwin who married the daughter of Edward Pier, Fond du Lac's first settler.

NORTH FOND DU LAC, Pop. 3,844

The Soo Line railroad desperately sought a new terminal in 1898. Seeking local help, the line looked to a few of Fond du Lac's leading citizens. Those citizens bought land for the Soo in Friendship where the level ground was suitable for freight yards. After the railroad shops moved in, housing became a necessity and subdivisions were platted to include buildings for the workers.

Not to be outdone, the Chicago Northwestern Railroad announced similar designs on this area, and built an 18-stall roundhouse, the state's largest, in 1901. By 1913 the Soo Line and the Northwestern each employed more than 1,000 men.

VAN DYNE

On the Wisconsin map of 1830, this little town was known as Smoker's Village, a Winnebago Indian enclave of eight lodges and 150 inhabitants. Smoker was the son of Sarrachou, the Winnebago Chief who lived in Taycheedah.

Platted by Daniel R. Van Dyne in 1866, the town was laid out in lots and soon contained a grocery store, grist mill, blacksmith shop, cheese factory, hotel and a few farms. It was also a stop on the Soo Line railroad, halfway between Fond du Lac and Oshkosh.

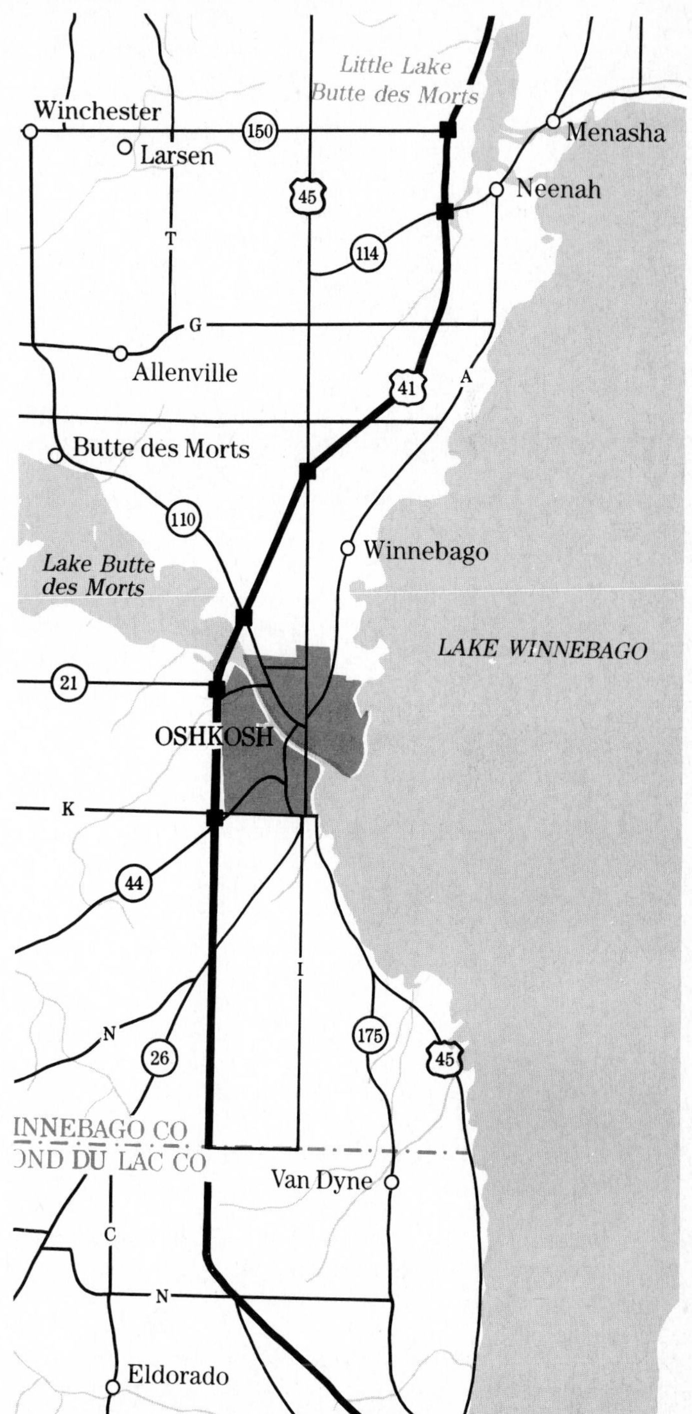

WINNEBAGO COUNTY, Pop. 131,732

Until 1842 Winnebago County was nothing but wilderness. Bounded on the east by Lake Winnebago, it resembled a vast park of prairie, forests, lakes and rivers.

The shores of Lake Winnebago consisted of a timber belt which extended two-five miles inland and included oak, sugar maple, hickory, elm and basswood. Frequent fires kept the undergrowth down, creating large open areas among the tall burr oaks. Many early Indians maintained villages at these oak openings, primarily on lakes Butte des Morts, Winneconne and Poygan.

Winnebago County, with abundant game, fish and fur bearing animals and a shallow lake that provided ample wild rice supplies and easy canoe portages, became the natural center of Wisconsin's Indian population. The Winnebagoes came first, making their home on Doty Island where Neenah and Menasha now stand. The oldest Wisconsin map, drawn in 1632, refers to these Indians as Puans, after the Lac des Puans (Lake Winnebago) that they lived on. These French words are roughly translated as "stinking waters." However, the Winnebagoes, a Dakota tribe of the Algonkian Indians, referred to themselves as Ho-changa-ra, or "people speaking the original language." Meanwhile, the Eastern Algonkian tribe referred to their western brothers as Ouinipegou, or "People of the Sea".

Winnebago County's first white settler was Augustin Grignon who moved here in 1818 and established a trading post with James Porlier near present day Butte des Morts. It was here that the Indian trail between Fort Winnebago in Portage and Fort Howard, near Green Bay, crossed the Wolf River.

White settlement in Winnebago County was slow while vast numbers of people migrated to southern Wisconsin for the many lead mining jobs. A few hardy families appeared in 1836, including the Piers at Fond du Lac and the Gallups and Stanleys at Oshkosh, but they were the only settlers between Neenah and Milwaukee, a distance of more than 100 miles.

SHSW

Oshkosh, 1890.

Four years after Winnebago was organized in 1842, only 732 persons lived here. However, this beautiful lake and river country soon attracted rapid growth. The population jumped from 732 to 2,787 in one year and it is still growing.

OSHKOSH, Pop. 49,678

Webster Stanley, who moved here in 1836, is generally considered the founder of the City of Athens as Oshkosh was originally called. Stanley, employed by the government to transport supplies from Fort Howard to Fort Winnebago, was impressed by the area's natural beauty and advantages. Consequently, in July of 1836, he left his home in Neenah, loaded a boat with a year's provisions, lumber, tools and furniture, and set out with his family and a small crew.

The journey was rough and hampered by indecisiveness. After capsizing once along the way, the crew finally reached Garlic Island, now Island Park, where they decided to stay until morning. The following day, after a short period of confusion, the pioneers finally landed on the south side of the Fox River. Upon exploring, they found Coon's Point where they unloaded and built a shanty. A short while later Stanley met James Knaggs, an Indian trader who lived across the river, and went into partnership with him. Together they ran Knaggs tavern and ferry business.

About mid-August, Stanley was joined by his brothers-in-law, August Henry and Amos Gallup. In a short time, the three pioneers claimed a large tract of land north of the mouth of the Fox River. Gallup claimed 170 acres at the mouth of the Fox and Lake Winnebago. Stanley's 117 acres

SHSW

A fresh start. Photo/C.J. Van Schaick.

adjoined Gallup's to the west. Here they built a house where they lived together until the following November when Gallup built a log house on his own land. The city of Oshkosh had begun.

When Winnebago County organized in 1840, Stanley's tavern became its political center—all elections and important meetings were held there. It was there that trader Robert Grignon, interested in maintaining good will with the Indians, insisted that the village be named for Oshkosh, a Menomonee chief and friend of most white settlers. The proposition was strongly supported by those who favored the Indians and opposed by those who preferred a more classic name. Gallup insisted it remain Athens. However, Grignon and his followers prevailed in an assembly meeting that fall and the name Oshkosh was voted in. Although the name's meaning is disputed, it has generally been translated as "brave," a description worn well by the Menomonee chief who took a fatherly interest in the town named after him.

FOX RIVER VALLEY

In general, the towns along Lake Winnebago's western shore have become known as the Fox River Valley. This area began around 10,000 years ago when the Wisconsin glacier swept into the state, advancing in the form of icy tongues called lobes. When this ice and snow mountain hit the tip of Door County, it ran into an ancient geological formation, the Niagara Escarpment, and split into two more lobes. One of these, the Lake Michigan lobe, formed Lake Winnebago. The other, the Green Bay lobe, sculpted the Fox River Valley.

Meltwater impounded from the retreating ice lobes formed Glacial Lake Oshkosh, which then drained southeast to Lake Michigan. Most of Lake Oshkosh drained in time, although certain irregularities on the lake's floor created other water bodies, including Lake Winnebago, the state's largest inland lake which still drains down the Fox River to Green Bay.

FOX RIVER

The Fox River, which originated with Glacial Lake Oshkosh, was a major part of Wisconsin's natural waterway for the early settlers. Marquette and Joliet explored the entire Fox in 1673, before portaging to the Wisconsin River and traveling on to the Mississippi.

However, 10,000 years before the explorers traversed this free-flowing river, Glacial Lake Oshkosh was impounded behind a dam of glacial drift. The lower Fox, downstream from Lake Winnebago, cut through this barrier into the underlying bedrock, creating a drop of 15 feet per mile from Neenah-Menasha to Kaukauna. Eight rapids mark the Fox's course between those twin cities and DePere and spurred early settlement.

Unfortunately, hydroelectric dams and associated industrial developments, primarily paper mills, have turned the free flowing Fox of Nicolet, Marquette and Joliet into one of the nation's more polluted rivers. Serious efforts are being made to clean up the Fox before it destroys all of Green Bay.

NEENAH, Pop. 23,272

For many years Menominee Indians occupied this site as part of the Winnebago Rapids reservation. However, they were forced to give up all land north of the Fox River and west of Lake Winnebago on September 3, 1836 when they ceded nearly four million acres in a treaty signed at Cedar Rapids, near Appleton. The Menominees continued to live on their Winnebago Rapids reservation, occasionally working in the government-run saw and grist mills, but the work

SHSW

Winnebago Indians Coo-Nu-Gah (First Boy) and Big Bear.

was ill-suited to their way of life and they didn't always show up for work. Without help, the project had to be abandoned. In 1838 a smallpox epidemic killed one-third of the Indians. Those who survived soon left the dying reservation. The buildings fell into decay and the government soon advertised the sale of all reservation land and buildings.

Hearing of the sale through his good friend, Governor James Duane Doty, Milwaukee newspaperman Harrison Reed made a bid. The Secretary of War approved the sale in 1844 and Harrison got 562 acres of land, including 34 log houses, a blacksmith shop, saw and grist mill and all the waterpower to operate it, tools, logs, timber, glass, carts and wagons. The price of this land, which became Neenah, was $4,760.

Reed solicited the help of a New Yorker, Harvey Jones, to cover bonds filed on the bid, and thus formed Neenah-Menasha's trio of founding fathers (Doty, Reed and Jones).

Needing someone to help repair the abandoned mills, Harrison hired George Mansur, a Buffalo, New York native. Mansur's family had lived in Kaukauna for a year but decided to move on in April, 1844. They located their claim on the Lake Shore road and became Neenah's first permanent white settlers. The town was officially incorporated and named Neenah, a Menomonee word meaning "water" on March 28, 1856.

THE PAPER CITY

Originally known as Flour City, (see route 45) it wasn't long before Neenah claimed another title which has been synonymous with its name ever since.

Although this Paper City got into the game long after the Milwaukee, Whitewater and Appleton mills had declined, Neenah was really the springboard for this thriving new industry. According to the "Paper Mill Directory," Neenah had the second highest number of mills operating anywhere in the country by 1900.

It all began in an old, red frame building in 1865. The Neenah Paper Company, the town's first paper mill, is now the site of the famous Kimberly-Clark Company, manufacturers of "Kleenex." The Neenah mill was built by a stock company, composed of Hiram Smith and his brother, Nathan Cobb, Dr. Robinson, John Jamison and Moses Hooper, with $10,000 in capital stock.

The mill's paper stock was rags; no wood pulp was then used. The rags came from Milwaukee, were sorted by women and girls, then processed into print paper which sold at 11 and one-half cents per pound. The mill produced 3,500 pounds of paper in a 24-hour day.

Hiram and Edward Smith leased the mill in 1867 but Edward sold his interest to D.C. Van Ostrand before the year ended and the firm became Smith & Van Ostrand until they sold it to Kimberly, Clark & Company in 1874. Five years later, J. Alfred Kimberly, Charles B. Clark, F.C. Shattuck and Havilah Babcock formed a four-way partnership. The Fox River mill was the first paper mill venture of that partnership which has become the state's largest papermaker. Its head office is still in Neenah.

MENASHA, Pop. 14,728

The U.S. government originally offered the Menasha site for sale on August 31, 1835. Lots were bid off at prices ranging from five to ten dollars per acre. The Hon. James Duane Doty, Governor of Wisconsin, convinced of the tremendous waterpower available here, bought a large portion on what became known as Doty Island. The restored Grand Loggery is open to visitors.

SHSW

Neenah mills on the Lower Fox River.

In 1847, when this area was still wilderness and the Fox River ran wild over the rapids, John L. Kimberly (later of Kimberly Clark & Company) bought all the mill and store land for $100. It was subsequently sold for $838 and was platted six years later.

The site, known then as Waupakun, was still a dense forest in 1848 when Cornelius Northrup built a slab house at the intersection of Milwaukee and Sixth streets. He hauled slabs for the house over Doty Island from the mission at Winnebago Rapids (Neenah) two miles away and formed the cabin by placing the slabs upright and battening the ragged edges up against one another, flat sides together. This dwelling, the first in Menasha, has long since rotted away.

The real inducement for settling here was the availability of hydraulic power for operating milling and manufacturing industries. However, before these enterprises could be erected the river had to be improved by damming the water and excavating a canal to carry the increased head of water to the mill site. The water forming Lake Winnebago, gathered by 5,000 miles of rivers and creeks, discharges through two channels, one at Menasha, the other at Neenah. The Menasha channel is about two miles long and connects Lake Winnebago with Little Lake Butte des Morts below.

The state contracted Curtis Reed, whose father had settled Neenah, to build the dam and retain all rights for future use of the waterpower for hydraulic purposes. Reed moved here from Fond du Lac in 1848 and built a log dwelling near the site of the proposed canal.

In Reed's house, the town was named Menasha. Always fond of Indian names, Doty had suggested Menashay after the Indian village of Four Legs which had originally been located on Doty Island. Cutting off the y, the assemblage voted for Menasha, the Indian word meaning "settlement on the Island," which distinguished their village from another nearby.

A short time later, Reed began work on the canal. Although much was done that first year, it eventually fell back to the state to complete. When it was finished in 1850, a number of saw mills located near the dam at the river's edge, created a manufacturing site which has distinguished this area ever since.

By 1860 Menasha was a major center for manufacturing products defined as lumber and timber derivatives. The Menasha Pail Factory, operated by Elisha D. Smith, produced 20,000 dozen pails, 1,500 tubs, 500,000 broom handles, 500,000 feet of lumber and sundry articles worth $5,000. Ten years later that count had increased to include 240,000 pails, 14,400 churns, 50,000 butter tubs, 95,000 fish buckets, 800,000 broom handles and wash day items, 60,000 wash tubs, 12,000 washboards and six million clothes pins. In 1869 the "Sentinel" reported that, "The Menasha Wooden Ware Factory…is one of the largest of its kind in the U.S. and the magnitude of its business is truly astonishing. It keeps in constant employment 150 hands and consumes annually 4,000,000 feet of pine lumber and one million feet of hardwood lumber… with yearly business aggregates at $300,000."

Early clothespin maker. Photo/Helgesen.

OUTAGAMIE COUNTY, Pop. 128,726

Some 300 years ago Outagamie County was the hunting ground of the Winnebago, Menominee and Outagamie Indians. The Winnebago, whose villages were mostly southwest of this county, were an eastern branch of the Sioux. The Menominee belonged to an altogether different Indian group, the Algonkian, which held most of the area east to the Atlantic. The Outagamie, also known as the Fox, were an extremely independent Indian nation and natural enemies of the Winnebago. Nonetheless, the county and the river were named for them.

The Fox began drifting into this area about 1630 and settled near the Wolf River. Fifty years later they moved to a village on the Fox River near Little Lake Butte des Morts on the west side of Menasha, where they controlled white trade on the river for many years. By the late 17th century, the Fox began open warfare against the whites, due largely to frauds perpetrated on them by early French traders. They demanded tribute from any trader's boat approaching the village. The whole Fox village met a tragic end in a battle that created the meaning of Lake Butte des Morts, or "Hill of the Dead." (See Route 45) Eventually, the tribe left this part of the state and later merged with the Sauk.

The name Outagamie, meaning "dwellers on the other side

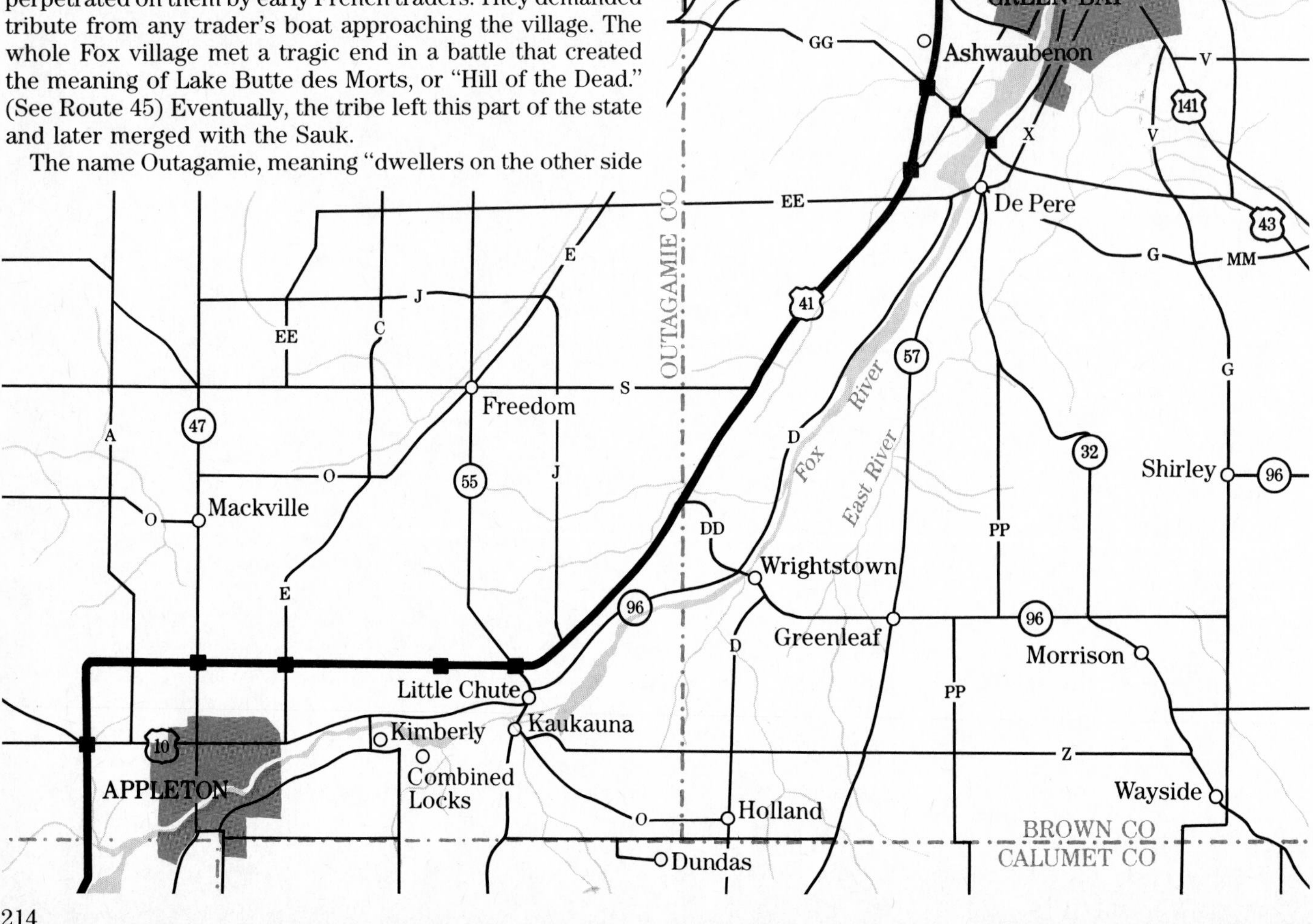

of the stream," came from the Chippewa who used it when referring to the Fox.

WHITE SETTLEMENT

The Fox River meant waterpower and transportation and became a magnet drawing settlers here. For many years French explorers traveled the Fox, trading with the Indians, settling disputes and opening new fields of fur trade. The first permanent settlers located around Kakalin Falls, the present town of Kaukauna. A log house built there in 1837 by the town's first settler, Charles Augustin Grignon, has been restored and can be visited Tuesday through Sunday, Memorial Day to Labor Day, from 1-5 p.m.

The greatest influx of settlers came in the 1840's when Lawrence University was established at Appleton. By the turn-of-the-century Outagamie County's population had risen to 46,247 people, with Germans prevailing.

APPLETON, Pop. 53,531

In the fall of 1848, John F. Johnston and his family moved here from Menasha and their home became the village's first permanent settlement. More than just a home, the Johnston establishment soon served as a hotel, hospital, church and post office.

One year before the Johnston's moved in, Lawrence University had been chartered with money from Boston's Amos A. Lawrence. Johnston knew well the men who started Appleton, named for Amos Lawrence's father-in-law, and he watched proudly as the town prospered with men of good will and capital. It incorporated on April 14, 1853 and continued to grow as a new paper mill, established that year to make wrapping paper, ran night and day to fill orders. The establishment, originally called the Edwin Atkinson Mills, was soon known as the Appleton Mills of C.P. Richmond. Appleton's first newspaper, the "Crescent," began operations later in 1853 but was dismayed that the new mill could not produce newsprint. It was three years before the Crescent stopped importing paper stock from Beloit.

Paper mills continued their rapid growth here after the Fox River Paper Corporation began business in 1883.

KIMBERLY, Pop. 5,881

Although highway 41 only skirts this little town, it is interesting to note its development. Early government maps refer to Kimberly as Smithfield, a mission town located along an Indian trail on the Fox River's south bank. It is almost directly across from where the Menominee Indians ceded their remaining lands in the 1836 Treaty of Cedars. A marker notes that site one mile west of Little Chute on highway 96.

Kimberly-Clark & Company acquired rights to this area and built a pulp and paper mill here in 1889. The old trail became a road and a village grew up around the mill. It incorporated in 1910 as Kimberly.

LITTLE CHUTE, Pop. 7,907

Early French explorers passing here named this spot La Petite Chute but it was platted years later as Nepomuc. That name came from a Catholic Church here,

St. John Nepomuc, only a small wigwam when erected in 1836 near the old mill site, long before Outagamie County was organized. One year later, a new frame church was built and Rev. Theodore Van Den Broek was appointed pastor.

Van den Broek, a wilderness missionary priest, came from Holland and soon convinced his Dutch countrymen to migrate to this land of promise. The Fox River Development Company, desperate for workers, offered free transportation to foreigners who would settle in the valley and help build canals on the Fox. With Van den Broek's assistance, three boatloads of Hollanders sailed from Rotterdam on March 10, 1848. Following a stormy voyage, they landed at New York's Ellis Island two months later and finally arrived at Little Chute on June 20.

The Forty-Eighters were greeted by the little frame church near the river, a number of log huts and a frightening wilderness. Nine families moved several miles southeast, since there weren't enough houses in town and founded a colony called Franciscus Bosh, now known as Hollandtown. (Ed.note: The author's father was born here.) The families at the church site established the neat and thrifty community of Little Chute where many residents still speak the native language.

KAUKAUNA, Pop. 11,310

The Indians originally named this town Ogag-kane or O-gau-gau-Ning, which the French changed to Cacalin and later Grand Kaukaulin. The present city was actually two villages at one time, Kaukauna or Grand Kakalin on the north side of the river and Ledyard on the south. Father Claude Jean Allouez passed along these riverbanks in 1669 to serve as a missionary among the Indians. An important portage here gave Allouez a chance to walk the banks of Kaukauna where he "found apple trees and vine stocks in great numbers."

A huge rock, resembling a face, hung over the rapids here but was destroyed when missionaries learned that the natives worshipped it as an idol. Rolling the boulder into the river, the naive priests destroyed one of the most important Indian relics of the time.

Dominick and Paul Ducharme and Augustin Grignon were the first permanent white settlers in Kaukauna, landing there in the 1790's. The log house Grignon built is the oldest house in the state and is still open to visitors. A post office was established in 1832 and Grignon appointed postmaster. Two years later, Kaukauna had become the area's main trading post.

In 1880-81, the Milwaukee, Lake Shore & Western Railroad created the Kaukauna Waterpower Company which constructed a 2,400-foot-long canal to help channel water above the government built dam on the Fox River. Its success led to the building of a stave, pulp and paper, flouring, planing and shingle mill which in turn brought prosperity to the town.

Kaukauna became a part of Outagamie County in 1851 and incorporated in 1885.

BROWN COUNTY, Pop. 175,280

This county, rich in state history, once covered nearly half of Wisconsin stretching as far south as Illinois. Although 22 counties were eventually carved out of the original county, the territory now known as Brown County always contained the land between De Pere and Green Bay where Wisconsin's history began.

When Samuel de Champlain, Governor of New France, was looking for a water route to China, he heard about a People of the Sea in the west who occupied a strategic position along the route. Quickly, he sent Jean Nicolet to find them. Landing at Green Bay in 1634, Nicolet discovered the lodges of the Menominee (People of the Sea) Indians at the mouth of the Fox River and claimed the area for the King of France.

Excited by Nicolet's reports, Jesuit missionaries decided to explore this area in search of a westward passage to the Pacific. Father James Marquette and Louis Joliet joined in this pursuit, landing at Green Bay in June, 1673. Passing from there through the Fox and Wisconsin rivers, Marquette finally reached the Mississippi on June 17, thus charting the first continuous natural waterway between the St. Lawrence and the Gulf of Mexico. For two centuries the new Fox-Wisconsin waterway created the region's most absorbing commercial interest—fur-trading. Begun in 1634 with the first French explorers, it continued until 1844 when no valuable fur-bearing animals were left.

The county's first permanent settlers were the DeLanglades who arrived in 1745 from Mackinaw, Michigan. (For more information on DeLanglade, see Green Bay, page ?.) The county was later named for Major-General Jacob Brown, a successful army leader in the War of 1812.

WRIGHTSTOWN, Pop. 1,169

The Fox River divides this village into two parts: East and West Wrightstown. The land rises gently from either shore, creating a picturesque setting.

Noel S. Wright, for whom the town was later named, came here from Vermont in 1833 and became the town's first permanent settler. Rumor has it that cats were at a premium among early settlers and Wright purchased his first 40 acres of land at $1.25 per acre by selling felines for $2.00 each.

Wright established a ferry here in 1836 for the convenience of travelers on the Military Road cut from Ft. Howard to Ft. Winnebago. Wright's Ferry was a well-known crossing for many years.

DE PERE, Pop. 14,892

De Pere began as a mission founded by the Jesuit missionary Claude Allouez in 1668. At the the Potawatomi Indian's invitation, Allouez said his first mass at the foot of George Street on December 3, the day of St. Francis Xavier after whom he named the mission. Indians later destroyed the mission in the Fox wars and it was never rebuilt. A memorial stands there today.

The title of De Pere's first permanent settler went to General William Dickinson who moved his family here in April, 1829. The move to this unbroken wilderness was very painful for Mrs. Dickinson and was aggravated by her three-year-old daughter who constantly cried that she didn't like the trees. A short time later Mrs. Dickinson's parents moved here and helped combat her loneliness. By 1847, only six families lived here.

Communications with the outside world improved when a plank road was built in 1853. The road, from Green Bay to DePere, connected Brown County with adjacent communities and increased settlement. The Chicago & Northwestern railroad snorted through the Lower Fox region in August, 1862, providing access all the way to Chicago and making this area much more desirable.

De Pere is split into two distinct parts—De Pere and West De Pere—which are separated by the Fox River but connected by a 1500-foot bridge. An eight-foot waterfall creates waterpower equivalent to 12,000 horsepower and provides good manufacturing opportunities.

ASHWAUBENON, Pop. 14,486

A part of West De Pere extends into this small, irregularly-shaped town along the Fox River's west bank.

John H. Peterson, the town's first settler, owned the only oxen team, and was soon busy hauling logs, day in and day out, for the new homes, church and school that were built. Early Ashwaubenon had only 35 families, chiefly of Scandinavian or Holland-Belgian descent, who laid out their farms in a complete circle, creating its irregular shape.

GREEN BAY, Pop. 87,899

Just as all roads led to ancient Rome, so too did all Brown County roads lead to Green Bay. In winter the highways were lined with oxen teams as far north as Little Suamico and as far south as Little Chute. With few exceptions, these teams brought in lumber or shingles. At one time, the county had 150 saw and shingle mills. By 1870 Brown County was the world's leading shingle market, producing 500 million in Green Bay alone.

Green Bay was the first area of Wisconsin discovered by white explorers, in 1634. A memorial five miles northeast of Green Bay on highway 57 marks the spot of Joliet's discovery. One hundred years later Augustin DeLanglade and his son Charles became the first permanent settlers when they moved to the east side of the Fox River near Green Bay and opened a trading post. Most of the Indians they encountered were friendly, but one band frequently threatened to break into the store and help themselves. As was his fashion, DeLanglade responded daringly, "Well, my friends, if you have come to fight, we will cross to the prairie on the other side of the river and have a little fun." The Indians never took him up on his offer and the DeLanglades lived out their days in peace.

FORT HOWARD

In the summer of 1816 the U.S. government decided to build a fort at Green Bay. Four companies of soldiers were dispatched and landed at Green Bay where they visited the Menominee chief, Tomah, to ask his consent. He said that the government was too strong for him to refuse and they could build the fort wherever they wished.

The original garrison was four miles above Green Bay on the Fox River. To obtain the soldiers' business, a few traders opened a liquor store which the soldiers named Shanty Town, an army phrase for "house where liquor is sold." As a consequence, all of the county's businesses soon centered there.

The actual fort was built in 1820 near the present city of Green Bay. Hewn timbers about a foot square were used in its construction and the entire structure was painted white and surrounded by gardens and grain fields. The parade grounds and drill gardens were located at the present city of Howard. The soldiers' arrival stimulated the county's growth and settlers began moving here in increasing numbers.

The Fort Howard Hospital Museum, located on Kellogg and N. Chestnut Ave., was the site of the first fort hospital and contains articles used by the soldiers. It is open daily from May through November.

SHSW

Fort Howard, Green Bay, 1865.

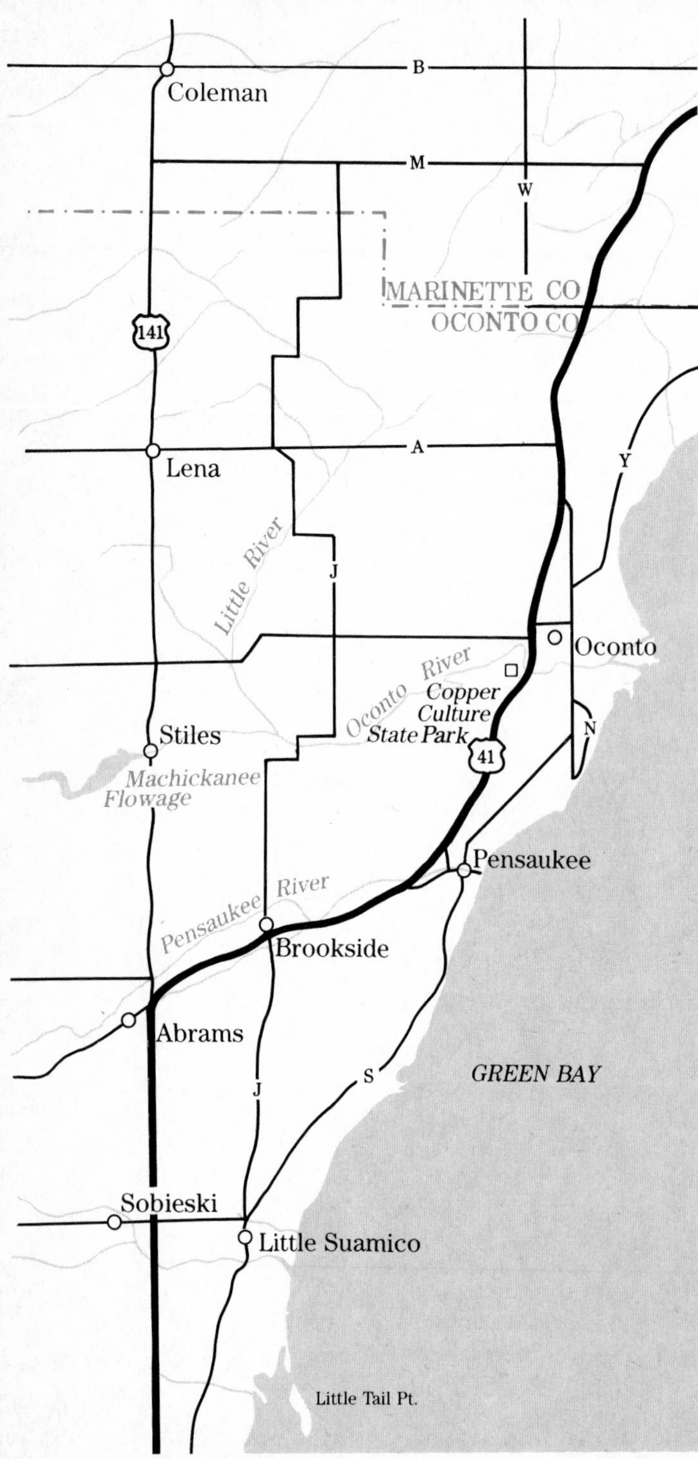

SUAMICO, Pop. 4,003

The first settlements here were made in 1846 and 1850 at or near the Suamico River. A. Sensiba, Stephen Burdon and Willard Lamb were among the first settlers. Before long, the town had eight mills, including three at the mouth of the river and one owned by Lamb.

Suamico's sandy and fertile soil produces abundant crops of wheat, rye, oats, barley, corn, peas and potatoes. However, these natural farming conditions were neglected until after the mills ceased operations.

OCONTO COUNTY, Pop. 28,947

In the last three centuries, Oconto County, like many Wisconsin counties, was ruled by four different nations. The Menominee Indians of the Algonkian tribe ruled first, followed by the French who explored the area in 1634 and finally lost control during the French and Indian War. The English followed when Capt. Balfour sailed up Green Bay with a small company of Redcoats and planted a Union Jack flag over Green Bay Territory. Finally, in 1816, the United States came to Oconto County in the person of Col. John Miller and four vessels of American troops.

Ten years later J.P. Arndt began the earliest settlement and one of the county's most profitable industries—lumber. Arndt obtained a lease from the Menominee tribe through the U.S. government to cut timber on the Pensaukee River. He built the area's first mill and dam, and Oconto County's lumber barons prospered until the virgin timber regions were diminished.

George Lerwick, Mr. Langden and Mr. Ehrie began the county's first permanent settlement when they built a dam on the present site of Oconto around 1835. Although the dam was later carried away by rains, the men remained in town for another ten years.

SOBIESKI

Polish settlers named this town after King John Sobieski of Poland. Little is known about the community before 1895 except that a few saw mills were located on the Suamico River. About that time, J.J. Hoff from the J.J. Hoff Land Company of Milwaukee, traveled here to establish a farm community. He established his first land office in Sobieski, selling land for $15 per acre. Polish settlers cleared the land and built log cabins, and the town that began with 20-40 acres has expanded to about 160.

ABRAMS, Pop. 1,181

When Richard B. Yeaton, Abram's first settler, came to town he bought much of the land on which the village now

SHSW

Farm of Rolla Shufelt. Vicinity of Oconto.

stands. Arriving in 1857, Yeaton started the first blacksmith shop, making tools for settlers from miles around and establishing trade with the Indians. One Indian known as No Nose because his nose was bitten off in a fight slept on the floor near Yeaton's cabin stove. The cabin and blacksmith shop have stood in Abrams for almost a century, a symbol of its early pioneers.

Many settlers moved to Abrams to work in the mills which had located here because of a five-mile strip of timber called Pumpkin Pine near by. Trees in the patch grew four to five feet in diameter, had very little grain, and were a high quality pine.

Several boarding houses and homes sprang up when the railroad came through town in 1881.

BROOKSIDE

Although little is known of its past, Brookside is located along a brook which may account for its name.

PENSAUKEE, Pop. 1,000

Oconto County's first saw mill was located here in 1827. Homes were built for the workers and a few years later, Pensaukee (from the Menominee Indian word Paissacue meaning "inside the mouth of a river") became a booming mill town, competing with others nearby.

The Pensaukee River had seven dams, with at least three mills operating at one time during logging's peak. As the timber was cleared, settlers turned to farming and fishing which later became Pensaukee's principal business.

Then, in 1877, a disastrous tornado ruined this once prosperous town. Sad tales were told—of a bale of straw that tore through a heavy door; a sewing machine blown through a cow; and a baby snatched from its mother's arms by the fierce wind and never seen again. The tornado destroyed all of the mills and most of the homes and the town never recovered.

OCONTO, Pop. 4,505

Oconto is located at the mouth of the Oconto River, midway between Marinette and Green Bay. Incorporated in 1869, the town was called Oak-a-toe by the Indians, meaning "river plentiful with fish." Indians once hunted game, fished and riced where white men now have river homes.

In the winter of 1669, the Jesuit priest Allouez established the Mission of St. Francis Xavier at Oconto, the first white man's post in northeastern Wisconsin.

The first permanent settlers, the Thomas Lindsey family, came here by boat on June ten, 1846. They lived in a tent for the first ten days, then built an overnight lodge for other newcomers who flocked into the village to work in the flourishing lumber industry.

From 1850 to 1900, Oconto was a typical lumber town—wild and rugged. The muddy, sawdust-filled streets were lined with wooden sidewalks, scarred and chipped by the rivermen's calked boots. Frequent fights broke out between the rivermen and the lumberjacks.

SHSW

Destructive fires and unsound logging practices left much of northern Wisconsin devastated.

While busy mills were turning out pine lumber, John Stein from Norway began building sail boats and setting nets in Green Bay, beginning the commercial fishing industry which is still practiced in Oconto.

MARINETTE COUNTY, Pop. 39,314

This county, like so many in northern Wisconsin, developed out of the great lumbering industries. From its headwaters at Marinette, the Menominee River provided a natural boundary between Wisconsin and part of the Upper Peninsula and served a dozen tributaries and a dozen lumber barons.

The first saw mill appeared on the Menominee in 1832. It was unsuccessful, however, and was sold at a sheriff's sale a few years later for 18 barrels of whitefish. Several years later, Isaac Stephenson came to Marinette and established the N. Ludington Company to whom the Menominee was most generous. In the following years, the river was choked with logs en route to 23 mills along its banks and mouth. By 1888, 650 million feet of lumber came from this great timber region annually and the boom lasted until 1911.

The county's name came from Marinette, the half-breed wife of William Farnsworth who helped him run a successful trading post for the American Fur Trading Company.

PESHTIGO, Pop. 2,807

For most travelers, Peshtigo will always be considered the site of the greatest disaster in Wisconsin's history. It was here, on October 8, 1871, the same day as the great Chicago fire, that a fire raged out of control, taking an incredible toll of human life and property.

The stage had probably been set almost a year before in a conspiracy of earth and air. The previous winter had seen little snow, the spring had few showers and July brought a drought to most of the land. Everything north and west of Green Bay was parched and cracked. Even the tamarack swamps were dry.

The pine forests were like tinder and tongues of flame soon darted among the roots and licked the brush. The forest was surrounded by fire and the entire nearby area was in flames. In early September, a dark pall of smoke was noticeable on the shores of Green Bay. Farmers gathered their families and goods and headed for Peshtigo where they hoped to make an effective stand against the fire.

By mid September, forest fires raged up and down the shores of Green Bay, encompassing Sturgeon Bay, Little Suamico, Pensaukee, Oconto, Peshtigo and all settlements in between. By latter September, telegraph communication was severed with Green Bay and thus the rest of the state. By the end of September, the people of five counties waited in dread for the fearful enemy to approach.

Finally, on Sunday, October 8, a tornado formed within the fire, sweeping away most of the northern towns. Fearing the worst, many people committed suicide. Peshtigo, a town of 300 families, was doomed. Everything was on fire. Frightened citizens ran for the river to escape the blaze, but debris from the burning town fell into the river and those who didn't drown were killed by shooting timber and bricks. Seventy persons rushed to the local boarding house and their charred bodies were found days later. In less than one hour, Peshtigo and its 800 people were annihilated. Only one building was left standing. The property loss was estimated at a quarter of a million dollars.

More important than the first settler or the origin of the town's name, the Peshtigo fire will remain with the town forever. A museum is open daily to inform visitors of the tragic event.

MARINETTE, Pop. 11,965

Marinette's first settler, Indian trader Louis Chappee, established a fur-trading post on the Wisconsin side of the river in 1796.

Chappee, a bold, energetic man, was a trader by instinct and he maintained a trade monopoly for many years. However, a stronger man named William Farnsworth came to town in 1822, saw the flourishing trade and seized the post by force when Chappee was away. Too weak by then to resist, Chappee loaded his goods on a canoe and moved to the foot of the rapids.

A beautiful and intelligent woman named Marinette, who later leant her name to the town and the county, came with Farnsworth. She lived with him for several years, raising their children and running the trading post with a strong business sense seldom seen by women of that day. Although Farnsworth found her help invaluable, he left her unexpectedly one day and never returned. Marinette later moved to Green Bay where she died on June 3, 1865 at the age of 73.

The terrible fire of 1871 which destroyed Peshtigo also spread toward Marinette. Fortunately, townspeople saved the town by bravely hauling water, digging trenches, wetting down buildings and putting blankets on them to protect against falling cinders. The small farming community of Birch Creek, about 12 miles away, bore the brunt of the firestorm as it swept away property and killed 19 residents. The tornado of fire finally exhausted itself at Birch Creek, leaving in its wake a path of destruction 40 miles long and ten miles wide. The devastating fire had destroyed millions of dollars in property and 1,200 human lives.

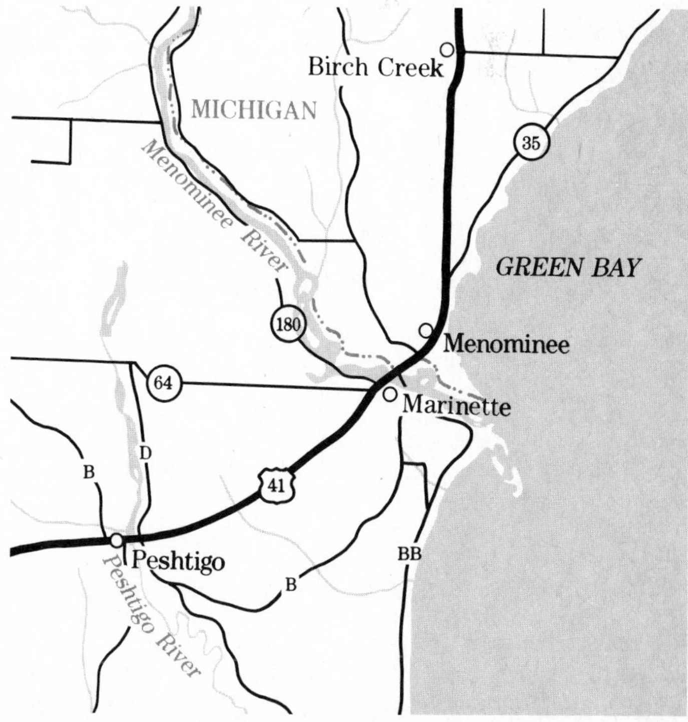

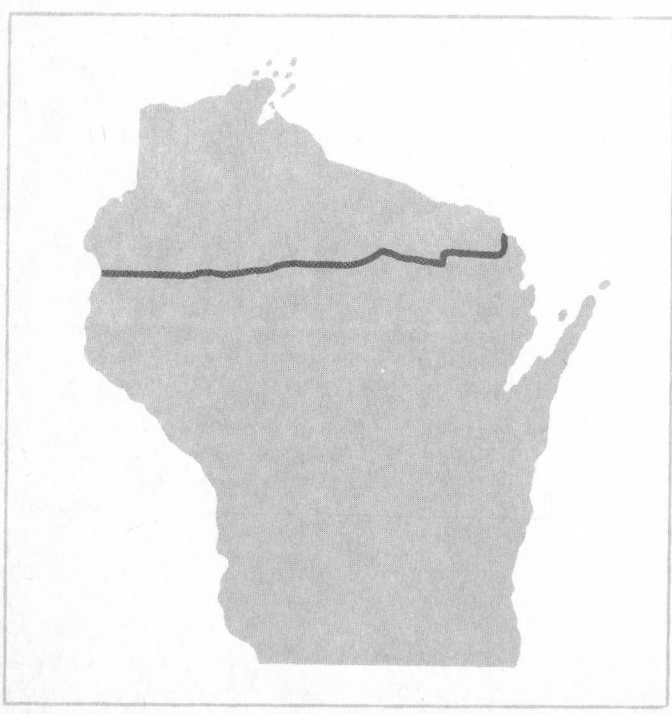

U.S. 8 travels 250 miles through northern Wisconsin. After leaving the deep valley of the St. Croix River, a valley carved by the drainage of glaciers, the road passes through a land which was once the domain of Indians and loggers. U.S. 8 also follows the important railroad route of the Soo Line, first built to bring the wheat from the prairies of Minnesota to the docks of Sault St. Marie.

ROUTE 8, ST. CROIX FALLS TO NIAGARA

SHSW

Shell Lake Cycle Club at the Dells of the St.Croix.

POLK COUNTY, Pop. 32,351

The St. Croix River, one of the major outlets of Glacial Lake Duluth, the glacial lake that preceded Lake Superior, has cut a deep scenic valley along the western border of Polk County. It was here that the Dakota and Ojibwe fought for control of hunting and ricing lands and that the first whites explored as they sought fur trade with the Indians. The Ojibwe pushed into Wisconsin and Minnesota from the Chequamegon Bay of Lake Superior beginning in the latter 1600's.

In 1681, explorer Daniel Greysolon Sieur Duluth and five other French Canadians came down from Lake Superior along the important Bois Brule and St. Croix rivers. Duluth was most likely the first white to see the beautiful St. Croix Valley which was covered with thick forests of pine, birch, oak and maple.

The Indians had used this river highway for many years but the French were the first to exploit the region by trading knives, blankets, guns, powder and other items for Dakota and Ojibwe furs. The furs, shaped into hats, coats and other garments, were in great demand in Europe. This land passed from the French to the British in 1763 and then to the Americans in 1783. The British and Americans developed important trade companies, such as the Northwest, Hudson Bay and American Fur Trading Companies. Trade was conducted throughout the valley and an occasional trader built a crude cabin, but the constant fighting between the Dakota and Ojibwe made it dangerous.

However, as the white man's need for land and timber grew, he was attracted to Polk County's rivers and white pine.

The Ojibwe, who had gained control of northern Wisconsin through years of hard fought battle with the Dakota, gave up their lands to the U.S. government in 1837 in a treaty signed at Fort Snelling in St. Paul. With this treaty, the whites began to move in. Mills sprang up along the St. Croix, from Stillwater to St. Croix Falls. Lumbermen left the almost barren pineries of New England and headed west for the virgin forests of Wisconsin and Minnesota. Throughout the last half of the 1800's, lumber choked the St. Croix River as it headed for markets along the Mississippi.

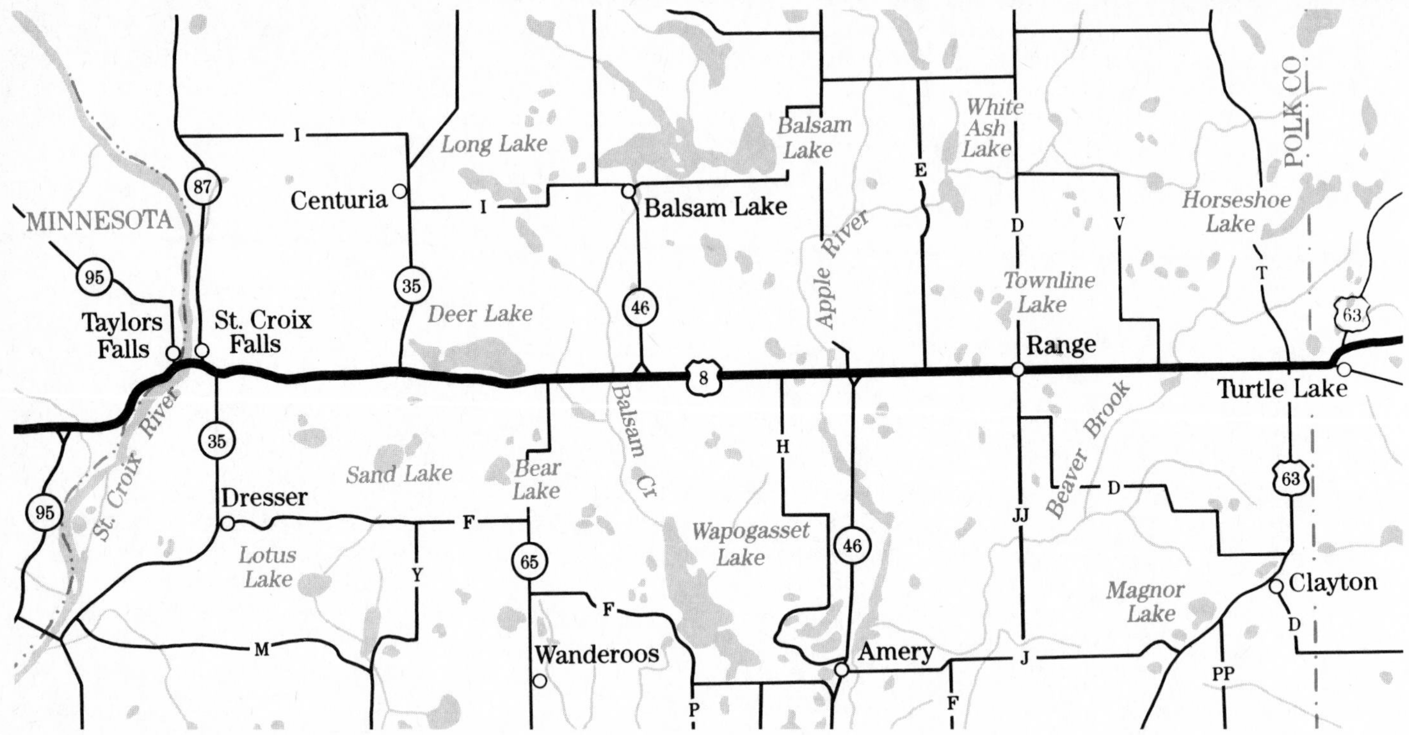

Outside of lumbering interests, settlement didn't take hold in Polk County until after the Civil War. New homestead laws then made this state appealing for a war veteran who wanted to clear land for farming. The county was actually formed in 1853 from St. Croix County and named after James Polk, the 11th President of the United States. The village of St. Croix Falls was made the county seat, but a few months later people living around Osceola Mills voted a change and moved the county seat there. City fathers weren't sure how long the county seat would remain in Osceola Mills and bought a portable safe for the records, rather than spend money on a permanent vault. Elections were held often, but it wasn't until 1898 that the county seat was finally moved to Balsam Lake. Today, dairying, tourism and small manufacturing are the mainstays of this region's economy.

ST. CROIX FALLS, Pop. 1,497

St. Croix Falls is located at a place the Ojibwe called "Ka-ba-kong," meaning "waterfall." Here the St. Croix river has cut through sandstone and lava to form a spectacular gorge called the Dalles of the St. Croix. Dalles is French for "slab of rock."

The incredible flow of glacial waters from Lake Superior rushed through here cutting circular holes or kettles, isolating rock pinnacles, and etching unusual formations in a gorge that runs from St. Croix Falls south to Osceola. The road off State 35, just south of St. Croix Falls, leads into the 1,325-acre Wisconsin Interstate Park which includes most of the dalles of the St. Croix. Citizens from both Taylors Falls and St. Croix Falls formed committees as early as 1895 to persuade their legislatures to establish a park here. The park, including both sides of the river, was established in 1900 as Wisconsin's first state park. It has good camping sites and roads and trails make it easy to explore the dalles, including Devil's Chair and Devil's Kitchen, two of the more spectacular formations within the gorge. If you visit the park, look for the rock known as the Old Man of the Dalles, a face-like profile in rock. The Ojibwe felt that this image was that of Winneboujou, their mythical god who lived in the St. Croix-Bois Brule region. Legends tell of many Dakota Indians, enemies of the Ojibwe, who were killed in the icy waters that flowed below.

The new interpretative center of the Ice Age National Scientific Reserve is also located in the park. This center, one of nine in Wisconsin, was the dream of Raymond Zillmer of Milwaukee who wanted to preserve areas in Wisconsin which best showed the effects of the glaciers. In 1971 nine reserves totaling almost 40,000 acres were set aside, some connected by trails that closely follow the outermost ridges left by the last glaciers. Five units are now open to the public, including Devils Lake, Interstate, Mill Bluff, and the Kettle Moraine and Horicon Wildlife Area. The center at Interstate Park features a 20-minute film and a display describing the ice age's effects on the St. Croix Valley. Additional information on the reserves is available from the Department of Natural Resources, Madison.

SETTLERS AT ST. CROIX FALLS

The first white to claim land in the Falls area was a storekeeper and developer named Franklin Steele. In 1837, Steele left his store at Fort Snelling in Minnesota and settled on land along the river, not yet surveyed by the government. The site was ideal for a lumber mill. While getting supplies for this new town down river at St. Louis, Steele and George Fitch formed the St. Louis Lumber Company, chartered a steamboat called Palmyra, headed back to the Falls with equipment for a mill and lumbering operation. Shortly after the Falls had a dam, saw mill, store and about 20 homes. They struggled to keep this remote operation going for several years but eventually went broke. Not to be defeated, Steele became one of the prime developers of the Minnesota lumber industry. In the meantime, lumbermen wrote of being "demoralized by the threatening behavior of the Indians" during these early days. Ownership of the bankrupt St. Louis Lumber Company, also known as the St. Croix Lumber Company, passed to Caleb Cushing, but it burned in 1848.

So much energy was spent on lumbering along the St. Croix that little effort went into farming. Most food was brought from Stillwater or St. Paul. In 1844, when heavy snow cut off St. Croix Falls from its supplies, few settlers had enough food and many went hungry for two months. Some became so desperate that they worked their way to Fort Snelling and traded shingles for Army pork.

Regular mail delivery began coming up the river in 1840. Boats were used during the summer but during winter the mail was dragged up the treacherous ice by sled. The Planter's House hotel was built, followed by the Cushing Hotel. An historian describing night life at the Cushing said "the boys with the fair ones of those days would trip the light fantastic toe, to the wee-sma'hours."

The growth of St. Croix was slowed by lawsuits and disagreements over land ownership which lasted for nearly 50 years. A compromise was finally reached in 1856 with formation of the St. Croix Manufacturing and Improvement Company. New buildings went up and the village grew. A company run by Swedes, the Great European and American Land Company, also tried to entice settlers here, but records show that the company's owners found it "convenient to

SHSW

Thousands of logs choked the St.Croix River during the late 1800's. Lumbering activity had peaked by the turn-of-the-century.

SHSW

A lazy summer day. Photo/C.J. Van Schaick

absent themselves from the country" due to broken promises and lacking funds. The first bridge spanning the St. Croix was built in 1856 shortly after an unusual marriage on the river. A Minnesota man wished to marry a Wisconsin girl living in St. Croix Falls, but the only available justice was in Taylor's Falls, Minnesota. Since the girl would not cross to Minnesota for the ceremony and the justice's authority was limited to Minnesota, the whole group rafted out on the river to the state line and married.

A short distance south, Warren Kent and his brothers built a mill in 1844 which was known as Osceola Mills and later just Osceola, named after a Seminole Chief from Florida. It was one of the largest flour mills on the St. Croix and ground wheat for the lumber camps. Boat building was also big: the Osceola, built there in 1854, was a steamboat which worked the St. Croix between the Falls and Stillwater.

NEVERS DAM

Ten miles north of St. Croix Falls was the Nevers Dam, built in 1889, and reputed to be the largest pile-driven dam in the world. When the massive log jam of 1886 choked the St. Croix's narrow passage for almost two months, the decision was made to construct a dam to better regulate the river. The logging interests at Stillwater couldn't afford another large jam.

The dam's prime usefulness ended with logging on the St. Croix at the turn-of-the-century, although Northern States Power Company used it to regulate water flow over their hydro- electric plant at the Falls. The wooden structure withstood many spring floods until 1954, when some of it washed away. NSP tore it down in 1955. Some rotted pilings and earth causeways are all that remain of this engineering feat.

Located just north of the hydro dam is the headquarters for the St. Croix National Scenic Waterways system. It includes an excellent interpretive center with information on area history and natural resources. The St. Croix National Scenic Riverway, which includes the Namekagon River, was established in 1968 as one of the original eight rivers protected under the National Wild and Scenic Rivers Act. The system includes nearly 260 miles of some of the most undeveloped river areas in the Midwest.

NAMING THE ST. CROIX

The Dakota called this river Hoganwahnkay-kin, or "place where the fish lie." Their legend tells of a brave who stopped here to drink from the river and was suddenly transformed into a large fish. Father Hennepin, one of the first explorers of this region in the early 1680's, called this the "river of the tomb" because of the dead left here after a battle with the Ojibwe. French explorer Le Sueur first called this the St. Croix, French for "Holy Cross," supposedly because he discovered a cross over a voyageur's grave near the river. It is approximately 170 miles in length, beginning in marshes near Solon Springs and emptying into the Mississippi at Prescott.

BALSAM LAKE, Pop. 749

East of St. Croix Falls, the road climbs out of the valley and along a rolling countryside where farms and hardwood forests compete for space. The highway passes the old Deer Lake School, a township school from 1930 to 1957. This highway extended only a few miles east of the St. Croix Falls until the 1930's when U.S. 8 was constructed to provide an east-west link to the state.

The village of Balsam Lake is located four miles north of U.S. 8. While St. Croix Falls was developing as a milling town, trade was also thriving along the shores of Balsam Lake, which was named by the local Ojibwe Indians. Maurice Samuels started trading here around 1845, about the same time Edward Worth and his family settled at the mouth of Balsam Creek. Worth and a man named Webster built a dam and made shingles for the settlers who began trickling in. In 1846, Worth began cutting a road between Balsam Lake and St. Croix Falls which soon became known as the Broadway. He also carried mail on a pony from Point Douglas to St. Croix Falls until 1848. Maurice Samuels started another mill as well as a trading post. Samuels also ran a post at the Falls and was reportedly the first to introduce whiskey into the area: he would let his stock sell out except for generous supplies of rot gut which "caused great trouble."

By 1870, 300 people lived in Balsam Lake, kept busy by two mills which cut large quantities of lumber near the shores and floated it across the lake. From there, lumber was hauled to St. Croix Falls and rafted down the St. Croix. In 1872, a mail route was established between St. Croix Falls, Balsam and Turtle Lakes. Since the village is near the center of the county, a movement was successful in moving the county seat from Osceola in 1898. Balsam Lake today is dairying center and tourist area. The Polk County Historical Museum has three floors of interesting exhibits in the old county courthouse.

DAM SITE

The Ridler Mill and Dam which operated during the latter 1800's, was located where U.S. 8 crosses the Apple River. The dam turned generators which supplied electricity to the nearby Apple River School and area farms. The Apple River was once a channel for the pre-glacial St. Croix River, accounting for the deepening of its valley beginning in the Somerset area. Like many streams that drained this part of Wisconsin, the Apple River was important to the logging of white pine which once forested this area. During the winter of 1873-74, 13 million feet of pine were cut and floated down to the St. Croix and within a few years 15 logging camps were working along the Apple River. Dams were opened when waters ran high in the spring, sending logs down river to Stillwater.

A county park is now situated where the first wooden bridge spanned the Apple River in 1877. Take County Rd. H south to the Mains Crossing road and then east to the new bridge. It is a quiet, out of the way place to picnic and speculate about the loggers who traveled this river in those early days.

RANGE

A post office was established at Range in 1898, with Hans Hagstad as postmaster. Hagstad also took over a cooperative store first opened in the late 1890's by a well-driller named Alfred Ekegren. The post office was discontinued in 1911. Today the old post office, store, and creamery stand vacant and heavily vandalized. They will probably soon be torn down.

BARRON COUNTY, Pop. 38,730

Numerous glaciers crossed over Barron County during an on-again, off-again, period lasting for more than a hundred thousand years. The latest glacier to affect portions of Barron County, the Wisconsin Stage of glaciation, ended 10,000 to 12,000 years ago. Only certain sections of the glacier extended here: one area of northwest Barron County was covered by the St. Croix Lobe; the northeast part was covered by the Chippewa Lobe. Irregular hills, called terminal moraines, were formed along the edges of these glacial flows.

Before the whites established themselves here, the Dakota and Ojibwe fought bitterly for the important hunting and ricing lands. The Treaty of 1825, signed at Prairie du Chien, gave the Ojibwe this land and the Dakota land to the west. Unfortunately, the treaty didn't end trouble between the two nations and fighting continued for years.

The name Knapp, Stout & Company is inseparable from the early history of Barron County. The logging company began in 1846 when Captain Wilson and John Knapp bought a small mill at what later became Menomonie. Others joined the partnership, including Henry Stout, and the company made massive land purchases from the government at $1.25 an acre. In 1879 they purchased 100,000 acres in the area from Cornell University and the Northwestern & Omaha railroads. Wilson eyed the Barron County land, recognized the need for raising wheat, pork, potatoes and vegetables for the crews, and founded Prairie Farm in the southcentral part of the county. When Knapp, Stout & Company reached its peak, they were farming 6,000 acres of land in Barron and Dunn counties. They soon expanded logging operations into Barron County, starting a logging camp at today's city of Barron in 1860. Eight years later they had a camp at what is now Rice Lake and a few years later, one at Chetek.

In the 1870's, Knapp, Stout & Company were considered the largest logging operation in the world. They left in their wake devastated forests whose stumps and slash provided fuel for fires which raged across the region.

Shortly after 1890 lumbering declined and Knapp, Stout & Company began disposing of their cut-over land by advertising bargain prices in Scandinavian countries and eastern cities. Many people jumped at the chance to farm and agriculture became increasingly important. Wheat and potatoes dominated at first, but dairy farming and dairy products eventually sustained the Scandinavian and German farmers who settled here.

The county was known as Dallas County until 1869, when it was named in honor of Henry D. Barron, a St. Croix Falls politician who represented the region. Unfortunately, the county's early records were lost when County Treasurer James Bracklin and his files fell out of a boat into the Red Cedar River. Bracklin was saved, but the files weren't! (This county description is repeated on U.S. 53 and 63.)

TURTLE LAKE, Pop. 762

This fertile region of farms and dairy herds was once surrounded by a vast pine forest that drew lumbermen to the Red Cedar and Yellow rivers to the east. However, with the coming of the St. Paul, Minneapolis, Chicago & Omaha Railroad, this location seemed a good place to erect a mill. By Summer, 1878, the line was constructed from Turtle Lake to Cumberland. In the next few years, the Omaha line connected the important ports of Superior and Ashland. Turtle Lake then became an important shipping point for area farmers and for wood cut on the steam-powered mill built by Richardson. His operation attracted a number of loggers to Turtle Lake, almost half of whom were Indians who lived in wigwams at Upper and Lower Turtle lakes. In addition there was some intermarriage between the lonely white loggers and Indians. After becoming a stop on the Omaha, the hamlet acquired a hotel built by C.W. Haskins. The only other buildings in town were two saloons. Mail began to arrive and Richardson became post master. For a short time, the village was known as Skowhegan, after Richardson's home town in Maine.

By this time the giant lumber company known as Knapp, Stout & Company began logging near Upper & Lower Turtle lakes. From these lakes, they floated logs down Turtle and Hay creeks to their mills in Menomonie. With supplies coming from St. Paul by train, they requested a train stop at their camp on Turtle Lake, and Skowhegan subsequently took the name Turtle Lake.

Richardson sold the mill to his brother Joel in 1884, the year work began on the Soo Line. The Soo was to connect the important shipping center at Sault Ste. Marie with the river town of St. Paul. Long winters with wheat stranded at the frozen ports of Duluth and Superior on Lake Superior, gave incentive for the development of an east-west connection where wheat from the Minneapolis mills could find an outlet. Turtle Lake became the railroad's temporary center as they built the line both east and west from here. The village grew around a junction point of two important lines which stretched across northern Wisconsin. The Omaha and Soo lines shared a depot but not without problems. In April, 1901, trains from each line plowed into each other at the crossing, rammed the depot and burned it down. A few people were injured, but no one was killed. A new depot was built and a better signaling system was developed.

About 1890, the Richardson mill, which had gone bankrupt, and a shingle factory built by J.W. Stone were bought and moved to the growing city of Barron. With the mills gone and logging declining, farming became more important to Turtle Lake's economy. A creamery was established in 1900, but farming was not well-organized and the business failed. The creamery at Almena also took milk from the Turtle Lake area. However, a new owner of the Turtle Lake creamery bought a carload of milk separators and gave them to farmers in return for cream. His ploy worked and faith in the Turtle Lake Creamery grew. In 1916 the Turtle Lake Co-op Creamery began by buying out that industrious owner for $14,000.

Turtle Lake also had a pea canning company. Gedneys, a pickle company located near Minneapolis, established a pickle station here in 1911 to collect cucumbers from local gardens. The village at one time had five hotels, two banks, two oil supply depots, two photograph galleries, a harness and shoe shop, tailor, livery barn, theater, and other small shops.

An unusual man named John Till came to the Turtle Lake area in 1902 and became quite famous healing people with a mysterious plaster sauve. Trains brought patients from the East to be cured by this man known as the bare-foot doctor. His operation expanded to other villages and he built a sanatorium at Turtle Lake in 1918 to house his growing number of clients. When the train came to town, buggies lined up to pick up passengers headed for Till's place. In 1919, he was convicted of practicing medicine without a license and, after years of litigation, moved back to Austria. His two-story clinic burned in 1933. The local library has an interesting collection of historical pictures from the village.

Turtle Lake Library

Turtle Lake, ca.1880

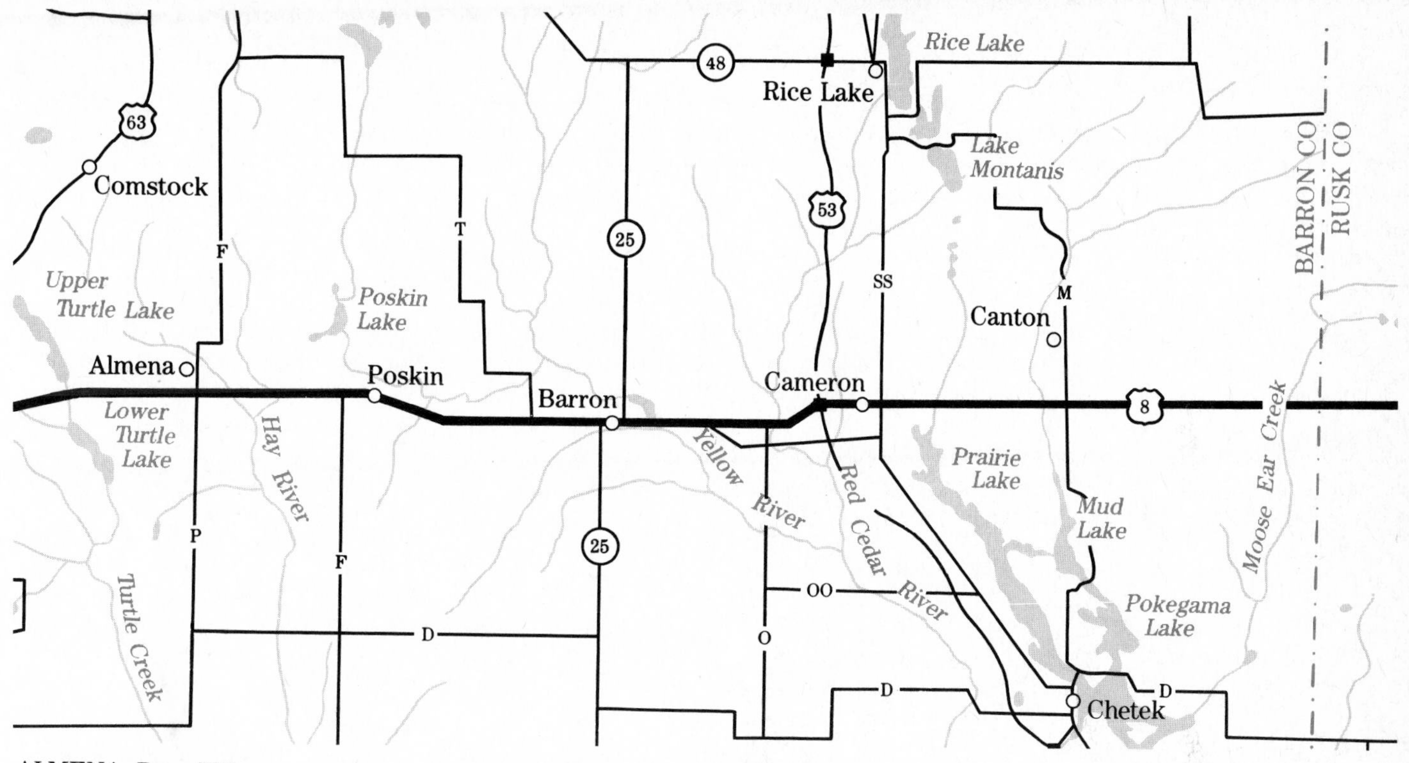

ALMENA, Pop. 526

The small village of Almena is situated on rolling land of glacial sand and gravel. An Ojibwe Indian camp, located near Almena, was one of the largest and last to exist before the Ojibwe were forced to their reservation near Couderay in 1878, because the Indians were troublesome to whites as settlement increased in the area. Many women were afraid to be alone with their children while their husbands were off in the woods. There was some begging by Indians and rumors spread of drunken orgies. The county board finally petitioned the U.S. Government to force them onto the reservation.

Meanwhile, Turtle Lake was already growing around its lumber mill when Theodore Hamm of St. Paul encouraged a few of his relatives to establish a city in Wisconsin. Albert Koehler and S.W. Sparlin got off the Soo and wandered around a bit before clearing land here for a new village in the summer of 1887. That fall they applied to the government for a post office name. This clearing, located by Lightning Creek, inspired them to call this Lightning City. However they were asked to drop the word City, so chose a new name instead. Albert combined his name with that of Wilhelmina, his wife. Koehler's friend Sparlin opened the first store and Almena grew as a supply center for area farmers.

POSKIN

This was once known as Cosgrove, after Peter Cosgrove who settled here in the summer of 1883. Cosgrove built a log store, and sold supplies to loggers working at Poskin Lake. Several years later, C.H. Strand came to Cosgrove and started a mill and another store. When the railroad came through in 1884 it began calling this spot Poskin Lake after Mary Poskin, the Indian wife of Capt. Andrew Tainter, one of the principle holders in the Knapp, Stout & Company lumber concern. Eventually lake was dropped from the name.

At one time, Poskin was the site of creameries, grain elevators and an insurance company called the North Wisconsin Farmers Mutual Cyclone Insurance Company which had 4,250 members with $6 million in property insurance in 1907.

BARRON, Pop. 2,595

In 1848 Knapp, Stout & Company moved into southern Barron County in the Prairie Farm area and began large farms to grow potatoes, wheat and vegetables for the lumber camps which were expanding into the area from their Menomonie mills.

However it was another 12 years before John Quaderer, a foreman with Knapp, Stout, came to the spot now known as Barron. He settled along a creek, which would be named after him, just a short distance from the Yellow River. Quaderer felt this was an excellent place for a lumber camp. His reputation for cutting logs was already known along the Red Cedar River, so he had little trouble rounding up men to work. For the next 20 years, Barron was little more than a logging center with only a few shacks and one store. In 1863, when still known as Dallas County (it became Barron County in 1869), the county government located in John Quaderer's house and he became the town constable.

Though 30 years had passed since the last armed conflict with Black Hawk along the Wisconsin River, whites still feared the Indians living in the area. In fact, the Sioux Uprising took place in Minnesota in 1862. When two of the first white women settlers died suddenly, they were thought to have been poisoned by jealous Ojibwe squaws.

Bear hunters in front of the Barron County courthouse.

A number of new businesses were started when the Soo line came through in 1884, including another saw and flour mill. Run by the Parr, Post & Company, the mill consisted of a double water-wheel which cut 30,000 feet of lumber and 35,000 shingles daily. Barron also had a woolen mill that in 1887 was dying and preparing 8,000 yards a month for manufacture into cashmere coats, dress goods, mackinaws, blankets, hosiery and yarn. Salesmen left Barron in wagons and called door to door throughout the rural communities.

By 1887, Barron had grown into a manufacturing and business center with a population near 800. With much of the available pine gone by the late 1800's, farmers began clearing the remaining stands of hardwoods. They brought these to Barron for the barrel and stave factory run by George Parr & Son. On cold winter mornings many sleds, piled high with logs, filed into Barron to be unloaded at Parr's mill.

CAMERON, Pop. 1,115

This village was first settled about one mile south of the present town at a place called Holman's Crossing near the tracks of the Chicago, St. Paul, Minneapolis & Omaha Railroad. In 1884 the Soo Line built in an east-west direction, passed Holman's Crossing just to the north. Eventually the buildings were moved on sleds and wagons to the junction of the two railroads. The new village became known as Cameron. The old village known as "Old Cameron," both named by L.C. Stanley, the original owner of the village land, after a friend who was a state senator from La Crosse. At one time, residents of North Cameron had a choice of 12 passenger trains they could take in any direction.

In the last half of the 1800's the Cameron area was heavily settled by Scandinavians who first came to work in the logging camps. Many supplemented their meager incomes by farming during the summer when the ground was too soft and the streams too low to float logs. With the frost, many headed back to the remote lumber camps or signed up for railroad construction.

BARRON HILLS

East of Cameron lie the Barron Hills, a rolling tree-covered region which rises 600 feet above the surrounding plains of northern Wisconsin. These hills are called monadnocks, a geologic term which describes them as remnants of a former highland or mountain range that once crossed Wisconsin. This range formed millions of years ago, being one of the first land areas to rise out of the sea which once covered the North American Continent. These mountains were much like the Rocky Mountains of today. Over time, the mountains eroded away, forming the relatively level plains of Wisconsin with these hills as an example of the erosive power of wind and rain over long periods of time.

CANTON

This small village along the Soo Line tracks had its beginning about three miles south where Pokegama Creek empties into Mud Lake. About 1872 a few homes sprang up and a post office began under the name of Sumner. That name was dropped because another Wisconsin town had already chosen it and the village called itself Sioska. Two town promoters named Edgbert and Hutchinson platted Sioska and built a dam and mill on Pokegama Creek. Others settled around the mill and soon built a school and store.

When the Soo line was being built from Turtle Lake, villagers were sure it would pass through Sioska. But instead, the tracks laid in 1884 passed three miles north across an open area of land called the Pokegama Prairie. Not to be defeated, the village loaded up its stores and belongings and moved north to its present location. Canton was officially platted in 1884 and became a small railway station.

RUSK COUNTY, Pop. 15,589

Organized 1901, Rusk County was the last county to be formed in Wisconsin. It was originally called Gates County, after a Milwaukee lumberman who was a promoter for the county's organization and who owned large tracts of area real estate. In 1905 the county was renamed after General Jeremiah Rusk, Wisconsin's governor from 1882 to 1889.

When the United States land office for northwestern Wisconsin opened at St. Croix Falls in 1848, most of northwest Wisconsin was surveyed for settlement. Yet it took another eight years before surveyors made it into Rusk County. When surveying teams arrived in 1856 they reported the region devoid of people except for a small group of French Canadians and Indians gathered near a Catholic church built along the Flambeau River.

Logging started about 1860 when Daniel Shaw began working the area along the Flambeau. Shortly after, settlers and loggers began moving up the valleys of the Chippewa, Flambeau, Thornapple and Jump rivers. Rough trails and tote roads were the only means of travel into the back country until the Soo Line was built across the center of the state in 1884-85. From then on, small mills and shipping points formed along the tracks, eventually growing into small towns. The railroad was also interested in developing the area adjacent to the tracks, hoping to make their line more profitable. North of Weyerhaeuser and Glen Flora, 40,000 acres were purchased by the railroad and promoted to Swedish immigrants through their consul in St. Paul. By 1926, so much of the county had been logged that locals estimated that 88 percent of the land was now unproductive. Advertising campaigns tried to entice farmers from the crowded east to move here and work the cut-over land.

WEYERHAEUSER, Pop. 313

Like most other villages in the county, Weyerhaeuser formed because it was to be a shipping point on the Soo Line. The crude shacks first built there were named for Fredrick Weyerhaeuser, the lumber magnate who made much of his wealth in northern Wisconsin. A German immigrant, Weyerhaeuser started as a saw mill worker and eventually bought land either alone or with railroad companies to develop the largest lumber concern in the world. He was considered brilliant in his ability to get everything possible out of the white pine forests. His Mississippi River Logging Company soon became

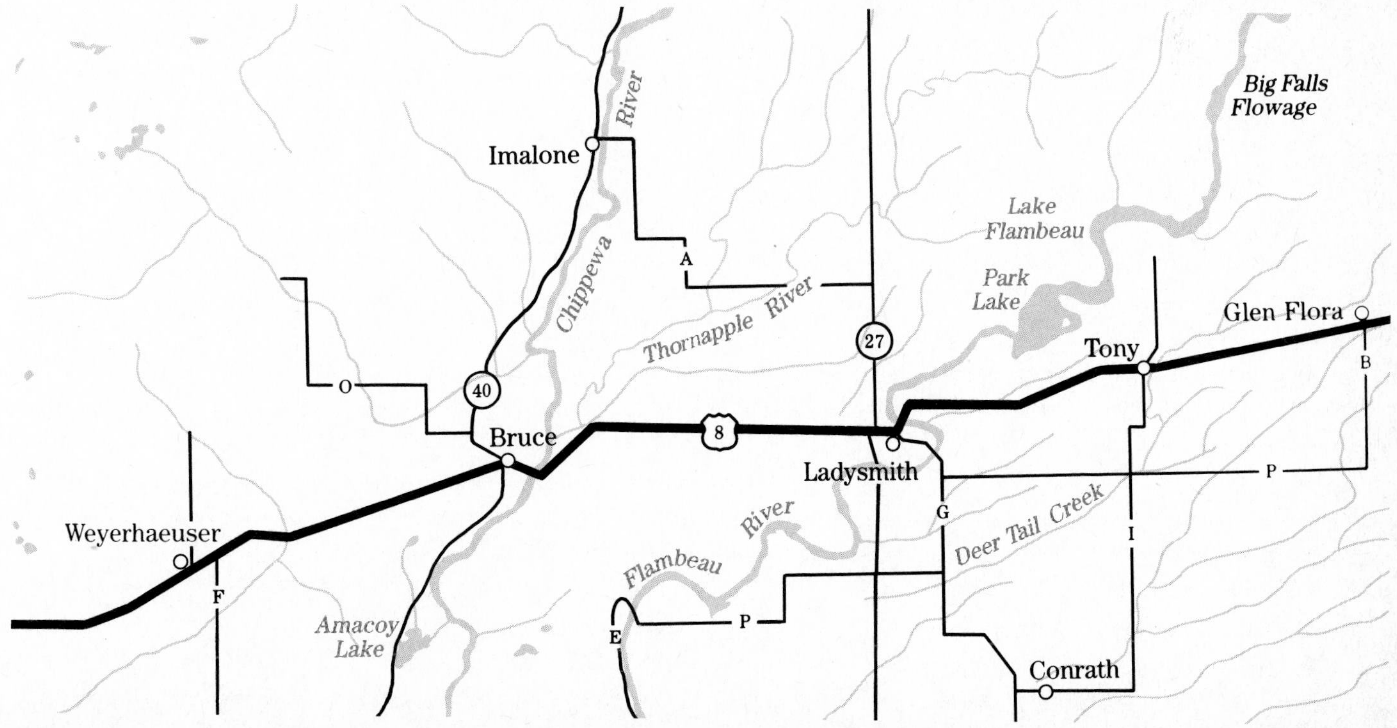

SHSW

Looking north on Second St. W., Ladysmith, WI, ca. 1880's.

one of the largest lumber syndicates of all times: camps and connecting railroads spread over northwestern Wisconsin like a spider web, but the Chippewa River Valley was his focus. Weyerhaeuser's business methods have been heavily criticized over the years because his concern was only for lumber. After reducing the Wisconsin and Minnesota forests to stubble, he moved to the Pacific Northwest, leaving new immigrants and out-of-work loggers to contend with the cut-over land.

During the logging boom, the village of Weyerhaeuser had two hotels, four general stores, two saw mills, a creamery and even a Montana sheep rancher who purchased 1000 acres to graze sheep. An early pamphlet bragged that "the businessmen of this place are live and up-to-date." The Hardwood Lumber Company was one of the largest companies in this small hamlet, cutting 25,000 feet of lumber a day and employing up to 60 men. For a number of years the village spelled its name Weyerhauser. Only recently did the village add a fourth "e", giving it the proper spelling. The depot is now boarded up and a caboose stands in front as a memorial.

BRUCE, Pop. 905

Named after A.C. Bruce, a major area landowner and son of Fredrick Weyerhaeuser, Bruce was established in 1884 along the Soo Line tracks. The Chippewa River & Menomonie Railroad ended here for a time during the height of logging. Bruce's location along these railroads and its proximity to the Chippewa River attracted lumber mills which employed 200 men and provided the town's economic base. The Chippewa railroad, basically a logging line, also built engine stalls and a roundhouse here so they could reverse their trains' direction. As logging increased, so did the number of hotels, saloons and other businesses. One historian noted that the nearby lumber camps provided housing for "ladies of scarlet fame." When these flowery ladies came to town, the other women pulled down their window shades!

A village called Apollonia formed where the Chippewa line crossed the Soo a mile west of Bruce. It clustered around the railroad shops and most rail workers built their homes here. From Apollonia, which was named for Weyerhaeuser's daughter, trains hauled logs down to the "big bend" in the Chippewa River, where they were dumped and rafted down to the mills of Chippewa Falls. Farming replaced the camps and lumberjacks after logging ended in the late 1800's. Businesses like the Bruce Co-op Dairy provided farmers with an outlet for their milk and cream.

LADYSMITH, Pop. 3,826

The busy city of Ladysmith is built between the Flambeau River and the Soo Line, the two factors which determined its beginning and subsequent growth. The Flambeau River winds down through the forests of northern Wisconsin and provided an early highway for the trappers and missionaries who ventured into this pine-covered wilderness. A logger named Bruno Vinett cleared an area along the falls of the Flambeau and his small farm became a resting spot for river travelers.

When the Soo Line was built through here in 1885 a 40-acre tract was platted and called Flambeau Falls. However, when the railroad built a small depot here they called the station Warner.

There was little at Warner when Robert Corbett moved his logging business over from Cumberland in 1886. Corbett did his part for the town's progress by building warehouses, a hotel, a barn for his logging horses, and a large boarding house for his crew known as the beehive. Logging was done in the village proper until the land was cleared. Developers were soon selling regular lots for $15 and corner lots for $25, stumps and all. For awhile school was held in front of Corbett's hotel and the post office was stuck in a corner.

The large Menasha Woodenware Company quietly started buying land and waterpower rights in the village in 1900, but word leaked out and many people moved to Warner to share in the expected boom. Village fathers were so anxious to please E.D. Smith, the company's owner, that they renamed the town Ladysmith. Reportedly Mrs. Smith never intended to visit her city. When the county was formed in 1901, Ladysmith was located in its center, was the largest city, and the obvious choice as county seat. Up to that point the county was proud of the fact that it had no attorneys or courts. An historian wrote that "they got along without courts and attorneys, settling their differences by compromise or with fists." In the following years, the village grew around its lumber industry, creamery, and canning plant.

During the Civil War in 1861, a bald eagle was captured along the Flambeau River and used as a mascot for a Wisconsin regiment. The eagle was called Abe and was carried into 39 battles. A romanticized history reports that Abe would "scream and spread his wings" as he was carried on a standard into battle. He died in 1881 and is on display at the state capital.

TONY, Pop. 146

Located along Deer Tail Creek, this small village was once known as Deer Tail but was renamed Tony after Anthony Hine, a manager of the John Hine Lumber Company. Tony at one time had a population of 400, with more than 150 working the stave and saw mills. There was a hotel, wagon factory, blacksmith, school, branch office of the Leinenkugel Brewery of Chippewa Falls, and a 500-seat opera house. Long winter evenings featured performances by the town's six-person orchestra and a 16-member band played during the summer. Tony promoted itself as having electric lights, a long distance connection, and "all the social features of an ambitious city." As with many towns in the Chippewa and Flambeau valleys, the mills shut down when the trees were gone and people moved on. There is little in Tony now except for the school, a small feed mill and a few homes.

GLEN FLORA, Pop. 83

This town began as a lumbering village along the Soo Line named Miller's Siding, but settlers who moved in and dreamed of a metropolis felt the name sounded like a rail spur. It was reportedly renamed by O.K. Otis who suggested Flowery Glen because of the wild flowers in the nearby forest. The name was modified to Glen Flora.

The village eventually grew to 400 people and included four churches, three saw mills, a hotel, newspaper, charcoal kiln, photograph gallery, school, lawyer, doctor and real estate agent.

INGRAM, Pop. 61

Ingram began in 1885, the same year the Soo Line came through and the Lawrence Lumber Company established their mill here. The mill used waterpower from the Middle Fork of the Main Creek. City fathers were proud of the three hotels, stores, church and public hall but wanted the town of 400 to grow much larger and offered reduced train fares to anyone who would stop and look over the land. Some cut-over farm land was selling for as little as $6 an acre. When people wanted to move here, the town kept moving costs low by subsidizing a portion of their freight. Today, the creek is overgrown with brush, hiding all traces of the old mill. The depot has been torn down and only the foundation remains.

SHSW

1876 photo of "Old Abe," mascot of 8th Wisconsin Civil War regiment, captured near Ladysmith, 1861.

HAWKINS, Pop. 407

As the Soo Line extended across Main Creek, several logging companies used this area as their center of operations. They either hauled logs to the creek to be floated to the Chippewa River or used the Jump River to the east. It is unclear whether the town was named for a logger or a railroad official. A boarding house was built in Hawkins in 1885 to house men who came looking for work in the camps. The small village grew around the train depot and soon included a general store, post office, school and hotel.

The Ellingson Lumber company bought the old Crosby Mill in 1902 and started a colonization company to bring more people here. Hawkins continued to grow during the early 1900's with the addition of a box factory and a sash and door company. Even as late as 1923 a new brick hotel was built on Main Street. Today a huge pine log lays in front of the Lutheran Church as a memorial to C.K. Ellingson.

PRICE COUNTY, Pop. 15,788

In Spring, 1879, the Wisconsin Legislature formed the county of Price, named after William T. Price who served in the state senate during the 1850's and died while serving in the U.S. House of Representatives in 1886.

The many streams which drain the county aided its development as an important logging region during the late 1800's. Major Isaac Stone, the county's first white settler, started logging along the Spirit River in southeastern Price

County in 1860. When the Wisconsin Central reached here in 1872, several families located near Stone's house in what became known as the Spirit River Settlement.

Eventually logging extended from the Wisconsin River and upwards of 5,000 men came into the county during the winters to cut pine. Settlements really began to take hold after the Civil War in the late 1870's. Families tried to survive on small farms by raising oats, potatoes and other root crops and working in the woods during the winter. Only 785 people lived in the county in 1880 but the railroads and land companies heavily promoted the region. By 1890 had attracted enough Czechoslovakians, Poles, Germans and Finns to make the population 5000.

Phillips was named county seat when the county was formed in 1879. At that time, the Phillips Lumber Company, the only major company in town, was logging the region by an extensive system of rails that reached into the woods using two locomotives and 60 flat-bed cars. Phillips was named after the president of the Wisconsin Central, a railroad which reached from Lake Michigan to the harbor of Ashland.

KENNAN, Pop. 194

When the census was taken in 1890, only 20 voters lived in this township. Though a village called Ripley was platted along the Soo Line in 1886, the only building here in 1890 was the saw mill run by the Rickett brothers. After 1890 a post office was built and people began to settle. Named Kennan after K.K. Kennan, who originally platted the village in 1886, the village today consists of several small homes and a portable saw mill operation.

CATAWBA, Pop. 205

The name Catawba was taken from an Indian word meaning "divided." The old cheese factory, no longer in production, is located on the south side of town. It is still a collection point for local dairy farmers. The building in back is the boiler where whey is separated during cheese making.

PRENTICE, Pop. 605

In 1877 there was nothing here except trees, shrubs, and the Wisconsin Central railroad tracks which connected Ashland, the Penokee-Gogebic Iron Range and Milwaukee. But the trains brought lumbermen and Prentice, with an ideal location on the Jump River, became the operations center of the Jump River Lumber Company. The Company's owner, O.D. Van Dusen, bought land here, built a steam saw mill in 1882 and soon followed with a store and some houses for employees. A planing mill, which had the capacity to finish 100,000 feet of lumber per day, was built a few years later.

In 1887, when the Soo Line was finally completed between Minneapolis, St. Paul and Sault Ste. Marie, Prentice was at

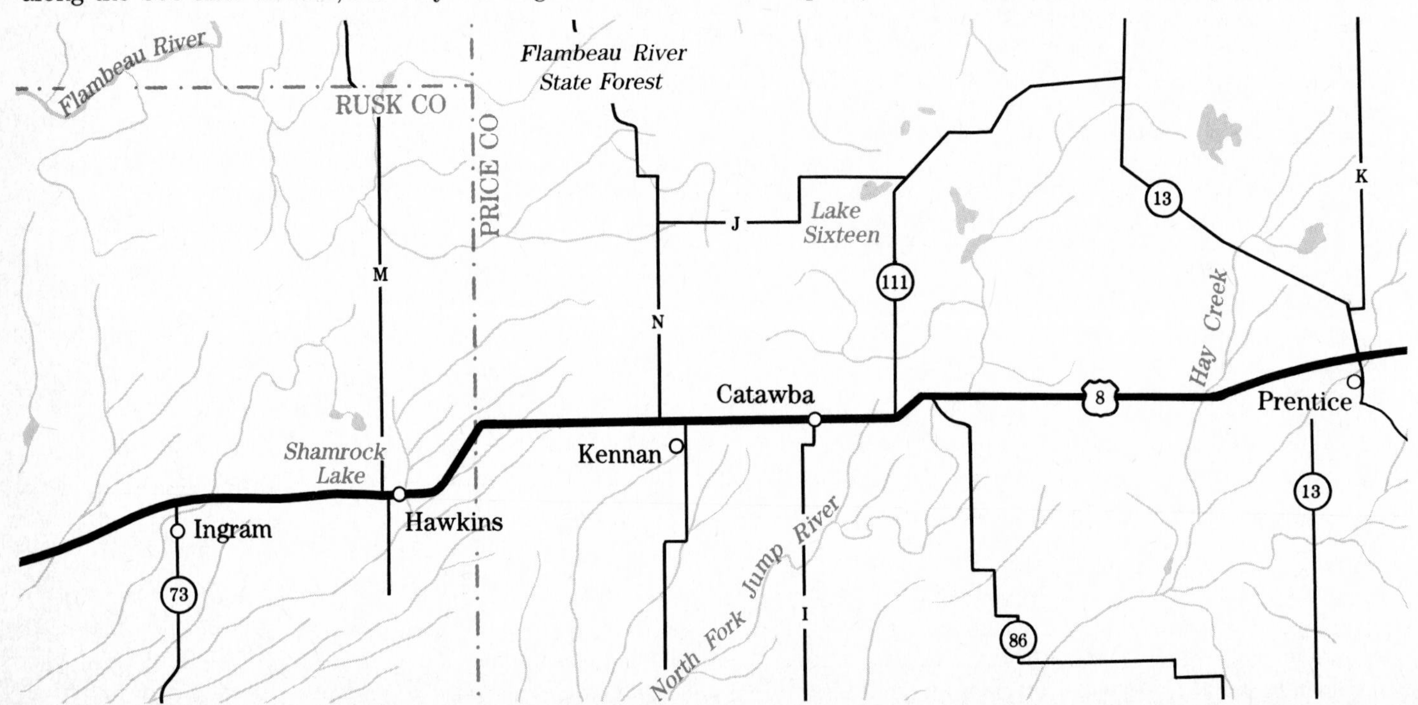

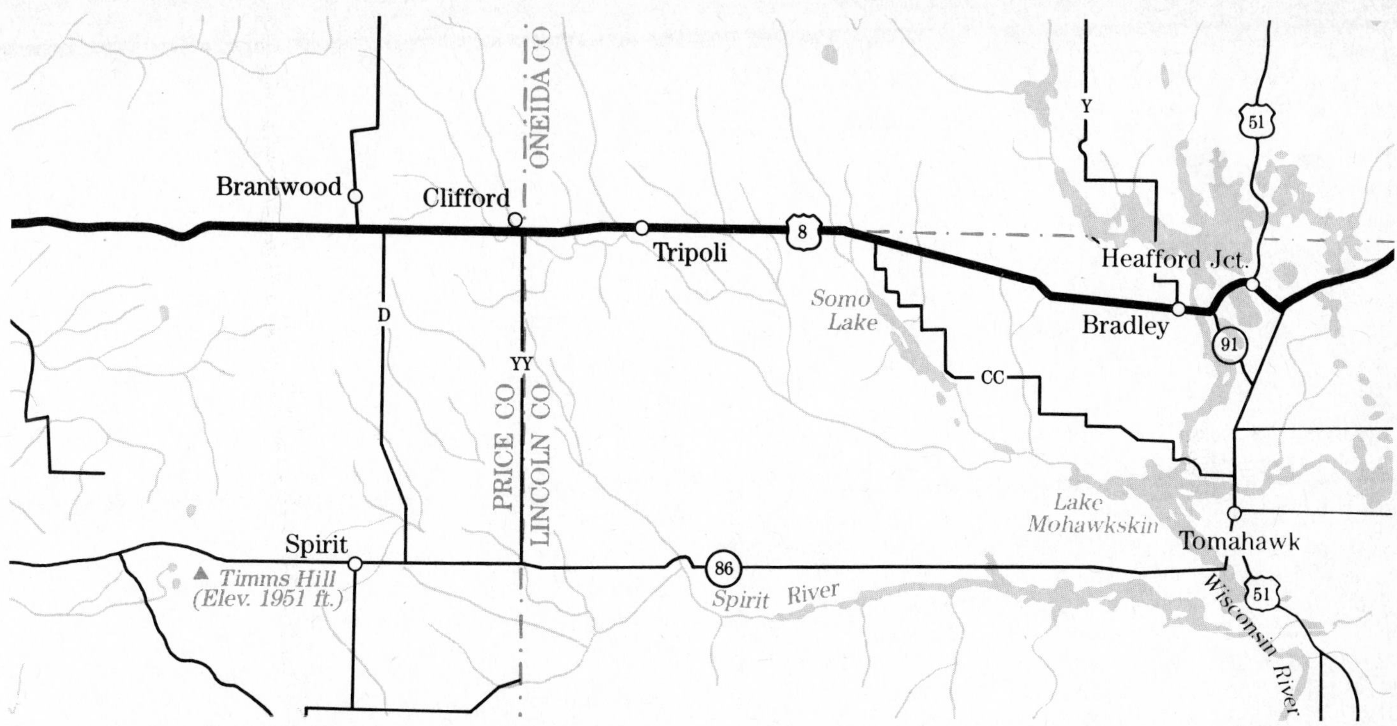

the crossroads of two important lines. During the winter months when Lake Superior was choked with ice, Minneapolis millers needed a way to get their flour east. The Soo was considered a miller's railroad: soon thousands of barrels of flour were passing through Prentice. When Alexander Prentice became the first postmaster in 1883, the village was named after him.

The 1890 census lists the population at 750 residents. A large tanning company, built in 1891, had buildings, vats, boilers, and workers' tenements covering 30 acres. It tanned 200,000 sides of leather a year, but burned down and was never rebuilt.

Prentice was one of the Wisconsin villages which developed a strong cooperative movement. At one time or another, the town included the Prentice Co-op Supply Company, Price County Co-op Oil Assoc., a credit union, and an educational group called the Prentice Co-operative League.

BRANTWOOD

Brantwood was originally the site of a mill known in 1894 as Brant's Landing. With a population of 150 in the early 1900's, it became a small retail center for the Finnish farmers who came to work the cut-over land. During the winter months they supplemented their income by working in the woods, cutting cordwood that sold at $2.50 a cord.

Many of the farmers continued to take Finnish saunas: they built small rooms out of logs and laid stones in the corner around a stove to provide dry heat. South of Brantwood is Tim's Hill, the highest point in Wisconsin and a remnant of an ancient mountain range which crossed this area millions of years ago.

TRIPOLI

Logging began here in 1866 when an Indian known as Israel Stone ran a mill at the nearby Somo River. When the Soo Line built a siding here in 1887 the small hamlet took the name Tripoli, Greek for "three cities," because it bordered three counties. The mills closed after logging ended in the late 1800's and many settlers moved away. Times were extremely tough during the depression and one-third of the small frame houses were sold and carted away.

LINCOLN COUNTY, Pop. 26,311

Lying in the midst of Wisconsin's rolling hills along the Wisconsin River, Lincoln County was established in 1874 and named for President Abraham Lincoln.

Several hundred lakes stud more than half of the county. The lakes of the Lac du Flambeau Indian Reservation form the headwaters of the Wisconsin River which flows south into the Mississippi. Waterpower from these lakes and river

SHSW

Skidding white pine over frozen ground, ca. 1913. Smith Coll.

provided the county's first and most important industry, logging.

The courthouse, located in Merrill, is one of the county's more unique features. Land was purchased in 1900, ground broken in 1901, and the courthouse completed in 1902 following widespread labor trouble from the industries which furnished the building materials. It cost $119,882. Built in colonial style, the ground dimensions are 98X125 and the tower height is 156 feet. Entrances open into a beautiful rotunda, 32 feet in diameter and 50 feet high. A handsome tile floor is laid out in a mosaic design.

HEAFFORD JCT.

The Soo Line was the first train that ran through this railway junction village in 1885. Tracks were later laid for the Marinette, Tomahawk & Western railroad from near Heafford to Tomahawk, originally the Grand Trunk railway, but the financier died, and the project was never completed.

The Chicago, Milwaukee and St. Paul railroad came through in 1890 and the town was named after its first depot agent.

ONEIDA COUNTY, Pop. 31,216

Like most northern Wisconsin counties, Oneida developed primarily because of the lumber industry. It was lumbermen who cleared the primeval forest which covered most of the vast territory and opened the way for the farmer.

The first logging north of the Tomahawk River was done in the winter of 1857-58 at Rhinelander. The heaviest stand of white and Norway pine lay just north of here in a belt 18 miles wide and 40 miles long, believed to have contained nearly 700 million feet of pine and 300 million feet of hemlock. In addition, 12 miles northeast of Rhinelander, a large tract of birch, birdseye maple and curly maple tempted the new hardwood mills. In later years, a stand of more than 50,000 acres of spruce attracted pulp and paper industries.

The lumber business began, appropriately, on New Year's Day, 1858, when a crew from Helms & Company in Stevens Point cut out the first tote road from Grandfather Bull's Falls to Eagle Lake on the Eagle River. That winter they banked 20,000 logs and drove them to Mosinee for sawing. With each season, the work gathered momentum and during the winter of 1885-86 some 20 camps procured supplies at Rhinelander. In the Eagle River district the cut was estimated at 58 million feet. By 1908 the great northern pineries were all but depleted and by 1931 less than 15 percent of the logs and lumber used in Oneida County came from within its borders.

Oneida County took its name from an Indian word meaning "granite people," and was officially formed in January of 1887. The population then was 5,010, with 3,665 native-born and 1,345 foreigners, with Canadians and Scandinavians most represented.

SHSW

Inspecting Soo Line RR tracks at Rhinelander, ca. 1908.

WOODBORO, Pop. 547

This small village was founded by George E. Wood of Chicago who bought a tract of timber and began logging operations in 1890. He built a saw mill the following year. When everything was in full swing, Wood employed 150 men and started a village, building some 50 houses, a boarding house, store and post office. The town, named after Wood, was a prosperous lumbering headquarters for 14 years, until May 1904 when a fire destroyed the planing mill and several hundred thousand feet of lumber.

RHINELANDER, Pop. 7,873

This northern Wisconsin town's greatest asset originally lay in its location—deep in the heart of one of the world's finest timber regions on a convenient, natural waterway. It wasn't long before Anderson Brown of Stevens Point, often called the "Father of Rhinelander," brought these attractions to everyone's attention.

Brown traveled here by birch bark canoe in 1871, looking for timber stands below the Eagle River that could be easily logged. Boom Lake's fine waterpower and great log-storing capacity were instantly apparent and Brown took the initial steps which led to a prosperous lumbering trade. Three years later he and his father bought about 1500 acres, fronting on both the river and the lake.

When the Milwaukee Lake Shore & Western Railway began building a railroad line from Milwaukee to Ontonagon on Lake Superior in 1878, the Browns saw a chance to start a settlement and they offered the railroad half of their land to make a rail connection in this area, then known as Pelican Rapids. Accepting the offer, the railroad sent in engineers to lay out the town. The first train arrived on November 9, 1882, and the town was platted 18 days later. The name was soon changed to Rhinelander in honor of F.W. Rhinelander of New York City, president of the railroad.

The town prospered. In the early 90's, eight large mills operated day and night. Businesses went up everywhere. Hotels, drug stores, a post office, bank, boarding houses, dry goods stores—everything but saloons. As part of Brown's agreement with the railroad, all property deeds contained a five year restriction on the sale of liquor. Nonetheless, the drug store reportedly sold out its stock of 1,800 bottles of Hostetter's bitters in record time!

By World War I, Rhinelander handled a record 700 million board feet of pine and 300 million feet of hardwood. The last log drive down the Pelican River occurred in 1923.

For information on the Wisconsin River see Routes 51, 14 and 61.

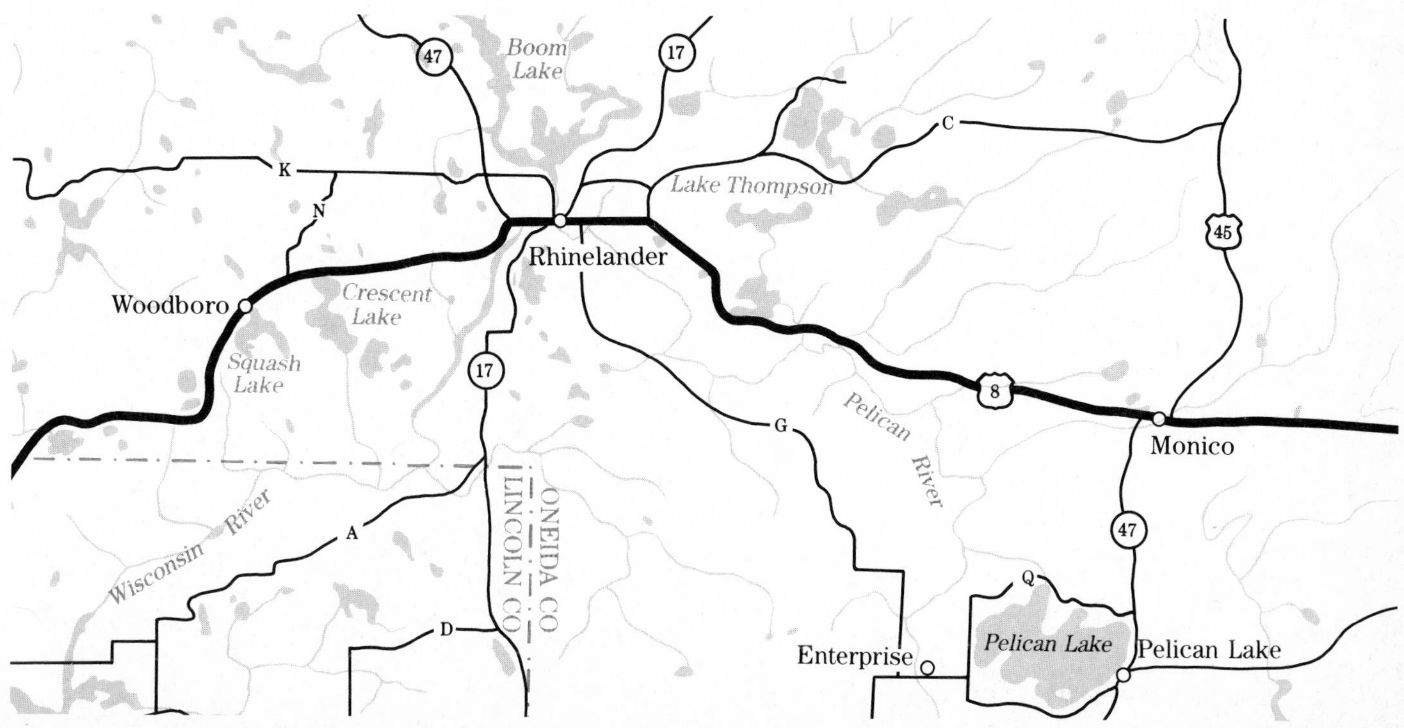

MONICO, Pop. 291

The crossing known as Monico Junction was little more than a few railroad shanties in 1882 when the Milwaukee, Lake Shore & Western Railway was building into Rhinelander. But a year later the Wisconsin Sulphite Fibre Company bought most of the town site and built a factory which was to remove bark and decay from pulpwood and ship it to Appleton's pulp mills. The town's prospects looked bright when it was platted on April 24, 1883.

The sulphite plant was torn down that fall and a new one was established with five rotary boilers. Early intentions were to develop a paper mill. Prospects again looked bright but the mill burned down a few years later. Instead of rebuilding, the company gave up its plans, sold its interests and left the village. Ed Squier of Rhinelander bought the site and sold lots to various parties.

Fire was the village's chief enemy, destroying many of the local establishments which were never rebuilt. As late as October, 1920, fire destroyed two stores, the post office, restaurant and seven or eight residences. Three years later, the railway depot burned to the ground.

An early surveyor, B.F. Dorr, reportedly named the town after Monaco, the principality on the French Riviera. Better at surveying than spelling, Dorr missed the correct name by one letter.

FOREST COUNTY, Pop. 9,044

Officially organized in 1855, Forest County was once a vast timber region and continues its importance in that once-vital industry. The Connor Mill in Laona is the world's largest hardwood mill and just a few miles north of Highway 8 near Newald is the world's largest white pine. The MacArthur Pine is 420 years old and has a circumference of 17 feet, two inches. Towering 148 feet into the sky, it is heads above any other tree in the heavy hardwood forest from which the county took its name.

POTAWATOMI INDIANS

In the early 1800's, the hills and villages of this densely forested county, became the permanent home of the Potawatomi ("Keeper of the Fire") Indians. Because of the tribe's depressed conditions, Congress appropriated $150,000 to purchase more land and an additional $100,000 to build new homes. The acquired property, originally owned by lumber companies, was mostly useless cutover land, purchased in staggered sections among white settlers to promote faster assimilation. Scattering their homes over 20 miles, the Potawatomi settled along the hills of Crandon, Laona, Wabeno and Townsend in dwellings which could only reached by path or trail. Originally the Potawatomi owned 14,439 acres. As of 1978 the tribe still controlled 11,267 acres.

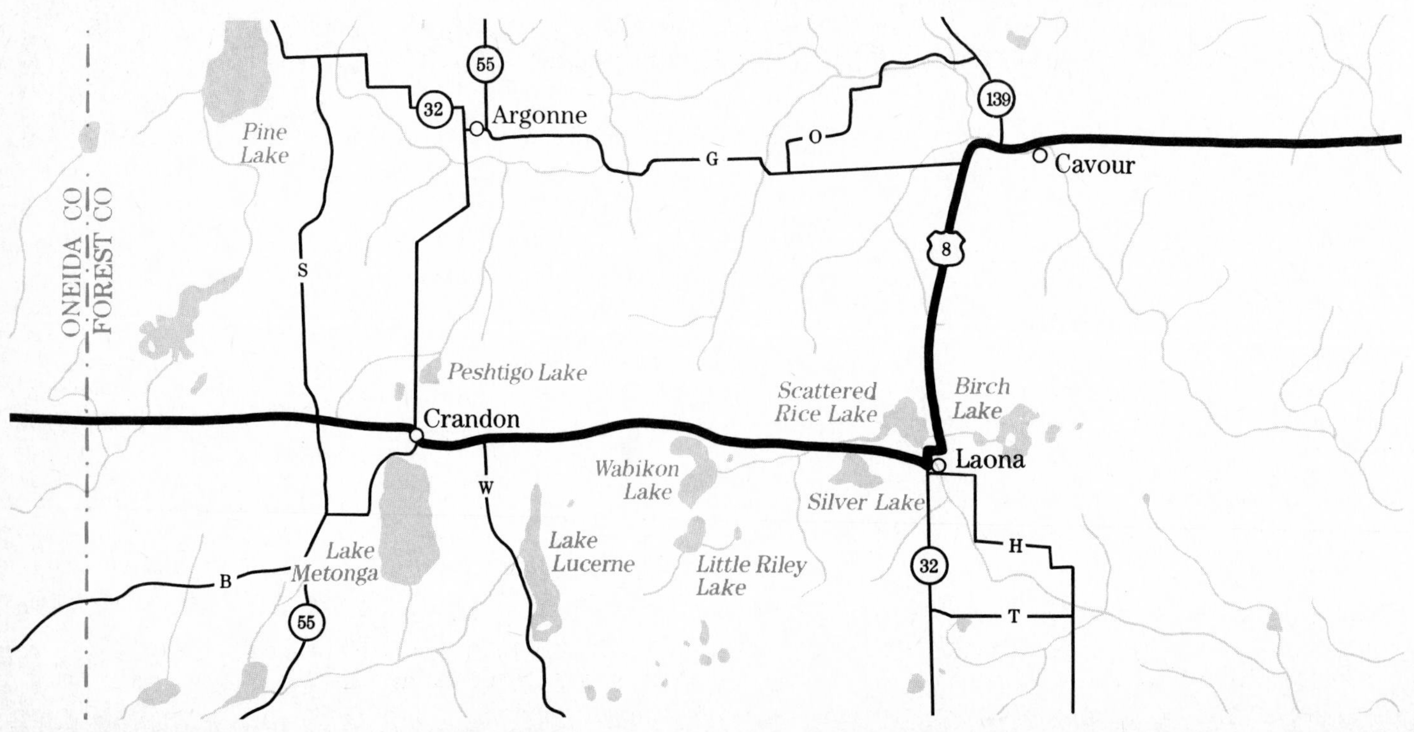

The Potawatomi fought the Sioux tribes in 1806 in an effort to remove the Sioux from an area known as Mole Lake. Bows, arrows, tomahawks and war clubs were used and more than 500 warriors were killed including Chief Yellow Thunder who had once fought the famous Chief Black Hawk.

CRANDON, Pop. 1,969

One of Forest County's best known residents, Samuel Shaw, founded Crandon in 1885. At the time, the area was surrounded by a heavy hardwood forest and high moraine ridges and was soon nicknamed Little Kentucky by many of the early residents from Kentucky. The town's official name honored Major Frank P. Crandon, tax commissioner of the Chicago and Northwestern Railroad, who helped create the new county and assisted in platting the town.

By the turn-of-the-century, Crandon had seven saloons, a beer warehouse, music store, three hotels, two doctors, a dry goods store and 250 people. Ten years later, it boomed with scores of new mills and more than 2,000 people. The county seat of Forest was officially organized on January 28, 1909.

Highway 8 still follows the path of the early Crandon-Laona road which was laid out originally in a rather crooked pattern. In the early days, the road was just a rough wagon trail from Crandon to Wabikon Lake and merely an Indian path from there to Laona.

LAONA, Pop. 1,474

Much of the area's original land was bought by the Spencer Lumber Company of southern Wisconsin. The pine was then cut and hauled to Roberts Lake by wagon or sled. Seeking more efficient transportation, a railroad bed was later laid, a project which took three years to complete. When it was finished in 1872 a party was held at a cabin on Silver Lake, the first known dwelling erected on the present site of Laona. Barney McKinley, who was largely responsible for the railroad project, was given the honor of naming the town and named it after the first white child born in the territory, Leona Johnson.

About the time the Wisconsin Central Railroad came through town, three Scottish brothers, Robert, John and James Connor, started a partnership and moved here to farm, establish a trading post and buy lumber. The result is the present Connor Forest Industries which includes the world's largest hardwood saw mill and headquarters at Laona.

CAVOUR

When the Soo Line was finished from Minneapolis to Michigan in 1887 this became a stop named after a railroad timekeeper, Count Cavour.

MSHS

MacArthur Pine, largest white pine in the world. Over 380 years old.

ARMSTRONG CREEK, Pop. 501

Around 1900, there was little here except a few rugged trails through cutover woods. Hoping to increase settlement, a land company sent an advertisement to people in Poland telling them of the attractive farming land here. They included pictures of the area, taken in winter when snow covered the dead stumps. Offering to pay transportation, the company seduced many Polish families to cross the ocean and settle here, sight unseen. When spring came and the snow melted, the harsh reality set in: stumps and rocks were everywhere. Still the Polish people stayed, erecting houses in their own style and farming the poor land. Today, the Polish community is still the town's backbone, though many descendants have left for better jobs in the city.

The town was reportedly named after a lumber baron and the creek that runs through town.

SHSW

Fall Hunting party, northern Wisconsin.

MARINETTE COUNTY, Pop. 39,314

Marinette County was formed in 1879 from what was previously eastern and southeastern Oconto County. An American Fur Trading post was established on the Wisconsin side of the river near Marinette in 1796, but it was 26 years before the first settler arrived.

Louis Chappee, a bold and energetic Indian trader, was the original agent and well suited to his profession. Consequently, there was a struggle when William Farnsworth, another fur company agent, came in 1822 to take control. Farnsworth got the Chippewa Indians on his side by arranging the release of two Chippewa chiefs who had been imprisoned at Fort Howard at Chappee's request. One day when Chappee was gone Farnsworth and his followers took forcible possession of the post. Unable to rebuff them, Chappee packed his belongings and re-established himself at the foot of the rapids now bearing his name.

Farnsworth's helpmate at the post was his wife, a beautiful and intelligent woman named Marinette. Her reputation as the best Indian trader in the northwest was well-founded. During her husband's absences, she kept the books to the penny. Farnsworth later left her for reasons unknown but she stayed on at the post. She died in Green Bay on June 3, 1865 at the age of 73. The county and city of Marinette were named for her.

GOODMAN, Pop. 803

James B. Goodman and family were the first and by far the most important settlers of this small town which was founded in 1908. As part of their initial settlement, the Goodmans purchased a large tract of timber land where they built a saw mill and houses which they rented to their employees. Later, the Goodmans also built a planing mill, dry kiln, chemical plant and veneer mill. In fact, the Goodman's owned the whole town until 1955 when they sold the mill to Calumet and Hecla, Inc. and the houses to private individuals.

DUNBAR, Pop. 522

When logging camps and lumber mills filled this area in the late 1800's, the township population was 2,000. A camp cook named Dunbar was in charge of all supplies unloaded here. When the train neared his camp, the crew would yell, "What's for Dunbar today?" and the town was subsequently named after him.

"Long Dan Bartlett" surveyed Dunbar in 1888 for the Girard Lumber Company. After successfully operating for almost 40 years, the company was destroyed by fire in 1919. Most residents speculated that the fire happened at a good time since area timber was depleted by then.

PEMBINE, Pop. 773

When the Milwaukee and Northern Railroad and the Minneapolis and Atlantic Railroad came through here in the 1880's this area was just a crossing called Pemene Junction. Slowly, the name evolved to Pembine Junction and finally, Pembine. A Green Bay man, hearing that the town's small stream was especially good for trout fishing, asked a French Canadian for directions. The Frenchman pointed toward the stream and said "La Pemene c'est bon won," meaning "La Pemene, it is a good one." In 1847 government surveyors named the stream Pemene-Bon-Won.

Pembine took its name from an Indian word meaning "water berries" or "cranberries." It's the same name given a stream flowing into the Menominee River and the falls on that river.

NIAGARA, Pop. 2,079

Although trader Chappie was probably the first to move here, the earliest recorded settlement was in 1889 when John Stoveken built a small pulp mill adjacent to Lower Quinnesec Falls. A lumber company, blacksmith shop, store and two frame houses later completed the settlement.

Stoveken's pulp mill was one of the first in Wisconsin. The pulp was rafted across the river above the Falls, then hauled five more miles by horse and wagon to the closest railroad line in Quinnesec, Michigan. The expense and difficulties of this method ended in 1894, when the Chicago and Northwestern Railroad built its line into Niagara from Quinnesec.

In 1898 the mill was sold to Kimberly-Clark and Company of Neenah. A year later they razed the building, replacing it with a two-machine operation. Currently the Niagara mill, still using one of its two original machines, produces 450 tons of paper each day and remains the town's major employer.

Niagara grew rapidly and incorporated in 1914 with a population of 1,247. Its name is an Indian word meaning "thundering waters," referring to the lower Quinnesec Falls.

MENOMINEE RIVER

The Menominee, with its headwaters in Florence County, cascades more than 100 miles to its mouth at Marinette, a natural boundary between Wisconsin and this part of the Upper Peninsula. For many years this river was king over a beautiful tract of virgin timber and many saw mills sprang up along its path. The first appeared in 1832, but was sold a few years later at a sheriff's sale for 18 barrels of whitefish.

When logs were rolling, the Menominee was choked for ten miles each spring with lumber headed for 23 dust-spitting mills. In 1888, a record year, 650 million feet of lumber came out of this great timber region.

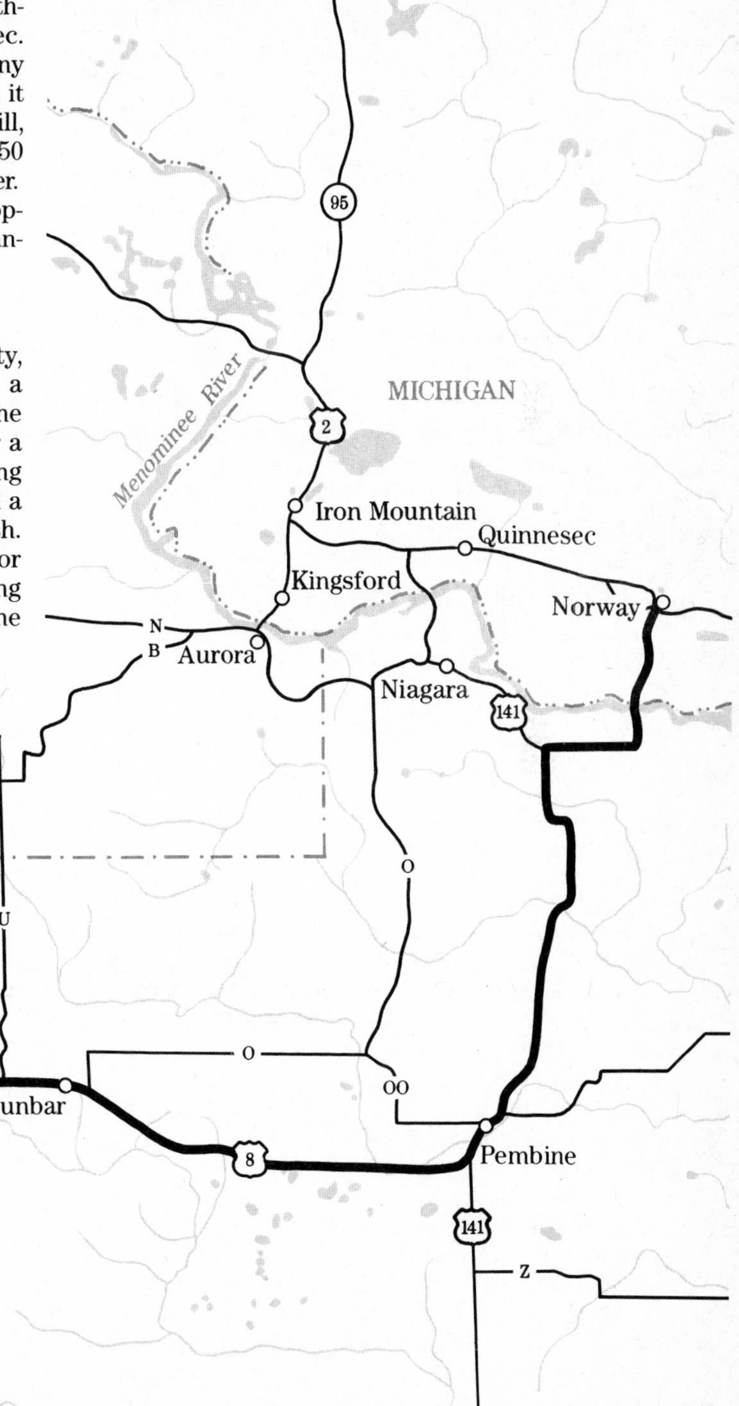

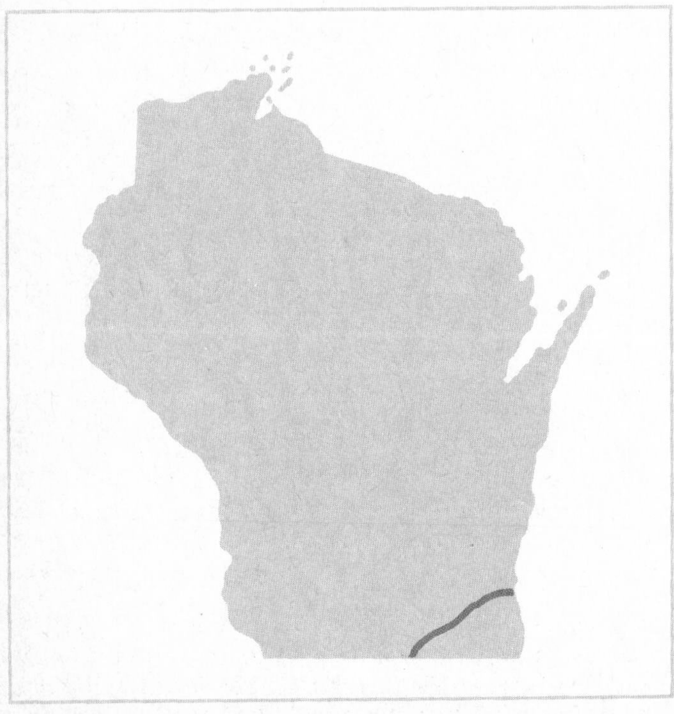

State 15 is a divided highway running 55 miles from the bustling, college town of Beloit to the thriving metropolis of Milwaukee. This short but beautiful route will take you through many lovely lake areas filled with wonderful old estates and summer homes. A short detour near Mukwonago, brings you to Old World Wisconsin, the only multinational, multicultural, outdoor museum in the world.

ROUTE 15, BELOIT TO MILWAUKEE

MSHS

Early Indian tribes maintained camps along the Rock River.

ROCK COUNTY, Pop. 139,420

There was once an almost continuous line of Indian villages and camp sites from northern Rock County near the south end of Lake Koshkonong to the state line at Beloit on the Rock River. Before the first white settlers came in 1835, a Winnebago village stood on the site of Beloit at the junction of Turtle and Rock rivers. The Winnebago shared this county with Sauk, Foxes and Potawatomi Indians and eventually it was given away by treaty; the first on January 30, 1816 and the last in 1837 when the Winnebago ceded all remaining land east of the Mississippi.

The ceding gave rise to the first white settlement in Rock County although French Canadian fur trapper Joseph Thibault claimed to have lived near Beloit for 12 years before he was visited by Caleb Blodgett in 1836. A year before that visit John Inman and William Holmes of Milwaukee established themselves as the first permanent settlers by building a small cabin on the Rock River's southern bank, near the present city of Janesville.

Twenty years later Rock County was covered from one end to the other by a network of railroads. Most came through around 1852 and four years later the Racine, Janesville, Beloit and Mississippi completed its line to Beloit. Janesville became the central point of eight rail lines, Beloit of six, affording ample facilities to transport surplus produce to Eastern markets. In return, the railroads brought in a variety of manufactured goods and opened the area to travel and immigration.

Rock County's early pioneers were mostly Norwegian and many settled near Plymouth and Avon in a beautiful area they called Luther Valley. From here the immigrants ran a printing office which published the "Emigranten," for many

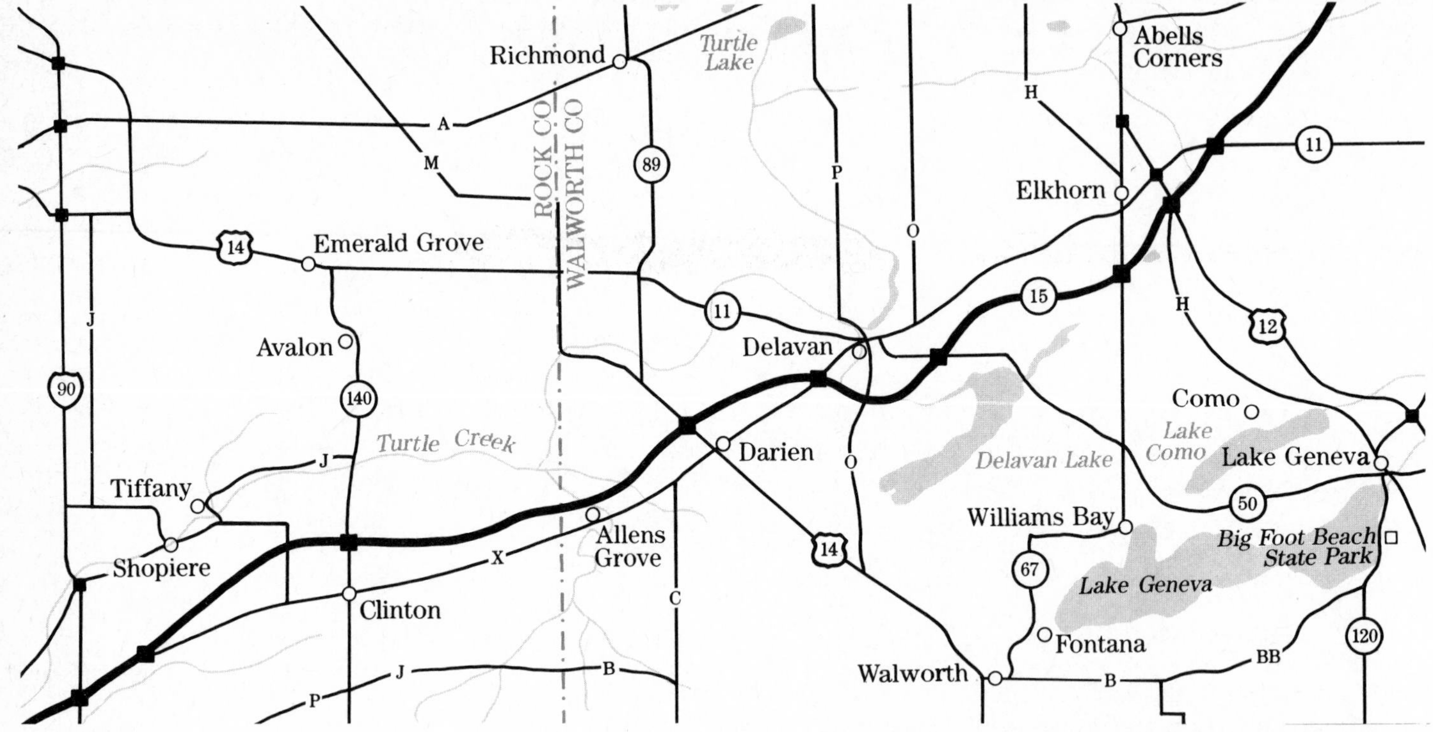

years the only permanent Scandinavian newspaper in the United States.

The Rock River and the county get their names from the rocky nature of the area's soil. According to one story, the river was first named by French explorers who called it Riviere des Kickapoo after a Kickapoo Indian tribe living along its shore. In the 1700's the name was changed to Riviere de la Roche, meaning "river of the rock."

BELOIT, Pop. 35,207

When Caleb Blodgett came here in 1835 he discovered fur trader Thibault in sole possession of the area. Deciding to settle here, Blodgett purchased Thibault's claims on the east side of Rock River, about ten sections of land, for $250. A year later he brought his wife and two children here. With his son-in-law, John Hackett, Blodgett built a log cabin of two rooms separated by a passageway; one for his family, the other for prospectors and help. He then sold one-third of his property to Charles F. Goodhue who helped him build a saw mill. The following spring they sawed their first boards and built a dam on Turtle Creek. About a year later, Blodgett built the state's first grist mill on the same creek. Some customers traveled more than 100 miles to get there.

The city's most important growth began in 1837 with arrival of the New England Emigration Company, organized by 14 people to assist in emigration and founding of agricultural communities, similar to the ones in Colebrook, New Hampshire, where the company organizers had previously lived. Dr. Horace White, the company's agent, selected sites for homes, including some which belonged to Caleb Blodgett. On March 14 White bought one-third of Blodgett's claim for $2,500. Much of Colebrook's population immediately followed and Beloit began to blossom.

The many Eastern immigrants demanded a Christian institution of higher learning. In 1843, 28 members of the General Presbyterian and Congregational Convention discussed plans for a college. After much consultation and prayer, and a little help from their Eastern brethren, Beloit College was conceived. The town pledged a ten-acre site and raised $7,000 to erect the first building. Although one building was not yet completed, the first class was admitted November 4, 1847. One of the college's first professors, Deacon Hinman, father of eight children, received an annual salary of $500.

The town residents didn't like any of the names by which it was known, including Turtle, Blodgett's Settlement and New Albany. In 1857 a name committee was formed and one of its members, L.G. Fisher, selected Beloit.

In 1886, when Beloit had a hard time financially, a businessmen's association was formed to promote the city and encourage new businesses. The following year, the Berlin Machine Works (now Yates American Machine Company) moved in. By 1937 it employed 500 workers to manufacture 200 types of woodworking machines.

CLINTON, Pop. 1,751

Some of Beloit's early pioneers, in search of good farm land, eventually moved to and organized a settlement they called Jefferson Prairie after their original home in New York. This area, at the present intersection of Highway 15 and J, was later known as Clinton Corners. Officially organized in 1842, the name of Clinton was adopted at the first town meeting in honor of DeWitt Clinton, the mayor of New York.

Clinton's first residents lived in a dwelling made of four crutches set in the ground with poles thrown across, a brush heap for a roof, Indian blankets for the sides, and a wagon box for a floor. This structure served as a house for eight days and nights, before the men built a 12X16 log house which sheltered many of Clinton's early settlers.

Two railroads, the Racine and Mississippi and the Chicago/Fond du Lac, raced to be the first into Clinton in 1856. Construction crews worked hard to arrive first to avoid buying the expensive hardware needed to join their rails to those laid first. The Chicago road won by ten minutes and 1,000 people turned out to see the outcome. Subsequently, Clinton was moved to the railroad junction. In 1857 the name was changed to Ogden, after the president of the Chicago line, but residents objected and the post office approved the change back to Clinton in 1864.

Eighteen years later the little settlement around the railroad tracks incorporated with a population of 800.

WALWORTH COUNTY, Pop. 71,507

Proximity to the big city and scores of beautiful wooded lakes make this county a popular, recreational center year-round.

Walworth's history dates back to the days of the Mound Builders, early

Indians who left behind prehistoric mounds in animal formations. Early settlers located several mounds in the southeastern lake district. No white man ever visited or lived in this region prior to 1830 and permanent settlement began primarily after the Black Hawk War.

Mrs. John Kinzie, wife of the Fort Winnebago Indian agent, was the first white to visit this area when she came in the fall of 1832. Three years later, the first permanent settlers were surveyors John Brink, John Hodgson and the brothers Ostrander who staked out claims in the present city of Lake Geneva in October, 1835.

Indian trails were the only roads in the early days of Walworth County, with the principal trail leading from Big Foot Lake (now known as Lake Geneva) through La Fayette and East Troy to Mukwanago. It was commonly known as the Army Trail because of its heavy use by soldiers marching from Fort Dearborn to Fort Howard. White men built the first permanent county road by dragging an oak tree 12 miles from a settlement in Spring Prairie to what is now Delavan. A stage route was established over this route in 1836 and mail was carried once a week on horseback. It later became part of State Highway 20.

A different type of road also became widely known in this county. The Underground Railroad which operated between Milwaukee and Canada in 1843 ran through the heart of Walworth and citizens were proud that no slave was ever captured within its boundaries.

The Yerkes Observatory, built in 1895 in Williams Bay, houses the world's largest (40-inch aperture) refracting telescope.

DARIEN, Pop. 1,152

According to "The Wisconsin Place Names Book," Darien was settled by John Bruce of New York, who came here in 1837 and bought up most of the land which was later named Bruceville in his honor. Bruce set aside a three-acre strip for a commons similar to those in the early New England towns he had known. That strip is now known as Bruce Park or Darien Village Park.

SHSW

Beloit developed early into an industrial city.

Baraboo Circus Museum

Winter months were used to prepare next season's circus acts.

Many settlers came here in 1838 from Darien, New York and decided to change the town's name. By 1860 Darien was reportedly the largest shipping point for stock, grain and pine between Milwaukee and the Mississippi River.

The Wisconsin School for the Deaf in Delavan grew from a small private school for deaf mutes here. It began in 1852 at the home of Ebenezer Cheesebro who wanted to educate his deaf daughter. He lobbied the legislature to pass a law founding the state institution.

DELAVAN, Pop. 5,684

The Phoenix brothers, Samuel and Henry, moved here in early 1836 dreaming of a settlement dedicated to temperance, religion and racial tolerance. Their claim, near Lawn Lake Lodge at the outlet of Delavan Lake on Turtle Creek, was chosen to utilize the lake's waterpower and with the hope that a federal road would one day pass here.

Many of their dreams came to pass. The brothers built a saw mill and Samuel preached the first sermon in the county. In time the federal road came through and the settlement grew to 200 people by year end. Samuel, known locally as "Colonel," was credited with naming the county Walworth and the town Delavan, in honor of Edward Delavan, a prominent temperance leader from New York. The dream of temperance lasted only nine years when it became unconstitutional to enforce.

Despite the temperance issue, Delavan's claim to fame was the circus, or rather, circuses. Between 1847-1894, 28 circuses winter quartered in Delavan. For almost 50 years, Walworth Avenue was a winter magic land as elephants, tigers and circus performers marched down its cobble streets.

America's largest circus at the time, the U.S. Olympic Circus, owned by Edmund and Jeremiah Mabie, arrived first, choosing this area because Delavan's abundant pasture land, pure lakes and four-season climate were all important for their horses, valuable assets to the circus. The Mabies purchased 400 acres for its winter quarters and performers flocked to the area. Although the famous Barnum and Bailey Circus began here, the magical circus era in Delavan ended as abruptly as it had begun when the E.G. Holland Railroad Circus left town in 1894. Circus barns and familiar landmarks are now gone but not forgotten. A marker in the town park commemorates the exciting era.

LAKE GENEVA, Pop. 5,607

Many of Walworth County's "firsts" happened in Geneva, now a very active tourist town not far from Highway 15. The first white settlement began at the foot of Lake Geneva (see Walworth County) in 1835 and was followed by the first saw and grist mill and the county's first school house.

In February, 1836, Christopher Payne and two companions, arrived at the foot of the lake, sensed the valuable waterpower here, and staked out a claim by cutting and blazing trees. They began a cabin, mill and dam in March and a month later families moved in from Illinois. Payne, a typical woodsman, had been a scout and courier during the Black Hawk War. He remained in Geneva for only one year, then traveled the county in search of new challenges, blazing paths for new pioneers and homesteaders.

ELKHORN, Pop. 4,605

Elkhorn's founder, Le Grande Rockwell, a native of Otsego County, New York, discovered this location when searching for the center of Walworth County. He believed that the center would be a strategic and beneficial place to live. Accompanied by a friend named Coleman, Rockwell left his Milwaukee home in 1837 on his search and met Hollis Latham.

Continuing westward over the trail made by the Phoenix brothers, the three eventually came to a point near Elkhorn's city park. They noticed a large oak tree with a pair of elk horns hanging from a branch and decided they must be near the center. Exploring a bit further, they finally determined the exact center and each took claims cornering it. These sections now embrace the city limits of Elkhorn, Walworth's county seat.

This area was also the home of Joseph Webster, author of the Civil War camp song, "Lorena" and the popular hymn, "In the Sweet Bye and Bye."

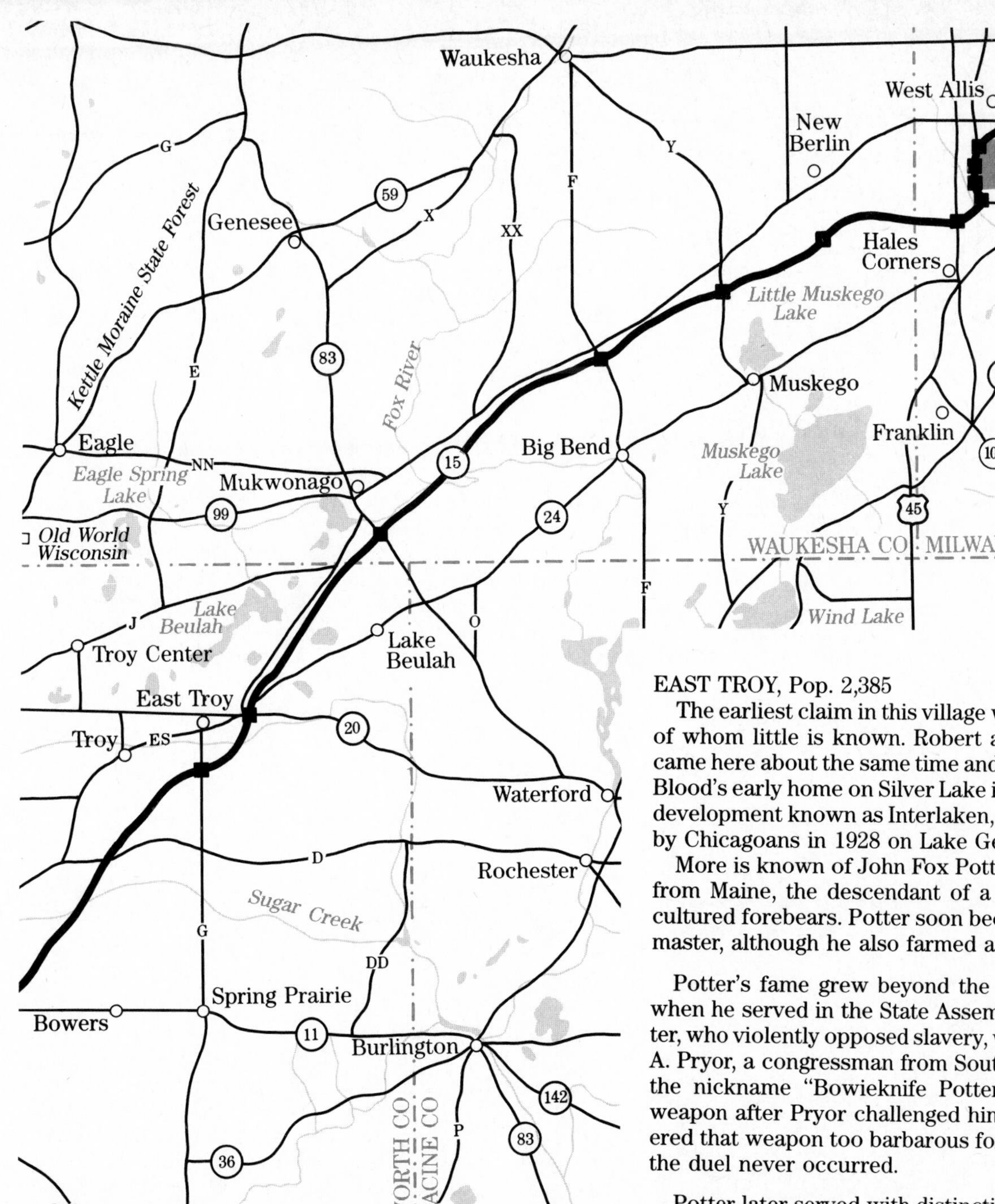

EAST TROY, Pop. 2,385

The earliest claim in this village was staked by a Mr. Robert of whom little is known. Robert and Asa Blood apparently came here about the same time and lived on adjoining claims. Blood's early home on Silver Lake is now part of an extensive development known as Interlaken, a summer colony planned by Chicagoans in 1928 on Lake Geneva.

More is known of John Fox Potter who came here in 1836 from Maine, the descendant of a long line of brilliant and cultured forebears. Potter soon became the first village postmaster, although he also farmed and practiced law.

Potter's fame grew beyond the boundaries of Wisconsin when he served in the State Assembly. During this time Potter, who violently opposed slavery, was an adversary of Roger A. Pryor, a congressman from South Carolina. Potter gained the nickname "Bowieknife Potter," when he choose that weapon after Pryor challenged him to a duel. Pryor considered that weapon too barbarous for a man of his stature and the duel never occurred.

Potter later served with distinction as Consul at Montreal. His farm home on Potter's Lake, where he died in 1899, was the site of an exclusive summer colony, Miramar, for many years.

LAKE BEULAH

Formerly known as Crooked Lake, Beulah owes its beginning to Harold Rogers who built a summer resort here and opened an amusement park about 1880. At one time, Rogers had a steamer on the lake called the Lady Anna.

WAUKESHA COUNTY, Pop. 280,326

Waukesha, like all northern and eastern Wisconsin counties, was formed through the early glacial action of the Superior, Chippewa, Green Bay and Michigan glaciers. The Green Bay and Michigan accumulated drift along a 150-mile line which is seen today in the tumultuous ridge known as the Kettle Moraine which passes through the beautiful lake region of southwestern Waukesha County. Landforms from this glacial period can still be seen in the beautiful Kettle Moraine State Forest (southern unit). More than 50 miles of trails offer hikers a good sampling of the water-filled kettle lakes, conical-shaped hills (kanes) and large ridges of gravel (moraines). The Scuppernong Trail covers a variety of landscapes and its lookout point has a breathtaking view.

The name Waukesha was chosen by Joshua Hathaway who selected this location for a future town site. Hathaway claimed the name was taken from a Potawatomi Indian word Wauktsha, meaning "fox" or "little fox," which also applied to the river along which Waukesha is located.

SHSW

Threshing the important wheat crop.

The county's first permanent white settlers were the Cutler brothers and their employees, John Manderville and Henry Luther, who settled Waukesha on May 7, 1834. Arriving on horseback from LaPorte, Indiana, they were enchanted with the Fox valley which offered them a blooming prairie, scattered oak groves, timber, springs and waterpower. The brothers and their companions blazed out a claim, embracing the river's rapids. That first summer they raised a few potatoes and a little buckwheat.

OLD WORLD WISCONSIN

This 576-acre historic site, operated by the State Historical Society, offers visitors an unique glimpse into the past. More than 40 buildings including homes, farms, churches, and schools, originally constructed by immigrant settlers, have been gathered from all over Wisconsin, making this the world's only multinational, multicultural outdoor museum.

All buildings and ethnic customs have been preserved and are recreated by costumed interpreters who go about daily chores much as the settlers did a century ago. Special events highlight the changing seasons and visitors are included in the activities. Old World Wisconsin is open daily from May 1-October 31 and s easily reached off Highway 15 or Highway 67 near Eagle. An admission fee is charged to anyone over 5 years old.

MUKWONAGO, Pop. 4,014

Prior to white settlement, Mukwonago was a large Potawatomi Indian village. Situated on Mukwonago Creek, not far from the Fox River, it was a desirable spot for a hunting tribe. The valley, with its lakes, streams and heavy forests, was very good to them and they raised corn in abundance. Teepees were sturdily built and an ample council house was built of poles and covered with the bark of large trees. The village was still standing when the first white settlers moved here in 1836.

About June 15 of that year, Sewall Andrews and Henry Camp selected the Indian village site for their future home. The Potawatomi objected, although they had previously relinquished title to the land by treaty. Despite the objections, Camp and Andrews built the area's first white home about a mile and a half northwest of the village. Later the men traded two barrels of flour for the privilege of building another house within the village limits. It became the lodging place for most white residents until the following winter.

The pioneers chose the name given by the Indians, meaning "a place where bears are killed." In Potawatomi, Mukwa was the name for bear.

BIG BEND, Pop. 1,345

The first pioneers named Putnam built a saw mill here in 1841, then opened a tavern and established the first store. The settlement grew slowly until the electric railway pushed through town in 1907.

MUSKEGO, Pop. 15,277

Luther Parker, whose son became the state's lieutenant governor, was Muskego's first settler. His log house was built in 1836 near the south end of Little Muskego Lake where it stood for 40 years. Early settlers estimated that the house sheltered 40 families, many of whom were only looking for temporary quarters.

Parker faced all the hardships of any pioneer; a dense forest, marshes too wet for cultivation, neighbors miles away and no permanent roads. He was forced to follow Indian trails for 20 miles to Milwaukee to purchase supplies for his family which he then carried home on his back. The sorrow of that first winter was increased when a daughter died soon after birth in those harsh surroundings. A colony of Norwegians moved in in 1839 but were almost wiped out ten years later by a widespread cholera epidemic.

Little Lake Muskego, where Parker built his home, is located in northern Muskego and is about a mile and a quarter long and three quarters of a mile wide. Its outlet is a small stream which flows into the bigger Lake Muskego, the county's largest lake. These two lakes provide ample quantities of sunfish which the town honors with its Indian name Muskego.

NEW BERLIN, Pop. 30,529

Although Germans were numerous among the early pioneers, New Berlin was settled by Yankees who named the town after their home in New York. Like most of Waukesha County, this area was first settled in 1836. Sidney Evans built the first house, but sold it to his brother John a few years later and moved to Milwaukee County.

A few settlers came here late that year and built a dam and the county's first saw mill which soon provided lumber for homes. Although several Irishmen moved in around 1840, settlement was slow until five years later when Jacob Korn brought in the first group of Germans from Rhenish-Bavaria.

MILWAUKEE COUNTY, Pop. 964,988

Long before the white man came to this county, the Potawatomi Indians had their council grounds at the junction of the Menomonee and Kinnickinnic rivers. Their name, Mahn-a-waukee, meant "gathering place," and was the basis for the name Milwaukee.

Permanent settlement began about 1833 when increasing numbers of New England settlers came here. A year later, with Wisconsin still a part of Michigan Territory, the Michigan legislature passed an act laying out Milwaukee County. Since settlement was still scarce, the county didn't officially organize until August 25, 1835 when Milwaukee was named county seat. By 1836 the county population was 2,893, with half concentrated around the mouth of the Kinnickinnic River.

Although fur trading and farming were the main occupations of early settlers, Milwaukee's lakes and rivers rapidly made it the county's most important trading and industrial center. Many pioneers moved into this booming town for job opportunities in flour milling, brick making, meat packing and brewing and

Milwaukee once again became known as a great gathering place.

SHSW

Monthly stock fair at Hales Corners, 1915.

HALES CORNERS, Pop. 7,110

A New Englander named William Hale made the first claim here in 1837 and became postmaster when the post office was established later. His home and other buildings in town soon became known as Hales Corners. A convenient stopping point for the stage between Milwaukee and southern and western Wisconsin, Hales Corners and the Hales Hotel and Tavern prospered from 1848 to 1884. After the railroad bypassed here, the town became just another quiet country village. Today it is a bedroom community for Milwaukee workers.

GREENFIELD, Pop. 31,467

Today's thriving community of Greenfield began with the Chicago-Northwestern Railroad station in 1880. Until then, this area was relatively uninhabited. The railroad also brought the first permanent settlers, Fred W. and Stutley I. Henderson, whose lots were officially platted on April 12th, 1887. The Homestead Company soon platted other lots and the settlement became known as North Greenfield.

Transportation lines continued to expand into this little community, primarily due to a heated debate over development of a state fairgrounds here. After several years of contention the location was secured, assuring a foundation for Greenfield's later growth.

For Milwaukee information, see Route 94 page 5.

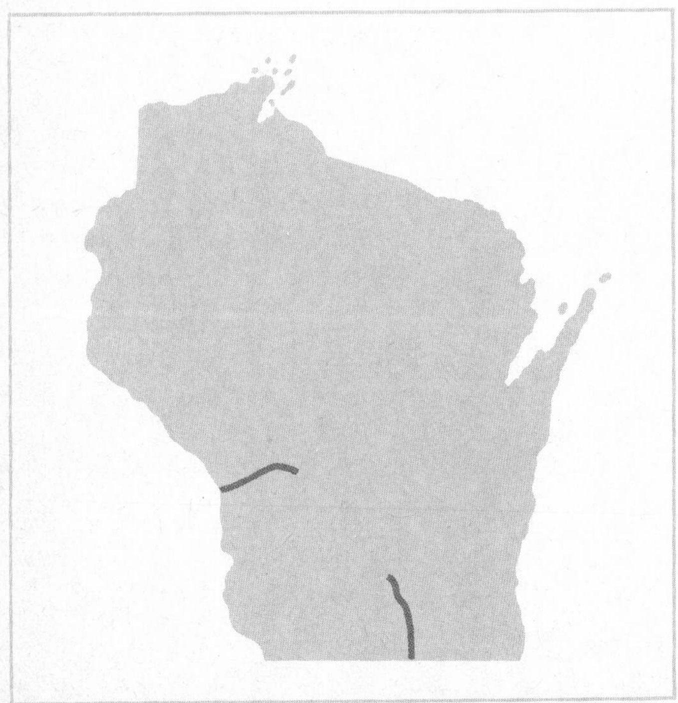

Interstate 90 passes through the rich farmland of southern Wisconsin, where important industrial towns such as Beloit and Janesville grew. On the stretch from Tomah to La Crosse, the freeway descends to the Mississippi River along the valley of the La Crosse River.

ROUTE I-90, BELOIT TO LA CROSSE

SHSW

A fashionable rider posing for photographer C.J. Van Schaick.

ROCK COUNTY, Pop. 139,420

Rock County once had an almost continuous line of Indian villages and camps from the south end of Lake Koshkonong to the state line at Beloit along the Rock River. Before the first white settlers came in 1835, a Winnebago village was located at the junction of Turtle and Rock rivers where Beloit stands today. The Winnebago shared this county with Sauk, Fox and Potawatomi Indians and eventually their lands were signed away by treaty in 1837.

This gave rise to white settlement in Rock County, although a French Canadian fur trapper, Joseph Thibault, claimed he lived near Beloit for 12 years before Caleb Blodgett visited him in 1836. However, in 1835 John Inman and William Holmes of Milwaukee established themselves as the first permanent settlers by building a small cabin on the Rock River's south bank near present day Janesville.

Twenty years later, a network of railroads crossed Rock County from one end to the other. Most railroads came through about 1852 and the Racine, Janesville, Beloit and Mississippi completed its line to Beloit four years later. Janesville became the central point of eight rail lines, Beloit of six, and afforded ample facilities for transporting large quantities of surplus produce to Eastern markets. In return, the railroads brought in a variety of manufactured goods and opened the area to travel and immigration.

Rock County's early pioneers were mostly Norwegians and many settled near Plymouth and Avon in a picturesque area they christened Luther Valley. From here the immigrants published the "Emigranten" which was the only permanent Scandinavian newspaper in the United States for many years.

The river was named by French explorers who called it Riviere des Kickapoo after a Kickapoo Indian tribe that lived along it. In the 1700's the name was changed to Riviere de la Roche, meaning "river of the rock," which referred to a large rock located at an Indian fording place in Janesville township.

BELOIT, Pop. 35,207

When Caleb Blodgett came here in 1835, he found Joseph Thibault trading with the Indians at the confluence of Turtle Creek and the Rock River. Deciding to settle here, Blodgett purchased all of Thibault's claims on the east side of Rock River using the standard Indian measurement of what could be seen in three looks. He paid about $250 and a year later brought his wife and two children here. With the help of his son-in-law, John Hackett, Blodgett built a log cabin of two rooms separated by a passageway; one for his family, the other for prospectors and help. He then sold one-third of his property to Charles F. Goodhue and Goodhue helped him build a saw mill. They built a dam on Turtle Creek and the

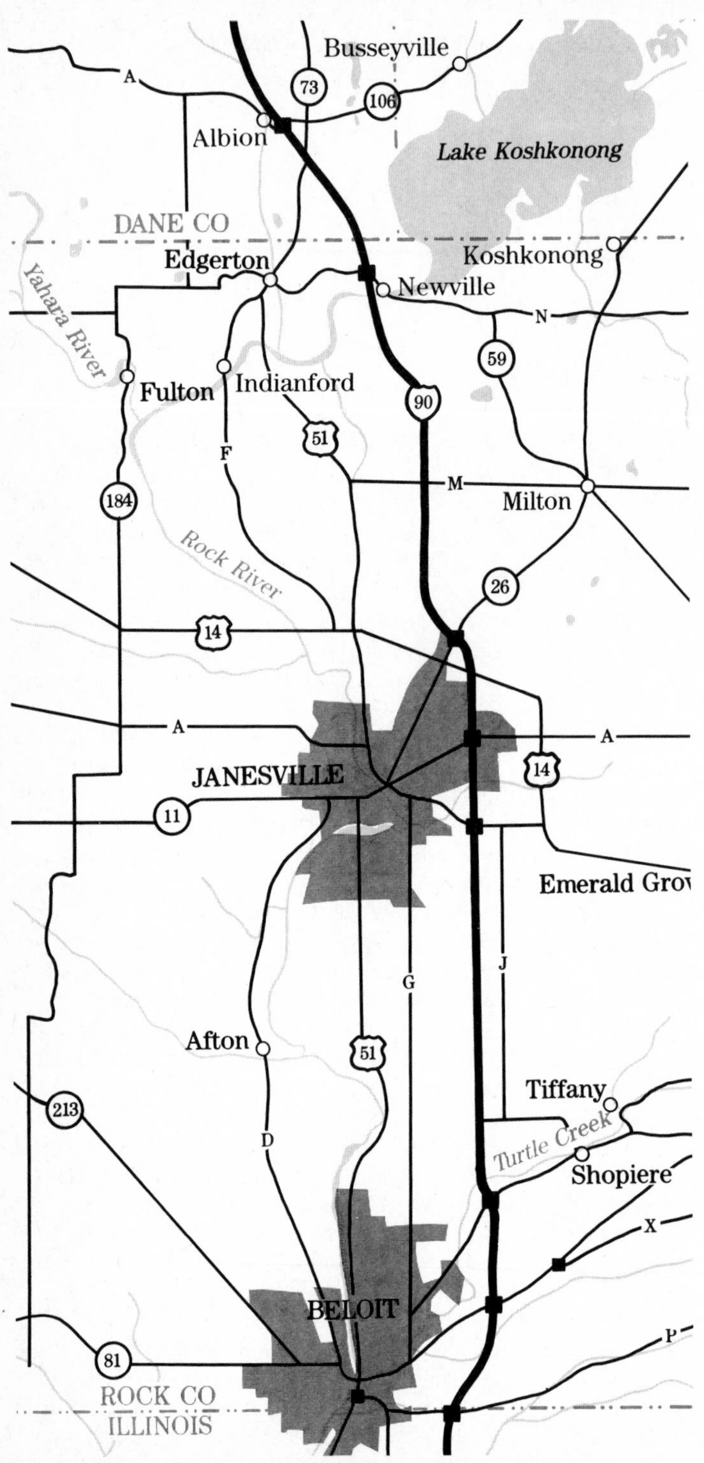

following spring they sawed their first boards. About a year later, Blodgett built the state's first grist mill on the same creek; a few customers traveled more than 100 miles to get there.

The city's most important growth began in 1837 when the New England Emigration Company arrived. Fourteen members organized the company to assist in emigration and the founding of agricultural communities similar to their homes in New Hampshire. An agent, Dr. Horace White, selected sites for company homes, some of which belonged to Caleb Blodgett. On March 14, White bought one-third of Blodgett's claim for $2,500, and many from the east followed, and Beloit began to blossom.

Many eastern immigrants demanded a Christian institution of higher learning. In the Fall of 1843, 28 members of the General Presbyterian and Congregational Convention discussed plans for a college, located away from the influence of commercial cities on the East Coast. They chose Beloit as the location and city fathers pledged 10 acres and $7,000 to erect the first building which was not yet completed when the first class was admitted November 4, 1847. For the privilege of teaching here, one of the college's first professors, Deacon Hinman, father of eight children, received $500 per year.

Although the village was variously known as Turtle, Blodgett's Settlement and New Albany, its citizens weren't happy with any of the names. They formed a committee in 1857 and selected Beloit because many residents identified with Detroit and the names were similar.

SHOPIERE

Lying along Turtle Creek a few miles north of Beloit is Shopiere, a small village which was begun by three Beloit men in 1836. The Meeker family came shortly after and built a shanty. They had ten children and the whole family was reportedly quite heavy, averaging about 200 pounds each. Settled on the opposite side of Turtle Creek was a small colony from Connecticut. The two groups were quite different in habits and appearance and a feud soon developed over the cutting of hay along the river bottoms. Fearing no hay for their cow, John Meeker armed his wife and five daughters with pitchforks and fish spears and sent them to cross the river and chase the New Englanders away. The Meekers won the conflict and left for home with three new rakes, a jug of whiskey and three johnny cakes.

When the post office was established, it took the name Waterloo from this encounter. But the village's name was changed to Shopiere, from the French word Chaux-pierre, meaning limestone, because the region around Turtle Creek has numerous limestone outcroppings. A mill with three stones was built along the creek to grind the local flour. A brewery was also located here for a time.

From 1851 to 1859 Shopiere was the home of Louis Harvey who became Governor of Wisconsin in 1862. Shortly after being elected to office, Harvey led a relief group to Wisconsin troops who had suffered badly in the Battle of Shiloh. Harvey drowned in April 1862 when he fell from a boat on the Tennessee River en route home.

JANESVILLE, Pop. 51,071

Janesville, located around a ford in the shallow Rock River, got started when soldiers who had passed here during the Black Hawk War returned to settle. In October, 1835, four men built a cabin near the river by the Big Rock. By winter, eleven people were sharing the 18 x 16 foot cabin. Henry Janes heard about this new land along the Rock River and on his arrival he carved his initials on a tree. He built a tavern and hotel on the river's east bank and ran a ferry across the shallow water.

The post office was established by placing a cigar box at the end of Jane's bar and the town was eventually named after him. However, when others began settling here, the town became too crowded for Janes. He sold his interests, moved west and soon had towns in Iowa and Minnesota named after him. By 1849, Janes was on the West Coast boasting he had never seen a railroad or telegraph. Janesville became the county seat for Rock County when it was organized in 1839 and by 1842 the court house was ready to be used. In 1849, a school for the blind was established at Janesville. Abraham Lincoln visited Janesville in 1859 when he took the prairie road up from Beloit to speak to Republicans.

Janesville continued to grow. Nine stagecoach and mail lines crossed the river here to other parts of the state. Flat-bottomed boats were pulled up the shallow Rock River and even a few steamboats docked near Janes' old tavern. An academy, the Janesville Collegiate Institution, opened in 1844. By 1845, more than 800 people lived here. The homogeneous community prospered in farming and light industry during the next 75 years and the population reached 1,300 by 1850. The following year, the first state fair was held in Janesville. By 1860, the city had grown to 7,000 people. In the 1880's railroads brought new life to the city, along with new industries such as the James Harris' safety oil lamp and the Janesville Barbed Wire Company.

George Parker incorporated his pen company here in 1892 and steadily increased his operation until it was one of this country's most popular pens. Today Parker Pen is second only to General Motors in workers employed in Janesville. During the 1920's, the General Motors Corporation began building tractors, cars and Fisher automotive frames. More than half of the city's workers depended on General Motors until the plants closed during the depression in the early 1930's. What many had feared became reality, 75 percent of Beloit's work force was unemployed. After the depression, General Motors, Parker Pen and some 60 other industries provided the industrial base for the city. Today many of Janesville's stores and homes are being restored, adding to the unique flavor of this old river town.

EDGERTON, Pop. 4,335

In 1836, two brothers, Robert and Daniel Stone, left Michigan and traveled up the Rock River Valley to the mouth of the Yahara River where they made their claims and planted beans and corn. Two years later they built a log cabin in what is Edgerton and others soon joined them in farming the rich soil. Ferries were established across the river, including the Goodrich ferry at Lake Koshkonong. A saw mill was built at the base of the lake in 1845 and was later converted to a grist mill. The first bridge the Rock River in this area was built at Indianford.

The train followed in 1854 and passed a few miles away from the small village of Fulton because the land owners there were asking more than the railroad was willing to pay. Other area settlers donated 23 acres for the new depot which was first known as Fulton's Station and the early village consisted of only a post office and a small tavern. The collection of homes built by railroad workers and settlers eventually took its name from Benjamin Edgerton, the surveyor who placed the route to Madison. Soon the village boasted two hotels—the Exchange and United States. About this time, area farmers began growing tobacco and the broad-leafed plants and slatted drying sheds could be seen across the countryside. Most of the tobacco farmers were Norwegians. Edgerton soon became one of the largest American cigar-wrapper markets and tobacco buyers became as important to Edgerton as the cotton buyers were to the South.

Early tobacco crops were stored in grain elevators and sheds along the railroad, but large brick warehouses began to be built along the tracks in 1869. A surface clay was discovered nearby and many yellow brick buildings were built with the bricks made by local factories. So much cash changed hands each December when the tobacco was baled and brought to town, that the Tobacco Exchange Bank was formed. Today the old warehouses still line the tracks and most of the tobacco grown here is sold as chewing tobacco.

INDIANFORD

Named because the Winnebago Indians crossed the Rock River at this shallow place, Indianford was settled around 1837 by William Foster who came to start a village and run a ferry. It was known as Foster's Ferry for a time. Foster built an 85-foot steamboat called the Star of the West, which he hoped to navigate along the Rock River to Lake Koshkonong. However, the railroad bridge south of Edgerton was an obstacle and a running feud developed between Foster and the railroad. His boat disappeared one day and was found years later at the bottom of the river filled with stones. Foster could never prove the railroad was responsible.

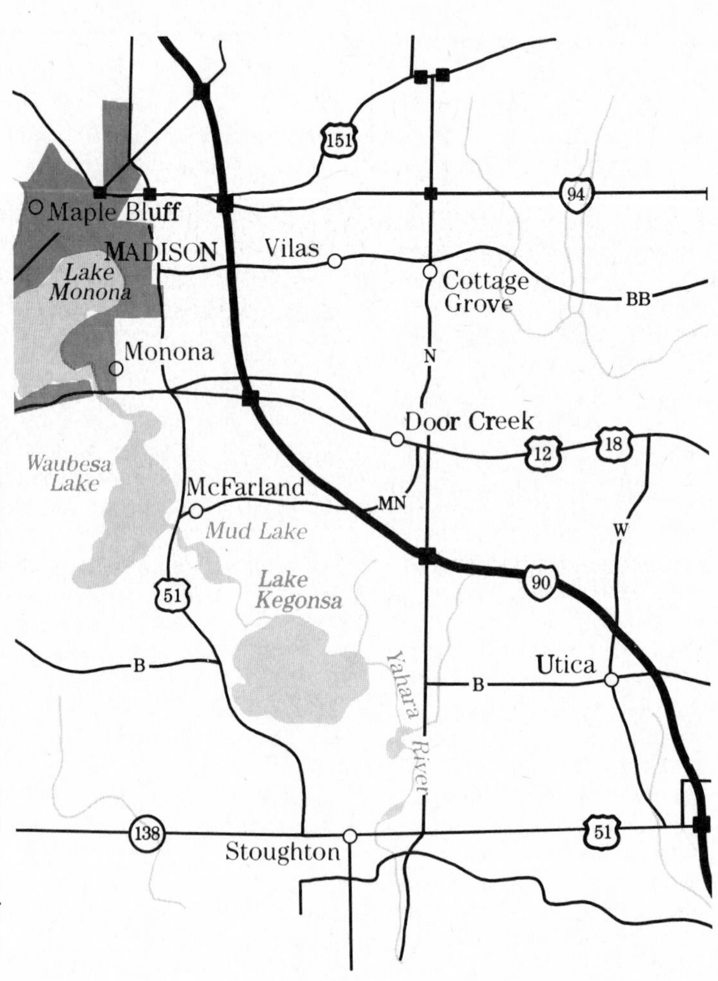

LAKE KOSHKONONG

Once a vast marsh through which the Rock, Crawfish and Bark rivers flowed, Lake Koshkonong provided waterfowl with natural habitat and Indians with wild rice and celery. When Thibault, Beloit's first settler, moved up to the shores of Koshkonong to live, he left his shaving razor on a rock by the marsh. The Winnebago called the lake Koshkonong, meaning, "place where we shave."

This marshy region had so many ducks that travelers joked they could shoot all they wanted from the porch of Edgerton's United States Hotel. When dams were built on the Rock River at Indianford in 1846, the water level was raised several feet, creating a 10,400 acre lake. Today this shallow lake reportedly provides excellent fishing for walleye, bass and crappies. It has 11 public and commercial accesses.

ALBION

Albion's first settlers were Jesse Saunders and Duty Green who came from New York in 1841. The small village was soon populated by Norwegian and New England families. Baptists arrived and built a church in 1843. Ten years later they chartered the Albion Academy and Normal Institute and ran it until 1901 when Norwegians took it over and ran it as a Lutheran school. During the Civil War, meetings were reportedly held in a room under the church to identify and harass Southern sympathizers. The church was also part of the Underground Railroad, which helped slaves escape to the North.

The Academy closed its doors in 1914 and today only two structures remain. One, a museum, has a room dedicated to Sterling North, an author of children's books who was born in Edgerton. The spired white church stands on one side of the old campus grounds.

(For the continuation of Interstate 90 from Madison to Tomah, follow Interstate 94, beginning on page 16.)

SHSW

Chicago, Milwaukee & St. Paul R.R. roundhouse at Tomah, 1900.

ANGELO

Just west of Sparta is the small village of Angelo, named after Dr. Seth Angel, the first settler in 1852. Angel had supposedly been tipped off that this was a good mill site on the La Crosse River and that another man, Searl, was heading for Mineral Point to finalize the claim. Angel rode his horse for Mineral Point, while Searl rode the stage. Angel beat Searl to town by one hour and made the claim.

Angel's new saw mill was the only one in the area other than Esau Johnson's on the Kickapoo and settlers often had to wait hours to get boards for their new buildings.

SPARTA, Pop. 6,934

In July 1851, William Petit purchased 160 acres along the La Crosse River where two pioneer roads intersected. One road, opened in 1849, crossed between Hudson on the St. Croix River and Prairie du Chien, by passing through Eau Claire and Black River Falls. Another road followed on old Indian trail from Portage, along the La Crosse River down to the Mississippi River. Petit felt there were enough travelers crossing the intersection of these roads to warrent a small hotel and tavern. It was crude enough, with only one room and a loft. The floors were only slabs of wood covering the ground and those that wanted to sleep had only the floor for a bed. Supplies came from La Crosse which had only the land office and a few other stores.

Petit's brother, Franklin, had tried to settle a few miles north of Sparta in 1850 but found the Winnebago unfriendly. According to Franklin, the Indians appeared at his door, ordered food to be cooked and then occupied his cabin during the night, telling him he had no business being in the region. He joined his brother the following year at Sparta. William laid out the courthouse square in 1851, with a number of lots surrounding it. His mother named the village after the ancient Greek city. Petit promoted the town by giving lots to anyone who would settle here.

By then, logging had increased along the La Crosse River. Several settlers took up Petit's offer of free land but by 1854 only 14 houses were located in the town. However, when the Milwaukee and St. Paul Railroad was surveyed up the river near Sparta in 1858, the small village got a boost. Grist mills, a paper mill, ironworks and other factories were established. In 1865, a La Crosse man played a cruel hoax on the residents of Sparta. Oil fever had reached Wisconsin and many hoped they would become rich if oil was found nearby. At night, a man named Tichnor buried a number of oil barrels to give the appearance of producing wells. He sold shares in his "Gem Petroleum Company," and then disappeared. It didn't take long for shareholders to realize they had been taken.

Shortly after, the same well-drilling machinery was used

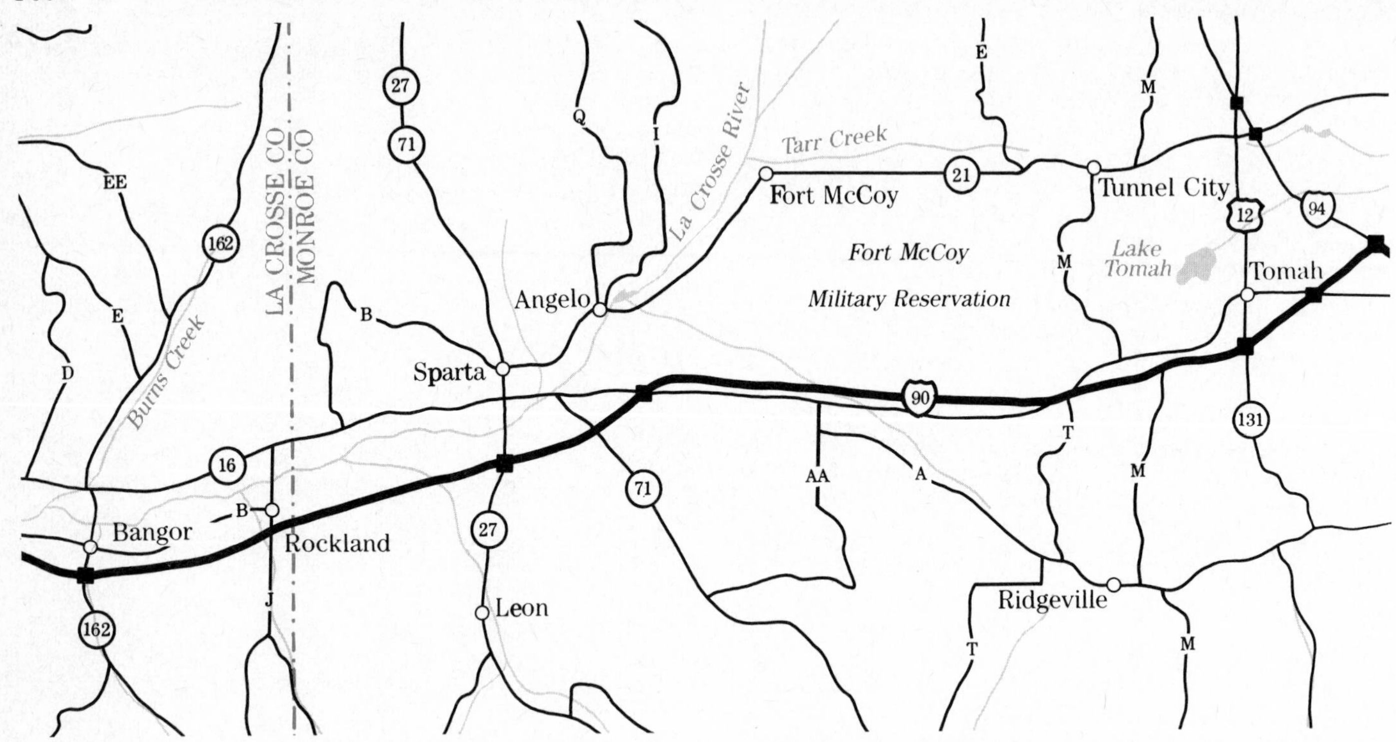

to drill for water. The well contained mineral water which attracted people seeking a cure for their ailments. Several more wells were sunk and during the 1870's, Sparta became a busy health resort area which had Russian, Turkish and other types of baths. The water was thought to cure malaria, gallstones, anemia, infections and tuberculosis.

More recently, Donald (Deke) Slayton, an astronaut in the Apollo-Soyuz test project in July of 1975, grew up near Sparta and has become the town's local hero. He was the docking pilot on the historic flight where a manned Russian and U.S. spacecraft joined in orbit for scientific experiments. One of the nation's original seven Mercury astronauts, Slayton was flight manager for the first flight of the multi-billion dollar space shuttle.

The Elroy-Sparta State Trail, 100 feet wide by 32 miles long, also begins here. The trail follows the abandoned Chicago & Northwestern Railroad right-of-way and passes through three tunnels, including one which is 3/4 miles long.

CAMP MCCOY

In 1906, Secretary of War William Taft tried to establish a federal military camp in each section of the country. The northern camp was to be located next to the state camp at Camp Douglas. That effort failed and 7,000 acres were purchased near Sparta for artillery practice. Battery C from Fort Snelling was the first to use this land and the first wireless message sent to St. Paul, Minnesota originated from here in 1909. In 1910, the camp, first called Camp Robinson, was renamed Camp Bruce E. McCoy in honor of a Civil War veteran who originally owned the property.

In the early 1920's, Camp McCoy was used to store thousands of tons of powder and pyrex gun cotton. Over the years it has also been used by the Department of Agriculture and the Civilian Conservation Corps during the depression. In World War II is was used as an internment camp for Japanese and German nationals. Camp McCoy is now used as a summer training camp for Army Reserve units.

LA CROSSE COUNTY, Pop. 91,056

La Crosse County is a hilly, unglaciated land with deep fertile valleys draining into the Mississippi or La Crosse rivers. The bluffs lining the Mississippi range from 400 to 500 feet high and consist mostly of limestone and sandstone. These sedimentary rocks contain shells and remnants of ancient animals and fish—evidence that this area was under a sea that once covered most of the North American Continent. During the glacial melting at the end of the last ice age 10-12,000 years ago, the La Crosse and Mississippi rivers began to cut their valleys through the rock. At one point, the Mississippi valley was at least 300 feet deeper then it is today, but when the glaciers retreated and the waters slowed, the river silted back to its present level.

Father Hennepin, a French missionary and explorer was the first white person to pass up into the Upper Mississippi region, arriving in 1680. Except for traders who occasionally camped along the river, La Crosse County wasn't settled until 1841. At that time the nearest towns were Prairie du Chien and Galena, Illinois. Milwaukee was in its early days and Chicago had a population of only 5,000. La Crosse County wasn't formed until 1851, and it wasn't until 1918 that its present boundaries were finally set.

The name La Crosse was given by French traders who watched the Indians play a game with sticks and a deerskin ball. Jonathan Carver passed here in 1766 and noted that the goals were 600 yards apart and up to 300 men participated in this game. Carver said the Indians played the game with such ferocity that many were injured or broke bones.

ROCKLAND

Named after a large nearby rock, this village formed when the railroad was built up from La Crosse during the late 1850's. It was once known as Rockland Station.

BANGOR, Pop. 1,012

The old village of Bangor is situated in the broad valley of the La Crosse River. In the fall of 1853, John Wheldon, his wife and seven children came here from Oneida, New York and built a log house near Dutch Creek. Over the years Wheldon served as postmaster, Justice of the Peace and the village's Notary Public. Before the hamlet was allowed a post office, mail came twice weekly on the Baraboo-La Crosse stage. Wheldon named the town after his Welsh birthplace when he became postmaster in 1854.

One of the farmer's early problems was to make flour from their grain. Hauling grain to La Crosse and flour back was slow and difficult. Wheldon and another settler, Jenkins, decided to build a mill on Dutch Creek. They hauled logs by oxen down to the stream where a dam and grist mill slowly took shape. By 1855 flour was being ground. Between 1855 and 1860, the valley was flooded with new immigrants.

Jenkins became the next Justice of the Peace and was occasionally paid in potatoes when he performed marriages. The Welsh farmers who settled here found it important to define those who were not Welsh. A Massachusetts man named Williams was referred to as Yankee Williams, to avoid confusing him with a Welshman of the same name.

Before the railroad came up the La Crosse Valley, Bangor was located on the west side of the creek that runs through the town. In 1858 when the Chicago, Milwaukee & St. Paul railroad was completed, the depot was placed on the creek's east side, forcing the town to move across. In 1864, the Bangor Woolen Mills was established along the creek. It employed 12 men working four looms, a spinning jack and a carding machine and manufactured 25,000 yards of flannel,

SHSW

La Crosse inter-state Fair. Photo/ C.J. Van Schaick.

10,000 yards of cashmere, 150 blankets and 2,000 pounds of stocking yarn during 1880.

WEST SALEM, Pop. 3,276

In 1855, Monroe Palmer felt this location along the La Crosse River would be an ideal place for a new town in the valley. He hired a surveyor, Isaac Thompson of La Crosse, to lay out a town called Neshonoc, after an Indian name. Fifteen acres were surveyed and a small hotel was built, followed by other buildings and a mill owned by Palmer. His dam created the mill pond now called Lake Neshonoc. By 1858, 100 people lived here.

When the railroad was surveyed up the valley, residents offered the railroad 10 acres to build their depot south of Neshonoc at Salem Station. The depot was built there in 1858 and most of the merchants moved their buildings from Neshonoc down to the new village along the railroad. After mail became confused with Salem in Kenosha County, the village changed its name to West Salem. Norwegian and German immigrants settled here and founded a creamery in 1891 that averaged one million pounds of butter annually. In the meantime, the abandoned village of Neshonoc was planted in corn and potatoes.

The home of Hamlin Garland, a well-known author who spent 22 years (1893-1915) living and writing here, is located on the town's northwest side. Garland is best known for his realistic portrayal of Midwestern rural life, including his short stories in "Main-Traveled Roads." He won the 1922 Pulitzer Prize for biography with his book, "A Daughter of the Middle Border."

In 1878, four miles south of West Salem, a young boy hunting raccoons found a small hole leading into a hillside cave that came to be known as picture rock cave. He found the walls covered with crude drawings of elk, lynx, rabbit, a bison and other figures that were difficult to interpret. The following year Rev. Edward Brown, a geologist, excavated and discovered layers of ashes and sand that revealed at least four distinct periods of occupancy in the cave. At one time this cavern was 15 feet wide at its opening with the inside about 30 feet long and 13 feet high.

LA CROSSE, Pop. 48,347

Winnebago Indians were the first to live here at the confluence of the Mississippi and La Crosse rivers. During the early 1800's they camped here to trade their furs for guns, powder, knives, blankets , shirts and whiskey. A tragic period began for the Winnebago in 1837 when they ceded all their land east of the Mississippi for reservations in Iowa and Long Prairie, Minnesota. Many refused to leave and in 1841, 18-year-old Nathan Myrick came to the terraced land of "Prairie La Crosse" to trade with the Indians who had stayed. Myrick arrived with only ten cents and a load of goods. He waited ten days before Indians came but finally "we had plenty good trade." Myrick built a crude trading post on Barron's Island, which is now Pettibone Park and with a partner named Eben Weld, he traded and cut cord-wood for steamers. The next year Myrick built a new cabin on the main land at Prairie La Crosse, a sandy, treeless prairie about ten miles long and three miles wide.

Myrick wrote about one cold winter morning when, "The weather was cold and that night a blizzard sprung up. (The next) morning was the bluest I ever experienced; I was sick, and homesick, and it was the only time I wished myself back home in the East (New York)."

Despite that homesickness, Myrick made his post at Prairie La Crosse the central trading spot from the Black River to the Bad Axe on the south and traded with such important Indians as Chief Winneshiek and Chief Decorah. In 1841 a group of Mormons began working the forest of Black River Falls. In 1844 Myrick and "Scooter" Mills went up to the Black River pineries to cut and float logs down to La Crosse. From there the lumber was floated down river to help in the

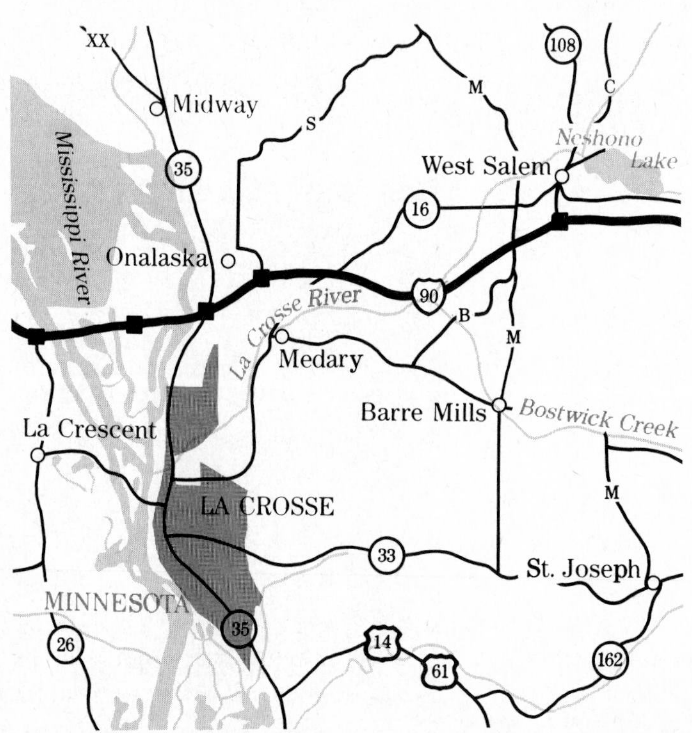

SHSW

The "Mary Morton" lying at the La Crosse levee, 1881.

building of St. Louis. Up until then, all traveling was done along the Mississippi. It wasn't until 1845 that the first overland trip was made in eight days from Prairie du Chien. In 1848 when the Winnebago were forcibly removed from this region, the white population at Prairie La Crosse still numbered only 30.

That same year the government made land available in the area, but settlement was slow. Then in the early 1850's, a number of settlers from New York and Vermont came and established grist mills, saw mills and a newspaper which helped promote this new town. In 1851 Prairie La Crosse was made the county seat and was an important lumber town for the next 40 years. Lots were sold for about $40 in 1851 and a number of buildings were constructed. Yet the growth of Prairie La Crosse from this once desolate, sand-heaped river terrace was a slow process.

U.S. 61 passes through the quiet farming region which thrives along the ridge of the Mississippi River Valley. Today there is little hint that Wisconsin's early settlement focused in this region which was once rich in lead. During the 1820's, thousands swarmed here, living like badgers in the sides of hills, more intent on finding lead than establishing towns. U.S. 61 crosses the Wisconsin River into the coulee country, a hilly region with deep valleys which was untouched by the glaciers.

ROUTE 61, IOWA BORDER TO READSTOWN

SHSW

Mining crew in southwestern Wisconsin, 1895.

GRANT COUNTY, Pop. 51,736

Grant County was organized in 1836 and named for the Grant River, a winding stream which flows through the center of the county and empties into the Mississippi near Potosi. The river itself is named after Cuthbert Grant, an obscure fur trader who was one of the first white settlers. Although there is some question as to his real name, most agree that it was Grant and he lived near the river. In 1810 Grant lived at the Indian village of Chief Pascanans, near Potosi, and supposedly encountered a party of Winnebago unhappy that he was in their territory. Giving chase, one of the Indians caught Grant and struck him over the head with a tomahawk. Since Grant always wore his cooking kettle under his hat, he felt little pain. Amazed by this the Indians apparently never bothered Grant again.

Drained by the Grant, Little Grant and Platte rivers, Grant County is also one of several southwest Wisconsin counties untouched by glaciers during the last ice-age. The region's soil is formed by the weathering of rocks and by soil carried from Minnesota by the prevailing westerlies. The county is also part of a 13,000 square mile area called the Western Uplands which has an average elevation 1200 feet above sea level. The most pronounced topography, deep valleys and coulees, have been eroded by the Mississippi and Wisconsin rivers and their tributaries over many years. The centrally located Grant River flows from the county's uplands down to the Mississippi near Potosi. The "Military Ridge" is a well-known topographic feature, formed along the headlands eroded away by streams which drained into the Wisconsin River. A road was built along this ridge in 1835 to connect Fort Crawford at Prairie du Chien with Fort Howard at Green Bay. Today U.S. 18 to Madison follows the ridge.

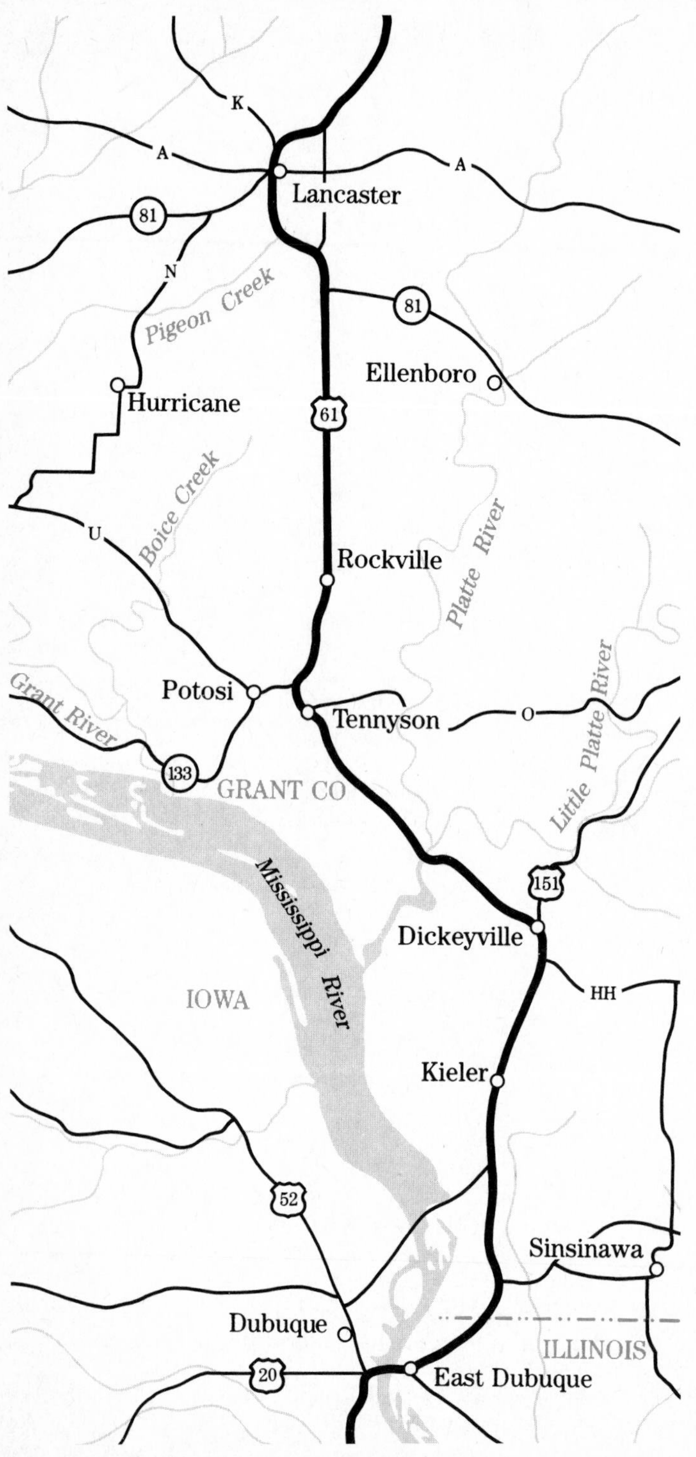

DISCOVERY OF THE MISSISSIPPI

Grant County was one of the earliest regions in Wisconsin to be explored. In 1673 Frenchmen heard Indians talk of a great river (Mississippi), but no whites had seen it. The French in Quebec commissioned Louis Joliet to search out this great river in May of 1673. Joined by Father James Marquette, Joliet and five other men descended the Wisconsin River in "two birch-bark canoes."

On June 17 their canoes crossed out into the Mississippi and Joliet "had a joy he could not express." They were the first whites to see these rugged bluff regions where limestone cliffs rise 500 feet above the broad Mississippi valley. That valley was carved thousands of years ago by glacial rivers draining Lake Agassiz in northwest Minnesota and Glacial Lake Duluth (Lake Superior).

Seven years later, in 1680, Father Louis Hennepin came across Lake Michigan, down the Fox and Wisconsin Rivers and finally out to the Mississippi. The first white to explore the Upper Mississippi, Hennepin intended to convert the Indians and bring this area under French rule. However, he was captured by Dakota Indians near Lake Pepin and brought to an important Indian camp at Lake Mille Lacs in Minnesota before being rescued by Sieur DuLuth. Duluth was exploring the Lake Superior region when he heard that a white prisoner was being held near Mille Lacs.

EARLY SETTLEMENT IN GRANT COUNTY

In the late 1600's the southwest portion of Wisconsin (Grant, Iowa & Lafayette Counties) was known to contain lead deposits. Jonathan Carver noted Indians working numerous small lead mines near present day Grant County when he passed through here in 1766. Lead deposits were also found near Dubuque, Iowa and Galena, Illinois. A French fur trader, Julien Dubuque, heard rumors about the area's lead in 1788 and he and his miners gained the Indians' confidence and worked a smelter south of present day Dubuque.

Dubuque's men probably ranged into Grant County long before there was a permanent settlement here. However, by June, 1827, Chief Red Bird of the Winnebago and his braves were upset by the influx of whites into their land and killed some settlers east of Prairie du Chien. The small number of settlers in the lead region feared a general uprising and built log stockades, but Red Bird surrendered several months later. With his capture and a promise of peace, men streamed into the area seeking their fortune in lead. They spent their energy prospecting for lead and had little time for building houses. The state nickname "badger" come from the fact that many men fashioned temporary living space by digging badger-like dens into the hillside.

LEAD MINING

Indians probably didn't mine in Grant County until the French of the eastern Great Lake region established the need for lead shot during the 1700's. One of Louis Hennepin's maps showed a lead mine in 1687 and in 1690 Nicholas Perrot started a trading post in southwestern Grant County to take advantage of the lead trade. However, Indian hostility checked growth in the Grant County area until 1820. The only exception was for Capt. John Shaw, who convinced the Winnebago to allow him to ship ore from Prairie du Chien for trade at St. Louis.

Major ore exploitation began in 1824 when a mine was opened at a place called Hardscrabble, which became one of Grant County's first white settlements. The mining camp received its name after there was a problem deciding the proper owner. The apparent winner was named Hardy, making it "Hardy's scrabble." The town was renamed Hazel Green in 1838 by residents who wanted a more pleasant name.

Just east of U.S. 61 and a short distance west of Hazel Green, another promising lead deposit was found at Sinsinawa. After the Winnebago scare in 1827, the region attracted many miners from Missouri, Kentucky and Illinois. In 1828, when Milwaukee was still a small trading outpost and Racine was only a sandbar, 10,000 men worked the southwestern Wisconsin mines. Land that once sold for $1.25 an acre climbed to $10,000 when lead was discovered. The region between Hazel Green, Potosi and Beetown contained some of the most productive lead mines. Between 1839 and 1849 the annual production of the lead district was estimated at 40 million pounds. More than 3,000 men were employed. The lead region's peak year was 1847.

Zinc was found along with the lead ore, but it wasn't until the 1860's that two German chemists developed an effective way of extracting the metal. In fact, from 1872 to 1882 zinc production in the mining district was double that of lead. A form of zinc called sphalerite is occasionally mined today.

The lead, which extended 30 miles north and south of the Illinois-Wisconsin border and 60 miles east and west of the Mississippi River, was deposited by the vast preglacial seas that covered the continent. When searching for lead deposits, the Indians usually found it under a plant called mineral weed which resembled sage, grew to about 18 inches in height, and developed large red tassels. Heavy concentrations of wire grass was also considered a sign of nearby lead deposits. White miners found that the more successful ore deposits were located in the county's prairie areas: ravines, irregular swells, and hills ranging up to 100 feet high were the best places to find lead.

SINSINAWA

One of the area's interesting features is a rounded mound that rises nearly 290 feet near Sinsinawa. During the 1830's, Father Samuel Mazzuchelli, an Italian-born Dominican priest, spent much time traveling around Wisconsin trying to bring Christianity to the Indians and whites. He eventually made

SHSW

Lead mine interior near Cassville, 1900.

his way into the lead region, building churches at Dubuque and Galena. In 1844 he purchased the picturesque Sinsinawa mound which housed a small stockade built by General F. Jones. Mazzuchelli built a church and began plans for a men's college, a convent, a missionary school and a training school for Dominican sisters called St. Clara's Academy. Sinsinawa meant "rattlesnake" to the Winnebago and "a place of young eagles" to the Dakota. The collection of old and new buildings beautifully situated on the hillside is now the mother house and training center for the Dominican Order of Sisters. The beautiful chapel is open to the public.

DICKEYVILLE, Pop. 1,156

This village, formed later than most in the county, was named after a Mr. Dickey, first postmaster and shopkeeper. The unusual Grotto of "Christ The King and Mary His Mother" and the adjacent "Holy Ghost Park" are located here. Built by Father Mathias Wernerus and his cousin Mary Wernerus from 1920-30, these sermons in stone have attracted many visitors, including 40,000 people who traveled here in 1937. The grotto contains religious figures carved from Italian marble and non-religious figures constructed of broken pieces of glass, china, shells and petrified wood. The interior is of Arizona onyx and the ceiling is covered with stalactites.

TENNYSON, Pop. 476

This small village wasn't incorporated until 1940, although a number of Dutch settlers had called it Dutch Hollow earlier.

POTOSI, Pop. 736

By 1828 nearly 13 million pounds of lead had been shipped to smelters along the Mississippi and villages were sprouting across Grant County. Shortly after 1829 Snake Hollow became important when Willis St. John discovered a productive vein in an old Indian cave. Lead ore was shipped a short distance down the hill to the Mississippi and Snake Hollow rivaled the port of Galena, Illinois for a time. The town eventually became known as Potosi. From its riverport, called Potosi Station, barges floated downstream for smelting along the Mississippi.

In 1855 a Bavarian named Gabriel Hail built the Potosi brewery for $10,000 and paid his eight employees a total of $50 a week. Hail's Potosi beer became widely known throughout the Mississippi Valley and during prohibition his near-beer was considered the best around. The crumbling brewery is on county 133, on the west side of this interesting old town. Down by the Mississippi a road leads under the railroad bridge to a spit of land that extends out into the river, an excellent spot to see the broad river valley.

RAILROADS

Probably more than any other county in Wisconsin, Grant County suffered from rail routes which were proposed but never came to be. In 1836 the Belmont & Dubuque proposed a line through the county from Belmont to the Mississippi, but it was never built. A line from Potosi to Milwaukee was planned in 1844, but was never built. Around 1845, the Pensacola Railroad (now the Illinois Central) proposed a line from Pensacola to Potosi, but this never reached Potosi. Historians have counted at least 26 attempts to bring the iron horse into Grant County, and Potosi residents were the first to buy bonds in the undertaking. They claimed that Potosi's harbor was the best location along the Mississippi. The local paper in promoting the town said "the hollow was sufficient to accommodate any reasonable population that might wish to borough together..say forty or fifty thousand."

In October, 1856, the Milwaukee & Mississippi finally crossed through the northern part of the county en route from Madison to Prairie du Chien. Today the Burlington Northern passes through western Grant County along the Mississippi River.

VANISHED TOWNS

Several towns that thrived during the mining boom have since faded away. Paris (also known as De Tantabaratz) was once a town of 1,300 residents at the junction of the Platte rivers where Tou Le Jon tied up his boat in 1828. Platted after Paris, France, the town was a center of early smelting and shipping and boasted a public boarding house, a hotel, store, wharf, warehouse and many homes. Nothing remains today except some indentations in the ground.

Osceola, located east of the Burlington station at Potosi, was near an Indian town called Pascanans. The first post office between Galena and Prairie du Chien was at Mississippi City, a small village located where Indian Creek enters the Platte River. Loring Wheeler was the postmaster and storekeeper. In 1829 Mississippi City had one of the state's first saw and grist-mills and a Mr. Hough, who ground wheat and corn.

Ellendale, located not far from Burton on the Grant River, also vanished during the late 1800's. Some boat building was done in Ellendale and ore was shipped from the Muskalunge mines. British Hollow, located between Potosi and Lancaster on U.S. 61, was another small hamlet.

TELEGRAPH LINE OF GRANT COUNTY

In 1849 a promoter named Henry O'Reilly collected $8,000 to build a telegraph line so Grant County might be the "disseminator of news for the teeming thousands and unborn millions." Subsequently the line was stretched from Dubuque

SHSW

First Territorial Capitol near Leslie, 1836.

to Potosi and then on to Lancaster, Platteville and Mineral Point in Iowa County where it ended. O'Reilly soon went bankrupt and stockholders tried vainly to carry on the project. The experiment in telegraphy failed and the galvanized wires were used as clotheslines for many "whose hearts were heavy at their loss, but whose hands were light when it came to recovering anything whether legally or otherwise."

SEAL OF WISCONSIN

The lead industry's impact on Wisconsin's early days is evident in the state seal. The emblem includes a crossed pick and shovel for lead mining, a hand holding a hammer for manufacturing, an anchor for all the state's waterways and a plow for agriculture. The shield rests upon a pyramid of pig lead and the two figures in the emblem are a sailor and a miner. A badger symbolizes the early miners who lived like badgers. The emblem was designed and approved during the administration of Nelson Dewey, Wisconsin's first governor.

END OF THE MINING ERA

The lead mining region was always dependent on the price of lead. Initially lead prices were high because wood and white paint were in demand for new construction throughout the eastern seaboard. Lead was used in paint, bullets and many areas of manufacturing. However the price of lead dropped 80% to $1 a hundred pound in 1830 and many miners left the area. The price recovered two years later and the lead region boomed for the next decade. Lead production peaked in 1847, then declined. When gold was discovered in California, many miners packed up and headed for this new land to find their fortune. The "Grant County Herald" wrote in 1852 that, "Grant County will loose more than a fourth of her adult population to California, like the whale that swallowed Jonah." Property values dropped and the Potosi ferry was so backlogged that west-bound travelers often had to wait four to five days to cross the Mississippi.

Tragedy struck here in the late summer of 1850 when Asiatic cholera hit at Beetown, Fennimore and Wingville. In two weeks forty-one people died at Beetown alone.

WILD BILL HICKOK

James Butler Hickok was reportedly born on Mitchell Hollow Road, one mile east of Platteville, in 1837. A United States Marshal of Deadwood, South Dakota and a famous Black Hills personality, Hickok died in 1876.

LANCASTER, Pop. 4,076

Nahem Dudley and Henry Bushnell became the Lancaster area's first settlers in 1828. Dudley stayed on for a year or two, then sold his land to Aaron Boice. Abram Miller erected a mill a few miles west on Pigeon Creek in 1835.

When Grant County was formed in 1836, Cassville lobbied to be county seat but its location on the western side of the county was against it. Major Glendower Price anticipated the need for a central location, purchased 80 acres from Aaron Boice, and donated land and $1,000 to help the county commissioners chose Lancaster as the county seat. At the time, Aaron Boice and his cabin were the only things in Lancaster. The town was named after Lancaster, Pennsylvania by a Price relative and the prairie south of town became known as Boice's Prairie. Boice soon left the region and reportedly died fighting Indians in Texas.

The courthouse was finished in 1838 and a number of buildings went up that year. The present courthouse was completed in 1902 and the business district grew around it. A colony of freed slaves called the Pleasant Ridge Colony emigrated five miles west of Lancaster in 1848. They had more than 100 members by the end of the Civil War but only a cemetery remains today.

Nelson Dewey, who became Wisconsin's first governor when it was admitted into the Union as the 30th state in 1848, is buried at the cemetery just east of the junction of highways 61, 35 and 81. Dewey, who died in 1889, acquired 2000 acres west of here at Cassville and established a plantation which he called Stonefield. It is part of Nelson Dewey State Park at Cassville.

PRAIRIE AREAS

Most of Wisconsin was covered with pines and hardwoods before the whites came and began logging, but some sections of Grant and Iowa County were extensions of the great tall grass prairies of Illinois. The road from Lancaster to Fennimore passes through one of these early prairie areas, although farmers have removed all traces of the tall waving grasses that provided tillable land for Grant County's early settlers.

FENNIMORE, Pop. 2,212

John Fennimore decided to farm here because of a large spring located along a ridge of land. He offered water to travelers during the height of the Black Hawk War in 1832 and disappeared one day, never to be heard from again. When the village formed a few years later, it was named Fennimore Center. "Center" was eventually dropped.

John G. Perkins moved the first house into Fennimore in April 1862, but it was six years before the village was laid out into a 16-block area. A well was dug and two oak buckets provided the only drinking water. A windmill constructed over the well was torn down in 1878. Fennimore is located on the Military Ridge which extends east and west, separating drainage north into the Wisconsin River from that which flows south into the Rock and Mississippi rivers. The Blue and Green rivers flow from Fennimore Township north into the Wisconsin while the Grant and Platte flow south into the Mississippi.

Fennimore residents eagerly anticipated plans to connect them to the outside world by rail. A line reached Fennimore in 1878 and the Chicago & Northwestern extended eastward along the Military Ridge in 1880. A narrow gauge line of the Chicago & Tomah Company ran between Woodman on the Wisconsin River and Fennimore from the 1880's until it closed in 1926. In 1889 the town started publishing a small paper on a hand press called "The Fennimore Times." Electricity wasn't connected until 1904 or 1905. Until then Daniel Decker lighted the town's lamps from a short ladder, except when the moon was bright. During Halloween, local boys put chickens in the lamps.

MILITARY ROAD

Before 1835, Grant and Crawford counties had nothing that could be called a road. Trails crisscrossed, connecting mines, small hamlets and favorite hunting spots. The United States didn't get possession of this region until 1796 when the British turned over their western posts at Green Bay, Portage and Prairie du Chien to the new government. The posts were dependent on the Wisconsin and Fox Rivers for communication and travel.

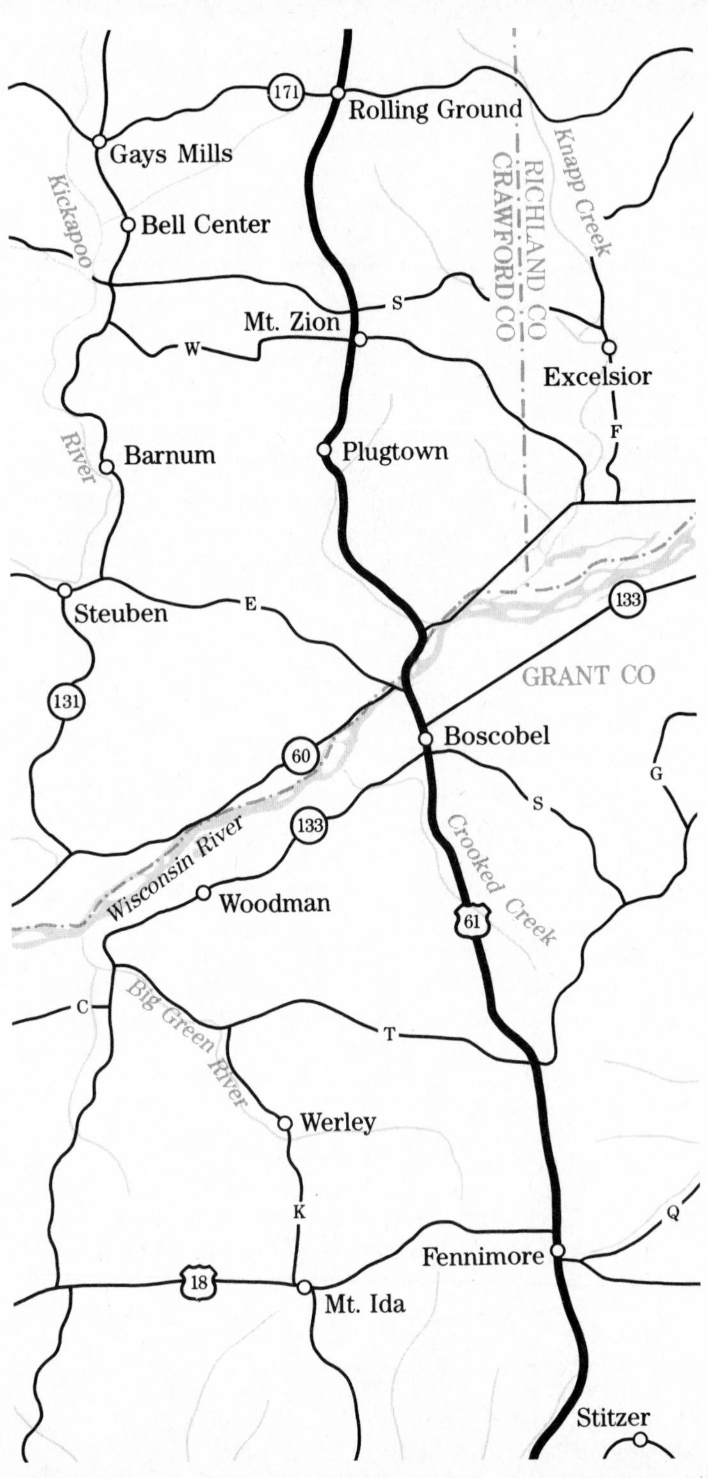

In 1835 Secretary of War Lewis Cass ordered that a road be constructed between Green Bay and Prairie du Chien. Soldiers at Prairie du Chien were responsible for the section to Fort Winnebago at Portage. Very crude and about 33 feet wide, the road had mile-markers and logs were placed side-to-side to form a corduroy road over marshy areas.

The road was named for the Military Ridge that it traversed to Portage. The ridge separates the streams that flow north to the Wisconsin River from those that flow south to the Rock and Mississippi rivers. Many settlers who pushed west during the 1850's used this road and the Chicago & Northwestern railroad was built along it between 1880 and 1881, connecting Fennimore to Mt. Horeb.

BOSCOBEL, Pop. 2,662

Boscobel is situated on the Wisconsin River bottoms, in the shadow of the wooded river bluffs. The village's name is a French-Indian word meaning "beautiful woods." The village formed later than most in Grant County and Thomas Sanders is credited with becoming the first settler in 1846. Sanders spent most of his time cutting and floating logs down to the Wisconsin River on the creek that bears his name and runs through town. When lead production peaked in 1847, Boscobel was tried as a shipping point. The idea was to circumvent the overland trip down the Mississippi by shipping lead up the Wisconsin and Fox rivers to New York via the Great Lakes. The plan proved ineffective and Boscobel later catered to lumbermen along the Wisconsin River. The town began to grow after the Milwaukee & Mississippi tracks reached here in September, 1856, and it incorporated eight years later.

Boscobel became a stopping point for steamers traveling upstream from the Mississippi to Sauk City and Portage, and stages brought travelers here from the lower counties to continue their trip up the Wisconsin. Wheat and other produce also made its way to Boscobel, making it an important agricultural shipping point.

One evening in September, 1898, two unacquainted traveling salesmen spent the night in room 19 of the Hotel Boscobel. They discovered they were both devout Christians when one began reading the Bible. They talked about the lonely traveler who often had nothing to read but outdated papers and worn-out telephone books and wondered if they could do something to solve the problem. The following year the two men, John Nicholson and Samuel Hill, met at Janesville and organized the Gideons Commercial Travelers' Association of America, a non-denominational organization which soon boasted 23,000 members. Their goal of placing Bibles in every hotel room in the U.S. has long been realized. Today the Gideons are based in Nashville,Tennessee. The Hotel Boscobel, currently being restored, has 17 rooms for guests, including room 19.

SHSW

Boscobel covered bridge across the Wisconsin River, ca. 1900.

SHSW

One-room schoolhouse. Photo/ C.J. Van Schaick.

SHSW

"Big Mill" of Chippewa Lumber & Boom Co. ca. 1900.

WISCONSIN RIVER

From its source in the Lac Vieux desert near the Michigan border, the Wisconsin River winds its way 430 miles through the state to the Mississippi River at Prairie du Chien, making it Wisconsin's longest river. From the summer of 1673 when Joliet and Marquette passed along its shallow waters on their way to discovering the Mississippi, the Wisconsin River provided the explorer, missionary and fur trader with a major water route between the Great Lakes and the Mississippi.

The Winnebago and Sauk Indians used this river to travel and hunt many hundreds of years before the white man and referred to it as the stream of a thousand isles. Father Marquette called the river Meskousing and wrote that "it was a wide river with a sandy bottom and shoals that renders its navigation very difficult." For this reason alone, large steamboats rarely ventured up the Wisconsin. Today, the shifting sand bars caused by silt from the farmlands, make boat traffic past Boscobel very difficult for all but canoes.

The Wisconsin River drains more of the state than any other river and was the only natural highway through the rolling and hilly Western Uplands of southwest Wisconsin. It provided the best canoe route, outside of the Illinois River, for explorers to cross between the Mississippi and Great Lakes. Many wonder why Green Bay, Portage, Prairie du Chien and other cities located along such an important river highway never became the Chicago or St. Louis of the Midwest.

While the broad fertile prairies of Illinois and Iowa provided the farmer with a resource to grow food, logging soon became one of the leading industries of this new state called Wisconsin. Northern Wisconsin's unlimited pineries employed thousands of men and provided the capital and incentive to the railroads to crisscross the state and bring out the wood that would help build America. Before the railroads, rivers such as the Wisconsin echoed with calls from the rivermen as they guided raft after raft of logs down to the Mississippi. The many rapids in the northern section of the Wisconsin made the job difficult and the rivermen needed much skill to keep the rafts intact.

According to early records, lumber was first cut for Fort Winnebago at Portage in 1828. Until 1876, most lumber cut on the upper Wisconsin was sent in large rafts down the Mississippi and on to St. Louis. If the water level was high enough the trip took 24 days. The railroads that crisscrossed the state in the later 1800's finally eroded the Wisconsin River's commercial importance. Today the river is an excellent recreational stream for canoeists, fishing enthusiasts, and those who enjoy the river's isolated beauty.

EARLY CRAWFORD COUNTY

In 1818 old Crawford County was part of the vast Territory of Michigan that stretched across Lake Michigan and into the area that would become Wisconsin. Crawford County encompassed all the present day counties of southwestern Wisconsin and was one of only three counties in this new western region—Michilimackinac (formed across northern Wisconsin), Crawford (south and western Wisconsin) and Brown (east of Portage, Wisconsin). During the 1820's the U.S. Government began to take an interest in this region. Before 1823, settlers with legal claims above $1000 had to make the long trip to the district court at Detroit. James Doty first held district court at Prairie du Chien in May, 1823.

The county began increasing in population in 1825, when whites were attracted by the lead mining to the south. Though the Sauk and Fox Indians had given up claims to land south of the Wisconsin River in 1804 (for $2234.50 and $1000 per year respectively), the Winnebago had not. In June of 1827, the Winnebago committed a number of hostile acts against settlers. The Prairie du Chien militia, along with volunteers from Galena, headed up the Wisconsin River and put an end to what was called the Winnebago War. The Winnebago signed a treaty at Prairie du Chien in August, 1829, turning over eight million acres south of the Wisconsin River to public domain.

SHSW

Men digging foundations for Soldier's Grove water tower, 1898.

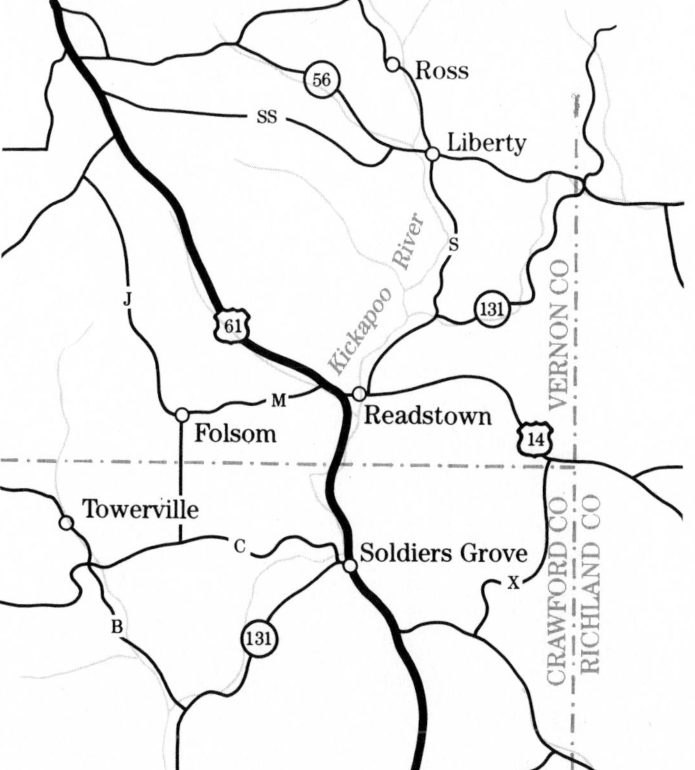

During the summer of 1836, when the Wisconsin Territory was set apart from the huge Territory of Michigan, only 11,680 whites had land claims. Most were situated west of the Mississippi in the Green Bay area: Crawford County claimed only 850 residents. However, during the mid-1800's, a large number of settlers flocked into Wisconsin from New England, Ohio, Pennsylvania, the Carolinas and Virginia. The immense area of Crawford County was reduced by the formation of Grant, St. Croix and Sauk counties during 1836-1840, and by the formation of Richland and Chippewa counties in 1842.

Coulee Country

The area of Wisconsin which borders the Mississippi is known as Coulee Country. It is a region of steep-sided hills which have been eroded away by streams and creeks that drain into the Mississippi, Wisconsin, Kickapoo, and Chippewa rivers. Highway 61 runs parallel to and approximately five miles east of the 65-mile-long Kickapoo River. This rugged country is also part of the large Driftless Area: an area untouched by glaciers during the last ice age. Today this area appears much of what the rest of Wisconsin was like before the glaciers ground and leveled the land.

U.S. 61 between the Wisconsin River and Soldiers Grove travels the early route of the Boscobel Road, the road which connected the lead region with Viroqua in Vernon County. A local historian wrote that this area, "has no villages, no stores or hotels, but abounds in hospitality. It never had a licensed saloon within its (township) borders and is made up of intelligent, moral class people whose time and attention is absorbed in agriculture."

Plugtown

Just northwest of Plugtown (4 miles north of the Wisconsin River on U.S. 61) was the site of the area's first settlement. In 1845 William and Randolph Elliott came to what later became section 19 of Scott township. They felled some trees, made a squatters claim, and left. William didn't return with his family until the fall of 1850. Unfortunately, one of the Elliott children died three years later after its clothing caught fire. The child was buried in what became a cemetery two miles west of Mt. Zion. Burril McKinney built the first log cabin a mile north and west of Plugtown in 1849.

Mt. Zion

In 1866 one of the earliest town halls in the state was erected near the center of Scott township. Mt. Zion Church was built in 1881 for $1,000 under the leadership of Rev. Isaac Adrian. The first person buried in the cemetary near Mt. Zion was a Prussian soldier who fought in the 1815 battle of Waterloo.

GAYS MILLS, Pop. 627

John Gay emigrated from Indiana to this place along the Kickapoo River in 1848. Gay was a civil engineer and the Kickapoo provided power for him to build saw and flour mills which were heavily used by area farmers. Gay died in 1859, but his brother John continued the saw mill until 1878 when the area's lumber became scarce. The saw mill was torn down, but the flour mill continued under various owners until 1924.

About 1890, when the post office was established, the hamlet took the name of Gays Mills. It experienced a boom when the railroad came through in 1892. After the turn-of-the-century, John Hays and Ben Twining exhibited area apples at the State Fair. After the apples won first prize at the State Fair and in New York, apple growing at Gays Mills took off.

In 1908, the Wisconsin Horticultural Society needed a site to experiment with growing apples and Hays donated land east of Gays Mills at High Ridge. The Society planted a variety of apple trees and the experiment proved so successful that the area became known as the Kickapoo Apple Region. Many people still come to see apple blossoms in spring and to buy apples in the fall. The drive west along state 171 on the high ridge is beautiful, with the deep Kickapoo Valley providing a backdrop to numerous orchards.

SHSW

Apple trees bloom in the Kickapoo River Valley, 1940.

SHSW

Flooding on the Kickapoo River causes Kickapoo and Northern R.R. derailment near Soldier's Grove.

BELL CENTER, Pop. 124

Bell Center received its name after Dennis Bell bought some land here from Silas Anderson about 1852. Bell hired a surveyor named C.D. Bellville to lay out the town, then sold a portion of land to his brother, Elias Bell. When it was time to name the town, there was little discussion.

KICKAPOO RIVER

This river begins in Monroe County and flows 65 winding miles to the Wisconsin River at Wauzeka. Although there is some confusion about how the river was named, several writers agree that it is based on an Indian word (Kiwiganawa) meaning "he stands about or moves about." Surprisingly, no Kickapoo Indians lived in this area. In 1889, the Kickapoo Valley and Northern Railway Company organized to build a railroad up the Kickapoo River Valley and the first trip was made from the Wisconsin River to Soldiers Grove in 1892.

SOLDIERS GROVE, Pop. 622

The topography around Soldiers Grove is irregular and broken by springs and streams that feed into the picturesque Kickapoo River. Farms are situated on ridges and the valleys are forested in maple, oak, ash and elm. Clayton Township, in which Soldiers Grove is located, was first settled by Simeon Tyler and his wife who came from New York in 1850 and built a 10 x 14 foot log cabin. Unfortunately they died three years later.

In 1856, Joseph Brightman homesteaded 80 acres along the Kickapoo and built a frame house, barn and water-powered saw mill. For several years Brightman's buildings were the only ones in Pine Grove, as the settlement was known. In 1866, the small hamlet was platted into 4 square blocks and Brightman was named postmaster. Samuel Hutchins built a hotel and store in 1866. The U.S. Post Office asked Pine Grove to change its name in 1873, because mail was being delivered to Pine Grove in Brown County. Residents decided on Soldiers Grove since a contingent of soldiers had camped here when pursuing Chief Black Hawk in 1832.

Soldiers Grove, built on the flood plain of the Kickapoo River, has suffered from a series of devastating floods. The most recent, in 1978, destroyed homes and businesses and the decision was finally made to move the town to higher ground. Today the village is south of where the old main street stood. Many of the new buildings are solar heated, an innovation for a small town.

Route U.S. 61 continues northward with U.S. 14 starting at Reedstown. (See page 283).

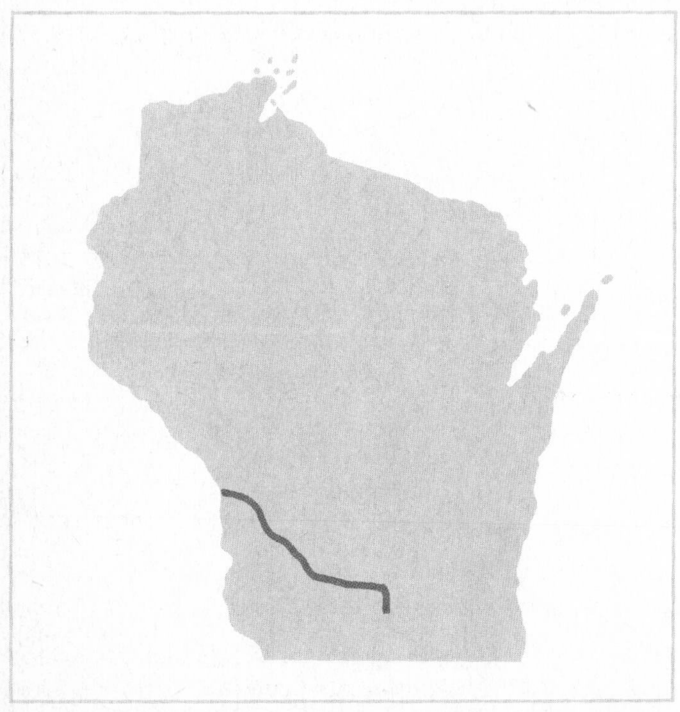

U.S. 14 passes from the Four Lake Region, into the rich Wisconsin River Valley. The rolling hills and rich farmland attracted many immigrants during the early years of this territory. As the road leaves the Wisconsin River Valley, it enters the coulee country, a region untouched by the last glaciers that pushed across Wisconsin 12,000 years ago. Early farmers used this land of steep hills and narrow valleys for raising wheat, tobacco and corn.

ROUTE 14, MADISON TO LA CROSSE

SHSW

An 1865 view looking down State St. toward the University of Wisconsin. Photo taken from the state capitol.

MADISON, Pop. 170,616

The city of Madison, the capital of Wisconsin, is built on a narrow strip of land between Lakes Monona and Mendota. Early explorers found this lake region, "beautiful, but uninhabitable" so while southwest Wisconsin was being settled and mined for its lead, the Madison area was left to the Winnebago.

When James Doty lost his appointment as a federal judge in 1832, he became involved in land speculation here. Doty appreciated the value of the Four Lakes area from previous explorations and began buying land. Together, Doty and Steven Mason, Governor of Michigan Territory, owned most of the land between Lake Mendota and Monona. They platted the city, and named it after James Madison, fourth President of the United States. Madison died in 1836, the year the new town was platted.

After Black Hawk's capture and the death of many of his warriors in 1832, fears of Indians lessened and whites began settling in this new area west of Lake Michigan. In 1836, the Territory of Wisconsin was created and the first Territorial Congress was held in a small frame building at Belmont in southwest Wisconsin. Doty was there and lobbied hard to move the capitol to his newly-created town. Ironically, this was several months before the first settler had even moved into the city.

Eban Peck, who moved here with his wife and son and built three log buildings, is credited as Madison's first settler. His buildings stood where 122 Butler Street is today, and became the center of activity in Madison for a time. When work started on the capitol, Peck's small hotel and tavern provided workers with rest and refreshment. It also became a stopover on the stage between Portage and Mineral Point. In the 11 years before the first capitol was completed many meetings were held upstairs in the American Hotel. Legislators often complained about meeting in the partially-completed state house, telling of ice on the walls, frozen inkwells, poor accommodations (many had to sleep on crowded floors) and noise from squealing pigs kept in the basement. There were several attempts to move the state government to Milwaukee where it was more civilized.

Madison grew slowly and was a little village of about 40 buildings and 700 residents when Wisconsin became a state in 1848. Pigs, chickens, and cows reportedly strolled the capital grounds by day and residents stalked bear, wolves and deer by night. In 1847 Leonard Farwell of Milwaukee arrived in Madison and pledged to shape it into what a state capital should be. Streets were laid out and improved, thousands of shade trees were planted, marshes drained and the decaying wood sidewalks were replaced. A canal was opened between Lakes Mendota and Monona where Farwell built a dam and grist mill. His projects eventually led him into the Governor's seat in 1852.

The Territorial Government of Wisconsin passed a law in 1838 incorporating the "University of the Territory of Wisconsin," but the university wasn't opened until Wisconsin became a state. In 1849 the first 20 students entered the old Madison Female Academy building for training. That same year 157 acres were purchased along Lake Mendota as the future university site, although the rolling hills overlooking the lake were only a tangle of bushes and trees. The first permanent building, North Hall, was erected in 1851 and served as a dormitory, classroom, mess hall and faculty living quarters for several years. In 1855 a new dormitory, South Hall, was completed.

The school added buildings and courses, but a financial problem developed because of insufficient funding by the state. Since most students withdrew from school to fight in the Civil War, only one qualified to graduate in 1864 and commencement was canceled. The university almost went bankrupt and professors were asked to work at half-pay. By 1866, the university was reorganized and acquired more than 300,000 acres of land from the federal government. Today the University of Wisconsin in Madison has an enrollment of 43,000 students.

After 1850, the railroads replaced the stage lines that led in and out of Madison and the city grew as a service center for the state. Steamboats plied Lake Mendota, parks were developed, and some 26 hotels were built to handle the many visitors. By 1916, this quiet area where the Winnebago once hunted and fished, had a city of 32,000 people. That same year the new granite capitol was completed, replacing the second capitol which had burned in 1904. The capitol, with sections pointing to the four points of the compass, is topped by a dome that can be seen for many miles. (For more information on the Madison area, see page 17.)

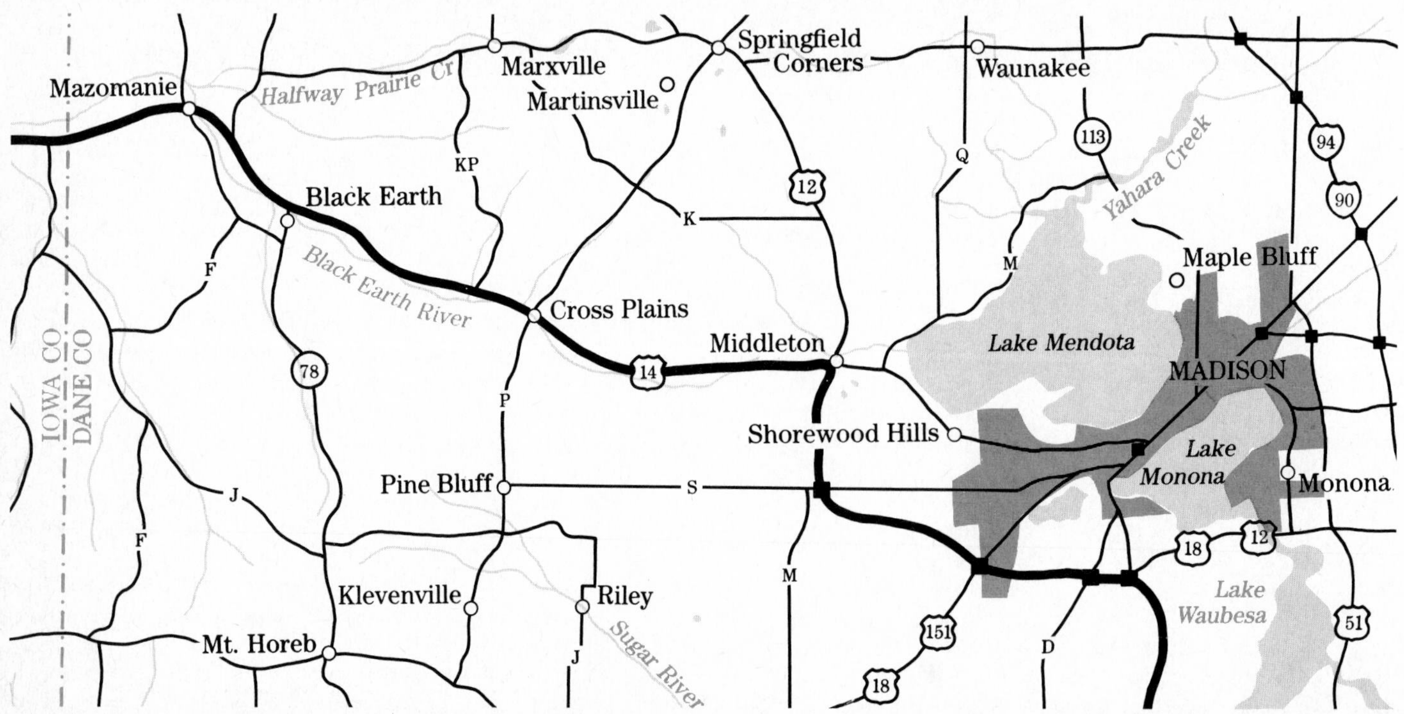

MIDDLETON, Pop. 11,779

Middleton began as a mill in 1838 and is now one of Madison's fastest growing suburbs. When Madison was settled, much of the lumber came from the mill of Thomas Whittlesey who located here in 1838 near a large white oak forest.

Many German immigrants farmed the rolling hills overlooking Lake Mendota and had to travel to Blue Mounds to have their grain milled. They rested here at a stop built along the Military Highway. Later, another inn, the Junction House, was built. The small collection of homes, taverns and a shoe shop was known as Junction. When Harry Barnes was appointed postmaster, he ran the post office from his hotel and named the town for one in Vermont. In 1847, Sandford built a log schoolhouse. Lucinda Rhodes, the first teacher, was paid $2 a week.

An attempt was made to commercially work the large peat beds near the village, but was called off after much time and money had been spent draining the marsh. The Milwaukee & Mississippi came through here in 1856, connecting Madison with Prairie du Chien.

CROSS PLAINS, Pop. 2,156

When Berry Haney built a double log house along the Military Road in 1836, he let travelers sleep on his floor if there was room. This hotel of sorts was known as Haney's Stand. Haney later ran a stage between Mineral Point and Fort Winnebago until he claimed land at what became Sauk City. His colorful life ended when he was shot in Arkansas.

Cross Plains was settled by many veterans of the War of 1812 who were given land here after 1832. It took its name from its location at the intersection of two military highways. In 1852, a wealthy German named Peter Mohr platted a nearby town and named it after his wife Christina. He built 30 stone buildings and named the streets, Celina, Eulalia, Jovina and Gerda after his children. He even named two streets Julius and Caesar. Cross Plains and Christina eventually merged. Chief Black Crow was reportedly buried in an Indian burial ground just south of Cross Plains. His body had been placed on a platform to keep it away from wolves and foxes, but two men climbed the scaffold and took the skull for a trophy.

BLACK EARTH, Pop. 1,145

This area was first known as Farmerville, but was changed to Black Earth in 1851 because farmers considered the rich black earth the best in the state. One of the town's first settlers was Henry Wilson who arrived late in the fall of 1843. Since he had little time before winter he built a rounded frame from saplings and covered it with marsh grass. His family survived the winter cooking outside to avoid setting the house on fire. For years, area settlers referred to Wilson and his "haystack" home.

The village was platted in 1850 and a grist mill was one of the first mills to operate west of Madison. It had three stones, two for wheat and one for corn. The flour was known as Sunbeam and Minnesota Patent. The Patrons' Mercantile Company, one of the state's oldest cooperatives, was also located here. After the Milwaukee and Mississippi came though in 1856, Black Earth became a shipping point for area farmers. According to a shipping report, 85 carloads of cattle, 90 cars of hogs and 38,000 bushels of wheat left Black Earth in 1876.

MAZOMANIE, Pop. 1,248

Located on Black Earth Creek, Mazomanie is near the site of the Black Hawk War's Battle of Wisconsin Heights. Mazomanie is derived from a Winnebago word that means, "iron that walks." Manzemoneka was a Winnebago who became infamous in the area after he shot and killed an Indian agent at Fort Winnebago at Portage. Members of the British Temperance Emigration Society first settled the town in 1843, purchasing large amounts of government land and adopting the Indians' name. Later in 1856, when the first railroad connected Lake Michigan with the Mississippi River, the name was changed to Mazomanie. The British Temperance Society eventually built Dover, a small town west of Mazomanie which consisted of three stores, a blacksmith shop, cooperage, mill and the Dover Hotel. However, the train missed Dover and most settlers moved east to Mazomanie a few years later. A young Dover inventor, John Appleby, designed a binding machine in 1860 that was eventually used around the world to bind wheat.

In 1856, a New York minister founded Haskell University at Mazomanie. A building was erected and Latin, French, mathematics, drawing and music were taught to about 50 students. Unfortunately, there wasn't enough money to pay instructors and maintain the building. The university closed three years later and the building became a store.

BLACK HAWK WAR

In the spring of 1832, a band of Sauk and Fox Indians crossed the Mississippi after a miserable winter on their reservations in Iowa. They believed life would return to normal if they returned to their homeland in Illinois and peacefully raised crops. The whites, however, saw them only as invaders who were breaking a treaty. A series of tragic events followed, fueled by the Indians' naivete and a militia eager to pull the trigger. Realizing their mistake, the Indians feared for their lives and fled up the Rock River into Wisconsin, led

SHSW

The Wisconsin River Valley near Prairie du Sac.

by an aging Chief Black Hawk. The inept soldiers soon lost Black Hawk's trail in the marshy and largely uncharted Four Lakes Region, but some soldiers heading to Portage for supplies discovered Black Hawk and his band by chance.

The Army renewed the chase, trying to save face for having lost Black Hawk's trail. In July, 1832, the soldiers finally caught up with the band as they tried to cross the Wisconsin River near present day Sauk City. The Indians held off the soldiers long enough to allow most of the aged, women and children to cross the river. Women and children were put in canoes, while the braves followed along the shoreline. This battle at Wisconsin Heights was the beginning of the end for the near-starving band. The sick, old and starving were reportedly left along the way, unable to keep up.

This hungry, pathetic force eventually ended up at the mouth of the Bad Axe River on the Mississippi, surrounded on all sides by their pursuers. Black Hawk tried to surrender to the steamboat Warrior standing off shore, but his white flag was met with cannon fire, killing 23. Hoping someone would take pity on the women and children, Black Hawk sent them out in canoes or rafts. Sparing no one, the soldiers killed 150 women, men and children on the river. Black Hawk escaped, but was later captured and imprisoned for a time at Fort Crawford at Prairie du Chien, then paroled at St. Louis. He was quoted as saying, "I loved my towns, my cornfields, and the home of my people..I fought for it." The Black Hawk War, as it was called, was the only real confrontation in Wisconsin between the Indians and whites.

IOWA COUNTY, Pop. 19,802

By 1829, so many settlers had come to the lead region, a land the Indians called the Smokey Mountain Region that the area south of the Wisconsin River was formed into Iowa County. Much of the settlement could be attributed to the use of steamboats on the Mississippi after the Virginia made its historic trip up to St. Paul in 1823. The beginning of mail service (1826), the end of the Black Hawk War (1832) and the opening of lands for public sales (1834) were other important factors that led to the region's settlement. With the Indian danger eliminated and roads developed so supplies could be purchased at Prairie du Chien, new homes and farms began to spring up throughout the county. But the lure of lead and immediate wealth attracted most of the early settlers. Major Dodge, who came to Iowa County in 1827 to work his mine (which would become the city of Dodgeville,) gave this account of the area. "The soil on the prairies is of the richest and finest kind. From May to October they are covered with tall grass. In the time of strawberries, thousands of acres are reddened with the finest quality." Dodge also talked of the prairie fires. "The flames rush through the long grass with a noise like thunder; dense clouds of smoke arise and the sky itself appears almost on fire. Travelers crossing the prairie are sometime in serious danger, which they can escape only by setting fire to the grass around them and taking shelter in the burnt part."

Most of the early roads were Indian trails that were improved and widened by early miners hauling their ore to either the Mississippi or up to Helena on the Wisconsin River. When the land office was located at Mineral Point, the roads became naturally widened by those racing across the prairie to file a new claim.

After the Welsh, Scottish, English and Norwegians immigrants broke sod for farms, they began raising wheat as their main cash crop. But plant disease, cinch bugs, and one-crop farming eventually forced the farmers into diversifying their crops. For a period during the late 1800's, sheep farming for wool was popular.

When it came time to form a county government, Helena, a lead mining village on the Wisconsin River was the first choice for the county seat. But at the first gathering of the territorial court there, they couldn't find enough men to sit on the jury. Subsequently the court was held down at Mineral Point. There was considerable competition between Dodgeville and Mineral Point for the county seat; legal battles continued in the state courts until Dodgeville finally won control in 1860.

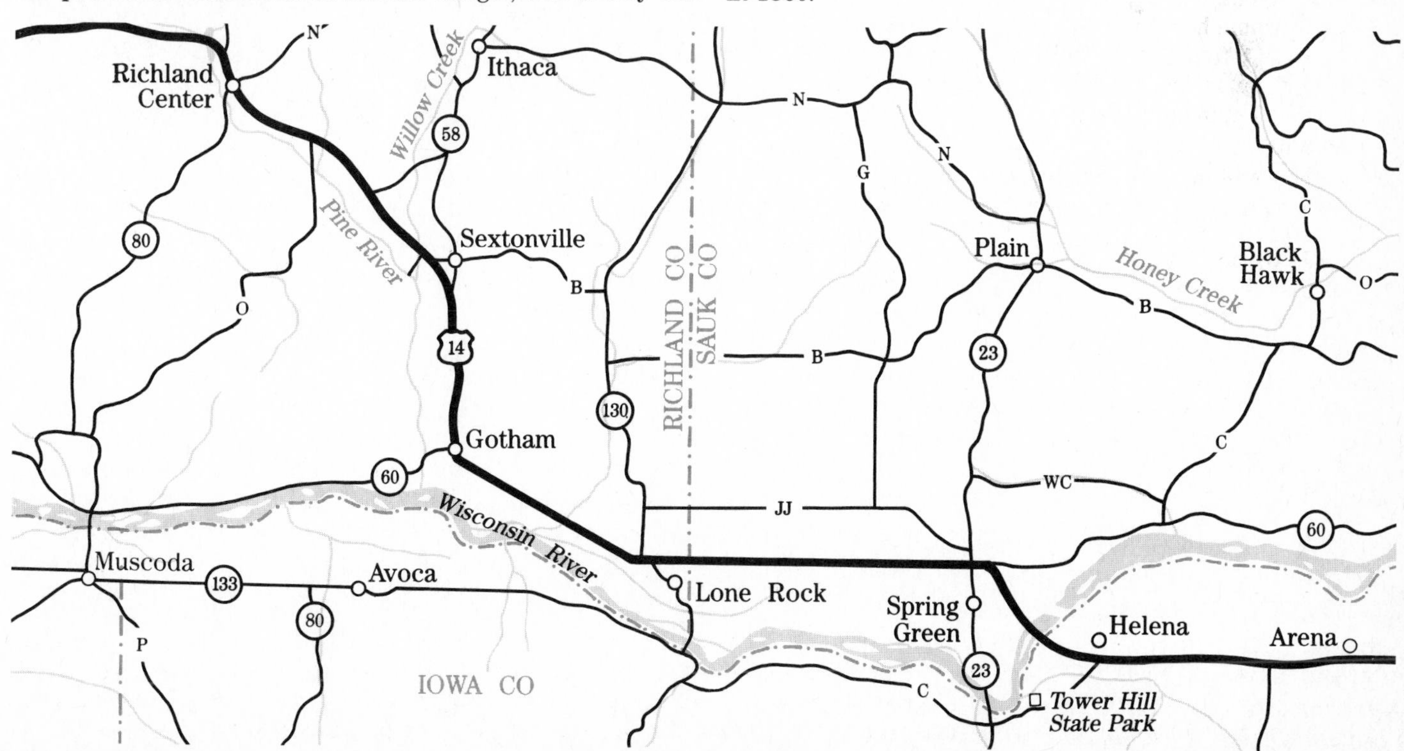

ARENA, Pop. 451

Old Arena and a settlement named Hayworth originally formed along the Wisconsin River a few miles west. Farmers brought their cattle and hogs here to market and returned with lumber that was rafted down river from Wisconsin Dells. However, when the railroad came in 1856 connecting Madison, Milwaukee and Prairie du Chien, settlers turned their backs on Arena and Hayworth. Oxen hauled the buildings to the railroad tracks and a new town was begun.

OLD HELENA & TOWER HILL STATE PARK

In 1828, settlers dreamed that a village next to the Wisconsin River here would rival the great mining and shipping depot of Galena, Illinois. With lead mining increasing in southwestern Wisconsin, a major shipping point had to be established. A few buildings were raised in 1828, followed by a hotel and a government building for storing lead and supplies. Talk was that Helena would even be the state capital.

But residents panicked and deserted the town when news reached here that Black Hawk and his band were entering the territory from Illinois. Houses were torn apart to make rafts so soldiers could cross the river in pursuit of the Indians. Though Helena was finished as a village, Whitney, Platte & Company came here to construct a shot-tower to make lead bullets. A 120-foot shaft was blasted and bored through the sandstone where lead was dropped from a tower into a pool of water. When the molten lead hit the water from this height, it created a perfectly round shot. The shot was sorted by size, put into kegs and loaded on steamboats at Mill Creek. At peak efficiency, 10,000 pounds of shot were processed each day.

Lead was hauled here from the southwestern Wisconsin mines from 1835 to 1841. A post office was established again, as well as a five story warehouse and a tavern owned by Alvah Culver. The bullet business and the town's buildings suffered from the lead markets highs and lows and the tower was permanently closed in 1861 when many workers left to fight in the Civil War. Some of the buildings were moved up to Helena Station two miles northeast where the railroad crossed the Wisconsin River.

Today the Tower Hill State Park occupies the area with facilities for camping, hiking and picnicking. A steep walk uphill to the shot tower brings you to the edge of a bluff looking over the beautiful Wisconsin River Valley.

SAUK COUNTY, Pop. 43,469

Formed as a part of Dane County in 1840, Sauk County was named after the Sauk, Sac, or Ozaukee Indians who once occupied this region. One source says their name means, "people living at a river mouth." Another says it means "yellow earth" because they painted themselves in yellow ochre. Sauk County is bounded by the Wisconsin River and rugged dells region on the east and by unglaciated valleys and hills on the west. The county's most conspicuous feature is the Baraboo Range, hills which rise gently from the great bend in the Wisconsin River.

SHSW

Spring Green, 1913. Photo/S. Gillett

SPRING GREEN, Pop. 1,265

The first woman to live on the southern Sauk County prairie named this township and village. She was a widow named Turner who left a teaching job in Massachusetts to head west with her two children. She stopped in the Wisconsin River Valley and soon married a man named Williams. When surveyors stopped at their farm, she asked them to name the area Spring Green because of a nearby hollow which each spring turned green before the surrounding area.

Before the railroad crossed the Wisconsin River, only brush and tall grass grew here. Old Helena and the shot-tower were two and one half miles south, but few ever traveled north through this prairie area. Farmers began breaking ground about 1850 and the village got started when a few railroad workers built some simple shacks to live in while they worked on the Milwaukee & Mississippi Railroad. The little hamlet became the first in the county to have connecting railway service and farmers brought their flour, hops and livestock here for shipping.

It was a proud sight when the train crossed the river into Spring Green that summer of 1856. The first freight, a Case threshing machine, was loaded on a flat-bed and the owner, Uncle John Jones, rode proudly on the flat-car as the train pulled into town. The Spring Green depot was built soon after. Though the train connected Spring Green to Prairie du Chien and Milwaukee, Alexander Stewart opened a stage line between Spring Green and northern Sauk County in 1859. Eventually the route ran only to Sauk City. An academy was moved here by oxen from Richland Center in the 1860's and placed on a nearby hill. Mr. Silsby taught a small group of children until he joined the Army and the school was closed. Spring Green was soon filled with stores and the Strong Hotel.

One thing villagers would not tolerate was the sale of liquor. Landowners banded together and refused to sell property to those intending to sell the devil's brew. Nonetheless, someone had the nerve to build a saloon on the other side of the tracks in 1857. It was written that "it had no right to live, so its days were few." Another tavern opened in conjunction with a small hotel and the owner was arrested and sent packing. It wasn't until after the Civil War that the temperance movement faded and saloons appeared in town.

A woman, Maurice Cavanaugh, operated a saw mill here and became known as the Lady Logger. She ultimately acquired 11 mills. From 1860 on, Spring Green developed as a shipping point for area farmers.

TALIESIN (Frank Lloyd Wright)

Located two miles south of Spring Green, is the home of the late Frank Lloyd Wright. Wright, born in Richland Center in 1869, came to love the rich rolling countryside along the Wisconsin River while working on his uncle's farm during the summers. As Wright grew older, he became one of the world's leading architects and ran his business from Oak Park, Illinois. Though a midwesterner, Wright's flamboyant clothes, long hair and other eccentricities set him apart from most architects.

Wright inherited 200 acres from his grandfather in 1911 and built a house just south of the Wisconsin River. Spring Green residents were upset because Wright had left his wife and family in Chicago to live here with his mistress, Mamah Borthwick. Some even petitioned the sheriff to evict Wright because of his immoral living situation. Wright's house was built of sandstone and earth-colored materials and was designed to exist naturally with the countryside. The house was called Taliesin, Welsh for "shining brow." As Wright later wrote, he wanted to build "a house a hill might marry and live happily with ever after." A complex man, Wright vacillated between indifference to critical comment and defending his lifestyle by writing lengthy letters to newspapers or holding press conferences.

Tragedy struck Taliesin on August 14, 1914, when Wright was away on business. Wright's disgruntled chef set fire to Taliesin, then struck down Mamah and her visiting children with an axe as they tried to escape. By the time Spring Green citizens had put out the fire, Mamah, her two children and four employees were dead. Julian Carlston, the chef, was found cowering in the furnace room.

The house was rebuilt, but was almost destroyed by lightning in 1924 when it sustained $300,000 in damage, only $30,000 of which was insured. Wright had by then married an artist, Miriam Wright, but that marriage was soon tangled in divorce lawsuits that dragged on until 1927. Another fire broke out at Taliesin in February 1927, damaging valuable blueprints, books and Wright's studio.

Wright soon went broke trying to pay his debts, alimony payments and the high maintenance expenses at Taliesin. The banks foreclosed on him in 1927. Friends rallied and helped Wright incorporate his estate in order to sell stock to pull him and Taliesin out of debt. One of Wright's goals was realized in 1923 when he organized the Taliesin Fellowship, which enabled approximately 23 architect students to apprentice under Wright and his associates. Though Spring Green was always wary of Wright's eccentric lifestyle, after he died in the spring of 1959 everyone was proud of the man who put the village on the map.

Wright's grave is located within sight of Taliesin at the small Unity Chapel graveyard. Mamah and members of his family are also buried here with simple markers of sandstone, the same stone in Taliesin.

HOUSE ON THE ROCK

A few miles south of Spring Green and Taliesin on State 23, is the House on the Rock, one of the more unusual offerings in this part of the county. The house, started in the early 1940's by an eccentric named Alex Jordan of Madison, is constructed on, over and around a rocky ledge that looks out over the rolling hills of the Wisconsin River Valley. It took more than 5,000 tons of stone to build its 13 rooms, each on a different level. After so many requests to tour the house, Jordan opened it to the public in 1961. The home and adjacent buildings house one of the world's largest collections of automated music players as well as an impressive array of guns, dolls, china and oriental art. If you make the journey to the House on the Rock, allow a few hours to take it all in.

RICHLAND COUNTY, Pop. 17,476

Richland County is made up of steep hills and fertile valleys whose black earth and history of abundant crops gave rise to its name. During the ice age, glaciers passed east of the county, allowing the rivers and creeks to cut deep valleys through the land over thousands of years. The result is a more rugged appearance than the eastern part of the state. Richland County is nearly in the center of Wisconsin's driftless area and many consider it the most beautiful part of the state. Edward Daniels, the first state geologist, wrote that the "scenery combines with every element of beauty…giving us sunlite prairie with waving grass, a thousand flowers and also the sombre depths of forests."

These forests of red and white oak, sugar maple, elm, ash, walnut, cherry and pine, broke the winds from the Minnesota prairies and attracted settlers who left the lead mines to farm. Bear, deer and elk ranged in and about the forest openings and along the sandy river bottoms. The early Indians, called Mound Builders, developed a post ice age civilization here which was in many ways more sophisticated than that of the Indians who followed. Archaeologists have found many mounds in the southern part of the county bordering the Wisconsin River and a particularly large number around Lone Rock. When the first settlers came, many mounds still had distinct animal shapes and were called effigy mounds, but time and farming have erased these early records. The Winnebago were the last Indians to occupy Richland County before the whites showed interest in this region.

John Coumbe, the first settler credited with coming to Richland County, immigrated from England and eventually made his way to the Grant County lead mines. In 1838, a year after the Winnebago had signed a treaty giving up their Wisconsin lands, Coumbe headed north and crossed the Wisconsin River to claim land. He built a shack at what later became known as Port Andrew and called his place Trip Knock. Much to Coumbe's chagrin, he discovered a number of Winnebago living here who refused to leave their old hunting grounds. Fearing for his life, John Coumbe left but returned two years later to farm. In 1840, by the time other settlers came north across the Wisconsin River, most of the Winnebago had moved or been forced to their Minnesota reservation.

SHSW

Tobacco was an important crop to Richland and Vernon County farmers.

James Andrews and Captain Smith recognized the growing need for a ferry to handle immigrants wanting to cross north of the Wisconsin River and started a service to their newly platted town of Savannah (now Muscoda). The first professional services were provided by Robert Boyd, a blacksmith. One frigid day while Boyd was shoeing a horse in the comfort of his cabin, the unhappy animal broke loose. It eventually punched a hole in the floor and fell into Boyd's root cellar where it became mired in the cabbages, rutabagas, onions and turnips. A platform and hoist had to be built to lift the animal out.

During the winter of 1843-44, many men came to work the forests along the Pine River. Some took advantage of a natural rock bridge and used it for a time as a home (at a town now named Rockbridge.) On their excursions along Pine River the loggers named many of the county's features.

The county was named in 1841, when only seven families held what they termed a "mass meeting" to petition the territorial Legislature to create a new county. When picking a name, the settlers thought of the abundance of wild strawberries, gooseberries, raspberries, wild plums, apples, grapes, honey, walnuts, butternuts, hickory, hazel nuts and maple sugar, and Richland seemed the logical choice. However, it wasn't until nine years later that the state legislature approved the formation of Richland County.

LONE ROCK, Pop. 577

When the railroad came through here in 1856, the small depot was known as Lone Rock because of an unusual pile of sandstone rock just south of the village. Loggers rafting down the Wisconsin River to the Mississippi probably first used the name.

Lone Rock had only one house when the train first reached here, but several hotels, a general store and a blacksmith shop were soon built. The hotels were small, however, since the Haskell House was carted down from Richland Center and the Union House was ferried across the Wisconsin River.

GOTHAM

This small village was once located closer to the Wisconsin River and known as Richland City. When steamers carried supplies and people between the Mississippi and Portage, Richland City was the most important stop along the way. Platted in 1849, this river town soon had a school, blacksmith, shoemaker, cabinet maker, general store and post office. In 1853, Professor Silsby built and ran an academy for four years, before closing it down. The building was later moved to Spring Green. Ephraim Brown built a saw mill in 1855, providing area settlers with building lumber. A large steam grist mill was also built, but was unprofitable in this size town. The mill was eventually moved to Milwaukee.

In 1856, when the railroad was built through the area, Richland City's leaders were confident tracks would be laid through the village. On weekends, people picnicked at the construction site. One Sunday some Richland City businessmen went down to Lone Rock and found workers driving pilings into the river, meaning the line would cross the river and miss the village. A railroad official informed the businessmen that the town was bypassed because of their greedy attitude and that someday corn would grow where their businesses now stood. He was correct. Richland City's importance as a riverport faded overnight. When the village started rebuilding up the hill along the railroad, its name was changed to Gotham to end the confusion with Richland Center. The new name came from Captain M.W. Gotham, a Great Lakes captain who lived in the village for a time. Gotham and his two sons later died in a shipwreck on Lake Erie.

SEXTONVILLE

New Englanders began settling here around the county's first grist mill in 1851. Before that, farmers had to make the long trip to Prairie du Chien to have flour and corn ground into meal. Named after a man called Sexton, the town's early pride was its high school, the county's first. After the railroad passed west of the city, the village's growth stopped. Today the school is boarded up and may be converted to apartments.

RICHLAND CENTER, Pop. 4,923

This city was first settled in 1850 by Ira Haseltine who came to know this area along the Pine River during his early travels through the county. He decided to buy the land and build a mill where the river rushed down at a good rate. When he platted the village, the streets were made too narrow for the cars which would one day pass here. The waterpower and thick forests along the steep slopes of the Pine River drew a number of timber related industries. Barrel makers found perfect ash and oak. A bed frame factory began, along with a tannery, cabinetmakers, tobacco warehouses, a woolen mill, butter tub and cheese box factories, brickyards and creameries. Because of its geographical center Richland Center was named county seat.

SHSW

Richland Center locomotive en route, 1876.

When the railroad passed south of the village on its way to Prairie du Chien, a feeder line was built down to it. Plans got underway in 1875 and the unique road had rails made of maple. Since the saw mills were in Richland Center, construction began there instead of up from the existing line. As a result, the heavy steam locomotive was hauled on a flatbed, pulled by horses and oxen, and all the bridges had to be reinforced. The spectacle drew crowds and the wooden tracks were finally laid to Lone Rock in 1876. Eventually the Pine River & Stevens Point Railroad was bought out by the Chicago, Milwaukee, and St. Paul, which replaced the wooden rails with iron ones.

Richland Center continued to thrive as a dairy processing center for milk and cheese, and as home to a coffee roasting company, a button manufacturer and what was one of the state's largest cooperative livestock shipping organizations. Frank Lloyd Wright was born there in 1869 and designed a grocery warehouse which has an unusual pattern of glass strips rising to an ornate cement frieze that borders the roof. The village was an active center for the woman's suffrage movement and narrowly missed adding a suffrage clause to its charter when it incorporated in 1887.

Nine miles north of Richland Center at Rockbridge is a natural rock bridge where a tributary of the Pine River has cut a 12 by 20 foot arch. West of Richland Center, the highway begins to cross into coulee country, a region of narrow valleys where early farmers tried raising dairy cattle or growing tobacco.

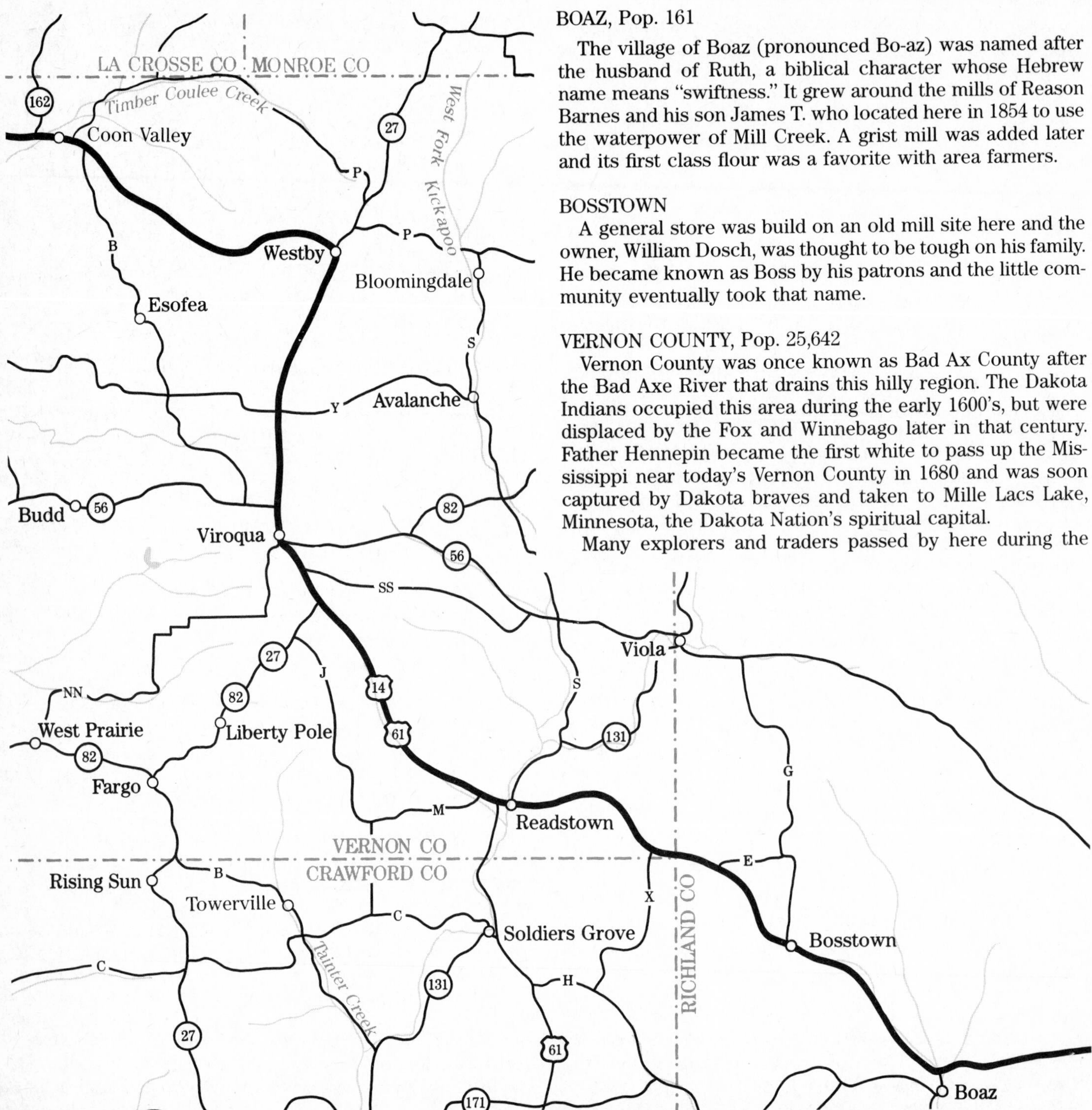

BOAZ, Pop. 161

The village of Boaz (pronounced Bo-az) was named after the husband of Ruth, a biblical character whose Hebrew name means "swiftness." It grew around the mills of Reason Barnes and his son James T. who located here in 1854 to use the waterpower of Mill Creek. A grist mill was added later and its first class flour was a favorite with area farmers.

BOSSTOWN

A general store was build on an old mill site here and the owner, William Dosch, was thought to be tough on his family. He became known as Boss by his patrons and the little community eventually took that name.

VERNON COUNTY, Pop. 25,642

Vernon County was once known as Bad Ax County after the Bad Axe River that drains this hilly region. The Dakota Indians occupied this area during the early 1600's, but were displaced by the Fox and Winnebago later in that century. Father Hennepin became the first white to pass up the Mississippi near today's Vernon County in 1680 and was soon captured by Dakota braves and taken to Mille Lacs Lake, Minnesota, the Dakota Nation's spiritual capital.

Many explorers and traders passed by here during the

1700's, and a few maintained posts along the Mississippi. In 1817, Joseph Brisbois had a post at the mouth of the Bad Ax River. However, white settlement didn't begin in Vernon County until after the Winnebago ceded this land by a treaty signed at Washington in 1837. In that document, the Winnebago ceded all lands east of the Mississippi and were to remove themselves to an Iowa reservation within the next eight months. Since it was difficult for the Winnebago to give up their longtime hunting grounds, groups of Indians crossed the Mississippi, back to their old Wisconsin lands, for the next several years.

Bad Ax County was organized out of Crawford County in March of 1851 and a log cabin at Viroqua built by Moses Decker in 1850 served as the first courthouse. As time passed residents of Bad Ax County began to feel uncomfortable with their county name. Many state legislators in Madison were reportedly startled whenever the speaker called on the "gentleman from Bad Ax." The name was often the object of satire at Madison theaters and a movement began to change it to Winneshiek. Vernon was chosen in 1862 to associate the county with the green fields of Mount Vernon, home of George Washington, this country's first President. The first whites to explore the eastern side of the county were two men who reached Camp Creek near Viola in 1843. Tired of hacking their way through the woods, they carved their initials and date on a tree which settlers discovered when they began to move here in the 1850's.

READSTOWN, Pop. 396

In the midst of coulee country, where the steep-sided hills have been worn by streams, is Readstown. When Daniel Reed moved to Wisconsin from New York, he soon discovered the Kickapoo Valley's beauty and moved here from Liberty Pole. Reed built a saw mill on the river in 1849 and others soon began to settle around him. Orin Wisel helped Read build his mill and for many years they logged the nearby forests. When the railroad was built up the valley in the late 1800's, many of the rail ties came from Readstown. The new settlers needed to grind their wheat, so Read added a flour mill to his operation saving the locals a 16-mile trip to the next closest mill. A bridge was built across the Kickapoo around 1853 and Wisel ran it as a toll bridge. It cost three cents to walk across, and another seven cents if you had a horse.

Mail delivery eventually became a priority so Bill Austin started a post office in 1857. His route lay between Orion and Viroqua, up and down steep hills and along narrow coulees. Austin made the trip in a few days, with mail sacks that had been brought up the Wisconsin to Orion. He also ran a brewery in the village, but it burned. He rebuilt but gave up after it was washed down the Kickapoo in a flood. At one time, villagers built a dam to harness the river and make electricity, but they abandoned the project after powerlines reached town. Read remained a bachelor for many years until he found a younger woman to marry him. Shortly after she became ill and died.

For many years the town prospered along the railroad tracks built up from Soldiers Grove in 1897. Hotels were constructed, as was a tobacco warehouse, a creamery and other stores and shops.

VIROQUA, Pop. 3,716

Viroqua is situated on a plateau overlooking a valley. It is named as the legend is told, for an Indian woman who jumped to her death from a nearby cliff after her father forbid her to marry a white trapper.

Moses Decker, who explored this region in 1846, found a place to settle in an opening in the oak forests. His sons helped build a crude shack and broke a small plot of land to raise vegetables. Fearing the cold winter, they left and returned in the spring. Decker platted a town in 1850, but only three families were calling this home in August of 1851.

The first hotel, the Buckeye House, was built in 1852 from lumber cut at Read's Mill on the Kickapoo. The Buckeye also housed a tavern, a law office and a general store. The village soon grew from three log houses to 60 houses and 350 inhabitants. The first school began in the log courthouse in 1851 with 16 students who paid two dollars for three months of lessons.

Jeremiah Rusk and his family came here in a covered wagon in 1853 and bought a hotel and stage line. He became active in politics, became the sheriff and was influential in starting the Republican Party here in Viroqua. In 1861 he was elected to the legislature as the "Gentleman from Bad Ax." He was the brunt of Bad Ax jokes at Madison and pushed for a new county name in 1862. Rusk also led the Bad Ax Tigers in the Civil War, a group that returned with "many honorable scars." He eventually served three terms as state governor beginning in 1882.

As the county seat, Viroqua was serviced by daily stages that ran to Black River Falls, Prairie du Chien, Muscoda and La Crosse. The village was hit hard during the national monetary crisis of 1857 and the editor of the local paper advertised that it "would take wheat, corn or oats as payment for the paper." The paper was filled with notices of tax delinquent land, but the village continued to grow after the Civil War with the arrival of easterners and Norwegians. Many were dairy farmers, while others raised tobacco.

In June of 1865, a tornado crossed the county and destroyed a third of the village. Homes and farms were destroyed and the schoolhouse was hit, killing six of the 24 children. Dozens were seriously injured. Only two hours after the storm had passed, Jeremiah Rusk returned home from the Civil War.

Money poured into the stricken village from as far as Milwaukee and Chicago, and the village was rebuilt. When tracks were laid down to Viroqua from Sparta, the town experienced a boom. "The number of hogs and railroad ties marketed here is simply amazing," wrote a reporter in the 1880 local newspaper. Tobacco also continued to play a part in the area economy. At one time Viroqua had three sorting houses which selected the choicest binder leaves around.

Some unusual rock formations are located nearby. One formation typical of an unglaciated area, Monument Rock, is located seven miles south of town. This 40 foot pinnacle was formed by a long process of weathering by wind and rain and a more resistant sandstone that formed a protective cap.

WESTBY & COON VALLEY

A running joke in Viroqua was that you could tell anyone from Westby by the twang in their voice. For many years more Norwegian than English was heard on Westby's streets because 90 per cent of the early population came from western Norway. Autumn lutefisk dinners were important celebrations. Early farmers grew tobacco. Westby had a warehouse which employed 120 men to sort and stack the leaves used in wrapping cigars. The town was named after Ole Westby, one of the first settlers.

Coon Valley, in the heart of coulee country, was founded by Norwegians and Bohemians who raised tobacco and cows. The Coon Valley Soil Project was the first of its kind in the nation when established in 1933. It was created to control the terrible erosion affecting area farming. Much of the top soil was being washed down Coon Creek into the Mississippi. The project, including dams, reforestation and strip-farming was so successful that it served as an example to farmers across the nation.

SHSW

Wisconsin family poses for photographer C.J. Van Schaick.

SHSW

Fountain City, 1885. Photo/G. Gesell

LA CROSSE COUNTY, Pop. 91,056

La Crosse County is a hilly, unglaciated land of deep fertile valleys which drains into the Mississippi or La Crosse rivers. The sandstone and limestone bluffs that line the Mississippi, range from 400 to 500 feet high and contain shells and remnants of ancient animals and fish—evidence that this area was covered by a sea which covered most of North America. It was during the melting of the glaciers at the end of the last Ice Age 10-12,000 years ago, that the La Crosse and Mississippi rivers began to cut down through the rock. At one point, the Mississippi valley was 500 feet deeper then it is today. When the glaciers retreated and the waters of the Mississippi slowed, the river basin silted back to its present level.

Father Hennepin, a French missionary, was the first white person to pass up into the Upper Mississippi Valley in 1680. Except for traders who occasionally camped along the river during those following years, La Crosse County wasn't settled until 1841. The nearest towns then were Prairie du Chien and Galena, Illinois. Milwaukee was in its early days and Chicago had a population of only 5,000. La Crosse County was formed in 1851, but its present boundaries weren't set until 1918.

La Crosse was a name given by French traders who watched the Indians play a game with sticks and a deerskin ball.

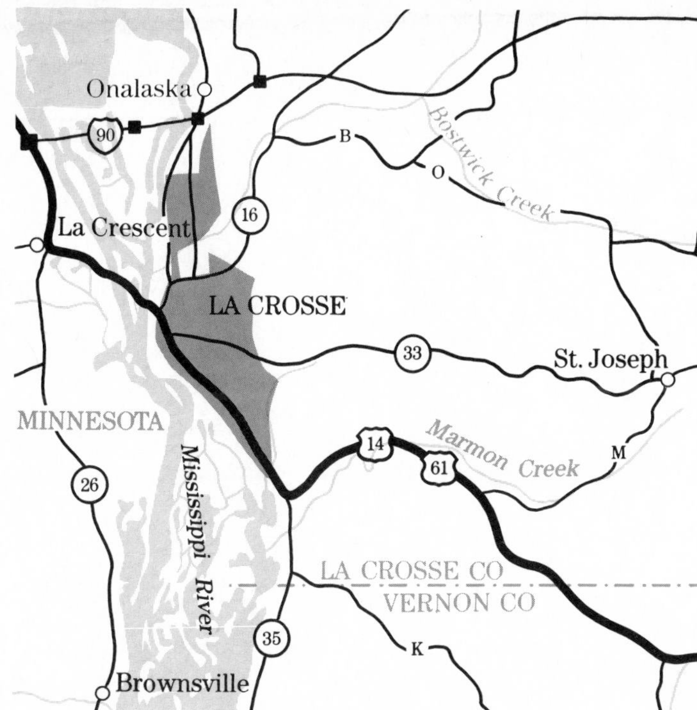

Jonathan Carver noted in his travels past here in 1766, that the goals were 600 yards apart and up to 300 men participated in this game. Carver said they played with such ferocity that many suffered broken bones.

LA CROSSE, Pop. 48,347

Winnebago Indians were the first to live here at the confluence of the Mississippi and La Crosse rivers. During the early 1800's they camped here to trade their furs for guns, powder, knives, blankets, shirts and whiskey. In 1837 a tragic period began for the Winnebago when they ceded all their land east of the Mississippi for reservations in Iowa and Long Prairie, Minnesota. However, many refused to leave and 18-year-old Nathan Myrick came up to the terraced land of Prairie La Crosse in 1841 to trade with those who had stayed. He arrived with only ten cents and a load of goods and had to wait ten days before Indians came. Finally "we had plenty good trade" and Myrick built a crude trading post on Barron's Island, now Pettibone Park. Here with a partner named Eben Weld, Myrick traded and cut cord-wood for steamers. The next year he built a new cabin on the mainland at Prairie La Crosse, a sandy treeless prairie about ten miles long and three miles wide.

Myrick wrote about one cold winter morning where, "The weather was cold and that night a blizzard sprung up. (The next) morning was the bluest I ever experienced; I was sick, and homesick, and it was the only time I wished myself back home in the East (New York)."

But Myrick hung on and over the next few years the post at Prairie La Crosse became the central trading spot from the Black River to the Bad Axe River on the south. Myrick traded with important Indians such as Chief Winneshiek and Chief Decorah. In 1841, a group of Mormons began working the forest of Black River Falls. Some moved down to a place they named Mormon Coulee in 1844, but left after a year because of differences with other settlers. In 1844 Myrick and and a man named Scooter Mills went up to the Black River pineries to cut and float logs down to La Crosse. From there the lumber was floated down to St. Louis. Up until then, all traveling was done along the Mississippi. It wasn't until 1845 that the first overland trip was made in eight days from Prairie du Chien. In 1848 when the Winnebago were forcibly removed from this region, the white population at Prairie La Crosse was still only 30.

That same year the government made land available in the area, but settlement was slow until the early 1850's when a number of settlers from New York and Vermont came here and established grist mills, saw mills, and a newspaper which helped promote the new town. In 1851, Prairie La Crosse was made the county seat and was an important lumber town for the next 40 years. Lots were sold for about $40 in 1851 and many buildings were constructed, but it was a slow transition from this once desolate, sand-heaped river terrace.

A number of German and Norwegians immigrated here during the late 1850's, attracted by the Black River's pine forests. The Germans promptly established a singing society and a club called the Maennerchor and Turnverein respectively. By 1856 this village of Germans, New Englanders and Norwegians had grown to 3,000 and became sophisticated enough to drop Prairie from its name. Historian J.A. Renggly wrote in those early days, "that drifting down the great (Mississippi) on a radiant morning, the voyager will recall nothing more varied in his travels than the city of La Crosse. The home of savages less than 50 years ago, it is now the home of wealth, enterprise, education and refinement."

Being a good river port (1,569 boat arrivals in 1857) and a lumber center wasn't enough for La Crosse. It was the addition of the La Crosse and Milwaukee Railroad in 1858 that assured the city's success. When the Civil War stopped river traffic below Ohio, La Crosse became an important link for western Wisconsin and points westward. By the turn-of-the-century lumbering dropped off drastically but other industries, including four large breweries, developed to sustain the town. Today La Crosse is a diversified industrial and agricultural center.

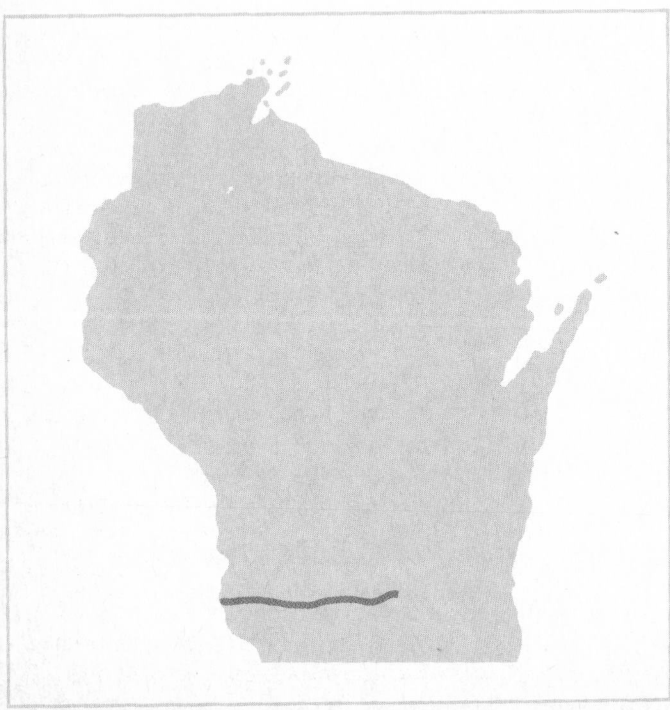

U.S. 18 leaves the beautiful city of Madison and crosses the rolling farmland of southern Wisconsin. For the most part, the road runs along a ridge of land known as the Military Ridge, named after one of the first roads to connect the early forts located at Prairie du Chien and Portage. The road also passes the Blue Mound, a hill which served as a landmark for Indians and early explorers traveling across the prairie.

ROUTE 18, MADISON TO LA CROSSE

SHSW

Madison grocery wagon loads supplies on Bassett St., ca. 1890.

DANE COUNTY, Pop. 323,545

As U.S. 18 leaves Madison (for information on Madison see page 17) it passes into a farming region where the soil was laid down by glaciers thousands of years ago.

The first Indians to inhabit Dane County came after the last glaciers some 10-12,000 years ago. They preceded the more recent Indian nations and are known only by the mounds they built throughout the state. Many of these mounds resembled animals and were used for religious and burial ceremonies. Unfortunately, most mounds have been obscured over the years by time, weathering and farming. Subsequently, the Fox, Miami, Illinois, Sauk and Winnebago Indians hunted and lived in Dane County. However, with strong pressure from the whites, the Winnebago signed a treaty with the U.S. Government in 1837, ceding all their hunting and farming rights east of the Mississippi.

The Yahara Valley and beautiful Four Lakes Region remained isolated during the early 1800's, except when an occasional miner crossed from Green Bay to the lead mines of Galena and southwestern Wisconsin. These miners and explorers used well-worn Indian trails that crossed the region, but a need for roads soon developed. More important than the miners' needs, the U.S. Army needed a supply road to connect Fort Howard at Green Bay with the military outpost of Prairie du Chien on the Mississippi. The Military Road started through Dane County about 1839 and followed a well-worn Indian trail along a ridge south of the Wisconsin River from Prairie du Chien to Blue Mounds. From there it followed a trail northwest of Lake Mendota en route to Portage. The road even had mile-stakes to keep travelers aware of their progress.

The Territory of Wiskonsin (its early spelling) was created in 1836 and Dane County was established shortly after. James Doty, Madison's developer, named the county for Nathan Dane, creator of the Ordinance of 1787 which established the Northwest Territories of which Wisconsin was a part.

BLACK HAWK WAR

In the spring of 1832, a band of Sauk and Fox Indians crossed the Mississippi into Illinois after spending a miserable winter on reservations in Iowa away from their original lands. They believed life would return to normal if they returned to their Illinois homeland and peacefully raised crops. But the whites saw them only as invaders, breaking a treaty. A series of tragic events followed, fueled by the Indians' naivete and a militia more eager to pull the trigger then negotiate. Realizing their mistake, the Indians feared for their lives and fled up the Rock River into Wisconsin led by an aging Chief Black Hawk. The inept soldiers soon lost Black

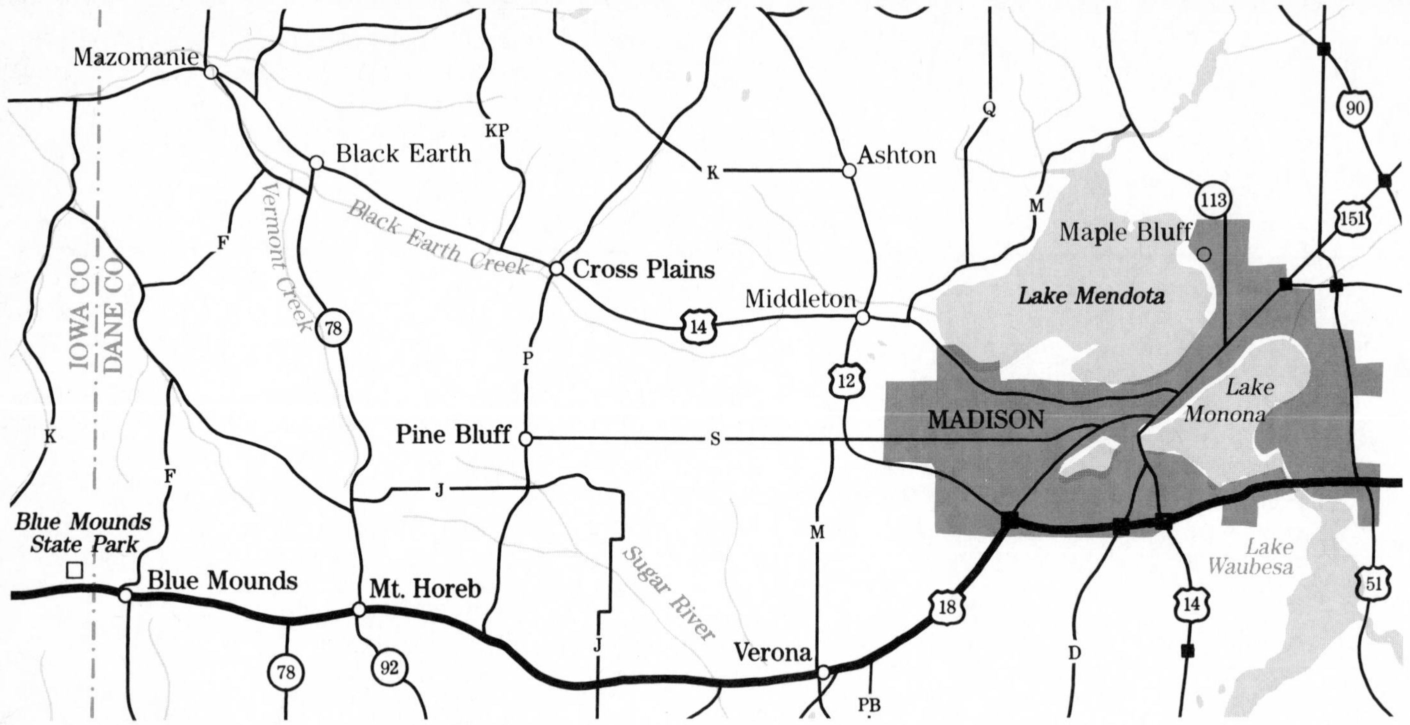

Hawk's trail in the marshy and largely uncharted Four Lakes Region, but some soldiers heading to Portage to obtain supplies discovered Black Hawk and his band by chance.

The Army started the chase anew, trying to save face for the humiliation they had suffered in losing Black Hawk. In July, 1832, the soldiers finally caught up with Black Hawk as the band tried to cross the Wisconsin River near today's Sauk City. The Indians held off the soldiers long enough to allow most of the women, children and aged to cross the river, but this battle at Wisconsin Heights was the beginning of the end for the near-starving band. The sick, old and starving were left along the way, unable to keep up. Women and children were put in canoes, while the braves followed along the shoreline as they tried to escape down the Wisconsin River.

This hungry, pathetic force eventually ended up at the mouth of the Bad Axe River on the Mississippi, surrounded by their pursuers. Black Hawk tried to surrender to the steamboat Warrior standing off shore, but his white flag was met with cannon fire, killing 23. Hoping someone would take pity on the women and children, Black Hawk sent them out in canoes or rafts. Sparing no one, the soldiers killed 150 women, men and children on the river.

Black Hawk escaped, but was later captured and imprisoned for a time at Fort Crawford at Prairie du Chien and before his imprisonment at St. Louis. He was quoted as saying, "I loved my towns, my cornfields, and the home of my people..I fought for it." The Black Hawk War, as it came to be called, was the only real confrontation between the Indians and whites of Wisconsin.

VERONA, Pop. 3,336

Situated along Badger Mill Creek, the Verona region was first settled in 1837 by James Young and Thomas Stewart. On their arrival they noted the numerous Indian mounds that dotted the area. Their first home was built into the hillside, with a roof constructed of grass. Verona was named by two early settlers, George and William Vroman, for their old hometown, Verona, New York. For a while, the small settlement was known as Verona Corners, because of its location at the junction of two pioneer roads. One ran north from Galena, Illinois to Green Bay and the other was used to haul iron ore west to Mineral Point. About 1850, the name was shortened to Verona. In 1844, William Wheeler and Vroman built the county's first mill, eliminating the long slow trip elsewhere.

The Chicago & Northwestern railroad came from the west along the Military Ridge during the early 1880's, reaching across Dane County from Blue Mounds into Verona, providing an economic boost to the village. Unfortunately the railroad has found the route unprofitable and recently vacated their right-of-way and torn up the tracks.

Nineteen miles south of Verona on State 69 is New Glarus, a town which grew out of a crop failure and hard times in Switzerland in 1844. Those events lead to formation of a Swiss immigration society and Judge Nicholas Duerst and Fridolin Streiff traveled to America to find suitable farmland for the society. They traveled for two months before they came to this valley and purchased 1,200 acres of farmland and a half section of woods. In the meantime, 193 men, women and children left for the United States on an Atlantic crossing that took 93 days. They traveled to St. Louis where they were to meet Duerst and Streiff, but found only word that the men were in Illinois looking for land. Some became discouraged and returned home, but slightly more than 100 continued their search for new land.

Two men searched for Duerst and Streiff, while the rest of the group moved up the Mississippi to the Galena, Illinois lead region. Four months after being in America, they discovered Duerst and the new Swiss colony was founded after a difficult overland trip to New Glarus Valley.

The colony wheat farmed but took to dairying after the Civil War. They started a cheese factory in 1870 and other businesses such as a lace-making plant followed and is still operated to this day. New Glarus has retained a Swiss flavor by constructing a number of its buildings in traditional Swiss fashion. The local historical society has also preserved nineteenth century life in New Glarus in a two-acre museum that contains 12 buildings and memorabilia from area homes and farms. A state park and the Sugar River Trail, a 23-mile path which follows an old railroad right-of-way, are also located here.

MOUNT HOREB, Pop. 3,251

The agricultural center of Mt. Horeb, a community settled by Swiss and Norwegians, is located on a rise overlooking the rich farmland of the Blue Mounds area. A church was established here in 1848, when the stop was known as Horeb Corners. G. Wright, the first postmaster, reportedly named the village after the mountain from which Moses received the Ten Commandments (also known as Mount Sinai).

Just west of Mount Horeb is Little Norway or Nissedahle, Norwegian for "valley of the elves." This collection of buildings and displays was founded in 1926 by Isak Dahle, a Norwegian businessman from Chicago. Dahle purchased 160 acres and constructed an outdoor museum which includes a stave church whose dragon heads were to ward off evil spirits, as well as other displays to preserve the area's strong Norwegian heritage.

BLUE MOUNDS, Pop. 387

U.S. 18 traverses the rolling farm land to Blue Mounds, a small village named after the large hills that rise above the countryside. The Blue Mounds were noticed in 1766 by English explorer Jonathan Carver who left his canoe at the Ouisconsin (Wisconsin) River and crossed south 15 miles to examine these strange mounds. He climbed to the top of West Blue Mound and surveyed the treeless prairie that faded into the autumn haze. Carver also noticed that the Sauk Indians extracted large quantities of lead from these hills with a quality as "good as other countries." Beside mining lead, they also used the flint found in the hills for making arrows and scraping tools. The Indians developed a tradition around these hills and believed the haze covering the hills during the summer was from the pipe of their god, Wakanda, the maker of the earth.

SHSW

Blue Mounds, ca. 1910. Photo/S. Gillett

Blue Mound, 1,716 feet above sea level, was formed by the erosive action of wind and water over millions of years. The hills' limestone had been slowly changed to quartzite, which formed a protective cap slowing the weathering process.

The lead the Indians mined at Blue Mounds attracted the county's first settlers. Ebenezer Brigham came to Blue Mounds in 1828 with several yoke of cattle and a companion Jeremiah Lycan. Brigham's search for lead paid off as he soon discovered a rich deposit in sections 5 and 7. The claim made Brigham the county's first permanent white resident. More than four million pounds of lead ore was lifted from Brigham's mine with only a windlass and bucket. He hauled it across the prairie to Green Bay and Chicago by oxen, taking 15 days to reach Chicago. On one occasion he was offered a choice Chicago lot in exchange for his dog.

SHSW

Waiting for the stage. Photo/E. Bass

Brigham soon built a small public house known as Brigham's Place along the soon to be built Military Road. He had no shortage of business, taking care of miners and those traveling between Green Bay and Prairie du Chien. During the Black Hawk War, a small fort was built here to protect the miners. After the war, lead mining at Blue Mound slowly waned.

BLUE MOUNDS STATE PARK

This 1,100 acre park is situated on Blue Mound, a hill that rises several hundred feet above the neighboring landscape. Originally, this mound was used by Indians and travelers along the Military Highway as a point of navigation. Today 78 campsites, a swimming pool, and picnic area are located on the flat-topped hill. Observation towers on the east and west sides view the rolling valleys of the Wisconsin River watershed, the distant Baraboo Range in which Devils Lake is located, the Pecatonica River Valley and on a clear day the distant Platte, Belmont and Sinsinawa mounds. Also located nearby is Cave of the Mounds, a large limestone cavern discovered in 1939 when an explosive charge in a quarry opened up the side of the cave. It was opened to the public in 1940 and draws many tourists.

MILITARY ROAD

Before 1835, little in Grant or Crawford Counties could be called a road. Trails crisscrossed, connecting mines, small hamlets and favorite hunting spots. The United States didn't get possession of this region until 1796, when the British turned their western posts over to the United States. The military posts established at Green Bay, Portage and Prairie du Chien, were dependent on the Mississippi, Wisconsin and Fox Rivers for communication and supplies.

In 1835 Secretary of War Lewis Cass ordered that a road be constructed between Green Bay and Prairie du Chien. Soldiers at Prairie du Chien were responsible for the section to Fort Winnebago at Portage. The road, very crude and about 33 feet wide, had posted mile-markers to inform travelers of their progress. Over marshy areas, logs were cut and placed side to side to form a corduroy road.

The road followed the ridge or divide that separates the streams that flow north to the Wisconsin River and those that flow southward to the Rock and Mississippi rivers. This ridge was named Military Ridge because of the road. Many new settlers pushed west during the 1850's, using this road. The Chicago & Northwestern railroad was built along this ridge between 1880 and 1881, connecting Fennimore to Mt. Horeb.

IOWA COUNTY, Pop. 19,802

By 1829, so many settlers had come to this lead region, a land the Indians called the Smokey Mountain Region, that the area south of the Wisconsin River was formed into Iowa County to provide local government. Much of the settlement could be attributed to the use of steamboats on the Mississippi after the Virginia made its historic trip up to St. Paul in 1823. The beginning of mail service (1826), the end of the Black Hawk War (1832) and the opening of lands for public sales (1834) were other important factors that led to the area's settlement. After the danger of Indians was eliminated and roads were developed so supplies could be purchased at Prairie du Chien, new homes and farms sprang up throughout the county. However, it was the lure of lead and sudden wealth that attracted most early settlers. Major Dodge came to Iowa County in 1827 to mine lead. His mining camp would become the city of Dodgeville.

"The soil on the prairies is of the richest and finest kind. From May to October they are covered with tall grass. In the time of strawberries, thousands of acres are reddened with the finest quality," wrote Dodge. He also wrote of the prairie fires. "The flames rush through the long grass with a noise like thunder; dense clouds of smoke arise and the sky itself appears almost on fire. Travelers crossing the prairie are sometimes in serious danger, which they can escape only by setting fire to the grass around them and taking shelter in the burnt part."

Most of the early roads were Indian trails that had been improved and widened. The early travelers were miners hauling their ore to the Mississippi or Helena on the Wisconsin

River. When the land office was opened at Mineral Point, the roads were widened naturally by those racing across the prairie to file a new claim. In 1857, the Illinois Central reached into the county from the south.

When the Welsh, Scottish, English and Norwegian immigrants broke the root-bound sod for farming, they raised wheat as their main cash crop. But plant disease, cinch bugs, and the problems of one-crop farming eventually forced the farmers to diversify their crops. For a period during the late 1800's, raising sheep for wool was popular.

When a county government was formed, Helena, a lead-mining village on the Wisconsin River, was the first choice as the county seat. At the first gathering of the territorial court, there weren't enough men to sit on the jury. Subsequently the court was moved to Mineral Point. Over the years competition between Dodgeville and Mineral Point grew over the choice of the county seat; legal battles were dragged out in the state courts until Dodgeville finally won control in 1860.

POKERVILLE

The small hamlet of Pokerville used to exist just inside the Iowa County Line. It began when an English bachelor, Thomas Champion, built a small cabin just west of Blue Mounds in 1845. The following year, two others built a small hotel. One of them, Giblett, was a professional gambler and in a short time this place was known as Pokerville. During the days of lead mining and up to the Civil War, poker was the hamlet's main industry. In addition to gamblers, the village had three stores, two hotels, a schoolhouse, harness maker, and doctor.

BARNEVELD, Pop. 579

When the Milwaukee & Madison Railroad was surveyed through the county in the early 1880's, a Dutch railroad surveyor named the proposed station Barneveld after Jonna Barneveld, a leader in the Dutch independence movement. Barneveld was later condemned as a traitor and executed in 1619. Each spring, thousands of tulips bloom here—a gift from Barneveld, Netherlands.

RIDGEWAY, Pop. 503

U.S. 18 enters this small village as it follows the Military Ridge across the county. Before 1832, a considerable amount of mining was done in the vicinity by transient diggers. During the Black Hawk War, miners headed for the Blue Mounds fort located on Brigham's place. Ridgeway actually got its start in 1836 when George Hickcox immigrated from Utica, New York to build a mill. For several years, his log cabin served as a resting place for travelers along the Military Highway.

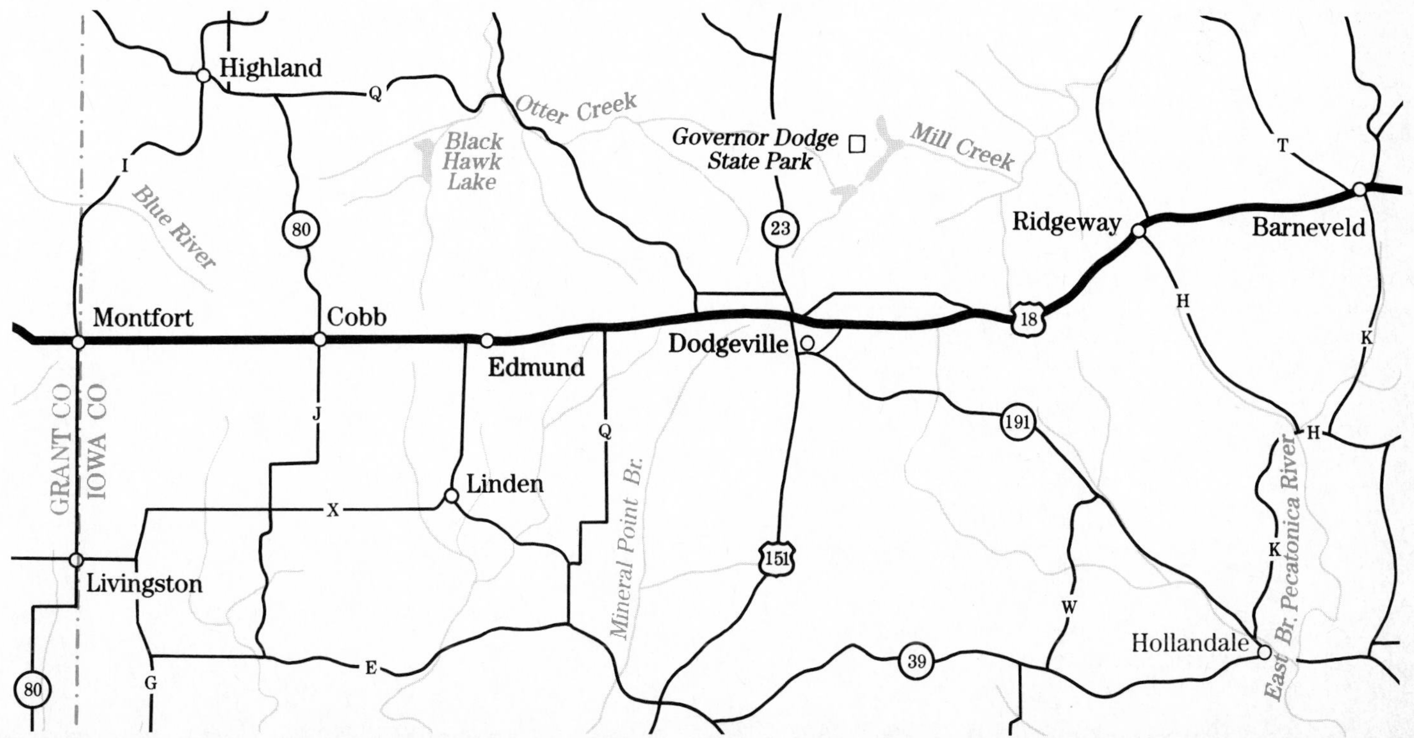

With the help of Joseph Roulette, a noted scout and area trader, Hickcox built a saw and grist mill in 1839. It was one of the first mills in this part of the state and customers came from 40 miles away. For many years after the mill's completion, the roar of the machinery could be heard day and night. One of the county's early roads led from Ridgeway to the shot-tower at Helena where lead ore was smelted and made into lead shot.

Ridgeway is also the home of the Ridgeway Ghost. The ghost, a man killed in a fire, supposedly traveled area roads during the latter 1800's. There were many stories of travelers seeing strange apparitions and being chased along the ridge.

DODGEVILLE, Pop. 3,458

Dodgeville is named after Henry Dodge, one of early Wisconsin's colorful characters. Dodge came from the south where he was a major in the Louisiana militia and illegally settled here with his family in 1827. He built a substantial home to protect his family from the Indians. This was at the same time the Winnebago Indians became angry with the large number of miners coming onto their lands.

Dodge struck a rich lead deposit here and soon had a smelting furnace built. An Indian agent who was sent from Prairie du Chien to tell Dodge he couldn't settle here, reported that there were 130 men working the mines, each armed with rifles and pistols. In 1827 the Winnebago ceded their land in southwestern Wisconsin as a fine for taking action against whites who had encroached upon their lands.

SHSW

Southwestern Wisconsin lead miners.

SHSW

A young couple photographed by C.J. Van Schaick.

Lead mining was early Dodgeville's only industry, but from 1827-1829 Dodgeville was the metropolis of the mining region with stores, taverns, shops and miners digging in every direction. The bottom fell out of the lead market in 1829 and Dodgeville lost many of its businesses almost overnight. In 1836 only six buildings were occupied. Neighboring Mineral Point was the more important of the two villages for the next 30 years, but in 1859, boundary changes in Iowa County made Dodgeville more centrally located and it became the county seat. Litigation slowed the process and for one temporary victory Mineral Point residents fired a 12-inch cannon, letting Dodgeville know they had won. The courts finally settled on Dodgeville as the county seat in 1860 and the courthouse was completed. The oldest in the state, the Greek Revival courthouse was constructed by Cornish masons using limestone from a nearby quarry. Appropriately, it sits over an old lead mine shaft. In fact, much of the city was built over the old mines.

Dodgeville grew slowly over the years boosted by Cornish, Welsh and other immigrants and by the approach of the railroad which made it a regional marketing center for the new farmers. In 1876, a slag furnace was built in Dodgeville to extract the remaining lead left in the slag from the smelting process. Slag was hauled to this furnace from as far away as Galena, Illinois and the reclaimed lead was then shipped to buyers in Chicago. This old slag furnace still sits on the town's east side. Several old stone homes built by early Cornish immigrants are located on North Main Street.

Three miles north of Dodgeville on State 23 is the 5,000 acre Governor Dodge State Park, a combination of valleys, lakes and prairie openings where picnic and more than 260 camping spots are nicely dispersed. Located in Wisconsin's driftless area, untouched by glaciers, the small streams here have had millions of years to wear down the landscape into steep valleys and coulees.

Five miles further north on State 23 is one of Wisconsin's more unusual tourist attractions, the House on the Rock. The house, started in the early 1940's by Alex Jordan of Madison, is constructed on, over and around a rocky ledge that looks out over the rolling hills of the Wisconsin River Valley. Jordan used more than 5,000 tons of stone to build its 13 rooms, each on a different level. After many requests to tour the house, he opened it to the public in 1961. The home and adjacent buildings contain one of the world's largest collections of automated music players in addition to displays of guns, wooden horses, dolls, toys, electric trains, china and oriental art. The world's largest carousel, opened in 1981, contains 16,400 lights and 269 animals—but no horses. An admission fee is charged. Allow plenty of time if you stop.

EDMUND

When the railroad was surveyed along the Military Ridge, Edmund Baker offered land to have the depot named after him. The town was once busy with a grain elevator and stockyards which shipped area cattle and hogs, but there is little here today except for the post office, a bank branch office and some homes. Even the depot has been removed from the vacated railroad right-of-way. One of the last lead mines to operate in this part of southwest Wisconsin was located in Linden, four miles south, but finally closed in 1975. Though mining is over in Iowa County, some of the miners' early habits still survive. The miners' meal—meat and potato baked in a crust so they could eat in the mine—can still be found in some area restaurants. Ask for a pasty.

COBB, Pop. 381

The old railroad town of Cobb is situated at the headwaters of the Pecatonica River. The town has also been known as Danville, Cross Plains (because the Military Highway passed along the level plain), and Village of Eden. Settlement began here in 1847 when John Meeker and E. Prichett cleared 880 acres for farming. General Amos Cobb became fond of the area when he camped in the vicinity during the pursuit of Chief Black Hawk in 1832. He helped establish a post office here in 1850. In 1880, the Madison branch of the Chicago & Northwestern Railroad was built through the small village. A canning factory was built on the town's north side in 1923 and still operates today as Oconomowoc Canning Company, canning sweet corn and peas from local farms. Every August the annual Corn Boil attracts more than 8,000 to this small village. Located 3.5 miles north of Cobb is the beautifully clear 200-acre Black Hawk Lake. Full camping and recreational facilities are available at the lake which is surrounded by 1,800 acres of bluffs, meadows and valleys.

SHSW

Montfort, ca. 1911. Photo/S. Gillett

MONFORT, Pop. 616

This village located in a valley, got started as a mining town in 1827. Richard Palmer was searching for water for his oxen, when he discovered a stream down in this ravine where he found pure lead-crystals pushed to the surface by badgers. Palmer started to mine here and was soon followed by others. Crude shacks and mining pits were scattered about the small hamlet which was known for a time as Wingville because someone caught a pheasant with their hands. It became known as Montfort after miners built a stockade to protect themselves during the Black Hawk scare in 1832.

Montfort was hit with a severe cholera outbreak in the summer of 1850. Many communities of Iowa and Grant Counties contracted the dreaded disease. Many lonely miners were found dead at their claims. Settlers thought the low areas bred the infectious disease, so they camped up on the high prairie until the epidemic was over. Dodgeville lost 100 people to cholera that year.

Between Montfort and Fennimore, is the 300-foot high Platte Mound which can be seen 15 miles to the south near Platteville. While the rest of the region was eroded down, it has withstood the weathering effect of wind and rain because of a resistant cap of limestone, .

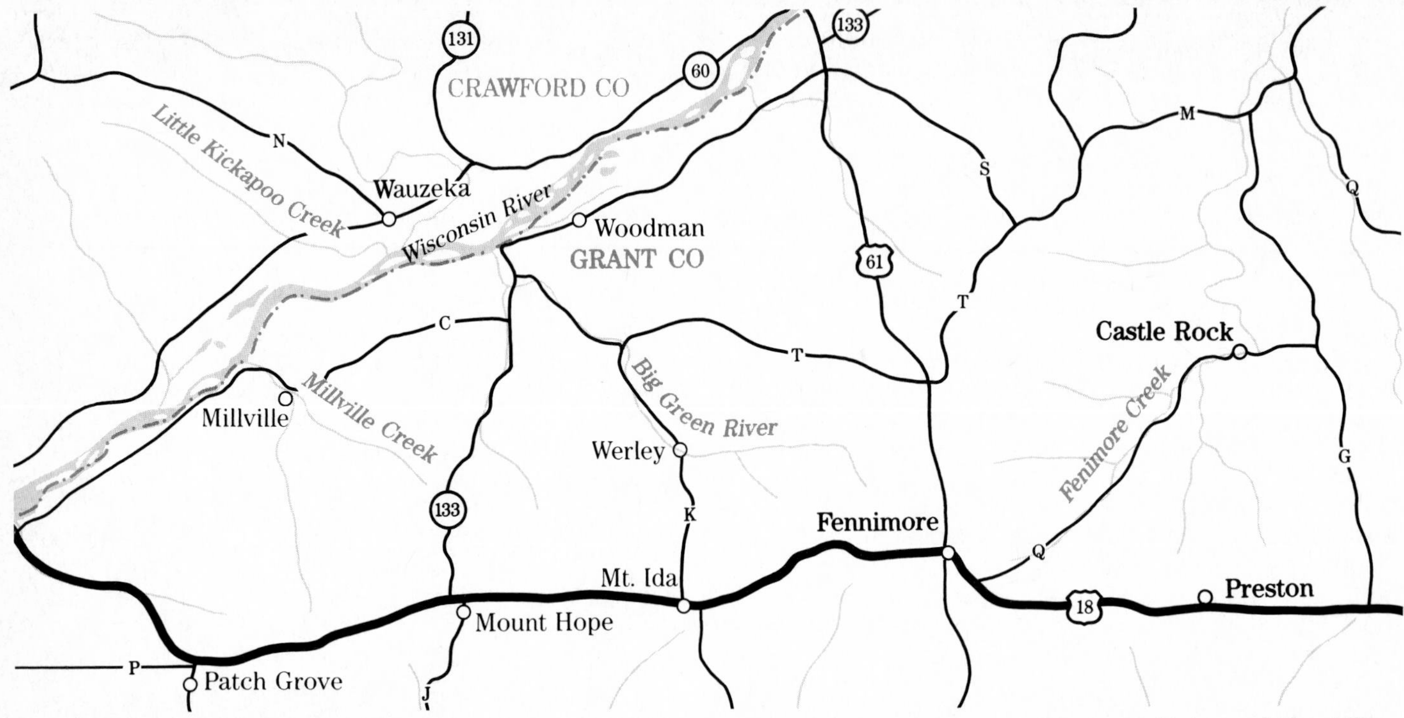

GRANT COUNTY, Pop. 51,736

Grant County was organized in 1836 and named from the Grant River which winds through the center of the county and empties into the Mississippi near Potosi. The river itself is named after an obscure fur trader, Cuthbert Grant, one of the area's first white settlers. There is some question about his real name, but most agree that it was Grant and he lived near the river. In 1810 he supposedly spent some time living at the Indian village of Chief Pascanans, near Potosi. A story tells of Grant encountering a party of Winnebago unhappy about his cabin in their territory. Giving chase, one of the Indians caught Grant and struck him over the head with a tomahawk. Since Grant always wore his cooking kettle under his hat, the blow had little affect. Amazed by this, the Indians apparently never bothered Grant again.

Grant County is drained by the Grant, Little Grant and Platte Rivers. It is also one of the several southwest Wisconsin counties that was not crossed by glaciers during the last ice age. The region's soil is formed by the weathering of its rocks and the wind-blown soil carried from Minnesota by the prevailing westerlies. Grant County is also part of a 13,000 square mile area called the Western Uplands which has an average elevation 1200 feet above sea level. The most pronounced topography includes the deep valleys and coulees formed by the Mississippi and Wisconsin rivers and their tributaries over many years. The centrally-located Grant River flows from the county's uplands down to the Mississippi near Potosi. A well-known feature of Grant County is the Military Ridge, formed along the headlands that were eroded by streams draining into the Wisconsin River. In 1835, a road was built along this ridge to connect Fort Crawford at Prairie du Chien with Fort Howard at Green Bay. Today U.S. 18 follows the route to Madison.

EARLY SETTLEMENT IN GRANT COUNTY

In the late 1600's the southwest portion of Wisconsin (Grant, Iowa & Lafayette Counties) was known to contain lead deposits. Jonathan Carver passed through this region in 1766 and noted numerous small lead mines worked by Indians in and around today's Grant County. Lead deposits were also found near today's Dubuque, Iowa and Galena, Illinois. A French fur trader, Julien Dubuque, heard rumors about the region's lead in 1788 and came here with several miners who assisted him in gaining the Indians' confidence and working a smelter just south of present-day Dubuque.

Dubuque's men probaby ranged into Grant County long before any permanent settlement had taken place here. In June, 1827, Chief Red Bird of the Winnebago and his braves became upset by the white settlement on their lands and killed some settlers east of Prairie du Chien. As a result, the small number of settlers in Wisconsin's lead region built log stockades in fear of a general uprising. Red Bird surrendered several months later. With his capture and a promise of peace, fortune seekers streamed into the region. The energy spent prospecting for lead left little time for building houses and the state nickname badger came from the fact that many of these miners fashioned temporary living space by digging badger-like dens into the hillsides.

LEAD MINING

It is unlikely that lead mining by Indians was started here until need for lead shot was established by the French of the eastern Great Lakes region. One of Louis Hennepin's maps showed a lead mine in 1687. In 1690, Nicholas Perrot started a trading post in southwestern Grant County to take advantage of the lead trade. However, the Indians' hostility checked any rapid growth in this area until 1820, except for Capt. John Shaw who convinced the Winnebago to allow him to ship ore from Prairie du Chien for trade at St. Louis.

The real ore exploitation began in 1824 when a mine was opened in souther Grant County at Hardscrabble, making it one of the county's first white settlements. The Hardscrabble mining camp was named after some difficulty developed identifying the proper owner. The apparent winner was named Hardy and thus it was Hardy's scrabble. The village was renamed Hazel Green in 1838 by residents who wanted a more pleasant name.

After the Winnebago scare in 1827, the region attracted miners from Missouri, Kentucky and Illinois. In 1828, when Milwaukee was still a small trading outpost and Racine was only a sandbar, 10,000 men worked the southwestern Wisconsin mines. Land that once sold for $1.25 an acre climbed to $10,000 when lead was discovered. The region between Hazel Green, Potosi and Beetown contained some of the most productive lead mines. Between 1839 and 1849, the lead district's annual production was estimated at 40 million pounds and more than 3,000 men were employed. The lead region's production peaked in 1847.

FENNIMORE, Pop. 2,212

John Fennimore started to farm here because of a large spring located near the Military Ridge, an east-west ridge of land which divides the Wisconsin River watershed from the streams that flow south into the Rock and Mississippi rivers. Since he was near the Military Road, Fennimore offered water to those traveling. This was during the height of the Black Hawk War in 1832 and one day Fennimore disappeared, never to be heard from again. When the village formed a few years later, it was named Fennimore Center. Center was eventually dropped.

John G. Perkins moved the first house into Fennimore in April, 1862, but it was six years before the village was actually laid out into a 16-block area. A well was dug and two oak buckets provided the only drinking water. A windmill over the well was torn down in 1878.

Fennimore residents greatly anticipated plans to connect them by rail to the outside world. A line reached Fennimore in 1878 and the Chicago & Northwestern company extended eastward along the Military Ridge in 1880. A narrow gauge line run by the Chicago & Tomah Company was in use between Woodman on the Wisconsin River and Fennimore from 1880's until 1926, when it was closed down. In 1889 the town started publishing a small paper, "The Fennimore Times," which was turned out by a hand press. Electricity wasn't connected until 1904 or 1905. Until then Daniel Decker lighted the lamps from a short ladder, except when the moon was bright. During Halloween, local boys gave Decker a hard time by putting chickens in the lamps.

MT. IDA & MOUNT HOPE

These villages and their townships were organized in 1877 and 1865 respectively. Mount Hope wasn't incorporated as a village until 1919.

SHSW

Small mining operation in Beetown.

PATCH GROVE & BRIDGEPORT

Originally this village was known as Finntown after Enos Finn, one of the early settlers. However, when Henry Patch came here in the mid-1830's and built his cabin near a grove of trees, the post office took the name Patch Grove. From here, the road descends down the long grade into the Wisconsin and Mississippi River Valleys.

Just across the Wisconsin River, under the bridge is the old river village of Bridgeport. During the late 1800's and early 1900's, Bridgeport was an important cattle and produce shipping point along the river. A fire almost destroyed the village in 1936 and only a few aging homes remain.

WISCONSIN RIVER

From its source in the Lac Vieux desert near the Michigan border, the Wisconsin River winds its way 430 miles through the state to the Mississippi River at Prairie du Chien, making it the state's longest river. From the summer of 1673 when Joliet and Marquette passed along its shallow waters on their way to discovering the Mississippi, the Wisconsin River provided the explorer, missionary and fur trader with a major water route between the Great Lakes and the Mississippi. The Winnebago and Sauk Indians used this river to travel and hunt many hundreds of years before the white man and referred to it as the stream of a thousand isles. Father Marquette called the river Meskousing and wrote that, "it was a wide river with a sandy bottom and shoals that renders its navigation very difficult." For that reason, large steamboats rarely ventured up the Wisconsin. Today, because of the silt from the farmlands, the shifting sand bars make boat traffic very difficult past Boscobel, except for canoes and shallow-draft boats.

The Wisconsin River drains more of the state than any other river and was the only natural highway that led through the rolling and hilly Western Uplands of southwest Wisconsin. It provided the best canoe route, outside of the Illinois River, for explorers to cross between the Mississippi and Great Lakes.

SHSW

Photograph by Dr. Joseph Smith

SHSW

Main St., Patch Grove, 1908. Photo/S. Gillett

While the broad fertile prairies of Illinois and Iowa provided the farmer with a resource to grow food, logging soon became one of the leading industries of this new state called Wisconsin. The unlimited pineries of northern Wisconsin provided the resource, employed thousands of men, and gave the railroads incentive to crisscross the state to bring out the wood that helped build America. Before the railroads, rivers such as the Wisconsin echoed with the rivermen's calls as they guided raft after raft of logs down to the Mississippi. The many rapids in the river's northern section made it difficult for rivermen and they needed much skill to keep the rafts intact.

According to the earliest records, lumber was first cut for Fort Winnebago at Portage in 1828. Until 1876, most of the lumber cut on the upper Wisconsin was sent in large rafts down to the Mississippi River and on to St. Louis. If the water level was high enough, the trip could be made in 24 days. The railroads that spread across the state during the latter half of the 1800's, reduced the Wisconsin River's commercial importance. Today the river provides an excellent recreational stream for canoeists, fishing enthusiasts, and those who enjoy the isolated beauty of this river.

SHSW

Stock day at Bridgeport. Photo/S. Gillett

DISCOVERY OF THE MISSISSIPPI

Grant County was one of the earliest regions in Wisconsin to be explored. In 1673, French explorers heard Indians talk of a great river (Mississippi), but no whites had seen its upper reaches. The French in Quebec commissioned Louis Joliet in May of 1673 to search out this river that supposedly emptied into the Sea of California. Joined by Father James Marquette, Joliet and five other men descended the Wisconsin River in two birch-bark canoes.

Their canoes passed into the Mississippi on June 17 and Joliet "had a joy he could not express." They were the first whites to see the rugged bluffs of the broad Mississippi Valley, where limestone cliffs rise 500 feet high. This valley was carved out thousands of years ago by glacial rivers draining Lake Agassiz in northwest Minnesota and Glacial Lake Duluth (early Lake Superior).

Seven years later, in 1680, Father Louis Hennepin came across Lake Michigan, down the Fox and Wisconsin Rivers and finally out to the Mississippi River. The first white to explore the Upper Mississippi, he intended to convert the Indians and bring this region under French rule. Instead, Hennepin was captured by Dakota Indians near Lake Pepin and brought to an important Indian camp at Lake Mille Lacs in Minnesota. He was later rescued by Sieur DuLuth, another Frenchman, who was exploring the Lake Superior and St. Croix region when he heard that Hennepin was being held prisoner near Mille Lacs.

(For information on Wyalusing State Park, Crawford County and Prairie du Chien, this route continues on page 299.)

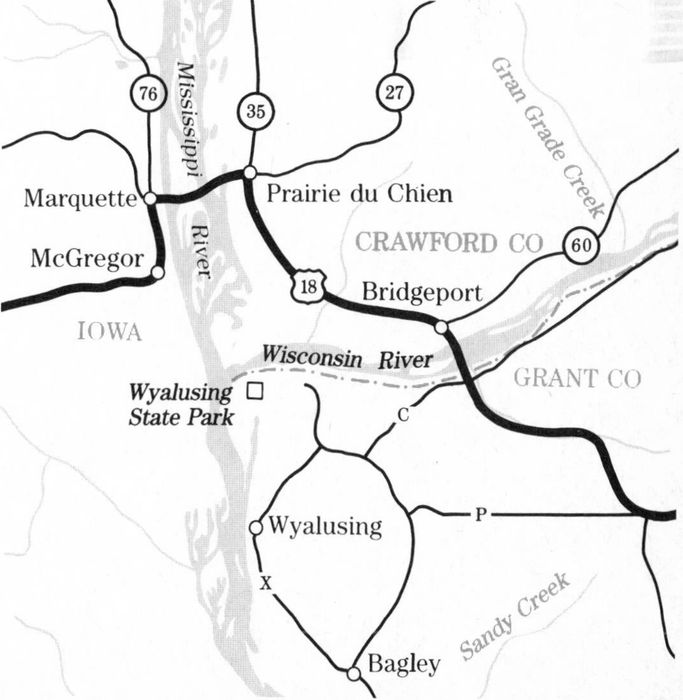

State 35 passes along the broad Mississippi River Valley, a valley eroded by the rush of glacial water thousands of years ago. The Mississippi provided the Indians, traders and settlers with a passage into the forested regions of Wisconsin and Minnesota. For many years during the late 1800's, huge rafts of logs floated quietly by Prairie du Chien and La Crosse as the forests of Wisconsin were cut. Other important rivers such as the Wisconsin, Chippewa and Black rivers carried the logs of Wisconsin to the Mississippi River.

ROUTE 35, PRAIRIE DU CHIEN TO RIVER FALLS

SHSW

Mississippi River excursion steamer.

WYALUSING STATE PARK

Situated on the bluffs overlooking the confluence of the Wisconsin and Mississippi rivers, the site of Wyalusing State Park was once considered a prime location for a city. In fact, in the early 1800's, an eastern group proposed to build a city here. One Pennsylvania man likened the area to a town in his home state named for the Indian Wyalusing. The Indian word means "home of the hoary veteran."

The 2,500-acre park is situated on a 500-foot bluff overlooking the broad Mississippi and Wisconsin valleys, their islands and backwater channels. These valleys were carved by the rush of glacial water draining Glacial Lake Agassiz (larger than the combined area of today's Great Lakes) and Lake Duluth, a larger version of Lake Superior. At one time the valley floor was several hundred feet deeper than it is today. Easing of the meltwaters allowed the valley to silt back up and rivers such as the Wisconsin and Chippewa still contribute large amounts of sediment to the Mississippi. In 1924, 200,000 acres between Wabasha, Minnesota and Rock Island, Illinois were designated as the Upper Mississippi Wildlife and Fish Refuge. This great waterway is the home of thousands of varieties of birds, fish and waterfowl and becomes one of the major flyways for birds exiting south in the fall.

There are ten miles of trails in the park, most self-guided. Numerous Indian mounds from the Effigy Mound culture are located here and local legend has it that $50,000 of gold is buried in the park, stolen from Fort Crawford at Prairie du Chien. There also 132 camping sites and four dormitories that hold up to 108 persons. Many of the campsites face out on the bluff, giving a spectacular view of the Mississippi and Wisconsin river valleys.

WISCONSIN RIVER

The Wisconsin River, the longest in the state, begins near the Michigan border at Land O'Lakes and travels 430 miles to its confluence with the Mississippi at Prairie du Chien. From the summer of 1673, when Joliet and Marquette passed by on their way to discovering the Mississippi, the Wisconsin provided explorers, missionaries and fur traders with the

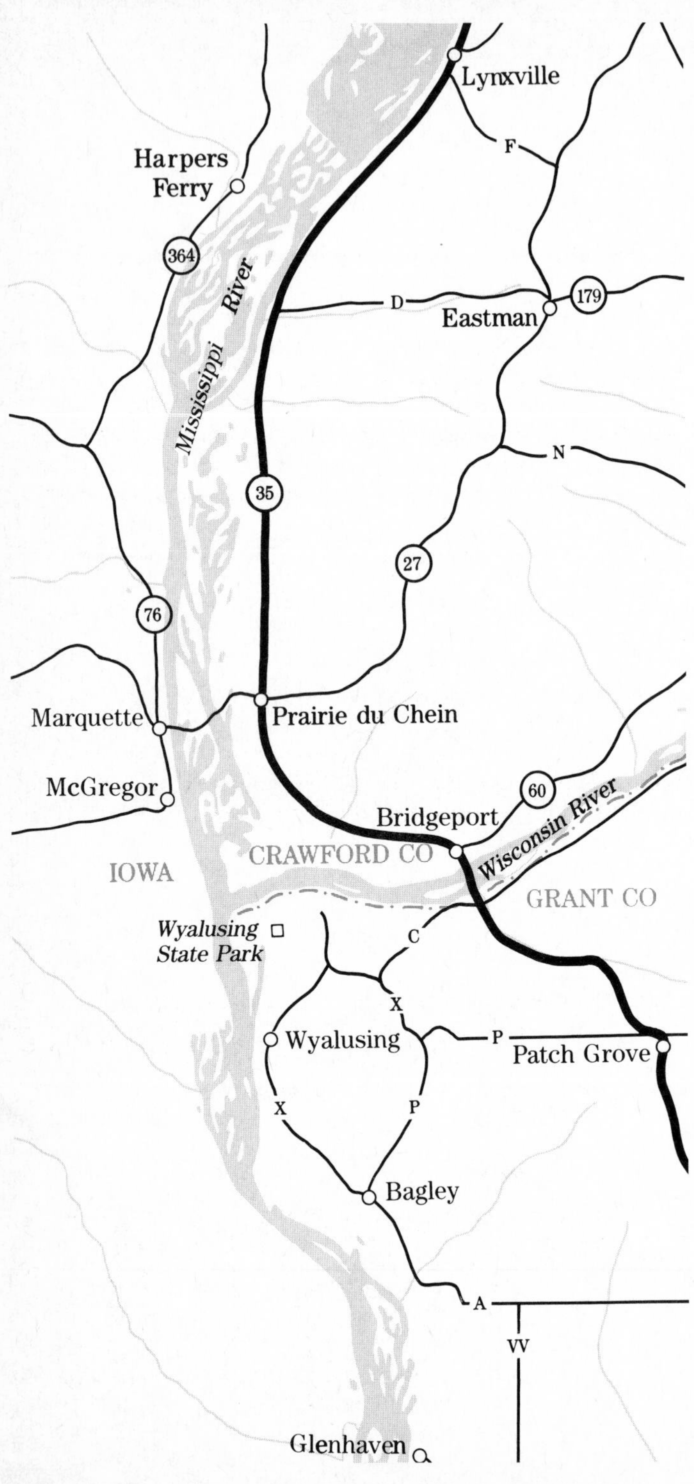

only route connecting them with the Great Lakes and the Mississippi River. The Winnebago and Sauk Indians, who used this fluid highway to travel and hunt hundreds of years before the white man, referred to it as "the stream of a thousand isles." Father Marquette called the river Meskousing and wrote that it was "...a very wide river with a sandy bottom and shoals that renders its navigation very difficult." For this reason alone, large steamboats rarely ventured up the Wisconsin. Even today, silt from the farmlands causes shifts in the sand bars making traffic past Boscobel very difficult except for shallow draft boats.

The Wisconsin River cut a wide gorge through the rolling and hilly Western Uplands of southwest Wisconsin and provided the best canoe route, outside of the Illinois River, for explorers to cross the region.

Lumber was obviously one of the leading industries of this new state. The broad fertile prairies of Illinois and Iowa enabled farmers to grow food, but the unlimited pineries of northern Wisconsin provided the capital, employed thousands of men and gave railroads incentive to crisscross the state bringing out the wood to help build America. However, before the railroads, rivers such as the Wisconsin echoed with the rivermen's calls as they guided raft after raft of logs. The Wisconsin, with its many tributaries, drains more of the state than any other river. Its many rapids in the northern section made it difficult for rivermen.

Records show that lumber was first cut for Fort Winnebago at Portage in 1828. Up to 1876, most lumber cut on the upper Wisconsin was sent in large rafts down to the Mississippi River and on to St. Louis. If the water level was high enough, the trip could be made in 24 days. Railroads built across the state during the latter 1800's reduced the Wisconsin River's commercial importance, but it thrives today as an excellent recreational stream for canoeists, fishing enthusiasts, and those who simply enjoy its isolated beauty.

According to Winnebago legend the Wisconsin River was formed by a large serpent who lived in the northern part of the state. One day the serpent traveled southward to the great sea and its body pushed down through the earth, making the riverbed. When it moved its tail, water splashed from the channel forming the thousands of lakes and swamps that cover the land.

CRAWFORD COUNTY

In 1818, Old Crawford County was part of the vast Territory of Michigan that stretched across Lake Michigan and into what would become Wisconsin. Crawford County, with its county seat at Prairie du Chien, encompassed all the present-day counties of southwestern Wisconsin. In fact, Crawford was one of only three counties in this new western region.

These were Michilimackinac (formed across northern Wisconsin), Crawford (south and western Wisconsin) and Brown (east of Portage, Wisconsin). During the 1820's settlers in Old Crawford had a growing feeling that the U.S. Government was taking an interest in their region. A postmaster was appointed as well as an Indian agency to handle claims. In addition, a yearly session of district court was held at Prairie du Chien though settlers with legal claims above $1000 had to make the long trip to the district court at Detroit until 1823. James D. Doty held the first district court at Prairie du Chien in May, 1823.

White settlement in Crawford County rapidly increased starting in 1825 as word spread of the lead mining to the south. The Sauk and Fox Nations had given up their claims to land south of the Wisconsin River in 1804 for a small amount of money, but the Winnebago had not. In June, 1827, some Winnebago Indians led by Red Bird, carried out a number of hostile acts against settlers, including some killings. The Prairie du Chien militia, along with volunteers from Galena, headed up the Wisconsin River and put an end to what was called the Winnebago War. The Winnebago eventually signed a treaty at Prairie du Chien in August, 1829, turning eight million acres of land south of the Wisconsin River over to public domain.

In the summer of 1836, when the Wisconsin Territory was set apart from the huge Territory of Michigan, only 11,680 whites claimed land in this region. Most lived west of the Mississippi or in the Green Bay area: Crawford County had only 850 residents. However, during the mid-1800's, a large number of settlers moved into Wisconsin from New England, Ohio, Pennsylvania, the Carolinas and Virginia. The immense area of Old Crawford County was shaved down by formation of Grant, St. Croix and Sauk counties from 1836-1840 and Richland and Chippewa counties in 1842.

Coulee Country

The area of Wisconsin bordering the Mississippi has been called the Coulee Country and includes Crawford County. It is a region of steep-sided hills eroded away by streams that drain into the Mississippi, Wisconsin, Kickapoo, and Chippewa rivers. This rugged country of high bluffs and steep valleys is part of a large area called the Driftless Area, a 13,000 square mile unglaciated region bounded by Blue Mounds on the east, the Chippewa River on the north and the Mississippi to the west. Since the grinding and leveling action of the glaciers did not occur here, this area looks much like it did before the ice age. Increased melting from the glaciers carved the valleys deeper, forming a beautiful region where limestone outcroppings protrude from hillsides forested in hardwoods.

In 1854, Edward Daniels, the state's first geologist, described this driftless region as one of prairies and woods, dotted and belted with beautiful groves and oak openings. He said, "...the scenery combines every element of beauty and grandeur-giving us the sunlit prairie...waving grass...the sombre depths of primeval forests and castellated cliffs rising hundreds of feet."

SHSW

Eight thousand foot, pile pontoon bridge built to cross the Mississippi at Prairie du Chien.

SHSW

Kane's Hotel built around 1839 by Ezekiel Tainter at Prairie du Chien.

SEAL OF WISCONSIN

The impact of the lead industry on Wisconsin's early days is apparent in the state seal. Chosen during the administration of Nelson Dewey, Wisconsin's first governor, it includes a crossed pick and shovel for lead mining, a hand holding a hammer for manufacturing, an anchor for all the waterways in the state, and a plow for agriculture. The shield rests upon a pyramid of pig lead. Figures include: a sailor and miner as well as a badger, a symbol for early miners who lived like badgers.

PRAIRIE DU CHIEN, Pop. 5,859

Prairie du Chien lies on a level area of prairie surrounded by river bluffs just north of where the Wisconsin River joins the Mississippi. Many years before Marquette and Joliet glided out of the Wisconsin River in 1673 to the broad Mississippi valley, a prehistoric people lived here. Little is known of these early people except for mounds they fashioned after the shapes of animals.

Father Hennepin and Sieur DuLuth explored the Mississippi a few years after Marquette and Joliet. They were followed by Nicholas Perrot in 1685. Perrot built the first structure in the county and called it Fort Saint Nicholas. From Lake Pepin in the Mississippi he claimed this area west of Lake Michigan for France in May, 1869. Next came Le Sueur, Jonathan Carver and nameless others. Indians living here referred to these explorers and traders as "men with hats." Traders referred to the Indian village near the mouth of the Wisconsin as Prairie du Chien, which was French for "Prairie of Big Dog." Big Dog (his Indian name was Alim) was chief of the village where thousands of Indians visited to unload their winter catch of furs in exchange for the white man's goods.

This distant river post became the early trade link for the French colonies at Quebec on the St. Lawrence and New Orleans at the Gulf of Mexico. From Prairie du Chien, many of the furs that flowed out of the uncharted Northwest found their way to Europe. France gave up all its lands to the English after the French and Indian War ended in 1763, but that did not deter the French traders who lived in Prairie du Chien. The French continued to trade with Indians, along with a growing number of English and American born traders. Early historians report that these Americans were of a different breed, not satisfied to trade for furs but more interested in taking the Indian land.

The first permanent white settlement started here in 1781 when Augustin Ange, Pierre Antaya and Basil Giard paid the Indians for some land. The only other significant settlement in Wisconsin at this time was a trading post at Green Bay with about 50 families. The French and Indians traded peaceably at Prairie du Chien and intermarried. When France gave up this territory in 1763, the British took over and trade continued in the French tradition. Harmony existed between the Indians here and the voyageurs who were proud to be known as "the men of the north."

Lt. Zebulon Pike passed through Prairie du Chien when exploring the Upper Mississippi after the United States took control of both shores of the Mississippi in the Louisiana Purchase of 1803. He reported that the village had 370 inhabitants. Pike crossed the river here, located a site he thought favorable for a fort, and it became known as Pike's Peak. Pike's Peak of the Rockies was named on a later expedition.

Despite the Louisiana Purchase, the residents of Prairie du Chien considered themselves British subjects until 1813. That year, the American government, concerned about securing this new outpost or gateway to the northwest, sent a gun boat up from St. Louis under the command of Joseph Perkins. He established the first American Army Post in Wisconsin, named Fort Shelby, and raised an American flag over Wisconsin soil for the first time.

The British retook Fort Shelby the following year and held it until news reached the post that the War of 1812 had ended. Since British influence was entrenched and the Indians were rumored to be uncooperative, a new fort was built at the Prairie. Named Crawford after William Crawford, a member of President James Madison's Cabinet, it was completed in 1817. Those next years were miserable ones for the residents of Prairie du Chien. The American soldiers and officers viewed the villagers with disdain and questioned their loyalty to the Union. Many citizens were arrested for the smallest provocation and whipped or otherwise punished. This same year Rev. Marie Joseph Dunand, a Trappist monk from St. Louis,

SHSW

Old Prairie du Chien graveyard.

SHSW

Fort Crawford Hospital, Prairie du Chien, 1880-90.

came to Prairie du Chien and established the first Catholic parish in Wisconsin. Dunand left 30 days later and it was ten years before another priest came to Prairie du Chien. Also in 1817, the American Fur Company, owned by John Jacob Astor, started operations here. Astor's agent was Joseph Rolette, a colorful man known from Quebec to St. Louis who is buried in the old French cemetery north of the city on county road F.

In 1821 Prairie du Chien was incorporated into a borough. Joseph Rolette was named warden in Crawford County's first attempt at self government. Early ordinances were concerned with collecting taxes and keeping order. "Every person arriving within the limits of this village in a trading capacity shall pay for every keel boat one dollar, and every flat bottomed boat or piroque fifty cents for each and every time." Fines were levied for smoking chimneys, houses with straw roofs, hitching horses to main street fences and for people "sneaking about after ten in the evening."

In 1823, Prairie du Chien residents saw the first steamboat, the Virginia, ascend the upper Mississippi on its way up river with supplies for Fort Crawford and Fort Snelling at St. Paul. Joseph Rolette went along for the ride, helping cut wood for the boilers. The first post office was established in the village in 1824 with James Doty as its postmaster, although regular mail service didn't arrive until 1832.

SHSW

Dousman Hotel, Prairie du Chien, 1862.

One of the larger Indian councils was held here in the summer of 1825 with territorial governor Lewis Cass and Gen. William Clark. The council lasted 14 days with leaders of the Dakota (Sioux), Sauk, Fox, Ojibwe (Chippewa), Winnebago, Menominee, Iowa, Ottawa, and Potawatomi tribes taking part. Some historians consider this one of the great Indian councils ever held in the Northwest. Its purpose was to create a lasting peace in this region and to better define the boundaries of individual Indian nations. Fortunately, a massacre didn't occur even though some of the nations, including the Dakota and Ojibwe, had such a longstanding mutual hatred that most could not remember when or why it began. Four years later, in 1829, the Winnebago, Ojibwe and Ottawa held another council and turned over eight million acres of land south of the Wisconsin River to the U.S. government.

General Gaines inspected Fort Crawford and found it "so decayed and one quarter of the 44 man garrison ill," that plans were made for moving the fort a mile southeast, away from low ground where it was subject to flooding. The new fort, completed in 1834, was rectangular with high pine stockades on the north and south sides. It also had a library, auditorium and a nearby hospital where Dr. William Beaumont did research on the human digestive system which was the bulwark of digestive physiology for many years. Life at the new fort was no easier than life at the old. Some 100 soldiers died during a cholera outbreak in 1832, and fighting between the Winnebago and Sacs added to the tension.

When Chief Black Hawk crossed into the Kickapoo Valley during the Black Hawk War, Fort Crawford soldiers massacred a boatful of helpless Indian women and children he had sent down the Mississippi in hopes someone would pity them. Black Hawk was captured and taken to Prairie du Chien, where he was jailed until his transfer to another prison. Fort Crawford soldiers also helped build the Military Highway that connected Prairie du Chien with Fort Winnebago at Portage in 1835. One of the fort's main objectives was to control a homesick and discontented Winnebago nation which was finally forcibly removed from Wisconsin in 1840, only to be shuttled from reservations to reservation. Fort Crawford was abandoned in 1856 and its buildings torn down or removed.

During the 1850's, Prairie du Chien continued to grow as raft after raft of lumber moved downstream from the rich pineries of the St. Croix River valley. When the railroad reached here in 1857, a new trade link with the town of Milwaukee was soon established. In a few years Prairie du Chien was shipping a hundred carloads of Minnesota wheat a day to Milwaukee. A pontoon railway bridge spanned the Mississippi in 1874, opening new markets to the west. However, despite its location on the river crossroads, the Military Highway, and development of the railway system linking it with the Great Lakes, Prairie du Chien never became the metropolis many had expected.

Today it is a quiet river town giving little hint of its rich pioneering history. St. Feriole Island, where Prairie du Chien got its start, has had most of its homes removed because of continued flooding problems. But the Brisbois House and the old stone fur warehouse are still there. Villa Louis is also located out on St. Feriole Island. Another point of interest is the old Fort Crawford Military Cemetery, one of the smallest military cemeteries maintained by the U.S. government.

VILLA LOUIS

Hercules Dousman came to Prairie du Chien in 1826 to assist the aging Joseph Rolette in running this outpost of the American Fur Company. Dousman amassed a large fortune here and was considered by 1838 "the most valuable man on the Upper Mississippi." By the late 1820's, Prairie du Chien was a thriving settlement. Most problems involving the French and British loyalists were over and Astor's American Fur Company was one of the major powers of the Northwest.

When Fort Crawford was relocated from along the Mississippi in 1829, Dousman bought the old site. He had by than married his dead partner's widow, Jane Rolette, and he built her a red brick Georgian home on the fort site. In 1870, he had that house torn down and built the present cream-colored brick mansion. Named Villa Louis, the Dousmans decorated the house with expensive furniture, art objects, Waterford crystal, rare books and many other items. After Dousman died the house remained in the family and was restored by family members in the 1930's, making it one of the more authentically furnished Victorian homes in the United States. The house and 80-acre park was donated to the city in 1935 and the State Historical Society of Wisconsin has owned Villa Louis since 1952. Tours are given (admission is charged) from May through October.

EARLY TRANSPORTATION

For several decades after traders began gathering around Prairie du Chien, Indian trails and natural waterways were the only routes settlers traveled. Then in 1835, Fort Crawford soldiers began to construct a highway from Prairie du Chien to Fort Winnebago at Portage. It then continued on, connecting Portage with Fort Howard at Green Bay.

The road basically follows U.S. 18 to Madison. It was a crude road cut through timber and across swamps before climbing up on a ridge of land that became know as the Military Ridge. This rise of land divides the Wisconsin River watershed from the rivers that drain into Illinois.

One of the earliest highways to reach north from Prairie du Chien was built by Alfred Brunson to connect with the lumber camps along the Black River. It took Brunson and his 14 man crew 12 days to cut through the forests up to a Mormon community at Black River Falls, then another 52 days to cut a path further north to Lake Superior at La Pointe. The road became known as the Black River Road.

LYNXVILLE, Pop. 174

In 1846 two brothers immigrated from Poland, settled here for two years to trade with the Indians, then left for reasons unknown. Their names have been lost and a ravine near Lynxville named Polander's Hollow is the only reminder of their presence. In 1848 the Haney brothers crossed over from the Kickapoo Valley and built a log cabin at a bend in the river known as Devil's Elbow. They cut wood and bought furs from the Indians and Haney's landing became known as one of the best spots on the river for steamboats to take on firewood from the abundant timber that covered the islands, hills and ravines. In 1857 the village was laid out by surveyors who arrived on the steamboat Lynx, from which the town took its name.

SHSW

Main St., Lynxville. ca. 1880.

Lynxville was a favorite fishing spot for many years. In fact, legend has it that one commercial operation from Dubuque, Iowa drew out 80,000 pounds of fish in one seine. Such over-fishing and general mismanagement of the Mississippi's natural resources resulted in establishment of a fisheries station here as part of the Upper Mississippi Wildlife and Fish Refuge. The refuge is a 200,000-acre stretch from Rock Island, Illinois north to Wabasha, Minnesota.

A stockyard was once located north of the old Burlington railroad depot and a popular hotel hugged the steep hillside overlooking town. The largest river raft on the Mississippi was to have been assembled in Lynxville in 1896. It was 260 feet wide by 1550 feet long and contained 2,250,000 board feet of lumber.

FERRYVILLE, Pop. 227

This small village is situated on a plateau above the Winneshiek Bottoms, an area of backwater lakes and sloughs. The name Winneshiek comes from Chief Winneshiek, a bearded Indian who used to trade along the Mississippi. The Indian meaning for Winneshiek is "dirty, brackish." A large Winnebago village existed north of Ferryville before the Winnebago were moved to reservations in Iowa and Minnesota.

The town was platted in 1859 and named Ferryville because its owners intended to run a ferry between it and Lansing, Iowa. Once a ferry began several years later, it was used to ship grain, stock and produce to Lansing where it was loaded on to the Chicago, Milwaukee and St. Paul Railroad. The ferry was discontinued when the Burlington Railroad reached Ferryville during the early 1880's. For several years after, livestock and grain were shipped from the stockyards and warehouse maintained by the depot. A local story explains that Ferryville's generous boundaries were created after city fathers passed an ordinance requiring that the village be a mile long before liquor licenses would be granted. True or not, the village is exceptionally long for its population.

SENECA

The small settlement of Seneca developed around the country inn of William Philamalee who came here in 1851. A few years later Samuel Langdon bought the inn and laid out the village. The village school here was said to be the best outside of Prairie du Chien. Seneca was a tribe of the Iroquois nation of New York. Its name translates as "place of stone."

DESOTO, Pop. 318

The small river town of Desoto straddles the counties of Vernon and Crawford. This area was once known as Winneshiek's Landing since Chief Winneshiek traded furs here with the early French traders. For many years after this region was settled, a band of Winnebago had a village three miles south of Desoto at a place once known as Wyburn's Glen. Chief Winneshiek and a number of his tribe are reportedly buried at the top of Mt. Winneshiek, a nearby bluff overlooking the Mississippi. Other nearby bluffs carry the names of Indians who once lived in this region. Mt. Moo-na-pa-ga, which separates the twin valleys, was named for a well-known Winnebago brave who was named Jim Brown by white settlers. Further south is a bluff called Wee-hun-ga, named after Moo-na-pa-ga's wife. Finally there is a bluff called Mt. Carrickmore, a rounded hill with a single massive rock resting at its top.

Two French men moved here shortly after the Black Hawk War ended in 1832 and traded with the Indians for Astor's

American Fur Company. However, there was little growth here until 1854 when Dr. Simeon Powers, Dr. Houghton and Dr. Osgood laid out the village. They purposed to develop a closed colony of people of New England extraction, excluding foreign settlers and businessmen. Rumor has it that an Englishman was refused dinner at one of the inns. When he insisted that it was a public place, they took his silverware away. In 1857 N.S. Cate broke Desoto's exclusivity by establishing a large saw mill here. Cate employed as many as 50 men, most of whom were not New Englanders. The mill cut an average of 50,000 board feet of lumber daily until it failed in 1861.

VERNON COUNTY, Pop. 25,642

Vernon County was once known as Bad Ax County after the Bad Axe River which drains this hilly region. The Dakota Indians occupied this region during the early 1600's, but were eventually displaced by the Fox and Winnebago nations later in that century. In 1680 Father Hennepin became the first white to pass up the Mississippi near today's Vernon County. He was soon captured by Dakota braves and taken to Mille Lacs Lake, Minnesota, the spiritual capital of the Dakota nation.

Many explorers and traders passed by this region during the 1700's, and a few maintained posts along the Mississippi including Joseph Brisbois who had a post at the mouth of the Bad Axe River in 1817. But white settlement didn't begin in Vernon County until after the Winnebago ceded this land by a treaty signed at Washington in 1837. In that treaty, the Winnebago ceded all lands east of the Mississippi and were to remove themselves to an Iowa reservation within eight months. However, it was difficult for the Winnebago to give up their long-held hunting grounds: for several years groups crossed the Mississippi to their old Wisconsin lands.

SHSW

Ferryville, 1909. Photo/S. Gillett

Bad Axe county was organized out of Crawford County in March, 1851, and a log cabin built by Moses Decker in 1850 at Viroqua became the first courthouse. As time passed, residents of Bad Axe County became uncomfortable with their county name. State legislatures in Madison were reportedly startled whenever the speaker called on the "gentleman from Bad Ax" and the name was an object of satire at Madison theaters. A movement began to change the name to Winneshiek but Vernon was chosen in 1862 to associate the county with the green fields of George Washington's home, Mount Vernon.

BAD AXE RIVER

The Bad Axe River has been the site of two important and bloody battles between whites and Indians. The first took place in 1827. Chief Red Bird, a Winnebago, became displeased with whites occupying Indian land in the southwest lead regions. He led a raid that ended in the murder of a farmer and hired hand just west of Prairie du Chien. Hostilities continued, upsetting the new settlers and miners of southwestern Wisconsin. Shortly after, Red Bird escaped to a Winnebago encampment at the mouth of the Bad Axe River. As the Indians celebrated, two keel-boats innocently tried to land. The Indians opened fire, killing several men on the boats, but the boats escaped to spread the story and terror along the river communities. Red Bird was captured by a large force of volunteer soldiers who came to quell the uprising and he died in prison.

The next battle came in 1832 at the end of the Black Hawk War. Black Sparrow Hawk, a Sauk Indian, refused to give up his lands near Rock Island, Illinois, because he did not accept the treaties negotiated by other tribes. As a result his village was burned and he and his band were forced west across the Mississippi. In the spring of 1832, Black Hawk's band crossed the Mississippi and headed northward along the Rock River. There were deaths on both sides and white settlers constructed stockades all across southern Wisconsin. Chased by soldiers, Black Hawk and his band of braves, women and children escaped down the Wisconsin River.

The hungry, pathetic band eventually ended up at the mouth of the Bad Axe, surrounded by their pursuers. Black Hawk tried to surrender to the steamboat Warrior standing off shore, but his white flag was met with cannon fire, killing 23. Hoping someone would pity the women and children, Black Hawk put a group out in canoes and rafts. Sparing no one, the soldiers shot down 150 women, men and children. Black Hawk escaped, but was later captured and returned to Fort

Crawford at Prairie du Chien. He was eventually paroled from imprisonment at St. Louis. Black Hawk was quoted as saying, "I loved my towns, my cornfields, and the home of my people..I fought for it."

VICTORY

A trader named Patwell once traded here, supplied by Hercules Dousman of the American Fur Company at Prairie du Chien. But Ira Stevens is considered the first pioneer here, settling in 1849. The town and area didn't really attract settlers until it was platted in 1852. Named after the victory over Black Hawk at the Bad Axe River, the town had a good boat landing which was handling a fair amount of grain in 1860. The town boasted a hotel, store, blacksmith, shoe shop, school house and a population of 300.

GENOA, Pop. 283

In 1848 a number of Italians immigrated here from the lead region of Galena, Illinois. A few years later the village, which had called itself Bad Axe City, was officially laid out and renamed Genoa because residents thought the growing village of fishermen and farmers resembled Genoa, Italy. For a time, huge flocks of wild pigeons nested off shore on the numerous islands on the Mississippi. Villagers reportedly went after these pigeons with nets and returned with barrels full. A post office was established here in 1854 and St. Charles' Catholic Church began services under Father Marko in 1862.

STODDARD, Pop. 762

The region around Stoddard was farmed in 1852 by Norwegians Halver Jorgenson and Andrew Emberson. Sixteen years later Henry H. White, traveling west from Vermont, climbed a bluff overlooking the Mississippi and decided to settle. He built a frame house, and after purchasing enough land, laid out the village on the side of a gently sloping bluff. He named it after a former mayor of La Crosse.

This region along the Mississippi once had a number of river pirates who stole lumber from rafts and resold it to Minnesota farmers. Today, the maze of lakes and sloughs are part of a backwater lake system created by Lock & Dam No. 8 at Genoa. The system is included in the Upper Mississippi National Wildlife and Fish Refuge which extends down to Rock Island, Illinois.

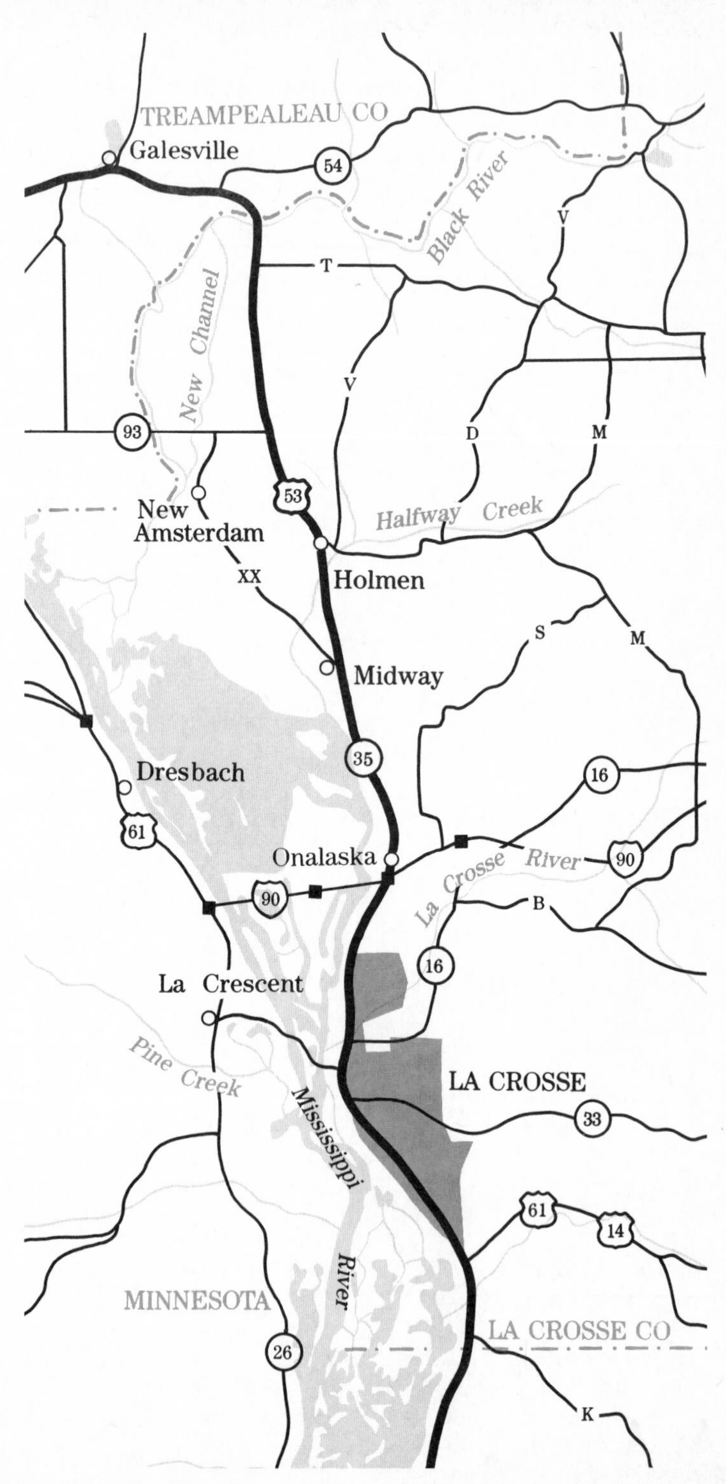

LA CROSSE COUNTY, Pop. 91,056

La Crosse County is a hilly, unglaciated land of deep fertile valleys which drains into the Mississippi or La Crosse rivers. The sandstone and limestone bluffs that line the Mississippi, range from 400 to 500 feet high and contain shells and remnants of ancient animals and fish—evidence that this area was covered by a sea which covered most of North America. It was during the melting of the glaciers at the end of the last Ice Age 10-12,000 years ago, that the La Crosse and Mississippi rivers began to cut down through the rock. At one point, the Mississippi valley was 500 feet deeper then it is today. When the glaciers retreated and the waters of the Mississippi slowed, the river basin silted back to its present level.

Father Hennepin, a French missionary, was the first white person to pass up into the Upper Mississippi Valley in 1680. Except for traders who occasionally camped along the river during those following years, La Crosse County wasn't settled until 1841. The nearest towns then were Prairie du Chien and Galena, Illinois. Milwaukee was in its early days and Chicago had a population of only 5,000. La Crosse County was formed in 1851, but its present boundaries weren't set until 1918.

La Crosse was a name given by French traders who watched the Indians play a game with sticks and a deerskin ball. Jonathan Carver noted in his travels past here in 1766, that the goals were 600 yards apart and up to 300 men participated in this game. Carver said they played with such ferocity that many suffered broken bones.

SHSW

Riverboats anchored at the La Crosse levee.

LA CROSSE, Pop. 48,347

Winnebago Indians were the first to live here at the confluence of the Mississippi and La Crosse rivers. During the early 1800's they camped here to trade their furs for guns, powder, knives, blankets, shirts and whiskey. In 1837 a tragic period began for the Winnebago when they ceded all their land east of the Mississippi for reservations in Iowa and Long Prairie, Minnesota. However, many refused to leave and 18-year-old Nathan Myrick came up to the terraced land of Prairie La Crosse in 1841 to trade with those who had stayed. He arrived with only ten cents and a load of goods and had to wait ten days before Indians came. Finally "we had plenty good trade" and Myrick built a crude trading post on Barron's Island, now Pettibone Park. Here with a partner named Eben Weld, Myrick traded and cut cord-wood for steamers. The next year he built a new cabin on the mainland at Prairie La Crosse, a sandy treeless prairie about ten miles long and three miles wide.

Myrick wrote about one cold winter morning where, "The weather was cold and that night a blizzard sprung up. (The next) morning was the bluest I ever experienced; I was sick, and homesick, and it was the only time I wished myself back home in the East (New York)."

But Myrick hung on and over the next few years the post at Prairie La Crosse became the central trading spot from the Black River to the Bad Axe River on the south. Myrick traded with important Indians such as Chief Winneshiek and Chief Decorah. In 1841, a group of Mormons began working the forest of Black River Falls. Some moved down to a place they named Mormon Coulee in 1844, but left after a year because of differences with other settlers. In 1844 Myrick and and a man named Scooter Mills went up to the Black River pineries to cut and float logs down to La Crosse. From there the lumber was floated down to St. Louis. Up until then, all traveling was done along the Mississippi. It wasn't until 1845 that the first overland trip was made in eight days from Prairie du Chien. In 1848 when the Winnebago were forcibly removed from this region, the white population at Prairie La Crosse was still only 30.

That same year the government made land available in the area, but settlement was slow until the early 1850's when a number of settlers from New York and Vermont came here and established grist mills, saw mills, and a newspaper which helped promote the new town. In 1851, Prairie La Crosse was made the county seat and was an important lumber town for the next 40 years. Lots were sold for about $40 in 1851 and many buildings were constructed, but it was a slow transition from this once desolate, sand-heaped river terrace.

A number of German and Norwegians immigrated here during the late 1850's, attracted by the Black River's pine forests. The Germans promptly established a singing society and a club called the Maennerchor and Turnverein respectively. By 1856 this village of Germans, New Englanders and Norwegians had grown to 3,000 and became sophisticated enough to drop Prairie from its name. Historian J.A. Renggly wrote in those early days, "that drifting down the great (Mississippi) on a radiant morning, the voyager will recall nothing more varied in his travels than the city of La Crosse. The home of savages less than 50 years ago, it is now the home of wealth, enterprise, education and refinement."

Being a good river port (1,569 boat arrivals in 1857) and a lumber center wasn't enough for La Crosse. It was the addition of the La Crosse and Milwaukee Railroad in 1858 that assured the city's success. When the Civil War stopped river traffic below Ohio, La Crosse became an important link for western Wisconsin and points westward. By the turn-of-the-century lumbering dropped off drastically but other industries, including four large breweries, developed to sustain the town. Today La Crosse is a diversified industrial and agricultural center.

ONALASKA, Pop. 9,249

During its early days this area was occasionally inhabited by traders and loggers. But it wasn't until 1851 that William G. Rowe purchased a small house already framed and moved it here from La Crosse and ran it as a tavern for loggers working the Black River. Soon a number of people had settled around Rowe's tavern and by the late 1800's the town boasted 300 people, a post office, school house, and train depot.

The meaning of the town's name is unclear, although Rowe frequently quoted a line of poetry which referred to an Alaskan fishing village named Oonalaska.

MIDWAY

Once known as Midway Station, this small village formed around the railroad which came through in the early 1870's. The hamlet once had a blacksmith shop, a frame hotel, a store and a grain elevator.

HOLMEN, Pop. 2,411

This spot along Halfway Creek had been a resting stop for travelers on the trail to Black River Falls. But the village got its real start when Frederick Anderson built his blacksmith shop here in 1867. It was first known as Frederickstown and Cricken before the new postmaster asked that it be named after a Mr. Holmen who surveyed this region in 1851. Holm is also a Norwegian word referring to land that is low, rich and borders water.

In 1876 the Caseberg Mill Company rebuilt a dam across Halfway Creek and for several decades ground wheat, corn and buckwheat into flour for local farmers. A rafting pin factory also located here manufacturing pins used to connect rafts of logs together on their journey down the Mississippi. As Holmen grew, the town boasted new shops, a two-story hotel, a meat market, a creamery, ice harvesting and its first doctor who came in 1883.

TREMPEALEAU COUNTY, Pop. 26,158

This beautiful region is part of the Upper Coulee County, a land of high prairie where streams have cut deep coulees through the sandstone on their run down the Mississippi Valley bluffs.

Although many trappers passed through here, Nicholas Perrot was the first to reside in this county. He reportedly spent the winter of 1685 camped two miles above the present village of Trempealeau, then moved up to Lake Pepin the following spring.

The French were determined to establish a post among the Dakota Indians and in 1731 sent Rene Godefrey sieur de Linctot to winter near a large bluff situated in the Mississippi River bottoms. The Dakota called this bluff Pah-hah-dah or "mountain separated by water." The French called it la montagne qui trempe a l'eau, meaning "the mountain which is stepped in water." From this French phrase came the word Trempealeau.

The Dakota and Winnebago occupied these lands and traded with the French, followed by the English and finally the Americans. From these Mississippi bluffs the Indians watched the rapid change and new technology the whites brought up the river. The first steamboat, the Virginia, steamed past Trempealeau Mountain in the spring of 1823 on its journey up to Fort Snelling.

James Reed, James Dousville and a colorful trapper named Augustin Rocque are considered the first settlers to move into the county. James Reed brought his family up from Prairie du Chien in 1840 and settled at what was first known as Reed's Landing, then as Montoville and later as Trempealeau. Trempealeau County was officially formed in 1854 with the county seat at Galesville, but the county government later moved to Arcadia and finally to Whitehall in 1877.

GALESVILLE, Pop. 1,239

During the summer of 1853 Judge Gale became frustrated with his attempts to establish a college in La Crosse and decided to develop a new town and college. He traveled the rolling coulee country 17 miles north of La Crosse looking for a place to start his town, build a mill and establish his school. Fording the Black River, he journeyed up Beaver Creek to where the waterpower would be ideal for his mill, purchased 2,000 acres, and platted Galesville. Gale's brother-in-law, Dr. William Young, the town's first doctor, actively promoted Galesville throughout the area. When Trempealeau County was organized in 1854, the town was named the county seat despite the fact that only rugged trails led to it.

A number of settlers came here in 1854 as work began on the mill. Unfortunately it was destroyed in a flash flood and another was started. A year later, Galesville's population was only 30. A writer describes Galesville's early days as ones of "strange scenes, queer characters, eccentric experiences and sadness." However, it grew rapidly over the next several years. The Commercial Hotel was built, as well as a courthouse, flour mill, blacksmith and general store.

During this time, Judge Gale was busy looking for subscribers to his college which he had tentatively named Yale University. In 1858 there was enough money to lay the foundations for what would be called Gale College. Early historians noted that the university grounds rested on the edge of Beaver Creek valley and included two Indian mounds that were 35 and 75 feet in length. One mound resembled a bear, the other a horse.

Gale College was closed in 1903 and the buildings housed a two-year Lutheran college until 1939. The Brothers of Mary bought it as a training school in 1941 and run it today as an ecumenical retreat house.

TREMPEALEAU, Pop. 956

Trempealeau is another small village on the Mississippi located near a large bluff which rises out of the river. Father Hennepin passed here in 1680, but Nicholas Perrot was probably the first white person to slide his canoe up on shore. The Dakota called the bluff Pah-hah-dah or "mountain separated by water." The French called it la montagne qui trempe a l'eau, meaning "the mountain which is stepped in water," and from this came the word Trempealeau.

Though Perrot only lived here the winter of 1685, he traded in the region for the next 20 years. In 1731, the French wanted to establish a post among the Dakota Indians and sent Rene Godefrey sieur de Linctot to winter here. The following year Linctot went to Fort Beauharnois at Lake Pepin to help rebuild that post, but he maintained the small post near Trempealeau for six years before Indian troubles forced him to torch the fort and leave in 1737. It wasn't until 1840, 103 years later, that permanent settlement began at what would later become Trempealeau village. A man named James Reed brought his family up from Prairie du Chien and built a log cabin which became known as Reed's Town. Reed was a soldier at Fort Crawford, a courier during the Black Hawk War, and an eyewitness to the Bad Axe Massacre. Accompanied by his brother-in-law James Dousville (who actually

SHSW

Boating in the shadow of Mt. Trempealeau.

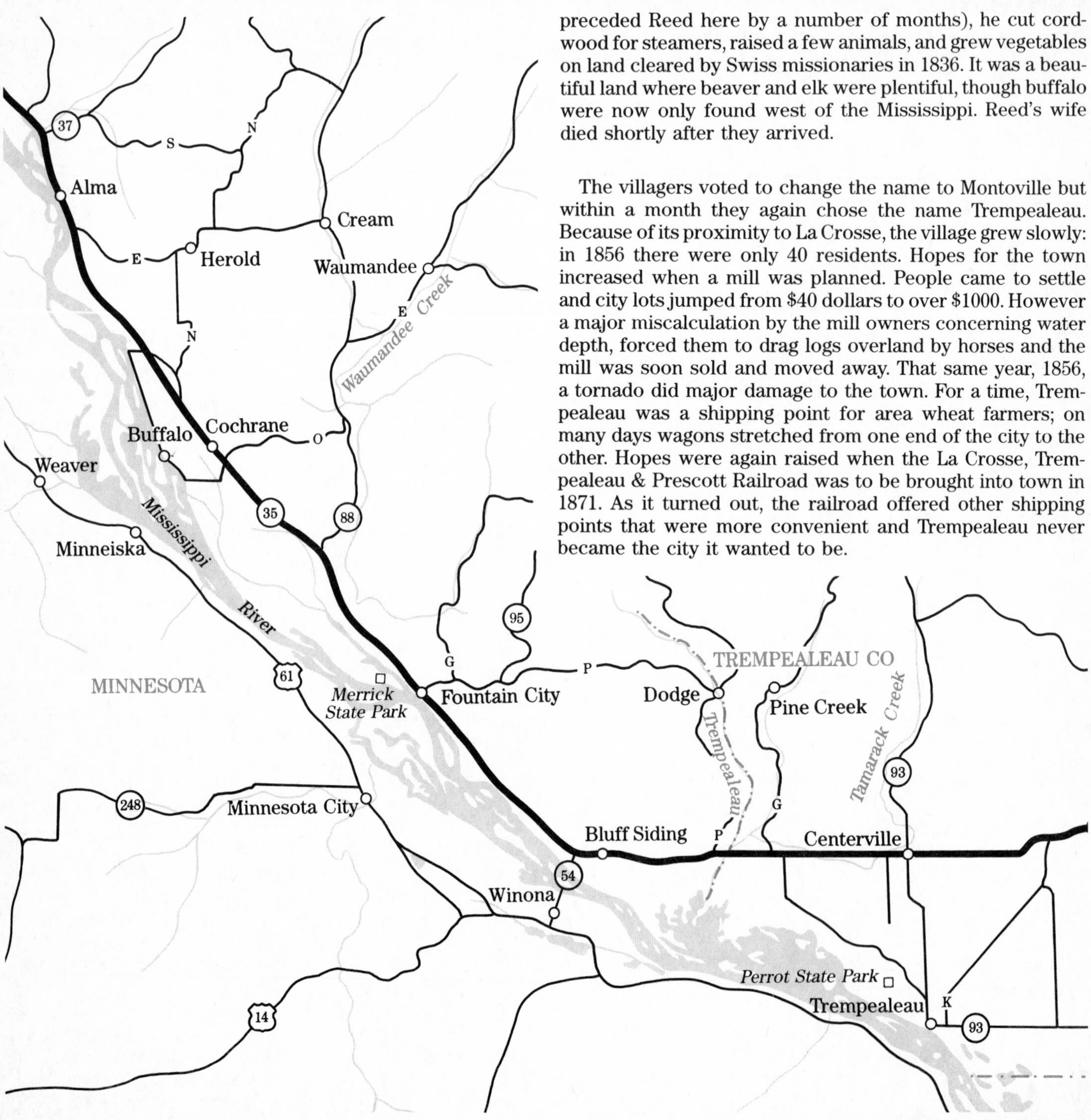

preceded Reed here by a number of months), he cut cordwood for steamers, raised a few animals, and grew vegetables on land cleared by Swiss missionaries in 1836. It was a beautiful land where beaver and elk were plentiful, though buffalo were now only found west of the Mississippi. Reed's wife died shortly after they arrived.

The villagers voted to change the name to Montoville but within a month they again chose the name Trempealeau. Because of its proximity to La Crosse, the village grew slowly: in 1856 there were only 40 residents. Hopes for the town increased when a mill was planned. People came to settle and city lots jumped from $40 dollars to over $1000. However a major miscalculation by the mill owners concerning water depth, forced them to drag logs overland by horses and the mill was soon sold and moved away. That same year, 1856, a tornado did major damage to the town. For a time, Trempealeau was a shipping point for area wheat farmers; on many days wagons stretched from one end of the city to the other. Hopes were again raised when the La Crosse, Trempealeau & Prescott Railroad was to be brought into town in 1871. As it turned out, the railroad offered other shipping points that were more convenient and Trempealeau never became the city it wanted to be.

PERROT STATE PARK

This state park situated along the Mississippi, rests in the shadows of Mount Trempealeau. From the top of a bluff within the park, one supposedly can see the tree-lined valleys of the Black, Mississippi, Trempealeau and La Crosse rivers.

The park is the location where Nicolas Perrot spent the winter of 1685-86 before continuing up the Mississippi to establish Fort St. Antoine where he claimed this remote wilderness for France in 1689. Sieur de Linctot, also maintained a post here until he abandoned it in 1736. Time and nature quickly covered the rubble of the old post and it was many years later before the ruins were discovered, including the old fireplace hearth that warmed Perrot 200 years before.

CENTERVILLE

Located just east of the Tamarack Creek is the small crossroads hamlet of Centerville. At first known as Martin's Corners, the name was changed to Centerville because the town is located on a broad terrace of the Mississippi.

TREMPEALEAU RIVER

The Trempealeau River valley winds up through the Mississippi River bluffs to the central plains of Wisconsin, a 13,000 square mile area of gently rolling land. The gentle topography however is disrupted occasionally by the eroding action of rivers and streams and the effects of glaciers. The Trempealeau Valley provided the perfect route for building the Green Bay and Wisconsin Railroad up from the Mississippi valley on its journey east to the Lake Michigan harbor of Green Bay. When Stephen Long came up the Mississippi in a six-oared skiff in 1817 he was overcome by the region's beauty. He wrote about the, "hills marshaled into a variety of agreeable shapes, some towering into lofty peaks while others present broad summits embellished with contours and slopes in the most pleasing manner."

BUFFALO COUNTY, Pop. 14,309

This county of steep bluffs and sloping valleys was organized in 1853, and named from the Buffalo River which drains into the Mississippi north of Alma. The county is bordered by three other important rivers; the Chippewa, Trempealeau and Mississippi. Its lush hills are covered with poplar, birch, elm, hickory and many other varieties of hard and soft woods.

The first county seat was located at Sand Prairie, a narrow strip of land on the Mississippi three miles above Fountain City, but no meetings were held there, mainly because it was under water much of the time. Fountain City became the county seat until 1860, then moved to the more centrally located village of Alma. Before whites arrived, this area was a disputed territory and many battles were fought for its control. In fact, a number of bones and skeletons were reportedly found in Fountain City in its early days. In roughly sectioned territories with few stable boundaries, the Dakota Indians ranged the western side of the Mississippi, the Ojibwe pushed down from the north, and the Winnebago held the land extending eastward from Lake Michigan. Despite tension and fighting between the Dakota and Ojibwe, early traders and settlers were drawn to this area because of the Indians' desire to trade their furs.

MARSHLAND

This railroad junction was once an important shipping point for furs and fish brought down to the Mississippi from the Trempealeau River Valley. When farming began to take over the area, many acres were reclaimed from draining the extensive marshes located here. Marshland once consisted of a store, hotel and two saloons, and residents hoped its location on the railroad would ensure growth. Today Marshland contains a single gas station and dried sedge grass covers the foundation of the old hotel.

BLUFF SIDING

A large lime burning industry was once located along this small siding on the Chicago & Northwestern Railroad. It also had a store, hotel, school and two saloons.

FOUNTAIN CITY, Pop. 963

Shortly after the Winnebago signed away their Wisconsin lands in 1837, a man named Holmes pushed up the Mississippi in search of trade with the Indians. In late 1839, as winter began, he stopped at a Dakota Indian camp on the Minnesota side which would later become the town of Winona. It looked like a good place to trade, but the Indians persuaded Holmes that the east side of the river was the only good place for a white man. Taking the hint, he and his small group crossed to the shelter of the Waumandee bluffs, an area which later became Fountain City.

Holmes carried on trade from 1839-41, helping his income by cutting cordwood for steamboats traveling the Mississippi. This spot became known as Holmes' Landing, but Holmes felt crowded by his new neighbors so he "stole away in the night with his squaw and children never to be heard from again."

Real settlement began in 1842 when a boatfull of Swiss landed here from Galena, Illinois. They built their cabins along the shore and like Holmes began cutting wood for steamboats traveling between Galena and Fort Snelling. They made a good income because this was one of the few good stopping spots along the river for steamers. For many years Holmes' Landing was the only development in the county and most travel was by river, except for an occasional hardy soul that ventured overland from Milwaukee. The county's first store, post office and newspaper began here.

In 1854, when the village was actually platted, a movement succeeded in changing the name to Waumandee, a Dakota word meaning, "beautiful stream." However, Waumandee never caught on and Fountain City was chosen because of the numerous springs that seep from nearby Eagle Bluff. According to a writer, "...the Indian trails gave way to public roads, the slippery log across the creek was thrown aside..and the village assumed a civilized appearance." So civilized in fact that a German singing society called Turnverein was organized in 1858. Fifteen years later, a soda water plant was built, as well as the Eagle Brewery with a yearly capacity of 1000 barrels. Today Fountain City is a small village built up on the steep hills that line the river.

MERRICK STATE PARK

This 291-acre park, located just north of Fountain City, was named after George B. Merrick, a Mississippi river pilot, who wrote many stories about the Upper Mississippi. The park has swimming, camping and offers boat access to the Mississippi. Waumandee Creek empties here into a small lake of the same name which was created much like Lake Pepin: sedimentation blocked the creek, backing up the waters to create a lake. Today, it is filled with an overgrowth of aquatic plants.

COCHRANE, Pop. 512

A St. Paul land company began selling lots here in 1886 when it was apparent that the Chicago, Burlington & Northern line would begin carrying freight between St. Paul and Prairie du Chien. The company named the new village after a director of the railroad. In the village's early days, several village men started the Cochrane Basket Factory, but couldn't make ends meet. The Pepin Pickle Company also maintained a pickling station here for a time. At the turn-of-the-century, this small community supported three musical bands; the Excelsior Band, Fireman's Band and the Cadet Band.

BUFFALO, Pop. 894

The village of Buffalo is situated on a terrace of the Mississippi about 20 feet above the flood plain. This terrace and others like it were formed when the Mississippi's water level fluctuated during the melting of glaciers 10,000 years ago.

Records show that two men named Hammer and John Wecker were the first to call this spot home in 1853. They cut cordwood for the steamboats as did many early residents along the Mississippi. It wasn't until 1856 that scouts of the Colonization Society of Cincinnati, Ohio came here to establish a town. The society, made up of laborers who wanted to move west, first intended to move to Kansas, but decided on Buffalo instead. Their first job was to clear the trees and lay out the town. Instead of laying out the town along the river's natural contours, they laid it out to true north, causing many unusable lots and spaces in town. Blame for this was given to the number of surveyors in the Society. A few years later a saw and flour mill, brewery, store and post office were constructed. The mill was the first combined grist and saw mill built in the county.

Buffalo never really grew to the size the residents envisioned, mainly because steamboats could only reach here during high water. In its desire for growth, Buffalo unsuccessfully tried to have the county seat moved here in 1861. For many years it was Wisconsin's smallest incorporated village.

ALMA, Pop. 848

Alma is squeezed in between the river and a bluff once topped by a large rock. The river captains used this rock as a landmark to navigate, since they could see its form silhouetted against the sky even at night. It became known as Twelve Mile Bluff because it was located about 12 miles from the mouth of the Chippewa River. Victor Probst and John Weckler arrived here in 1848, followed shortly by several others, including John and Nicolas Marty. Their activity centered around cutting cordwood and making shingles for roofs. For mail, they boated to the Minnesota side of the river 12 miles upstream to a village called Reed's Landing. When it was time to resupply with such items as pork, flour, clothing and tools, they contacted steamboats to take their orders to Galena, Illinois.

The first recorded business at Twelve Mile Bluff was a saloon run by a man known simply as Beyer. There was nothing fancy about it, only a shed attached to the Marty house. Activity increased at Alma in 1855 when two hotels called the Alma & Wisconsin Houses were built. A brewery was also built and the town was platted.

About this time a storekeeper named Gates suggested the town pick a name other than Twelve Mile Bluff because few enjoyed taking time to pronounce the name. Gate suggested Alma after a Russian River where an important battle of the Crimean War took place in the 1850's. Before the railroads, Alma was the most important wheat shipping point on the Wisconsin side between St. Paul and La Crosse. The county seat was established here in 1860 and the Beef Slough Boom Company began lumbering operations at the mouth of the Chippewa River in 1867. At one time this river town had five

SHSW

Alma

general stores, five blacksmiths, two breweries, three shoe shops, six wheat warehouses, two hardware stores, three hotels, two saw mills and three wagon shops. Fredrick Fischer constructed the town's first sawmill in 1870.

In late April, 1881, an event which had been predicted for many years finally happened: the giant boulder on Twelve Mile Bluff crashed down the hill in a thunderous rush. It broke into hundreds of pieces and narrowly missed destroying an important mill.

NELSON, Pop. 389

Little is known abouth the Englishman James Nelson except that he settled near the mouth of the Chippewa River in 1844. At first his name marked a landing on the Mississippi, an ideal stopping place for travelers along the Mississippi and Chippewa rivers. During the late 1800's a ferry carried passengers between Nelson and Reads Landing, an active logging town on the Minnesota side.

When the railroad was surveyed through here, it picked a path on higher ground to avoid flooding. A new village began developing under Rattlesnake Bluff near the proposed route. When the line was completed in 1866 this new siding became known as Fairview and a rivalry existed between the two towns for a time. Eventually most moved up from Nelson on the river and the little village of Fairview renamed itself Nelson.

CHIPPEWA RIVER & BEEF SLOUGH

The Chippewa River begins in northwest Wisconsin's forest and lake region and eventually finds its way to the Mississippi River at the base of Lake Pepin. For thousands of years, the faster-moving Chippewa has deposited rich sediment from the farms and forests into the slower-moving Mississippi, creating a natural dam of sand and silt which backs up the Mississippi here, forming the 25-mile long Lake Pepin.

A low, marshy backwater area called Beef Slough was once the Chippewa River's main channel. During the 1860's, Beef Slough became a massive log harbor for hundreds of thousands of white pine from Wisconsin's northern forests. The Chippewa, which drains approximately seven million acres in Wisconsin, was once a river valley with an estimated 20 billion feet of lumber. The scramble began during the mid-1800's to remove as many trees as rapidly and efficiently as the lumbermen knew how. The Chippewa River was their answer.

Before long a rivalry developed between the Chippewa River mills at Eau Claire and those along the Mississippi. A Mississippi River group formed in 1867 at Alma as the Beef Slough Manufacturing, Booming, Log-Driving and Transportation Company. Its main purpose was to construct a boom across the mouth of the Chippewa to collect logs coming down the river. They tallied the logs as they directed them into the slough, referring to the brand lumbermen placed on each log when the trees were cut. This was done to credit the loggers upstream so they might be paid.

However, this new boom across the Chippewa threatened to cut off boat traffic and necessary trade to Durand, Eau Claire, Menomonie and Chippewa Falls. When the state legislature granted a charter to the Slough Company, it specifically required that the boom be movable to allow for the free passage of river traffic. The conflict was called the Beef Slough War, but in reality it was more tension between the Mississippi and Chippewa lumbermen than open conflict.

After the first log drive to the Beef Slough Boom was completed, a tough crew went down to Alma to be paid. There wasn't enough money to go around and the lumbermen took over the town and "...indulged in riotous acts." A temporary militia was formed to keep the men at bay until they were paid. The Chippewa River is rich with stories about the crude, robust lumbermen, the lumber mills, companies, and speculators who worked the Chippewa Valley until the white pine flowed no more. Ownership of the slough, mills and other river companies changed hands many times. A number became rich, while others lost everything to the river. Beef Slough peaked in 1888, as huge log rafts were formed here and sent down the Mississippi to St. Louis. Shortly after 1889, however, operations at Beef Slough had to be abandoned because of uncontrollable silting in the slough. Today, the Beef Slough area is part of the 9,000 acre Tiffany Wildlife Area which includes deer, beaver, eagles, turtles and is an important nesting area for wood ducks.

PEPIN COUNTY, Pop. 7,477

This county with its irregular shape was formed from Dunn County in February of 1858. The county seat was first established at the growing village of Pepin, but was soon moved up the Chippewa River to Durand.

Before whites began making claims here, Chief Wabasha and his Dakota braves controlled this region. Nevertheless, the Ojibwe, an Indian nation that began exerting its force from the Lake Superior region during the early 1700's, led many deadly raids against the Dakota by traveling the Chippewa River. Over the following century, whites made claims to these lands and rapidly overwhelmed the native Americans and their culture.

It was here at Lake Pepin that Father Hennepin, the first white to pass along the Upper Mississippi, was captured by the Dakota in 1680. Seven years later a Frenchman named Le Sueur ventured up the Mississippi in search of furs and copper. But it wasn't until 1689 that Nicholas Perrot claimed the Upper Mississippi region for France from Lake Pepin's

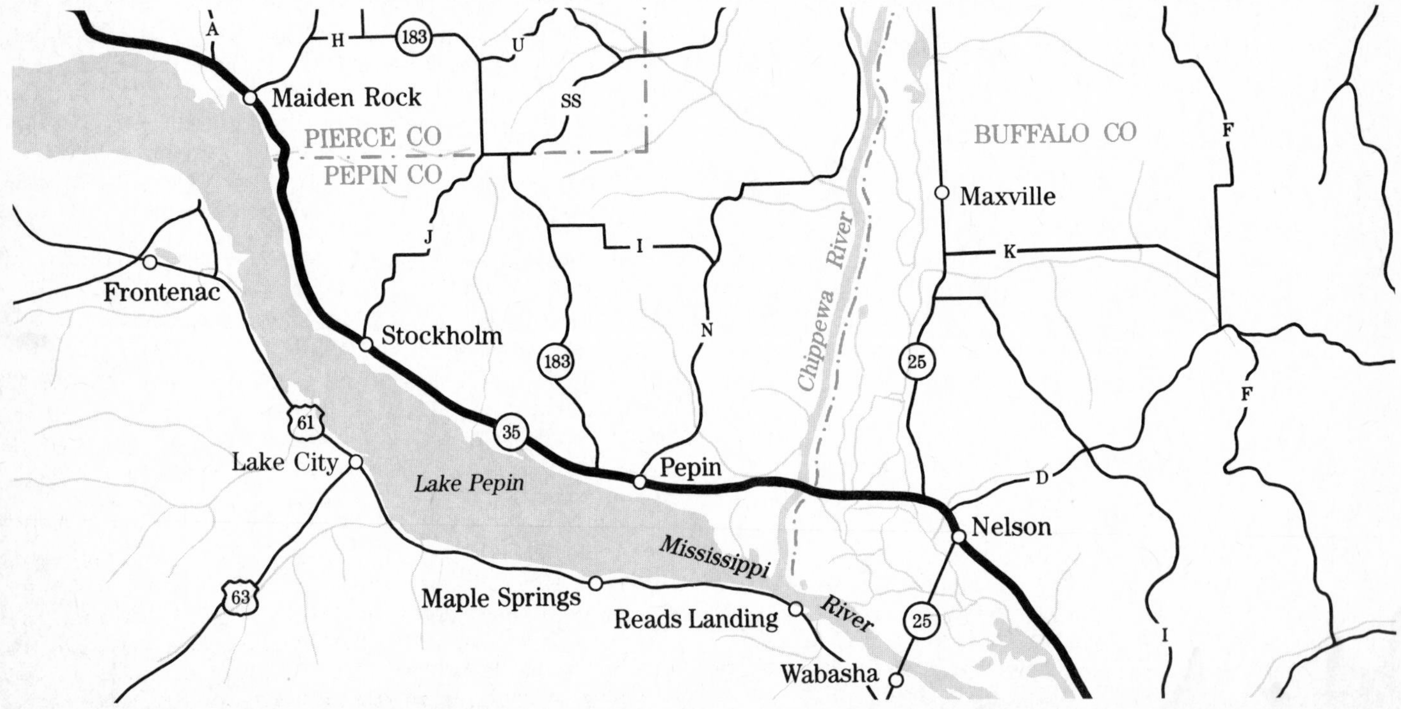

shore. The French traded here with the Indians for the next 74 years before the British took control in 1763. Claim to this rich fur trading region changed hands between Britain and the United States in 1783 and then again during the War of 1812. When the British were finally removed from Prairie du Chien in 1814, settlements began to slowly spread up the river. However, settlement didn't begin in earnest until after the Dakota and Ojibwe gave up claims to their Wisconsin lands in 1837.

PEPIN, Pop. 890

Bounded by wooded bluffs on one side and by the expansive Lake Pepin on the other, is the old fishing village of Pepin. John McCain, a river pilot for many years, became familiar with this part of the Mississippi and decided to make this area his home. In 1841 he selected a site slightly north of today's Pepin, but put off building until 1846. Another river pilot and cousin of McCain, Bill Newcomb, came the same year and built his cabin south of McCain's in what later became Pepin village. Over the years, this place has been known as Newcomb's Landing, North Pepin, Kansas and finally Pepin.

With development of the Chippewa pineries during the early 1850's, other settlers saw this spot as a perfect location for a new town. A road soon connected with Chippewa Falls and a stage line began operating, traveling between the two towns in two days for only three dollars. During the winter of 1854 a post office was opened, and the town was platted as North Pepin the following spring.

Pepin grew rapidly with the addition of stores, warehouses, a blacksmith, hotel, newspaper and grain elevator. The county's first church, the Methodist Episcopal church, began in 1856. When Pepin County was officially formed in 1858, Pepin became the county seat. But the village was at a disadvantage from the beginning. During low water, which was most of the summer and fall, Pepin was inaccessible to river boats. Shallow draft boats began servicing Durand and Chippewa Falls, hurting the once lucrative stage routes that came up from Pepin. A short time later, in 1861, the county seat was moved to Durand. When the railroad was built on the Minnesota side in 1870, the town lost more business and by the time the Chicago, Burlington & Northern entered Pepin in 1886, little benefit was felt. If anything, Pepin's winter fishing industry was its most stable economic element since 1893 when the annual catch totaled $250,000.

Laura Ingalls Wilder, an author of children's books who began writing when she was 65, was born in a log cabin not far from Pepin. Her first book, "Little House in the Big Woods," is an account of her life along the bluffs of the Mississippi Valley.

SHSW

Fishing boats tied on Lake Pepin. Photo/Denison

FORT ST. ANTOINE

Here, at the mouth of Bogus Creek, Nicholas Perrot bent over the Mississippi, poured oil into it, and lit it to the astonishment of the Indians. With this action, he claimed all of the Upper Mississippi and region west "no matter how remote" for the King of France. The year was 1689 and Perrot built a small fort to trade with the Indians. The fort was occupied for about two years, then abandoned, and forgotten until 1855 when its remains were discovered.

STOCKHOLM, Pop. 104

Eric Peterson, an immigrant from Varmland, Sweden, came here to live in 1851. He claimed this spot, then returned to Sweden to find a wife to bring back to America. He soon married and returned to this homesite on the Mississippi in 1854. The trip was long and difficult and his wife gave birth to a girl, Maltilde, on the day they arrived here.

That spring, Eric's brother and several other Swedes came up the river from Illinois and built a community house to live in until each had a cabin. This was a prosperous Swedish community for many years with a hotel, steam feed mill, farm produce, and flour mill. The post office was established in 1860. When Wisconsin was a great wheat state, the grain warehouse here stored 30,000 bushels. Lake Pepin's natural resources also helped the town's economy. As kosher markets developed along the East Coast, many tons of river carp were seined from the water and breeding ponds were eventually constructed along the river bottoms. Dredging for clams to sell for button-making was also done here. When the railroad came through in 1886, cities on the Mississippi's west shore already captured most of the river trade and all the wheat coming from the Minnesota and Dakota fields. In 1890, Stockholm's population was only 711. Sixteen years later a fire destroyed a good portion of the town.

The summer of 1938 was one of the most important for this small community. Crown Prince Gustav of Sweden, Princess Louise and other members of the royal family visited Stockholm on the Mississippi to acknowledge its strong Scandinavian heritage.

LAKE PEPIN

Pepin is one of the oldest names to appear on the early maps of Wisconsin. There are at least three explanations for the name of this expansive widening of the Mississippi. The first is that it was named after Pepin le Bref, a King of France. Another historian writes that explorer Duluth noted that the Pepin brothers lived in this vicinity during the late 1600's. In 1680 Father Hennepin was captured somewhere along the lake and subsequently named this body of water, Lac des Pleurs or "Lake of Tears." He chose that name from the evening he spent here as prisoner of Dakota braves who, Hennepin recalled, cried though the night in an emotional plea to their chief to let them kill him. Their pleas were unheeded and Hennepin was taken to the main Dakota village, Kathio, at Lake Mille Lacs in Minnesota.

The 25-mile-long Lake Pepin is bordered by high bluffs. A massive flow of glacial water carved out the broad deep river valley during the glacial run-off that dates back 10-12,000 years ago. The Mississippi valley was even deeper than today. As glacial run-off slowed, sedimentation filled the riverbed back to its present level. The faster-moving Chippewa River has carried down sand and gravel from the Wisconsin farmlands and deposited it at its confluence with the Mississippi. This creates a bottleneck across the Mississippi forcing it to back up and fill the shallow basin of Lake Pepin. The U.S. Army Corps of Engineers, the government unit which maintains a nine-foot deep shipping channel up the Mississippi, is continually plagued by the shifting sands dumped by the Chippewa River.

Lake Pepin has supported commercial fishing and during the early 1900's a considerable amount of clamming was also done in the area to supply button factories on the Minnesota side of Lake Pepin at Lake City. Lake Pepin is also the site of the first water skiing attempt, done by Ralph Samuelson in 1922.

PIERCE COUNTY, Pop. 31,149

Bordered on the west by two great waterways, the Mississippi and St. Croix, Pierce County's early white settlement began at Prescott when a contingent of officers at Fort Snelling claimed 1,200 acres in 1827. They built a cabin and established a trading post. Philander Prescott took possession of this land and, along with a man named Reed, kept others from settling here until 1841. The county developed slowly at first, and there wasn't any great move to settle here until the St. Croix pineries began producing in the 1840's. The county wasn't formally organized until it was separated from St. Croix County in 1853, with the county seat located at Prescott. The total value of personal property in the county that year was only $28,000. The county seat was moved to Ellsworth in 1860.

MAIDEN ROCK, Pop. 172

At one time, many steamboats passed here and sounded their whistles in memory of an Indian maiden who committed suicide from this bluff. Legend has her name as Winona, a Dakota Indian name often given to the first born girl. Her father, Chief Red Wing, one of a series of chiefs by that name, wanted her to marry, but Winona was in love with another man and climbed to the ledge of the bluff, sang her deathsong, and threw herself from it rather than marry her father's choice.

SHSW

1915 log raft passing down the Mississippi River.

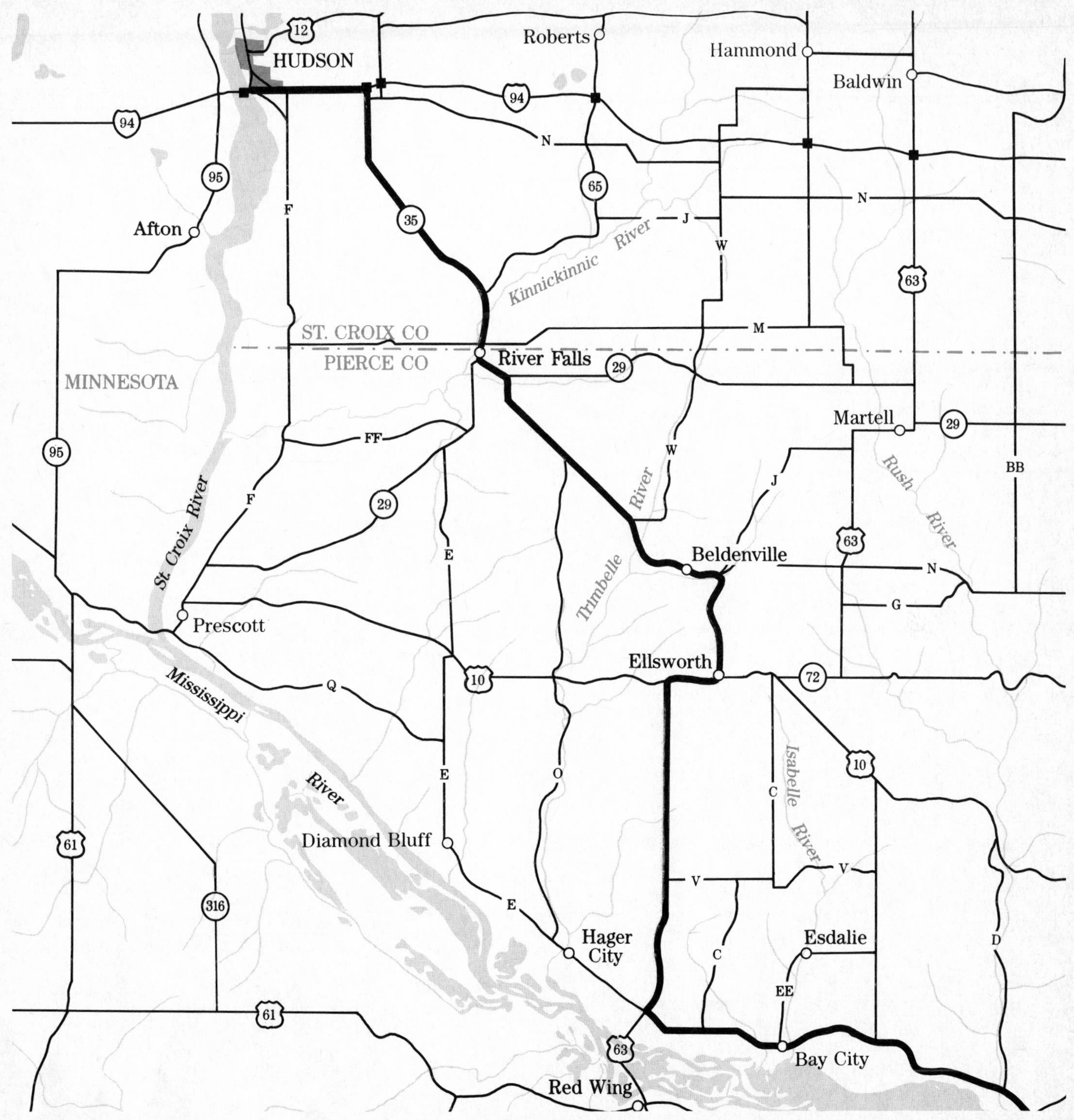
HUDSON
Roberts
Hammond
Baldwin
12
94
N
65
95
Afton
F
35
J
Kinnickinnic River
W
N
63
M
ST. CROIX CO
PIERCE CO
River Falls
29
MINNESOTA
Martell
29
95
FF
W
Rush River
BB
River
J
F
29
E
63
Beldenville
St. Croix River
Trimbelle
N
G
Prescott
Ellsworth
10
72
Mississippi
Q
River
10
Isabelle River
E
O
C
Diamond Bluff
V
V
61
316
E
Hager City
Esdalie
D
C
EE
61
63
Bay City
Red Wing

J.D. Trumbull and his 24-horsepower saw mill came from Stillwater, Minnesota and was the first to settle here. Others came shortly after, mostly to work at Trumbull's mill. He soon added a shingle mill to his operation, built the first hotel and became post master in 1856, collecting a grand total of $11 his first year. The first sailboat to be used in trade at Lake Pepin was constructed here in 1856. However, like other towns on the Wisconsin side of the Mississippi, Maiden Rock was penalized economically because it wasn't close enough to the Mississippi's main river channel. Undaunted, Trumbull built a steamboat and tried to bring some commerce to Maiden Rock.

Northwest of Maiden Rock where Cave Creek joins Rush Creek, early settlers found ancient Indian drawings at a place called Cave Creek Ledge. Many thought these drawings were done before the Dakota and Ojibwe occupied this region, since they don't reflect the hostilities that existed between the two nations. It is doubtful these markings still exist today.

BAY CITY, Pop. 543

Sitting at the head of Lake Pepin on a terrace of the Mississippi is the small village of Bay City. The spot's initial attraction was the Isabelle River which enabled two brothers named Phillips to build a mill here in 1853. Like most towns where waterpower was an asset, other settlers were also attracted here. A man named Morton bought a tract of land and hoped to profit by selling lots. He hired a surveyor to lay out a town to be named Saratoga. Unfortunately, a short-tempered squatter named Dexter objected and shot the surveyor. Dexter was convicted of murder, the first in the county, and spent ten years in prison. Morton lost money on his venture and the plans for Saratoga were soon dropped. Charles Tyler paid the back taxes on Morton's property and planned a new town named Bay City.

Thomas Nelson started a brick kiln, turning out 100,000 bricks per year, supplying settlers with materials for their chimneys.

ELLSWORTH, Pop. 2,143

This town is located in an area of hills and valleys along the eastern border of what came to be known as the Big Woods. According to early records, Anthony Huddleson came to the Ellsworth area to clear land in 1855. Like other New Englanders, he was looking for relief from expensive overworked eastern land. Other farmers soon followed and area land was quickly cleared. As Pierce County became settled, many, especially those in River Falls, were unhappy with the long trip to the county seat at Prescott. They felt the county had a better chance to thrive if it had a centrally-located government. When the lines were drawn to find the county's geographic center, they converged on a wooded ridge which was to become Ellsworth. The county commissioners met in the basement of Bill Crippin's small hotel in April, 1861. The following year a town hall was erected and the township name was changed from Perry to Ellsworth, after a Union Colonel killed in the Civil War.

When the Sioux City Railroad was extended down from River Falls to Ellsworth during the early 1880's, railroad officials asked the city fathers where they wanted the tracks to run. As this story goes, the request was to "be within one mile of the courthouse." When the tracks were laid, it came within four feet under a mile from the courthouse. Because of this, Ellsworth began a new development over at the station site. One of the village's important early industries was a barrel factory, started in 1874 to supply Minneapolis, St. Paul and Red Wing.

A man named Cairnes experimented with Russian apples here, trying to make a variety that could withstand the frigid climate. For many years Cairnes' apples showed up at the county fair.

BELDENVILLE

When the Civil War broke out in 1861, Pierce County had only 5,000 residents and the largest villages were Prescott, River Falls and the new town of Ellsworth. However, a number of small hamlets such as Beldenville grew up around mills located on streams that wound their way down the St. Croix or Mississippi rivers. Other early towns similar to this one included El Paso, Sunrise (now Martell), Forestville and Trimbelle. Other mills and a veneer plant joined Belden's mill on a branch of Trimbelle Creek and there was much activity here for many years.

RIVER FALLS, Pop. 9,036

This village is built around the Kinnikinnic River which leaves the open valleys to the east and begins to drop here through a narrow gorge that channels its last eight miles to the St. Croix. The river enters the St. Croix a few miles north of Prescott, where it has created a pronounced sand delta. Kinnikinnic is a Potawatomi Indian word that pertains either to the willows that grow along the river's banks or to the tobacco the Indians smoked.

Joel Foster heard stories about the beautiful Kinnikinnic River valley when he was in Stillwater in 1848. With several others he traveled here and took claims close to the river. They were interested in the river's waterpower and had no doubt that this would be a great location for a manufacturing center. This small community first called itself Kinnikinnic,

Pierce County feed grinding mill, ca. 1900's.

but choose Greenwood when the town was platted in 1854. The village thrived on the numerous mills that lined the river. Stores opened and many services got started in the growing town. However, the post office soon found itself exchanging mail with another Greenwood in Clark County, so the name was changed to River Falls in honor of the falls on the Kinnikinnic here.

In 1856 River Falls became one of the first towns in northwestern Wisconsin to establish an academy. It was eventually replaced in 1870 by Hinckley's Military Academy, a coeducational boarding school, but the residents of River Falls had their minds set on a larger institution. Congress had allocated funds for establishing state normal schools in the early 1870's and River Falls was the fourth Wisconsin city to have a such a school. It opened in 1874 with 10 professors and 200 students with a goal to prepare teachers for public education. Today the school is part of the University of Wisconsin system.

The railroad came here in 1878, carrying away local timber and flour from mills with names like Clifton Hollow, Prairie Flour, and Cascade. A major event in the town's history was the fire of 1876 which began on a January morning when gale-force winds were blowing. The fire started in a home next to the post office and since there wasn't an organized fire department most of the important businesses were destroyed. The docile Kinnikinnic has flooded from time to time and caused damage along its path. One of its worst floods ravaged the town in 1894, carrying away some of the eight bridges that connected the two sides of the city.

River Falls organized as a city in 1885 with A.D. Andrews as mayor. Unfortunately, Andrews died a few months later.

(Information on St. Croix County and Hudson can be found on Route 94, page 44.)

BIBLIOGRAPHY

American Sketch Book, The. La Crosse: Sketch Book Co., 1876.

Around the Shores of Lake Superior. A guide to Historic sites. Madison: Univ. of Wis. Board of Regents, 1979.

Auburndale. Compiled by Residents. Helbach Printing, Inc., Amherst, WI: 1971.

Bailey, Judge William. History of Eau Claire County Wisconsin. Chicago: C.F. Cooper & Co., 1914.

Bailey, Mrs. Sturges. Eau Claire County History Indexes., Index To The Historical And Biographical Album Of The Chippewa valley, 1979.

Bailey, W.F., History of Eau Claire County, Past And Present. Chicago: C.F. Cooper & Co., 1914.

Barrett, Sam. Ancient Aztalan, Milwaukee: Board of Trustees, 1933.

Basinger, Carl. The Luxembourg Community of Ozaukee County, Madison: (Term Paper), 1952.

Bayfield, Comm. H.W. Outlines Of The Geology Of Lake Superior.

Biographical History Of Clark And Jackson Counties. Lewis Publishing Co., 1891.

Biographical Record Of Rock, Green, Grant, Iowa, and Lafayette Counties, Beers & Co., Chicago: 1901.

Boyer, David S. National Geographic 1977, P 30-37 v152, No.1

Brown, Charles Edward; French Pathfinders. Madison: State Historical Society, 1934.

Brown, Charles Edward; The Pictured Cave Of La Crosse Valley Near West Salem.

Brown, Dorothy. Wis. Indian place names, Chicago: S.J. Clarke, 1924.

Buchen, Gustave. History of Sheboygan Co., Sheboygan: 1944.

Burnham, Guy M. The First House, 1931.

Burnham, Guy M. Lake Superior Country in History and in Story. Boston: 1930.

Butterfield, C.W. History of La Crosse County. Chicago: Western Historical Company, 1881.

Butterfield, C.W. History of Columbia County, Chicago: Western Historical Co., 1880.

Canfield, W.H. 1873 Guide-book To The Wild Romantic Scenery Of Sauk Co. Wisconsin, Republic Print Co.

Century of Faith, A. First Reformed Church of Oostburg, WI: 1950.

Chapman, Earl and Assocociates. U.S. Highway 53, The Gateway Route, 1941.

Chapman, Silas. Handbook of Wisconsin, Milwaukee: Chapman, 1855.

Chappelle, Ethel. The Why Of Names In Washburn Co., Birchwood WI: 1965.

Chappelle, Ethel. Around the Four Corners, Rice Lake, Wisconsin: Chronotype Pub. Co., 1975.

Christiansen, Ruth Bunker, Polk County County Place Names. Frederic, Wi: 1975.

Civic Century, A. Clintonville Harvest Festival, Inc., 1955.

Clark County Centennial. Neillsville, WI: 1953

Clark, Giles. Historic Tales of the Fox River Valley, Menasha: Educational Enterprises, 1973.

Clark, James I. Chronicles Of Wisconsin, State Historical Society Of Wisconsin, 1955 (16parts).

Cole, H.E. Baraboo, Dells And Devils Lake Region; Scenery, Archeology, Geology, Indian Legends And Local History.

Cole, H.E. Baraboo and other Place Names in Sauk County, Baraboo, WI: The Baraboo News Publishing Co., 1912.

Cole, Harry Ellsworth. History of Sauk Co., Chicago & New York: Lewis Pub. Co., 1918.

Cole, H.E. Stagecoach and Tavern Days in the Baraboo Region, Baraboo, WI, 1923.

Connor, Mary Roddis. A Century With Connor Timber, Stevens Point, WI: Worzalla Publishing Co., 1972.

Corrigan, Walter, Sr. History of the Town of Mequon, Pub. by the Mequon Club, 1870.

Current, Richard Nelson. Wisconsin, A History, New York: W. W. Norton & Co., Inc., 1977.

Curtis-Wedge, Franklyn. History of Buffalo and Pepin Counties, Winona, MN: H.C. Cooper & Co., 1919.

Davis, Andrew Mcfarland. A Preliminary Railroad Survey In Wisconsin, 1857, The Madison Society.

Dawes, Clara & William. History of Oshkosh, Pub. unknown, 1938.

Dawes, William. History of Winnebago County, Oshkosh: Service Print Shop, 1938.

Day, Genevieve Cline. Hudson in the Early Days, Hudson, WI: Star-Observer, 1963.

Decker, A. Along the Wisconsin River, Milwaukee: Eve. Wi Co., 1940?

Derleth, August William. Sauk County, A Centennial History, 1948.

Dessureau, Robt. History of Langlade County, Antigo: Berner Bros. Pub. Co., 1922.

Doty, James. Northern Wisconsin in 1820, Madison: SHSW, 1876.

Drury, John. This is Dane County, Chicago: Inland Photo Co.

Easton, Augustus. History Of The Saint Croix Valley, Chicago: H.C. Cooper, Jr. & Co., 1909.

Eau Claire, Sawdust City, A History Of Eau Claire From Earliest Times To 1910, Stevens Point: Worzalla Pub. Co. 1960.

Ellis, Albert. Upper Wisconsin Country, Madison: SHSW, 1857.

Engel, Pastor Armin L. Nearly a Century for Christ. 1950.

Falge, Dr. Louis. History of Manitowoc Co., Chicago: Goodspeed Historical Assn., 1913.

Field, Martin. History of the town of Mukwonago, Pub?

Forrester, George. Historical and Biographical Album of the Chippewa Valley, Chicago: A. Warner Publisher, 1891.

Fox, Edgar B. & Dudley, W.T. History & Directory of Green Lake and Waushara Counties, Berlin, WI: Courant Book Co., 1869.

Fox, Philip Marvin. The Link Between Three Hundred years Of Travel: The Brule-st. Croix Portage, Minneapolis: 1968

Frazier, Gertrude & Poff, Rose. The Kickapoo Valley, Frazier & Poff, 1896.

Freeman, Samuel. Emigrant's Handbook and Guide to Wisconsin, Milwaukee: Sentinel and Gazette Power Press Plant, 1851.

Gagnon, Evan. Neshota, the Story of Two Rivers, Stevens Point: Worzalla Pub. Co., MCMLXIX.

Gard, Robt. and Sorden, L. Romance of Wisconsin Place Names, New York: October House Inc., 1968.

Gard, Robert. Wild Goose Marsh, Madison: Straus Printing & Pub. Co., WI, 1972.

Garvaglia, Carolyn. Early Days of Niagara, The Niagara Journal, 1976.

Gibbs, T. Choice Of Farming Land In The St. Croix Valley, Atwood & Culver, 1875.

Gordon Centennial Book. Gordon, Wisconsin, 1960.

Gould, Whitney & Wittman, Stephen. Brownstone & Bargeboard.

Gregory, John Goadby. Sw Wis. Hist Of Old Crawford County, Chicago: S.J. Clarke Pub. Co. 1932.

Gregory, John & Brown, Chas. Scenic & Historic Wisconsin, Madison: State Historical Museum, 1934.

Guernsey, Orrin & Willard, Josiah. History of Rock County and Transactions of the Rock County Agricultural Society, Janesville, WI: 1856.

Haight, Theron W. Memoirs of Waukesha County, Madison: Western Hist. Assn, 1907.

Harris, Lucille & Schuh, Dorthea. Elcho Centennial, Summer 1959.

Harney, R.J. History of Winnebago Co., Oshkosh: Allen & Hicks, 1880

Heritage Areas of Iron County, Madison: U. of W., 1977.

Hill, Elmer. Golden Anniversary Year Book of Rusk County, 1951.

History of Crawford and Richland Counties, Springfield: Union Publishing Co., Il., 1884.

History of Dane County, Chicago: Western Historical Co., 1880.

History of Delavan. 1982.

History of Dodge Co, Chicago: Western Historical Co., MDCCCLXXX

History Of Iowa County, Chicago: Western Historical Co.

History of Northern Wisconsin, Chicago: The Western Historical Co., 1881.

History Of St. Croix Valley (polk #5) Minneapolis: North Star Pub. Co., 1881.

History Of Sauk Co. Wis, Settlement, Growth, And Development. Chicago: Western Historical Company. 1880.

History of Stevens Pt. Stevens Point: Portage County H.S., 1958.

History Of Vernon County, Union Pub. Co. 1884.

History of Waukesha County. Chicago: Western Historical Co., 1880.

History of Wisconsin Highway Development. State Highway Commission of Wisconsin. Madison: 1947.

Hjalmar, Holand. Old Peninsula Days, Ephraim: Pioneer Pub. Co., 1934.

Hocking, Grace Gilmore. The Memorable Kickapoo Valley, Richland Center, WI: Richland County Publishers Inc., 1977. !!!

Holand, Hjalmar R. History of Door Co., Chicago: S.J. Clarke Pub. Co., 1917.

Hubell, Homer. Dodge County, WI–Past & Present, Chicago: S.J. Clarke Pub. Co., 1913.

Hudson's Heritage, A Guide To The Historic Sites Of Hudson. St. Croix Co. Historical Society.

Hunt, N. Jane. Brevets Wisconsin Historical Markers & Sites Brevet Press, 1974

Huntley, Sidney J. Sparta Up To Date, 1899. Souvenir Supplement Of The Monroe County Democrat.

Incidents in the History of Brown County. Teachers, Brown County, 1948.

Island View Hotel Company, The Most Famous Pleasure Resort In Northern Wisc. Bayfield Co. Press. 1890.

Jenkins, Paul B. The Book of Lake Geneva, Chicago: Univ. of Chicago Press, 1922.

Jones, J.E. History of Columbia County, Chicago: Lewis Pub. Co, 1914.

Keathley, Clarence R. Iron County Brought Into Focus, Ironton, MO: 1976.

Kemper, Jackson. A Trip Through Wisconsin, Madison: Magazine of History, 1925.

Keyes, Elisha. Early days in Jefferson County, Madison: SHSW, 1888.

Kingston, J.T. Early Exploration and Settlement of Juneau

County, Wisconsin Historical Society Collections, Vol 8, 1908.

Kohler, Ruth Miriam De Young The Story of Wisconsin Women. 1948.

Krueger, Lloyd C., Coordinator. Fairchild Centennial, Eau Claire Printing Co., 1972.

La Crosse County Historical Society Sketches Series, 1-8. 1931-55.

Land of the Fox. Appleton: State Centennial Committee, 1949.

Landscapes Of Wisconsin, American Association Of American Geographers, 1975.

Lapham, Increase. Wisconsin: Its geography and topography. Milwaukee: I.A. Hopkins–New York: Paine & Burgess, 1864.

Lapham, Increase A. Old Settler's Club of Milwaukee County, Milwaukee: Daily Commercial Times Printers, 1875.

Lawson, Publius. History of Winnebago County, Chicago: C.F. Cooper & Co., 1908.

Leberman, J. 100 years of Sheboygan, Sheboygan: 1946.

Ledgler, Henry Eduard. Wisconsin- Leading Events In Wisconsin History. Milwaukee Sentinel Co., 1898.

Lomira Centennial. Compiled by Citizens of Lomira. 1976.

Lyman, Frank H.. The City of Kenosha, Kenosha County, Chicago: S.J. Clarke Pub. Co., 1916.

Marple, Andrea. Country of the Shining Pines. A manual on Sawyer County's history and development.

Marple, Eldon. The Visitor Who Came to Stay, Hayward: The County Print Shop, 1971.

Marshall, Albert M. Brule Country, St. Paul: North Central Publishing

Co., 1954.

Marshfield Highlights of History. Compiled by Marshfield Residents, 1972?

Martin, Deborah B.. History of Brown Co, Chicago: S.J. Clarke Pub. Co., 1913.

Martin, Charles. History of Door County, Sturgeon Bay: Expositor job print, 1881.

Mather, Cotton, Upper Coulee Country, Prescott, WI: Trimbelle Press, 1975.

Mcmillan, Morrison, Early Settlement Of La Crosse And Monroe Counties, Wisconsin Historical Soc. Report, 1859.

McVean, Norman S. & Jones, George O. History of Wood Co., Minneapolis: H.C. Cooper, Jr. & Co., 1923

McVean, Norman S. & Jones, Geo. O. History of Lincoln, Oneida & Vilas Counties,

Minneapolis: H.C. Cooper, Jr. & Co., 1924.

Memories of Forest County. YCC Improvement Program, NEWCAP, Inc., 1980.

Metz, James I., Ed. Prairie, Pines, and People, Menasha, WI: George Banta Co., 1976.

Morley, Albert. Brule Country Marshall, St.Paul: North Central Publishing, 1954.

Necedah Centennial Program. Necedah, WI: Centennial Steering Comm., 1953.

Neill, Edward D. History Of St. Croix Valley, Polk Co., Pierce County, North Star Pub. Co., 1881.

Novak, Jerry. History of the Moquah Area. Northland College, Ashland, WI.

Oconto County Centennial Program, 1948.

O'Neill, Margaret. Early History of The Friendly Valley and Falls of St. Croix, St. Croix Falls, MN: Standard Press, 1937.

Osseo Centennial Publication, 1957.

Ott, John Henry. Jefferson County Wisconsin and its People, Chicago: S.J. Clarke Pub. Co., 1917.

Paul, Barbara & Justis, eds. The Badger State, Grand Rapids, Mich: Wm. B. Eerdmans Publishing, 1979.

Paull, Rachel and Richard. Geology of Wisconsin and Upper Michigan, Dubuque, IA: Kendall/Hunt Publishing Co., 1977.

Patterson, Betty. Index To Crawford And Richland Counties History, Wisconsin State Genealogical Soc., 1981.

Pen and Sunlight Sketches of the Principle Cities in Wisconsin,

Wisconsin: Phoenix Publishing, 1893.

Plumb, Ralph G.. History of Manitowoc Co., Brandt Printing & Binding Co., 1904.

Pond, Alonzo W. Interstate Park And Dalles Of St. Croix, Taylors Falls, Mn., The Standard Press, 1937.

Portrait of the Past/A photographic journey through Wisconsin, Wisconsin Trails. 1971.

Quaife, Milo. Wisconsin, its history & its people, Chicago: S.J. Clarke, 1924.

Quickert, Carl. The Story of Washington County, Chicago: S.J. Clarke Pub. Co., 1912.

Raihle, Paul. The Valley Called Chippewa. Cornell, WI: The Chippewa Valley Courier, 1940.

Reimann, Lewis C.. Hurley–Still No Angel, Michigan: Northwoods Publishers, 1954.

Reuss, Henry S. On the Trail of the Ice Age, Milwaukee: Raintree Publishers, Inc., 1981.

Rosholt, Malcolm L. The Battle Of Cameron Dam.

Ross, Hamilton Nelson. La Pointe-Village Outpost. H.M. Ross, 1960.

Rudolph, Robt. Wood County Place Names, Madison: Univ. of Wis. Press, 1970.

St. Croix Standard Press, Supplement. 1915.

Sanford, A.H. and Hirshheimer, H.J. A History Of La Crosse.

Scarborough's Road Map And Motor Guide To Wisconsin, The Scarborough Company 1912.

Schafer, Joseph. The Wisconsin Lead Region, Madison: SHSW. 1932.

SE Wis: A History of Old Milwaukee County. Vols. 1 & 2, Chicago: S.J. Clarke Pub. Co., 1932.

Sorden, L.F. & Gard, Robt. E. Wisconsin Lore, New York: Duell, Sloan and Pearce, 1962.

Sorensen, George P. The History of Waushara Co., Wautoma: Judge Geo P. Sorensen, Pub., 1932.

Stark, William F. Ghost Towns of Wisconsin. Sheboygan WI: Zimmerman Press, 1977.

Stewart, Jim & Shirley. Easy Going (A comprehensive guide to Grant, Iowa and Lafayette Counties), Madison: Tamarack Press, 1976.

Stone, Fanny S. Racine and Racine Co., Chicago: S.J. Clarke Pub. Co., 1916.

Stouffer, A.L. The Story of Shell Lake, Washburn Historical Society. 1961.

Straub, A.G. History of Marathon, WI, Marathon: Marathon Times, 1957.

Tourists' Guide To The Health And Pleasure of the Golden Northwest.

Chicago, Milwaukee & St. Paul Railway, 1879.

Town of Oulu. Historical Sketches of the Town of Oulu, Bayfield County.

Tlachac, Mathew. The history of the Belgian Settlements, Algoma: Belgian American Club, 1974.

Umhoefer, Jim. Guide to Wisconsin's Parks, Madison: Litho Productions, Inc., 1982.

Ware, John M. History of Waupaca Co., Chicago & New York: Lewis Pub. Co., 1917.

Way, Royal. The Rock River Valley, Chicago: S.J. Clarke Pub. Co., 1926.

Webster, Clement Lyon. Ancient Mounds in Iowa and Wisconsin, Smithsonian Inst. Rept. 1887.

Wakefield, Joseph. History of Waupaca County, Waupaca: D.L. Stinchfield, 1890.

Weatherhead, Harold. Westward To The St. Croix, St. Croix Hist. Soc. 1978.

Wheeler, Adele G. Historical Album of Niagara, WI, Pub. by Adele Wheeler, 1961.

Whyte, Bertha Kitchell. Wisconsin Heritage Boston: Chas.T. Branford Co., 1954.

Wisconsin–Description And Travel Guide To Towns Along The Mississippi River. St. Paul, Ward & Young 1857.

Wisconsin Historical Markers and Sites, Sioux Falls: Brevet Press, 1974.

Wisconsin Magazine of History. Madison: SHSW, assorted dates.

Wisconsin Then and Now. Madison: SHSW, Assorted dates.

Worthing, Ruth. History of Fond du Lac County, Published by author, 1976.

Zillier, Carl. History of Sheboygan Co., Chicago: S.J. Clarke Pub. Co, 1912.

Negative Numbers for State Historical Society of Wisconsin

P. 5, WHI (X3) 20666; P. 7, WHI (X3) 20687; P. 9, WHI (X3) 39832; P. 10, WHI (X3) 31290; P. 11, WHI Class. File 32 & WHI (X3) 23310; P. 13, WHI (V22) 1250; P. 14, WHI Class. File 1486; P. 15, WHI (X3) 23168; P. 17, WHI (X22) 4491; P. 19, WHI (X3) 34460; P. 21, WHI (X3) 30785; P. 23, WHI (X3) 24628; P. 24, WHI (X3) 26525; P. 25, WHI (X3) 9554; P. 26, WHI 7286; P. 27, WHI 1004 & WHI Class. File 6062; P. 29, WHI (X3) 39584; P. 33, WHI (V2) 3 & WHI (V24) 1748; P. 34, WHI (X3) 2541; P. 37, WHI (X3) 1390; P. 40, WHI (K6); P. 41, WHI (X3) 18781; P. 43, WHI (V24); P. 44, WHI (X3) 39833; P. 47, WHI (X3) 38811; P. 49, WHI (X3) 38812; P. 50, WHI 53206; P. 53, WHI (X31) 9745 & WHI (X3) 39813; P. 54, WHI (X3) 39814; P. 56, WHI Class. File 52303; P. 58, WHI (X3) 29605; P. 59, WHI (X96) 17801 & WHI (X3) 39815; P. 63, WHI (X3) 17093; P. 66, WHI (D478) 91 11976; P. 68, WHI (X3) 39810; P. 69, WHI Class. 53208; P. 70, WHI (W63) 6119; P. 71, WHI Class. File 18355; P. 73, WHI (X3) 31156; P. 75, WHI (3489); WHI (X3) 39803; P. 78, WHI ((X313) 2729; P. 80, WHI (W6) 11668; P. 85, WHI H44 (89) 4106; P. 86, WHI (X3) 39804; P. 88, WHI (Classified #185); P. 91, WHI (V2) 1102; P. 93, WHI (X32) 3823; P. 95, WHI (X3) 7903; P. 97, WHI (X3) 3287 & WHI (S65) 79; P. 98, WHI (X3) 23313; P. 101, WHI (X3) 39826; P. 103, WHI (X3) 39827; P. 104, WHI (X28) 2827; P. 105, WHI (V2) 729; P. 107, WHI (V2) 363; P. 109, WHI (X3) 12370; P. 110, WHI (X3) 20917 & WHI U.of W. 3987-E; P. 113, WHI (X3) 14697; P. 115, WHI Class. File Indian 4 & WHI (V2) 179; P. 116, WHI (X3) 28608; P. 118, WHI (X3) 39828; P. 119, WHI (X3) 18374; P. 121, WHI (X3) 34849 & WHI (X3) 12656; P. 124, WHI Class. File 57; P. 126, WHI (X3) 39829; P. 127, WHI (X31) 5659; P. 129, WHI (S65) 9; P. 140, WHI (D489) 6298; P. 143, WHI (W6) 11673; P. 146, WHI (X3) 129; P. 147, WHI (X2) 20175 & WHI (X28(2754; P. 153, WHI (X323362); P. 154, WHI (W64527315); P. 159, WHI (3307); P. 165, WHI (X#) 19029; P. 167, WHI (X3) 39822; P. 170, WHI (X3) 39823; P. 176, WHI (X3) 39824; P. 178, WHI (X3) 24507 & WHI (X3) 39825; P. 180, WHI (X3) 29356; P. 183, WHI (H44) 40; P. 185, WHI (X2) 13552; P. 188, WHI (X3) 39816; P. 189, WHI (X3) 39817; P. 191, WHI (X3) 39818; P. 192, WHI (V2) 213 2400; P. 195, WHI (X3) 39819; P. 196, WHI (X3) 39820; P. 198, WHI (X3) 39821; P. 201, WHI 4106; P. 203, WHI Class. File 202; P. 204, WHI (X3) 18454; P. 207, WHI (X3) 33874; P. 208, WHI (X2) 20260; P. 210, WHI (X3) 29851; P. 211, WHI (X3) 23189; P. 212, WHI (X3) 20676; P. 213, WHI (X3) 32151; P. 217, WHI (W64) 21049; P. 219, WHI (X3) 23303; P. 220, WHI (X3) 25419; P. 223, WHI (X3) 39800; P. 225, WHI (X3) 8856; P. 226, WHI (V2) 1064; P. 233, WHI (X3) 39801; P. 236, WHI (S65 74) & WHI (X3) 39802; P. 239, WHI (9728 Classified 17); P. 243, WHI (X3) 24120; P. 245, WHI (X3) 37063; P. 248, WHI (54848); P. 249, Classified 6445; P. 251, WHI (V24) ; P. 255, WHI (X3) 38773; P. 257 WHI (X3) 39831; P. 259, WHI (X3) 10122; P. 261, WHI (X3) 25071; P. 263, WHI (F4) 303; P. 265, WHI (X3) 20952; P. 267, WHI (X3) 39830; P. 268, WHI (V2) 813 & WHI (X3) 30862; P. 270, WHI 5472; P. 271, WHI (X3) 36532; P. 273, WHI (X3) 1498; P. 276, WHI (C69) 6482; P. 278, WHI (G5) 1895; P. 280, WHI (5375 Classified); P. 281, WHI (X3) 39805; P. 284, WHI (X3) 30773 (G473) 120; P. 287, WHI (X3) 39596; P. 289, WHI (G5) 253; P. 290, WHI (B35) 28; P. 292, WHI (C3) 688 Class. File 35 & WHI (F4) 303 Class. File 57; P. 293, WHI (G5) 1476; P. 295, WHI (X92) 59 Class. File 57; P. 296, WHI (X3) 39806; P. 297, WHI (G5) 369; P. 299, WHI (X3) 39807; P. 301, WHI (X32) 3814; P. 302, WHI (X3) 15034; P. 303, WHI (X3) 39808 & 39809; P. 304, WHI (X3) 18585; P. 305, WHI (G5) 1283; P. 307, WHI (G5) 809; P. 309, WHI (X3) 24949; P. 311, WHI (X3) 32069; P. 315, WHI (X3) 29812; P. 317, WHI Class. File 12 18016; P. 318, WHI 4048; P. 321, WHI (X3) 20964.

INDEX

Book Designed by Richard Olsenius
Edited by Margaret Nelson
Type set by Type House/Duragraph, Minneapolis, in 10 pt. century book.
Paper is coated 65# matte
Book Printed at North Central Publishing, St. Paul